P9-BTN-655

PSYCHOLOGICAL ASSESSMENT IN CLINICAL PRACTICE

PSYCHOLOGICAL ASSESSMENT IN CLINICAL PRACTICE

A PRAGMATIC GUIDE

Edited by
MICHEL HERSEN, Ph.D.

Brunner-Routledge
Taylor & Francis Group

NEW YORK AND HOVE

Cover designed by Elise Weinger

Published in 2004 by
Brunner-Routledge
270 Madison Avenue
New York, NY 10016
www.brunner-routledge.com

Published in Great Britain by
Brunner-Routledge
27 Church Road
Hove, East Sussex
BN3 2FA
www.brunner-routledge.co.uk

Brunner-Routledge is an imprint of the Taylor & Francis Group.
Printed in the United States of America on acid-free paper.

10 9 8 7 6 5 4 3 2 1

Library of Congress Cataloging-in-Publication Data

Psychological assessment in clinical practice : a pragmatic guide /
editor, Michel Hersen.
        p. cm.
Includes bibliographical references and index.
    ISBN 0-415-93502-4 (Hardback)
   1. Psychodiagnostics. 2. Clinical psychology. 3.
Psychotherapy—Evaluation. I. Hersen, Michel.
RC469.P767 2004
616.89'075—dc22

                                              2003025614

CONTENTS

v

110148

PREFACE

Numerous books have dealt with psychological assessment. These books have ranged from the theoretical to the clinical. However, most of the pragmatics involved in the day-to-day activities of the psychological assessor often have been neglected in press. Also, very often, particularly in the case of motoric behavioral assessment, strategies carried out have required use of instrumentation and research assistants. This is a luxury most of us do not have. In light of the above, the primary objective of *Psychological Assessment in Clinical Practice: A Pragmatic Guide* is to provide the reader (students and practitioners alike) with the realities of conducting psychological assessment in clinical settings that lack a plethora of research assistants and staff. Indeed, most individuals become solo practitioners or at best work in settings where they must conduct assessment themselves. This multi-authored book, then, details the specifics as to how this is done.

The book is divided into three sections. Following the two introductory chapters on "Pragmatic Issues of Assessment in Clinical Practice" and "Ethical Issues in Assessment" in section 1, the bulk of the book consists of the second section (Evaluation of Adults: eight chapters) and section 3 (Evaluation of Children: six chapters). Each chapter in sections 2 and 3 has a similar format:

1. Description of the disorder or problem
2. Range of assessment strategies available
3. Pragmatic issues encountered in clinical practice with this disorder
4. Case illustration
   a. Client description
   b. History of the disorder or problem
   c. Presenting complaints
   d. Assessment methods used
   e. Psychological assessment protocol (results to be presented)
   f. Targets selected for treatment
   g. Assessment of progress
5. Summary

ACKNOWLEDGMENTS

Many individuals have contributed to this final product. First, I thank the contributors who were willing to share their expertise with all of us. Second, I thank Dr. George Zimmar, former classmate in graduate school, longtime colleague, and an editor at Brunner/Routledge, for understanding the rationale and need for this volume. Third, I once again thank Carole Londerée, the best editorial assistant one might wish to have, for keeping the project on track. And fourth, I thank Tamara Tasker and Cynthia Polance for their fine technical help.

Michel Hersen
Forest Grove, Oregon

THE EDITOR

Michel Hersen, Ph.D., ABPP (State University of New York at Buffalo, 1966) is professor and dean, School of Professional Psychology, Pacific University, Forest Grove, Oregon. He completed his postdoctoral training at the West Haven VA (Yale University School of Medicine Program). He is past president of the Association for Advancement of Behavior Therapy. He has co-authored and co-edited 139 books and has published 224 scientific journal articles. He is co-editor of several psychological journals, including *Behavior Modification, Aggression and Violent Behavior: A Review Journal, Clinical Psychology Review, and Journal of Family Violence.* Dr. Hersen is editor-in-chief of the *Journal of Developmental and Physical Disabilities*, and the *Journal of Anxiety Disorders, and Clinical Case Studies*, which is totally devoted to description of clients and patients treated with psychotherapy. He is editor-in-chief of the 4-volume work entitled: *Comprehensive Handbook of Psychological Assessment* and the 2-volume work entitled: *Encyclopedia of Psychotherapy.* He has been the recipient of numerous grants from the National Institute of Mental Health, the Department of Education, the National Institute of Disabilities and Rehabilitation Research, and the March of Dimes Birth Defects Foundation. He is a diplomate of the American Board of Professional Psychology, fellow of the American Psychological Association, distinguished practitioner and member of the National Academy of Practice in Psychology, and recipient of the Distinguished Career Achievement Award in 1996 from the American Board of Medical Psychotherapists and Psychodiagnosticians. Finally, at one point in his career, he was in full-time private practice and on several occasions he has had part-time private practices.

THE AUTHORS

Vincent J. Adesso, Ph.D., ABPP, is professor of psychology at the University of Wisconsin-Milwaukee. His research interests focus on understanding the role of social learning in the causes and consequences of alcohol consumption. Much of his work has examined the effects of alcohol expectancies on behavior after drinking. Currently, he is working to develop a college-level intervention for binge drinking.

Maria E. A. Armento is a graduate student in the clinical psychology program at the University of Tennessee, Knoxville. Her main research interest is in depression most specifically in the area of treatment outcome. She is presently working on a project exploring the effectiveness and feasibility of a brief behavioral activation treatment for depression for clinically depressed cancer patients within a primary care setting.

Todd C. Buckley, Ph.D., is a research scientist at the VA Boston Healthcare System and an assistant professor in the department of psychiatry at the Boston University School of Medicine. His research interests include the interface between psychopathology and physical health, with a particular focus on posttraumatic stress disorder (PTSD). In addition, he has completed descriptive psychopathology studies and treatment outcome trials with PTSD patient populations. He has authored/coauthored 33 journal articles and book chapters in these areas of investigation.

Robert Bare currently is a graduate student in the clinical psychology program at the University of Tennessee and is completing his internship at the Federal Correctional Instution in Butner, North Carolina. His research interests are in the areas of psychopathy and the relation of psychopathic behaviors to anxiety and depressive mood states.

Ron A. Cisler, Ph.D., is an associate professor of Health Sciences and director of the Center for Urban Population Health at the University of Wisconsin-Milwaukee. He also is affiliated with the University of Wisconsin Medical School and Aurora Healthcare, Inc. His research interests lie broadly in assessment and intervention of alcohol problems.

John F. Clarkin, Ph.D., is a professor of clinical psychology in psychiatry at the Weill Medical College of Cornell University and director of psychology for NewYork Presbyterian Hospital. Dr. Clarkin is the codirector of the Personality Disorders Institute. He is on the Research Faculty at the Columbia Psychoanalytic Institute. Dr. Clarkin's academic writing has focused on the phenomenology and treatment of personality disorders, and the theoretical underpinning for differential treatment planning of psychiatric patients. His research activities have focused on the phenomenology of the personality disorders and the treatment of patients with borderline personality disorder and bipolar disorder. He is the author of numerous articles and books on psychopathology, treatment planning, and personality disorders. Two recent and relevant books include: John F. Clarkin and Mark Lenzenweger, *Major Theories of Personality Disorder,* and John F. Clarkin, Frank Yeomans, and Otto F. Kernberg, *Psychotherapy of Borderline Personality.*

Lara Delmolino, Ph.D., is a research assistant professor at Rutgers, the State University of New Jersey. She also serves as the assistant director for research at the Douglass Developmental Disabilities Center, a program for children and adults with autism. Dr. Delmolino has experience in the assessment and treatment of children with autism, and pursues her research interests in applied behavior analysis and autism.

Brad B. Evans, M.S., received his B.S. in psychology from Southern Oregon University and his M.S. in clinical psychology from Pacific University. He is currently in the 4th year of the Psy.D program at Pacific University and is preparing to start an internship in the summer of 2004 with the U.S. Air Force at Wilford Hall Medical Center.

Sydney Ey, Ph.D., received her B.A. in 1985 from Yale University, her Ph.D. in clinical psychology at the University of Vermont in 1993, and completed her internship at Judge Baker Children's Center/Children's Hospital in Boston. Before coming to Pacific University, Dr. Ey was at the Medical University of South Carolina and University of Memphis. Her research interests are in the areas of resilience in children and adults with a particular focus on the development and importance of optimism and effective coping responses. Currently, as director of the school of professional psychology's primary practicum site, the Psychological Service Center, Dr. Ey is involved in teaching, supervision, and research on client outcomes and therapeutic alliance within a training clinic setting.

Tamara Fahnhorst, M.P.H., is a grant coordinator in the Division of Child and Adolescent Psychiatry at the University of Minnesota. She received her master's degree in maternal and child public health from the University of

Minnesota in 2000. For 15 years Ms. Fahnhorst has implemented prevention and intervention initiatives for children with disruptive behavior. Ms. Fahnhorst's areas of special interest include cognitive-behavioral skills training for children with disruptive behavior and brief intervention for adolescents who abuse substances.

Kurt A. Freeman, Ph.D., is an assistant professor in the Department of Pediatrics, Child Development and Rehabiliation Center, Oregon Health & Science University. He serves as the director of the neurobehavioral clinic and the coordinator of the behavioral pediatric treatment service. Dr. Freeman's research focuses on common and severe behavior problems in children and adolescents. In addition to conducting his own research, Dr. Freeman serves on the ediorial boards of *Aggression & Violent Behavior: A Review Journal, Behavior Modification,* and *Journal of Developmental and Physical Disabilities*.

Jacinda C. Hammel, M.S., is currently a doctoral student in clinical psychology at Auburn University. She received the B.S. in business and the B.S. in psychology from Indiana University in 1994 and 2001, respectively, and the M.S. in psychology from Auburn University in 2004. Her current interests include anxiety disorders, psychophysiology, and psychotherapy.

Sandra L. Harris, Ph.D., is a board of governors distinguished service professor at Rutgers, the State University of New Jersey, and the executive director of the Douglass Developmental Disabilities Center, which she founded in 1972 at the university. The Center has programs for people of all ages with autism. Professor Harris writes and lectures extensively on meeting the needs of people with autism using ABA teaching methods.

Clifford V. Hatt, Ed.D., NCSP, is coordinator of psychological services, Virginia Beach City Public Schools. He is adjunct associate professor of psychology at the College of William & Mary and at Norfolk State University. Dr. Hatt is a licensed clinical psychologist, a nationally certified school psychologist, and a fellow and diplomate of the American Board of Medical Psychotherapists. He received his doctoral degree in school psychology from the University of Northern Colorado.

Brandon B. Hayes, M.S., is a doctoral student in the department of psychology at the University of Wisconsin-Milwaukee.

Derek R. Hopko, Ph.D., is an assistant professor at the University of Tennessee. He graduated from West Virginia University and completed his residency and postdoctoral training at the University of Texas Medical

School in Houston. In general, his research and clinical interests focus on mood and anxiety disorders. Specifically, Dr. Hopko conducts treatment outcome research as it pertains to the behavioral treatment of clinical depression, also addressing coexistent medical conditions (i.e., cancer) that may be involved in the etiology and maintenance of depressive syndromes. Recent research has addressed the practicality of extending a brief behavioral activation approach to treating depression within a primary care environment. In the area of anxiety disorders, Dr. Hopko studies attentional processes among individuals with performance-based anxiety disorders, seeks to quantify the impact of anxious-responding on behavioral tasks, and conducts psychometric work evaluating the validity and reliability of current methods of assessing the construct of anxiety.

Heather Jennett, M.S., received her master's degree in psychology from Rutgers University in 2002 and is working on her Ph.D. in clinical psychology under the mentorship of Sandra Harris, Ph.D. Her clinical and research interests include the behavioral treatment of children with autism. She is currently completing a predoctoral internship at the Kennedy Krieger Institute at Johns Hopkins University.

Danny G. Kaloupek, Ph.D., is deputy director of the behavioral science division of the National Center for PTSD at VA Boston Healthcare System and associate professor in the departments of psychiatry and behavioral neuroscience at Boston University School of Medicine. Dr. Kaloupek's areas of interest include application of psychophysiological measurement to stress and anxiety disorders, and study of the health-related impact of traumatic stress. Dr. Kaloupek is active in the trauma field as a member of journal editorial boards and scientific review panels, and through governance of professional societies.

B.J. Larus, Ph.D., is associated with Aurora Sinai Medical Center and the Center for Addiction and Behavioral Health Research. Her research and clinical interests are in the area of addictions.

Carl W. Lejuez received his Ph.D. in 2000 from West Virginia University. After serving as faculty in the Brown University School of Medicine and as the director of Laboratory Research in the Addictions Research Group at Butler Hospital, he joined the Clinical Psychology Program at the University of Maryland in 2001. Dr. Lejuez's clinical and research interests focus on the development of ecologically valid laboratory analogues of addiction and their use to better understand the active ingredients of treatment. His most recent projects involve (1) the creation and validation of a behavirol task to predict adolescent risk-taking behaviors (e.g., drug use, unsafe sexual practices) and (2) the application of distress tolerance and behavioral activation strategies to smoking cessation.

Barbara Lopez, M.S., is a doctoral candidate at Florida International University. Ms. Lopez has received a National Institute on Drug Abuse Minority Supplement to conduct her dissertation research on anxiety and affective disorders and their associated risk for drug-use disorders. Ms. Lopez participates in ongoing research aimed at developing and evaluating psychosocial interventions for reducing phobic and anxiety disorders in children at the Child and Family Psychosocial Research Center.

Barry M. Maletzky, M.D., P.C., received a bachelor's degree from Columbia University in 1963 and a medical degree from the State University of New York in 1967. Following completion of his residency in psychiatry at the Oregon Health Sciences University in 1971, he has been in the private practice of psychiatry in Portland, where he also teaches psychiatry, both at Oregon Health Sciences University and at Pacific University. Dr. Maletzky has been conducting research in a variety of areas within psychiatry for the past 30 years, has authored over 60 scientific articles and 3 books in this field, and has been principal investigator in a number of clinical trials. Hobbies include mountain climbing and hiking. Dr. Maletzky is currently writing a book on mountain wildflowers in the Pacific Northwest.

Megan Martins, M.S., is a doctoral student in clinical psychology at Rutgers, the State University of New Jersey and the research coordinator at the Douglass Developmental Disabilities Center. Her primary clinical and research interests are the efficacy of behavioral treatments for children with autism.

Joel F. McClough, Ph.D., received his doctorate in clinical psychology from the University of Illinois at Chicago, and completed his clinical internship at the Payne Whitney Clinic of New York-Presbyterian Hospital/ Weill Medical College of Cornell University. He is a former fellow of psychology in psychiatry at the Personality Disorders Institute at New York-Presbyterian Hospital, Westchester Division. Dr. McClough is currently senior staff associate in the department of psychiatry, Columbia University College of Physicians and Surgeons, as well as research director at Hall-Brooke Behavioral Health Services in Westport, CT. Dr. McClough is also in private practice in New York City.

F. Dudley McGlynn, Ph.D., is a native of the Kansas City area in Missouri. He was graduated from Missouri Valley College in 1963 and received a Ph.D. in clinical psychology from the University of Missouri-Columbia in 1968. His academic career has included posts at Mississippi State

University, the University of Florida, the University of Missouri-Kansas City, and Auburn University. He has published mostly in the areas of behavior therapy, anxiety disorders, and topics along the interface of psychology and dentistry. He has served on the editorial boards of 7 journals.

Catherine Miller, Ph.D., is an assistant professor in the School of Professional Psychology at Pacific University, teaching ethics courses and supervising clinical training. She received her Ph.D. from West Virginia University and has worked as a court clinician, a community mental health therapist, and a private practitioner specializing in forensic issues.

Susannah L. Mozley, Ph.D., is a postdoctoral fellow in clinical psychology at the National Center for PTSD, affiliated with Boston VA Healthcare System and Boston University School of Medicine. She obtained her doctoral degree from Auburn University, including internship training at the Durham, North Carolina VA Medical Center. Her research interests include meaning-making processes in adjustment to trauma, assessment of PTSD, and the relationship between PTSD and externalizing behaviors (specifically substance abuse/dependence and antisociality).

Michael D. Newcomb, Ph.D., is professor of counseling psychology and former chair of the Division of Counseling Psychology and director of the Marriage and Family Therapy Program in the Rossier School of Education at the University of Southern California. He is also research psychologist and scientific director of the Substance Abuse Research Center in the Psychology Department at the University of California, Los Angeles (UCLA). He received his Ph.D. in clinical psychology from UCLA in 1979 and is a licensed clinical psychologist in the state of California. Dr. Newcomb is fellow in several divisions of the American Psychological Association and also fellow in the American Psychological Society. He is principal investigator on several grants from the National Institute on Drug Abuse. Professor Newcomb has published over two hundred papers and chapters and written three books: two on drug problems (*Consequences of Adolescent Drug Use* [with Bentler published by Sage] and *Drug Use in the Workplace* [published by Auburn House]), and the third on sexual abuse and development of women (*Sexual Abuse and Consensual Sex: Women's Developmental Patterns and Outcomes* [with Wyatt and Riederlie published by Sage]). Dr. Newcomb has served on several journal editorial boards including the *Journal of Personality and Social Psychology, Cultural Diversity and Ethnic Minority Psychology, Health Psychology, Journal of Counseling Psychology, Experimental and Clinical Psychopharmacology, Archives of Sexual Behavior, Journal of Addictive Diseases,* and *Journal of Child and Adolescent Substance Abuse.* His research interests include: etiology and consequences of adolescent drug abuse; cultural diversity; structural equation modeling, methodology, and multivariate analysis; human sexuality; health psychology; attitudes and affect related to nuclear war; etiology and consequences of childhood trauma; and cohabitation, marriage, and divorce. He has served on several national review and advisory committees for such groups as the National Academy of Science, National Institute on Drug Abuse, National Institute of Mental Health, Office of Substance Abuse Prevention, and various research centers around the country.

Helen Orvaschel, Ph.D., is a professor at the Center for Psychological Studies of Nova Southeastern University. She received her Ph.D. from the Graduate Faculty, New School for Social Research in New York and completed a postdoctoral fellowship in psychiatric epidemiology and population genetics from Yale University School of Medicine. She serves on the editorial boards of several journals, reviews manuscripts for a dozen others, served as a grant reviewer for the National Institute of Mental Health and the William T. Grant Foundation, and presented her work at national and international meetings. Dr. Orvaschel has published extensively and is the author of a diagnostic interview used internationally.

Allen G. Sandler, Ph.D., is an associate professor in the Special Education Program at Old Dominion University, Norfolk, Virginia. He coauthored this chapter while serving as a Fulbright Scholar in the Department of Psychology and Education at Hue University, Vietnam, where he established classroom programs for children with intellectual disabilities and developed assessment strategies for identifying children with mental retardation.

Steven L. Sayers, Ph.D., received his doctorate in clinical psychology from the University of North Carolina, Chapel Hill, in 1990. He is currently assistant professor in the Department of Psychiatry of the University of Pennsylvania. His research and clinical interests include the assessment and treatment of couples and families, as well as the role of family members in the outcome of psychiatric and medical problems.

Wendy K. Silverman, Ph.D., is professor of psychology and director of the Child and Family Psychosocial Research Center at Florida International University, Miami. Dr. Silverman has received several grants from the National Institute of Mental Health (NIMH) to conduct research on developing and evaluating psychosocial interventions for reducing phobic and anxiety disorders in children. She has published over 125 scientific articles and book chapters, and has coauthored four books. Dr. Silverman is editor of the *Journal of Clinical Child and Adolescent Psychology*, the flagship journal for Division 53 (clinical child and adolescent psychology) of the American Psychological Association, and is on the editorial board of ten other scientific journals.

Todd A. Smitherman, M.S., is currently a doctoral student in clinical psychology at Auburn University. He received the B.S. in psychology from Samford University in 2000 and the M.S. in psychology from Auburn University in 2002. His current interests include anxiety disorders, empirically supported treatments, and the science of clinical psychology.

Cynthia Steinhauser, Ph.D., received her Ph.D., L.C.S.W. in social service adminstration from the University of Chicago and is a licensed clinical social worker in Oregon. She has more than 25 years of experience in the fields of mental health and corrections including appointments for the Correctional Services of Canada. Dr. Steinhauser specializes in the cognitive/behavioral treatment of sexual offenders. Her work includes an arousal reconditioning workbook and a comparative treatment outcome study of the effectiveness of cognitive and behavioral methods in reducing deviant sexual arousal in groups of incarcerated pedophiles. Dr. Steinhauser is particularly interested in the development of techniques for the treatment of sexual offenders with developmental disabilities.

Tiffany M. Stewart, Ph.D., earned her Ph.D. from Louisiana State University. She completed a one-year internship at the Medical University of South Carolina in 2002. She is now a faculty member at the Pennington Biomedical Research Center and Our Lady of the Lake Regional Medical Center in Baton Rouge, Louisiana. Her research has focused upon eating disorders and obesity with a special emphasis on body image and mindfulness. She has published research journal articles and book chapters on the topics of eating disorders, dieting, behavior therapy, and the assessment and treatment of body image.

Donald A.Williamson, Ph.D., earned his Ph.D. from the University of Memphis. He completed a one-year internship at Western Psychiatric Institute and Clinic, University of Pittsburgh, in 1978. He is now chief of health psychology at the Pennington Biomedical Research Center, where he has been employed in a full-time position since 1999. His research has focused upon obesity and eating disorders. He has published research journal articles, book chapters, and one book on the topics of obesity, eating disorders, behavior therapy, behavioral medicine, and health psychology. He has been program director for the Eating Disorders Program at Our Lady of the Lake Regional Medical Center since 1991.

Kenneth C. Winters, Ph.D., is the director of the Center for Adolescent Substance Abuse Research and an associate professor in the department of Psychiatry at the University of Minnesota. He received his B.A. from the University of Minnesota and a Ph.D. in clinical psychology from the State University of New York at Stony Brook. His primary research interest is the prevention and treatment of adolescent drug abuse. Dr. Winters has published numerous research articles in this area, and has received several research grants from the National Institute of Health and various foundations. He is on the editorial board of the *Journal of Child and Adolescent Substance Abuse* and is an associate editor for the *Psychology of Addictive Behaviors*, the *Journal of Substance Abuse Treatment*, and the *Journal of Gambling Studies*. He was also the lead editor for two recent *Treatment Improvement Protocol Series* (numbers 31 and 32) published by the Center for Substance Abuse Treatment (SAMHSA) that focused on adolescent drug abuse assessment and treatment. He is a frequent invited plenary and workshop speaker, and is a consultant to many organizations, including the Hazelden Foundation, National Institute on Drug Abuse, Center for Substance Abuse Treatment, World Health Organization, and the Mentor Foundation (an international drug abuse prevention organization).

General Issues

Sydney Ey
Michel Hersen

Pragmatic Issues of Assessment in Clinical Practice

On the first day of a graduate psychology class in diagnostic interviewing, students are asked to describe what it takes to be a great detective. Keen observation, curiosity, strategic questions, perseverance, and deductive reasoning are some of the many qualities attributed to Sherlock Holmes, Miss Marple, Colombo, and Inspector Morse. The instructor then asks the class to consider how these same qualities might be applied in clinical practice — especially in relation to assessment and case conceptualization. Many parallels are drawn, as being a good clinician often calls for similar skills and experiences as a detective. In fact, some cognitive behavioral therapists even describe therapy to their clients as a collaborative investigation of the problem and search for possible solutions as in the case of detectives or scientists (e.g., Beck, 1995).

Regardless of clinicians' orientation, the ability to carry out a thorough investigation of a client's presenting problem is key to psychotherapy (e.g., Morrison, 1995). Clinicians use assessment to understand what brings the client to therapy, what types of treatment might be appropriate, and monitor whether interventions are helpful. In particular, there is a growing emphasis on the benefits of one aspect of assessment in clinical practice — ongoing evaluation of client progress in therapy or formal treatment outcome assessments (e.g., Lambert et al., 2001; Truax, 2002). Yet there are many challenges in clinical practice to carrying out initial and ongoing assessment with all clients. For example, in a recent survey of APA-accredited graduate psychology training programs, only 56% of clinic directors indicated that formal treatment outcome assessments were routinely conducted at their facilities (Tyler, Busseri, & King, 2002). Common barriers to assessment include lack of agreement on what to measure and anxiety regarding clinician evaluation, lack of interest, and fears of additional paper work burdening clients and therapists (e.g., Tyler et al. 2002). By contrast, sites that incorporated formal outcomes assessment into clinical practice reported benefits such as improved quality of care, training implications, and research possibilities (Tyler et al., 2002; Lambert et al., 2001). Clearly, the benefits to clients and clinicians warrant a close look at how to incorporate more formal and systematic assessment of treatment outcomes into practice.

In this chapter, key decision points in designing a treatment outcome assessment protocol will be outlined. The current context of assessment in practice as well as the types and purposes of assessment will be described. Finally, a case example of a treatment outcomes protocol developed in a large psychology training clinic will be used to demonstrate some of the possibilities and challenges.

☐ Context

A number of forces have influenced use of assessment by clinicians including theory, efficacy of therapy research, managed care, funding initiatives, and clinical training issues. There is a rich historical emphasis on scientific inquiry through careful assessment and observation in the field of clinical psychology as evidenced by such popular training models as the scientist-practitioner model (Benjamin & Baker, 2000) and local clinical scientist model (Stricker & Trierweiler, 1995). In all of these models, clinicians incorporate theory and research into their assessment, diagnosis, case conceptualization, and treatment planning. Specifically, the scientific aspect of psychology suggests that clinicians should be capable of measuring systematically what they do in session and whether their clients are making progress. In addition, clinicians use assessment to understand their clients' presenting problem and determine diagnosis if applicable.

A substantial literature exists showing that clinicians have used assessment to systematically evaluate whether their clients are benefiting from therapy (e.g., Weisz, Weiss, Alicke, & Klotz, 1987; Seligman, 1995). It must be acknowledged, however, that many initial studies of treatment outcomes were done in university or research-oriented settings, with additional resources such as grants, technical support (e.g., computer database, analyst), and research assistants to facilitate data collection, entry, and interpretation. The typical private practitioner or even clinician in an agency does not have the same resources to easily implement one of these formal treatment protocols (e.g., Plantz, Greenway, & Hendricks, 1997).

But managed care in the area of medical and mental health services and local and national funding sources for nonprofit agencies are increasingly calling for service providers in all settings to be accountable; service providers are being asked to use brief empirically validated interventions regardless of resources to carry out these evaluations (e.g., Chambless & Ollendick, 2001; Plantz et al., 1997). In other words, mental health care providers are required to document whether they are providing the best possible treatment to clients in the most efficient manner (i.e., least timely and expensive). Certainly, such additional scrutiny from funding sources and managed care case managers has encouraged clinicians to look for ways to clearly communicate the effectiveness of their services. Formal assessments at the beginning, during, and after therapy are crucial within these settings.

Assessment of client satisfaction and attitudes about seeking help is critical in order for clinicians to make the necessary changes in their practice to meet their clients' needs (e.g., Ey, Henning, & Shaw, 2000; Miller, Duncan, & Hubble, in press). Critical to the success of treatment is the client's willingness to even seek therapy in the first place. Unless clinicians have a sense of what the barriers might be to someone seeking help from them, they will be unable to address the concerns. For example, clinicians at a student counseling center speculated that potential consumers (distressed health professional students) were less likely to come to the center for help due to the location of the center next to financial aid and other well frequented offices (Ey et al., 2000). A survey of potential clients (students in the medical university) found that students were highly concerned about being seen by faculty or fellow students on their way into therapy and this concern was predictive of less willingness to seek help at the counseling center (Ey et al., 2000). Assessment of potential clients' perceptions of barriers to treatment can then influence service delivery to future clients and help clinicians be aware of changing trends in clinical practice.

Finally, as is evident in self-study requirements by the American Psychological Association Accreditation Committee (2003), graduate psychology programs and internships are being urged to collect systematic data on whether they are meeting their training objectives. An obvious training objective of clinical and counseling psychology programs is the preparation of master's or doctoral level clinicians who competently assess and treat their clients. Including formal treatment outcome evaluations in sites with clinicians-in-training would be one way to document the success of a training program's objective. Unfortunately, only one clinic reported looking at student clinicians' effectiveness in terms of client outcomes in the most recent study of formal treatment outcome research in training clinics; no one reported looking at supervisor's effectiveness in terms of their trainees' success with clients (Tyler et al., 2002).

To summarize, clinicians today are often trained in a model of psychology that is based on scientific and/or systematic evaluation of clients' concerns and treatment response. More recently, systems of care and funding sources are forcing clinicians to be clear about what they are providing clients and how their clients are responding. Additionally, clients are more likely to be asked to provide their perspectives on what brought them to therapy, what they were satisfied with, and what they found to be problematic. Marketing and service delivery are then influenced by feedback from clients and other referral sources. In short, most clinicians must be prepared to incorporate some formal assessment and evaluative component in their practices in order to be successful.

☐ Types and Purposes of Assessment

The function of assessment in clinical practice varies greatly and can include any and all of the following objectives:

- Diagnosis and/or evaluation of clients' reason for seeking treatment
- Case conceptualization
- Treatment planning
- Monitoring of client response to treatment
- Change clients' behavior or cognitions through increased self-awareness (e.g., self-monitoring, behavioral experiments)
- Program evaluation or individual clinician evaluation of effectiveness (e.g., Callaghan, 2001)

Not surprisingly, there is a great deal of variability in what assessments are used to achieve these multiple purposes (e.g., Morrison, 1995; Bufka, Crawford, & Levitt, 2002).

Interview

The most common form of assessment in practice is the initial interview with the client – also known as the intake or diagnostic interview (Summerfeldt & Antony, 2002). A mental status examination of affect, mood, thought and language processes, risk issues, concentration, and memory also may be incorporated within the interview. In the interview, clinicians typically assess the following: (a) client's current symptoms, history of presenting problem, duration, onset, intensity, frequency, and context, (b) client's coping strategies, strengths, resources, (c) family, educational, and relationship history, (d) medical and mental health history, (e) risk issues, (f) prior trauma or abuse history, (g) substance abuse issues, (h) past treatment, (i) client expectations of therapy, and (j) co-occurring or comorbid psychological symptoms not initially mentioned in presenting problem. Clients without a recent physical exam are often encouraged to have a medical examination to rule out possible medical conditions that mimic mental health problems (e.g., Morrison, 1997).

A large literature is available on the benefits and drawbacks of structured diagnostic interviews versus semistructured or unstructured interviews (see review by Summerfeldt & Antony, 2002). In brief, researchers such as Spitzer and his colleagues (1974) have noted that there is less agreement among clinicians about diagnosis of a particular client when the clinicians rely upon unstructured interviews rather than a structured protocol. Structured interviews such as the Anxiety Disorders Interview Schedule (ADIS-IV) for the *Diagnostic and Statistical Manual of Mental Disorders*, 4th edition (DSM-IV) (Brown, Di Nardo, & Barlow, 1994) and *Structured Clinical Interview for DSM-IV Axis I Disorders* (SCID-CV; First, Spitzer, Gibbon, & Williams, 1997) standardize how questions are asked, what questions are asked, and how diagnostic criteria are applied to yield a final diagnosis. Interviews are designed for trained mental health professionals to administer and vary in length from 45 to 60 minutes on average. Although reliability and validity vary across interviews and types of disorder, structured interviews yield better results in terms of diagnostic accuracy than unstructured interviews (Summerfeldt & Antony, 2002). Yet a structured protocol may miss some key aspects of a client's presentation and is typically atheoretical in orientation.

Some clinicians are concerned that the structured format may interfere with rapport building in this vital first session with clients. Rogers (2001) warns against this "either/or fallacy" about structured interviewers coming across as cold to their clients. He argues that skilled interviewers can use structured questions in such an expert manner that the structure is less obvious and the client feels comfortable and heard. Nonetheless, Rogers (2001) does acknowledge that even the most skilled interviewer must be careful to not miss important clinical data outside the structured interview. "Premature closure" is cited as a common error among inexperienced clinicians who rush to apply a diagnosis or wrap up an interview without taking into consideration all the data — especially discrepant data (Rogers, 2002, p. 4). Semistructured interviews usually include a structured protocol regarding psychological symptoms but may include more open-ended questions to incorporate other information besides diagnosis such as client expectations and strengths.

Standardized Questionnaires

Clinicians may incorporate in their initial and subsequent meetings with clients some additional measures for clients to complete before and after therapy sessions. Standardized questionnaires that have been evaluated to be reliable and valid in the measurement of a particular area of concern are recommended. Use of standardized measures facilitates the clinician and client evaluating how the client's symptoms compare to other clients across a number of settings and allows the clinician to more systematically monitor progress in sessions. In addition, the use of brief standardized questionnaires completed by clients facilitates screening for mental health issues in primary care medical settings where mental health issues often go undetected (Bufka, Crawford, & Levitt, 2002).

Measures vary in terms of length and content. Commonly used questionnaires include broad-band measures of psychological distress such as the Brief Symptom Inventory (BSI; Derogatis & Melisaratos, 1983) or Outcome Questionnaire-45 (OQ-45.2; Lambert et al., 1996). Child clinicians often use measures of child and adolescent emotional and behavior problems such as the parent-completed Child Behavior Checklist (Achenbach, 1991a) or teacher-report or teen self-report versions (Achenbach, 1991b; Achenbach, 1991c respectively). Clinicians also may incorporate narrow-band measures of specific symptoms or diagnosis within their practice to get more focused information on client presenting problems and progress in treatment. For example, clients may complete psychometrically sound questionnaires of specific symptoms such as depression (e.g., Beck Depression Inventory; Beck & Steer, 1987) or anxiety (e.g., Beck Anxiety Inventory, Beck & Steer, 1990).

Partners, roommates, parents, and other collateral sources also may be asked to complete questionnaires on the client's symptoms to provide another perspective on the client's situation. For example, in a study on problem drinking among undergraduates, researchers asked roommates also to report on subjects' drinking episodes (Marlatt et al., 1998). Data from roommates were helpful in determining accuracy of reporting by undergraduates who were at high risk for problem drinking (Marlatt et al., 1998). Similarly, child clinicians are familiar with the range in perspectives that parents, teachers, and children have about the child's problem. For example, Achenbach and his colleagues (1993) found that there was very little agreement between parents' ratings, teachers' ratings, and teen's self-report ratings on parallel measures of youth emotional and behavioral problems. All perspectives are important to take into consideration as behavior certainly varies by context and by informant; treatment planning needs to take these differences into consideration. For example, a child who is rated as highly oppositional by one parent and not by the other may have different relationships with each parent and need different types of intervention from each parent. Or perhaps the discrepancy in parental ratings is due to different expectations and attitudes about child behavior — a potentially rich topic in treatment.

Observation

Although clinicians with a behavioral emphasis (e.g., Truax, 2002) are likely to incorporate observational procedures in their assessment and treatment planning, many clinicians are unlikely to regularly include formal observation of clients in contexts outside of the therapy setting. Observation of a client's behavior in settings such as the classroom, work setting, social arena, or home may provide the clinician with "clues" into the relevant antecedents and consequences of a client's behavior that the client is unable to detect and report on in session. In addition, contextual factors such as a teacher's way of communicating, the noise level in a classroom, and other children's behavior can be important factors to consider in evaluating a child with reported "off task" and inattentive behavior. Students trained to do classroom observation of children are often encouraged to clearly define the behavior of concern ahead of time and then record how often the target child and other comparison children nearby engage in this behavior (e.g., Sattler, 1988). When the results are similar, an environmental explanation for the child's school problems may be more appropriate than a diagnosis for the child. Of course there are constraints with observation including the time and cost of traveling to settings to observe, the possibility of changing the behavior due to being present and observing, and issues related to confidentiality.

Therapy Process

How clients feel about the therapeutic alliances or relationships with their therapists is moderately but reliably related to positive therapy outcomes (Horvath & Symonds, 1991). Specifically, relationship factors such as feeling good about the tasks of the session, goals of treatment, and emotional bond with the therapist account for a significant proportion of the variance in treatment gains (Horvath & Symonds, 1991). Furthermore, such alliance appears to be established quickly — perhaps within the first three sessions of therapy (Horvath & Greenberg, 1989). If this perspective by clients is so closely linked to success in treatment, it is essential that clinicians early on and throughout therapy monitor client perspectives on therapeutic alliance. Psychometrically sound measures such as the short and long versions of the Working Alliance Inventory (Horvath & Greenberg, 1989; Tracey & Kokotovic, 1990) allow clinicians and their clients to evaluate and address therapeutic alliance in a systematic fashion.

Additionally, therapy process is influenced by the clinician's assessment of client's motivational level or readiness to change (Miller, Duncan, & Hubble, in press). There are measures of readiness to change, including the University of Rhode Island Change Assessment (URICA; McConnaughy, DiClemente, Prochaska, & Velicer, 1989) stages of change measure that clients can complete at the beginning of therapy and throughout treatment. Clinicians also can regularly assess client's expectations and motivation to address issues through direct inquiry in session. Common barriers to treatment progress such as client resistance and hopelessness can be overcome through direct but nonjudgmental discussion of motivation issues in treatment (Miller et al., in press).

Therapy Progress: Outcomes

Although this chapter is not an extensive and exhaustive review of the substantial literature on conducting treatment outcomes studies (see Chambless & Ollendick, 2001), several recommendations can be applied to clinical practitioners. First, clinicians and clients can use standardized broad and narrow-band questionnaires (described earlier) to regularly assess and discuss progress (or lack of it) in treatment. Second, therapists and clients can develop idiographic measures particular to the client's targets (e.g., treatment objectives) and monitor progress in those areas (e.g., 0 = no progress to 100% = success). For example, a client with severe anxiety about dating might rate each week how much progress he has made toward his treatment objective to initiate conversations with members of the opposite sex. This kind of information focuses the therapy session and helps the client and therapist identify areas where interventions may need to be modified to increase treatment gains. Third, lack of psychological symptoms may be insufficient to fully evaluating client growth. Seligman and his colleagues writing in the area of positive psychology (e.g., Seligman & Csikszentmihalyi, 2000) have argued that absence of depressive symptoms, for example, does not mean the person is necessarily happy. Perhaps clinicians need to systematically assess the presence of positive behaviors as well as the disappearance of negative behaviors. For example, there are measures of positive affect (e.g., the Positive and Negative Affect Scale (PANAS) Watson, Clark, & Tellegen, 1988) and optimism (Life Orientation Test-Revised [LOT-R]; Scheier, Carver, & Bridges, 1994). Additionally, the client's ability to initiate positive relationships with others (the desired behavior) may be more relevant to treatment evaluation than a decrease in their social anxiety scores on the Beck Anxiety Inventory (BAI; Beck & Steer, 1990).

Finally, evaluating the client's ability to maintain treatment gains at follow-up is crucial to knowing whether an intervention has lasting effects (e.g., Kazdin & Weisz, 1998). Exit interviews, surveys, and client satisfaction measures may be administered in the last session and in follow-up assessments often at 6 months or 1 year after treatment has ended. Exit interviews often assess whether the clients believes they have made progress, what they liked and disliked about therapy, and how hopeful they are about being able to maintain the changes.

Comment

Clinicians are faced with a wealth of choices in terms of assessment in practice. A large literature exists that supports use of semistructured or structured interviews and standardized broad and narrow-band questionnaires for diagnosis, case conceptualization, and treatment planning and monitoring. Furthermore, additional factors linked to treatment outcomes, such as client ratings of therapeutic alliance, readiness to change, motivation, and optimism may be systematically evaluated during treatment. Finally, the measurement of treatment gains may be based upon ongoing standardized measures of psychological symptoms as well as more idiographic ratings by therapists and clients of client progress on specific treatment objectives.

☐ Key Decision Points

The development and implementation of an assessment protocol for one's clinical practice need not be intimidating but it can require time and careful planning in order for changes to be meaningful. The process of developing and implementing formal assessment in practice typically requires at least 4 steps: (1) planning and design, (2) feasibility evaluation, (3) piloting and implementing, and (4) evaluating.

To demonstrate some of the decisions made during this process, a case example will be used of a large psychology training clinic in which the staff revised the psychotherapy assessment process for adult clients. The Psychological Service Center serves as the primary training site for first and second year practicum students in the School of Professional Psychology's doctoral psychology program at Pacific University. Each year, approximately 40 new doctoral psychology student clinicians are assigned to the clinic to work with some of the 700 clients seen annually at the clinic. Ten faculty supervisors and a small administrative staff oversee clinical and administrative operations of the clinic. The mission of the training clinic is threefold: training, clinical service to the community (many of them who lack adequate resources to see private practitioners), and research. The clinic director determined that a committee of supervisors, staff, and student clinicians was needed to evaluate clinician concerns about excessive paper work, unstructured and awkward intake interviews, vague phone screening protocols, and a lack of standardized treatment outcome measures and research opportunities.

Planning and Design

The first step of a new protocol is to put together a working group of clinicians and relevant staff to address the following questions:

- What do we want to accomplish with an assessment protocol?
- How will this information be used and by whom?
- Who will be responsible for administering, entering, scoring, and interpreting assessment data?

At the training clinic, committee members made recommendations after reviewing the current protocols in these areas and the literature on diagnostic interviews, treatment outcome measures, and client satisfaction questionnaires and exit surveys. An outside consultant who is a clinical psychologist with expertise in the design of forms, ACCESS databases, and program evaluation was hired to assist in developing and implementing the protocol.

The clinic committee decided that the purpose of the assessment should be to improve initial diagnostic interviewing to inform treatment planning, to increase therapist awareness of treatment progress in order to improve treatment, and to evaluate client satisfaction and progress at the end of treatment. An underlying goal of all of these changes was to improve the training of future doctoral level clinicians by providing them with more feedback and guidance on their clinical efforts.

With these purposes in mind, a decision was made to shift the intake interview to being semistructured to increase clinicians' thoroughness in evaluating clients at the initial meeting. Of note, the phone screening for individuals calling to make an initial intake appointment was structured and more comprehensive in order to reduce the number of clients who came for intake and were immediately found to be ineligible for services due to limitations of the training clinic services. This level of structure helped create a standard approach to working with initial clients and fully informing them of the procedures at the training clinic before their appointment.

In the diagnostic intake interview less experienced clinicians seemed to need the prompts to address a range of Axis I disorders rather than solely inquire about the client's presenting problem. As described earlier by Rogers (2001), inexperienced interviewers are prone to rush to conclusions without considering all of the data gathered from the interview and other measures. Standardized measures with normative data to compare clients' symptoms to were added at intake and subsequent therapy sessions. Specifically, as part of the intake assessment all adult clients also completed a well-validated measure of psychological distress (OQ-45.2; Lambert et al., 1996), a short version of a stages of change measure (URICA; McConnaughy et al., 1989), a measure of alcohol abuse (Alcohol Use Disorder Identification Test [AUDIT]; Barbor, De La Fuente, Saunders, & Grant, 1989), and a survey of relationship satisfaction and history of domestic violence.

In addition, clients completed a redesigned, more user-friendly questionnaire that included questions about the client's reason for seeking help, exposure to domestic violence, abuse, and other forms of trauma as a child and recently as an adult, medical issues, risk issues, substance abuse history, expectations for therapy, and prior treatment experiences. Prior to the modified protocol, interviewers did not routinely assess for commonly seen issues in mental health settings such as domestic violence, substance abuse, and past and recent trauma (e.g.,

Morrison, 1995). Failure to address these issues had immediate implications for proper treatment planning.

Another change in the clinic operations was in the area of monitoring treatment gains and process variables. To monitor progress in treatment, all adult clients complete the OQ-45.2 every session for the first four sessions and then every fourth session afterward and at the last meeting. The decision to administer the OQ-45.2 the first four sessions every time was made to capture a large number of clients who typically left within the first through third sessions and quickly identify clients who were highly distressed and not experiencing much relief since beginning treatment. Clinicians who were informed about clients who were highly distressed early on in treatment were more likely to retain the clients in therapy than clinicians who did not know the results of their clients' OQ-45.2 scores (Lambert et al., 2001).

To increase specificity of treatment outcome monitoring, supervisors were encouraged to work with their supervisees to include narrow-band measures, such as the BDI or BAI, to assess for changes in particular symptoms throughout treatment and the end of treatment. A form was created in which the client and clinician could chart weekly progress on specific client objectives (treatment goals).

In order to monitor and address a vital factor in treatment, therapeutic relationship, all clinicians and clients filled out the therapist and client versions of the short form of the Working Alliance Inventory (Tracey & Kokotovic, 1989) at the fourth session and every fourth session afterward. Therapeutic alliance is believed to be established by at least the third session (Horvath & Greenberg, 1989). Therapists were encouraged to enter and score their OQ-45.2 and WAIs in the customized database soon after administration and share the results with their clients using visual means (graphing out the results each week) and/or discussion.

As no exit surveys of client satisfaction, attitudes about progress made in treatment, and overall evaluation of progress could be found to meet the specific interests of the clinic (i.e., reasonable cost, comprehensive), a new questionnaire was designed. Clients were asked to complete the exit survey at the last session (or surveys were mailed to them following ending of therapy). In particular, researchers at the clinic interested in evaluating the reasons clients end treatment wanted to know how therapist and client ratings of the reason for ending therapy would compare. For example, although a therapist might identify that a client was prematurely ending treatment, a client might see treatment as fully successful and therefore ending on time as expected. The literature on premature termination (e.g., Wierzbicki & Pekarik, 1993) shows that there is ongoing debate about the definition of premature termination and the necessity of directly assessing clients' perspectives about progress in treatment and reasons for ending.

Overall administration of the new protocol was primarily by the clinic director with the help for a graduate research assistant. Each clinician was assigned responsibility for administering the measures to their clients prior to the assigned session, entering the data in the database, and scoring it. Clinicians were encouraged to include the scored data in their supervision meetings, therapy sessions, and charts, as appropriate. The database consultant designed a customized ACCESS database that scores the measures and even generates full text reports for the intake interview and scored measures and termination report.

Feasibility Evaluation

During the first phase of the project, feasibility issues often arise as the realists at the table ask "who is going to pay for these changes?" and "do we really have the resources to pull these ideas off?" All of these concerns are valid. Certainly, clinicians in any setting must consider the cost of copyrighted questionnaires and scoring programs or hiring a computer database consultant. Often if a copyrighted questionnaire is too expensive to purchase for a practice, the clinician may be able to search journals for other measures that are in the public domain or more affordable. Some measures can be purchased at a reduced rate by training clinics or researchers.

The training clinic could not have implemented these changes without the funding to hire the consultant to design the database that clinicians use to enter and score the measures, create intake and termination reports, and develop a potential database for training and research purposes. Plantz and his colleagues in the nonprofit sector (1997) argue that nonprofits typically lack the technical expertise to quickly and easily put in place an outcome evaluation protocol; hiring a consultant to assist with this technology may be critical.

Even prior to the arrival of the federal law, Health Insurance Portability and Accountability Act (HIPAA), clinicians have operated under strict legal and ethical guidelines regarding protecting the confidentiality of the clinical charts. Clinicians must ensure that any clinical information that can be traced back to a specific client due to personal health information (PHI) such as name, address, client file number, and date of birth is protected and cannot be accessed by others without permission. Databases on computers that are linked to a network could be vulnerable to breaches in confidentiality if the network does not have an adequate "firewall" or protection against unauthorized user access. As a result of these concerns, a decision was made to take the computer with the clinic database offline so that no one could access the database via a network. Proper passwords were put in place and the computer is in a secured location.

Another factor to consider in feasibility is the time and burden to clients, staff, and clinicians using these new protocols. For example, the initial paper work at intake was taking some clients 30–45 minutes to complete prior to a 90-minute intake interview. Several questionnaires were eliminated to make the paper work less burdensome to clients. Clinicians were assigned to administer and enter the questionnaires, as it was believed that they would be more invested in the results than a staff person assigned to enter all measures. There are pros and cons to having staff members versus clinicians carry out this aspect of the assessment protocol. The ACCESS database fields, however, are user-friendly and make it easy and quick for clinicians to enter their data and even text paragraphs when writing up their intake report. This database design has allowed clinicians to create professional looking, typed reports that are immediately applicable to their practice.

Piloting and Implementing

Even the best detectives know that "the best laid plans" or initial deductions can be off base. Part of being a detective/clinician is testing out hypotheses and modifying in response to data. The same holds true for developing an assessment protocol. It is critical that questionnaires be piloted with "pseudo-clients," clinicians and several clients in order to identify areas that are unclear, too lengthy, or problematic. The reading level of the measures must be checked in order to assess whether the clinical population being seen will be able to easily understand and complete the measures. Reading level can be easily checked in software programs such as Microsoft Word (in the Tools menu).

The pilot protocol can then be modified before being fully implemented. Of course as more data comes in and clinician's interests or objectives for the protocol change, the measures can be changed. In particular, at the training clinic the pilot stage demonstrated the importance of getting clinicians, staff, and supervisors fully oriented to the purpose of the protocol and ways of administering, scoring, and interpreting the results. A series of training/orientation meetings was held to walk everybody through the procedure. Individual teams of clinicians then met with a graduate research assistant who was familiar with the database to receive extra hands on training. The assistant was available to provide additional training and consultation. A manual was created to explain the computer database fields and the assessment measures to clinicians. A log was created for each chart to remind clinicians of the sessions in which they needed to remember to administer particular questionnaires. The database needed to be modified to make certain menus easier to read.

Evaluation

Finally, ongoing assessment of the utility of the assessment protocol is needed. Formal evaluations can be conducted (e.g., see reviews by Schalock, 1995) to determine if objectives of the protocol are being met. Less formal evaluations might be conducted through a committee of clinicians and staff reviewing the use of the measures and identifying areas needing additional work. For example, the director of the clinic has noted that some student clinicians are starting to incorporate into psychotherapy sessions and notes client and therapist ratings of therapeutic alliance and overall distress into psychotherapy sessions — one of the stated goals of the committee. Furthermore, student feedback regarding the usefulness of the measures suggests that they are finding the intake format and questionnaires to be a great improvement and helpful in their efforts to diagnose and conceptualize the case at the initial session. It must be acknowledged that, like other sites, noncompliance with administering and entering all measures during treatment and at the end is a problem — especially among more advanced clinicians who are having to adjust their way of doing assessment. Newer clinicians have been more open to the changes and all subsequent years of clinicians are being trained in these procedures in their first year of classes — even before they come to the training clinic.

As the new protocol has been implemented for only 7 months, formal analyses of the data are just being scheduled. Several students are using the database for master's theses research. In addition, the director will be looking for ways to use the data to inform training. For example, would supervisors respond differently (and more effectively) if they received regular, systematic data on how their supervisees' clients are progressing and describing the therapeutic alliance? Are there differences in how clinicians respond to their clients' ratings? What are the treatment implications? Some of these questions will be addressed as more information is adduced.

☐ Summary

Clinical practice has a long tradition of scientific inquiry in treatment settings. Managed care, funding initiatives, and consumer groups demand that clinicians be clearer about what they are trying to accomplish in treatment. Clinicians are being asked to engage in thoughtful assessments that evaluate a client's presenting problem, treatment needs, and response to treatment. This chapter has provided an overview of some of the pragmatic issues related to assessment in clinical practice. Subsequent chapters will include more detailed information about narrowband measures and focused assessments.

The development of structured and semistructured interviews has lead to improved diagnostic accuracy (e.g., Rogers, 2001). The large literature on treatment outcomes provides examples of ways of systematically evaluating treatment gains with standardized, psychometrically strong measures. In addition, for the clinician who wants additional or different information than that yielded by standardized measures, there are ways of creating idiographic measures of progress such as client weekly ratings of progress on specific objectives.

Although many measures are readily available to clinicians, feasibility issues such as computer database resources, cost of measures, and time to administer and score measures must be considered. Most importantly, clinicians need to feel as if the data generated is directly applicable and helpful to their work. Perhaps "process is as important as the product," (Plantz et al. 1997, p. 88). The process of asking clients how they perceive their treatment and progress may be more important than the actual results in the end. Clinicians are sending a clear message that clients' perspectives count and will be systematically evaluated.

☐ References

Achenbach, T. M. (1993). *Empirically based taxonomy: How to use syndromes and profile types deprived from the CBCL/4–18, TRF, and YSF*. Burlington: University of Vermont, Department of Psychiatry.

Achenbach, T. M. (1991a). *Manual for the Child Behavior Checklist/4–18 and 1991 Profile*. Burlington: University of Vermont, Department of Psychiatry.

Achenbach, T. M. (1991b). *Manual for the Teacher Report Form and 1991 Profile*. Burlington: University of Vermont, Department of Psychiatry.

Achenbach, T. M. (1991c). *Manual for the Youth Self-Report Form and 1991 Profile*. Burlington: University of Vermont, Department of Psychiatry.

American Psychological Association (2003). *Self-Study Instructions for Internship Programs*. Washington, DC: American Psychological Association.

Barbor, T., De La Fuente, J. R., Saunders, J. & Grant, M. (1989). *The Alcohol Use Disorders Identification Test: Guidelines for use in primary health care* (WHO Publication No. 89:4). Geneva: World Health Organization.

Beck, A. T., & Steer, R. A. (1987). *Manual for the revised Beck Depression Inventory.* San Antonio, TX: Psychological Corporation.

Beck, A. T., & Steer, R. A. (1990). *Manual for the revised Beck Anxiety Inventory.* San Antonio, TX: Psychological Corporation.

Beck, J. S. (1995). *Cognitive therapy: Basics and beyond.* New York: Guilford Press.

Benjamin, L. T., & Baker, D. B., (2000). Boulder at 50: Introduction to the section. *American Psychologist, 55,* 233–235.

Brown, T. A., Di Nardo, P. A., & Barlow, D. H. (1994). *Anxiety Disorders Interview Schedule for DSM-IV (ADIS-IV).* San Antonio, TX: Psychological Corporation.

Bufka, L. F., Crawford, J. I., & Levitt, J. T. (2002). Brief screening assessments for managed care and primary care. In M. M. Antony & D. H. Barlow (Eds.). *Handbook of assessment and treatment planning for psychological disorders* (pp. 38–63). New York: Guilford Press.

Callaghan, G. M. (2001). Demonstrating clinical effectiveness for individual practitioners and clinics. *Professional Psychology: Research and Practice, 32,* 289–297.

Chambless, D. L., & Ollendick, T. H. (2001). Empirically supported psychological interventions: Controversies and evidence. *Annual Review of Psychology, 52,* 685–716.

Derogatis, L. R., & Melisaratos, N. (1983). The Brief Symptom Inventory: An introductory report. *Psychological Medicine, 13,* 596–605.

Ey, S., Henning, K., & Shaw, D. L. (2000). Attitudes and factors related to seeking mental health treatment among medical and dental students. *Journal of College Student Psychotherapy, 14,* 23–39.

First, M. B., Spitzer, R. L., Gibbon, M., & Williams, J. B. W. (1997). *Structured Clinical Interview for DSM-IV Axis I Disorders (SCID-I)-Clinician version.* Washington, DC: American Psychiatric Press.

Horvath, A. O., & Greenberg, L. A. (1989). Development and validation of the Working Alliance Inventory. *Journal of Counseling Psychology, 36,* 223–233.

Horvath, A. O., & Symonds, B. D. (1991). Relationship between working alliance and outcome in psychotherapy: A meta-analysis. *Journal of Counseling Psychology, 38,* 139–149.

Kazdin, A. E., & Weisz, J. R. (1998). Identifying and developing empirically supported child and adolescent treatments. *Journal of Consulting and Clinical Psychology, 66,* 19–36.

Lambert, M. J., Hansen, N. B., Umphress, V., Lulnnen, K., Okiiskhi, J. Burlingame, G. M., & Reisinger, C. W. (1996). *Administration and scoring manual for the OQ-45.2.* Stevenson, MD: American Professional Credentialing Services LLC.

Lambert, M. J., Whipples, J. L., Smart, D. W., Vermeersch, D. A., Nielsen, S. L., & Hawkins, E. J. (2001). The effects of providing therapists with feedback on patient progress during psychotherapy: Are outcomes enhanced? *Psychotherapy Research, 11,* 49–68.

Marlatt, G. A., Baer, J. S., Kirvlahan, D. R., Dimeff, L., Larimer, M., Quigley, L. A., Somers, J. M., & Williams, E. (1998). Screening and brief intervention for high-risk college student drinkers: Results from a 2-year follow-up assessment. *Journal of Counseling and Clinical Psychology, 66,* 604–615.

McConnaughy, E. A., DiClemente, C. C., Prochaska, J. O., Velicer, W. F. (1989). Stages of change in psychotherapy: A follow-up report. *Psychotherapy: Theory, research, practice, training, 26,* 494–503.

Miller, S. D., Duncan, B. L., & Hubble, M. A. (in press). Client-directed, outcome-informed clinical work: Directing attention to "what works" in treatment. Retrieved April 28, 2003 from http://www.talkingcure.com.

Morrison, J. (1997). *When psychological problems mask medical disorders: A guide for psychotherapists.* New York: Guilford Press.

Morrison, J. (1995). *The first interview revised for DSM-IV.* New York: Guilford Press.

Plantz, M. C., Greenway, M. T., & Hendricks, M. (1997). *Outcome measurement: Showing results in the nonprofit sector. New directions for evaluation, 75.* New York: Jossey-Bass.

Rogers, R. (2001). *Handbook of diagnostic and structured interviewing.* New York: Guilford Press.

Sattler, J. M. (1988). *Assessment of children* (3rd ed). San Diego, CA: Jerome M. Sattler Publishing.

Schalock, R. L. (1995). *Outcome-based evaluation*. New York: Plenum Press.

Scheier, M. F., Carver, C. S., & Bridges, M. W. (1994). Distinguishing optimism from neuroticism: A reevaluation of the Life Orientation Test. *Journal of Personality and Social Psychology, 67,* 1063–1078.

Seligman, M. E. P., & Csikszentmihalyi (2000). Positive psychology: An introduction. *American Psychologist, 55,* 5–14.

Seligman, M. E. P. (1995). The effectiveness of psychotherapy: The Consumer Reports Study. *American Psychologist, 50,* 965–974.

Spitzer, R. L., & Fleiss, J. L. (1974). A re-analysis of the reliability of psychiatric diagnosis. *British Journal of Psychiatry, 125,* 341–347.

Stricker, G., & Trierweiler, S. J. (1995). The local clinical scientist: A bridge between science and practice. *American Psychologist, 50,* 995–1002.

Summerfeldt, L. J., & Antony, M. M. (2002). Structured and semistructured diagnostic interviews. In M. M. Antony & D. H. Barlow (Eds.). *Handbook of assessment and treatment planning for psychological disorders* (pp. 3–37). New York: Guilford Press.

Tracey, T. J., & Kokotovic, A. M. (1989). Factor structure of the Working Alliance Inventory. *Psychological Assessment: A Journal of Consulting and Clinical Psychology, 1,* 207–210.

Truax, P. (2002). Behavioral case conceptualization for adults. In M. Hersen (Ed.). *Clinical behavior therapy: Adults and children.* New York: John Wiley & Sons (pp. 3–36).

Tyler, J. D., Busseri, M. A., & King, A. R. (2002). Treatment outcome assessment practices of psychology training clinics. *The Behavior Therapist, 25,* 144–147.

Watson, D., Clark, L. A., & Tellegen, A. (1988). Development and validation of brief measures of positive and negative affect: The PANAS scales. *Journal of Personality and Social Psychology, 54,* 1063–1070.

Weisz, J. R., Weiss, B., Alicke, M. D., & Klotz, M. L. (1987). Effectiveness of psychotherapy with children and adolescents: A meta-analysis for clinicians. *Journal of Consulting and Clinical Psychology, 55,* 542–549.

Wierzbicki, M., & Pekarik, G. (1993). A meta-analysis of psychotheraphy dropout. *Professional Psychology: Research and Practice, 24,* 190–195.

Catherine Miller
Brad B. Evans

Ethical Issues in Assessment

Assessment may be defined as "a conceptual, problem-solving process of gathering dependable, relevant information about an individual, group, or institution to make informed decisions" (Turner, DeMers, Fox, & Reed, 2001, p. 1100). The importance of assessment to psychology cannot be overstated, as psychological testing may be considered "a defining practice of professional psychology since the field's inception" (Camera, Nathan, & Puente, 2000, p. 141). The outcomes of psychological assessment may be life-altering, such as placing a child in special education classes, denying an applicant a job, or altering treatment of a patient.

Given the importance of assessment, it is not surprising that there are numerous ethical pitfalls for the assessor (Welfel, 1998). This chapter reviews the main ethical issues inherent in assessment, including competence, informed consent, and confidentiality. In addition, the impact on assessment practices of federal statutes such as the Americans with Disabilities Act (ADA, 1990), the Civil Rights Act (1964, 1991), and the Individuals with Disabilities Education Act (IDEA, 1975) is discussed.

☐ Ethical Issues in Assessment

Competence

By far, the most important ethical issue in assessment is that of competence. Weiner (1989) concluded that "competence is prerequisite for ethicality," stating that "although it is . . . possible in psychodiagnostic work to be competent without being ethical, it is not possible to be ethical without being competent" (p. 829). Competence in assessment implies that the psychologist has the requisite knowledge and training to determine appropriate tests and how to administer them.

The most recent American Psychological Association (APA) Ethics Code emphasized the importance of competence in Standard 2.01, stating that psychologists provide services only within the boundaries of their competence, based on their education, training, supervised experience, consultation, study, or professional experience (APA, 2002). However, the 2002 Code does not clearly define the professional qualifications necessary for competence in assessment generally. Given that there are thousands of published psychological assessment devices, it is not possible to be competent to administer every one of them. With few guidelines available on qualifications of testers, "psychologists are generally left to address this matter on the basis of their own awareness of their competencies and limitations" (Koocher & Keith-Spiegel, 1998, p. 156).

It should be noted that competence is not dependent on the specific degree obtained, but rather is based on relevant training and supervised experience (Anastasi, 1976). A brief review of training and supervision recommendations should aid psychologists in the examination of their assessment qualifications.

First, training in assessment should include courses in psychometrics, statistics, and test interpretation. According to APA Guidelines for Test User Qualifications (Turner et al., 2001), to be considered competent in assessment, a psychologist should have general psychometric knowledge and skills, which serve as the bases for most typical uses of tests. The following three main knowledge areas are considered essential for all test users: (a) psychometrics, including reliability, validity, and norms; (b) effects of ethnic, racial, cultural, gender, age, and linguistic variables on administration of tests and interpretation of scores; and (c) effects of disabilities on administration of tests and interpretation of scores (Turner et al., 2001). At a minimum, psychologists administering tests should understand the various types of reliability (inter-rater, test-retest, internal consistency, and alternate forms) and validity (content, criterion-related, and construct) (Cronbach, 1960). Psychologists also should understand the impact that changing standardized administration to accommodate cultural differences or disabilities might have on reliability and validity estimates.

In addition to training in core skills and knowledge, psychologists should obtain supervised experience on the administration and scoring of *each* test, as "competence in the use of one test or one group of tests [does not] imply competence in any other test" (Welfel, 1998, p. 226). Clearly, the amount of time required to become competent in administration and scoring will vary, as some tests, such as the revised Wechsler Adult Intelligence Test (WAIS-III; Wechsler, 1997) or the Rorschach Inkblot Test (Rorschach, 1921/1942) are more difficult to learn. Therefore, "a specific prescribed format or mechanism for supervision cannot be described for each test user" (Turner et al., 2001, p.1104). What is clear is that supervision should be continued until the supervisor judges that mastery of the test is obtained.

The previous discussion clearly demonstrates the need for both training and supervision to become competent in assessment. However, to *maintain* competence in assessment, examiners should ensure that the following five principles are followed each time testing is conducted. First and foremost, competent assessment practice requires psychologists to employ tests that are psychometrically sound. It is important that psychologists only use tests that are reliable and that have been validated for the purpose at hand, as "a test that is reliable, valid, and quite useful for one purpose may be useless or inappropriate for another" (Koocher & Keith-Spiegel, 1998, p. 149). To ensure that reliability and validity coefficients retain their meaning, psychologists should do two things: (a) follow standardized administration procedures of each test and (b) maintain strict security with testing protocols. Test security is important in maintaining that responses to tests are genuine, unrehearsed, and a sample of the individual's behavior at the time of testing. Prior knowledge of test questions and understanding of test scoring and interpretation can serve to compromise the utility and validity of test results. A lack of test security results in "very concrete harm to the general public — loss of effective assessment tools" (APA, 1996, p. 646). While many secure tests can be accessed to at least some extent by tenacious searching of university libraries or the Internet, protecting assessment instruments should remain a high priority for examiners.

A second principle of competent assessment practice requires that psychologists employ only tests that meet a standard of relevance to the needs of a particular client (Anastasi, 1988). A client's right to privacy must be respected, as the "process of arriving at the diagnosis, of prodding the client for details of his or her experience, is in many ways an invasion of privacy no less severe than a physical examination by a medical doctor or an audit by the IRS" (Welfel, 1998, p. 218). In other words, testing must be given for a good reason, as "testing for its own sake, or because of an institutional mandate, is inappropriate" (Welfel, 1998, p. 226).

Third, competent assessment practice requires that psychologists assess only within a defined relationship (APA, 2002). In other words, psychologists should resist any temptation to assess persons casually in social situations or to provide a diagnosis without having conducted an in-person evaluation.

Fourth, competent assessment practice requires the integration of multiple sources of data rather than reliance on test scores as the sole criterion on which clinical or other decision are made. Interviews with collateral sources, reviews of prior records, and direct observations are necessary for a competent evaluation.

Finally, competent assessment practice requires that examiners carefully supervise test administration and scoring. Regardless of who administers and scores tests, only trained and competent professionals should supervise the assessment process. Students or assistants may administer tests, and automated services may score tests; however, the trained professional is still responsible for appropriate administration and interpretation of scores (APA, 2002).

In summary, a competent assessor is one who employs psychometrically sound and relevant tests, along with other data sources, to answer specific assessment questions within a defined relationship. Ultimately, "knowing what one's tests can do — that is, what psychological functions they describe accurately, what diagnostic conclusions can be inferred from them with what degree of certainty, and what kinds of behavior they can be expected to predict, is the measure of the [psychologist's] competence" (Weiner, 1989, p. 829).

Informed Consent

The term informed consent is commonly used throughout the field of psychology; for example, consent to treatment, consent to participate in research, and consent to release information are but a few of the contexts in which consent is given and sought. Consent, however, is a legal term, and care should be given to its application within the realm of psychological assessment. While the intent here is to provide a general understanding of informed consent, the information presented should not be used in substitution for state law or ethical guidelines.

Informed consent in assessment implies that the test taker (or his or her legal guardian) has agreed to be evaluated prior to testing and after being informed of reasons for testing, intended uses of data, possible consequences (including risks and benefits), what information will be released (if any), and to whom the information will be released (APA, 1996). The APA Committee on Psychological Tests and Assessment (1996) indicated that informed consent may be desirable to obtain even when not required (e.g., court-ordered assessment). Further, even when informed consent is not required, it is advisable to inform test takers of the testing process, including who may have access to the report, unless such information will threaten the psychometric properties of the instrument or test (APA, 1996).

Typically, consent consists of three separate aspects: voluntariness, competence, and information (Bersoff, 1995; Everstine et al., 1980). First, voluntariness implies that the examiner must obtain the test taker's consent "without exercising coercion or causing duress, pressure, or undue excitement or influence" (Koocher & Keith-Spiegel, 1998, p. 417).

Second, the test taker must be considered legally competent to grant consent. Unless legally deemed incompetent, all adults are assumed competent to give consent. Children, however, generally are not presumed to be competent, although the legal age to give consent varies by state. In assessing children or adults deemed legally incompetent, substitute consent should be obtained from parents, legal guardians, or from the court as applicable. Everstine and colleagues (1980) recommended obtaining consent from both the required substitute and from the incompetent person whenever possible. At the very least, information about testing in developmentally-appropriate language should be given to the legally incompetent person, and assent, or agreement, should be obtained (Keith-Spiegel, 1983).

Finally, the test taker must have the requisite information to consent. Sufficient information must be provided to the test taker to allow the individual the opportunity to make an informed decision regarding his or her participation in assessment. While it is unnecessary (and perhaps impossible) to review all possible outcome scenarios with the client, it is necessary to provide facts a reasonable person would need in arriving at an informed decision. Whether test results will be used in decision making, if copies of test reports will be kept in the client's file, and the right to refuse testing or to withdraw at any time are examples of information that should be given to each potential test taker (Welfel, 1998). In addition, policies on feedback about testing results and removal of outdated or obsolete testing data should be reviewed.

Information on feedback policies is particularly important, as it appears that psychologists do not routinely provide feedback to test takers. As recently as 1983, Berndt's survey of psychologists found that a majority favored only limited feedback to test takers, suggesting that most examiners viewed full disclosure on a regular basis as an unrealistic goal. However, APA (1996) clearly has stated that test takers have the right to feedback about testing results, unless this right is waived by the test taker prior to testing or prevented by law (e.g., when courts mandate testing for competency to stand trial). A feedback session is recommended to serve two main purposes (Welfel, 1998). First, a feedback session allows the test taker an opportunity to respond to incorrect or misleading conclusions. Second, feedback may be therapeutic for the client, promoting symptom reduction and improved client-therapist rapport. However, special care should be given in how information is presented to the individual client. Many psychological assessment instruments are complex, even for the professional trained in its usage, psychometric properties, and interpretation. Therefore, summary reports may be more beneficial to clients than raw test data. Reports should be written in a manner that is clear and simple and free from technical language in order to avoid misinterpretation and misunderstanding. As Koocher and Keith-Spiegel (1998) noted, "It is wisest to write reports with a directness and clarity that makes it possible to give copies of the report to the client" (p. 165). Examiners should be available to answer specific questions about assessment results and to clarify questions raised by the client. In summary, a good rule of thumb is "to provide as full a description as time, interest, and test security allow, [only] omitting or postponing review of results that the counselor judges would be harmful to the client's current well-being" (Welfel, 1998, p. 230). Regardless of the method of feedback utilized, a description of the examiner's feedback policy should be reviewed during informed consent procedures.

Information on obsolete data policies should also be reviewed with each test taker. APA (2002) requires that examiners refrain from basing recommendations or decisions on obsolete or outdated testing data. How long a psychologist may rely on certain test results depends primarily on the construct being measured (Welfel, 1998). Tests that measure rapidly changing constructs, such as depressed or anxious moods (e.g., Beck Depression Inventory–II; Beck, Steer, & Brown, 1996; Beck Anxiety Inventory; Beck & Steer, 1990) may be valid only for several days or weeks. Other tests that measure more stable personality constructs (e.g., Minnesota Multiphasic Personality Inventory-2; Butcher, Dahlstrom, Graham, Tellegen, & Kaemmer, 1989) may be valid for several months. Regardless of the tests employed, examiners should inform potential test takers of their policies on removal of such data.

Clearly, much information should be provided to test takers prior to examination. Following the presentation of this information, common practice entails asking the client to state the concept in his own words. This practice gives the examiner some degree of certainty regarding the client's understanding of consent.

Use of written documents to record the terms of consent is standard. Both client and clinician can benefit from a written contract specifying client rights and responsibilities, limitations of confidentiality, and fees for services. Documentation of informed consent should be reviewed verbally with the client in language appropriate to the client's level of understanding and free from technical jargon or colloquial terminology (Mann, 1994; Welfel, 1998). As a rule of thumb, consent forms should be written at no higher than a 7th grade reading level (Miller, 2002). Additionally, the client should be given an opportunity to look over such documentation and ask questions before signing, in order to ensure understanding. Research conducted on the effects of written informed consent forms generally has found positive effects. For example, Handelsman (1990) found that the use of written consent forms increased clients' positive judgments of therapists' experience, likeability, and trustworthiness.

Confidentiality

Koocher and Keith-Spiegel defined confidentiality as "a general standard of professional conduct that obliges a professional not to discuss information about a client with anyone" (1998, p. 116). Confidentiality between clinician and client cannot be overstated as a critical ingredient for candid and cooperative participation. It can be argued that confidentiality is what allows psychological services to be effective, since without candid client participation assessment results can be invalid, diagnoses inaccurate, and therapy ineffective (DeKraai & Sales, 1982). The basis for most clients agreeing to receive psychological services is an understood agreement of confidentiality, and is among the primary reasons why informed consent is requested and documented.

It is important to ensure that clients have an understanding of the limits of confidentiality. For example, all 50 states have legal statutes which mandate disclosure of various information, including child abuse, elder abuse, suicide, and/or imminent harm to others. In addition, assessment and testing are frequently conducted for third parties that have a vested interest in the outcome of test data. For example, insurance companies and health maintenance organizations (HMOs) can and do request assessment information in order to determine eligibility for coverage or reimbursement for services rendered. Furthermore, employers, legal representatives, and schools often request testing results to aid in decision-making. The amount of information requested can vary widely from complete and full disclosure of all test data in legal proceedings to summary reports prepared for prospective employers.

Releasing information to individuals or entities other than the client presents a myriad of ethical and legal obstacles. Psychologists should refer to the APA Ethics Code (2002) for guidance, as well as the newly enacted federal law known as the Health Insurance Portability and Accountability Act (HIPAA, 1996). This comprehensive law sets a federal floor on confidentiality, requiring explicit client authorization for release of information to third parties. To comply with both the Ethics Code and federal law, psychologists should inform test takers, prior to assessment, of any mandatory, as well as any likely, releases of information. In addition, when requests from third parties are received, psychologists should have test takers sign their consent to release specific testing information. Finally, psychologists, once granted consent, should exercise extreme caution in releasing only the necessary information to satisfy the inquiry of the third party rather than releasing the entire contents of the client's chart. As stated previously, examiners should not release secure test materials (e.g., protocols, test items) unless permission is granted from the testing publisher.

Child test takers pose special dilemmas for examiners. As previously discussed, unless granted by law, children are not considered capable of consenting to assessment. Therefore, testing results may be shared with the legal guardian who consented to the child's participation in assessment. However, a good rule of thumb is to follow the same procedures utilized for release of information to third parties. In other words, examiners must clarify limits of confidentiality with the child and legal guardian at the outset of testing and should only release relevant information to the legal guardian.

In summary, psychologists should inform all potential test takers of the concept of confidentiality as well as the limits to this concept. Although psychologists should safeguard assessment results as much as is legally possible, they should also have frank discussions with test takers of possible disclosures of information prior to beginning the assessment process.

☐ Legal Issues in Assessment

Educational Law

In 1975, Congress passed Public Law 94-142, also known as the Individuals with Disabilities Education Act (IDEA). This federal law requires states, through their local school districts, to provide appropriate individualized educational plans in the least restrictive environment for all children identified with disabilities. Two landmark cases on assessment illustrate the difficulty examiners have in identifying such children, specifically those with learning disabilities.

First, in *Larry P. v. Riles* (1979), plaintiffs were several African-American elementary school children who were placed in special education classes due to their low scores on standardized intelligence tests. Plaintiffs claimed that intelligence tests were biased against the culture and experience of African-American children as a class. To prove their case, plaintiffs demonstrated racial imbalances in special education classrooms, showing that while African Americans made up only 29% of all students in the San Francisco school district, a full 66% of students in special education classrooms were African American. The federal court ruled that, whether intentionally or not, the result of utilizing standard intelligence tests was unequal placement. Therefore, the court ruled that intelligence tests could not be used with African-American children to make educational placement decisions.

In contrast, in *People in Action on Special Education (PASE) v. Hannon* (1980), the court ruled that standardized intelligence tests may be used in educational decision-making, as long as resulting scores are not the sole criterion for placement decisions. Currently, most school districts allow the use of standardized intelligence tests in decision-making but do not allow the scores to be used in isolation.

Employment Law

In 1964, Congress passed Public Law 88-352, also known as the first Civil Rights Act. As one of its many features, Title VII of this act prohibited employment discrimination on the basis of race, gender, ethnicity, religion, and national origin. As a result, many employers began requiring that potential or current employees pass standardized intelligence tests before they were offered jobs or promotions. In *Griggs v. Duke Power Company* (1971), 13 African-American men brought a class action suit against their employer, alleging that the use of a standardized intelligence test was racially discriminatory. To prevail in their suit, plaintiffs demonstrated that the power company implemented the testing requirement on the same day that Title VII went into effect. Plaintiffs also demonstrated that the power company, with a workforce of 95, hired only 14 African-American employees. The Supreme Court ruled that the intelligence test requirement had an adverse or disparate impact (i.e., it negatively affected African Americans more than other racial groups) and that such impact was illegal. The Court introduced the idea of job relatedness, stating that, in order to utilize intelligence or other standardized tests, companies must demonstrate how the attributes measured in each test are relevant to subsequent job performance (Koocher & Keith-Spiegel, 1998). Rather than barring companies from using such tests, this ruling mandated that companies demonstrate the utility of such tests prior to their use.

In 1991, Congress passed Public Law 102-166, an update of the original Civil Rights Act. Title I of this act banned any form of test score adjustment based on race, color, religion, gender, or national origin. This process of score adjustment, sometimes referred to as subgroup norming, makes it illegal for employers to use differential test cutoffs by race in decision-making (Koocher & Keith-Spiegel, 1998).

Finally, a recent congressional act that greatly impacted psychological testing in the workplace is Public Law 101-336, better known as the Americans with Disabilities Act (ADA, 1990). Specifically, the ADA prohibits pre–job offer medical examinations, which may have the effect of discriminating against otherwise qualified disabled individuals. These medical examinations may include psychological testing if such testing is designed or used to reveal impairment or the state of an individual's mental health. The ADA does allow such examinations to be utilized post–job offer. However, similar to the mandate in *Griggs v. Duke Power Company*, the statute clearly requires that such examinations show demonstrable relationships to successful job performance.

As an overview, several legal issues must be considered before utilizing psychological or intelligence tests in either educational or employment settings. First, examiners must demonstrate that each proposed test is related to successful performance in that setting. The idea of job relatedness first introduced by the U.S. Supreme Court in *Griggs v. Duke Power Company* is that the attributes measured by each test must be clearly relevant to the particular work required (Koocher & Keith-Spiegel, 1998). Second, examiners should demonstrate that there are no significant differences in rejection or placement rates for different groups. Most importantly, as with all assessment situations, examiners should never rely on test results in isolation to make employment or educational placement decisions. Instead, comprehensive assessments with multiple sources of data should be conducted before any educational or employment recommendations are made.

□ Summary and Recommendations

For psychologists conducting assessments, both ethical and legal issues must be considered. Psychologists should be familiar with the main ethical issues of competence, informed consent, and confidentiality as they relate to assessment. Remaining competent as an assessor implies psychologists should regularly seek consultation and education opportunities, as the field of assessment continues to expand and develop. Those conducting psychological assessments are encouraged to vigilantly revisit the components of informed consent and continue exploring techniques to effectively communicate the aspects of consent to their clients.

Psychologists should also be aware of state and federal laws that pertain to assessment and seek clarification and consultation for legal questions as needed. Before conducting assessments, psychologists are advised to seek further discussions of ethical and legal issues in the following guidelines: (a) the newly revised American Psychological Association's Ethics Code (APA, 2002), (b) the report by the American Psychological Association's Committee on Psychological Tests and Assessment (1996), (c) the Standards for Educational and Psychological Testing (Joint Committee of the American Educational Research Association, American Psychological Association, & the National Council on Measurement in Education, 1999); and (d) the Guidelines for Test User Qualifications (Turner et al., 2001).

□ References

American Psychological Association. (2002). Ethical principles of psychologists and code of conduct. *American Psychologist, 57*(12), 1060–1073.

American Psychological Association Committee on Psychological Tests and Assessment. (1996). Statement on the disclosure of test data. *American Psychologist, 51*(6), 644–648.

Americans with Disabilities Act (ADA), 42 USCA 12101–12213 (1990).

Anastasi, A. (1976). *Psychological testing* (4th ed.). New York: MacMillan.

Anastasi, A. (1988). *Psychological testing* (6th ed.). New York: MacMillan.

Beck, A. T., Steer, R. A., & Brown, G. K. (1996). *Beck Depression Inventory – II (BDI-II) manual.* San Antonio, TX: Psychological Corporation.

Beck, A. T., & Steer, R. A. (1990). *Manual for the revised Beck Anxiety Inventory.* San Antonio, TX: Psychological Corporation.

Berndt, D. J. (1983). Ethical and professional considerations in psychological assessment. *Professional Psychology: Research and Practice, 14*(5), 580–587.

Bersoff, D. N. (Ed.). (1995). *Ethical conflicts in psychology*. Washington, DC: American Psychological Association.

Butcher, J. N., Dahlstrom, W. G., Graham, J. R., Tellegen, A., & Kaemmer, B. (1989). *Minnesota Multiphasic Personality Inventory-2 (MMPI-2): Manual for administration and scoring*. Minneapolis: University of Minnesota Press.

Camera, W. J., Nathan, J. S., & Puente, A. E. (2000). Psychological test usage: Implications in professional psychology. *Professional Psychology: Research and Practice, 31*(2) 141–154.

Cronbach, L. J. (1960). *Essentials of psychological testing* (2nd ed.). New York: Harper & Row.

DeKraai, M. B., & Sales, B. D. (1982). Privileged communications of psychologists. *Professional Psychology, 32*, 372–388.

Everstine, L., Everstine, D. S., Heymann, G. M., True, R. H., Frey, D. H., Johnson, H. G., et al. (1980). Privacy and confidentiality in psychotherapy. *American Psychologist, 35*, 828–840.

Griggs v. Duke Power Company, 401 U.S. 424 (1971).

Handelsman, M. M. (1990). Do written consent forms influence clients' first impressions of therapists? *Professional Psychology: Research and Practice*, 21(6), 451–454.

Health Insurance Portability and Accountability Act (HIPAA), Pub. L. No. 104–191 (1996).

Individuals with Disabilities Education Act (IDEA), Pub. L. No. 94–142 (1975).

Joint Committee of the American Educational Research Association, the American Psychological Association, & the National Council on Measurement in Education. (1999). *Standards for educational and psychological testing*. Washington, DC: AERA.

Keith-Spiegel, P. (1983). Children and consent to participate in research. In G. B. Melton, G. P. Koocher, & M. J. Saks (Eds.), *Childrens' competence to consent* (pp. 179–211). New York: Plenum Press.

Koocher, G. P., & Keith-Spiegel, P. (1998). *Ethics in psychology: Professional standards and cases* (2nd ed.). New York: Oxford University Press.

Larry P. v. Riles, 343 F. Supp. 1306 (1979).

Mann, T. (1994). Informed consent for psychological research: Do subjects comprehend consent forms and understand their legal rights? *Psychological Science*, 5, 140–143.

Miller, C. A. (2002, November). *Update on ethical and legal issues*. Workshop presented at Pacific University.

People in Action on Special Education v. Hannon, 506 F. Supp. 831 (N.D. Ill. 1980).

Rorschach, H. (1921/1942). *Psychodiagnostics: A diagnostic test based on perception* (P. Lemkau & B. Kronenberg, Trans.). Berne: Huber (U.S. distributor., Grune & Stratton).

Title I of the Civil Rights Act, Pub. L. No. 102-166, 105 Stat. 1071 (1991).

Title VII of the Civil Rights Act, Pub. L. No. 88–352, 78 Stat. 253–266 (1964).

Turner, S. M., DeMers, S. T., Fox, H. R., & Reed, G. M. (2001). APA's guidelines for test user qualifications. *American Psychologist, 56*(12), 1099–1113.

Wechsler, D. (1997). *Wechsler Adult Intelligence Scale-III*. San Antonio, TX: Psychological Corporation.

Weiner, I. B. (1989). On competence and ethicality in psychodiagnostic assessment. Journal of *Personality Assessment*, 53(4), 827–831.

Welfel, E. R. (1998). *Ethics in counseling and psychotherapy*. Pacific Grove, CA: Brooks/Cole Publishing.

II

SECTION

Evaluation of Adults

F. Dudley McGlynn
Todd A. Smitherman
Jacinda C. Hammel

CHAPTER

Panic, Agoraphobia, and Generalized Anxiety Disorder

☐ Description of the Disorders or Problems

Panic attacks are sudden periods of extreme biological and cognitive fearfulness that typically peak within 10 minutes then gradually subside. According to the *Diagnostic and Statistical Manual of Mental Disorders*, 4th edition, revised text (DSM-IV-TR; American Psychiatric Association [APA], 2000), the symptoms of panic attacks include at least four of the following: tachycardia or palpitations, sweating, trembling/shaking, shortness of breath or smothering, sensations of choking, chest pain or discomfort, nausea or stomach distress, feeling dizzy or faint, derealization or depersonalization, fear of losing control or of going crazy, fear of dying, numbing or tingling sensations, and chills or hot flushes. Panic disorder (PD), in turn, is characterized by presence of recurring, unexpected panic attacks. Formally the attacks must be accompanied by a month or longer of continuing concern about having additional attacks, by worry about implications of such attacks or their consequences, or by an adaptively significant change in behavior as a result of the attacks.

The core feature of agoraphobia is anxiety about being in places or situations from which escape might be difficult, impossible, or embarrassing, or in which help might not be available, in the event of panic. Thus, agoraphobia involves fear of experiencing panic in one or more situations, not fear of the situations themselves. Common panic situations include public places, public transportation, and crowded areas. Usually the fear of panic eventuates in avoidance of the troublesome situations.

Of those who present agoraphobia clinically, 95% or so also merit a diagnosis of panic disorder (APA, 2000). Of those who present panic disorder clinically, the majority also show agoraphobia. The diagnosis of panic disorder with agoraphobia (PDA) is used when the individual meets the diagnostic criteria for both disorders. Unless otherwise stated, PDA is of interest here.

Epidemiological studies estimate that lifetime prevalence of PDA is between 1.5% and 3.5%; one-year prevalence rates range from 1% to 2% (APA, 2000). Comorbidity figures for Axis I diagnoses among patients who have PDA according to DSM-III-R (APA, 1987) have ranged from 51% to 91% of patients (Beck & Zebb, 1994). Comorbidity patterns for PDA and PD are much the same; comorbid diagnoses include specific phobia and social phobia, dysthymia and major depression, and alcohol use/dependence. Major depression is more often comorbid with PDA than with PD alone (Starcevic, Uhlenhuth, Kellner, & Pathak, 1993).

Mixed panic and agoraphobia cohorts have typically been used in studies of Axis II comorbidity. Rates of personality-disorder diagnoses among these patients have been 25% to 60% (Beck & Zebb, 1994). Cluster C is overrepresented among comorbid Axis II designations. Some evidence suggests that rates of both Axis I and Axis II comorbidity increase as agoraphobia worsens and as patients' lives become increasingly constrained.

Since the late 1980s theorists concerned with PDA have arranged biological and psychological factors into multielement etiologic models (see McNally, 1994). The model proposed by Barlow (1988, 2002) is a satisfactory exemplar. The development of PDA begins when biological and/or psychological diatheses combine with life stress to produce unusual bodily sensations that are benign but detectable. The bodily sensations, in turn, become cues for fearful catastrophizing. Next the fearful catastrophizing prompts increased attention to such sensations along with behavioral avoidance of events or situations wherein the sensations are expected to occur.

While the various etiologic models of PDA are similar to one another, important disagreements exist at virtually every theoretical choice point. There is disagreement, for example, about the physiological underpinnings of the focal sensations, about how focal sensations become cues for fearful catastrophizing, and about how fear-motivated avoidance is established (Barlow, 2002; McNally, 1994). It is doubtless true that multielement models afford the best hope for explaining PDA satisfactorily but much work remains.

Generalized anxiety disorder (GAD) is characterized by uncontrollable, excessive worry accompanied by chronic anxiety. For at least 6 months, worry about a number of life events or activities is accompanied more days than not by at least three of six symptoms: restlessness, fatigue, impaired concentration, irritability, muscle tension, and sleep disturbance (APA, 2000). The focus of worry is not associated with another disorder such as worry about contamination (obsessive-compulsive disorder), worry about experiencing a panic attack (panic disorder), or worry that one's physical ailments signify a life-threatening illness (hypochondriasis).

The most recent large-scale epidemiological study, the National Comorbidity Survey, obtained a lifetime prevalence rate for GAD of 5.1% and a current prevalence rate for GAD of 1.6%, using DSM-III-R criteria (Wittchen, Zhao, Kessler, & Eaton, 1994). Also utilizing DSM-III-R criteria, the Epidemiologic Catchment Area study estimated a one-year prevalence rate of 3.8% for GAD (Blazer, Hughes, George, Swartz, & Boyer, 1991). As with PDA, there is high comorbidity of GAD with mood disorders and other anxiety disorders. Approximately 75% of individuals with a principal DSM-III-R diagnosis of GAD had a comorbid anxiety or mood disorder (Brawman-Mintzer et al., 1993; Brown & Barlow, 1992; Massion, Warshaw, & Keller, 1993). Utilizing DSM-IV criteria, Brown, Campbell, Lehman, Grisham, and Mancill (2001) reported significant comorbidity with posttraumatic stress disorder (23%), PD (19%), PDA (16%), social phobia (13%), and obsessive-compulsive disorder (12%). Beyond anxiety and mood disorders, there is significant comorbidity of GAD with health care utilization for physical complaints and with alcohol and drug-related problems (cf. Ballenger et al., 2001; Brown, Campbell, et al., 2001; Wittchen et al.). Indeed, 82% of individuals with GAD in the National Comorbidity Survey reported significant impairment in lifestyle and physical functioning (Wittchen et al.).

Compared to PDA there are few etiologic modes of GAD that are well developed. However, some consensus is beginning to emerge regarding the general diathesis-stress etiology and regarding the role of worry in GAD (see Barlow, 2002; Borkovec & Roemer, 1995). According to that consensus, generalized biological and psychological vulnerabilities combine to form a pervasive diathesis for the development of emotional disorders. The biological domain entails a genetic vulnerability for negative affect that predisposes people to anxiety and related emotional disorders (such as depression). The psychological domain entails the effects of early experiences of uncontrollability and unpredictability usually vis-à-vis actions of caregivers. The consensus seems to be that both biological and psychological vulnerabilities are necessary to the genesis of GAD and other emotional disorders.

At the next level, the emerging consensus holds that the above vulnerabilities magnify responses to negative life events so that individuals with GAD become overly sensitive to even minor stresses and relatively likely to think of stressful events as unrealistically probable, unpredictable, and uncontrollable. Worry enters the picture as a means of coping with catastrophic images and with the aversive affect that cognitive catastrophizing would otherwise engender. Worry then becomes chronic because it is negatively reinforced in at least two ways: worry about improbable events is usually followed by the absence of such events, and worry forestalls the (aversive) affective correlates of the imaging that worry displaces (see Borkovec & Roemer, 1995). Worry is maladaptive in the long run; by forestalling emotional imaging it forestalls emotional processing, and by suppressing sympathetic arousal it contributes to autonomic inflexibility. Thinking of stressful events as unpredictable and uncontrollable is maladaptive also because it fosters negative self-evaluation and slows the development of realistic problem-solving skills.

☐ Range of Assessment Strategies Available

Assessment of Panic Disorder with Agoraphobia

In assessing PDA, the clinician thinks in terms of four major domains of assessment: situational antecedents, interoceptive anxiety, panic-related cognitions, and agoraphobic avoidance. In principle, self-report, behavioral, and physiological assessment methods can be used to specify problems and monitor progress during treatment. Since most physiological assessment tools are not readily available to clinicians in private practice, a narrative about psychophysiological assessment is withheld here. Readers who are interested in psychophysiological assessment of PDA, including ambulatory psychophysiological recording, can consult Papillo, Murphy, and Gorman (1988) and Barlow (2002), among other sources. Instrumentation for recording heartbeats is straightforward to use and readily available, thus heart-rate recording as part of anxiety-disorder assessment is becoming more common. Yartz and Hawk (2001) have provided an excellent clinical guide for heart-rate measurement. Clinicians should, however, review information about basic physiology such as that provided by Papillo and colleagues before interpreting heartbeat records.

Self-Report Strategies

Self-report methods afford the only means available for understanding panic phenomenologically. Such understanding is important given contemporary attention to cognitive models of anxiety and, in particular, to catastrophic misappraisals of bodily sensations in PDA (e.g., Barlow, 2002). Self-report methods are also practical and cost efficient. Self-report methods can be broken down into structured interviews, questionnaires, self-monitoring, and situational fear ratings.

Structured Interviews

When assessing for PDA and other anxiety disorders, the structured or semistructured interview of choice is the Anxiety Disorders Interview Schedule for DSM-IV: Lifetime Version (ADIS-IV-L; Di Nardo, Brown, & Barlow, 1994). The ADIS-IV-L assists in determining both lifetime and current PDA diagnoses. In addition, the ADIS-IV-L provides information about the history of the anxiety problems, about maladaptive thinking, about situational antecedents to PDA symptoms, and about the symptoms themselves. The ADIS-IV-L is composed of modules specific to each of the anxiety disorders; it also provides interview data about depression, psychosis, drug abuse, and organic symptoms. The ADIS-IV-L can be administered in its entirety, or modules may be selected that are germane to the presenting problems and referral questions.

The ADIS-IV-L and its prior editions were developed so as to keep pace with the diagnostic nomenclature as it evolved. Over the years, the ADIS has demonstrated good psychometric properties. There have been reports of good interrater reliabilities, particularly for those disorders with frequent behavioral markers. For example, Brown, Di Nardo, Lehman, and Campbell (2001) reported interrater reliabilities of DSM-IV diagnoses based on the ADIS-IV-L among 362 patients selected randomly from among those who presented to their anxiety disorders specialty clinic. For 83 patients who received at least one PDA principal diagnosis, the kappa coefficient was .77. There have also been favorable reports regarding the various issues of validity (Barlow, 2002).

Questionnaires

The narrative here provides an overview along with some details. More complete and helpful information is available in an excellent sourcebook by Antony, Orsillo, and Roemer (2001). Several questionnaires have been developed to assess aspects of PDA, including interoceptive anxiety, panic-related cognitions, and agoraphobic avoidance. Interoceptive anxiety can be assessed by administration of the Anxiety Sensitivity Index (Reiss, Peterson, Gursky, & McNally, 1986). The 16-item Anxiety Sensitivity Index is a popular and well-researched questionnaire that quantifies a construct known as anxiety sensitivity, the tendency of a person to evidence catastrophic thinking in the presence of certain bodily sensations (Reiss & McNally, 1985). While the matter is controversial, the Anxiety Sensitivity Index appears to have one higher-order factor and three lower-order factors, the latter reflecting physical concerns, social concerns, and concern over loss of cognitive capacity (Zinbarg, Barlow, & Brown, 1997). The Anxiety Sensitivity Index has been shown to have strong psychometric properties (Peterson & Reiss, 1993) and has been shown to afford prediction concerning variables such as response to challenge and response to treatment (see Taylor, 1999). Recently, the Anxiety Sensitivity Index was revised and lengthened to 36 items, in an effort to more thoroughly measure the dimensions of anxiety sensitivity. Research with the revised index has demonstrated strong internal consistency and is ongoing (Taylor & Cox, 1998).

The 18-item Body Sensations Questionnaire (Chambless, Caputo, Bright, & Gallagher, 1984) is available for assessing the bodily sensations present when the client is anxious or fearful. The Body Sensations Questionnaire was developed in conjunction with the 15-item Agoraphobic Cognitions Questionnaire (Chambless et al.), which is used for assessing the prominence of various panic-related cognitions, particularly those related to the themes of physical/bodily concern and loss of control. Both scales have been found to have satisfactory internal consistency and test-retest stability. Both have also shown good discriminant and construct validity, and sensitivity to effects from treatment (Chambless et al.; Chambless & Gracely, 1989).

The above questionnaires are among the most common and well-researched tools for assessing feared bodily sensations and panic-related cognitions. Additional instruments exist for assessing fear when in situations that are often avoided. The 27-item Albany Panic and Phobia Questionnaire (Rapee, Craske, & Barlow, 1995), for example, contains an agoraphobia subscale, an interoceptive subscale, and a social phobia subscale. It has shown adequate internal consistency and test-retest stability; its agoraphobia and interoceptive subscales have been shown to distinguish between those with PDA, those with other anxiety disorders, and those without a diagnosis (Rapee et al.). Antony (2001) and Bouchard, Pelletier, Gauthier, Côté, and Laberge (1997) have provided comprehensive reviews of several other questionnaires sometimes used to assess PDA.

Self-Monitoring

Self-monitoring entails self-recording certain features of the behavior(s) of interest, for example, the location, intensity, and duration of panic attacks. Typically, self-monitoring is performed close in time to the behavior of interest with the assistance of a record form, although some professionals (e.g., Taylor, Fried, & Kenardy, 1990) provide clients with hand-held computers that, at regular intervals, prompt and store ratings related to panic. Local forms can be generated easily by the clinician, but standardized self-monitoring forms are available (see Barlow, 2002). Many standardized forms prompt the client to record whether he or she was alone or accompanied by someone else during the attack, whether the attack occurred in a stressful situation, and whether the attack was expected. Bodily sensations experienced and catastrophic cognitions are often listed as well. The main benefit of self-monitoring is that it allows the clinician to know something about the details of panic as the client experiences it in his or her everyday world. Accuracy of self-monitoring is always an issue but is enhanced when the record forms are turned in regularly and checked for completeness (McGlynn & Rose, 1998). Some have argued that the ecological validity of data from self-monitoring is enhanced when hand-held computers are used (Shiffman, 2000).

Situational Fear Ratings and Self-Efficacy Ratings

Situational fear ratings occur during self-monitoring (above) and in the context of behavioral assessment (below). That is, when a client self-monitors or is instructed to attempt behaviors linked to PDA, he or she is asked to rate the concurrent levels of fear and/or distress. Such ratings are generally obtained on a 0–100 scale, with zero meaning no anxiety and 100 meaning the most intense anxiety imaginable. Some clinicians provide clients with visual analogue rating scales; usually there are 100-cm lines with anchor points at every 25 cm.

Assessment of self-efficacy (Bandura, 1977) follows a similar procedure as situational fear rating. The client is asked to rate from 0–100 his or her confidence (level of efficacy) in successfully performing a task such as remaining in a situation where panic is likely to occur. Oftentimes the client provides additional ratings (0–100) of his or her confidence in the self-efficacy judgments. Situational fear ratings and self-efficacy ratings are beneficial in that the former provide numerical scales by which the clinician can understand the severity of the client's fear, and the latter enable the clinician to predict the likely vigor and persistence of self-change efforts. Self-efficacy ratings can be used also to develop exposure hierarchies, as when the client is instructed to confront situations that occasion panic or that prompt increasingly likely avoidance. A 25-item scale intended to measure self-efficacy for controlling panic was reviewed by Bouchard and colleagues (1997). It affords measurement of self-efficacy for panic control in the face of panicogenic thoughts, somatic events, and situations. Psychometric work is limited, but it is a good example of self-efficacy assessment in the PDA arena.

Behavioral Assessment Strategies

Behavioral assessment of PDA allows for direct observation of a client's behavior vis-à-vis feared events or situations. Behavioral assessment strategies are most useful in characterizing agoraphobic avoidance, but can also be combined with self-monitoring and with situational fear ratings to evaluate cognition, fear intensity, and physical sensations during exposure to panic cues. Behavioral assessment strategies for PDA are generally of three types: (1) behavioral avoidance tests (sometimes called behavioral approach tests), (2) symptom induction tests, and (3) biological challenge tests.

Behavioral Avoidance Tests

In relation to PDA, a behavioral avoidance test (BAT) involves instructing a client to enter various contexts in which panic, avoidance, or both may result and to remain until he or she anticipates that no further progress will be made or until he or she is too distressed to continue. As such, BATs provide objective data about behavior when confronting the targeted situation. Naturalistic BATs involve exposure to an actual context in the "real" environment, and thus attenuate the external validity problem inherent in many types of clinical assessment (McGlynn & Bates, 1999); contrived BATs involve exposure to an artificial situation, typically in a laboratory or clinician's office. Conclusions derived from BATs are generally at risk of being influenced by demand characteristics and limited content validity. Conclusions derived from contrived BATs are, in addition, weakened by suspect external validity. However, contrived BATs are valuable substitutes when naturalistic BATs are not feasible (see McGlynn & Rose, 1998).

Naturalistic BATs are valuable in the assessment of agoraphobic avoidance. One commonly used technique is to instruct clients to walk as far as possible along a specified outdoor path and return when they feel they can go no farther (see Vermilyea, Boice, & Barlow [1984] for a description of a standardized "behavioral walk"). Ordinarily the client supplies fear ratings at various points along the route. One noteworthy benefit of a BAT is that it allows the clinician to assess the client's utilization of safety signals. Safety signals include objects, people, or both that the client keeps nearby in order to ease anxiety, such as medication, cellular telephones, family members, and so on (see Rachman [1984] for an early discussion of the role of safety signals in agoraphobia).

Symptom Induction Tests

Symptom induction tests and biological challenge tests are used to reproduce panicogenic symptoms so that the symptoms and catastrophic responding to the symptoms can be evaluated. Symptom induction tests entail having the client engage in exercises that promote the feared bodily sensations of panic. For example, feelings of dizziness can be arranged by having the client spin in a chair for a short period of time; heart-rate increase can be produced by instructing the client to run in place for a few minutes; shortness of breath can be produced by having the client inhale solely through a straw for 1 minute (see Barlow, 2002). The degree of relevant fear can be quantified concurrently via situational fear ratings. By using a variety of these exercises, and structuring them so as to minimize overlap between the symptoms from one exercise to the next, the clinician can assess which bodily sensations are feared by the client.

As with other assessment modes, symptom induction tests can be used periodically both as a form of exposure treatment and as a means of ongoing treatment evaluation. Additionally, symptom induction tests can be used to construct exposure hierarchies that prioritize bodily sensations according to the level of fear they engender. Finally, symptom induction tests may be combined with BATs (e.g., instructing the client to walk around briskly while in a crowded mall) in an attempt to mimic the client's feared bodily sensations in targeted situations (Antony & Swinson, 2000).

Biological Challenge Tests

Symptom induction tests likely produce symptoms that are relatively weak by contrast with the somatic events of clinical interest. For that reason, some psychologists have become interested in biological challenge tests in which somatic events are produced pharmacologically (see Rapee, 1995). In particular, carbon dioxide challenge has received interest recently because it can be done safely without medical oversight (Forsyth & Karekla, 2001). There are variations in carbon dioxide delivery procedures regarding factors such as duration and mixture (cf. Bourin, Baker, & Bradwejn, 1998); optimal procedure is not yet known.

Assessment of Generalized Anxiety Disorder

For GAD, assessment is directed mainly toward delineating the self-reported content and function of a client's worry, but might also entail attempts to characterize factors such as intolerance of uncertainty and avoidance of aversive affect. Content relates to the topics of worry, such as finances, health, occupation, and family. Themes of worry might, for example, be "What if my electricity gets turned off because I do not pay the bill?"; "What if my husband has a heart attack?"; "What if I don't finish this project for my boss?"; or "What if my child is hit by a bus?" Function of worry relates to the purpose worry serves from the client's perspective, such as fending off danger or acting as a motivator. As noted earlier, self-report, behavioral, and physiological assessment methods are commonly used for anxiety disorders. However, GAD does not lend itself to behavioral assessment given that worry is not available for direct observation. Physiological methods, in turn, are not discussed here for reasons mentioned earlier.

Self-report methods available for assessing GAD include structured interviews, questionnaires, and self-monitoring. Questionnaires can be meaningfully subdivided within the domains of diagnostic screening, worry content, and the functions of worry.

Structured Interviews

The International Consensus Group on Depression and Anxiety (Ballenger et al., 2001, p. 54) recommends asking two screening questions for GAD: "During the past 4 weeks, have you been bothered by feeling worried, tense, or anxious most of the time?" and "Are you frequently tense, irritable, and having trouble sleeping?" Affirmative responses to these questions can prompt further assessment.

The ADIS-IV-L (Di Nardo et al., 1994) is suitable for lifetime and current diagnosis of GAD as well as PDA (and other anxiety disorders). In their study of interrater reliability of DSM-IV diagnoses mentioned earlier, Brown, Di Nardo, et al. (2001) obtained a kappa coefficient of 0.67 for 76 patients who had at least one GAD diagnosis. The ADIS-IV-L is particularly useful in differential diagnosis of GAD and obsessive compulsive disorder (OCD). The worries of GAD superficially resemble the obsessions of OCD. However, obsessional thoughts in OCD are ego-dystonic intrusions that differ in precipitants and content from the exaggerated everyday worries of GAD (cf. Turner, Beidel, & Stanley, 1992). Additionally, the ADIS-IV-L provides information about physical symptoms unique to GAD, content of worry, level of distress and functional interference, precipitants, and maintaining factors.

Questionnaires

Two questionnaires can be used to screen for GAD: the Generalized Anxiety Disorder Questionnaire-IV (Newman et al., 2002) and the Penn State Worry Questionnaire (Meyer, Miller, Metzger, & Borkovec, 1990). The Generalized Anxiety Disorder Questionnaire-IV is a 9-item self-report diagnostic instrument for GAD that provides scores from 0 to 33 when used as a continuous measure. As a continuous measure or dichotomous diagnostic tool, it affords a diagnosis of GAD based on DSM-IV criteria and provides the clinician with the client's major worry themes in their own words. Because it is relatively new, the Generalized Anxiety Disorder Questionnaire-IV has not been evaluated adequately in psychometric terms. Data cited by Roemer (2001b) point to good internal consistency and test-retest stability in a college sample. This author also cites evidence of strong correlations between the Generalized Anxiety Disorder Questionnaire-IV and the Penn State Worry Questionnaire as well as independent agreement for diagnoses based on the Generalized Anxiety Disorder Questionnaire-IV and the ADIS (kappa of 0.70).

The Penn State Worry Questionnaire is a 16-item self-report questionnaire that assesses the intensity and excessiveness of worry. It is widely used and has shown good to very good internal consistency, test-retest stability, and demonstrable construct validity (cf. Molina & Borkovec, 1994). Discriminant validity for GAD versus other anxiety-disorder groups was shown in a fairly large-scale study by Brown, Antony, and Barlow (1992), who also provide normative data from clinic patients in various anxiety-disorder categories.

Content of Worry

After establishing a diagnosis of GAD, the next step is characterizing the content of the client's worry: what does he or she worry about? Common themes of worry include interpersonal confrontation, competence, social acceptance, and concern about others, in addition to various minor matters (Breitholtz, Johansson, & Öst, 1999). The 25-item Worry Domains Questionnaire (Tallis, Eysenck, & Mathews, 1992) can be used to supplement other assessment data by quantifying worry in five domains: relationships, lack of confidence, aimless future, work, and finances. Among nonclinical samples, the Worry Domains Questionnaire has shown good test-retest stability overall and for most subscales, excellent internal consistency overall, and adequate to good internal consistency for the subscales (Stober, 1998). Factor-analytic results have been inconsistent. The developers of the Worry Domains Questionnaire recommend administering the Anxious Thoughts Inventory (Wells, 1994) in order to characterize worry related to health concerns. By addressing social worry and meta-worry (below), as well as health worry, the 22-item Anxious Thoughts Inventory provides the clinician with information about these other worry topics and about the extent to which a client worries about worrying. As with the Worry Domains Questionnaire, validity-related research with the Anxious Thoughts Inventory is in its early stages. Given that GAD is one of the most commonly-diagnosed anxiety disorders in late adulthood (Blazer, George, & Hughes, 1991), a specialized 35-item scale for the elderly has been developed. The Worry Scale for Older Adults (Wisocki, 1988) quantifies worries about social, financial, and health concerns. Psychometric studies have shown that the Worry Scale for Older Adults has excellent internal consistency, fair test-retest stability, and convergent validity.

Function of Worry

Recently, clinicians and researchers have studied clients' beliefs about their worry. Meta-worry, positive and negative beliefs about worry, might have a functional role in GAD. Positive beliefs reflect "the ways in which GAD clients think that their worrying actually serves a positive, adaptive function" (Borkovec, Hazlett-Stevens, & Diaz, 1999, p. 126). In particular, positive beliefs about worry might serve as maintaining factors in the disorder. Common positive themes include: worry avoids or prevents negative events (superstitious belief), worry prepares for the worst, worry distracts from more emotional topics, worry serves as a motivator, and worry aids in problem solving. (For a more detailed description of these beliefs see Borkovec et al. [1999].)

Several self-report questionnaires are available to assess a client's beliefs about worry. The 65-item Meta-Cognitions Questionnaire (Cartwright-Hatton & Wells, 1997) assesses beliefs about worry and intrusive thoughts via five factor-analytically derived subscales: positive worry beliefs, beliefs about controllability and danger, beliefs about cognitive competence, general negative beliefs (e.g., those related to responsibility, superstition, and punishment), and cognitive self-awareness or introspective preoccupation. The 29-item Consequences of Worrying Scale (Davey, Tallis, & Capuzzo, 1996) assesses beliefs about the functions and consequences of worry. The scale provides five factor-analytically derived subscale scores that quantify the strengths of negative beliefs that worry disrupts performance, exaggerates a problem, and causes emotional distress, as well as the strengths of positive beliefs that worry motivates and helps analytical thinking. The revised 25-item Why Worry Scale-II (Freeston, Rhéaume, Letarte, Dugas, & Ladouceur, 1994) quantifies the extent to which the client believes that worry aids in problem-solving, helps to motivate, prevents negative outcomes, protects the individual from negative emotions in the event of negative outcomes, and is regarded as a positive personality trait. (For psychometric characterization, see Roemer [2001a] for the Meta-Cognitions Questionnaire and Roemer [2001b] for the Consequences of Worrying Scale and the Why Worry Scale-II.)

In addition to assessing clients' beliefs about their worry, assessment of worry in GAD sometimes is concerned with the psychological functions worry might be serving. As noted earlier, avoidance of uncertainty and avoidance of negatively-valenced affect are conceptualized as major sources of negative reinforcement in the maintenance of chronic worry (Borkovec & Roemer, 1995; Dugas, Gagnon, Ladouceur, & Freeston, 1998). The 27-item Intolerance of Uncertainty Scale (Freeston et al., 1994) provides relevant information about how a client reacts to uncertainty. It does so by characterizing the emotional and behavioral consequences of uncertainty (e.g., how uncertainty affects self-perception, expectations about the predictability of the future, and frustration from unpredictable events). The 42-item Affective Control Scale (Williams, Chambless, & Ahrens, 1997) provides relevant information about avoidance of affect. It does so via four subscales assessing fear of anxiety, depression, anger, and strong positive affect. Both the Intolerance of Uncertainty Scale and the Affective Control Scale have shown good psychometric properties in work to date. Both questionnaires are of potential interest to clinicians who are impressed by aversions to uncertainty and to affect as features of GAD.

Self-Monitoring

Some aspects of pathological worry can be differentiated from normal worry via self-monitoring the amount of time spent worrying (Dupuy, Beaudoin, Rhéaume, Ladouceur, & Dugas, 2001). In one use of self-monitoring, for example, the client ends the day by recording the number of hours spent worrying. Additionally, self-monitoring is useful in assessing the severity, content, and outcomes of worry. Borkovec and colleagues (1999) describe how to utilize a Worry Outcome Diary wherein clients record worries and feared outcomes each week. After the actual worry-related outcome is evident, the client records that outcome, rates his or her actual coping ability, then makes comparisons to the feared outcome and to the expected coping ability. This process places worries along a realistic-unrealistic dimension. Additionally, self-monitoring can aid in identifying behavioral cues that signal worry, such as pacing, nail-biting, or hair-twirling. Behavioral cues can then be utilized to identify even earlier cues. For example, the client notes that pacing signifies worry, records the time spent worrying, and reflects on their behavior prior to pacing. This reflection is used to identify behavioral cues for pacing (and worrying) such as wiggling toes or to identify specific event triggers such as notification of deadlines.

The Worry Record (Craske, Barlow, & O'Leary, 1992) provides for self-recording the triggering events and various cognitive accompaniments of worry before and during cognitive-behavior therapies for GAD. Initially, it provides for recording of automatic thoughts, anxiety ratings, and estimated probabilities of adverse outcomes. Then it prompts recording of countering evidence, revised or realistic estimates of adverse outcomes, and anxiety levels after applying cognitive restructuring techniques. Ideally, the client learns to apply cognitive restructuring techniques to reduce the anticipated likelihood and adversity of worry-related outcomes (Brown, O'Leary, & Barlow, 2001).

Pragmatic Issues Encountered in Clinical Practice: Panic Disorder with Agoraphobia

Symptoms of PDA occur also in disorders of endocrine, neurological, respiratory, and cardiovascular function, and in substance-related disorders (Dattilio & Salas-Auvert, 2000). Thus, a complete medical evaluation is recommended for any client suspected of having panic disorder, and the clinician should be aware of medical conditions that might contraindicate the use of challenge or symptom induction tests. As noted earlier, symptoms of PDA overlap also with those of other psychological disorders, particularly other anxiety disorders and depression. Thus differential diagnosis is sometimes difficult.

The differential diagnosis of PDA is generally guided by understanding the thematic focus of the client's anxious apprehension and avoidance behavior. In PDA, the theme is "fear of fear," or fear of having unexpected panic, as well as avoidance of activities and situations wherein panic is expected. Sudden spikes of fear and habitual avoidance are common in other anxiety disorders as well, but generally are related to certain contexts and are not experienced as unexpected. In social phobia, fear and avoidance are related to social or performance situations that have a potential for negative evaluation. In specific phobias, fear and avoidance are associated with tangible events or situations other than those at issue in social phobia. Avoidance that is similar to agoraphobic avoidance is observed also among obsessive-compulsive clients seeking to avoid contamination and among those with posttraumatic stress disorder seeking to avoid trauma reminders.

Cost is another pragmatic concern in assessing PDA. While most of the aforementioned assessment strategies are generally inexpensive, they do take time. Encouraging the client to complete self-assessment activities outside the office reduces some of the allocated time and associated costs. Some BATs and symptom induction tests can, for example, be done as homework. Some clinicians recoup the costs of administering copyrighted documents (such as the ADIS-IV-L). Frequently, a fixed amount is billed dependent upon which assessment instruments are used, determined by whether or not there are copyrighted documents, time spent scoring and interpreting, computer software scoring costs, and the like. The administration, scoring, and interpretation of most of the aforementioned assessment instruments can be subsumed under the heading "psychological testing," and will be reimbursed by many third party payers, even when completed outside of the clinic.

Pragmatic Issues Encountered in Clinical Practice: Generalized Anxiety Disorder

A number of medical conditions can mimic the anxiety symptoms of GAD, and some chronic illnesses are associated with GAD. As with PDA, therefore, a medical evaluation for concomitant disorders such as cardiovascular diseases, irritable bowel syndrome, and hyperthyroidism is needed prior to diagnosing and treating GAD.

Worry is relatively difficult to assess because it is private behavior. Factors that initiate and reinforce or otherwise maintain worry are difficult to assess for the same reason. The questionnaires and self-monitoring protocols described earlier are valuable in characterizing worry and its maintaining conditions in the individual client, and additional questionnaires are described in Antony and colleagues (2001). In the final analysis, however, worry is sufficiently private and idiosyncratic to require in-depth clinical interviewing. Careful assessment of worry, therefore, ultimately introduces the various weaknesses of interview data.

Assessment of anxiety in GAD is not straightforward either because anxiety in GAD differs from that of other anxiety disorders. Anxiety in GAD does not involve abrupt sympathetic arousal and associated indicators such as tachycardia, breathlessness, and dizziness. Rather, as noted earlier, it involves restlessness, irritability, fatigue, impaired concentration, and other indicators of a guarded approach to living and apprehensiveness. Therefore, many of the commonly used measures of anxiety will underestimate the magnitude of the problem.

Because of the characteristic features of anxiety in GAD, it is especially important to consider possible confusion between symptoms of anxiety and symptoms of depression, as well as the possibility of comorbid depression which often follows GAD (cf. Ballenger et al. 2001). Roemer and Medaglia (2001) note correctly that the inherent potential for confusion is augmented by the fact that some popular questionnaire measures confound the measurement of anxiety and depression.

☐ Case Illustration

(Portions of this case are from a client; others are added for expository purposes.)

Client Description

Amanda was 31 when she presented for treatment. She was a sophomore at a local 2-year college, having decided to return after a long hiatus from school. Amanda was residing with her husband and four children in a nearby rural town. She was referred after her youngest daughter underwent a psychological evaluation. Amanda was advised by the clinician who tested her daughter to seek help for her own anxiety and seemingly constant worrying.

History of the Disorder or Problem

When asked about her difficulties, Amanda reported that she remembered having been "nervous" since the first grade. After she began having children at age 21, her anxiety symptoms reportedly worsened and her worry reached out to include her children. She also recounted a fear of tornadoes that she had when she was younger, and stated that she later developed an extreme fear of thunderstorms. Subsequently, she went to her physician because she thought that a constant heavy feeling in her chest and constriction of her breathing were related to a medical condition such as bronchitis. In addition, she reported constant headaches. Her physician diagnosed her with PD and GAD and prescribed Buspar®, which she continued to use even though it did not significantly reduce her symptoms. Finally, episodes of extreme fear began to occur in situations other than those involving violent weather, and she reported that these attacks sometimes appeared to "come out of the blue."

Presenting Complaints

Amanda's current difficulties centered on her growing fear of panic and constant worry. She reported that she worried about her grades and schoolwork, about the safety of her children, and about the nature of her relationship with her husband (who was rarely home due to his job and his passion for activities such as hunting and fishing). She had become suspicious that her husband was "cheating" because he was so rarely at home. When asked about her panic symptomatology, Amanda reported that her fear of panic was causing her to avoid more and more situations in which she thought an attack might occur. At the same time, concern for the safety of her children prompted frequent contacts with them and with those involved in their care. Her fear of panic attacks and constant worrying had culminated in reliance on safety signals — she would not leave the house unless she had her cellular telephone and medication with her.

Assessment Methods Used

In addition to a standard intake interview (from which the information above was gathered) and Mental Status Exam, Amanda was administered the ADIS-IV-L modules for panic disorder, agoraphobia, and generalized anxiety disorder. Amanda also completed four self-report measures germane to her panic symptomatology (the Anxiety Sensitivity Index, the Agoraphobic Cognitions Questionnaire, the Body Sensations Questionnaire, and the Albany Panic and Phobia Questionnaire) and three measures to assess GAD-related worry (the Penn State Worry Questionnaire, the Worry Domains Questionnaire, and the Why Worry Scale-II). She also engaged in selected symptom induction tests to assess fears of physical sensations. Outside of the office, she completed self-monitoring forms pertinent to her panic and worry. Consultation with her physician helped rule out complicating medical conditions.

Psychological Assessment Protocol

The intake interview did not suggest that Amanda was experiencing any other psychological distress other than that related to PDA and GAD. She did not endorse depressive symptomatology or suicidal ideation. She denied recent changes in her eating and sleeping habits and use of illicit substances. She was oriented to person, place, and time. Short- and long-term memory appeared intact. She denied experiencing psychotic symptoms. A phone conversation with her physician indicated that, based on a recent physical exam, bloodwork, and presenting problems, he did not believe Amanda to be suffering from any medical conditions that would mimic or exacerbate her anxiety symptoms or interfere with exposure treatments.

Amanda's responses to the ADIS-IV-L indicated that she met criteria both for PDA and GAD. She reported that, over the last month, she had frequently worried and been severely apprehensive about having another panic attack (7 on a scale of 8). She endorsed moderate to severe symptoms of heart palpitations, shortness of breath, choking sensations, nausea, dizziness, tingling sensations, and a fear of dying as features of her panic attacks. She reported that fear of dying and fear of being unable to obtain assistance largely drove her avoidance of situations in which she feared she would experience panic.

Amanda's responses to the four PDA self-report measures were indicative of significant panic-related symptomatology. On the Anxiety Sensitivity Index, Amanda scored a 36, which approximates the mean score of 32.1 (SD = 11.3) for those who have panic disorder with moderate or severe agoraphobia (Rapee, Brown, Antony, & Barlow, 1992). On the Agoraphobic Cognitions Questionnaire, Amanda's mean score of 2.79 slightly exceeded the mean score of 2.32 (SD = 0.66) for a group of outpatients with agoraphobia reported by Chambless and colleagues (1984). Amanda scored a mean of 3.29 on the Body Sensations Questionnaire, again slightly exceeding the mean of 3.05 (SD = 0.86) for outpatients with agoraphobia (Chambless et al.). Her score of 29 on the agoraphobia subscale of the Albany Panic and Phobia Questionnaire far exceeded the mean of 12.8 (SD = 9.8) for a group of outpatients with PDA reported by Rapee and colleagues (1995). Her score of 17 on the interoceptive subscale of this measure also exceeded the mean of 9.6 (SD = 9.2) in the same PDA group (Rapee et al.).

On the three self-report measures related to GAD, Amanda's scores were indicative of chronic and excessive worry across several domains. On the Penn State Worry Questionnaire, Amanda scored a 74, slightly above the mean score of 67.66 (SD = 8.86) obtained by a group of GAD clients (Molina & Borkovec, 1994). On the Worry Domains Questionnaire,

Amanda scored a 65, well above the mean score of 40.03 (SD = 19.8) reported in a GAD sample (Tallis, Davey, & Bond, 1994). The overall score obtained on the Why Worry Scale-II was 55, which was slightly above the mean score of 46.9 (SD = 22.5) obtained by a group of individuals with a principal diagnosis of GAD via the ADIS-R (Ladouceur, Blais, Freeston, & Dugas, 1998) and well above the mean score of 43.3 (SD = 7.9) obtained by college students diagnosed by self-report questionnaires (Freeston et al., 1994).

The ADIS-IV-L modules and self-report measures confirmed that Amanda was suffering from both PDA and GAD, and helped the therapist characterize the phenomenology of her panic and worry. Her responses to the panic-related measures indicated that she was experiencing significant fear related to bodily sensations of panic, and that catastrophic thinking was tied to these bodily sensations. She also reported significant anxiety when in situations where she deemed panic likely, such as in the mall, in the supermarket, and while driving. Her responses to the three GAD measures indicated that her worry was chronic, excessive, and experienced as uncontrollable. A review of her responses suggested that she mostly worried about relationships and was pessimistic about the future. Reviewing her responses indicated also that she perceived her worry as preventing unpleasant outcomes, as protecting her from adverse emotions in the event of such outcomes, and as motivating her to action.

At the end of the first assessment session, Amanda was instructed to complete two self-monitoring forms throughout the following week. The first form was designed to identify the frequency of her panic attacks, bodily sensations, and cognitions experienced during each attack, whether the attack was experienced as unexpected or situationally-cued, and the maximum anxiety (0–8) experienced during each attack (Craske & Barlow, 2000). She was instructed to also note on the form the situation in which the attack occurred and which, if any, safety signals were present. Amanda was encouraged to complete the form even if she became afraid of having a panic attack but did not actually experience one. A second form, a Worry Outcome Diary (Borkovec et al., 1999), was provided to assess the frequency, content, and feared outcomes of her worry, as well as the actual outcome of the situation she had been worrying about. Her compliance in completing such forms was discussed as being crucial to developing an accurate picture of her problem and as an important predictor of treatment outcome.

One week later, her compliance and responses were reviewed. She reported having two panic attacks and four instances in which she was afraid of having an attack but did not. Her panic attacks and fear of panicking during the week primarily occurred when in large public places and when she was alone, and she reported carrying her medication and cellular telephone with her at all times. During the attacks, the primary physical symptoms reported were shortness of breath, heart palpitations, and dizziness. Her most frequently-reported cognitive themes were being afraid that she was going to die and losing control over her behavior. She reported that these symptoms and thoughts resulted in her feeling that she needed to escape the situation immediately. Not surprisingly, a significant portion of the worry noted on the GAD monitoring form was tied to her fear of having a panic attack. Additional sources of worry throughout the preceding week were related to her children's health, their performance in school, her relationship with her husband, and her fear of not graduating from college. It was helpful to contrast with Amanda the feared outcomes she noted and the actual outcomes of the situations she had been worrying about. In seven of the eight recorded instances, the feared outcome never occurred. The exception to this was that her son failed a math test, as she worried he might because he had not been doing all of his homework.

Following a review of her self-monitoring forms, the last half of the second assessment session was devoted to symptom induction tests designed around her reported fears of physical symptoms. Prior to each exercise, Amanda rated her self-efficacy (0–100) that she would be able to complete the exercise without having a panic attack; afterward she provided fear ratings (0–100) of the highest level of fear she experienced during each exercise. Three exercises were chosen to invoke the feared physical sensations: breathing solely through a straw for one minute (shortness of breath), running in place for 3 minutes (heart palpitations), and spinning rapidly in a swivel chair for one minute (dizziness). These exercises provided pretreatment measures for fears of physical sensations associated with panic.

Targets Selected for Treatment

The first targeted problem area was Amanda's fear of bodily sensations (interoceptive anxiety), which was treated via symptom induction exercises and was continuously evaluated with fear and self-efficacy ratings. A hierarchy was developed for increasingly feared bodily sensations, and Amanda reproduced the sensations at each level of the hierarchy via symptom induction exercises until she reported minimal fear. The second targeted problem was her agoraphobic avoidance and reliance on safety signals, which was treated via in vivo exposure in a shopping mall, two supermarkets, and other places in which she feared a panic attack might occur. At first, carrying her cellular phone and medication was permitted, but as in vivo exposure trials continued these safety signals were withdrawn. The final problem area related to PDA was her panic-related cognitions and tendency toward fearful catastrophizing, which were challenged using cognitive restructuring techniques.

Two problem areas related to GAD were identified for treatment. The first was anxiety symptoms per se, which were treated via muscular relaxation training and breathing retraining. The second GAD problem area was her irrational beliefs. Some targeted beliefs were about the functions of worry, such as her belief that worry served to prevent adverse outcomes. Other irrational beliefs were related to her tendency to overestimate the likelihood of feared outcomes. Treating such irrational beliefs involved cognitive therapy (restructuring, challenging automatic thoughts, etc.) and regular use of the Worry Outcome Diary to demonstrate that feared outcomes rarely occurred (and those that did occur had been largely out of her control).

Assessment of Progress

Amanda was readministered the ADIS-IV-L modules and the various self-report measures after 6 weeks and after 12 weeks of treatment. Her initial scores on these measures were used as standards for comparison. The symptom induction tests and associated efficacy and fear ratings were used throughout treatment both as a form of exposure therapy and as a way to monitor Amanda's lessening fear of physical panic symptoms. Follow-ups at 3 and 6 months included administering the self-report measures and having Amanda engage in both symptom induction and in vivo exposure exercises. The relevant ADIS-IV modules were readministered at follow-ups in order to determine whether she still met criteria for PDA and/or GAD.

☐ Summary

Comprehensive clinical assessment of both PDA and GAD should include a medical evaluation, assessment of potential comorbid conditions, and differential diagnosis based on a variety of self-report and behavioral methods. Self-report methods consist of semi-structured clinical interviews, questionnaires, self-monitoring, and situational fear and self-efficacy ratings. Behavioral methods include symptom induction tests, behavioral avoidance tests, and biological challenge tests. In assessing PDA, self-report and behavioral methods are used in concert to allow clinicians to understand relevant situational antecedents, bodily sensations experienced, interoceptive anxiety, and agoraphobic avoidance. GAD is assessed using self-report methods that allow clinicians to characterize the contents and functions of chronic worry. In general, these assessment strategies are used to identify and prioritize problems that warrant clinical intervention and to monitor progress in treatment. Assessment of PDA and GAD is described in the context of an idealized case report.

☐ References

American Psychiatric Association. (1987). *Diagnostic and statistical manual of mental disorders* (3rd ed., rev.). Washington, DC: American Psychiatric Association.

American Psychiatric Association. (2000). *Diagnostic and statistical manual of mental disorders* (4th ed., text rev.). Washington, DC: American Psychiatric Association.

Antony, M. M. (2001). Measures for panic disorder and agoraphobia. In M.M. Antony, S.M. Orsillo, & L. Roemer (Eds.), *Practitioner's guide to empirically based measures of anxiety* (pp. 95-125). New York: Kluwer Academic/Plenum.

Antony, M. M., Orsillo, S. M., & Roemer, L. (Eds.). (2001). *Practitioner's guide to empirically based measures of anxiety.* New York: Kluwer Academic/Plenum.

Antony, M. M., & Swinson, R. P. (2000). *Phobic disorders and panic in adults: A guide to assessment and treatment.* Washington, DC: American Psychological Association.

Ballenger, J. C., Davidson, J. R. T., Lecrubier, Y., Nutt, D. J., Borkovec, T. D., Rickels, K., Stein, D. J., Wittchen, H. -U. (2001). Consensus statement on generalized anxiety disorder from the International Consensus Group on Depression and Anxiety. *Journal of Clinical Psychiatry, 62* (suppl. 11), 53–58.

Bandura, A. (1977). Self-efficacy: Toward a unifying theory of behavioral change. *Psychological Review, 84,* 191–215.

Barlow, D. H. (1988). *Anxiety and its disorders: The nature and treatment of anxiety and panic.* New York: Guilford.

Barlow, D. H. (2002). *Anxiety and its disorders: The nature and treatment of anxiety and panic* (2nd ed.). New York: Guilford.

Beck, J. G., & Zebb, B. J. (1994). Behavioral assessment and treatment of panic disorder: Current status, future directions. *Behavior Therapy, 25,* 581–611.

Blazer, D., George, L. K., & Hughes, D. (1991). The epidemiology of anxiety disorders: An age comparison. In C. Salzman & B. D. Lebowitz (Eds.), *Anxiety in the elderly: Treatment and research* (pp. 17–30). New York: Springer.

Blazer, D. G., Hughes, D., George, L. K., Swartz, M., & Boyer, R. (1991). Generalized anxiety disorder. In L. N. Robins & D. A. Regier (Eds.), *Psychiatric disorders in America*: The *Epidemiologic Catchment Area study* (pp. 180–203). New York: Free Press.

Borkovec, T. D., Hazlett-Stevens, H., & Diaz, M. L. (1999). The role of positive beliefs about worry in generalized anxiety disorder and its treatment. *Clinical Psychology and Psychotherapy, 6,* 126–138.

Borkovec, T. D., & Roemer, L. (1995). Perceived functions of worry among generalized anxiety disorder subjects: Distraction from more emotionally stressing topics? *Journal of Behavior Therapy and Experimental Psychiatry, 26,* 25–30.

Bouchard, S., Pelletier, M. H., Gauthier, J. G., Côté, G., & Laberge, B. (1997). The assessment of panic using self-report: A comprehensive survey of validated instruments. *Journal of Anxiety Disorders, 11,* 89–111.

Bourin, M., Baker, G. B., & Bradwejn, J. (1998). Neurobiology of panic disorder. *Journal of Psychosomatic Research, 44,* 163–180.

Brawman-Mintzer, O., Lydiard, R. B., Emmanuel, N., Payeur, R., Johnson, M., Roberts, J., Jarrell, M. P., & Ballenger, J. C. (1993). Psychiatric comorbidity in patients with generalized anxiety disorder. *American Journal of Psychiatry, 150,* 1216–1218.

Breitholtz, E., Johansson, B., & Öst, L. -G. (1999). Cognitions in generalized anxiety disorder and panic disorder patients: A prospective approach. *Behaviour Research and Therapy, 37,* 533–544.

Brown, T. A., Antony, M. M., & Barlow, D. H. (1992). Psychometric properties of the Penn State Worry Questionnaire in a clinical anxiety disorders sample. *Behaviour Research and Therapy, 30,* 33–37.

Brown, T. A., & Barlow, D. H. (1992). Comorbidity among anxiety disorders: Implications for treatment and DSM-IV. *Journal of Consulting and Clinical Psychology, 63,* 408–418.

Brown, T. A., Campbell, L. A., Lehman, C. L., Grisham, J. R., & Mancill, R. B. (2001). Current and lifetime comorbidity of the DSM-IV anxiety and mood disorders in a large clinical sample. *Journal of Abnormal Psychology, 110,* 585–599.

Brown, T. A., Di Nardo, P. A., Lehman, C. L., & Campbell, L. A. (2001). Reliability of DSM-IV anxiety and mood disorders: Implications for classification of emotional disorders. *Journal of Abnormal Psychology, 110,* 49–58.

Brown, T. A., O'Leary, T. A., & Barlow, D. H. (2001). Generalized anxiety disorder. In Barlow, D. H. (Ed.), *Clinical handbook of psychological disorders: A step-by-step treatment manual* (3rd ed., pp. 154–208). New York: Guilford.

Cartwright-Hatton, S., & Wells, A. (1997). Beliefs about worry and intrusions: The Meta-Cognitions Questionnaire and its correlates. *Journal of Anxiety Disorders, 11,* 279–296.

Chambless, D. L., Caputo, G. C., Bright, P., & Gallagher, R. (1984). Assessment of fear of fear in agoraphobics: The Body Sensations Questionnaire and the Agoraphobic Cognitions Questionnaire. *Journal of Consulting and Clinical Psychology, 65,* 1090–1097.

Chambless, D. L., & Gracely, E. J. (1989). Fear of fear and the anxiety disorders. *Cognitive Therapy and Research, 13,* 9–20.

Craske, M. G., & Barlow, D. H. (2000). *Mastery of your anxiety and panic (MAP-3): Agoraphobia supplement.* San Antonio, TX: Psychological Corporation.

Craske, M. G., Barlow, D. H., & O'Leary, T. (1992). *Mastery of your anxiety and worry.* San Antonio, TX: Psychological Corporation.

Dattilio, F. M., & Salas-Auvert, J. (2000). *Panic disorder: Assessment and treatment through a wide-angle lens.* Phoenix, AZ: Zeig, Tucker, & Co.

Davey, G. C. L., Tallis, F., & Capuzzo, N. (1996). Beliefs about the consequences of worrying. *Cognitive Therapy and Research, 20,* 499–520.

Di Nardo, P. A., Brown, T. A., & Barlow, D. H. (1994). *Anxiety Disorders Interview Schedule for DSM-IV: Lifetime Version (ADIS-IV-L).* San Antonio, TX: Psychological Corporation.

Dugas, M. J., Gagnon, F., Ladouceur, R., & Freeston, M. H. (1998). Generalized anxiety disorder: A preliminary test of a conceptual model. *Behaviour Research and Therapy, 36,* 215–226.

Dupuy, J. –B., Beaudoin, S., Rhéaume, J., Ladouceur, R., & Dugas, M. J. (2001). Worry: Daily self-report in clinical and non-clinical populations. *Behaviour Research and Therapy, 39,* 1249–1255.

Forsyth, J. P., & Karekla, M. (2001). Biological challenge in the assessment of anxiety disorders. In M. M. Antony, S. M. Orsillo, & L. Roemer (Eds.), *Practitioner's guide to empirically based measures of anxiety* (pp. 31–36). New York: Kluwer Academic/Plenum.

Freeston, M. H., Rhéaume, J., Letarte, H., Dugas, M. J., & Ladouceur, R. (1994). Why do people worry? *Personality and Individual Differences, 17,* 791–802.

Ladouceur, R., Blais, F., Freeston, M. H., & Dugas, M. J. (1998). Problem solving and problem orientation in generalized anxiety disorder. *Journal of Anxiety Disorders, 12,* 139–152.

Massion, A., Warshaw, M., & Keller, M. (1993). Quality of life and psychiatric morbidity in panic disorder versus generalized anxiety disorder. *American Journal of Psychiatry, 150,* 600–607.

McGlynn, F. D., & Bates, L. W. (1999). Cognitive behavior therapy. In M. Hersen & A. S. Bellack (Eds.), *Handbook of comparative interventions for adult disorders* (2nd ed., pp. 225–255). New York: Wiley.

McGlynn, F. D., & Rose, M. P. (1998). Assessment of anxiety and fear. In A. S. Bellack & M. Hersen (Eds.), *Behavioral assessment: A practical handbook* (4th ed., pp. 179–209). Needham Heights, MA: Allyn & Bacon.

McNally, R. J. (1994). *Panic disorder: A critical analysis*. New York: Guilford Press.

Meyer, T. J., Miller, M. L., Metzger, R. L., & Borkovec, T. D. (1990). Development and validation of the Penn State Worry Questionnaire. *Behaviour Research and Therapy, 28,* 487–495.

Molina, S., & Borkovec, T. D. (1994). The Penn State Worry Questionnaire: Psychometric properties and associated characteristics. In G. C. L. Davey & F. Tallis (Eds.), *Worrying: Perspectives on theory, assessment, and treatment* (pp. 265-283). New York: Wiley.

Newman, M. G., Zuellig, A. R., Kachin, K. E., Constantino, M. J., Przeworski, A., Erickson, T., & Cashman-McGrath, L. (2002). Preliminary reliability and validity of the Generalized Anxiety Disorder Questionnaire — IV: A revised self-report diagnostic measure of generalized anxiety disorder. *Behavior Therapy, 33,* 215–233.

Papillo, J. F., Murphy, P. M., & Gorman, J. M. (1988). Psychophysiology. In M. Hersen (Ed.), *Handbook of anxiety disorders* (pp. 217–250). New York: Pergamon.

Peterson, R. A., & Reiss, S. (1993). *Anxiety Sensitivity Index Revised test manual*. Worthington, OH: IDS Publishing Corporation.

Rachman, S. (1984). Agoraphobia: A safety-signal perspective. *Behaviour Research and Therapy, 22,* 59–70.

Rapee, R. M. (1995). Psychological factors influencing the affective response to biological challenge procedures in panic disorder. *Journal of Anxiety Disorders, 9,* 59–74.

Rapee, R. M., Brown, T. A., Antony, M. M., & Barlow, D. H. (1992). Response to hyperventilation and inhalation of 5.5% carbon-dioxide enriched air across the DMS-III-R anxiety disorders. *Journal of Abnormal Psychology, 101,* 538–552.

Rapee, R. M., Craske, M. G., & Barlow, D. H. (1995). Assessment instrument for panic disorder that includes fear of sensation-producing activities: The Albany Panic and Phobia Questionnaire. *Anxiety, 1,* 114–122.

Reiss, S., & McNally, R. J. (1985). The expectancy model of fear. In S. Reiss & R. R. Bootzin (Eds.), *Theoretical issues in behavior therapy* (pp. 107–121). New York: Academic Press.

Reiss, S., Peterson, R. A., Gursky, D. M., & McNally, R. J. (1986). Anxiety sensitivity, anxiety frequency, and the prediction of fearfulness. *Behaviour Research and Therapy, 24,* 1–8.

Roemer, L. (2001a). Measures for anxiety and related constructs. In M. M. Antony, S. M. Orsillo, & L. Roemer (Eds.), *Practitioner's guide to empirically based measures of anxiety* (pp. 49–83). New York: Kluwer Academic/Plenum.

Roemer, L. (2001b). Measures for generalized anxiety disorder. In M. M. Antony, S. M. Orsillo, & L. Roemer (Eds.), *Practitioner's guide to empirically based measures of anxiety* (pp. 197–209). New York: Kluwer Academic/Plenum.

Roemer, L., & Medaglia, E. (2001). Generalized anxiety disorder: A brief overview and guide to assessment. In M. M. Antony, S. M. Orsillo, & L. Roemer (Eds.), *Practitioner's guide to empirically based measures of anxiety* (pp. 189–195). New York: Kluwer Academic/Plenum.

Shiffman, S. (2000). Real-time self-report of momentary states in the natural environment: Computerized ecological momentary assessment. In A. A. Stone, J. S. Turkkan, C. A. Bachrach, J. B. Jobe, H. S. Kurtzman, & V. S. Cain (Eds.), *The science of self-report: Implications for research and practice* (pp. 277–296). Mahwah, NJ: Erlbaum.

Starcevic, V., Uhlenhuth, E. H., Kellner, R., & Pathak, D. (1993). Comorbidity in panic disorder: II. Chronology of appearance and pathogenic comorbidity. *Psychiatry Research, 46,* 285–293.

Stöber, J. (1998). Reliability and validity of two widely-used worry questionnaires: Self-report and self-peer convergence. *Personality and Individual Differences, 24,* 887–890.

Tallis, F., Davey, G. C. L., & Bond, A. (1994). The Worry Domains Questionnaire. In G. C. L. Davey & F. Tallis (Eds.), *Worrying: Perspectives on theory, assessment, and treatment* (pp. 287–292). New York: Wiley.

Tallis, F., Eysenck, M., & Mathews, A. (1992). A questionnaire for the measurement of nonpathological worry. *Personality and Individual Differences, 13,* 161–168.

Taylor, S. (1999). *Anxiety sensitivity: Theory, research and treatment of the fear of anxiety.* Hillsdale, NJ: Erlbaum.

Taylor, S., & Cox, B. J. (1998). An expanded Anxiety Sensitivity Index: Evidence for a hierarchic structure in a clinical sample. *Journal of Anxiety Disorders, 12,* 463–483.

Taylor, C. B., Fried, L., & Kenardy, J. (1990). The use of real-time computer diary for data acquisition and processing. *Behaviour Research and Therapy, 28,* 93–97.

Turner, S. M., Beidel, D. C., & Stanley, M. A. (1992). Are obsessional thoughts and worries different cognitive phenomena? *Clinical Psychology Review, 12,* 257–270.

Vermilyea, J. A., Boice, R., & Barlow, D. H. (1984). Rachman and Hodgson (1974) a decade later: How do desynchronous response systems relate to the treatment of agoraphobia? *Behaviour Research and Therapy, 22,* 615–621.

Wells, A. (1994). A multi-dimensional measure of worry: Development and preliminary validation of the Anxious Thoughts Inventory. *Anxiety, Stress, and Coping, 6,* 289–299.

Williams, K. E., Chambless, D. L., & Ahrens, A. (1997). Are emotions frightening? An extension of the fear of fear construct. *Behaviour Research and Therapy, 35,* 239–348.

Wisocki, P. A. (1988). Worry as a phenomenon relevant to the elderly. *Behavior Therapy, 19,* 369–379.

Wittchen, H. -U., Zhao, S., Kessler, R. C. & Eaton, W. W. (1994). DSM-III-R generalized anxiety disorder in the National Comorbidity Survey. *Archives of General Psychiatry, 51,* 355–364.

Yartz, A. R., & Hawk, L. W., Jr. (2001). Psychophysiological assessment of anxiety: Tales from the heart. In M. M. Antony, S. M. Orsillo, & L. Roemer (Eds.), *Practitioner's guide to empirically based measures of anxiety* (pp. 25–30). New York: Kluwer Academic/Plenum.

Zinbarg, R. E., Barlow, D. H.., & Brown, T. A. (1997). Hierarchical structure and general factor saturation of the Anxiety Sensitivity Index: Evidence and implications. *Psychological Assessment, 9,* 277–284.

4
CHAPTER

Susannah L. Mozley
Todd C. Buckley
Danny G. Kaloupek

Acute and Posttraumatic Stress Disorders

☐ Description of the Disorders

The current psychiatric nomenclature, as delineated in the *Diagnostic and Statistical Manual of Mental Disorders*, 4th edition (DSM-IV; American Psychiatric Association, 1994), includes diagnostic criteria for two clinical disorders produced by exposure to traumatic events: acute stress disorder (ASD) and posttraumatic stress disorder (PTSD). Unlike most other psychiatric illnesses, these disorders are associated with precipitating events that are a necessary precondition for diagnosis. For an event to be defined as traumatic in this context, it may be directly or indirectly experienced (e.g., witnessed), but it must involve "actual or threatened death or serious injury," and result in a subjective response of "intense fear, helplessness, or horror" (DSM-IV, 1994, pp. 427–428).

Both disorders also require the expression of symptoms characterized as reexperiencing, avoidance, emotional numbing, and heightened arousal. Reexperiencing may include intrusive thoughts about the experience, trauma-related dreams, flashback episodes, a sense of reliving the trauma, or distress when exposed to reminders of the trauma. Avoidance refers to efforts to prevent thinking or speaking about the trauma, which may include involvement in specific behaviors that provide escape from trauma reminders. Numbing symptoms may include inability to remember important aspects of the trauma, diminished ability to experience emotion, diminished interest in previously enjoyed activities, social detachment, or a belief that one's life will be cut short. Symptoms of heightened arousal include difficulty sleeping, irritability, difficulty concentrating, feelings of being "on guard" and worried about safety, or exaggerated startle response. PTSD may be specified as "acute" when duration is 1 to 3 months, as "chronic" when duration is 3 months or more, or "with delayed onset" when PTSD symptoms do not occur until at least 6 months after the stressor.

There are two principal differences between the diagnosis of ASD and the diagnosis of PTSD: duration and dissociation. ASD is defined as occurring between 2 days and 1 month posttrauma, while PTSD cannot be diagnosed until at least one month has passed since the traumatic event. Additionally, ASD is defined by dissociation in the acute posttrauma phase, with a minimum requirement of three dissociative symptoms (numbing of emotional response, reduced awareness of surroundings, derealization, depersonalization, or dissociative amnesia). Although the PTSD diagnostic criteria also include dissociative flashback episodes, dissociative amnesia, and emotional numbing, an individual may be diagnosed with PTSD without presenting any of these symptoms.

Incidence

Lifetime risk for exposure to a potentially traumatic event is high, with estimated rates ranging from 60 to 90%, while lifetime rates for PTSD are much lower, ranging from 1 to 9% in the general population (Breslau et al., 1998; Helzer, Robins, & McEvoy, 1987; Kessler, Sonnega, Bromet, Hughes, & Nelson, 1995). Rates of ASD have been more difficult to determine, in part because of the lack of a "gold standard" diagnostic measure, but most studies have found ASD rates in the 10 to 20% range for various traumas (Harvey & Bryant, 2002). The percentage of individuals meeting PTSD criteria in the acute posttrauma phase (without the 1-month duration criterion) has been found to be similar or slightly higher than ASD rates (Blanchard et al., 1997; Patterson, Carrigan, Questad, & Robinson, 1990). Taken together, results of incidence rate studies reveal that while trauma exposure is common and a sizable minority of individuals shows high levels of symptoms in the first month, most trauma-exposed individuals will experience a remission of symptoms without formal psychiatric intervention.

Differential Diagnosis and Associated Features

Differential diagnosis is an important issue for both ASD and PTSD because of the broad array of possible posttrauma reactions. When evaluating for ASD, it is important to appreciate that even pronounced acute responses to extreme stress are not necessarily indicative of psychiatric disorder. In cases where there is sufficient impairment in important areas of functioning to warrant psychiatric diagnosis during the first month posttrauma, other diagnoses to rule out include: Adjustment Disorder, Mental Disorder due to a General Medical Condition, Substance-Induced Disorder, Brief Psychotic Disorder, or Major Depressive Episode. The individual's history might also suggest that the posttraumatic response primarily reflects an exacerbation of a preexisting mental disorder. Indeed, previous psychiatric problems are reliable, albeit modest, predictors of posttraumatic outcomes (Brewin et al., 2000). Even when symptoms persist past 1 month, it is important to recognize that not all observed psychopathology is necessarily attributable to PTSD given that many PTSD symptoms are similar to those of mood disorders and other anxiety disorders. In general, symptoms should link directly to trauma exposure in terms of onset and content (e.g., reexperiencing of trauma memories) before a PTSD diagnosis is made.

Research indicates a high rate of comorbidity such that 50 to 90% of individuals with chronic PTSD also meet criteria for another psychiatric disorder (Fairbank et al., 1993; Keane & Wolfe, 1990; Kulka et al., 1990). The most common comorbid disorders include Substance Abuse and Dependence, Generalized Anxiety Disorder, Major Depressive Disorder, and Dysthymic Disorder. PTSD has been found to be primary more often than not with respect to comorbid affective and substance use disorders (Kessler et al., 1995).

The aforementioned findings highlight the importance of differentiating symptoms due to trauma and those better accounted for by other psychiatric conditions. For example, feelings of despair, hopelessness, and guilt are common associated features for both ASD and PTSD, but also are associated with depressive and dysthymic disorders. As with many mood and anxiety disorders, PTSD is frequently associated with marital conflict and job loss related to symptoms of avoidance, social withdrawal, loss of interest in activities, and outbursts of anger (Byrne & Riggs, 2002; Riggs, Byrne, Weathers, & Litz, 1998; Zatzick et al., 1997). In some cases, avoidance of people, places, or activities that remind the individual of the traumatic event may resemble phobic avoidance or include panic attacks with agoraphobia. At the same time, physiological arousal accounted for by panic disorder can mistakenly resemble physiological reactivity to trauma cues.

The Acute Stress Disorder Debate

It is important to note that there is ongoing debate in the field of traumatic stress regarding the nature and utility of the ASD diagnostic category (Harvey & Bryant, 2002). Beginning with DSM-III, prolonged pathologic responses to extreme stressors could be defined in terms of PTSD, but the default option for diagnosis of traumatized individuals within the first month following exposure to trauma was an Adjustment Disorder. The primary arguments for developing the ASD diagnosis were to provide greater continuity with the PTSD diagnosis and to provide a means for formally recognizing the high levels of distress that are experienced by some individuals in the first month after trauma. Proponents of ASD have noted the importance of identifying individuals who are likely to develop prolonged difficulties (Koopman, Classen, Cardeña, & Spiegel, 1995), arguing that the ASD diagnosis will focus research attention on acute posttrauma reactions and their relationship to prolonged pathological reactions (e.g., PTSD; Solomon et al., 1996). It also has been argued that assessment of ASD can help direct immediate services to individuals in need and characterize the condition of traumatized communities (Koopman et al. 1995). Critics have pointed to the lack of evidence for the dissociative symptom criteria and have argued that one diagnosis should not exist primarily to predict another. Critics have further raised the concern that ASD pathologizes stress reactions that in most instances are transient and uncomplicated in their resolution (Harvey & Bryant, 2002).

The weight of current research on ASD suggests that high levels of general distress do occur within the first month posttrauma for a range of traumatic events, that early identification of individuals in distress is important, but that emphasis on dissociative symptoms unnecessarily limits the identification of at-risk individuals (Harvey & Bryant, 2002). With the jury still out on the clinical utility of the ASD diagnosis, we propose other known risk variables for use in clinical decision-making. Evidence suggests that ASD and acute PTSD symptoms (within the first month posttrauma) are equally effective for predicting the development of chronic PTSD (Brewin, Andrews, & Rose, 2003). Acute posttrauma symptoms of reexperiencing, avoidance, and arousal have all been shown to be predictive of PTSD (Brewin, Andrews, Rose, & Kirk, 1999; Bryant & Harvey, 1998; Harvey & Bryant, 1998; Shalev, Freedman, Peri, Brandes, & Sahar, 1997; Shalev, Peri, Canetti, & Schreiber, 1996). Other PTSD risk factors with current empirical support include history of prior trauma, low social support, younger age, low ambient cortisol levels, history of family instability, concurrent psychosocial stressors, and family history of anxiety, mood, or substance abuse disorders (Halligan

& Yehuda, 2000; Harvey & Bryant, 2002; Litz, Gray, Bryant, & Adler, 2002). The presence of increasing numbers of the aforementioned risk factors appears to increase the probability of an individual's developing PTSD in the aftermath of traumatic events.

☐ Range of Assessment Strategies Available

The challenges posed by trauma-related assessment often call for a multi-modal approach (e.g., Keane Wolfe, & Taylor, 1987). The measurement options may be among the best for any psychiatric disorder.

Assessment of Acute Trauma Reactions

Assessment of ASD has been limited by the lack of standardized ASD-specific measures and continuing debate about the utility of ASD diagnostic criteria (Bryant & Harvey, 1997). Currently two self-report measures and one structured clinical interview for ASD have demonstrated moderate reliability and validity: the Stanford Acute Stress Reaction Questionnaire (SASRQ; Cardeña, Koopman, Classen, Waelde, & Spiegel, 2000), the Acute Stress Disorder Scale (ASDS; Bryant, Moulds, & Guthrie, 2000), and the Acute Stress Disorder Interview (ASDI; Bryant, Harvey, Dang, & Sackville, 1998). These instruments are based on the ASD symptom clusters designated in the DSM-IV, criteria that were developed primarily on the basis of theory with limited empirical foundation or support (Bryant & Bird, 2001; Harvey & Bryant, 2002).

Practice guidelines for early posttrauma assessment and intervention developed by the National Institute of Mental Health (2002; also see Litz, Gray, et al., 2002) take a more empirical approach to the acute post-trauma reactions. These guidelines recommend foregoing formal ASD or PTSD diagnostic assessment in the first posttrauma week and, instead, emphasize evaluation of immediate practical needs, brief screening for risk factors (e.g. history of psychiatric illness, poor social support resources), and provision of information about eventual treatment options. Ideally formal assessment of symptoms can begin at least one week posttrauma, addressing a range of anxiety problems, depression, and substance use in addition to PTSD symptoms. Based on the risk factor research, the guidelines also emphasize the importance of using initial screening and early assessment to facilitate the individual's use of existing social supports. Early intervention, if warranted, might involve multiple components that include psycho-education, anxiety management, therapeutic exposure, cognitive restructuring, and relapse prevention (Bryant, Sackville, Dang, Moulds, & Guthrie, 1999; Echeburua, de Corral, Sarasua, & Zubizarreta, 1996; Foa, Hearst-Ikeda, & Perry, 1995). The guidelines note that for any level of intervention, informed consent should be obtained with a document that includes therapist credentials, information about the relationship between therapists and employers, and which emphasizes the voluntary nature of assessment and treatment.

Assessment of PTSD

A large number of standardized measures for PTSD assessment are available, and summaries of the available instruments and techniques can be found in numerous publications (e.g., Carlson, 1997; Litz, Miller, Ruef, & McTeague, 2002; Weathers & Keane, 1999). Despite their availability, measures of trauma exposure and PTSD are not routinely included in the assessment batteries used by clinicians working outside trauma research centers or PTSD-specific clinics (Dansky, Roitzsch, Brady, & Saladin, 1997). This state of affairs is surprising and troubling given evidence for the high incidence of trauma exposure in the general population.

Psychological assessment of PTSD is essentially a two-pronged process, with the assessment of trauma-related events being the first step, which in turn dictates whether or not comprehensive assessment of PTSD symptoms is necessary. That is to say, assessment of individual PTSD symptoms need not proceed any further if, in the course of a clinical assessment, it is determined that there are no traumatic events that meet Criterion A of PTSD as defined by DSM-IV (APA, 1994). If, however, traumatic events meeting the Criterion A definition are present, assessment should proceed accordingly. Individuals with a history of surviving or witnessing natural disasters, motor vehicle accidents, assault, abuse, other forms of violence, or sudden, unexpected death of a loved one should be evaluated to determine if their responses meet Criterion A for PTSD, and, if so, should be given a full PTSD evaluation. Given evidence for a high rate of trauma exposure in the general population (e.g., Kessler et al., 1995), assessment of trauma history also might be considered in cases where trauma exposure is not apparent or part of the presenting complaint, because individuals may not readily link their symptoms to a past event or may have experienced traumatic events such as child abuse, incest, rape, or suicide that have become deeply held secrets.

Assessment batteries for use with trauma-exposed individuals typically include some combination of self-report instruments and structured interviews that target both PTSD and comorbid symptoms. A multimethod approach is typically recommended for both theoretical and practical reasons. Theoretically, the construct of PTSD has multiple elements that are not captured by a single measure. Practically, there is considerable variation in the ways that individuals respond to stressful events, so that a range of measures is needed. The primary aims of assessment include identifying exposure to events that are potentially traumatizing, determining which events were traumatic, linking PTSD symptoms to traumatic exposure, identifying comorbid disorders, and assessing response bias (Weathers & Keane, 1999). While a single interview measure can often provide enough information to diagnose PTSD, a broader array of measures is recommended to address the range of symptoms, differential diagnoses, problematic behaviors, and impairments (Keane, Wolfe, & Taylor, 1987; Malloy, Fairbank, & Keane, 1983; Schlenger et al., 1992). In addition, combining different measurement techniques helps to minimize diagnostic errors.

Case-specific selection of tests is guided by both the purpose of the evaluation and information derived from initial screening. For example, it can be informative to inquire about how much time has passed since the index trauma, the range of lifetime exposures to traumatic events, whether there is evidence of comorbidity, previous psychiatric history, and the purposes for seeking the assessment. It is particularly important to know whether there are forensic or financial compensation considerations. This information helps shape the level of complexity of the assessment battery and the tools selected. Examples of cases representing increasing levels of complexity are presented below to illustrate how the selection of measures might proceed.

A prototypical case demonstrating minimal complexity in terms of PTSD evaluation is an adult with no history of childhood trauma, a single-incident trauma in adulthood that was not interpersonal in nature, absence of alcohol or drug dependence, and no involvement of monetary (e.g., compensation) or legal issues. Such a case might require only assessment of Criterion A traumatic exposure and PTSD symptom frequency and intensity using, for example, the Life Stressor Checklist–Revised (Wolfe & Kimerling, 1997), the PTSD Checklist (PCL; Weathers, Litz, Huska, & Keane, 1994), and the Clinician Administered PTSD Scale (CAPS; Blake et al., 1995). The CAPS interview is designed to address each PTSD symptom, when it first occurred, how often it occurs, and whether it causes distress and is disruptive to functioning. Effort should be made to establish that PTSD symptoms are attributable to the specific event even in relatively straightforward cases. Brief evaluation of current depression, phobic avoidance, and alcohol or drug abuse via structured or unstructured interview also is advisable if specific concern is noted about the potential presence of comorbidity during clinical or structured interviewing. Modules from the Structured Clinical Interview for DSM-IV (SCID; First, Spitzer, Gibbon, & Williams, 1997) may be used for this purpose.

Assessment becomes more complex with individuals who have experienced multiple traumas, particularly if one or more occurred during childhood, and when comorbid depression, alcohol or drug abuse, or symptoms of other anxiety disorders are markedly present. Other complicating factors might include anger difficulties, especially those associated with violent behavior, self-blame for victimization (e.g., feeling that one "deserved" abuse as a child for bad behavior), or survivor guilt associated with events that involved the deaths of others. Self-report measures are recommended to assess depression, such as the Beck Depression Inventory (BDI; Beck, Steer, & Garbin, 1988); violent behavior, such as the Conflict Tactics Scale (CTS; Straus, 1979); alcohol abuse, such as the Alcohol Use Disorders Identification Test (AUDIT; Saunders, Aasland, Babor, & de la Fuente, 1993); drug abuse, such as the Drug Abuse Screening Test (DAST; Skinner, 1982); or general anxiety symptoms, such as the State-Trait Anxiety Inventory (STAI; Spielberger, Gorusch, & Lushene, 1970). In addition to a structured PTSD interview, structured interviews for depression, substance abuse, and other anxiety disorders (e.g., SCID modules) can aid diagnosis of comorbid disorders. When response to trauma is complex, collateral information from friends or family members can be extremely valuable. This information is ideally obtained through face-to-face interview, but collateral self-report measures (e.g., the spouse/partner version of the Mississippi Scale for PTSD; Kulka et al., 1990) also can be used.

Another issue worthy of note is the interface between physical health and PTSD and how this affects clinical care. Many individuals who experience trauma suffer physical injuries and other biological insults as a result of the traumatic event itself. Therefore, in conjunction with mental health concerns, many individuals will have physical pain and role-functioning impairment as a result of their physical limitations. There is some evidence to suggest that recovery from physical injury and mental health recovery covary in meaningful ways (Blanchard et al., 1997). In addition, mounting evidence suggests that chronic PTSD serves as a risk factor for poor health and health outcomes (Buckley & Kaloupek, 2001; Friedman & Schnurr, 1995). PTSD may influence health via stress reactivity and comorbidity with adverse health behaviors such as smoking. Assessment of physical health and role-functioning limitations due to physical problems is often informative for case conceptualization and treatment planning (e.g., need to incorporate other disciplines in the treatment plan, need to track compliance with medical regimens). For this purpose, the SF-36 (Ware & Sherbourne, 1992; Ware, Snow, Kosinski, & Gandek, 1997) is often a useful adjunct for this purpose.

The most complex level of PTSD assessment includes cases that involve forensic issues, financial compensation related to trauma, co-occurring serious mental illness, a history of severe interpersonal trauma, or some combination of these issues. Establishing the veracity of reported symptoms and linking symptoms to a specific traumatic event becomes more difficult in each of these cases. Evaluation of PTSD for forensic purposes may be part of a legal defense involving diminished capacity or self-defense in a criminal case, a worker's compensation claim, or a personal injury tort, all of which include powerful competing demands that are likely to influence the presentation of symptoms. Financial incentives are a particular concern for worker's compensation, personal injury, or disability claims that are contingent upon a diagnosis of PTSD. Explicit documentation (e.g., verification from police reports) regarding the Criterion A event is especially important when such incentives are present.

Clinicians evaluating trauma in patients with serious mental illness must be alert to misdiagnosis, untreated trauma responses, and increased vulnerability to retraumatization associated with impaired functioning or impulsivity (Rosenberg et al., 2001). Dissociative symptoms, affect disregulation, and personality disorders are of specific concern when an individual has experienced prolonged interpersonal trauma, particularly when it occurred during childhood. Indeed, recent data reveal that many individuals treated for serious mental illness (e.g., schizophrenia) have extensive trauma histories and meet criteria for comorbid PTSD at greater rates than the general population (Mueser et al., 1998). Unfortunately, these same studies show that PTSD comorbidity goes largely undiagnosed and is thus not addressed in treatment plans that focus exclusively on the psychotic illness.

Several specific assessment methods including nondirective interviewing, use of multiscale inventories, use of collateral information, and psychophysiological evaluation are valuable additions to the assessment of complex cases. Beginning the assessment process with nondirective interviewing regarding general presenting problems can provide evidence relevant to the validity of specific symptom reports obtained by subsequent structured interviews (Sparr & Pitman, 1999). Expanding psychometric testing to include a multiscale inventory such as the MMPI-2 (Butcher, Dahlstrom, Graham, Tellegen, & Kaemmer, 2001) or the Personality Assessment Inventory (PAI; Morey, 1991) can provide information about a broad spectrum of symptom patterns as well as assessment of response validity. Adding to interview and testing by seeking corroboration from other sources, including collaterals, can help to connect the onset of specific symptoms to a traumatic event. Finally, when available, psychophysiological measures (heart rate, blood pressure, electrodermal activity, muscle activity, peripheral temperature, and/or electroencephalogram readings) can provide evidence about physical responses to trauma-related material when evidence from other measures is insufficient or contradictory (Blanchard & Buckley, 1999; Orr & Kaloupek, 1997).

☐ Pragmatic Issues in Clinical Practice with PTSD

Several factors that contribute to the complexity of PTSD assessment and treatment present special challenges for clinical practice. Highlighted here are issues related to response bias, substance abuse, PTSD chronicity and third-party reimbursement.

Potential Influences on Symptom Reporting

PTSD has become a compensable disorder for both veterans with military-related trauma and civilians who initiate litigation or worker's compensation claims as a result of traumatic injury. In addition, PTSD has been used as the basis for an insanity defense and as a mitigating factor in other criminal proceedings (Applebaum et al., 1993; Resnick, 1997). Pursuit of trauma-related financial compensation has become more commonplace leading to increased skepticism regarding malingering for personal gain, particularly given the subjective nature of psychiatric diagnosis. Financial incentives surrounding PTSD can be high and represent a level of secondary gain rarely encountered in relation to other types of mental disorder. Indeed, evidence suggests that compensation-seeking status does relate to performance on psychological testing for combat veterans seeking service connected disability (Gold & Frueh, 1998; Frueh et al., 2003) and individuals with personal injury cases (Youngjohn, Burrow, & Erdal, 1995; Youngjohn, Davis, & Wolf, 1997). This research indicates that individuals seeking trauma-related compensation are more likely to report extreme psychopathology and to have high scores on indices designed to assess malingering.

Malingering is not the only, or even the most prominent, concern in the assessment of PTSD. Response bias in the form of both overreporting and underreporting of symptoms is often suspected. Elevated symptom reporting in combat veterans seeking evaluation for PTSD is well documented (see Frueh et al., 2000). Various hypotheses have been proposed to explain this phenomenon, including the suggestion that this elevated reporting reflects an extreme disruption in psychological development during late adolescence, the age at which many veterans were exposed to combat (Talbert et al., 1994). Because of this response pattern, higher cutoffs or alternative scales have been recommended for several validity indices on the MMPI-2 when it is used with combat veterans (Frueh et al., 2003; Gold & Frueh, 1998; Elhai et al., 2002).

Diminished reporting also may be a concern with traumatized individuals, particularly for individuals who exhibit extreme avoidance of trauma-related cues. Victims of trauma may have difficulty communicating their intense emotions to others, may feel unwilling or unable to describe intensely personal experiences in public, or may believe that they should try to hide a horrifying experience from others (Kiev, 1993; McFarlane & van der Kolk, 1996). General guidelines for addressing response bias concerns in the assessment of PTSD include use of multiple sources of information to corroborate self-report, careful behavioral observation during interviews, use of instruments with response validity indices, and use of instruments designed to specifically assess malingering (Weathers & Keane, 1999).

Issues Related to Substance Abuse

The rates of alcohol use disorders range from 30% to 50% for individuals with a lifetime history of PTSD, and the rates of drug use disorders range from 25% to 35% (Kessler et al., 1995). Several hypotheses have been proposed to explain the PTSD-substance use disorder association including: self-medication of PTSD symptoms, a substance user's increased risk of trauma exposure, and increased vulnerability to PTSD following trauma exposure in substance users (Stewart, Pihl, Conrod, & Dongier, 1998). Although there is evidence indicating that the onset of PTSD often occurs prior to substance use disorders, the relationship between these disorders appears to be complex (Brady, Dansky, Sonne, & Saladin, 1998; Bremner et al., 1996; Chilcoat & Breslau, 1998). For example, there is evidence that the relationship is cyclical in some cases of physical and sexual assault, such that assault victims with PTSD who abuse substances are more vulnerable to subsequent assault (Kilpatrick, Acierno, Resnick, Saunders, & Best, 1997). Interviewing methods such as timeline followback (Sobell, Brown, Leo, & Sobell, 1996; Sobell & Sobell, 1996) may be useful for clarifying the pattern on a case-by-case basis.

Despite high rates of comorbid PTSD and substance use disorders, it is common for this comorbidity to be overlooked in treatment settings

(Brown, Stout, & Mueller, 1999; Dansky, Roitzsch, Brady, & Saladin, 1997; Ouimette & Brown, 2003). Specifically, substance abuse often is treated as primary while trauma-related features are not addressed. Several studies have suggested that substance use treatment programs should routinely screen for trauma exposure, because treatment is more successful when comorbid PTSD and substance-use disorders are addressed concurrently (Bastiaens & Kendrick, 2002; Crosby-Ouimette, Brown, & Najavits, 1998). The implications for not recognizing and treating both disorders can be serious. For example, both PTSD and substance-use disorders have been consistently found to be associated with increased anger, hostility, and perpetration of interpersonal violence (Beckham, Moore, & Reynolds, 2000; Chermack & Blow, 2002; Kubany et al., 1994; Kulka et al., 1990; Miller & Potter-Efron, 1989; Schonwetter & Janisse, 1991). In addition, intrusive symptoms of individuals with comorbid PTSD and active substance-use disorders appear to be especially resistant to treatment (Dansky, Brady, & Saladin, 1998). Substance use and substance-use disorders also have been found to be predictive of repeated victimization by means of interpersonal violence including sexual assault (Mears, Carlson, Holden, & Harris, 2001; Messman-Moore & Long, 2002). Overall, the research literature in this area clearly supports the recommendation that patients presenting with substance abuse or dependence should routinely be assessed for PTSD and vice versa.

Issues Related to Tracking Chronic PTSD

About one-third of individuals who develop PTSD will have a chronic, treatment-resistant condition (Kessler et al., 1995). Work with older trauma-exposed populations, including Holocaust survivors and combat veterans of both World War II and the Korean War, has indicated that persistent sleep disruption, intrusive memories, avoidance of stressors, and increased vulnerability to retraumatization can be present 40 to 50 years after the original trauma (Sadovoy, 1997). Many studies with treatment-seeking Vietnam War veterans have found chronic and unremitting symptoms 20 to 30 years after combat exposure (cf. Bremner et al., 1996; Davidson, Kudler, Saunders, & Smith, 1990; Kulka et al., 1990).

Because PTSD is so often a chronic condition, reassessment of PTSD symptom status over time is advisable. For older patients, symptoms that were managed well while the individual was working and raising a family often worsen following retirement, widowhood, decline in physical health, or some combination of these life events (Port, Engdahl, & Frazier, 2001; Potts, 1994; van Achterberg, Rohrbaugh, & Southwick,

2001). Many of the associated features of chronic PTSD (e.g., substance abuse, divorce, loss of a job, loss of social support due to social detachment) also are risk factors for the development of or worsening of PTSD symptoms and should be monitored. Reassessment over time also includes examination of intervening stressful and traumatic events that may exacerbate or reactivate PTSD symptoms. In fact, research evidence indicates that exposure to trauma increases vulnerability to further trauma, and symptoms that have remitted may be reactivated by further exposure to high stress or trauma (Arata, 2002; Christenson et al., 1981; Solomon, Garb, Bleich, & Grupper, 1987). For example, increased use of mental health services in Manhattan following the September 11 terrorist attacks was associated with a history of four or more lifetime traumatic events and two or more stressful events in the previous 12 months (Boscarino, Galea, Ahern, Resnick, & Vlahov, 2002). Studies such as this point to the value of ongoing PTSD/trauma assessment.

Reimbursement and Third Party Payment Issues

Because PTSD evaluations occur in many contexts, third party coverage may come from a variety of sources including government agencies (e.g., the Veterans Administration), legal firms (e.g., firms representing accident victims), and private companies (e.g., an auto manufacturer wishing to verify claims of injury due to faulty manufacturing), in addition to managed care and insurance companies. As with any type of psychological assessment or treatment, limits placed by third party payers on the number of billable hours is a central concern. Because the complexity and duration of PTSD assessment may vary considerably depending on the patient, it may be difficult to receive full remuneration for services. Often report writing is included in the time allotted for assessment, further limiting the amount of payment per hour of direct patient contact. Limitations to assessment or treatment sessions dictated by managed care requirements may create special problems for trauma survivors, particularly for those with histories of multiple or prolonged trauma that warrant a more extensive assessment battery. In addition, individuals who were victimized by a caretaker or other authority figure may be particularly sensitive to restrictions on mental health services imposed by managed care that may psychologically resemble their abuse (Shapard, 1997).

☐ Case Illustration

Client Description

Mr. X is a 27-year-old, married, Catholic, Caucasian male with no children. He has a high school education and works as a sales manager at an auto parts store. He has no previous psychiatric history by his report and is seeking services for the first time at the suggestion of his wife.

History of the Problem

Mr. X was in a severe motorcycle accident at age 23, prior to meeting his wife, which resulted in several broken bones, a punctured lung, and a 1-month stay in the hospital. The accident occurred when an oncoming truck swerved into his lane and he had to turn suddenly to avoid hitting it. Following this accident, Mr. X reported daily nightmares, irritability, withdrawal from friends and family, and increased alcohol use. He was fired from his job as an assistant manager at a convenience store due to frequent absences related to drinking. He then moved into his parents' home for several months while working various part-time jobs. The year following the motorcycle accident, Mr. X sold his motorcycle, secured a job at the auto parts store where he currently works, moved into an apartment, and met his wife at a local bar. Although he continued to drink heavily on weekends and to have occasional nightmares of the motorcycle accident, he was able to improve his work functioning and recently secured a promotion to manager. His symptoms have worsened over the past 4 months, since his wife began encouraging him to start a family.

Presenting Complaints

Mr. X was self-referred to the clinic, but stated that his wife had prompted him to come due to his sleep problems, depressed mood, and frequently missing work. He complained of feeling "too restless to sleep" and having nightmares related to the motorcycle accident several times per month. He stated that he was also concerned about losing his job due to arguments with his coworkers and using all of his sick days. Further inquiry during the first meeting revealed that he also suffers from chronic knee and back pain as a result of his accidents. The patient however, did not immediately report a connection between pain and his mental health status. He also stated that he avoids driving and that he is worried about starting a family because he does not want his child to ride in a car. (Comment: individuals suffering from even relatively severe trauma-related pathology may seek mental health care only after encouragement by another family member and then initially present with a few seemingly minor complaints.)

Assessment Methods

As described previously, recommended methods for PTSD evaluation begin with assessment of trauma history and the identification of any events meeting Criterion A. This is typically followed by self-report screening for PTSD symptoms, depression, and substance abuse, then a structured interview for PTSD and possibly other disorders. Collateral information from a spouse or other close family member is often valuable, though not always available.

Self-Report Measures

The self-report measures chosen assessed Mr. X's full history of trauma exposure (with the Life Stressor Checklist); screened for PTSD symptoms, depression, and alcohol abuse prior to interview (with the PCL, Mississippi Scale, BDI, and AUDIT); and assessed his response style and presentation of psychopathology in multiple domains (with the MMPI-2). His wife was asked to complete the collateral version of the Mississippi Scale with regard to her impression of her husband's symptoms, particularly given Mr. X's report that he had sought treatment at her request.

Interview

A CAPS interview and the SCID modules for depression, dysthymia, and drug and alcohol use were given to the patient. The CAPS interview was used to determine if Mr. X's immediate responses to the motorcycle accident met Criterion A requirements and to carefully assess each PTSD symptom in terms of its frequency and intensity. SCID modules were added to provide a thorough assessment of the depressive symptoms and substance use that Mr. X reported in the screening interview assessment of his presenting complaints.

☐ Psychological Assessment Protocol (Including Testing Results)

Results of the Life Stressor Checklist indicated that in addition to the motorcycle accident, Mr. X was the target of a robbery when he was working at a convenience store. During this episode, the robber displayed a gun, but did not fire it. No other potentially traumatizing events were indicated. In addition, Mr. X's score of 66 on the PCL is consistent with PTSD, although this scale also is highly correlated with measures of depression. A brief item-by-item query of the PCL indicated that most symptoms originated soon after the motorcycle accident. Mr. X's score of 110 on the Mississippi is above the empirically derived cutoff score for indicating PTSD. Results of the collateral Mississippi Scale completed by Mr. X's wife were generally consistent with his responses, but indicated that she perceives these symptoms as occurring with greater intensity than he does. BDI Results indicated a score of 22, consistent with a moderate level of depression. (Comment: moderate-to-high scores such as this are not uncommon for individuals with PTSD even in the absence of major depression.) At this point further inquiry was conducted to determine the onset of depressive symptoms vis-à-vis the trauma and to assess pretrauma history of depressive symptoms. This inquiry revealed evidence that significant depressive symptoms were present prior to thtrauma despite the initial negative report of the patient regarding premorbid psychiatric history.

His score on the AUDIT was 12, which is above the empirically derived threshold for predicting alcohol related problems. Thus, it was decided that the Alcohol Abuse/Dependence module of the SCID would be administered. Results confirmed the presence of alcohol abuse in the last year without dependence.

MMPI-2 scores for validity indices indicated average elevations for L, VRIN, and TRIN, suggesting that Mr. X responded consistently and openly. Scores for scale F and the F-K index were significantly elevated. However, an elevation of 62 on the F(p) scale suggested that elevations on the F and K scales were likely influenced by reported psychopathology and not indicative of an invalid profile. Mr. X produced a 7-2 profile on the clinical scales which is consistent with that of individuals who describe themselves as anxious, tense, depressed, and constant worriers. They tend to be guilt-ridden and preoccupied with their personal deficiencies despite evidence of their personal achievements. Because of their willingness to examine their own behavior, they tend to be excellent candidates for psychotherapy. On the supplementary scales, Mr. X's highest elevations were on scales designed to assess PTSD (PK & PS raw scores = 37 and 44, respectively).

Interview Assessment

Results of CAPS interview supported a current diagnosis of PTSD associated with the motorcycle accident. Regarding the previous month, Mr. X reported daily intrusive memories of the accident and three nightmares of the truck speeding toward him. After each nightmare, he remembered waking covered in perspiration and being unable to return to sleep. In the previous month, he reported that he has avoided talking about the accident with anyone, has avoided driving except to work and back, and that he has increased his alcohol use when he is upset by a memory of the accident. He also reported difficulty getting to sleep two to three times per week, irritability and sudden outbursts of anger two to three times in the past month, and excessive worry about his and his wife's safety associated with driving or riding in a car. CAPS results indicated that his current PTSD symptoms were primarily associated with the motorcycle accident, but that he also has intrusive memories of the robbery about once per month if he goes into a similar store or hears about an armed robbery in the news.

SCID results supported additional current diagnoses of Major Depressive Disorder, Recurrent, Moderate, and Alcohol Abuse. Mr. X endorsed depressed mood, loss of appetite, low energy, feelings of hopelessness, frequent thoughts of death (without current suicidal ideation), and insomnia as occurring most of the day, nearly every day for more than 2 weeks in the past month. He also described three previous similar episodes of depression since he was a teenager that each lasted 2 to 4 months. Regarding his current alcohol use, Mr. X stated that he has continued to drink even when it has led to arguments with his wife and difficulties at work. However, his alcohol-related difficulties did not meet full criteria for dependence.

Targets Selected for Treatment

Results of assessment indicated that Mr. X met criteria for current PTSD, recurrent Major Depression, and current Alcohol Abuse. His alcohol problems were targeted as the first stage of PTSD treatment in order to reduce the risk of his increasing his drinking in response to distress associated with exposure to trauma material in therapy sessions. Throughout treatment, his alcohol use and depressive symptoms were monitored as well as his PTSD symptoms.

Assessment of Progress

Following 6 weeks of weekly treatment focused on his alcohol abuse, Mr. X was able to reduce his drinking from an average of three to four drinks daily, to one drink every evening and no more than six on weekends. He was also able to attend work for one month without missing a day due to drinking or hangovers. However, he reported being late to work five times due to lack of sleep. Because his management of his alcohol consumption was improved, he was referred to the care of a psychiatrist to be evaluated for medication. He was ultimately prescribed Zoloft, which is one of the few FDA approved psychotropics for the treatment of PTSD. During the first six weeks of treatment, Mr. X's score on the BDI improved slightly, but his PTSD symptoms either remained at the same frequency and intensity or worsened (e.g., he reported fewer hours of sleep after reducing his evening alcohol consumption). Mr. X's PTSD symptoms were targeted in the next 10 weeks of treatment while monitoring of his drinking continued. He was trained in breathing and muscle relaxation techniques, and this was combined with guided imagery exposure to his traumatic motor vehicle accidents. At the end of this period of treatment, Mr. X reported a further reduction in his drinking and depressive symptoms, and reported improved sleep, which he attributed to the use of both relaxation techniques and medication.

☐ Summary

The current nosology of mental disorders includes two diagnoses tied explicitly to trauma exposure. PTSD has been included in the DSM since 1980, while ASD has been included since the inception of the DSM-IV in 1994. Both disorders also are defined by symptoms that reflect reexperiencing of the trauma, avoidance of trauma cues, numbing of emotional responsiveness, and hyperarousal. The distinction between ASD and PTSD is based on the amount of time that has elapsed since the trauma occurred (less than one month vs. one month or more) and a greater emphasis on dissociative symptoms in ASD. The ASD diagnosis remains controversial and the weight of current evidence suggests that the emphasis on early posttrauma dissociation is not warranted. Instead, recommendations based on research encourage early identification of risk factors for the development of prolonged difficulties, PTSD, or both, which may or may not include symptoms associated with ASD.

There are currently many PTSD-specific measures available to clinicians, but these measures are not typically included in assessment batteries outside of settings that specialize in trauma-related services. The general framework of PTSD assessment includes identification of traumatic events in the patient's history, self-report assessment of symptoms of PTSD along with symptoms of frequently comorbid conditions, and a structured PTSD interview. Several associated features and comorbid diagnoses are common to PTSD and are likely to influence the complexity of assessment procedures. These include guilt, depression, phobic avoidance, alcohol and substance abuse/dependence, interpersonal relationship conflict, and difficulty maintaining employment. PTSD resulting from prolonged interpersonal trauma, particularly if it occurs in childhood, is often associated with a complex PTSD presentation that includes dissociative symptoms, self-destructive behavior, extremely impaired relationships with others, mood instability, and personality changes. In addition, financial compensation or forensic considerations often found in trauma cases can significantly increase the complexity of the assessment process.

Practical issues in PTSD assessment include ongoing substance abuse and dependence, the potential influence of secondary gain due to financial compensation or forensic considerations, the value of multiple sources and formats for information gathering, the potential benefits of tracking chronic PTSD over time, and the increased risk for retraumatization of previously traumatized individuals. Finally, the complexity of PTSD assessment and the chronicity of PTSD itself have implications for third-party coverage that may restrict the number of sessions that will be remunerated.

☐ References

American Psychiatric Association. (1994). *Diagonistic and statistical manual of mental disorders*, (4th ed.). Washington, DC: American Psychiatric Association.

Applebaum, P. S., Jick, R. Z., Grisso, T., Givelber, D., Silver, E., & Steadman, H. J. (1993). Use of posttraumatic stress disorder to support an insanity defense. *American Journal of Psychiatry, 150,* 229–234.

Arata, C. M. (2002). Child sexual abuse and sexual revictimization. *Clinical Psychology Science and Practice, 9,* 135–164.

Bastiaens, L., & Kendrick, J. (2002). Trauma and PTSD among substance-abusing patients. *Psychiatric Services, 53,* 634.

Beck, A. T., Steer, R. A., & Garbin, M. G. (1988). Psychometric properties of the Beck Depression Inventory: Twenty-five years of evaluation. *Clinical Psychology Review, 8,* 77–106.

Beckham, J. C., Moore, S. D., & Reynolds, V. (2000). Interpersonal hostility and violence in Vietnam combat veterans with chronic posttraumatic stress disorder: A review of theoretical models and empirical evidence. *Aggression and Violent Behavior, 5,* 451–466.

Blake, D. D., Weathers, F. W., Nagy, L. M., Kaloupek, D. G., Gusman, F. D., Charney, D. S., et al. (1995). The development of a clinician-administered PTSD scale. *Journal of Traumatic Stress, 8,* 75–90.

Blanchard, E. B., & Buckley, T. C. (1999). Psychophysiological assessment of posttraumatic stress disorder. In P. A. Saigh & J. D. Bremner (Eds.) *Posttraumatic stress disorder: A comprehensive text.* Boston, MA: Allyn and Bacon.

Blanchard, E. B., Hickling, E. J., Forneris, C. A., Taylor, A. E., Buckley, T. C., Loos, W. R., & Jaccard, J. (1997). Prediction of remission of acute post-traumatic stress disorder in motor vehicle accident victims. *Journal of Traumatic Stress, 10,* 215–234.

Boscarino, J. A., Galea, S., Ahern, J., Resnick, H., & Vlahov, D. (2002). Utilization of mental health services following the September 11th terrorist attacks in Manhattan, New York City. *International Journal of Emergency Mental Health, 4,* 143–156.

Brady, K. T., Dansky, B. S., Sonne, S. C., & Saladin, M. E. (1998). Posttraumatic stress disorder and cocaine dependence: Order of onset. *American Journal on Addictions, 7,* 128–135.

Bremner, J. D., Southwick, S. M., Darnell, A., & Charney, D. S. (1996). Chronic PTSD in Vietnam combat veterans: Course of illness and substance abuse. *American Journal of Psychiatry, 153,* 369–375.

Breslau, N., Kessler, R. C., Chilcoat, H. D., Schultz, L. R., Davis, G. C., & Andreski, P. (1998). Trauma and posttraumatic stress disorder in the community. *Archives of General Psychiatry, 55,* 626–632.

Brewin, C. R., Andrews, B., & Rose, S. (2003). Diagnostic overlap between acute stress disorder and PTSD in victims of violent crime. *American Journal of Psychiatry, 160,* 783–785.

Brewin, C. R., Andrews, B., Rose, S., & Kirk, M. (1999). Acute stress disorder and posttraumatic stress disorder in victims of violence crime. *American Journal of Psychiatry, 156,* 360–366.

Brown, P. J., Stout, R. L., & Mueller, T. (1999). Substance use disorder and posttraumatic stress disorder comorbidity: Addiction and treatment rates. *Psychology of Addictive Behaviors, 13,* 115–122.

Bryant, R. A., & Bird, K. (2001). Confirmatory factor analysis of acute stress disorder symptoms. Manuscript submitted for publication.

Bryant, R. A., & Harvey, A. G. (1998). Relationship between acute stress disorder and posttraumatic stress disorder following mild traumatic brain injury. *American Journal of Psychiatry, 155,* 625–629.

Bryant, R. A., & Harvey, A. G. (1997). Acute stress disorder: A critical review of diagnostic issues. *Clinical Psychology Review, 17,* 757–773.

Bryant, R. A., & Harvey, A. G., Dang, S. T., & Sackville, T. (1998). Assessing acute stress disorder: Psychometric properties of a structured clinical interview. *Psychological Assessment, 10,* 215–220.

Bryant, R. A., Moulds, M., & Guthrie, R. (2000). Acute Stress Disorder Scale: A self-report measure of acute stress disorder. *Psychological Assessment, 12,* 61–68.

Bryant, R. A., Sackville, T., Dang, S. T., Moulds, M., & Guthrie, R. (1999). Treating acute stress disorder: An evaluation of cognitive behavior therapy and supportive counseling techniques. *American Journal of Psychiatry, 156,* 1780–1786.

Buckley, T. C., & Kaloupek, D. G. (2001). A meta-analytic examination of basal cardiovascular activity in posttraumatic stress disorders. *Psychosomatic Medicine, 63,* 585–594.

Butcher, J. N., Dahlstrom, W. G., Graham, J. R., Tellegen, A., & Kaemmer, B. (2001). *MMPI-2 manual for administration and scoring.* Minneapolis: University of Minnesota Press.

Byrne, C. A., & Riggs, D. S. (2002). Gender issues in couple and family therapy following traumatic stress. In R. Kimerling & P. Ouimette (Eds.) *Gender and PTSD* (pp. 382–399). New York: Guilford Press.

Cardeña, E., Koopman, C., Classen, C, Waelde, L. C., & Spiegel, D. (2000). Psychometric properties of the Stanford Acute Stress Reaction Questionnaire (SASRQ): A valid and reliable measure of acute stress. *Journal of Traumatic Stress, 13,* 719–734.

Carlson, E. B. (1997). *Trauma assessments: A clinician's guide.* New York: Guilford.

Chermack, S. T., & Blow, F. C. (2002). Violence among individuals in substance abuse treatment: The role of alcohol and cocaine consumption. *Drug & Alcohol Dependence, 66*(1), 29–37.

Chilcoat, H. D., & Breslau, N. (1998). Investigations of causal pathways between PTSD and drug use disorders. *Addictive Behaviors, 23,* 827–840.

Christenson, R. M., Walker, J. I., Ross, D. R., & Maltbie, A. A. (1981). Reactivation of traumatic conflicts. *American Journal of Psychiatry, 138,* 984–985.

Crosby-Ouimette, P., Brown, P. J., & Najavits, L. M. (1998). Course and treatment of patients with both substance use and posttraumatic stress disorders. *Addictive Behaviors, 23,* 785–796.

Dansky, B. S., Brady, K. T., & Saladin, M. E. (1998). Untreated symptoms of PTSD among cocaine-dependent individuals: Changes over time. *Journal of Substance Abuse Treatment, 15,* 499–504.

Dansky, B. S., Roitzsch, J. C., Brady, K. T., & Saladin, M. E. (1997). Posttraumatic stress disorder and substance abuse: Use of research in a clinical setting. *Journal of Traumatic Stress, 10,* 141–148.

Davidson, J. R. T., Kudler, H. S., Saunders, W. B., & Smith, R. D. (1990). Symptom and morbidity patterns in World War II and Vietnam veterans with post-traumatic stress disorder. *Comprehensive Psychiatry, 31,* 1662–1170.

Echeburua, E., de Corral, P., Sarasua, B., & Zubizarreta, I. (1996). Treatment of acute post-traumatic stress disorder in rape victims: An experimental study. *Journal of Anxiety Disorders, 10,* 185–199.

Elhai, J. D., Ruggerio, K. J., Frueh, B. C., Beckham, J. C., Gold, P. B., & Feldman, M. E. (2002). The infrequency-post traumatic stress disorder scale (Fptsd) for the MMPI-2: Development and initial validation with veterans presenting with combat-related PTSD. *Journal of Personality Assessment, 79,* 541–559.

Fairbank, J. A., Schlerger, W. E., Cadell, J. M., & Woods, M. G. (1993). Postraumatic stress disorder. In P. B. Sutker & H. E. Adams (Eds.) *Comprehensive handbook of psychopathology* (2nd ed.) (pp. 145–165). New York: Plenum Press.

First, M. B., Spitzer, R. L., Gibbon, M., & Williams, J. B. W. (1997). *Structured clinical interview for DSM-IV Axis I disorders-clinician version (SCID-CV).* Washington, DC: American Psychiatric Press.

Foa, E. B., Hearst-Ikeda, D. E., & Perry, K. J. (1995). Evaluation of a brief cognitive-behavioral program for the prevention of chronic PTSD in recent assault victims. *Journal of Consulting and Clinical Psychology, 63,* 948–955.

Friedman, M. J., & Schnurr, P. P. (1995). The relationship between trauma, posttraumatic stress disorder, and physical health. In M. J. Friedman & D. S. Charney (Eds.) *Neurological and clinical consequences of stress: From normal adaptation to posttraumatic stress disorder* (pp. 507–524). Philadelphia: Lippincott, Williams & Wilkins.

Frueh, B. C., Elhai, J. D., Gold, P. B., Monnier, J., Magruder, K. M., Keane, T. M., et al. (2003). Disability compensation seeking among veterans evaluated for posttraumatic stress disorder. *Psychiatric Services, 54,* 84–91.

Frueh, B. C., Hamner, M. B., Cahill, S. P., Gold, P. B., & Hamlin, K. L. (2000). Apparent symptom overreporting in combat veterans evaluated for PTSD. *Clinical Psychology Review, 20,* 853–885.

Gold, P. B., & Frueh, B. C. (1998). Compensation-seeking and extreme exaggeration of psychopathology among combat veterans evaluated for posttraumatic stress disorder. *The Journal of Nervous and Mental Disease, 187,* 680–684.

Halligan, S. L., & Yehuda, R. (2000). Risk factors for PTSD. *PTSD Research Quarterly, 11*(3), 1–7.

Harvey, A. G., & Bryant, R. A. (1998). The relationship between acute stress disorder and posttraumatic stress disorder: A prospective evaluation of motor vehicle accident survivors. *Journal of Consulting and Clinical Psychology, 66,* 507–512.

Harvey, A. G., & Bryant, R. A. (2002). Acute stress disorder: A synthesis and critique. *Psychological Bulletin, 128,* 886–902.

Helzer, J. E., Robins, L. N., & McEvoy, L. (1987). Post-traumatic stress disorder in the general population: Findings of the Epidemiological Catchment Area survey. *New England Journal of Medicine, 317,* 1630–1634.

Keane, T. M., & Wolfe, J. (1990). Comorbidity in post-traumatic stress disorder: An analysis of community and clinical studies. *Journal of Applied Social Psychology, 20,* 1776–1788.

Keane, T. M., Wolfe, J., & Taylor, K. L. (1987). Posttraumatic stress disorder: Evidence for diagnostic validity and methods of psychological assessment. *Journal of Clinical Psychology, 43,* 32–43.

Kessler, R. C., Sonnega, A., Bromet, E., Hughes, M., Nelson, C. B. (1995). Posttraumatic stress disorder in the national comorbidity survey. *Archives of General Psychiatry, 52,* 1048–1060.

Kiev, A. (1993). Conveying psychological pain and suffering: Juror empathy is key. *Trial 29*(10), 16–21.

Kilpatrick, D. G., Acierno, R., Resnick, H. S., Saunders, B. E., & Best, C. L. (1997). A 2-year longitudinal analysis of the relationships between violent assault and substance use in women. *Journal of Consulting and Clinical Psychology, 65,* 834–847.

Koopman, C., Classen, C., Cardeña, E. & Spiegel, D. (1995). When disaster strikes, acute stress disorder may follow. *Journal of Traumatic Stress, 8,* 1995.

Kubany, E. S., Gino, A., Denny, N. R., & Torigoe, R. Y. (1994). Relationship of cynical hostility and posttraumatic stress disorder among Vietnam combat veterans. *Journal of Traumatic Stress, 7,* 21–32.

Kulka, R. A., Schlenger, W. E., Fairbank, J. A., Hough, R. L., Jordan, B. K., Marmar, C. R., et al. (1990). *Trauma and the Vietnam War generation: Report of findings from the National Vietnam Veterans Readjustment Study.* New York: Brunner/Mazel.

Litz, B. T., Gray, M. J., Bryant, R. A., & Adler, A. B. (2002). Early intervention for trauma: Current status and future directions. *Clinical Psychology: Science and Practice, 9,* 112–134.

Litz, B. T., Miller, M. W., Ruef, A. M., & McTeague, L. M. (2002). Exposure to trauma in adults. In M. M. Antony & D. H. Barlow (Eds.) *Handbook of assessment and treatment planning for psychological disorders* (pp. 215–258). New York: Guilford.

Malloy, P. F., Fairbank, J. A., & Keane, T. M. (1983). Validation of a multimethod assessment of posttraumatic stress disorders in Vietnam veterans. *Journal of Consulting and Clinical Psychology, 83,* 488–494.

McFarlane, A. C., & van der Kolk, B. A. (1996). Trauma and its challenge to society. In B. A. van der Kolk, A. C. McFarlane, & L. Weisaeth (Eds.) *Traumatic stress: The effects of overwhelming experience on mind, body, and society* (pp. 24–46). New York: Guilford.

Mears, D. P., Carlson, M. J., Holden, G. W., & Harris, S. D. (2001). Reducing domestic violence revictimization: The effects of individual and contextual factors and type of legal intervention. *Journal of Interpersonal Violence, 16,* 1260–1283.

Messman-Moore, T. L., & Long, P. J. (2002). Alcohol and substance use disorders as predictors of child to adult sexual revictimization in a sample of community women. *Violence and Victims, 17,* 319–340.

Miller, M. M., & Potter-Efron, R. T. (1989). Aggression and violence associated with substance abuse. *Journal of Chemical Dependency Treatment, 3*(1), 1–36.

Morey, L. C. (1991). *The Personality Assessment Inventory professional manual.* Odessa, FL: Psychological Assessment Resources.

Mueser, K. T., Goodman, L. A., Trumbetta, S. L., Rosenberg, S. D., Osher, F. C., Vidaver, R., Auciello, P., & Foy, D. W. (1998). Trauma and posttraumatic stress disorder in severe mental illness. *Journal of Consulting and Clinical Psychology, 66,* 493–499.

National Institute of Mental Health (2002). *Mental health and mass violence: Evidence-based early psychological intervention for victims/survivors of mass violence: A workshop to reach consensus on best practices.* NIH Publication No. 02-5138, Washington, DC, U. S. Government Printing Office.

Orr, S. P., & Kaloupek, D. G. (1996). Psychophysiological assessment of posttraumatic stress disorder. In J. P. Wilson & T. M. Keane (Eds.) *Assessing Psychological Trauma and PTSD* (pp. 69–97). New York: Guilford.

Ouimette, P., & Brown, P. J. (Eds.). (2003). *Trauma and substance abuse: Causes, consequences, and treatment of comorbid disorders.* Washington, DC: American Psychological Association.

Patterson, D. R., Carrigan, L., Questad, K. A., & Robinson, R. S. (1990). Post-traumatic stress disorder in hospitalized patients with burn injuries. *Journal of Burn Care Rehabilitation, 11,* 181–184.

Port, C. L., Engdahl, B., & Frazier, P. (2001). A longitudinal and retrospective study of PTSD among older prisoners of war. *American Journal of Psychiatry, 158,* 1474–1479.

Potts, M. K. (1994). Long-term effects of trauma: Post-traumatic stress among civilian internees of the Japanese during World War II. *Journal of Clinical Psychology, 50,* 681–698.

Resnick, P. J. (1997). Malingering of posttraumatic disorders. In R. Rogers, (Ed.) *Clinical assessment of malingering and deception* (2nd ed.) (pp. 130–152). New York: Guilford Press.

Riggs, D. S., Byrne, C. A., Weathers, F. W., & Litz, B. T. (1998). The quality of the intimate relationships of male Vietnam veterans: Problems associated with posttraumatic stress disorder. *Journal of Traumatic Stress, 11,* 87–101.

Rosenberg, S. D., Mueser, K. T., Friedman, M. J., Gorman, P. G., Drake, R. E., Vidaver, R. M., et al. (2001). Developing effective treatments for posttraumatic disorders among people with severe mental illness. *Psychiatric Services, 52,* 1453–1461.

Sadovoy, J. (1997). Survivors: A review of the late-life effects of prior psychological trauma. *American Journal of Geriatric Psychiatry, 5,* 287–301.

Saunders, J. B., Aasland, O. G., Babor, T. F., & de la Fuente, J. R. (1993). Development of the Alcohol Use Disorders Identification Test (AUDIT) WHO collaborative project on early detection of persons with harmful alcohol consumption II. *Addiction, 88,* 791–804.

Schlenger, W. E., Kulka, R. A., Fairbank, J. A., Hough, R. L., Jordan, B. K., Marmar, C. R., & Weiss, D. S. (1992). The prevalence of post traumatic stress disorder in the Vietnam generation: A multimethod, multisource assessment of psychiatric disorder. *Journal of Traumatic Stress, 5,* 333–363.

Schonwetter, D. J., & Janisse, M. P. (1991). Alcohol consumption, anger and hostility: A link to coronary heart disease. *Personality & Individual Differences, 12*(10), 1049–1055.

Shalev, A. Y., Freedman, S., Peri, T., Brandes, D., & Sahar, T. (1997). Predicting PTSD in trauma survivors: Prospective evaluation of self report and clinician administererd instruments. *British Journal of Psychiatry, 170,* 558–564.

Shalev, A. Y., Peri, T., Canetti, L., & Schreiber, S. (1996). Predictors of PTSD in injured trauma survivors: A prospective study. *American Journal of Psychiatry, 153,* 219–225.

Shapard, B. (1997). The human toll: Managed care's restriction of access to mental health services. *Psychoanalytic Inquiry* (1997 Suppl.), 151–161.

Skinner, H. A. (1982). The Drug Abuse Screening Test. *Addictive-Behaviors, 7,* 363–371.

Sobell, L. C., Brown, J., Leo, G. I., & Sobell, M. B. (1996). The reliability of the alcohol time-line followback when administered by telephone and by computer. *Drug and Alcohol Dependence, 42,* 49–54.

Sobell, M. B., & Sobell, L. C. (1996). *Problem drinkers: Guided self-change treatment.* New York: Guilford.

Solomon, Z., Garb, R., Bleich, A., & Grupper, D. (1987). Reactivation of combat-related post-traumatic stress disorder. *American Journal of Psychiatry, 144,* 51–55.

Solomon, Z., Laor, N., & McFarlane, A. C. (1996). Acute posttraumatic reactions in soldiers and civilians. In B. A. van der Kolk & A. C. McFarlane (Eds.) *Traumatic stress: The effects of overwhelming experience on mind, body, and society* (pp. 102–114). New York: Guilford Press.

Sparr, L. F., & Pitman, R. K. (1999). Forensic assessment of traumatized adults. In P. A. Saigh & J. D. Bremner, (Eds.) *Posttraumatic stress disorder: A comprehensive text* (pp. 284–308). Needham Heights, MA: Allyn & Bacon.

Spielberger, C. D., Gorusch, R. L., & Lushene, R. (1970). *Manual for the State-Trait Anxiety Inventory.* Palo Alto, CA: Consulting Psychologists Press.

Stewart, S. H., Pihl, R. O., Conrod, P. J., & Dongier, M. (1998). Functional associations among trauma, PTSD and substance-related disorders. *Addictive Behaviors, 23,* 797–812.

Straus, M. A. (1979). Measuring intrafamily conflict and violence: The Conflict Tactics Scales. *Journal of Marriage and the Family, 41,* 75–88.

Talbert, F. S., Albrecht, N. N., Albrecht, J. W., Boudewyns, P. A., Hyer, L. A., Touze, J. H., et al. (1994). MMPI profiles in PTSD as a function of comorbidity. *Journal of Clinical Psychology, 50,* 529–537.

van-Achterberg, M. E., Rohrbaugh, R. M., & Southwick, S. M. (2001). Emergence of PTSD in trauma survivors with dementia. *Journal of Clinical Psychiatry, 62,* 206–207.

Ware, J. E., Snow, K. K., Kosinski, M., & Gandek, B. (1997). *SF-36 health survey manual and interpretation guide.* Boston: The Health Institute, New England Medical Center.

Ware, J. E., & Sherbourne, C. D. (1992). The MOS 36-item short-form health survey (SF-36). *Medical Care, 30,* 473–481.

Weathers, F. W., & Keane, T. M. (1999). Psychological assessment of traumatized adults. In P. A. Saigh & J. D. Bremner (Eds.) *Posttraumatic stress disorder: A comprehensive text* (pp. 219–247). Boston: Allyn and Bacon.

Weathers, F. W., Litz, B. T., Huska, J. A., & Keane, T. M. (1994). *PTSD checklist civilian version.* Boston National Center for PTSD, Behavioral Science Division.

Wolfe, J., & Kimerling, R. (1997). Gender issues in the assessment of posttraumatic stress disorder. In J. Wilson & T. M. Keane (Eds.), *Assessing psychological trauma and PTSD* (pp. 192–238). New York: Guilford.

Youngjohn, J. R., Burrows, L., & Erdal, K. (1995). Brain damage or compensation neurosis? The controversial post-concussion syndrome. *Clinical-Neuropsychologist, 9,* 112–123.

Youngjohn, J. R., Davis, D., & Wolf, I. (1997). Head injury and the MMPI-2: Paradoxical severity effects and the influence of litigation. *Psychological Assessment, 9,* 177–184.

Zatzick, D. F., Marmar, C. R., Weiss, D. S., Browner, W. S., Metzler, T. J., Golding, J. M, et al. (1997). Posttraumatic stress disorder and functioning and quality of life outcomes in a nationally representative sample of male Vietnam veterans. *American Journal of Psychiatry, 154,* 1690–1695.

5
CHAPTER

Derek R. Hopko
Carl W. Lejuez
Maria E. A. Armento
Robert Bare

Depressive Disorders

☐ Description of Disorders

The predominant feature of mood disorders is the experience of dysphoric and/or euphoric states that deviate markedly from societal norms and create significant distress or impairment in functioning. The mood disorders encompass a variety of affective problems that include major (or unipolar) depression, bipolar disorder, cylothymia, dysthymia, and substance-induced mood disorder. Depressive disorders are a subset of the mood disorders and include major depression, dythymia, and depressive disorder (not otherwise specified [NOS]). The prevalence and functional impact of depressive disorders are substantial, necessitating an implementation of primary and secondary prevention (or assessment) strategies that facilitate efficient and effective recognition of clinical depression, assist in the selection of appropriate target behaviors, and help in designing intervention programs. Accurate detection of depressive symptoms and disorders requires a comprehensive assessment process that is based on awareness of diagnostic criteria, knowledge of risk factors, and utilization of a multimethod assessment strategy. Moreover, application of assessment strategies throughout the intervention process is essential for monitoring patient progress and facilitating clinical decision-making. Given the significance of the assessment process in recognizing and treating patients with depressive disorders, this chapter highlights characteristic symptoms and risk factors, elucidates a range of assessment strategies, focuses on pragmatic issues associated with assessing depressive disorders in clinical practice, and concludes with a case illustration depicting the use of assessment methods prior to and during psychotherapy.

Depression is in some respect an expression of normal human emotion that periodically may be experienced in the form of "sadness," "disappointment," "grief," or being "down in the dumps." It is not uncommon to periodically exhibit these feelings, particularly if environmental experiences are unrewarding, stressful, negative, or aversive. Indeed, factors such as the frequency and duration of stressful life experiences, atttributional style, degree of response-contingent positive reinforcement, and the extent of coping resources may greatly impact whether these normal human experiences become symptomatic and potentially evolve into a depressive disorder (Abramson, Metalsky, & Alloy, 1989; Beck, Rush, Shaw, & Emery, 1979; Cronkite & Moos, 1995; Lewinsohn, 1974). According to the *Diagnostic and Statistical Manual of Mental Disorders*, 4th edition, revised text (DSM-IV-TR; American Psychiatric Association, 2001), the two primary diagnostic criteria for major depressive disorder (MDD) are depressed mood and loss of interest or pleasure in most activities, at least one of which must occur for a duration of at least two weeks. Secondary symptoms include significant appetite change, weight loss, or both, sleep disturbance, psychomotor agitation or retardation, fatigue or energy loss, feelings of worthlessness or guilt, attentional or concentration difficulties, and recurrent thoughts of death or suicide. Of these diagnostic symptoms, dysphoric mood, appetite and sleep change, and thoughts of death are most common, while loss of interest in activities and psychomotor change appear to be less common (Weissman, Bruce, Leaf, Florio, & Holzer, 1991).

In contrast to MDD, dysthymia is a depressive disorder that is chronic in nature and requires that an individual experience a depressed mood on more days than not for at least 2 years. Dysthymia generally is characterized by fewer and less severe symptoms, with researchers indicating that symptoms such as decreased energy, suicidal ideation, concentration problems, and eating and sleeping disturbances are milder and not as prevalent compared with patients diagnosed with MDD (Klein et al., 1996). The term double depression has been used to refer to patients who experience a major depressive episode superimposed on a preexisting diagnosis of dysthymia. Compared with individuals with MDD, individuals with double depression may exhibit greater Axis I and II comorbidity (Pepper et al., 1995) and may be less likely to exhibit long-term treatment gains (Klein et al., 1998). The residual category of depressive disorder (NOS) is reserved for individuals who experience depressive symptoms but do not meet criteria for either MDD or dysthymia. Researchers recently have indicated that a subset of subsyndromal depressive symptoms may be characteristic of a minor depression, a diagnosis proposed for further study in DSM-IV (American Psychiatric Association, 1994). Although the definition of minor depression varies across studies and the distinction from depressive disorder NOS is somewhat unclear (Pincus, Davis, & McQueen, 1999), generally this label is applied to patients whose depressive symptoms fail to meet diagnostic criteria for a depressive disorder due to limited duration, intensity, or number of symptoms. Research with mixed-age and older adult samples has found that subsyndromal depression is more prevalent than diagnosable depressive disorders (Judd et al., 1998; Oxman, Barrett, Barrett, & Gerber, 1990) and is associated with increased disability, health care use, and risk for developing a formal diagnosable depressive disorder (Angst, Merikangas, & Preisig, 1997; Broadhead, Blazer, George, & Tse, 1990; Lyness, King, Cox, Yoediono, & Caine, 1999; Wagner et al., 2000). In addition, younger and older patients with minor depression typically are more similar to depressed patients than nonclinical groups on variables such as impaired social functioning and decreased quality of life (Koenig, 1997; Lewisohn et al., 2000; Wagner et al., 2000).

In assessing for depressive disorders and in conducting a differential diagnosis, it also may be useful to consider depressive symptoms within the domains of mood, cognition and perception, behavior, and somatic functioning (Rehm & Tyndall, 1993). Of these symptom domains, negative mood state generally is most stable, with depressed individuals frequently reporting immense sadness or feelings of hopelessness. The experience of anhedonia, or loss of interest in previously rewarding activities, may be reflective of this negative affect but often is exhibited in the form of decreased overt behaviors that may result in decreased exposure to environmental reinforcement and the onset and maintenance of depressive affect (Lewinsohn, 1974; Lejuez, Hopko, & Hopko, 2002). It also is common for depressed individuals to exhibit increased anger and irritability, which among adolescents may manifest as an externalizing problem or disorder (Pozanski, 1982). Impaired cognitive functioning also may be evident in the form of attentional deficits, poor concentration, and memory impairment (Williams et al., 2000), with some data to suggest attentional training procedures may be useful in alleviating depressive symptoms (Papageorgiou & Wells, 2000). Depressed cognitive styles or patterns of thinking may pervade the clinical picture, an assessment of which may assist in evaluating the severity of depressive symptoms (cf. Sacco & Beck, 1995). A subset of patients also may present with psychotic symptoms that are associated with increased depression severity, longer depressive episodes, greater incapacity, and more resistance to treatment (Coryell, 1998). Unlike other depressive subtypes, psychotic depressions tend to be only weakly associated with significant life events or stressors (Paykel & Cooper, 1992). Somatic symptoms traditionally include the vegetative symptoms of sleep and appetite disturbance as well as decreased energy. Most typically, depressed patients will exhibit decreased appetite and insomnia, although atypical symptoms (increased appetite and hypersomnia) may predominate characteristics linked with an increased likelihood of treatment response (Stewart, Rabkin, Quitkin, McGrath, & Klein, 1993). Appetite and sleeping patterns also are considered behavioral indices of depression, as are psychomotor behaviors, verbal or behavioral expressions of suicidality, and restricted activity patterns in the form of passivity or lethargy (Hopko, Lejuez, Ruggiero, & Eifert, 2002). Associated behaviors of social withdrawal and substance abuse may be considered in the same category, the former of which may represent an emotional avoidance strategy (Hayes, Strosahl, & Wilson, 1999).

Prevalence and Impact of Depressive Disorders

Approximately 30% of adult Americans have reported the experience of "dysphoria" for a duration of greater than 2 weeks at some point during their lifetime (Weissman et al., 1991). The experience of a major depressive episode is relatively less common, with Epidemiological Catchment Area (ECA) data suggesting a lifetime prevalence of 6.3% and a 1-year prevalence of 3.7% (Weissman et al., 1991). Comparatively, results of the National Comorbidity Survey suggested a lifetime prevalence of 17.1% and a 1-year prevalence of 10.3% (Kessler et al., 1994. See Kaelber, Moul, & Farmer [1995] for an explanation of differential rates). The American Psychiatric Association estimates the lifetime risk of MDD between 10–25% for women and 5–12% for men and the lifetime prevalence of dysthymia at about 6%, with females being twice as likely to develop both disorders (APA, 1994). A concerning discovery is that the incidence of depression and suicidal behavior appears to be progressively increasing across generations (Cross-National Collaborative Group, 1992). Interestingly, within primary care, and mindful of data indicating that clinical depression largely is unrecognized in this context, depression is among the most commonly experienced psychiatric problems, with as many as 10–29% of patients presenting with a depressive disorder (McQuaid, Stein, Laffaye, & McCahill, 1999). Depression also is the second most frequent psychiatric disorder among patients admitted to American mental hospitals (Olfson & Mechanic, 1996).

Functional impairment associated with depressive disorders also is quite extensive, including exacerbation of medical illness and negative effects on physical health (Stevens, Merikangas, & Merikangas, 1995), maladaptive cognitive processes (Beck, Rush, Shaw, & Emory, 1979), decreased engagement in pleasurable or rewarding behaviors (Lewinsohn, 1974), and problems with interpersonal relationships (Klerman, Weissman, Rounsaville, & Chevron, 1984). Compared with nondepressed students, depressed college students miss more classes, perform poorer in the classes they do attend, and have more relationship difficulties (Heiligenstein, Guenther, Hsu, & Herman, 1996). Moreover, the experience of a major depressive episode greatly increases the likelihood of future depressive episodes (Rohde, Lewinsohn, & Seeley, 1990) and is highly comorbid with other psychiatric problems such as anxiety disorders (Mineka, Watson, & Clark, 1998) and alcohol abuse (Regier et al., 1990). The direct (health care, medication) and indirect (lost wages, absenteeism) economic costs of treating depressive disorders are staggering (Booth et al., 1997). For example, Jonsson and Rosenbaum (1993) estimated that between $300–400 million in direct costs are spent annually on these disorders, and there is ample evidence to suggest that clinical depression is associated with increased use of medical health services (Simon & Katzelnick, 1997; Simon, Ormel, VonKorff, & Barlow, 1995).

Risk Factors

As mentioned previously, gender seems to be associated with development of clinical depression (for further discussion see Just & Alloy [1997] or Nolen-Hoeksema & Girgus [1994]). Other risk factors include Caucasian ethnicity, experiencing a separation or divorce, prior depressive episodes, poor physical health, and medical illnesses, (e.g., hypothyroidism, Cushing's syndrome), low socioeconomic status, adverse life events (e.g., unemployment, loss of loved one), and family history of depression (cf. Kaelber et al., 1995). Although major depression may develop at any age, the average age of onset is 15 to 19 years in females and 25 to 29 years for males (Burke, Burke, Regier, & Rae, 1990), with the average age of onset steadily decreasing over past decades (Weissman, Bruce, Leaf, Florio, & Holzer, 1991). It is important to note that earlier onset is associated with greater chronicity and poorer response to treatment (Akiskal & Cassano, 1997). Contrary to misconceptions, the elderly do not appear more susceptible to depression (Roberts, Kaplan, Shema, & Strawbridge, 1997). Although risk factors such as these should be considered in the assessment process, it is imperative to recognize that they are based on nomothetic data. Thus, it is unclear to what extent particular risk factors are causative, an associated epiphenomenon, or possibly a consequence of a depressive disorder (Kaelber et al., 1995). As such, we advocate an ideographic approach to assessment in which these generalizations are recognized within the context of a more extensive individualized assessment based on patients' unique clinical presentations and symptoms, severity of symptoms, and proximal and distal factors or events associated with the etiology and maintenance of symptoms (i.e., functional analysis). A broad range of assessment strategies for depression may facilitate this process.

☐ Range of Assessment Strategies Available

Numerous assessment strategies have been developed to assess for depression and related constructs such as attributional style, hopelessness, and depressive vulnerability. Approaches for assessing depression generally may be characterized as falling under the rubrics of unstructured or structured interviews, self-report measures, observational methods, and functional analysis (Thorpe & Olson, 1997). Although many resources are available, their appropriateness and clinical utility vary greatly across patient and assessment context (Alexopoulos et al., 2002). The level of skill and training required of the assessor to incorporate these strategies also is quite variable, ranging from minimal skill to administer a self-report measure, moderate skill to conduct a valid structured interview, and extensive skill to perform a comprehensive functional analysis of depressive symptoms. Indeed, a number of other logistical and procedural factors must be taken into account during the process of selecting an appropriate assessment tool or tools (Nezu, Nezu, & Foster, 2000). Prior to exploring these issues in greater detail, the present section outlines the primary methods of diagnosing clinical depression and assessing associated symptoms.

Unstructured and Structured Interviews

The structure of clinical interviews has tremendous variability, ranging from a primarily unstructured and completely flexible approach, to a semistructured approach that provides moderate direction while maintaining a degree of flexibility (e.g., intake form, Brief Psychiatric Rating Scale; Overall & Gorham, 1962), to structured methods that are more restrictive and goal-directed. A number of positive correlates may be associated with unstructured methods that include increased therapist-patient rapport, ability to assess how patients organize responses, and the potential to explore unique details of a patient's history. Most contemporary practitioners allow for some degree of flexibility, although most also make use of some type of intake form or checklist to facilitate the assessment process. Largely due to concerns about reliability and validity of unstructured interviews and efforts by managed care organizations to improve the efficiency and cost-effectiveness of assessment and treatment as well as the accountability of clinicians, increased focus has been placed on examining the utility of more structured procedures toward accomplishing these goals (cf. Groth-Marnat, 1997). The controversy over whether the use of more structured interviewing and assessment strategies is concomitant with managed care objectives continues, as does discussion over which assessment methods are most optimal. Indeed, managed care companies continue to exhibit marked variability in terms of preference for particular assessment strategies and documentation required to justify treatment for mental illness (Keefe & Hall, 1999). Acknowledging these ongoing issues, we present the most commonly used structured (clinician-rated) interviews.

The Structured Clinical Interview for DSM-IV — Patient Version (SCID-I/P; First et al., 1996) is a semistructured interview based on operational diagnostic criteria from the DSM-IV. It incorporates a categorical system for rating symptoms, and an algorithm for arriving at a final diagnosis. The SCID-I/P takes approximately 60–90 minutes to administer and requires fairly rigorous training. Administration begins with an open-ended interview that is followed by a systematic series of questions designed to facilitate an accurate differential diagnosis. Adequate interrater reliability and diagnostic accuracy have been demonstrated for the instrument (Ventura et al., 1998). Although this instrument has been utilized extensively in treatment outcome studies and is an invaluable research tool, clinicians in more applied settings may be reluctant to allocate the time required to conduct this more formalized assessment. In cases where a clinician suspects a depressive disorder is evident and wants to be more definitive, it may be feasible to streamline the approach by administering only the mood disorder module.

The Anxiety Disorders Interview Schedule (ADIS-IV; Brown, Di Nardo, & Barlow, 1994) is a semistructured interview designed primarily to provide a differential diagnosis of anxiety disorders. Likely due to the high level of overlap with anxiety disorders, the ADIS-IV also includes comprehensive modules for major depression and dysthymia, as well as screens for mania, somatization disorders, substance abuse, and psychosis. Many symptoms are rated on a (yes/no) nominal scale, several of which also include severity ratings that are established based on an anchored continuum of severity or interference. The ADIS-IV generally takes approximately 45–60 minutes to administer. A recently conducted reliability analysis using the ADIS-IV suggested that categories such as major depression, panic disorder, specific phobia, and social phobia had good to excellent reliability (i.e., $\kappa > 0.60$), while the category of dysthymia was associated with relatively poor agreement ($\kappa = 0.22$; Brown, Di Nardo, Lehman, & Campbell, 2001).

The Schedule for Affective Disorders and Schizophrenia (SADS; Endicott & Spitzer, 1978) is used to assess for over 20 major diagnoses, including major depressive disorder and the various subtypes. Based on individuals' responses to questions assessing current and past functioning, results can be used to assess the temporal nature (and severity) of psychological disorders. The SADS takes approximately 90–120 minutes to administer and requires extensive training. Spitzer, Endicott, and Robins (1978) reported excellent reliabilities for diagnoses including major ($\kappa = 0.90$) and minor depressive disorder ($\kappa = 0.81$).

The 17-item Hamilton Rating Scale for Depression (HRSD; Hamilton, 1960) was designed as a postdiagnostic measure to assess the severity of depressive symptoms and to measure changes in a patient's functioning over time. The recommendation is that the HRSD be completed (in about 10 minutes) following a clinical interview of at least 30 minutes duration in which the necessary information is obtained to accurately assess the patient (Hamilton, 1967). Interrater reliability coefficients of the HRSD generally are excellent ($\kappa > 0.84$) and data suggest moderate convergent validity with several self-report measures of depression (Nezu, Ronan, Meadows, & McClure, 2000). The HRSD is the most widely used and accepted outcome measure for the evaluation of depression and has become the standard outcome measure in clinical trials (Kobak & Reynolds, 1999). An additional benefit of this instrument is its availability at no cost via assessment resources (Nezu et al., 2000) and the Internet (www.glaxowellcome.com).

The Brief Psychiatric Rating Scale (BPRS; Overall & Gorham, 1962) was originally developed to assess 18 psychiatric symptoms and to evaluate change over time. Commonly used in inpatient settings and in treatment outcome research, the BPRS is completed based on observations obtained during a basic 20–30 minute clinical interview. Although the measure is used to assess clinical symptoms among patients with a broad range of problems, several scales are relevant to depression, including somatic concern, anxiety, emotional withdrawal, guilt, depressed mood, motor retardation, and blunted affect. Adequate interrater reliability, as well as discriminative and predictive validity of the measure has been documented (Faustman & Overall, 1999).

The Diagnostic Interview Schedule (DIS; Robins, Helzer, Croughan, & Ratcliff, 1981) is a 90–120 minute structured interview initially developed to estimate the prevalence and incidence of psychiatric disorders within the context of the National Institute of Mental Health's Epidemiological Catchment Area Program. As such, the DIS was designed to be conducted by laypeople who were provided with extensive training. Despite some evidence of instrument reliability and findings suggesting that lay interviewers formulate diagnostic impressions similar to those of psychiatrists (Robins et al., 1981), given the comparable time to administer the measure (90–120 minutes), the suggestion has been made that clinicians who use structured diagnostic interviews use those with more established psychometric properties (Nezu et al., 2000).

Self-Report Measures

Self-report measures of depression have proven useful as screening instruments, as auxiliaries in the diagnostic process, as tools for monitoring progress across treatment sessions, and as outcome measures for assessing the efficacy and effectiveness of various psychosocial and pharmacological interventions. Scales have been designed to assess a tremendous range of content areas, including affective, verbal-cognitive, somatic, behavioral, and social symptoms of depression. At present, there are at least 80 measures designed to assess depression and related constructs. The majority of these instruments have adequate to excellent psychometric properties (see Nezu et al., 2000 for a comprehensive review). A few of the most commonly utilized measures are presented here.

The Beck Depression Inventories (BDI; Beck & Steer, 1987; BDI-II; Beck, Steer, & Brown, 1996) assess the severity of depressive symptoms and each consists of 21 items, rated on a 4-point Likert scale. The instruments have excellent reliability and validity with depressed younger and older adults (Beck & Steer, 1987; Beck et al., 1996; Beck, Steer, & Garbin, 1988; Snyder et al., 2000). Among younger clinical and nonclinical adults, the instruments have substantial internal consistency ($\alpha = 0.73$–0.95) and adequate test-retest reliability for nonpsychiatric ($r = 0.60$–0.83) and psychiatric patients ($r = 0.48$–0.93) (Beck et al., 1988, 1996). Concurrent and construct validity among the Beck inventories and other indices of depression ranges from moderate ($r = 0.33$ with DSM III diagnosis of clinical depression; Hesselbrock et al., 1983) to strong ($r = 0.86$ with the

Zung SDS; Turner & Romano, 1984; see Beck et al., 1988, 1996 for comprehensive reviews).

The Hamilton Depression Inventory (HDI; Reynolds & Kobak, 1995) is a 23-item measure designed to assess for the presence and severity of depressive symptoms. A 17-item version also is available that is consistent with the HRSD in content and scoring. Strong internal consistency (α = 0.90–0.93), 1-week test-retest reliability (r = 0.95), and convergent validity with the HRSD (r = 0.94) and BDI (r = 0.93) have been demonstrated.

The Center for Epidemiological Studies' Depression Scale (CES-D; Radloff, 1977) is a 20-item self-report questionnaire of depressive symptoms (rated on a 0–3 anchored scale) that was designed as a survey instrument for assessing depressive affect in the general population. Although it was not intended for use as a diagnostic measure, CES-D totals have been shown to be moderately related to a diagnosis of clinical depression (Myers & Weissman, 1980) and some have argued for its utility as an initial depression screening measure (Roberts & Vernon, 1983). When used for screening, scores greater than 16 indicate that a patient may have clinical depression (Radloff, 1977). The CES-D has adequate psychometric properties in psychiatric and medical samples and is available at no cost (Nezu et al., 2000).

The Harvard Department of Psychiatry/National Depression Screening Day Scale (HANDS; Baer et al., 2000) is a 10-item screening measure that was derived using items from well-established instruments including the BDI (Beck & Steer, 1987) and the Zung SDS (Zung, 1965). Preliminary data indicate that the instrument has good psychometric properties, including adequate internal consistency (α = 0.87). The instrument also appears highly sensitive, with research indicating that over 90% of individuals who score 9 or higher on the instrument meet diagnostic criteria for major depression.

The Reynolds Depression Screening Inventory (RDSI; Reynolds & Kobak, 1998) is a 19-item measure (score range = 0–63) that assesses depressive symptom severity and is based on DSM-IV diagnostic criteria for major depression. Although scores greater than 24 indicate severe clinical depression, a cutoff score of 16 has been associated with sensitivity and specificity rates of 95% in identifying individuals with major depression. Internal consistency (α = 0.93) and test-retest reliability (r = 0.94) are strong. The instrument correlated strongly with the HRSD (r = 0.93) and the BDI (r = 0.93).

The Minnesota Multiphasic Personality Inventory 2 Depression Scale (MMPI-2-D; Butcher et al., 1989) is one of the 10 clinical scales on the MMPI-2 and consists of 57 true-false items that assess depressive symptoms (on more of a state level) as well as related personality features. Item responses on the MMPI-2-D are converted to a T-score, with elevations of 65 or greater considered clinically significant. Harris-Lingoes Depression Subscales provide additional information on several dimensions: subjective depression, psychomotor retardation, physical functioning, mental dullness, and brooding. Coefficient alphas on the MMPI-2-D range from 0.59 (males) to 0.64 (females) and the test-retest reliability is estimated at 0.75 (Nezu et al., 2000). In addition to limitations given the large number of items, caution should be exercised in using the MMPI-D-2 as researchers recently have indicated that the scale may be associated with problems with sensitivity and predictive power and may not be unidimensional as once theorized (Chang, 1996; Elwood, 1993).

The Personality Assessment Inventory (PAI; Morey, 1991) is a 344-item self-administered test of personality and psychopathology. Items are answered on a four-alternative scale, with the anchors "Totally False," "Slightly True," "Mainly True," and "Very True." The measure consists of 4 validity scales, 11 clinical scales, 4 treatment scales, 2 interpersonal scales, and several subscales. The depression clinical scale focuses on symptoms and phenomenology of depressive disorders and is broken down into three subscales that address the cognitive, affective, and physiological components of depression. Internal consistency of the full scales is satisfactory, with median coefficient alphas ranging from 0.81 (normative sample) to 0.86 (clinical sample). The depression scale is strongly convergent with the BDI ($r = 0.81$), HRSD ($r = 0.78$), and somewhat less so with the MMPI-D scale ($r = 0.66$; Morey, 1999).

Observational Methods

Observational methods of assessing depressive symptoms are used to measure the frequency and duration of observable (overt-motor) behaviors. Behaviors may include excesses such as crying, irritable/agitated behaviors, and even suicidal behaviors, or deficits such as minimal eye contact, psychomotor retardation, decreased recreational and occupational activities, as well as disruption in sleep, eating, and sexual behaviors (Rehm, 1988). Although direct behavioral assessment of depression should intuitively be a primary tool of behavioral (or cognitive-behavioral) therapists, remarkably minimal work has been done in this area subsequent to the pioneering research of the 1970s through the early 1980s.

Pertaining to verbal behavior (see Rehm [1988] for a comprehensive discussion), several studies have demonstrated that depressed individuals generally tend to exhibit a slower and more monotonous rate of speech (Gotlib & Robinson, 1982; Libet & Lewinsohn, 1973; Robinson & Lewinsohn, 1973). Individuals with depression also take longer to respond to the verbal behavior of others (Libet & Lewinsohn, 1973) and relative to nondepressed individuals, exhibit an increased frequency of self-focused negative remarks (Blumberg & Hokanson, 1983; Gotlib & Robinson, 1982) and use fewer "achievement" and "power" words in their speech (Andreasen & Pfohl, 1976). Nonverbal (motoric) differences between depressed and nondepressed individuals also are evident. In a pioneering investigation, Williams, Barlow, and Agras (1972) developed the Ward Behavior Checklist to assess smiling, motoric activities (e.g., reading, grooming), and "time out of the room" among a small group of depressed inpatients. These behavioral indices correlated moderately with scores on depression measures including the HRSD, but perhaps more interestingly, were more predictive of relapse at 1-year posttreatment. Depressed individuals also smile less frequently (Gotlib & Robinson, 1982), make less eye contact during conversation (Gotlib, 1982), hold their head in a downward position more frequently, engage in more self-touching (e.g., rubbing, scratching; Ranelli & Miller, 1981), and are rated as less competent in social situations (Dykman, Horowitz, Abramson, & Usher, 1991). There also is couples research that suggests when one partner is clinically depressed, interactions are more apt to be characterized by conflict and incongruity between verbal and nonverbal behaviors (Hinchliffe, Hooper, & Roberts, 1978). Finally, depressed mothers have been shown to be less active and playful and tend to exhibit shorter eye-gaze durations when interacting with their children (Field, Healy, Goldstein, & Guthertz, 1990; Livingood, Daen, & Smith, 1983).

Although many of these verbal and behavioral indices of depression have been used as pre-post outcome measures (see Rehm, 1988 for a review) and knowledge of these correlates may contribute to a more comprehensive assessment for clinical depression, systematic and structured analysis of these variables in the context of therapy (and/or home visits) may not be the most practical of assessment methods. Perhaps more useful in this regard, behavioral monitoring logs or diaries may be used to provide information about patients' sources of environmental reinforcement. For example, MacPhillamy and Lewinsohn (1971, 1982) developed the Pleasant Events Schedule to assess, monitor, and modify positive activities among individuals with depression. The measure also has been used as a treatment outcome instrument and appears sensitive to change following therapy. Along these same lines, our research group has used daily diaries to assess the frequency and duration of healthy nondepressive activities to assist in treatment planning and as a measure of treatment outcome (Lejuez, Hopko, & Hopko, 2001). Recent research has indicated that these daily diaries can be useful in assessing both immediate and future reward value of current behaviors, that reward value ratings correlate highly with self-report measures of depressive affect, and that mildly depressed and nondepressed students can be distinguished via response style (Hopko, Armento, Cantu, Chambers, & Lejuez, 2003).

Functional Analysis

Although many different definitions have appeared in the literature (Haynes & O'Brien, 1990), functional analysis generally refers to the process of identifying important, controllable, and causal environmental factors that may be related to the etiology and maintenance of depressive symptoms. Rooted in behavioral theory, functional analysis is a strategy fundamental to initiating an appropriate behavioral intervention. Applied to clinical depression, functional analysis involves the operational definition of undesirable (nonhealthy) depressive behavior(s) such as lethargy, social withdrawal, crying, alcohol abuse, and suicidality. Strategies for conducting functional analyses include interviews with the patient and significant others, naturalistic observation, the manipulation of specific situations that result in an increase or decrease of target behaviors, or some combination (O'Neill, Horner, Albin, Storey, & Sprague, 1990). Often incorporating some form of daily monitoring, depressed patients may be asked to record depressive (target) behaviors, the context (time, place, surroundings) in which they occur, and the consequences that follow. With all functional analytic strategies, the therapist is concerned with identifying the function (or maintaining reinforcers) that depressed behavior produces for an individual, or put more simply, why the depressed behavior occurs. According to behavioral theory, depressive behavior occurs because reinforcement for healthy behavior is minimal, because positive and negative reinforcement for depressive behavior is excessive, or both (Lewinsohn, 1974). In other words, depressed behavior may develop following extinction of "healthy" behaviors consequent to a decrease in response contingent positive reinforcement and may be maintained via the experience of pleasant consequences (e.g., other people completing responsibilities, attention, and sympathy), as a result of the removal of aversive experiences (e.g., unpleasant or stressful activities), or both.

In addition to using functional analysis techniques to understand more overt behavior, these strategies also may be useful for understanding maladaptive thought processes that more cognitively oriented therapists believe to be a critical feature in eliciting depressive affect (Beck, Shaw, Rush, & Emery, 1979). Indeed, through strategies that include the use of thought-monitoring logs or various thought sampling methods (Csikszentmihalyi & Larson, 1987; Hurlburt, 1997), functional analysis strategies can be used to identify specific thought patterns elicited by certain environmental events and how these cognitions may correspond with depressive mood states. These same methods also may be utilized to assess change during and following therapeutic strategies that focus on challenging and restructuring the maladaptive or irrational cognitions. Functional analysis methods may be useful in integrating assessment data, developing hypotheses about factors maintaining depressive behaviors, and may greatly assist in the formulation of a treatment plan. It also should be noted that from a pragmatic standpoint, the practice of conducting functional analyses requires extensive training and skill, is largely based on complex causal models of behavior disorders, and the compatibility of this strategy with the policies of managed care is at this stage undetermined. Because of these factors, it is unsurprising that the literature suggests that pretreatment functional analyses are only infrequently conducted (cf. Haynes & O'Brien, 1990). It also is evident, however, that functional analytic strategies may be quite useful in generating specific treatment goals and as a method of intervention (Haynes, 1998). More traditional (Ferster, 1973) and contemporary behavioral theories and interventions for depression (Lejuez, Hopko, & Hopko, 2002; Martell, Addis, & Jacobson, 2001; McCullough, 2000), as well as treatments for other psychiatric conditions (Hopko & Hopko, 1999; Linehan, 1993) to a greater or lesser degree incorporate functional analytic techniques.

☐ Pragmatic Issues Encountered in Clinical Practice with These Disorders

Various pragmatic issues are associated with assessing depressive disorders in clinical practice, which generally can be conceptualized in the broader context of assessment procedures and financial considerations. Some of the more fundamental issues surrounding the choice and implementation of assessment strategies include determining the goal(s) of assessment, conducting an ideographic multimethod approach to assessing behavioral problems, identifying and problem solving around obstacles to assessment, and evaluating whether assessment procedures are generating useful, reliable, and valid information (Nezu, Nezu, & Foster, 2000). These practical issues have nicely been summarized previously and thus only are briefly reviewed in the present context. The specific goals of assessment are quite diverse, and may include primary prevention screening strategies such as those provided during National Depression Screening Day (www.mentalhealthscreening.org/depression.htm), a program with documented effectiveness in identifying individuals with clinical depression and facilitating their access to the mental health care system (Greenfield et al., 1997). Several screening instruments (reviewed in the previous section) have demonstrated utility in expediting this process. A second goal of assessment might include the need to accurately diagnose patients, so as to facilitate appropriate patient-treatment matching, to generate confidence in research findings and generalizability of results, or both. Third, assessment may be necessary to better qualify and quantify problems and symptoms as well as maintaining contextual factors so as to assist in a clinician's case conceptualization (Goldfried & Sprafkin, 1976). Finally, assessment may greatly assist in the formulation of a treatment plan as well as comparative evaluations of the efficacy and effectiveness of various treatment modalities.

Regardless of the specific assessment goal, a multimethod, ideographic assessment will help to establish confidence in the validity of conclusions and recommendations. This means assessing across multiple response systems (i.e., behavioral, cognitive, physiological) using various methods (e.g., self-report, direct observation), and always with attention to unique environmental factors that may be involved in the etiology and maintenance of symptoms. Indeed, considering the numerous assessment strategies that may be beneficial in assessing and treating patients with clinical depression, clinicians will vary markedly in their knowledge and administration of these procedures. Without sufficient training and knowledge, clinicians may be unsuccessful in conducting a comprehensive psychological assessment and subsequently may provide ineffective treatment for their patients (Higgitt & Fonagy, 2002). In addition to skill level, many other factors may affect the reliability and validity of assessment results and clinical decision-making (Kaheman & Tversky, 1973; Arkes, 1981; Nezu & Nezu, 1989). Researchers have demonstrated, for example, that clinical decisions often are made out of habit rather than through systematically gathered information (Higgitt & Fonagy, 2002). Safeguards should be utilized to minimize the negative impact of such factors. Nezu and Nezu (1993) have forwarded a continuous and reciprocal problem-solving model that may assist the assessment process as it pertains to problem definition and formulation, generation of alternatives, decision making, and solution implementation and verification.

Addressing obstacles that may sabotage an otherwise informative clinical assessment also will be critical. Patient obstacles that may include logistical and motivational problems (particularly among depressed patients), therapist obstacles that may include lack of expertise, resources, or time, and common obstacles such as limited financial resources will be key problems to consider. Obstacles may necessitate the need for modification of assessment procedures, increasing clinician skill level (perhaps through continuing education), choosing other techniques that can be more effectively used, or both (Nezu, Nezu & Foster, 2000; Maruish, 1999). Finally, although assessment is most prominent at the outset of therapy, it also is a continuous process that begins with the initial patient visit and extends toward the maintenance phase at post-treatment, with periodic evaluation necessary to establish whether assessment strategies are accomplishing the goals for which they were designed.

Financial Considerations, Managed Care, and Assessment of Clinical Depression

A Substance Abuse and Mental Health Services Administration (SAMHSA) report estimated that approximately 22.3 million adults received mental health treatment in 2001, representing 11% of the population 18 years of age or older. The majority of these patients are treated within the context of primary care, in which major depression is one of the most common mental health problems (Spitzer et al., 1994; Ustun & Sartorius 1995). Intervention costs are staggering. The American Psychological Association (2000) reported, for example, that psychiatric disorders collectively accounted for approximately 15% of the nation's health care costs, with intervention costing in excess of $100 billion annually. Compounding this problem, indirect costs in the form of absenteeism, lost productivity, and employee turnover are significant, with estimates of depression-related costs exceeding $30 billion annually (Greenberg, Kessler, Nells, Finkelstein, & Berndt, 1996).

A further pragmatic consideration of assessing for clinical depression evolving out of this current zeitgeist is the necessity that clinicians be effective and efficient in assessment and intervention to meet the demands of managed care companies (Bieber et al., 1999; Johnson, 1995). Consistent with policies surrounding the cost-effectiveness of psychotherapy, managed care organizations (MCOs) have limited the reimbursement and subsequent use of psychological assessment procedures (Ficken, 1995; Werthman, 1995). Clinicians are consequently engaging in fewer testing procedures and are more restricted in their use of assessment instruments (Piotrowski, 1999).

So what does this mean for practitioners and the assessment of clinical depression? First, the impact of MCOs on various assessment strategies will be quite differential. In most cases, for example, clinicians will continue to receive monetary compensation for unstructured clinical interviews at the initiation of therapy. In community practice, the use of more timely structured interviews might be less feasible, as would the administration, scoring, and interpretation of lengthy personality assessment instruments (Piotrowski, 1999). Given the brevity of other self-report measures (such as the BDI or CES-D) and the feasibility of assessment occurring outside of the context of clinical practice (e.g., daily monitoring logs, self-report), there is no reason to suspect such strategies greatly would be affected by MCOs. Similarly, the process of conducting a functional analysis of depressive behavior generally is ongoing and is enmeshed within the context of psychotherapy. As long as therapeutic services are being reimbursed, so should this type of assessment.

Second, practitioners may have to learn to become more flexible and creative (Mays & Croake, 1997). This may involve assessment of depression via the training of nontraditional personnel such as nurses (Wells, 1999), using assessment instruments for multiple purposes (Hopko, Averill, Small, Greenlee, & Varner, 2001), incorporating family members into the assessment process (Lejuez, Hopko, & Hopko, 2001), writing briefer reports, and learning how to administer specific assessment instruments as required of MCOs. Third, as part of the need to increase efficiency, generation of educational opportunities to enhance understanding of clinical depression is warranted. A significant proportion of patients with clinical depression who present to primary care settings, for example, often are undiagnosed or misdiagnosed (McQuaid, Stein, Laffaye, & McCahill, 1999; Schuyler, 2000). Dissemination of effective and efficient assessment strategies to practitioners in this environment as well as utilization of technologically advanced assessment strategies (Sturges, 1998) therefore is exceedingly necessary. Fourth, managed care has necessitated that clinicians show increased accountability throughout the assessment and therapy process. Systems that monitor practitioner performance therefore will be critical toward meeting this demand and ensuring patient progress and improvement (Callaghan, 2001; Donabedian, 1985). Finally, it will become increasingly important for practitioners and managed care personnel to collaboratively work toward streamlining assessment processes and maximizing quality of care. For practitioners, this means learning about the philosophy and goals of MCOs, educating MCOs about the value of testing, and being conservative and discriminatory when requesting authorization and reimbursement for testing (Dorfman, 2000). These practices may ultimately result in more limited use of physician services and decreased medical costs, a phenomenon referred to as "medical cost offset" (Bieber et al., 1999; Simon et al., 2002).

☐ Case Illustration

Client Description

The patient (Anne) was a 38-year-old married Hispanic female. She had been married for 19 years and had three daughters, ages 5, 9, and 18. At the time of assessment Anne was a homemaker, but was previously employed in various secretarial positions. Anne had a tenth grade education. At intake she was oriented in all spheres, with adequate grooming and hygiene. Her mood was dysthymic and psychomotor retardation was evident. Anne's thought process was logical and goal-directed and there was no evidence of perceptual abnormalities. Her speech volume, rate, and tone were within normal limits. Anne presented with depressive symptoms that included depressed mood, decreased sleep and appetite, anhedonia, concentration difficulties, and feelings of guilt and low self-worth. She also reported several obsessive-compulsive symptoms that were related to a core fear of acquiring head lice.

History of the Disorder

Anne indicated that she had felt depressed for as long as she could remember, with the most severe symptoms manifesting over the past decade. Her history was unremarkable as far as significant psychosocial stressors. She had always resided in the same community, had positive peer and parental relationships, had no recollection of childhood abuse or neglect, and no significant medical history; however, she did report a family history of (maternal) depression. Anne reported that the last 2 years had been particularly difficult, following the loss of her job and subsequent financial problems. Anne's family moved into a low-income housing project that had deplorable living conditions, including rat and mice infestation as well as significant sewage problems. During their time at this residence, Anne indicated that her 9-year-old contracted lice from one of her schoolmates, which then quickly spread to other family members. When Anne first discovered lice in her daughter's hair she experienced her first panic attack and a marked worsening of depressive symptoms.

Anne reported no history of inpatient or outpatient psychological (or pharmacological) treatment. With the exception of her mother and aunt, Anne denied a family history of depression, anxiety, and psychosis. She did report a family history of polysubstance abuse, particularly with her brother and grandfather. Anne reported that she drinks wine infrequently (i.e., twice per month), smokes 1 pack of cigarettes per day, and drinks between 2–3 cups of coffee per day. She denied use of other psychoactive substances.

Presenting Complaints

Anne presented with coexistent depressive and anxiety symptoms. Depressive symptoms included anhedonia, dysthymic mood, insomnia, weight loss, and frequent crying spells. Physiological symptoms of anxiety included trembling, perspiration, increased heart rate, shortness of breath, nausea, and difficulty swallowing. Cognitive symptoms included a pronounced fear of "either myself or my daughters obtaining lice," the possibility of which was equated with a core fear of "being a bad and worthless mother." Behavioral symptoms involved avoidance of several situations that included movie theaters, restaurants, playgrounds, furniture (fabric), and contact with other children. When these situations could not be avoided, intense physiological and cognitive anxiety, as well as increased dysphoria was experienced. Ritualistic behaviors in the form of excessive hand washing, blowing, shaking, and tapping also were apparent. Such behaviors almost invariably resulted in marital conflict, a failure to maintain household responsibilities, and an associated increase in depressive symptoms. When anxiety-eliciting situations could successfully be avoided, Anne reported immense guilt and sadness related to the restrictions she was imposing on her children.

☐ Assessment Methods Used

- Clinician ratings
  - Anxiety Disorder Interview Schedule (ADIS-IV; Brown et al., 1994)
  - Hamilton Rating Scale for Depression (HRSD; Hamilton, 1960)
  - Unstructured clinical interview
- Self-report ratings
  - Beck Depression Inventory (BDI; Beck & Steer, 1987)
  - Beck Anxiety Inventory (BAI; Beck & Steer, 1993)

- PADUA Inventory (PI; Sanavio, 1988)
- Personality Assessment Inventory (PAI; Morey, 1991)
- Quality of Life Inventory (QOLI; Frisch, 1994)
- Behavioral observations (Lejuez et al., 2001)
  - Daily diaries, Value Assessment
  - Behavioral Checkout
  - Response Prevention Checklist
- Functional analysis.

Psychological Assessment Protocol

At the initiation of assessment/therapy, the patient underwent a brief unstructured clinical interview followed by administration of the ADIS-IV. Results of this interview suggested that Anne met DSM-IV-TR clinical criteria for major depression and obsessive-compulsive disorder. Further supporting the diagnosis of major depression, Anne received a score of 33 on the HRSD. Several self-report instruments also were completed during the initial assessment. Described in a previous section (see Range of Assessment Strategies) Anne scored a 38 on the BDI (severe depression). Anne also completed the Personality Assessment Inventory (PAI), an objective self-report measure of personality and psychopathological variables. Her profile was valid and interpretable. Significant elevations were noted on the depression (T = 72), Anxiety (T = 78), and Anxiety-Related Disorders (T = 82) clinical scales, as well as on all depression and anxiety subscales (i.e., cognitive, affective, physiological). The ARD-O (Anxiety-Related Disorder: Obsessive-Compulsive) subscale also was significantly elevated (T = 83). On the self-report anxiety measures, Anne scored a 34 on a measure of cognitive and somatic anxiety (BAI; Beck & Steer, 1993) and was significantly elevated on three of the four scales of the Padua inventory, which assess severity of obsessive-compulsive symptoms [impaired control of mental activities (24), contamination (33), checking (13), and worries of losing control over motor behaviors (2, ns). On the QOLI, which assesses life satisfaction on various life domains (e.g., health, relationships, money), Anne scored in the "low" range of life satisfaction (QOLI total = –4).

As a pretreatment assessment strategy and part of a brief behavioral activation treatment for depression (BATD; Lejuez et al., 2001, 2002), Anne also completed a daily diary for one week (Hopko et al., in press). This assignment was used to: (a) provide a baseline measurement by which to compare progress following treatment, (b) make Anne more cognizant of the quantity and quality of her activities, and (c) provide Anne with some ideas with regard to identifying potential activities to target during treatment. Daily monitoring revealed that Anne was leading a relatively passive lifestyle, characterized by such activities as television viewing, daytime napping, and aimless Internet surfing. When queried about the reward (or reinforcement) value of such activities, Anne indicated that minimal pleasure was being experienced. Her daily ratings of the reward value of activities confirmed this appraisal; On a Likert scale ranging from 1 ("minimally rewarding") to 4 ("extremely rewarding"), her average rating was 2.1 (SD = 1.3).

Following this monitoring exercise, the assessment process shifted to identifying Anne's values and goals within a variety of life areas that included family, social, and intimate relationships, education, employment/career, hobbies/recreation, volunteer work/charity, physical/health issues, and spirituality (Hayes et al., 1999). Based on this evaluation, an activity hierarchy was constructed in which 15 activities were rated ranging from "easiest" to "most difficult" to accomplish. These activities were outlined on a master activity log (maintained by the clinician) and a behavioral checkout (maintained by Anne) to monitor progress throughout each week of treatment. The behavioral checkout is presented in Figure 5.1. As part of the exposure and response prevention procedure that was implemented to treat Anne's obsessive-compulsive behaviors, she also was required to maintain a response prevention checklist. This checklist specified both appropriate and inappropriate behaviors (e.g., washing, checking) and required that Anne indicate on a daily basis whether she succeeded or did not succeed in following each of the recommendations.

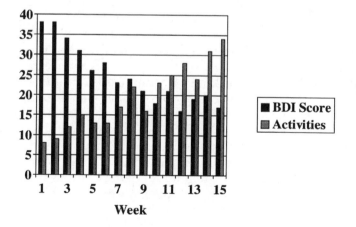

FIGURE 5.1. Weekly BDI scores and activity completion.

Finally, functional analytic procedures were conducted via unstructured interviews with the patient and significant others (i.e., parent, oldest daughter) to identify environmental factors that may be serving to maintain depressive symptoms/behaviors. These interviews revealed that Anne's depressive behaviors were at least partially maintained by positive consequences that followed. For example, when Anne would lie motionless on the couch, which periodically was accompanied by crying, her daughter frequently would provide a significant amount of sympathy and concern and would proceed to complete household tasks such as preparing dinner and washing dishes.

Targets Selected for Treatment

The first treatment goal was to systematically increase response contingent positive reinforcement by facilitating increased exposure to pleasant activities that were consistent with Anne's value/goal assessment. To accomplish this objective, Anne engaged in a brief behavioral activation treatment for depression (BATD; Lejuez et al., 2001). Anne moved through a constructed behavioral hierarchy in a progressive manner, moving from the easier behaviors to the more difficult. For each activity, Anne and the clinician collaboratively determined what the final goal would be in terms of the frequency and duration of activity per week. These goals were recorded on the master activity log that was kept in the possession of the therapist. Weekly goals were recorded on the behavioral checkout form that Anne brought to therapy each week. At the start of each session, the behavioral checkout form was examined and discussed, with the following weekly goals being established as a function of Anne's success or difficulty. Rewards were identified on a weekly basis as incentive for completing the behavioral checkout. A component of this treatment also included addressing rewards for depressive behavior as revealed through functional analysis. Through the use of behavioral contracting procedures, Anne and her daughter clearly specified how much time would be spent discussing Anne's negative affect and when this would occur (i.e., 15 minutes in the morning and 15 minutes before bedtime). Both individuals also agreed that it was better if Anne's daughter did not reward passive behavior by completing Anne's household responsibilities. As such, the agreement stated that her daughter would prepare dinner and wash dishes only twice a week (Monday and Thursday). For successful adherence to this contractual agreement, Anne was rewarded by being able to purchase a small amount of materials for her scrapbooking hobby.

The second treatment goal was to reduce Anne's avoidance behaviors (that resulted from anxiety eliciting stimuli and also increased depressive affect) through exposure and response prevention (ERP) strategies for OCD (Stanley & Averill, 1998). Through imaginal exposure strategies followed by in vivo techniques, Anne was encouraged to confront a variety of feared stimuli that included a pillowcase, comb, daughter's bed, furniture fabric, and her daughter's friends. Evident in the behavioral checkout, behaviors targeted for change were sometimes addressed via multiple treatment strategies. For example, taking the children to a movie or having lunch with a friend both were intended to increase exposure to rewarding activities and to alleviate depressive symptoms but also involved increasing contact with feared stimuli (e.g., fabric, other children) to extinguish anxiety-related responding.

Assessment of Progress

Progress was assessed via pre-post comparisons on the self-report and behavioral observation methods. As presented in Table 5.1, Anne made fairly robust improvement during the 15-week combined BATD-ERP

TABLE 5.1. Comparison of Pre- and Postassessment Measures

Assessment Measure	Pretest	Post-Test
HRSD	33	22
BDI	38	17
PAI (T-Scores)		
Depression Scale	72	57
Anxiety Scale	78	65
Anxiety-related Disorder Scale	82	64
BAI	34	21
PADUA		
Mental Activities	24	8
Contamination	33	14
Checking	13	6
Control	2	2
QOLI	−4	−2
Daily Diaries	2.1	2.7
Response Prevention Checklist		
Successful Behaviors	14 (week 1)	29 (week 15)

treatment intervention. Anne also completed a BDI on a weekly basis, which was plotted against her weekly behavioral checkout data (i.e., the number of activities she successfully completed during the previous week). These data suggested a strong relation between increased activity and alleviation of depressive symptoms (see Figure 5.2).

☐ Summary

Assessment of depressive disorders typically involves the use of interviewing strategies, self-report measures, behavioral observation methods, and functional analysis techniques, including the assessment of potentially maladaptive or irrational cognitions. Interviewing methods vary on the dimension of flexibility, with structured approaches more frequently utilized in research settings. Although the practicality of structured interviewing strategies in community practice is debatable, such methods may be useful in facilitating differential diagnosis and in documenting the need for psychological/psychiatric treatment, important considerations in the era of managed care. Similarly, utilization of self-report measures such as the BDI-II or CES-D may be a time-efficient method to facilitate the assessment process as well as monitor therapy progress and treatment outcome. Considering the outlined pragmatic concerns, increased flexibility of assessment methods may be necessary, such as using clinician-administered measures in non-traditional ways to facilitate differential diagnosis (Hopko et al. 2001). Practitioners and managed care personnel also will have to work collaboratively toward streamlining the assessment processes and maximizing quality of care while simultaneously ensuring that their responsibilities are not compromised. Although underutilized, behavioral observation and functional analysis techniques, including the assessment of dysfunctional cognitions, provide additional information that may be useful in identifying and modifying problematic behaviors or cognitions underlying a depressive disorder.

All of these strategies considered, we strongly advocate the importance of conducting a multimethod, ideographic assessment. However, we also acknowledge that the realities of clinical practice across a variety of settings often limit the feasibility of such a comprehensive approach. Accordingly, practitioners must evaluate potential restrictions and limitations (e.g., time, money, training, patient motivation) on a case-by-case basis and make a conscientious and well-informed decision on how well each of the available options meet both the therapist and patients' goals and needs. It certainly is the case that public and practitioner awareness of depression as a prevalent and treatable condition has grown in the

Activity	#	Time	Monday	Tuesday	Wednesday	Thursday	Friday	Saturday	Sunday
Tell daughters she loves them	5	UF	Y N G	Y N G	Y N G	Y N G	Y N G	Y N G	Y N G
Wake before 9:00 A.M.	6	UF	Y N G	Y N G	Y N G	Y N G	Y N G	Y N G	Y N G
Read chapter from Bible	7	UF	Y N G	Y N G	Y N G	Y N G	Y N G	Y N G	Y N G
Hug daughters	5	5–10s	Y N G	Y N G	Y N G	Y N G	Y N G	Y N G	Y N G
Groom garden/plants	3	30min	Y N G	Y N G	Y N G	Y N G	Y N G	Y N G	Y N G
Make dinner for family	5	UF	Y N G	Y N G	Y N G	Y N G	Y N G	Y N G	Y N G
Wash dishes	5	UF	Y N G	Y N G	Y N G	Y N G	Y N G	Y N G	Y N G
Telephone friend	2	20min	Y N G	Y N G	Y N G	Y N G	Y N G	Y N G	Y N G
Attend church on Sunday	1	UF	Y N G	Y N G	Y N G	Y N G	Y N G	Y N G	Y N G
Go for 20 min walk	3	UF	Y N G	Y N G	Y N G	Y N G	Y N G	Y N G	Y N G
To lunch with friend	2	1hr	Y N G	Y N G	Y N G	Y N G	Y N G	Y N G	Y N G
Attend Bible study	1	UF	Y N G	Y N G	Y N G	Y N G	Y N G	Y N G	Y N G
Take children to movie	1	UF	Y N G	Y N G	Y N G	Y N G	Y N G	Y N G	Y N G
Take children to Chucky Cheese	1	1hr	Y N G	Y N G	Y N G	Y N G	Y N G	Y N G	Y N G
Allow daughter to have friend over	1	2 hrs	Y N G	Y N G	Y N G	Y N G	Y N G	Y N G	Y N G

Note: UF = Until Finished, Y = Yes, N = No, G = Goal has been met

FIGURE 5.2. Behavior checklist

twenty-first century, an understanding that has translated into advances in the development of various assessment alternatives. Given these options and in consideration of patient welfare and competency of care, practitioners have a significant responsibility to educate themselves about available assessment resources and how these methods may assist in the clinical assessment and intervention processes. As health providers have become increasingly more accountable for the services they provide via standards and guidelines imposed by managed care companies, efficient and effective clinical assessment is vital. In response to this need, the primary purpose of this chapter has been to elucidate a variety of methods to assess for depressive disorders, outline important pragmatic issues that must be considered, and demonstrate how various methods may be applied in the context of clinical practice.

☐ References

Abramson, L. Y., Metalsky, G. I., & Alloy, L. B. (1989). Hopelessness depression: A theory-based subtype of depression. *Psychological Review, 96,* 358–372.

Akiskal, H. S., & Cassano, G. B. (1997). *Dysthymia and the spectrum of chronic depressions.* New York: Guilford.

Alexopoulos, G. S., Borson, S., Cuthbert, B. N., Devanand, D. P., Mulsant, B. H., Olin, J. T., & Oslin, D. W. (2002). Assessment of late life depression. *Biological Psychiatry, 52,* 164–174.

American Psychiatric Association. (1994). *Diagnostic and statistical manual of mental disorders* (4th ed.). Washington, DC: American Psychiatric Association.

American Psychiatric Association. (2001). *Diagnostic and statistical manual of mental disorders* (4th ed. text revision). Washington, DC: American Psychiatric Association.

American Psychological Association. (2000). Statistics from http://www.apa.org/topics/topic_depress.html.

Andreasen, N. J. C., & Pfohl, B. (1976). Linguistic analysis of speech in affective disorders. *Archives of General Psychiatry, 33,* 1361–1367.

Angst, J., Merikangas, K. R., & Preisig, M. (1997). Subthreshold syndromes of depression and anxiety in the community. *Journal of Clinical Psychiatry, 58* (suppl 8), 6–10.

Arkes, H. R. (1981). Impediments to accurate clinical judgment and possible ways to minimize their impact. *Journal of Consulting and Clinical Psychology, 49,* 323–330.

Baer, L., Jacobs, D. G., Meszler-Reizes, J., Blais, M., Fava, M., Kessler, R., Magruder, K., Murphy, J., Kopans, B., Cukor, P., Leahy, L., & O'laughlen, J. (2000). Development of a brief screening instrument: The HANDS. *Psychotherapy and Psychosomatics, 69,* 35–41.

Beck, A. T., Shaw, B. J., Rush, A. J., & Emery, G. (1979). *Cognitive therapy of depression.* New York: Guilford.

Beck, A. T., & Steer, R. A. (1987). *Beck Depression Inventory: Manual.* San Antonio, TX: Psychiatric Corporation.

Beck, A. T., & Steer, R. A. (1993). *Beck Anxiety Inventory: Manual* (2nd ed.). San Antonio, TX: Psychiatric Corporation.

Beck, A. T., Steer, R. A., & Brown, G. K. (1996). *Manual for the BDI-II.* San Antonio, TX: Psychological Corporation.

Beck, A. T., Steer, R. A., & Garbin, M. A. (1988). Psychometric properties of the Beck Depression Inventory: Twenty-five years of evaluation. *Clinical Psychology Review, 8,* 77–100.

Bieber, J., Wroblewski, J. M., Barber, C. A. (1999) Design and implementation of an outcomes management system within inpatient and outpatient behavioral health settings. In M. E. Maruish (Ed.), *The Use of Psychological Testing for Treatment Planning and Outcomes Assessment* (2nd ed.) (pp. 171–210). Mahwah, NJ: Lawrence Erlbaum.

Blumberg, S. R., & Hokanson, J. E. (1983). The effect's of another person's response style on interpersonal behavior in depression. *Journal of Abnormal Psychology, 92,* 196–209.

Booth, B. M., Zhang, M., Rost, K. M., Clardy, J. A., Smith, L. G., & Smith, G. R. (1997). Measuring outcomes and costs for major depression. *Psychopharmacological Bulletin, 33,* 653–658.

Broadhead, W. E., Blazer, D. G., George, L. K., & Tse, C. K. (1990). Depression, disability days, and days lost from work in a prospective epidemiologic survey. *Journal of the American Medical Association, 264,* 2524–2528.

Brown, T. A., Di Nardo, P. A., & Barlow, D. H. (1994). *The Anxiety Disorder Interview Schedule for DSM-IV.* Center for Stress and Anxiety Disorders. Albany: State University of New York.

Brown, T. A., Di Nardo, P. A., Lehman, C. L., & Campbell, L. A. (2001). Reliability of DSM-IV anxiety and mood disorders: Implications for the classification of emotional disorders. *Journal of Abnormal Psychology, 110,* 49–58.

Burke, K. C., Burke, J. D., Regier, D. A., & Rae, D. S. (1990). Age at onset of selected mental disorders in five community populations. *Archives of General Psychiatry, 47,* 511–518.

Butcher, J. N., Dahlstrom, W. G., Graham, J. R., Tellegen, A., & Kaemmer, B. (1989). *Minnesota Multiphasic Personality Inventory-2 (MMPI-2): Manual for administration and scoring.* Minneapolis: University of Minnesota Press.

Callaghan, G. M. (2001). Demonstrating clinical effectiveness for individual practitioners and clinics. *Professional Psychology: Research and Practice, 32,* 289–297.

Chang, C. H. (1996). Finding two dimensions in MMPI-2 depression. *Structural Equation Modeling, 3,* 41–49.

Coryell, W. (1998). The treatment of psychotic depression. *Journal of Clinical Psychiatry, 59,* 22–27.

Cronkite, R. C., & Moos, R. H. (1995). Life context, coping processes, and depression. In E. E. Beckham and W. R. Leber (Eds.), *Handbook of depression* (2nd Ed., pp. 569–587) New York: Guilford.

Cross-National Collaborative Group. (1992). The changing rate of major depression: Cross-national comparisons. *Journal of the American Medical Association, 268,* 3098–3105.

Csikszentmihalyi, M., & Larson, R. (1987). Validity and reliability of the experience sampling method. *Journal of Nervous and Mental Disease, 175,* 526–536.

Donabedian, A. (1985). *Explorations in quality assurance and monitoring: The methods and findings of quality assessment and monitoring: An illustrated analysis.* Ann Arbor, MI: Health Administration Press.

Dorfman, W. I. (2000). Psychological assessment and testing under managed care. In A. J. Kent and M. Hersen (Eds.), *A psychologist's proactive guide to managed mental health care* (pp. 23–39). Mahwah, NJ: Lawrence Erlbaum.

Dykman, B. M., Horowitz, I. M., Abramson, L. Y., & Usher, M. (1991). Schematic and situational determinants of depressed and nondepressed students' interpretation of feedback. *Journal of Abnormal Psychology, 100,* 45–55.

Elwood, R. W. (1993). The clinical utility of the MMPI-2 in diagnosing unipolar depression among alcoholics. *Journal of Personality Assessment, 60,* 511–521.

Endicott, J., & Spitzer, R. L. (1978). A diagnostic interview: The Schedule for Affective Disorders and Schizophrenia. *Archives of General Psychiatry, 35,* 837–844.

Faustman W. O., Overall J. E. (1999). Brief Psychiatric Rating Scale. In M. E. Maruish (Ed.), *The use of psychological testing for treatment planning and outcomes assessment* (2nd Ed., pp. 791–830). Mahwah, NJ: Lawrence Erlbaum.

Ferster, C. B. (1973). A functional analysis of depression. *American Psychologist, 28,* 857–870.

Ficken, J. (1995). New directions for psychological testing. *Behavioral Health Management, 20,* 12–14.

Field, T., Healy, B., Goldstein, S., & Guthertz, M. (1990). Behavior-state matching and synchrony in mother-infant interactions of nondepressed versus depressed dyads. *Developmental Psychology, 26,* 7–14.

First, M. B., Spitzer, R. L., Gibbon, M., & Williams, J. (1996). *Structured clinical interview for DSM-IV axis I disorders — Patient edition (SCID-I/P, Version 2.0)*. Biometrics Research Department. New York: New York Psychiatric Institute.

Frisch, M. B. (1994). *Manual and treatment guide for the quality of life inventory (QOLI)*. Minneapolis, MN: National Computer Systems.

Goldfried, M. R., & Sprafkin, J. N. (1976). Behavioral personality assessment. In J. T. Spence, R. C. Carson, & J. W. Thibaut (Eds.), *Behavioral approaches to therapy* (pp. 295–321). Morristown, NJ: General Learning Press.

Gotlib, I. H. (1982). Self-reinforcement and depression in interpersonal interaction: The role of performance level. *Journal of Abnormal Psychology, 91,* 3–13.

Gotlib, I. H., & Robinson, L. A. (1982). Responses to depressed individuals: Discrepancies between self-report and observer-rated behavior. *Journal of Abnormal Psychology, 91,* 231–240.

Greenberg, P., Kessler, R., Nells, T., Finkelstein, S., & Berndt, E. R. (1996). Depression in the workplace: An economic perspective. In J. P. Feighner and W. F. Boyer (Eds.), *Selective serotonin reuptake inhibitors: Advances in basic research and clinical practice* (pp. 327–363). New York: Wiley.

Greenfield S. F., Reizes, J. M., Magruder, K. M., Muenz, L. R., Kopans, B., & Jacobs, D. (1997). Effectiveness of community-based screening for depression. *American Journal of Psychiatry, 154,* 1391–1397.

Groth-Marnat, G. (1997). *Handbook of psychological assessment* (3rd Ed.). New York: John Wiley

Hamilton, M. (1960). A rating scale for depression. *Journal of Neurology, Neurosurgery, and Psychiatry, 23,* 56–62.

Hamilton, M. (1967). Development of a rating scale for primary depressive illness. *British Journal of Social and Clinical Psychology, 6,* 278–296.

Hayes, S. C., Strosahl, K. D., & Wilson, K. G. (1999). *Acceptance and commitment therapy: An experiential approach to behavior change*. New York: Guilford.

Haynes, S. N. (1998). The assessment-treatment relationship and functional analysis in behavior therapy. *European Journal of Psychological Assessment, 14,* 26–35.

Haynes, S. N., & O'Brien, W. H. (1990). Functional analysis in behavior therapy. *Clinical Psychology Review, 10,* 649–668.

Heiligenstein, E., Guenther, G., Hsu, K., & Herman, K. (1996). Depression and academic impairment in college students. *Journal of American College Health, 45,* 59–64.

Hesselbrock, M. M., Hesselbrock, V. M., Tenmen, H., Meyer, R. E., & Workman, K. L. (1983). Methodological considerations in the assessment of depression in alcoholics. *Journal of Consulting and Clinical Psychology, 51,* 399–405.

Higgitt, A., & Fonagy, P. (2002). Clinical effectiveness. *British Journal of Psychiatry, 181,* 170–174.

Hinchliffe, M., Hooper, D., & Roberts, F. J. (1978). *The melancholy marriage*. New York: Wiley.

Hopko, D. R., Armento, M., Chambers, L., & Cantu, M., & Lejuez, C. W. (2003). The use of Daily Diaries to assess the relations among mood state, overt behavior, and reward value of activities. *Behaviour Research and Therapy, 41,* 1137–1148.

Hopko, D. R., Averill, P. M., Small, D., Greenlee, H., & Varner, R. V. (2001). Use of the Brief Psychiatric Rating Scale to facilitate differential diagnosis at acute inpatient admission. *Journal of Clinical Psychiatry, 62,* 304–312.

Hopko, D. R., & Hopko, S. D. (1999). What can functional analytic psychotherapy contribute to empirically validated treatments? *Clinical Psychology and Psychotherapy, 6,* 349–356.

Hopko, D. R., Lejuez, C. W., Ruggiero, K. J., & Eifert, G. H. (2002). *Behavioral activation treatments for depression: Procedures, principles, and progress*. Manuscript submitted for publication.

Hurlburt, R. T. (1997). Randomly sampling thinking in the natural environment. *Journal of Consulting and Clinical Psychology, 65,* 941–949.

Johnson, L. D. (1995). *Psychotherapy in the age of accountability*. New York: Norton.

Jonsson, B., & Rosenbaum, J. (1993). *Health economics of depression*. New York: Wiley.

Judd, L. L., Akiskal, H. S., Maser, J. D., Zeller, P. J., Endicott, J., Coryell, W., Paulus, M. P., Kunovac, J. L., Leon, A. C., Mueller, T. I., Rice, J. A., & Keller, M. B. (1998). A prospective 12 year study of subsyndromal and syndromal depressive symptoms in unipolar major depressive disorders. *Archives of General Psychiatry, 55,* 694–700.

Just, N., & Alloy, L. B. (1997). The response styles theory of depression: Tests and an extension of the theory. *Journal of Abnormal Psychology, 106,* 221–229.

Kaelber, C. T., Moul, D. E., & Farmer, M. E. (1995). Epidemiology of depression. In E. E. Beckham and W. R. Leber (Eds.), *Handbook of depression* (2nd Ed., pp. 3–35) New York: Guilford.

Kahneman, D., & Tversky, A. (1973). On the psychology of prediction. *Psychological Review, 80,* 237–251.

Keefe, R. H., & Hall, M. L. (1999). Private practitioners documentation of outpatient psychiatric treatment: Questioning managed care. *Journal of Behavioral Health Services and Research, 26,* 151–170.

Kessler, R. C., McGonagle, K. A., Zhao, S., Nelson, C. B., Hughes, M., Eshleman, S., Wittchen, H. U., & Kendler, K. S. (1994). Lifetime and 12-month prevalence of DSM-IIIR psychiatric disorders in the United States: Results from the National Comorbidity Survey. *Archives of General Psychiatry, 51,* 8–19.

Klein, D. N., Kocsis, J. H., McCullough, J. P., Holzer, C. E., III, Hirschfield, R. M. A., & Keller, M. B. (1996). Symptomatology in dysthymic and major depressive disorder. *Psychiatric Clinics of North America, 19,* 41–53.

Klein, D. N., Norden, K. A., Ferro, T., Leader, J. B., Kasch, K. L., Klein, L. M., Schwartz, J. E., & Aronson, T. A. (1998). Thirty-month naturalistic follow-up study of early-onset dysthymic disorder: Course, diagnostic stability, and prediction of outcome. *Journal of Abnormal Psychology, 107,* 338–348.

Klerman, G. L., Weissman, M. M., Rounsaville, B. J., & Chevron, E. S. (1984). *Interpersonal psychotherapy of depression.* New York: Basic Books.

Kobak, K. A., & Reynolds, W. M. (1999). Hamilton Depression Inventory. In M. E. Maruish (Ed.), *The use of psychological testing for treatment planning and outcomes assessment* (2nd Ed., pp. 935–969). Mahwah, NJ: Lawrence Erlbaum.

Koenig, H. G. (1997). Differences in psychosocial and health correlates of major and minor depression in medically ill older adults. *Journal of the American Geriatric Society, 45,* 1487–1495.

Libet, J., & Lewinsohn, P. M. (1973). The concept of social skill with special reference to the behavior of depressed persons. *Journal of Consulting and Clinical Psychology, 40,* 304–312.

Linehan, M. M. (1993). *Cognitive-behavioral treatment of borderline personality disorder.* NewYork: Guilford.

Livingood, A. B., Daen, P., & Smith, B. D. (1983). The depressed mother as a source of stimulation for her infant. *Journal of Clinical Psychology, 39,* 369–375.

Lejuez, C. W., Hopko, D. R., & Hopko, S. D. (2001). A brief behavioral activation treatment for depression: Treatment manual. *Behavior Modification, 25,* 255–286.

Lejuez, C. W., Hopko, D. R., & Hopko, S. D. (2002). *The brief behavioral activation treatment for depression (BATD): A comprehensive patient guide.* Boston: Pearson Custom Publishing.

Lewinsohn, P. M. (1974). A behavioral approach to depression. In R. M. Friedman and M. M. Katz (Eds.). *The psychology of depression: Contemporary theory and research.* New York: Wiley.

Lewinsohn, P. M., Solomon, A., Seeley, J. R., & Zeiss, A. (2000). Clinical implications of "subthreshold" depressive symptoms. *Journal of Abnormal Psychology, 109,* 345–351.

Lyness, J. M., King, D. A., Cox, C., Yoediono, Z., & Caine, E. D. (1999). The importance of subsyndromal depression in older primary care patients: Prevalence and associated functional disability. *Journal of the American Geriatric Society, 47,* 647–652.

MacPhillamy, D. J., & Lewinsohn, P. M. (1971). *Pleasant events schedule.* Eugene: University of Oregon.

MacPhillamy, D. J., & Lewinsohn, P. M. (1982). The Pleasant Events Schedule: Studies on reliability, validity, and scale intercorrelations. *Journal of Consulting and Clinical Psychology, 50,* 363–380.

Martell, C. R., Addis, M. E., & Jacobson, N. S. (2001). *Depression in context: Strategies for guided action*. New York: W.W. Norton.

Maruish, M. (1999). Introduction. In M. E. Maruish (Ed.), *The use of psychological testing for treatment planning and outcomes assessment* (2nd ed., pp. 1–39). Mahwah, NJ: Lawrence Erlbaum.

Mays, M., & Croake, J. W. (1997). Managed care and treatment of depression. In R. S. Sauber (Ed.), *Managed mental health care* (pp. 244–278). Philadelphia, PA: Brunner/Mazel.

McCullough, J. P., Jr. (2000). *Treatment for chronic depression: Cognitive behavioral analysis system of psychotherapy*. New York: Guilford.

McQuaid, J. R., Stein, M. B., Laffaye, C., & McCahill, M. E. (1999). Depression in a primary care clinic: The prevalence and impact of an unrecognized disorder. *Journal of Affective Disorders, 55*, 1–10.

Mineka, S., Watson, D., & Clark, L. A. (1998). Comorbidity of anxiety and unipolar mood disorders. *Annual Review of Psychology, 49*, 377–412.

Morey, L. C. (1991). *The Personality Assessment Inventory professional manual*. Odessa, FL: - Psychological Assessment Resources.

Morey, L. C. (1999). Personality Assessment Inventory. In M. E. Maruish (Ed.), *The use of psychological testing for treatment planning and outcomes assessment* (2nd Ed., pp. 1083–1121). Mahwah, NJ: Lawrence Erlbaum.

Myers, J. K., & Weissman, M. M. (1980). Use of a self-report symptom scale to detect major depression in a community sample. *American Journal of Psychiatry, 137*, 1081–1084.

Nezu, C. M. & Nezu, A. M. (1989). Unipolar depression. In A. M. Nezu & C. M. Nezu (Eds.), *Clinical decision making in behavior therapy: A problem-solving perspective* (pp. 117–156). Champaign, IL: Research Press.

Nezu, A. M. & Nezu, C. M. (1993). Identifying and selecting target problems for clinical interventions: A problem-solving model. *Psychological Assessment, 5*(3), 254–263.

Nezu, C. M., Nezu, A. M., & Foster, S. L. (2000). A 10-step guide to selecting assessment measures in clinical and research settings. In A. M. Nezu, G. F. Ronan, E. A. Meadows, & K. S. McClure (Eds.), *Practitioner's guide to empirically based measures of depression* (pp. 17–24). New York: Kluwer Academic/Plenum.

Nezu, A. M., Ronan, G. F., Meadows, E. A., & McClure, K. S. (2000). *Practitioner's guide to empirically based measures of depression*. New York: Kluwer Academic/Plenum.

Nolen-Hoeksema, S., & Girgus, J. S. (1994). The emergence of gender differences in depression during adolescence. *Psychological Bulletin, 115*, 424–443.

Olfson, M., & Mechanic, D. (1996). Mental disorders in public, private, nonprofit, and proprietary general hospitals. *American Journal of Psychiatry, 153*, 1613–1619.

O'Neill, R. E., Horner, R. H., Albin, R. W., Storey, K., & Sprague, J. R. (1990). *Functional analysis of problem behavior: A practical assessment guide*. Sycamore, IL: Sycamore Publishing Company.

Oxman, T. E., Barrett, J. E., Barrett, J. B., & Gerber, P. (1990). Symptomatology of late-life minor depression among primary care patients. *Psychosomatics, 31*, 174–180.

Overall, J. E., & Gorham, D. R. (1962). The brief psychiatric rating scale. *Psychological Reports, 10*, 799–812.

Papageorgiou, C., & Wells, A. (2000). Treatment of recurrent major depression with attention training. *Cognitive and Behavioral Practice, 7*, 407–413.

Paykel, E. S., & Cooper, Z. (1992). Life events and social stress. In E. S. Paykel (Ed.), *Handbook of affective disorders* (2nd Ed., pp. 149–170). New York: Guilford.

Pepper, C. M., Klein, D. N., Anderson, R. L., Riso, L. P., Ouimette, P. C., & Lizardi, H. (1995). DSM-III-R Axis II comorbidity in dysthymia and major depression. *American Journal of Psychiatry, 152*, 239–247.

Piotrowski, C. (1999). Assessment practices in the era of managed care: Current status and future directions. *Journal of Clinical Psychology, 55*, 787–796.

Pincus, H. A., Davis, W. W., & McQueen, L. E. (1999). 'Subthreshold' mental disorders: A review and synthesis of studies on minor depression and other 'brand names.' *British Journal of Psychiatry, 174*, 288–296.

Pozanski, E. O. (1982). The clinical phenomenology of childhood depression. *American Journal of Orthopsychiatry, 52*, 3008–3013.

Radloff, L. (1977). The CES-D scale: A self-report depression scale for research in the general population. *Applied Psychological Measurement, 1,* 385–401.

Ranelli, C. J., & Miller, R. E. (1981). Behavioral predictors of amitryptaline response in depression. *American Journal of Psychiatry, 138,* 30–34.

Regier, D. A., Farmer, M. E., Rae, D. S., Locke, B. Z., Keith, S. J., Judd, L. L., & Goodwin, F. K. (1990). Comorbidity of mental disorders with alcohol and other drug abuse. *Journal of the American Medical Association, 264,* 2511–2518.

Rehm, L. P. (1988). Assessment of depression. In A. S. Bellack and M. Hersen (Eds.), *Behavioral assessment: A practical handbook* (3rd ed., pp. 313–364). New York: Pergamon.

Rehm, L. P., & Tyndall, C. I. (1993). Mood disorders: Unipolar and bipolar. In P. B. Sutker and H. E. Adams (Eds.), *Comprehensive handbook of psychopathology* (2nd Ed., pp. 235–261). New York: Plenum Press.

Reynolds, W. M., & Kobak, K. A. (1995). *Hamilton depression inventory (HDI): Professional manual.* Odessa, FL: Psychological Assessment Resources.

Reynolds, W. M., & Kobak, K. A. (1998). *Reynolds depression screening inventory: Professional manual.* Odessa, FL: Psychological Assessment Resources.

Roberts, R. E., Kaplan, G. A., Shema, S. J., & Strawbridge, W. J. (1997). Does growing old increase the risk for depression? *American Journal of Psychiatry, 154,* 1384–1390.

Roberts, R. E., & Vernon, S. W. (1983). The center for epidemiologic studies depression Scale: Its use in a community sample. *American Journal of Psychiatry, 140,* 41–46.

Robins, L. N., Helzer, J. E., Croughan, J. L., & Ratcliff, K. S. (1981). National Institute of Mental Health diagnostic interview schedule: Its history, characteristics, and validity. *Archives of General Psychiatry, 38,* 381–389.

Robinson, J. C., & Lewinsohn, P. M. (1973). Behavior modification of speech characteristics in a chronically depressed man. *Behavior Therapy, 4,* 150–152.

Rohde, P., Lewinsohn, P. M., & Seeley, J. R. (1990). Are people changed by the experience of having an episode of depression. A further test of the scar hypothesis. *Journal of Abnormal Psychology, 99,* 264–271.

Sacco, W. P., & Beck, A. T. (1995). Cognitive theory and therapy. In E. E. Beckham and W. R. Leber (Eds.), *Handbook of depression* (2nd Ed., pp. 329–351) New York: Guilford.

SAMHSA Prevalence and Treatment of Mental Health Problems. www.samhsa.gov.

Sanavio, E. (1988). Obsessions and compulsions: The Padua Inventory. *Behaviour Research and Therapy, 26,* 169–177.

Schuyler, D. (2000). Depression comes in many disguises to the providers of primary care: Recognition and management. *J S C Med Association, 96,* 267–275.

Simon G. E., Chisholm D., Treglia M., Bushnell, D. (2002). The LIDO study group: Course of depression, health services costs, and work productivity in an international primary care study. *General Hospital Psychiatry 24,* 328–335.

Simon, G. E., & Katzelnick, D. J. (1997). Depression, use of medical services and cost-offset effects. *Journal of Psychosomatic Research, 42,* 333–344.

Simon, G. E., Ormel, J., VonKorff, M., & Barlow, W. (1995). Health care costs associated with depressive and anxiety disorders in primary care. *American Journal of Psychiatry, 152,* 352–357.

Snyder, A. G., Stanley, M. A., Novy, D. M., & Beck, J. G. (2000). Measures of depression in older adults with generalized anxiety disorder: A psychometric evaluation. *Depression and Anxiety, 11,* 114–120.

Spitzer, R. L., Endicott, J., & Robins, E. (1978). Research diagnostic criteria. *Archives of General Psychiatry, 35,* 773–782.

Spitzer, R. L., Williams, J. B., Kroenke, K., Linzer, M., de Gruy, F. V., III, Hahn, S. R., Brody, D., & Johnson, J. G. (1994). Utility of a new procedure for diagnosing mental disorders in primary care: The PRIME-MD 1000 study. *Journal of the American Medical Association, 272,* 1749–1756.

Stanley, M. A., & Averill, P. A. (1998). Psychosocial treatments for obsessive-compulsive disorder: Clinical applications. In R. P. Swinson, M. M. Antony, S. Rachman, & M. A. Richter (Eds.), *Obsessive-compulsive disorder: Theory, research, and treatment* (pp. 271–297). New York: Guilford.

Stevens, D. E., Merikangas, K. R., & Merikangas, J. R. (1995). Comorbidity of depression and other medical conditions. In E. E. Beckham & W. R. Leber (Eds.), *Handbook of depression* (2nd Ed., pp.147–199). New York: Guilford.

Stewart, J. W., Rabkin, J. G., Quitkin, F. M., McGrath, P. J., & Klein, D. F. (1993). Atypical depression. In D. L. Dunner (Ed.), *Current psychiatric therapy*. Philadelphia: W.B. Saunders.

Sturges, J.W. (1998). Practical use of technology in professional practice. *Professional Psychology: Research and Practice, 29,* 183–188.

Thorpe, G. L., & Olson, S. L. (1997). *Behavior therapy: Concepts, procedures, and applications.* Boston: Allyn and Bacon.

Turner, J. A., & Romano, J. M. (1984). Self-report screening measures for depression in chronic pain patients. *Journal of Clinical Psychology, 40,* 909–913.

Ustun T., & Sartorius, N. (1995). *Mental illness in general health care.* New York: Wiley.

Ventura, J., Liberman, R. P., Green, M. F., Shaner, A., & Mintz, J. (1998). Training and quality assurance with the structured Clinical Interview for DSM-IV (SCID-I/P). *Psychiatry Research, 79,* 163–173.

Wagner, H. R., Burns, B. J., Broadhead, W. E., Yarnall, K. S. H., Sigmon, A., & Gaynes, B. N. (2000). Minor depression in family practice: Functional morbidity, co-morbidity, service utilization and outcomes. *Psychological Medicine, 30,* 1377–1390.

Weissman, M. M., Bruce, M. L., Leaf, P. J., Florio, L. P., & Holzer, C. (1991). Affective disorders. In L. N. Robins & D. A. Regier (Eds.), *Psychiatric disorders in America: The Epidemiological Catchment Area Study* (pp. 53–80). New York: Free Press.

Wells, K. B. (1999). The design of partners in care: Evaluating the cost-effectiveness of improving care for depression in primary care. *Social Psychiatry and Psychiatric Epidemiology, 34,* 20–29.

Werthman, M. J. (1995). A managed care approach to psychological testing. *Behavioral Health Management, 15,* 15–17.

Williams, J. G., Barlow, D. H., & Agras, W. S. (1972). Behavioral measurement of severe depression. *Archives of General Psychiatry, 27,* 330–333.

Williams, R. A., Hagerty, B. M., Cimprich, B., Therrien, B., Bay, E., & Oe, H. (2000). Changes in attention and short-term memory in depression. *Journal of Psychiatric Research, 34,* 227–238.

Zung, W. W. K. (1965). A self-rating depression scale. *Archives of General Psychiatry, 12,* 63–70.

Joel F. McClough
John F. Clarkin

Personality Disorders

☐ Description of the Disorders

The prevalence of personality disorders in the general population is approximately 10%–15% (Maier, Lichtermann, Klinger, & Heun, 1992). In clinical settings, the prevalence increases substantially (see Matia & Zimmerman [2001] for review). Personality disorders tend to co-occur with other more acute symptom-based (i.e. Axis I) disorders with great frequency (Maier, Minges, Lichtermann, & Heun, 1995). The Axis I disorders commonly associated with, and negatively affected by, comorbid personality disorders include (but are not limited to): major depression (Gunderson & Phillips, 1991; Shea, Widiger, & Klein, 1992), anxiety (Stein, Hollander, & Skodol, 1993), social phobia (Hirschfeld, Shea, & Weise, 1991), eating disorders (Godt, 2002), and schizophrenia (Hogg, Jackson, Rudd, et al. 1990). This substantial comorbidity is important, because the presence of a personality disorder often complicates proper diagnosis, interferes with effective treatment, and negatively contributes to the clinical course of many Axis I disorders (McGlashan, Grillo, Skodol et al., 2000).

Because of increasing concern over the cost, availability, and efficiency of mental health services in the United States, several large epidemiological studies have been conducted to assess treatment utilization by mental health consumers. Research has shown that personality disorder clients, especially those with borderline personality disorder, have exceptionally high rates of mental health service utilization, even exceeding that of major depression (Bender, Dolan, Skodol, Sanislow, et al., 2001). That is to say, clients with severe personality disorders have more frequent psychiatric hospitalizations, greater use of psychotropic medications, more emergency room visits, greater outpatient psychotherapy use, and greater failure to follow through with treatment plans. Individuals with personality pathology, especially borderline personality disorder, are notoriously difficult to treat due to the severe and persistent nature of their symptoms, and the adverse effect of their pathology on the therapeutic relationship. In fact, it is well established that individuals with personality pathology usually take much longer to improve in treatment (both psychotherapeutic and psychopharmacological) compared to those with more acute Axis I disorders without personality disorders (Kopta, Howard, Lowry, & Beutler, 1994; Gabbard, 2000). Obviously, the personality disorders represent important clinical challenges, and their presence can affect the outcome of many therapeutic endeavors.

In addition to their prominent role in most clinical settings, personality disorders make important contributions to larger societal and public health issues, often with very serious consequences. Research has demonstrated relationships between personality pathology and drug abuse (Links, Heslegrave, Mitton, et al., 1995), alcoholism (Nace, Saxon, & Shore, 1986), motor vehicle offenses, homelessness (Scott, 1993), increased risk of completed and attempted suicide (Paris, 1990), the transmission of HIV, divorce/marital discord (Zimmerman & Coryell, 1989), child neglect, unemployment (Drake & Vaillant, 1985), and criminal activity, including homicide (Tiihonen & Hakola, 1994). In fact, survey data have demonstrated that people with antisocial personality disorder represent a large proportion of individuals connected with the criminal justice system in many Western countries (Fazel & Danesh, 2002).

Given the ubiquitous impact of personality pathology in clinical practice, as well as society at large, one cannot underestimate the importance of properly identifying and treating personality disorders. However, there is strong evidence that clients with personality disorders are often underdiagnosed in clinical practice (Zimmerman & Mattia, 1999; Oldham & Skodol, 1991). This failure to properly identify personality disorders is most likely the result of their complicated clinical presentations, the limited time and resources of most clinicians, as well as the historical disagreement surrounding the constructs of personality and personality pathology. Unfortunately, it appears that the inherent complexity of the constructs, disagreements over definitions, as well as a paucity of practical guidance for practicing clinicians, have combined to contribute to this problem. This chapter is intended to aid in the proper identification and appreciation of personality disorders in clinical practice.

Definition

To understand personality disorders, it is important to briefly define the concept of personality. Although, there is great disagreement about the exact definition, simply put, personality is the combination or synthesis of our behaviors, thoughts, motivations, and emotions that make us unique individuals. Personality is what makes us "who we are" and impacts every aspect of our daily functioning. The basic units of personality are referred to as personality traits, in other words, the enduring patterns of perceiving, relating to, and thinking about ourselves (and the environment) that we exhibit across a diversity of personal and social contexts. In a healthy individual, these stable and enduring traits allow for consistency in behavior, so that those who know a person well can often predict his/her response to various situations with accuracy. In addition, normal personality individuals possess coping strategies or styles that are flexible in response to stressful or difficult situations. If one approach is not working, they will try another. Normal personality functioning requires role flexibility, in other words, knowing how and when to adapt to what the environment presents to you. If the environment places restrictions on one's behavior, the normal individual will typically adapt appropriately to what the circumstances require.

In contrast, it is the general lack of flexibility and the limited range of adaptive coping styles (resulting in subjective distress or impairment in functioning) that defines a person with a personality disorder. Personality disordered individuals typically implement the same or similar coping strategies over and over again without success. Instead of adapting appropriately and in proportion to the demands of the situation, the rigidity of the personality disorder client requires the environment or interpersonal situation to adapt to them. This pattern of inflexible and maladaptive response to the environment ultimately results in an exacerbation of stress and the consequent reduction of available opportunities to learn alternative and more adaptive coping strategies. Perhaps most importantly, these maladaptive patterns lead to the creation of interpersonal conflicts. According to Millon and Davis (2000), "… life becomes a bad one-act play that repeats over and over. They waste opportunities for improvement, provoke new problems, and constantly create situations that replay their failures, often with minor variations on a few related, self-defeating themes" (p. 13).

According to the *Diagnostic and Statistical Manual* of *Mental Disorders*, 4th Edition (DSM-IV, American Psychiatric Association, 1994)

> only when personality traits are inflexible and maladaptive and cause significant functional impairment or subjective distress do they constitute personality disorders. The essential feature of a personality disorder is an enduring pattern of inner experience and behavior that deviates markedly from the expectations of the individual's culture and is manifested in at least two of the following areas: cognition, affectivity, interpersonal functioning, or impulse control. This enduring pattern is inflexible and pervasive across a broad range of personal and social situations and leads to clinically significant distress or impairment in social, occupational, or other important areas of functioning. The pattern is stable and of long duration, and its onset can be traced back at least to adolescence or early adulthood. (p. 630)

DSM-IV Axis II Disorders

A complete description of the more than 100 criteria for all the personality disorders is beyond the scope of this chapter. The reader is referred to the DSM-IV (American Psychiatric Association, 1994) for a full listing. However, some defining characteristics, prevalence rates, and comorbidity patterns for each disorder are presented below. All prevalence rates are from Weissman (1993) and Mattia & Zimmerman (2001). All other information is from American Psychiatric Association (1994).

The DSM-IV lists diagnostic criteria for ten specific personality disorders. The personality disorders are grouped into three clusters based on descriptive similarities. Cluster A includes paranoid, schizoid, and schizotypal personality disorders. These people appear "odd or eccentric." Cluster B disorders include antisocial, borderline, histrionic, and narcissistic. These individuals often appear "dramatic, emotional, or erratic." Cluster C includes the avoidant, dependent, and obsessive-compulsive personality disorders. These individuals often appear "fearful or anxious."

Cluster A Disorders

Paranoid Personality Disorder (PPD)

The essential feature of PPD is a pervasive pattern of distrust and suspiciousness of the motives of other people. Individuals with PPD suspect, without sufficient basis, that others are exploiting, harming, or deceiving him/her. Prevalence is from 0.5% to 2.7% in the general population, 10% to 30% inpatient, and 2% to 10% outpatient settings. Axis I comorbidity includes: schizophrenia, delusional disorder, major depression, agoraphobia without panic attacks, and obsessive-compulsive disorder. Axis II comorbidity includes: schizotypal, schizoid, narcissistic, avoidant, and borderline.

Schizoid Personality Disorder (SPD)

The essential feature of SPD is a pervasive pattern of detachment from social relationships and a restricted range of expression of emotions in interpersonal settings. Prevalence varies from 0.3% to 0.9% in the general population and it is uncommon in clinical settings. It is more often diagnosed in men. Axis I comorbidity includes: schizophrenia and delusional disorder. These symptom-based disorders should always be considered as differential diagnoses. Axis II comorbidity includes: schizotypal, paranoid, and avoidant.

Schizotypal Personality Disorder (SCPD)

The essential feature of SCPD is a pervasive pattern of social and interpersonal deficits marked by acute discomfort with, and reduced capacity for, close relationships as well as by cognitive or perceptual distortions and eccentricities of behavior (e.g., ideas of reference, odd beliefs, odd thinking and speech). These individuals typically present with mild psychoticlike features, social isolation, and poor rapport. Prevalence varies between 0.3% to 5.6% in the general population. Axis I comorbidity includes: major depression, brief psychotic disorder, schizophreniform disorder, schizophrenia, and delusional disorder. Axis II comorbidity includes: paranoid, schizoid, avoidant, and borderline. Schizotypal personality disorder is unique in that it is the only Axis II disorder that was empirically defined based on its genetic relationship to an Axis I disorder (i.e., schizophrenia) (Siever, Bernstein, & Silverman, 1991). As a result, some researchers believe schizotypal personality disorder should be considered an Axis I disorder.

Cluster B Disorders

Antisocial Personality Disorder (ASPD)

The essential feature of ASPD is a pervasive pattern of disregard for and violation of the rights of others beginning in childhood or early adolescence and continuing into adulthood. This pattern has alternatively been referred to as psychopathy, sociopathy, or dyssocial personality disorder. In order to diagnose ASPD, the individual must be at least age 18 years old and have a history of conduct disorder with onset before age 15. Because of the manipulation, deceitfulness, and general egosyntonic quality of antisocial personality disorder, it is very important that collateral information from outside sources be integrated as part of the assessment.

Prevalence varies from 1.9% to 3.5% in the general population, much greater in forensic and substance abuse settings, and the diagnosis is much more often applied to males compared to females. Axis I comorbidity includes: major depression, anxiety disorders, and especially substance abuse/dependence. Axis II comorbidity includes: borderline, paranoid, histrionic, and narcissistic. Along with borderline personality disorder, ASPD is one of the most researched of all the personality disorders.

Borderline Personality Disorder (BPD)

The essential feature of BPD is a pervasive pattern of instability of interpersonal relationships, self-image, and affects, and marked impulsivity beginning by early adulthood. Patients with this diagnosis often exhibit frantic efforts to avoid real or imagined abandonment, feel chronic emptiness, alternate between extremes of idealization and devaluation in interpersonal relationships, engage in serious self-destructive behaviors (including suicide), have difficulty controlling their intense anger, and occasionally exhibit transient psychoticlike symptoms.Prevalence is 1% to 2% in the general population, about 10% in outpatient settings, even greater (about 20%) in inpatient settings, and the disorder is predominantly diagnosed in females. Axis I comorbidity includes: major depression, anxiety disorders, substance abuse/dependence, PTSD, and eating disorders. Borderline personality disorder is associated with substantial Axis II comorbidity, including histrionic, antisocial, schizotypal, and avoidant personality disorder. Borderline personality disorder is one of, if not, the most severe and complicated of the personality disorders to assess and treat, and therefore has garnered an enormous amount of research in the last several decades.

Histrionic Personality Disorder (HPD)

The essential feature of HPD is a pervasive pattern of excessive emotionality and attention seeking. Histrionic patients are often uncomfortable in situations in which they are not the center of attention, exhibit inappropriately sexually seductive and/or provocative behavior, are overly dramatic or theatrical, often use their physical appearance to draw attention to themselves, and are easily suggestible. Prevalence is approximately 2% in the general population, approximately 10%–15% in clinical settings; it is diagnosed more frequently in females. Axis I comorbidity includes: major depression, conversion disorder, and somatization disorder. Axis II comorbidity includes: borderline, narcissistic, antisocial, and dependent personality disorder.

Narcissistic Personality Disorder (NPD)

The essential feature of NPD is a pervasive pattern of grandiosity (in fantasy or behavior), need for admiration, and lack of empathy. NPD patients exaggerate achievements and talents; are often preoccupied with fantasies of unlimited success, power, and brilliance; exhibit a sense of entitlement; and are interpersonally exploitative. Prevalence is between 0% to 1% in the general population, 16% in clinical populations, and more than 50% of those diagnosed are male. Axis I comorbidity includes: major depression, bipolar disorder, substance abuse/dependence, dysthymia, and eating disorders. Axis II comorbidity includes: borderline, antisocial, paranoid, and histrionic. This particular disorder is unique in that most of the criteria are derived from psychoanalytic theory.

Cluster C Disorders

Avoidant Personality Disorder (APD)

The essential feature of APD is a pervasive pattern of social inhibition, feelings of inadequacy, and hypersensitivity to negative evaluation. These individuals avoid occupational activities that involve significant interpersonal contact; are unwilling to get involved with people unless certain of being liked; view themselves as socially inept, personally unappealing, or inferior to others; and are unusually reluctant to take personal risks or to engage in any new activities because they may prove embarrassing. Its prevalence varies between 0.4% to 1.3% in the general population, approximately 10% in outpatient mental health settings; it is equally common in men and women. Axis I comorbidity: There is a great amount of overlap between APD and Social Phobia, so much so that some view the two diagnoses as alternative conceptualizations of the same condition. Also commonly diagnosed with major depression and PTSD. Axis II comorbidities include all of the Cluster A disorders, as well as dependent and borderline personality disorder.

Dependent Personality Disorder (DPD)

The essential feature of DPD is a pervasive and excessive need to be taken care of that leads to submissive and clinging behavior and fears of separation. The submissive and dependent behaviors are believed to be designed to elicit caregiving from others and emanate from a self-perception of an inability to function properly without the aid of others. Prevalence is between 1.6% to 6.7% in the general population and appears to be equally common across gender. In outpatient mental health settings, DPD is considered to be one of the most common personality disorder diagnoses. Axis I comorbidity includes: major depression and most of the anxiety disorders (Hirschfeld et al., 1991). Axis II comorbidity includes: borderline, histrionic, and avoidant. Given the varying degrees of emphasis/discouragement of dependent behaviors in certain societies, it is especially important that the individual's behavior be judged in excess of cultural norms or expectations.

Obsessive-Compulsive Personality Disorder (OCPD)

The essential feature of OCPD is a pervasive pattern of preoccupation with orderliness, perfectionism, and mental and interpersonal control, at the expense of flexibility, openness, and efficiency. Despite the similarity in name, there is no etiological relationship between OCPD and the Axis I disorder obsessive-compulsive disorder and the two diagnoses do not co-occur with great frequency. Prevalence varies between 1.7% to 6.4% in the general population and appears to be twice as common in men. Its prevalence in outpatient mental health settings is approximately 10%. Obsessive-compulsive personality disorder may be unique among the personality disorders because some of its characteristic traits, such as excessive responsibility and perfectionism, are associated with high achievement. With regards to Axis II comorbidity, the relationship between OCPD and other Axis II disorders remains unclear.

Classification Systems

Attempts at creating typologies and characterizing personality can probably be traced back to Hippocrates in the fourth century B.C. with his identification of four basic temperaments based on the bodily humors (see Millon [1981] for a review). Since then, there has been passionate debate over how to classify and describe disorders of personality. Many argue that any attempt to represent the personality disorders as qualitatively discrete entities or clinical syndromes that can be diagnosed with prototypes (i.e., the DSM system) fails to capture the complexity and uniqueness of a person's personality, both the strengths and weaknesses. It is believed that this atheoretical and descriptive approach to the diagnosis of severe personality disorders may increase cross-sectional interrater reliability, but at the expense of the individual.

In response, several alternative approaches to the classification and diagnosis of personality disorders, outside of the categorical DSM system, have been proposed in the last few decades. These theory-guided approaches include dimensional (e.g., Widiger & Frances, 2002; Costa & McCrae, 1990), interpersonal (e.g., Benjamin, 1996), cognitive (e.g., Beck, Freeman, et al., 1990), psychoanalytic (e.g., Kernberg, 1984, 1996), biological (e.g., Cloninger, 1987), neurobehavioral (e.g., Depue & Lenzenweger, 2001), and evolutionary (e.g., Millon, 1996) models of personality and personality pathology. Most of these alternative approaches have developed a related assessment methodology that focus on dimensional traits (e.g., neuroticism, introversion vs. extroversion, affective reactivity, impulsiveness, harm avoidance, constraint, and identity diffusion).

There are clearly advantages to dimensional perspectives that view personality disorders as compositions of maladaptive traits located along a continuum from health to pathology. Some believe that any attempt to separate normality from pathology on a strictly objective basis is impossible, and that any distinctions are often the result of social and cultural forces, if not arbitrary. In fact, the authors of the various DSMs recognized that it was impossible to create an ideal classification system in clinical psychopathology. In their description of the DSM's history, Millon and Davis (1995) state that

> regardless of what advances were made in knowledge and theory, the substantive and professional character of mental health would be simply too multidimensional in structure and too multivariate in function ever to lend itself to a single, fully satisfactory system. It was acknowledged also that no consensus was likely ever to be found among either psychiatrists or psychologists as to how a classification might be best organized (e.g. dimensions, categories, observable qualities). (p. 16)

With that said, it is important to acknowledge the reality of current clinical practice in the United States. Personality disorders are established psychiatric diagnoses in the DSM-IV, and these disorders are presumed to be qualitatively distinct clinical syndromes. Whether or not one accepts this presumption, a working knowledge of the categorical personality disorder diagnoses is helpful in assisting clinicians with good treatment planning and clinical decision-making. Knowledge of an individual's personality disorder diagnosis will provide valuable information to the clinician about medication decisions, risk of suicide, treatment course, prognosis, interpersonal and occupational functioning, as well as etiological factors.

However, diagnosis is not assessment, and mastery of diagnostic criteria is not enough for a complete understanding of personality pathology. The DSM-IV Axis II categories are not an exhaustive list of all relevant personality constructs important to understanding an individual. They should be used as a starting point, from which the clinician can then add additional information (e.g., level of extraversion) to build a comprehensive understanding of the individual who seeks treatment. Diagnoses may be necessary (especially for communication, record keeping, and reimbursement), but they are not sufficient.

☐ Range of Assessment Strategies Available

Since the creation of Axis II, there has been an explosion of assessment instruments designed to measure personality disorders, dimensions, and maladaptive traits. Many of these instruments have come from the separate discipline of personality psychology with its emphasis on personality structure within the normal range, and it has become increasingly clear that these instruments offer clinically useful information in the area of psychopathology (see Watson & Clark, 1994). An exhaustive list of all possible instruments, along with a detailed discussion of their development, psychometrics, and relative merits, is beyond the scope of this chapter. Extended discussions of these issues are provided elsewhere (e.g., Kaye & Shea, 2000; Clark, Livesley, & Morey, 1997; Perry, 1992; Clark & Harrison, 2001; Zimmerman, 1994). We provide brief descriptions of the assessment strategies and instruments most useful to a practicing clinician, with special emphasis placed on the clinical interview, which is usually regarded as the criterion standard against which the validity of other assessment methods is judged. It is worth noting that projective tests (e.g., the Rorschach and Thematic Apperception Test) are very time-consuming, difficult to administer and interpret, and are no longer regarded as being as scientifically sound as self-report inventories or interviews, and their use has decreased considerably during the era of managed care. Therefore, they will not be included in this review.

Clinical Interview

Typically, clinical interviews can be categorized as structured, semistructured, or unstructured. Structured interviews are usually designed for research studies and not used in "normal" clinical work, and semistructured interviews will be discussed in the next section. The unstructured clinical interview, where the content of the interview is determined by the clinician/client interaction, is the most frequently used assessment strategy in clinical practice.

The clinical interview can take many forms because the theoretical predilection of the clinician will often dictate the focus of the clinical assessment. For instance, a psychodynamic clinician conducting an initial assessment of a borderline client would obviously be interested in symptomatic behaviors (e.g., number of suicide attempts, self-abusive acts, temper tantrums, and degree of substance use) necessary for diagnostic decisions. Additionally, this psychodynamic assessor would also be interested in the motivational structure that guides these behaviors: the extent of the client's superego development, the client's predominant transference themes, the client's use of primitive defensive mechanisms, and the quality of the client's object relations (for a description of such an assessment approach, see Kernberg [1981]). The goals of the assessment will be somewhat different if the clinician is a proponent of cognitive-behavioral theory, with its emphasis on maladaptive thoughts and the identification of overt behaviors to target in treatment. Nevertheless, regardless of one's theoretical orientation, there are some common guidelines that the clinician can follow when attempting to assess and identify personality disorders in a clinical interview.

First of all, the clinician needs to elicit a good history from the client that provides details about symptoms and symptomatic behavior from a developmental perspective, with special emphasis on the onset and progression of symptoms. This will aid in differentiating between an Axis I disorder and a characterological disorder. Axis I disorders tend to be of recent onset and episodic in nature. Pathological personality traits, although waxing and waning, surface throughout an individual's life and in many different contexts. To qualify as a personality trait, the behavior must be evident for at least 5 years. Needless to say, the clinician must have a good working knowledge of the Axis I and Axis II diagnostic criteria in order to make these distinctions.

In addition to a history of symptoms, it is crucial to obtain a detailed history of the client's interpersonal behavior and quality of relationships with others. In other words, the clinician needs to pay special attention to the client's pattern of perceiving, relating to, and thinking about his or her significant relationships, including family members, sexual partners, coworkers, as well as therapists. In fact, knowledge of any prior treatment attempts, the quality of the therapeutic relationship, and the reasons for treatment(s) termination will provide valuable information. For example, a client who simply describes his last three therapists as "idiots," or a client who states that her last therapist was uncaring because he wouldn't let her call him at 3:00 A.M., is providing the current clinician with important clues about that person's view of significant people in his or her life. A phone call (with permission) to previous therapists may be necessary.

We cannot overstate the importance of assessing interpersonal behavior and quality of relationships when working with personality disorder clients. Unlike many of the Axis I disorders, the essential feature(s) of all of the personality disorders are social or interpersonal in nature. Features can be described as: paranoid (distrust of others), schizoid (detachment from social relationships), schizotypal (discomfort in close relationships), antisocial (disregard for rights of others), borderline (interpersonal instability), histrionic (attention from others); narcissistic (need for admiration and lack of empathy), avoidant (social inhibition), dependent (submissive and clinging behavior and fear of separation), obsessive-compulsive (mental and interpersonal control). To get a good sense of the client's inner world, the clinician must know how the client interacts and functions in the outer world.

In addition to impairment in social functioning, an important (but often overlooked) requirement for a personality disorder diagnosis is significant distress or impairment in occupational functioning. Therefore, an assessment of the client's work history in the broad sense (work, profession, investment in work goals, and achievement) should be a standard part of the clinical interview.

The motivation of the person seeking treatment is an additional factor to consider when conducting the clinical interview that will provide the clinician with clues regarding personality pathology. When inquiring about the presenting complaint, it is important to determine if the symptoms are egosyntonic or egodystonic. In other words, is the client seeking help willingly because he or she is in distress or because a significant person in the client's life has suggested it, and failure to do so would result in some sort of negative consequence, such as divorce, loss of job, or punishment (possibly borderline, narcissistic, or antisocial).

Finally, in the clinical interview with a personality disorder client, there are three channels of communication that the clinician must attend to simultaneously. The first channel is the client's verbal communication, in other words, what the client actually says to you about their condition. The second channel is the client's behavior (e.g., dress, appearance, eye contact, social appropriateness, level of hostility or suspiciousness, etc.). The clinician's initial impressions of these factors can offer clues to help understand the person's personality traits. For instance, a client who avoids eye contact and appears extremely uncomfortable and suspicious may suggest a Cluster A disorder. A female client who shows up to her first appointment dressed in an inappropriately sexual manner and hugs the clinician may suggest a histrionic disorder. A client who responds to your friendly initial greeting with a dismissive or condescending smirk, may suggest borderline, antisocial, or narcissistic personality disorder. The third, and perhaps most important, channel of communication is the clinician's counter-transference, defined as all of the clinician's emotional responses to the client.

The clinician's emotional reaction to the client has important diagnostic and practical implications worthy of further discussion. Because many clients with personality disorders use primitive defense mechanisms, it is not uncommon for a clinician to feel as though the client is coercing him/her into behaving or feeling a certain way. For instance, with a client who presents as very helpless, the clinician may feel a pull to be more controlling and take charge during the session. However, this client will often frustrate the clinician's efforts to take the lead, resulting in the clinician feeling angry or frustrated. Clients who induce elements of their own internal world in the clinician are defending themselves against the intensity of feelings that such interactions invoke in the clinician. Instead of acknowledging feelings of anger or frustration, the severe personality disorder client will unconsciously coerce the clinician into experiencing those same feelings. In severe cases, the clinician may feel the pull to violate professional boundaries. As a rule, the more severe the personality pathology, the stronger the counter-transference reaction by the clinician. By paying close attention to these feelings, the clinician can use this information to better understand the client and clarify a possible diagnosis.

It is important to remember that with many of the Cluster B personality disorders, during the initial clinical interactions, more meaningful information is often communicated through the second and third channels, compared to the first. According to Clarkin, Yeomans, and Kernberg (1999), the clinician must always listen to the verbal material of the client in the context of his or her knowledge of the client's history, observation of the client's behavior, and appreciation of the clinician's counter-transference.

After a thorough unstructured clinical interview, the clinician should have enough information to raise the suspicion of the presence of one or more personality disorders, at which point the full DSM-IV criteria can be assessed and the diagnosis confirmed via a semistructured diagnostic interview or self-report inventory.

Semistructured Diagnostic Interviews

Semistructured interviews can be divided into two categories: those that are diagnostically based and those that are trait-based. Because the interviews below standardize the questions asked of clients, they have the benefit of greatly increasing interrater reliability, that is to say, the extent to which different interviewers agree about the diagnosis of the same subject. This is especially important with the personality disorders, since they appear to be a collection of overlapping constructs. There are currently five commonly used diagnostically based semistructured interviews designed to assess the full range of DSM-IV personality disorders:

- Structured Clinical Interview for DSM-IV Axis II Personality Disorders (SCID-II; First, Gibbon, Spitzer, Williams, & Benjamin, 1997).
- International Personality Disorders Inventory (IPDE; Loranger, 1995, 1999)
- Structured Interview for DSM Personality IV (SIDP-IV; Pfohl, Blum, & Zimmerman, 1997)
- Personality Disorder Interview-IV (PDI-IV; Widiger, Mangine, Corbitt, et al., 1995)
- Diagnostic Interview for DSM-IV Personality Disorders (DIPD-IV; Zanarini, Frankenburg, Sickel, et al., 1996).

Since each is designed to assess the same content (i.e., DSM-IV Axis II criteria), they share many of the same characteristics and their psychometric properties (i.e., interrater and test-retest reliability) are more or less similar (see Clark & Harrison [2001] for a review). They do, however, differ in regard to format, scoring, and the use of screening measures. These factors may ultimately influence the clinician's choice of which instrument to use, based on one's preference.

In terms of format, the DIPD-IV and the SCID-II group the questions according to diagnostic category. Arranging questions according to diagnosis could either facilitate or bias clinical judgments, depending on the clinician's level of objectivity (Clark & Harrison, 2001). It is believed that the grouping of questions according to diagnosis activates somewhat stereotypical self-schemas in the client, but it is not clear if this activation negatively affects the validity of the instrument (see Clark & Harrison, 2001). From a practical standpoint, this format provides the clinician an opportunity to choose a subset of diagnoses to assess with an individual, if time does not permit an omnibus evaluation. Of course, due to the enormous comorbidity among the personality disorders, this selective approach could be misleading.

The IPDE arranges the questions according to topics such as work, interpersonal relationships, affects, and reality testing. This arrangement tends to create a more natural discourse, and allows the client to reflect on his or her life according to the domains with which he or she is most familiar. This approach is also advantageous because it allows the interviewer to inquire about overlapping criteria in a single question. For example, inquiring once about a "reckless disregard for the safety of self or others" provides information relevant to both borderline and anti-social. The SIDP-IV and the PDI-IV provide versions with both types of format.

Despite slight variations in scoring (see Kaye & Shea, 2000), all the interviews allow for a presence or absence judgment, as well as a computation of a total score and the number of criteria met for each diagnosis (Clark & Harrison, 2001). The IPDE and SCID-II have the added benefit of a true or false screening questionnaire (the SIDP-IV has a brief clinician administered screening interview). If the client is below the designated threshold for the disorder, it is assumed that they do not have it, while scores above the threshold suggest the need for a full interview. Although there is debate regarding the ability of screeners to identify clients with a disorder, they are generally good at identifying those without a disorder (see Clark & Harrison, 2001), so these measures can be useful for guiding an assessment.

Trait-Based Interviews

There are four semistructured interviews for the assessment of personality pathology from a trait perspective. They are:

- Personality Assessment Schedule (PAS; Tyrer, 1988)
- Diagnostic Interview for Borderline Patients-Revised (DIB-R; Zanarini, Gunderson, Frankenburg, & Chauncy, 1989)
- Diagnostic Interview for Narcissism (DIN; Gunderson, Ronning-stam, & Bodkin, 1990)
- Psychopathy Checklist-Revised (PCL-R; Hare, 1991)

These interviews are designed to provide information on pathological personality traits, based on conceptualizations of personality disorders influenced by, but not entirely consistent with, the DSM concept (see Kaye & Shea, 2000; Clark & Harrison, 2001). With the exception of the PAS, each assesses only a single diagnostic category. These single category interviews go into much greater detail than the full-range diagnostic interviews, yielding rich clinical information, but can often be very time consuming, up to two hours for a single diagnosis. These trait-based interviews can be used for clinical purposes, especially in specialized settings where there is a specific interest in one psychopathological domain (e.g., forensic clinic, borderline inpatient unit), but are most commonly used in research.

Self-Report Inventories

In addition to clinical and semistructured interviews, self-report inventories are the other main information source that is available to the practicing clinician to aid in the assessment of personality disorders. Self-report instruments can be very helpful in quickly and efficiently identifying clinical problems prior to treatment. In addition, they can be used to evaluate progress throughout treatment, which has become very important in this era of managed care. Similar to semistructured interviews, self-reports can be divided into those that are diagnostically based and those that are trait-based.

Diagnostic Self-Reports

Diagnostic self-reports are

- Personality Disorder Questionnaire-IV (PDQ-4; Hyler, 1994)
- Coolidge Axis II Inventory (CATI; Coolidge & Merwin, 1992)
- Schedule for Nonadaptive and Adaptive Personality (SNAP; Clark, 1993)
- Wisconsin Personality Inventory (WISPI; Klein, Benjamin, Rosenfeld, et al., 1993)
- Minnesota Multiphasic Personality Inventory-Personality Disorder Scales (MMPI-PD; Morey, Waugh, & Blashfield, 1985)
- Millon Clinical Multiaxial Inventory-III (MCMI-III; Millon, Davis, & Millon, 1994)
- The Personality Assessment Inventory (PAI; Morey, 1991)

The PDQ-4, CATI, and SNAP were developed specifically to assess DSM Axis II criteria, while the MCMI and WISPI were developed to also assess the authors' unique conceptualizations of the Axis II disorders. The development of the MMPI-PD and PAI were not DSM criterion-based and therefore provide a more holistic or global assessment of personality pathology. The measures also differ in terms of length, reliability, validity, and amount of training necessary to interpret (see Kaye & Shea, 2000; Clark & Harrison, 2001 for review).

Although these diagnostic self-reports offer the advantage of speed and efficiency, they have been criticized on their ability to make categorical diagnostic distinctions when used alone. Some researchers believe that they are most useful as screening devices, especially the PDQ-4 (see Loranger, 1992; Zimmerman, 1994; Widiger & Sanderson, 1995).

Trait-Based Self-Reports

As previously discussed, many believe that the assessment of personality pathology should be focused on dimensional traits rather than diagnostic categories (see Widiger, Trull, Hurt, Clarkin, & Frances, 1987; Millon, 1981; Cloninger, 1987; Costa & McCrae, 1990; Clark, 1990; Siever & Davis, 1991). As a result, several trait-based self-report measures have been developed to measure pathological, as well as normal-range personality traits. These measures offer rich, detailed information about the individual that can supplement information gathered in the clinical interview. Some instruments measure multiple traits, while others focus on single dimensions. The choice of which measure to use depends on the specific goals of assessment. The measures designed to assess personality pathology do not directly assess the DSM-IV Axis II disorders, but rather components of those disorders, based on theory (e.g., Five-Factor Model). These instruments, despite their potential clinical utility, are mostly used in research settings and are uncommon in typical clinical practice. Therefore, the reader is referred to the primary sources, as well as two excellent reviews (Kaye & Shea, 2000; Clark & Harrison, 2001) for a detailed discussion of these measures. The range of trait-based instruments available are

- Schedule for Nonadaptive and Adaptive Personality (SNAP; Clark, 1993)
- Dimensional Assessment of Personality Pathology-BQ (Schroeder, Wormsworth, & Livesley, 1992, 1994)
- Personality Psychopathology-Five (PSY-5; Harkness & McNulty, 1994)
- Inventory of Personality Organization (IPO; Clarkin, Foelsch, & Kernberg, 2001)

- Inventory of Interpersonal Problems-Personality Disorder Scales (IIP-PD, Pilkonis, Kim, Proietti, & Barkham, 1996)
- Psychopathic Personality Inventory (PPI; Lilienfeld & Andrews, 1996)
- Schizotypal Personality Questionnaire (SPQ; Raine, 1991)
- Multidimensional Personality Questionnaire (MPQ; Tellegen, 1982)
- NEO Personality Inventory-Revised (NEO-PI-R; Costa & McCrae, 1992)
- Tridimensional Personality Questionnaire (TPQ; Cloninger, Przybeck, & Svrakic, 1991)

Problems with Direct Questions and Client Self-Report

Axis I disorders typically have the diagnostic advantage of being symptom-based and objective, resulting in less construct overlap and diagnostic comorbidity. However, it appears that the technology developed to aid in the assessment of Axis I disorders (e.g., semistructured interviews, self-reports) do not work equally well with the Axis II conditions.

With Axis I disorders, clients can usually respond accurately to direct questions about their symptoms. However, the reliance on direct questions and client self-report in personality assessment is problematic. First of all, recall of pervasive patterns of behavior over the course of several years can be unreliable. Second, the accurate description of personality traits can be negatively affected or biased by current mood state (i.e., depression), requiring assessment at different time points. Third, the Axis II criteria tend to be more subjective and internal (rather than behavior-based), so that the interviewer must rely on the individual's ability to accurately reflect on and report his or her subjective experience(s). However, many personality traits tend to be egosyntonic and unconscious, and acknowledgment of them requires a level of insight and self-awareness that is often impaired in certain personality disorders. In addition, many of the criteria are socially undesirable, making it easy for an individual to defend against or deny their presence (especially common in Cluster B).

Therefore, some believe that semistructured interviews and self-reports are not the ideal means of accurately assessing personality pathology in clinical practice. A clinical interview that allows the client to provide a narrative description of him or herself (with special emphasis on his or her interactions with others), combined with close observation of the client's behavior (especially with the clinician), and acute awareness of the clinician's emotional reactions to the client (counter-transference) is the preferred method. In fact, research confirms that this approach is most common in typical clinical practice, regardless of training (M.D., Ph.D., M.S.W.) or theoretical orientation (Westen, 1997).

☐ Pragmatic Issues Encountered in Clinical Practice with These Disorders

Many of the practical issues encountered in clinical practice with personality disorders have already been discussed above and center on the inherent difficulty in accurately assessing personality pathology (e.g., vague overlapping constructs, high rates of comorbidity, categorical vs. dimensional classification, unreliability of self-report, etc.). This appears to be a problem somewhat unique to the personality disorders. Two psychologists may disagree about the etiology or preferred treatment for depression, but will most likely agree on what constitutes a major depressive episode and how to recognize it.

Simply put, clients with personality pathology can be difficult to work with. In addition to the diagnostic complexity and subtlety of their presentations, their symptomatology and interpersonal style (e.g., suicide attempts, affective instability, irritability, self-abusive behavior, grandiosity, social withdrawal, etc.), can sometimes trigger strong reactions (e.g., feelings of helplessness, anger, frustration, resentment) in the clinician. Working with these clients, therefore, requires a good deal of personal patience and clinical acumen. A danger to avoid is the labeling of someone as borderline or narcissistic after only one session. Their clinical presentation may differ depending on the context in which the client is being assessed. Therefore, it is important to remember that not all difficult clients are personality disordered and not all personality disorder clients are difficult to deal with.

From a practical standpoint, that means that proper assessment of personality pathology requires time (several days or weeks), perhaps more time than most practicing clinicians can afford in today's economic climate. Unfortunately, the days of routine comprehensive psychological assessments, unlimited therapy sessions, and full reimbursement have been replaced by a managed care system centered on cost containment, accountability, diagnostic codes, and "medical necessity."

What does this mean with regard to reimbursement for assessment of personality disorders? Of course, the answer is not simple, since policies, procedures, and rates vary across states and insurance providers. Some excellent insurance companies will provide reimbursement regardless of diagnoses, while some managed-care companies simply do not recognize personality disorders (in the absence of an Axis I disorder) as a reimbursable condition. Some third-party payers believe (erroneously) that personality disorders are not responsive to time-limited psychotherapeutic interventions and are, therefore, not reimbursable. An added dilemma is that many practicing clinicians report that a majority of the clients that they see (60.6%) demonstrate personality pathology significant enough to require psychotherapeutic intervention, but are currently undiagnosable on DSM-IV Axis II (Westen & Arkowitz-Weston, 1998). Since a diagnosis is required for reimbursement, some clinicians may feel a pull to "justify" their treatment by providing an Axis I diagnosis that may or may not be in existence. This approach obviously has important ethical implications.

Despite the wide range of policies and procedures regarding reimbursement, there are some general guidelines that appear to be common among many managed-care companies that will affect a clinician's ability to be compensated for his or her services.

First of all, many (but not all) managed care companies make a distinction between an "assessment," an "evaluation," and "psychological testing." An "assessment" is often defined as the preliminary compilation of biopsychosocial information (derived from interviewing the client, family members, other informants) and reviewing past clinical records in order to make a determination about level of care. An "evaluation" is often defined as a comprehensive compilation of biopsychosocial information (derived from interviewing the client, family members, other informants), and a review of past clinical records that leads to a biopsychosocial formulation, determination of diagnoses, and a biopsychosocial treatment plan. "Psychological testing" is often defined as the use of professionally recognized standardized instruments that have been determined to be useful for a variety of diagnostic and treatment planning purposes. The administration of these instruments is regulated by ethics codes of professional organizations (e.g., APA) and state professional licensing laws. This psychological testing usually needs to be performed by or under the supervision of an appropriately credentialed psychologist or psychiatrist.

The "assessment," "evaluation," or both stages (as defined above) are usually considered part of routine clinical work and necessary for determining a diagnosis and developing an initial treatment plan. Most initial treatment plans require a description of the presenting problem, a mental status exam, diagnoses on all five Axes, the identification of targets for treatment, initial treatment goals, identification of a treatment modality, and proposed duration of treatment. A reviewer or case manager then decides how many sessions to authorize. These initial assessment activities are usually reimbursed as part of this authorized routine treatment.

Of course, a good clinical interview can often provide this requisite information with many clients. In fact, some of the more severe personality disorder clients present with identifiable targets for treatment, which third party payers easily recognize as medically necessary (e.g., suicide attempts, self-abusive acts, severe mood disturbance, etc.). In addition, because of the substantial comorbidity, many personality disorder clients present with clear Axis I pathology that can be legitimately diagnosed and targeted. However, as we have discussed, a comprehensive assessment of personality pathology usually requires more than one 45–50 minute encounter. What this means in practical terms is that a good portion of your initial allotment of sessions may have to be devoted to the formulation of your diagnosis and treatment plan. Unfortunately, since a thorough evaluation may require the use of standardized assessment instruments (e.g., semistructured interview, trait-based self-reports, etc.), and many providers specifically prohibit the use of the initial preauthorized visits for specialized "psychological testing," additional authorization may be required.

Additional "psychological testing" is not usually considered as a routine or normal procedure in an individual's treatment and therefore, requires proof of "medical necessity" and precertification with most insurers. Use of standardized psychometric instruments for diagnostic, personality functioning assessment, or both are usually considered to be potentially useful whenever a traditional assessment (unstructured clinical interview, review of records) is insufficient to generate an effective case formulation or behavioral health plan. Therefore, the clinician must make clear in the request for authorization that diagnostic clarity, assessment of personality functioning, or both is absolutely required for effective psychotherapy or psychopharmacology treatment planning, and that this information cannot be gained via traditional means. Of course, providers will impose their own criteria for eligibility. For example, some providers only reimburse for neuropsychological testing, some require documentation of the proposed instrument's validity and the existence of published norms, some automatically exclude certain instruments, some require the assessor to possess specific training or credentials, and so on. In addition, each provider will determine how long the testing should take and will place limits on number of hours that they will reimburse (e.g., a ceiling of 8 hours of psychological testing per calendar year, per customer).

Nevertheless, despite the vicissitudes of acquiring reimbursement for assessment of personality pathology, the information presented in this chapter regarding the important impact of personality disorders on clinical treatment of Axis I disorders, their potential lethality to the individual, and their cost to society will hopefully help the clinician prepare a convincing argument to a managed-care company for the "medical necessity" of proper diagnosis and identification of personality pathology in clinical practice.

☐ Case Illustration

Client Description

Elizabeth is a 23-year-old, unmarried Caucasian woman with a 2-year-old son. The client is working as a hostess at an upscale restaurant, while attending acting classes part-time at a local community college. She was somewhat overdressed, appeared younger than her stated age, displayed numerous piercings on her ears, and had a tattoo of a flower on her left ankle. Elizabeth arrived to the session 35 minutes late, appeared irritated, and offered no apology or explanation for the delay. When greeted in the waiting area, she refused to shake the clinician's hand and inquired, "How long is this going to take?" When informed of the length of the evaluation, she added angrily, "You know it is raining outside, don't you?" The client appeared dysphoric during the interview and was often teary while describing her situation.

History of the Disorder or Problem

Elizabeth reported being the only child of unmarried parents who separated when she was 5 years old. She described having a "very tumultuous" relationship with her mother throughout her lifetime and no contact with her biological father. She also described being sexually abused on two occasions by one of her mother's numerous boyfriends when she was 14 years old. She never revealed the abuse to her mother or the authorities because of feelings of embarrassment and guilt. Elizabeth began cutting her thighs with a razor when she left home for college at age 18 (and continues to do so weekly). During her first semester, she reported drinking excessively, occasionally binge eating, and engaging in several one night stands. One of the encounters resulted in a pregnancy and subsequent abortion. Her grades were terrible her first semester and she consequently dropped out. She returned home and found work as a waitress and part-time model. During the ensuing four years, Elizabeth lived in three different states as a result of short-lived relationships with men. She described each relationship as "very chaotic," "huge mistakes," and occasionally violent. She described being confused about why she stayed with these men since she knew they "were so bad for me." She reported overdosing on sleeping pills after the end of one of the relationships, although she denied that it was a suicide attempt. She also described difficulty controlling her anger, which has resulted in loss of employment. Elizabeth's son was the result of a short-lived affair with her former boss who was married with children. Elizabeth described three previous unsuccessful therapy attempts starting at age 18. She described two previous therapists as "incompetent," "uncaring," and incapable of understanding her. She described her first counselor in college as "the greatest." Despite this, she described being "very attached" to each of them and the termination of therapy as "totally traumatic." Elizabeth reported that she has been previously diagnosed with "depression," "anxiety," and "some sort of personality disorder."

Presenting Complaints

Elizabeth stated that she was seeking treatment because she saw an article about repressed memories of abuse in a women's magazine at work. In addition, she reported feeling "depressed and anxious all the time." She also stated that she always seems to "end up with the wrong guy" and that her professional and social lives are "a total mess." Elizabeth also gave a vague description of feeling like "I am going crazy." She stated that she wants to figure what is "wrong" with her and figure out what to do with her life.

Assessment Methods Used

The methods used to assess Elizabeth's case included

Unstructured clinical interview (with informants)
Semistructured diagnostic interview (select modules of IPDE)
Trait- and symptom-based self-report instruments (IPO, DAPP-BQ, AIAQ, BSI)

Psychological Assessment Protocol

The assessment of this client began with the scheduling of the appointment over the phone. Despite her insistence that she wanted (and needed) help, the client made it extremely difficult to schedule a time to meet. When offered several times from which to choose, she rejected each one and repeatedly accused the clinician of being inflexible and controlling. The clinician felt a pull to make special accommodations for her, making him feel as if he were being controlled by her. This feeling, combined with her intense anger and irritation, immediately alerted the clinician to the possibility of an Axis II condition. Her late arrival and reaction in the waiting area also provided important data about her possible diagnosis and personality structure.

The clinical interview was conducted in an unstructured manner, guided by hypotheses generated from the previous interactions with the client. It began with an attempt at gathering information about the client's current symptomatology, with special emphasis placed on determining the reasons for the client's suicidal and self-mutilating behavior. Special emphasis was also placed on determining the nature of the client's mood symptoms, which did not meet criteria for either major depressive episode or dysthymia. Her depressive symptoms were determined to be short-lived and reactive and did not include neuro-vegetative symptoms (e.g., sleep disturbance, weight gain/loss, psychomotor retardation) indicative of an Axis I disorder. She also denied feelings of worthlessness or guilt, although she did report chronic feelings of emptiness. It also became clear that her suicidal behavior did not occur during periods of depressed mood and were motivated by attempts to avoid abandonment by her boyfriends. A discussion of her continued substance use, eating disturbance, and sexual activity revealed marked impulsivity and appeared to be subthreshold for an Axis I disorder. Her concern about "going crazy" was addressed and she revealed mild, transient paranoia when under a great deal of stress. The clinical interview then focused on a discussion of her significant relationships, as well as her own conception of herself. This description of herself and others resulted in a picture of profound identity disturbance and a pervasive pattern of alternating between idealization and devaluation with her mother, boyfriends, therapists, and even her son. The information from the clinical interview strongly suggested borderline personality pathology.

Because of the client's late arrival, a second session was scheduled to continue the initial assessment. She willingly agreed to be seen the next day and offered no resistance regarding scheduling. She was asked (and granted) permission to speak to her most recent therapist. The client was given two self-report inventories (IPO and DAPP-BQ) to take home with her, fill out, and bring with her the next day. She was provided with instructions, as well as an explanation for the questionnaires. Elizabeth ended the first session by stating that she had never felt "so understood in my whole life."

TABLE 6.1. An Overview of the Patient's Assessment

Axis I	V71.09	No diagnosis or condition on Axis I
Axis II	301.83	Borderline Personality Disorder
	301.50	Histrionic Personality Disorder
Axis III	None	
Axis IV		Inadequate social support
Axis V	GAF=41	(Current)
	GAF=48	(Highest level in past year)

For the second session, the client arrived 10 minutes early, was very cheerful and overly familiar, referring to the clinician by his first name. In order to confirm the suspected diagnoses, the borderline, histrionic, and dependent criteria on the semistructured International Personality Disorder Examination were administered. The results of the semistructured interview revealed that Elizabeth did meet DSM-IV diagnostic criteria for borderline and histrionic personality disorder, but was subthreshold for dependent. A discussion with her previous therapist confirmed the interview findings and revealed additional suicidal gestures that Elizabeth did not report. Interpretation of the IPO self-report revealed Elizabeth to be highly identity diffused and predisposed to the use of primitive defensive mechanisms, but her level of reality testing appeared to be normal (see Table 6.1).

Targets Selected for Treatment

The following were the principal patient behaviors selected for treatment:

- Self-mutilating behavior
- Suicidal gestures
- Inappropriate anger
- Affective instability
- Identity disturbance

Assessment of Progress

Progress toward therapeutic goals was assessed with the periodic administration of symptom specific and personality structure self-report instruments including the Brief-Symptom Inventory (BSI: Derogatis, 1993), the Anger, Irritability, and Assault Questionnaire (AIAQ; Coccaro, Harvey, Kupsaw-Lawrence, Herbert, & Bernstein, 1991), and the IPO.

☐ Summary

Since the inclusion of personality disorders on a separate axis of the DSM-III in 1980, there has been passionate debate about their validity as distinct clinical entities, as well as the best ways to classify and measure them. Personality disorders appear to be somewhat unique in this regard. Despite the debate, it is clear that personality pathology is ubiquitous and has very important and far-reaching personal, clinical, and social implications. Until recently, these disorders have not been given proper attention in most mental health settings. It now appears that with proper instruction and guidance, personality disorders can be properly identified in clinical practice so that they can be properly treated.

☐ References

American Psychiatric Association. (1994). *Diagnostic and Statistical Manual of Mental Disorders* (4th Ed.) Washington, DC: American Psychiatric Association.

Beck, A. T., Freeman, A., & Associates. (1990). *Cognitive therapy of personality disorders*. New York: Guilford.

Bender, D., Dolan, R., Skodol, A., Sanislow, C., Dych, I., McGlashan, T., Shea, M., Zanarini, M., Oldham, J., & Gunderson, J. (2001). Treatment utilization by patients with personality disorders. *American Journal of Psychiatry, 158*, 295–302.

Benjamin, L. S. (1996). An interpersonal theory of personality disorders. In J. F. Clarkin & M. F. Lenzenweger (Eds.), *Major theories of personality disorder* (pp. 141–220). New York: Guilford.

Clark, L. A. (1990). Toward a consensual set of symptom clusters for assessment of personality disorder. In J. N. Butcher & C. D. Spielberger (Eds.), *Advances in personality assessment* (pp. 243–266). Hillsdale, NJ: Erlbaum.

Clark, L. A. (1993). *Manual for the Schedule for Nonadaptive and Adaptive Personality*. Minneapolis: University of Minnesota.

Clark, L. A., & Harrison, J. (2001). Assessment instruments. In J. W. Livesley (Ed.), *Handbook of personality disorders: Theory, research, and treatment* (pp. 277–306). New York: Guilford.

Clark, L. A., Livesley, W. J., & Morey, L. (1997). Personality disorder assessment: The challenge of construct validity. *Journal of Personality Disorders, 11*, 205–231.

Clarkin, J. F., Foelsch, P. A., & Kernberg, O. F. (2001). *The Inventory of Personality Organization*. White Plains, NY: Weill Medical College of Cornell University.

Clarkin, J. F., Yeomans, F., & Kernberg, O. F. (1999). *Psychotherapy for borderline personality*. New York: Wiley.

Cloninger, C. R. (1987). A systematic method for clinical description and classification of personality variants: A proposal. *Archives of General Psychiatry, 44*, 573–588.

Cloninger, C., Przybeck, T., & Svrakic, D. (1991). The Tridimensional Personality Questionnaire: U.S. Normative Data. *Psychological Reports, 69*, 1047–1051.

Coccaro, E. F., Harvey, P. D., Kupsaw-Lawrence, E., Herbert, J. L., & Bernstein, D. P. (1991). Development of neuropharmacologically based behavioral assessments of impulsive aggressive behavior. *Journal of Neuropsychiatry and Clinical Neuroscience, 3*, S44–S51.

Coolidge, F., & Merwin, M. (1992). Reliability and validity of the Coolidge Axis II Inventory: A new inventory for the assessment of personality disorders. *Journal of Personality Assessment, 59*, 223–238.

Costa, P., & McCrae, R. (1990). Personality disorders and the five-factor model of personality. *Journal of Personality Disorders, 4*, 362–371.

Costa, P., & McCrae, R. (1992). *Revised NEO Personality Inventory (NEO-PI-R) and NEO Five-Factor Inventory (NEO-FFI) professional manual.* Odessa, FL: Psychological Assessment Resources.

Depue, R. A., & Lenzenweger, M. F. (2001). A neurobehavioral dimensional model of personality disorders. In W. J. Livesley (Ed.), *Handbook of personality disorders: Theory, research, and treatment* (pp. 136–176). New York: Guilford.

Derogatis, L. R. (1993). Brief Symptom Inventory (BSI): *Administration, scoring, and procedures manual.* (3rd ed.). Minneapolis, MN: National Computer Systems.

Drake, R., & Vaillant, G. (1985). A validity study of axis II of DSM-III. *American Journal of Psychiatry, 142*, 553–558.

Fazel, S., & Danesh, J. (2002). Serious mental disorder in 23,000 prisoners: A systematic review of 62 surveys. *Lancet, 359*, 545–550.

First, M., Gibbon, M., Spitzer, R., Williams, J. B. W., & Benjamin, L. (1997). *User's guide for the Structured Clinical Interview for DSM-IV Axis II Personality Disorders.* Washington, DC: American Psychiatric Press.

Gabbard, G. (2000). Psychotherapy of personality disorders. *Journal of Psychotherapy Practice & Research, 9*, 1–6.

Godt, K. (2002). Personality disorders and eating disorders: The prevalence of personality disorders in 176 female outpatients with eating disorders. *European Eating Disorders Review, 10*, 102–109.

Gunderson, J., & Phillips, K. (1991). A current view of the interface between borderline personality disorder and depression. *American Journal of Psychiatry, 148*, 967–975.

Gunderson, J., Ronningstam, E., & Bodkin, A. (1990). The Diagnostic Interview for Narcissism. *Archives of General Psychiatry, 47*, 676–680.

Hare, R. (1991). *The Hare Psychopathy Checklist — Revised manual.* North Tonawanda, NY: Multi-Health Systems.

Harkness, A., & McNulty, J. (1994). The Personality Psychopathology-Five (PSY-5): Issues from the pages of a diagnostic manual instead of a dictionary. In S. Strack & M. Lorr (Eds.), *Differentiating normal and abnormal personality* (pp. 291–315). New York: Springer.

Hirschfeld, R., Shea, M., & Weise, R. (1991). Dependent personality disorder: Perspectives for DSM-IV. *Journal of Personality Disorders, 5*, 135–149.

Hogg, B., Jackson, H., Rudd, R., & Edwards, J. (1990). Diagnosing personality disorders in recent-onset schizophrenia. *Journal of Nervous & Mental Disease, 178*, 194–199.

Hyler, S. (1994). *Personality Disorder Questionnaire-IV (PDQ-IV).* New York: New York State Psychiatric Institute.

Kaye, A., & Shea, T. (2000). Personality disorders, personality traits, and defense mechanisms. In A. J. Rush, H. A. Pincus, & M. B. First (Eds.), *Handbook of psychiatric measures* (pp. 713–749). Washington, DC: American Psychiatric Press.

Kernberg, O. F. (1981). Structural interviewing. *Psychiatric Clinics of North America, 4*, 169–195.

Kernberg, O. F. (1984). *Severe personality disorders.* New Haven, CT: Yale University Press.

Kernberg, O. F. (1996). A psychoanalytic theory of personality disorders. In J. F. Clarkin & M. F. Lenzenweger (Eds.) *Major theories of personality disorder* (pp. 106–140). New York: Guilford.

Klein, M., Benjamin, L. S., Rosenfeld, R., Treece, C., Justed, J., & Greist, J. (1993). The Wisconsin Personality Inventory: Development, reliability, and validity. *Journal of Personality Disorders, 7*, 285–303.

Kopta, S., Howard, K., Lowry, J., & Beutler, L. (1994). Patterns of symptomatic recovery in psychotherapy. *Journal of Consulting & Clinical Psychology, 62*, 1009–1016.

Lilienfeld, S., & Andrews, B. (1996). Development and preliminary validation of a self-report measure of psychopathic personality traits in noncriminal populations. *Journal of Personality Assessment, 66*, 488–524.

Links, P., Heslegrave, R., Mitton, J., Van Reekum, R., et al. (1995). Borderline personality disorder and substance abuse: Consequences of comorbidity. Canadian *Journal of Psychiatry — Revue, 40*, 9–14.

Loranger, A. (1992). Are current self-report and interview measures adequate for epidemiological studies of personality disorders? *Journal of Personality Disorders, 6,* 313–325.

Loranger, A. W. (1995, 1999). *International Personality Disorder Examination manual.* Odessa, FL: Psychological Assessment Resources.

Maier, W., Lichtermann, D., Klingler, T., Heun, R., et al. (1992). Prevalences of personality disorders (DSM-III -R) in the community. *Journal of Personality Disorders, 6,* 187–196.

Maier, W., Minges, J., Lichtermann, D., & Heun, R. (1995). Personality disorders and personality variations in relatives of patients with bipolar affective disorders. *Journal of Affective Disorders, 53,* 173–181.

Matia, J., & Zimmerman, M. (2001). Epidemiology. In W. J. Livesley (Ed.), *Handbook of personality disorders: Theory, research, and treatment* (pp. 107–123). New York: Guilford.

McGlashan, T., Grilo, C., Skodol, A., Gunderson, J., Shea, M., Morey, L., Zanarini, M., & Stout, R. (2000). The Collaborative Longitudinal Personality Disorders Study: Baseline Axis I/II and II/II diagnostic co-occurrence. *Acta Psychiatrica Scandinavica, 102,* 256–264.

Millon, T. (1981). *Disorders of personality: DSM-III, Axis II.* New York: Wiley.

Millon, T. (1996). An evolutionary theory of personality disorders. In J. F. Clarkin & M. F. Lenzenweger (Eds.), *Major theories of personality disorder* (pp. 221–346). New York: Guilford.

Millon, T., & Davis, R. (1995). Conceptions of personality disorders: Historical perspectives, the DSMs, and future directions. In W. J. Livesley (Ed.), *The DSM-IV personality disorders* (pp. 3–28). New York: Guilford.

Millon, T. & Davis, R. (2000). *Personality Disorders in Modern Life.* New York: Wiley.

Millon, T., Davis, R., & Millon, C. (1994). *Manual for the Millon Clinical Multiaxial Inventory-III (MCMI-III).* Minneapolis: National Computer Systems.

Morey, L. (1991). *The Personality Assessment Inventory.* Odessa, FL: Psychological Assessment Resources.

Morey, L., Waugh, M., & Blashfield, R. (1985). MMPI scales for DMS-III personality disorders: Their derivation and correlations. *Journal of Personality Assessment, 49,* 245–256.

Nace, E., Saxon, J., & Shore, N. (1986). Borderline personality disorder and alcoholism treatment: A one-year follow-up study. *Journal of Studies on Alcohol, 47,* 196–200.

Oldham, J., & Skodol, A. (1991). Personality disorders in the public sector. *Hospital and Community Psychiatry, 42,* 481–487.

Paris, J. (1990). Completed suicide in borderline personality disorder. *Psychiatric Annals, 20,* 19–21.

Perry, J. C. (1992). Problems and considerations in the valid assessment of personality disorders. *American Journal of Psychiatry, 149,* 1645–1653.

Pfohl, B., Blum, N., & Zimmerman, M. (1997) *Structured Interview for DSM Personality IV (SIDP-IV).* Washington, DC: American Psychiatric Press.

Pilkonis, P., Kim, Y., Proietti, J., & Barkham, M. (1996). Scales for personality disorders developed from the Inventory of Interpersonal Problems. *Journal of Personality Disorders, 10,* 355–369.

Raine, A. (1991). The SPQ: A scale for the assessment of schizotypal personality based on DSM-III-R criteria. *Schizophrenia Bulletin, 17,* 555–564.

Schroeder, M., Wormsworth, J., & Livesley, J. (1994). Dimensions of personality disorder and their relationship to the Big Five dimensions of personality. In P. T. Costa & T. A. Widiger (Eds.), *Personality disorders and the Five-Factor Model of personality* (2nd ed., pp. 23–44). Washington, DC: American Psychological Association.

Scott, J. (1993). Homelessness and mental illness. *British Journal of Psychiatry, 162,* 314–324.

Shea, M., Widiger, T., & Klein, M. (1992). Comorbidity of personality disorders and depression: Implications for treatment. *Journal of Consulting and Clinical Psychology, 60,* 857–868.

Siever, L., Bernstein, D., & Silverman, J. (1991). Schizotypal personality disorder: a review of its current status. *Journal of Personality Disorders, 5,* 178–193.

Siever, L., & Davis, K. (1991). A psychobiological perspective on the personality disorders. *American Journal of Psychiatry, 148,* 1647–1658.

Stein, D., Hollander, E., & Skodol, A. (1993). Anxiety disorders and personality disorders: A review. *Journal of Personality Disorders, 7*, 87–104.

Tellegen, A. (1982). *Brief manual for the Multidimensional Personality Questionnaire*. Minneapolis: University of Minnesota.

Tiihonen, J., & Hakola, P. (1994). Psychiatric disorders and homicide recidivism. *American Journal of Psychiatry, 151*, 436–438.

Tyrer, P. (1988). *Personality disorders: Diagnosis, management and course*. London: Wright.

Watson, D., & Clark, L. (Eds.) (1994). Personality and psychopathology [Special issue]. *Journal of Abnormal Psychology, 103*.

Weissman, M. (1993). The epidemiology of personality disorders: A 1990 update. *Journal of Personality Disorders, 7* (Suppl.), 44–62.

Westen, D. (1997). Divergences between clinical and research methods for assessing personality disorders: Implications for research and the evolution of axis II. *American Journal of Psychiatry, 154*, 895–903.

Westen, D., & Arkowitz-Weston, L. (1998). Limitations of Axis II in diagnosing personality pathology in clinical practice. *American Journal of Psychiatry, 155*, 1767–1771.

Widiger, T. A., & Frances, A. J. (2002). Toward a dimensional model for the personality disorders. In P. T. Costa & T. A. Widiger (Eds.), *Personality disorders and the Five-Factor Model of personality* (2nd ed., pp. 23–44). Washington, DC: American Psychological Association.

Widiger, T., Mangine, S., Corbitt, E., Ellis, C., & Thomas, G. (1995). *Personality Disorder Interview-IV: A semistructured interview for the assessment of personality disorders*. Odessa, FL: Psychological Assessment Resources.

Widiger, T., & Sanderson, C. (1995). Toward a dimensional model of personality disorders. In W. J. Livesley (Ed). *The DSM-IV personality disorders: Diagnosis and treatment of mental disorders* (pp. 433–458). New York: Guilford.

Widiger, T., Trull, T., Hurt, S., Clarkin, J., & Frances, A. (1987). A multidimensional scaling of the DSM-III personality disorders. *Archives of General Psychiatry, 44*, 557–563.

Zanarini, M., Frankenburg, F., Sickel, A., & Yong, L. (1996). *Diagnostic Interview for DSM-IV Personality Disorders*. Laboratory for the study of adult development, McLean Hospital, and the Department of Psychiatry, Harvard University.

Zanarini, M., Gunderson, J., Frankenburg, F., & Chauncy, D. (1989). The Revised Diagnostic Interview for Borderlines: Discriminating borderline personality disorder from other Axis II disorders. *Journal of Personality Disorders, 3*, 10–18.

Zimmerman, M. (1994). Diagnosing personality disorders: A review of issues and research methods. *Archives of General Psychiatry, 51*, 225–245.

Zimmerman, M., & Coryell, W. (1989). DSM-III personality disorder diagnoses in a nonpatient sample: Demographic correlates and comorbidity. *Archives of General Psychiatry, 46*, 682–689.

Zimmerman, M., & Mattia, J. (1999). Differences between clinical and research practices in diagnosing borderline personality disorder. *American Journal of Psychiatry, 156*, 1570–1574.

Vincent J. Adesso
Ron A. Cisler
B. J. Larus
Brandon B. Hayes

Substance Abuse

☐ Description of the Problem

The assessment of substance use is a task the general clinician is likely to face regardless of the population with whom, or the setting in which, he or she works. Even the clinician who does not specialize in substance-abuse issues needs to have some knowledge of substance-abuse assessment because of the impact of drug use and dependence on diagnosis, treatment planning, and treatment outcome. Estimates based on epidemiological data suggest that, depending on the mental health setting, between 29% and 50% of individuals also have substance-use disorders (Caton et al., 1989; Drake & Wallach, 1989; Kanwischer & Hundley, 1990; Mueser et al., 1990; Regier et al., 1990; Safer, 1987). Due to the high frequency of comorbidity between behavior disorders and drug dependence (e.g., Kessler et al., 1994, 1996, 1997; Regier et al., 1990), every clinician has a considerable likelihood of encountering cases in which substance use is an important factor in diagnosis and treatment. Furthermore, drug use and abuse also may influence health, may mimic behavior disorders, and may interact with medications and produce untoward behavioral effects.

Drug use is widespread among Americans, with between 14 and 18 million meeting DSM-IV criteria for alcohol abuse or dependence (NIAAA, 1997). Between 4 and 6 million Americans abuse or are dependent on illegal drugs and more than 45 million of them are dependent on nicotine (NIDA, 1994). Many illicit drug users, of course, also abuse alcohol.

Substance abusers have been reported to experience more comorbid behavioral problems than people with any other psychiatric syndrome (Ross, Glaser, & Germanson, 1988; Wilson, Nathan, O'Leary, & Clark, 1996). In fact, Ball and Kosten (1994) estimate that the lifetime prevalence rates of other behavior disorders among substance abusers range from 75% to 85%. Comorbidity is greater among those dependent on illicit drugs than on alcohol, though the larger number of individuals who abuse alcohol than any illicit drug leads to greater representation of alcohol abusers among most samples. Little is known about comorbidity for nicotine dependence, although some recent work suggests rates for anxiety and depressive disorders among individuals dependent on nicotine that are similar to those for individuals dependent on illicit drugs (Kandel, Huang, & Davies, 2001). Among women who are substance abusers, the most common comorbid behavior disorders are depression (Hesselbrock & Hesselbrock, 1996) and anxiety (Skinstad et al., 1996). Among male substance abusers, the most common behavior disorder is antisocial personality disorder (Hesselbrock & Hesselbrock, 1996).

The symptoms of intoxication and withdrawal for many substances mimic the symptoms of other behavior disorders. To account for this fact, the *Diagnostic and Statistical Manual of Mental Disorders*, 4th edition, revised text (DSM-IV-TR; APA, 2000) details a number of disorders induced by substances. This reflects the bidirectional nature of the relation between behavior disorders and substance abuse: substance abuse may be both a cause and a consequence of behavior disorders; and, behavior disorders may be both a cause and a consequence of substance abuse. Nathan, Skinstad, and Langenbucher (1999) review much of the evidence for this bidirectional connection. Alcohol and other drugs can have important health effects that influence diagnosis as well as treatment progress and outcome. Many of these are reviewed in McCrady & Epstein (1999).

Assessment of substance use and abuse serves several purposes. This chapter divides substance abuse assessment into six levels to reflect the various functions that assessment may serve. The first of these is a case finding function, or screening to determine whether or not substance use or abuse is an issue for a particular client and how substance use or abuse might relate to the client's presenting problem. The second level involves developing a snapshot picture of the client's substance use and developing a preliminary treatment plan. The third level involves determination of the appropriate diagnosis, involving fuller assessment of which substances are used, the extent of their use, and the possible links with comorbid behavior disorders. The fourth level of substance use and abuse assessment entails developing a comprehensive understanding of the client's drug use and treatment history and of the psychosocial factors associated with drug use, and completing a functional analysis of the causes and consequences of drug use. The fifth level addresses the client's readiness to change the use of any or all of these substances, the client's attitudes toward treatment, barriers to treatment, goals, and the client's degree of treatment involvement. The final level of assessment of substance abuse is outcome evaluation after treatment completion.

To assess substance abuse, the clinician must have knowledge of the criteria used for diagnosing a substance use disorder. DSM-IV-TR (APA, 2000) divides problems due to alcohol and drug use into the substance-use disorders and the substance-induced disorders. Substance-induced disorders are those in which the presenting symptoms are phenomenologically similar to those of a behavior disorder but are attributable to use of a substance. There are ten substance-induced disorders listed: substance intoxication, substance withdrawal, substance-induced delirium, substance-induced persisting dementia, substance-induced persisting amnestic disorder, substance-induced psychotic disorder, substance-induced mood disorder, substance-induced anxiety disorder, substance-induced sexual dysfunction, and substance-induced sleep disorder.

The substance-use disorders are categorized in terms of either substance abuse or substance dependence. These diagnoses rely on a common set of criteria for the 11 classes of substances that are covered (alcohol; amphetamine or similarly acting sympathomimetics; caffeine; cannabis; cocaine; hallucinogens; inhalants; nicotine; opioids; phencyclidine [PCP] or similarly acting arylcyclohexylamines; and sedatives, hypnotics, or anxiolitics). Neither caffeine nor nicotine use can be diagnosed as substance abuse, and, further, caffeine use cannot be diagnosed as substance dependence.

Substance abuse is viewed as a less pervasive disorder than substance dependence. Therefore, fewer and less severe criteria are required to meet this diagnosis. However, this diagnosis should not be used to signify use, misuse, or hazardous use of substances. This diagnosis is thought to be more likely in individuals who have only recently started taking the substance and are experiencing problems due to its use.

Substance abuse is defined as a maladaptive pattern of substance use that causes recurrent and significant adverse consequences in the social, physical, legal, and vocational or educational realms of functioning repeatedly in the last 12 months. When the substance use poses a risk of physical harm (e.g., driving while intoxicated), its recurrent use is considered a part of the criteria. The criteria for substance abuse focus on the harmful consequences of repeated use and exclude tolerance, withdrawal, and a pattern of compulsive use as criteria included in this diagnosis. Thus, some individuals continue to have adverse consequences related to the use of a substance over a long period of time without developing substance dependence because they do not show evidence of tolerance, withdrawal, or compulsive use. It is worth repeating that this category of use is not applicable to caffeine and nicotine.

The diagnosis of substance dependence preempts the diagnosis of substance abuse if an individual's pattern of substance use has ever met the criteria for dependence for that particular class of substances. Substance dependence is characterized by symptoms from three realms of functioning: cognitive, behavioral, and physiological. These symptoms indicate that the individual continues to use the substance despite significant problems related to its use. A pattern of repeated use, which can result in tolerance, withdrawal, and compulsive drug-taking behavior, also must be present. Craving, defined as a strong desire to use the substance, is thought to be experienced by most individuals with substance dependence. The diagnosis requires that three or more of the symptoms occur concurrently at any time in the same 12-month period. The seven symptoms included are: tolerance, withdrawal, use of greater amounts or for longer periods than intended, persistent desire or unsuccessful efforts to control use, excessive time involvement, lifestyle change due to use, use continues despite knowing it causes other problems.

As many individuals may meet the criteria for substance dependence without giving evidence of having developed tolerance to the substance or of having withdrawal symptoms upon abstaining from the substance, DSM-IV-TR allows for assigning a diagnosis of substance dependence regardless of the presence of symptoms of tolerance or withdrawal. Therefore, two specifiers are used to indicate the presence or absence of tolerance or withdrawal. The specifier, "with physiological dependence," is used to indicate the presence of either tolerance or withdrawal or both. The absence of tolerance or withdrawal is indicated with the specifier, "without physiological dependence." There are six additional specifiers: four for course or remission status (requiring the absence of substance use for at least 1 month); one to indicate if the person is receiving agonist or antagonist therapy; and, one to indicate if the person is in an environment where access to the substance is controlled.

Finally, DSM-IV-TR accounts for use of any other substances with the diagnosis of other (or unknown) substance-related disorder to cover both substance use and substance-induced disorders. When during the same 12-month period an individual is repeatedly using at least three groups of substances, without one substance being predominant, the diagnosis of polysubstance dependence is used. Caffeine and nicotine are not included here.

The remainder of this chapter will review a variety of tools that may be used to assess substance abuse and problems the clinician is likely to encounter in the assessment of substance abuse. A case will be presented to illustrate the approach we have described and sample assessment results for this case will be presented. The manner in which the results of the assessment informed treatment also will be illustrated. The chapter will end with a summary statement regarding the assessment of substance abuse.

☐ Range of Assessment Strategies Available

Consideration should be given in any behavioral health, medical, or social agency setting to the range or levels of assessment strategies available to assist in identifying or characterizing the various problems, risk factors, comorbid issues, or combination thereof related to substance use, abuse, or dependence. Clinicians with limited background and training in substance abuse may choose to utilize only some of the levels of assessment presented and to refer a client to a specialist for more comprehensive assessment. This section reviews assessment methods associated with these varying levels, and considers their rationale and strategies for everyday clinical use. The subsequent broader section of this chapter deals with the practical issues related to assessing at these various levels.

Six conceptually distinct levels of assessment will be discussed, each representing a different purpose or target of assessment: (1) screening, (2) brief problem assessment and preliminary treatment planning, (3) diagnosis, (4) comprehensive pretreatment problem assessment, (5) treatment-related factors and within treatment assessment, and (6) outcome assessment. In addition, the issue of corroboration of assessment results will be discussed. Table 7.1 provides a summary of these six levels of assessment, including the purpose or rationale for each method of assessment and examples of commonly used or innovative measures representative of each assessment level. Generally speaking, these levels of assessment build upon each other, so that later levels require more extensive client and practitioner time, exchange of information, and follow-up, including administrative resource commitment.

Level 1 — Screening

Screening for substance-use disorders has gained popularity in the past 10–15 years with the realization that substance use is not a unitary disorder (Institute of Medicine, 1990; NIAAA, 1995a; NIAAA, 1997) and public health efforts at identification and "case finding" are important in

TABLE 7.1. Characteristics of Measurement Devices at Various Levels of Assessment

LEVELS OF ASSESSMENT		MEASURE				
Level	Purpose	Name	Items	Time(Min.)	Format	Administrator
1. Screening	To identify substance- use problems in non–substance use health and social services venues	Alcohol Use Disorders Identification Test (AUDIT; Babor et al. 1992)	10	3–5	Questionnaire or Interview	Trained Clinician or Assistant
		Drug Abuse Screening Test (DAST; Skinner, 1982)	10/20	3–7	Questionnaire or Interview	Trained Clinician or Assistant
		Rost Drug Abuse/Dependence Screener (Rost et al., 1993)	3	1	Questionnaire or Interview	Trained Clinician or Assistant
		Triage Assessment for Addictive Disorder (TAAD; Hoffman, 1995)	31	10	Questionnaire or Interview	Trained Clinician or Assistant
		Minnesota Multiphasic Personality Inventory- 2- Substance Abuse Scales (MMPI- 2; Butcher et al., 1989; Rouse et al., 1999; Stein et al., 1999)	567	90–120	Questionnaire or Interview	Trained Clinician
2. Brief Problem Assessment	To briefly assess substance- use problems, risk factors and involvement for use in motivational feedback, substance- use services engagement and preliminary treatment planning	Alcohol Dependence Scale (ADS; Skinner & Horn, 1984)	25	8–10	Questionnaire or Interview	Trained Clinician or Assistant
		Form 90- Quick (Form 90- Q; Miller, 1996)	10	5	Structured Interview	Trained Clinician or Assistant

Category	Purpose	Instrument	Items	Time	Format	Administrator
		Drinker Inventory of Consequences/Inventory of Drug Use Consequences (DrInC/INDUC; Miller et al., 1995)	15/50	5–15	Questionnaire or Interview	Trained Clinician or Assistant
		Readiness to Change Questionnaire (RTCQ; Heather et al., 1993)	12	3–4	Questionnaire or Interview	Trained Clinician or Assistant
3. Diagnosis	To provide definitive diagnosis of substance abuse or dependence	Structured Clinical Interview for DSM-IV Screen Patient Questionnaire (First et al., 1995a)	76	25	Computer-administered structured interview	Trained Clinician or Assistant
		Structured Clinical Interview for DSM-IV Axis I Disorders (First et al., 1995b)	Varies	45–90	Structured Interview	Masters level or above trained clinician
		Substance Dependence Severity Scale (SDSS; Miele et al., 2000)	Varies	15–25	Interview	Trained Clinician or Assistant
4. Comprehensive Pre-Treatment Problem Assessment	To assess substance-use, involvement, severity, family history, treatment history and psychosocial factors related to	Addiction Severity Index (ASI; McLellan et al., 1992; McLellan et al., 1980)	200	45–90	Structured Interview	Trained Clinician or Assistant
		Alcohol Abstinence Self-Efficacy (AASE; DiClemente et al., 1994)	40	12–15	Questionnaire or Interview	Trained Clinician or Assistant
		Drug History Questionnaire (DHQ; Sobell et al., 1995)	17	5	Questionnaire or Interview	Trained Clinician or Assistant
		Maudsley Addiction Profile (MAP; Marsden et al., 1998)	60	15–20	Questionnaire or Interview	Trained Clinician or Assistant
		Substance Abuse Relapse Assessment (SARA; Schonfeld et al., 1993)	39	60	Interview	Trained Clinician or Assistant

TABLE 7.1. (Continued)

LEVELS OF ASSESSMENT

MEASURE

Level	Purpose	Name	Items	Time(Min.)	Format	Administrator
		Desired Effects of Drinking (DED; NIAAA, in press)	16 37	5 10	Questionnaire or Interview Questionnaire or Interview	Trained Clinician or Assistant Trained Clinician or Assistant
5. Treatment-Related Factors and within Treatment Assessment	To assess treatment seeking, readiness, engagement, access and utilization factors and assess treatment, goals, goal attainment, therapeutic bond and service	Circumstances, Motivation, Readiness and Suitability Scales (CMRS; De Leon et al., 1994)	18	5	Questionnaire or Interview	Trained Clinician or Assistant
		Processes of Change Questionnaire (PCQ; Prochaska et al., 1988)	20/40	5- 10	Questionnaire or Interview	Trained Clinician or Research Assistant
		Alcohol and Drug Consequences Questionnaire (ADCQ; Cunningham et al., 1997)	29	10	Questionnaire or Interview	Trained Clinician or Assistant
		Reasons and Fears about Treatment Questionnaire (RFTQ; Oppenheimer et al., 1988)	27/54	10- 15	Questionnaire or Interview	Trained Clinician or Assistant
		Recovery Attitude and Treatment Evaluator (RAATE; Mee- Lee, 1988)	35/94	10- 30	Questionnaire or Interview	Trained Clinician or Assistant

	Treatment Services Review (TSR; McLellan, Alterman et al., 1992)	46	10-20	Structured Interview	Trained Clinician or Assistant
	Blood or Urine Chemical Markers	NA	5-30	Medical Procedure	Trained Clinician
6. Outcome Assessment	To assess substance abuse and dependence post-treatment outcome. Requires post-treatment follow-up of treatment participants				
	Form 90 Comprehensive Timeline of Alcohol and other drug use (Miller, 1996)	58	30-60	Structured Interview	Trained Clinician or Assistant
	Drinker Inventory of Consequences and Inventory of Drug Use Consequences (DrInC/INDUC; Miller et al., 1995)	15/50	5-15	Questionnaire or Interview	Trained Clinician or Assistant
	Psychosocial Functioning Inventory — Behavior and Role Functioning Subscales (PFI; Feragne et al., 1983)	14	5	Questionnaire or Interview	Trained Clinician or Assistant
	Short Form 36 (SF-36, SF-12; Ware et al., 1992; Ware et al., 1998)	12/36	3-10	Questionnaire or Interview	Trained Clinician or Assistant
Corroborative Assessment	To assess the veracity of self-reports through collaterals (e.g., significant other or professional), current use (e.g., urine or breathalyzer) or sustained use (e.g., blood level or urine tests) biological markers				
	Form 90-Collateral Self Report (Miller, 1996)	Varies	5-60	Questionnaire or Interview	Trained Clinician or Assistant
	Breathalyzer or Urine Drops	NA	1-30	Medical Procedure	Trained Clinician or Assistant

the secondary prevention of severe substance-use disorders (IOM, 1990; NIAAA, 1995a; NIAAA, 1995b). Screening for substance use can be accomplished effectively in non-substance-use-specialty medical and social service settings where individuals are seeking non-substance-abuse or dependence services. Screening for substance-use problems while individuals are seeking other medical or social services can be seen as an opportunistic event to engage individuals in primary or secondary substance-related programs (NIAAA, 1995b).

There are many measures available for screening of substance-use problems. A recent review of the literature has revealed over 30 such measures many of which have been developed in the past 5 years (McMurtry, Rose, & Cisler, 2003). An example of a recent screening measure for substance use is the revision of the Alcohol Use Disorders Identification Test (AUDIT; Babor, de la Fuente, Saunders, & Grant, 1992) to include other drugs (Alcohol Use Disorders Identification Test to Include Drugs — AUDIT-ID; Campbell, Barrett, Brondino, Cisler, Melchart, & Solliday McRoy, under review; Campbell, Barrett, Cisler, Solliday-McRoy, & Melchart, 2001). Other well-established measures are included in Table 7.1, including the Drug Abuse Screening Test (Skinner, 1982), the Rost Drug Abuse/Dependence Screener (Rost, Burnam, & Smith, 1993), and the Triage Assessment for Addictive Disorder (TAAD; Hoffman, 1995). These substance use screeners range from 3 to 30 or so items and require anywhere from 1 to 10 minutes for individuals to complete with the assistance of trained clinicians or research or administrative staff. Recent work (Rouse, Butcher, & Miller, 1999; Stein, Graham, Ben-Porath, & McNulty, 1999) suggests that clinicians may utilize MMPI-2 (Butcher, Dahlstrom, Graham, Tellegen, & Kaemmer, 1989) to screen substance-abuse problems.

Level 2 — Brief Problem Assessment

A fuller assessment of substance-use involvement is typically required once individuals are identified preliminarily as having a substance-use problem. However, all too often there are constraints on the amount of time clinicians can devote, how much time individuals with substance-use problems are willing to devote to problems assessment, or both. Recent developments in motivational interviewing and objective feedback of assessment results have shown promise in secondary prevention of further problem development (Bien, Miller, & Tonigan, 1993; Miller, 1985; Miller & Rollnick, 1991; Miller, Benefield, & Tonigan, 1993). The process of utilizing brief, standardized measures that have available nonclinical or subclinical norms can be a powerful strategy for providing objective feedback to individuals who may not be aware of how they compare with others in their level of substance use and related problems. Such data can be useful in the process of engaging the client in treatment.

Table 7.1 provides examples of measures that are brief yet characterize substance-use issues more fully than screening measures. For example, brief measures of alcohol use such as the Form 90-Quick (Miller, 1996) can characterize typical recent heavy drinking levels and compare clients' drinking to non-alcohol-disorder norms for heavy drinking. In addition, brief measures such as the Drinker Inventory of Consequences (DrInC) and its counterpart the Inventory of Drug Use Consequences (INDUC), both developed by Miller and colleagues (Miller, Tonigan, & Longabaugh, 1995), can provide a detailed picture of the types of consequences experienced by clients in relation to their alcohol and drug use, respectively. Measures such as the brief, 12-item Readiness to Change Questionnaire (RTCQ; Heather, Gold, & Rollnick, 1991; Heather, Rollnick, & Bell, 1993; Rollnick, Heather, Gold, & Hall, 1992) can provide a basis for discussing how ready (i.e., contemplation, action) or not (i.e., precontemplation) individuals may be for more formalized substance-use services.

Level 3 — Diagnosis

Although DSM-IV-TR (APA, 2000) diagnosis of substance abuse or dependence is required for insurance reimbursement, precise clinical diagnosis utilizing assessment tools such as the computer- or interviewer-administered structured clinical interview for DSM-IV (First et al., 1995a, 1995b) is rarely implemented in standard clinical practice.

A recent review of the literature revealed over 40 instruments targeting comprehensive substance-use or diagnosis assessment (McMurtry, Rose, & Cisler, 2003). The computer- or interviewer-administered structured clinical interview for DSM-IV (First et al., 1995a; 1995b) is a widely recognized, standardized assessment of substance-use disorders. A briefer, yet valid and reliable, option for substance-use disorder diagnosis is the Substance Dependence Severity Scale (SDSS; Miele, Carpenter, Cockerham, Trautman, Blaine, & Hasin, 2000). This measure still requires a trained clinician to assist in administration but takes substantially less time to complete.

Level 4 — Comprehensive Pretreatment Assessment

In order to understand the complex etiology, development, chronic, and debilitating nature of substance use, misuse, and dependence more fully, a comprehensive assessment of use, treatment history, bio-psycho-social factors, cultural and environmental contextual factors and potential mediating or moderating, effects of a range of intrapersonal, interpersonal, and environmental factors must be performed. Time constraints, however, preclude most clinicians from performing a comprehensive assessment, a practice more often accomplished in funded clinical trials on substance use.

This level of assessment is quite clearly the broadest of the 6 levels. A recent review of the substance-use literature found over 130 measures representing comprehensive pretreatment assessment such as substance use, use-related mediators and moderators, and comprehensive diagnosis (McMurtry, Rose, & Cisler, 2003). An example of a widely used measure that provides a more comprehensive picture of alcohol and drug involvement and associated problems is the Addiction Severity Index (ASI; McLellan, Kushner, Metzger, Peters, Smith, Grisson, Pettinati, & Argeriou, 1992; McClellan, Luborsky, Woody, & O'Brien, 1980), which assesses issues such as family history, legal issues, psychiatric comorbidity, and medical or health problems. Other measures that assess various alcohol or other drug-related issues include the Maudsley Addiction Profile (MAP; Marsden, Gossop, Stewart, Best, Farrell, Lehmann, Edwards, & Stang, 1998), Alcohol Abstinence Self Efficacy Scale (AASE; DiClemente, Carbonari, Montgomer, & Hughes, 1994), the Drug Avoidance Self-Efficacy Scales (DASES; Martin, Wilkonson, & Poulos, 1995), the Substance Abuse Relapse Assessment (SARA: Schonfeld, Peters, & Dolente, 1993), and the Desired Effects of Drinking (NIAAA, in press). Many of these measures are useful for developing a functional analysis of the client's substance use, relating causes and consequences to the substance use.

Level 5 — Treatment- Related Factors and Within Treatment Assessment

This level of assessment addresses client factors including reasons for seeking treatment, readiness, engagement, access, and utilization factors related to treatment. Another purpose of this level of assessment includes targeting treatment process factors, including treatment planning, goal attainment, and the therapeutic relationship between client and practitioner. Furthermore, this level of assessment can include assessing the fidelity and quality of the treatment approach provided. Much of these process-oriented assessments can offer the independent practitioner or agency administrators and stakeholders data for use in quality improvement of treatment initiatives.

The measures related to treatment initiation, access, and process are varied and can include client circumstances and treatment suitability (Circumstances, Motivation, Readiness and Suitability Scales [CMRS]; De Leon,

Melnick, Kressel, & Jainchill, 1994), client perceptions of self-change (Processes of Change Questionnaire [PCQ]; Prochaska, Velicer, DiClemente, & Fava, 1988), assessing the costs and benefits of changing alcohol or drug use problems (Alcohol and Drug Consequences Questionnaire [ADCQ]; Cunningham, Sobell, Gavin, Sobell, & Breslin, 1997), reasons and fears of treatment (Reasons and Fears about Treatment Questionnaire [RFTQ]; Oppenheimer, Sheehan, & Taylor, 1988), attitudes regarding recovery related to treatment (Recovery Attitude and Treatment Evaluator [RAATE]; Mee-Lee, 1988), or basic tracking of client utilization of services (Treatment Services Review [TSR]; McLellan, Alterman, Cacciola, Metzger, & O'Brien, 1992).

Level 6 — Outcome Assessment

Outcome assessment requires a before and during or a before and after treatment assessment of client status in order to determine either the change in relation to treatment (before and during), the change due to treatment (before and after), or both. Selection of outcome measures should be representative of the full array of dimensions related to the disorder being treated and assessed. For example, with respect to assessing alcoholism treatment outcome, practitioners should include measures of alcohol use (e.g., the Form 90 assesses the frequency and quantity of alcohol used on a daily basis; Miller, 1996), consequences of alcohol use (e.g., the DrInC assesses the intrapersonal, interpersonal, physical, impulse control, and social responsibility consequences related to alcohol use; Miller et al., 1995), potential mediators or moderators of outcome (e.g., AASE; DiClemente et al., 1994) as well as general non–alcohol specific functioning (e.g., Psychosocial Functioning Inventory; Feragne, Longabaugh, & Stevenson, 1983).

Too often practitioners have few administrative resources to conduct such lengthy and costly outcome assessments. However, developments in the science of assessment have made measuring outcomes more psychometrically sound and feasible (Bloom, Fischer, & Orme, 1995; Burnam, 1996). For example, Cisler and Berger (2001) demonstrated the utility of using a brief, easy-to-administer set of instruments to assess alcohol treatment outcome including the Form 90-Quick (Miller, 1996), the Short Index of Problems (Miller et al., 1995), two PFI subscales (Feragne et al., 1983) and the SF-12 (Ware, Kosinski, & Keller, 1998; Ware & Sherbourne, 1992). Outcome measures for substance-use services would in turn need to be broad enough to include daily use as well as the personal and social consequences of such use. A timeline follow-back approach to document daily illicit drug use and measures such as the Inventory of Drug Use

Consequences (Miller et al., 1995) could quite competently assess use and related consequence outcomes of substance-use services. However, briefer forms of these measures have not been developed for quick administration purposes making the assessment of substance-use outcomes more time consuming and cumbersome. For example, perhaps the most widely used measure for assessing substance-use outcomes is the Addiction Severity Index (McLellan et al., 1992; McLellan et al., 1980), which contains about 200 items and takes anywhere from 45 to 60 minutes to complete.

☐ Pragmatic Issues Encountered in Clinical Practice

As a general principle, the further along the continuum of assessment levels the practitioner engages his or her clients, the more resources she or he will require in terms of time and cost commitments. An exception is that, for example, a fairly informative treatment process evaluation (i.e., Level 5) can be conducted without conducting a comprehensive pretreatment problem assessment (i.e., Level 4). However, even though client time might be kept to a minimum in a treatment process evaluation, the amount of time required by the practitioner to collect data and then interpret findings and apply findings to treatment modification and improvement might be extensive. Clearly, outcome assessment (i.e., Level 6) is the most prohibitive level of assessment not only in terms of interview and medical procedure cost factors but also because of client confidentiality issues involved in these procedures. Outcome assessment requires extensive client monitoring and tracking procedures in order to gather follow-up data posttreatment.

A number of practical issues need to be considered when implementing screening measures in clinical practice. For example, identifying substance-use problems requires a fairly efficient, thorough, and responsive treatment system to meet the immediate or long-term service utilization needs of these individuals. All too often health and social service professionals fail to ask about substance-use problems because they have no means of addressing these concerns or know of proper resources for referring individuals for specialized services. Recent medically based strategies have shown promise in dealing with substance-use issues in nonspecialized settings including a simple model to "Ask," "Advise," and "Assist" for primary care physicians (Center for Substance Abuse Treatment, 2000). This model has potential for use in other medical or mental health settings (e.g., emergency rooms, outpatient psychiatric clinics) and social service settings (e.g., probation and parole, faith-based community programs, homeless shelters).

Administering brief measures to assess pretreatment client status and for use in providing feedback to facilitate client engagement into formalized treatment services is perhaps the most useful and practical level of assessment available to practitioners. With their brevity and focus, brief problem assessment measures can be used in everyday clinical practice without overburdening the practitioner and patient and yet still provide a useful service in comparing patient responses to general nonclinical or subclinical populations. For example, we have experienced clients reacting most to the feedback about the number of standard drinks they consume per week compared to other men or women in the United States. Patients have commented how this message on the quantity of their drinking "stayed with them" and was used as motivation to reduce their drinking to the level of the general population. Also, clients have stated that feedback on the magnitude of the estimated blood alcohol concentration on their heaviest drinking day and their average drinking day has served as strong indicator of the level of tolerance that they have developed to alcohol and the potential for problems that can occur under this intoxicated state. Clients also have communicated that feedback on the DrInC subscales provides a direct connection between drinking, becoming intoxicated, and the occurrence of subsequent problems. Most clients also find helpful the focus on how drinking has put them at risk for experiencing certain types of problems (i.e., the DrInC subscales of intrapersonal, interpersonal, physical, impulse control, and social responsibility consequences).

Sometimes, however, it has been our experience that clients are reluctant to complete measures. Oftentimes, it helps to reassure clients that no one response will "label" them as having a problem, that the measures are not meant to "trick" them in any way but rather the measures simply allow us to get a clear, concise picture of what their alcohol or drug use has been like. More importantly, we emphasize that the results of the assessment are designed to help them to decide what they want to do and stress that it is not the practitioner's role to make decisions for them.

Related to the feedback itself, clients sometimes react negatively to any individual piece of feedback or the feedback as a whole. It is important to "roll with" this resistance and try to reflect on their reaction (e.g., "Does that seem too high?" "Do you think that there's no way you drink that much in a week?" "It seems that only using cocaine one time in the past week is progress for you."). It has been helpful to encourage individuals to talk about their views or concerns regarding the data ("I don't drink more than anyone else," "All my friends drink more than me," "I'm not a skid row druggie," "I work, I care for my family"). However, once these statements are made by clients, it is helpful to move on to the next item and not spend time defending the instrument or explaining how it was developed. In this way, the therapist avoids putting clients at ease that might only dissipate the emotional reaction to the feedback. In these instances, therapists should acknowledge the client's reaction and move on. Encouraging discussion about thoughts, feelings, and concerns is perhaps the most powerful self-motivational strategy that might, in turn, reduce ambivalence regarding risky use and enhance the client's readiness to change alcohol- and drug-use practices.

Contrary to the belief that substance abusers underreport or "deny" use, researchers have shown that self-reports are accurate and can be reported with confidence if data are gathered under certain conditions (Babor, Brown, & Del Boca, 1990; Babor & DelBoca, 1992; Brown, Kranzler, & Del Boca, 1992; Del Boca & Noll, 200; Maisto & Connors, 1990; Sobell & Sobell, 1995; Sobell, Toneatto, Sobell, Gloria, & Johnson, 1992). According to Sobell and Sobell (1995), factors that enhance the accuracy of self-reported alcohol use include: (1) individuals should be alcohol free, (2) individuals are assured confidentiality, (3) the interview is conducted in a clinical or research setting promoting honest reporting, and (4) the interview questions are clear and understandable. For example, the validity of self-reported alcohol and substance use can be enhanced with the use of the Form 90 interview which, in part, uses a calendar method shown to enhance the accuracy of participants' memory of alcohol use (Babor & Del Boca, 1992; Miller, 1996; Sobell & Sobell, 1995). Other procedures should be implemented such as the use of a alcohol breathalyzer, to assure that subjects are alcohol-free when interviewed. Furthermore, corroborative measures such as blood and urine specimens can be used to enhance the veracity of self-reports although researchers have found high concordance between self-reports and biological measures (Babor & Del Boca, 1992; Babor, Steinberg, Anton & Del Boca, 2000).

Corroborative assessments, in terms of collateral information (e.g., reports of significant others or therapists/practitioners) or biological markers (e.g., blood or urine screens for alcohol or drug use), can serve as either verification of client self-reports or as an outcome indicator, or both (Litten & Allen, 1992). Random urine screens, for example, have been used traditionally in long-term residential or inpatient care facilities as a check for whether clients or patients are clean and sober from drugs and alcohol, which oftentimes is a requirement for program services. Other indicators such as a simple blood alcohol concentration breathalyzer reading can be used to assure that clients are not under the influence of alcohol during their clinic visit. Laboratory blood assays are useful indicators for assessing liver functioning complications due to long-term, chronic use (e.g., gamma-glutamyltranspeptidase, mean corpuscular volume) and shorter-term heavy alcohol consumption (carbohydrate deficient transferrin). Client or patient self-reports can also be corroborated by self-reported observations of substance use by significant others such as a spouse, partner, sponsor, or practitioner or by clinical judgments of client or patient functioning made by these same individuals.

☐ Case Illustration

Client Description

Ted is a 21-year-old, white male, referred by his physician because of continuing complaints of anxiety. Ted comes from an intact blue-collar family. His father is a factory worker and his mother is a housewife. He has two older brothers and one younger sister. He currently supports himself by working as a busboy at a high-end local restaurant. He has worked as a busboy for nearly 2 years. He also is trying to attend college. He lives alone in a rented apartment.

History of the Problem

Ted reported that he has always been uncomfortable around people other than his immediate family and one or two friends he has had since childhood. Ted describes himself as extremely shy. He has vivid memories of being teased as a child by his siblings and peers because he was so awkward in social situations. As a result, he spent most of his free time alone to avoid embarrassing himself in social situations and risk being teased. Since adolescence, he has realized that he is more fearful of social situations than others. Though he pushes himself to face the inevitable social encounters of school and work, he does so with marked and persistent anxiety and distress.

Presenting Complaints

Ted reported that he becomes very anxious in nearly all social situations. He is most anxious when meeting new people or talking to young women. He tends to avoid eye-contact and conversation with most people, except for family and close friends. At work, he stated that he experiences high levels of anxiety when he must enter the dining room and interact with customers. In fact, he begins to become anxious long before he begins work. When anxious, he feels his heart pounding and his thoughts racing, and becomes convinced that others will detect how anxious he feels.

Ted is also a student at a local technical college, but has dropped out each of the past three semesters after a few weeks of attending classes. He reported being extremely anxious walking down a crowded hall, interacting with other students, and especially when talking in class.

Although he avoids all social encounters at school and has never dated, Ted will join coworkers for a drink after work. He also goes out with his neighbor, a lifelong friend who has a large circle of friends and often invites Ted to join him. These outings usually involve going to a bar and Ted always drinks "a few beers" in order to feel more comfortable. Ted also reported that he will occasionally smoke marijuana when with his neighbor's group of friends.

☐ Assessment Methods Used and Psychological Assessment Protocol

Level 1: Screening

During the second session, Ted was given the Burns Anxiety Inventory (Burns, 1993) to evaluate the extent and nature of Ted's anxiety. He scored a 52, indicating extreme anxiety and panic. This measure was used to structure the discussion about his anxious symptoms. His highest scores related to racing, anxious thoughts ("I'll make a fool of myself" or "They'll think I'm stupid") and panic symptoms when in highly stressful situations. He had developed a mixed pattern of avoidant behaviors. At work, he pushed himself to complete anxiety-producing tasks but rushed through them. This often resulted in accidents, which reinforced his anxious beliefs. He began each of the last three school semesters enduring his anxiety but eventually fell behind in the class work and ended up dropping out. He avoided all social situations at school, and was able to tolerate going out with friends or coworkers only if he drank. Though he reported smoking marijuana, this did not help ease his anxiety but rather made him more "paranoid," more fearful of how others were judging him. As Ted reported drinking as a regular part of his involvement in social situations, his alcohol consumption seemed to warrant further investigation.

Level 2: Brief Problem Assessment

During the third session, Ted was asked to give a more detailed picture of his drinking. In response to questioning, he reported that on a typical evening out he would have 6 to 8 beers, and sometimes (once or twice a month) he would have 2 to 4 shots of whatever liquor the group was drinking in addition to the beers. Two or three times a week he went out for a drink after work and drank two or three beers in a 2-hour period. He also reported smoking marijuana once or twice a month but did not view this as a problem. He never bought marijuana himself, did not care for the way it made him feel, but would smoke when offered some in order to "fit in."

Levels 3 and 4: Diagnosis and Comprehensive Assessment

In addition to the social anxiety problems that brought Ted to treatment, further exploration of Ted's substance use seemed warranted. As Ted reported a pattern of binge drinking in social situations (that is, drinking more than 5 drinks at one sitting), he was asked to complete a battery of six instruments. His scores on these six instruments and their interpretation are given below:

1. On the Alcohol Use Disorders Identification Test (AUDIT; Babor et al. 1992), Ted scored 12, indicating a moderate level of problems compared to others seeking help for a drinking problem.
2. On the Alcohol Dependence Scale (ADS, Skinner & Allen, 1982), Ted scored 2, indicating a low level of problems due to his drinking.
3. On the Drinker's Inventory of Consequences (DrInC, Miller et al. 1995), Ted scored 4-0-0-6-2 (for the physical, relationship, personal, impulsive, and social responsibility scales, respectively), indicating few problems related to drinking except in the areas of physical health and impulsive actions.
4. On the Alcohol Abstinence Self-Efficacy (AASE; Di Clemente et al. 1994), Ted scored 15, 17, 19, and 2 (for the unpleasant emotions, positive social situations, physical concerns, and urges and temptations scales, respectively) confirming that he was most tempted to drink in social situations and to manage his feelings of anxiety and worry.
5. On the Desired Effects of Drinking (DED; NIAAA, in press), Ted scored high on three scales, indicating that he drank to feel good (6), to

facilitate social situations (8), and to manage negative feelings (9). On all other scales he scored 0 to 2.

6. On the Readiness to Change Questionnaire (RTCQ; Heather et al., 1993), Ted scored highest on the precontemplative scale, indicating he did not see his drinking as a problem and was not currently thinking about quitting.

Ted completed these measures in the last half hour of the third session and the therapist took 10 to 15 minutes to score and complete the feedback form. In addition, 5 to 10 minutes were used to gather the specific information on his drinking and marijuana use in order to provide feedback specific to his pattern of drinking (using a modified Form 90). An additional 5 minutes were needed to convert this information into standard drinks per week and estimated blood alcohol level using the BACCHAS (Markham, Miller, & Arciniega, 1991) computer program. All these assessments were billed as part of the third session.

Based on these assessment data, Ted was given the following diagnoses:

Axis I: 300.23: Social Phobia, Generalized
    305.00: Alcohol Abuse
    292.89: Cannabis Intoxication
Axis II: None
Axis III: No health problems reported
Axis IV: Stress of school, work, social encounters
Axis V: GAF 55

Level 5: Feedback and Treatment Selection

Feedback was presented in the fourth session and used to structure the discussion of his drinking and how it related to his anxiety. As Ted was in the precontemplative stage of change (i.e., did not see his drinking as a problem and was not considering changing his drinking behavior), the therapist focused on enhancing his readiness to change his drinking behavior as well as providing basic information about alcohol and drinking problems, including: binge drinking, tolerance, dependence, and alcohol's biphasic effects on anxiety.

The feedback provided information in three areas: drinking, problem severity, and a functional analysis.

Drinking

In a typical month, Ted drank 14 out of 30 days. On 8 of these days he drank heavily (5 or more drinks) and on 6 he reported light drinking. In a typical week, Ted drank 21.6 standard drinks; at this rate, he was drinking more than 91% of other men in the United States (this comparison was made utilizing data from the National Alcohol Survey; Caetano & Tam, 1995). His estimated BAL was 0.084 mg/% on his typical heavy drinking days and 0.149 mg/% on the heaviest drinking day that he reported. Ted reacted most strongly to the total number of drinks he had each week and how this number compared with other American men.

Problem Severity

Ted scored 12 on the AUDIT, indicating a moderate level of problems compared to others seeking help for a drinking problem, and 2 on the ADS, indicating a low level of problems. His scores on the DrInC indicated few problems related to drinking except in the area of physical health and impulsive actions. When discussing these findings, Ted related an incident where, after excessive drinking, he had been kicked out of a bar for harassing female customers. He admitted that his drinking contributed to his problems at school: after a night of drinking he would miss classes the following day and fall behind in his homework.

Functional Analysis

The AASE showed that Ted was most tempted to drink in social situations and to manage feelings of anxiety and worry. The DED found that he drank to feel good, facilitate social situations, and manage negative feelings. The RTC indicated that Ted did not see his drinking as a problem and had not thought of changing his drinking. Ted agreed that he drank primarily in social situations and that he used alcohol to help him manage his anxiety. He was reluctant to give up drinking because it helped him function in social situations that he would otherwise avoid. This led to a discussion of the biphasic effect of alcohol on anxiety. Finally, the treatment of social anxiety was discussed. The therapist shared concerns that drinking would interfere with Ted's learning new skills to manage anxiety and building his confidence when using these skills in social situations.

The feedback session was billed as the fourth treatment session.

Target Selected for Treatment

Ted agreed to abstain from alcohol while in treatment for social anxiety. He was asked to keep an anxiety log, in which he would record his anxiety level in a variety of situations using a score from 0–100 and describe the situation. His marijuana use was not addressed directly, though Ted agreed to continue to monitor both drinking and marijuana use as part of his anxiety log. In this way, he and his therapist could see if his marijuana use interfered with treatment and could keep track of his compliance with his abstinence goal. Ted also agreed to a psychiatric consultation for medication as he had been using alcohol to manage his anxiety. Lastly, Ted and his therapist agreed that, after anxiety treatment, therapy would focus on helping Ted develop skills to moderate his drinking and to identify behaviors that might indicate his drinking was becoming a problem (i.e., that he was not able to moderate his use of alcohol).

Assessment of Progress

Ted initially was able to abstain from alcohol, but had three episodes of drinking as he began in vivo exposure to anxiety-provoking social situations. He reported no use of marijuana during his treatment, stating that this was relatively easy because he had not been drinking when he was offered marijuana. Functional analyses of each of his three drinking episodes showed that Ted was using alcohol to manage his anxiety. In addition, in one incident he did not attempt to use the anxiety-reducing skills he had learned in session and in two incidents he did not persevere in his attempts to utilize these skills. Based on these analyses, Ted was able to recommit to his decision to abstain during the course of treatment. After 4 months, he was able to reduce his anxious symptoms successfully in a variety of social situations. He had enrolled in classes and was confident that he would be able to complete the semester. Although he did return to drinking, Ted was able to moderate his use. He reported drinking once or twice a week and drinking one to three drinks any time he drank. When he first came to treatment, Ted's GAF was 65. At the end of treatment, his GAF was 80.

Ted was given this diagnosis at termination:

Axis I: 300.23: Social Phobia, Generalized, in early remission
    305.03: Alcohol Abuse, in remission
    292.89 Cannabis Intoxication, in remission
Axis II: None
Axis III: No health problems reported
Axis IV: Stress of school, work, social encounters
Axis V: GAF 80

☐ Summary

As most, if not all clinicians will probably be faced with clients with substance-use and abuse issues comorbid with behavior disorders, this chapter attempted to provide the clinician with a multilevel approach to the assessment of substance abuse. The six levels of assessment presented in this chapter provide the clinician with choices about assessment tools and about the extent of assessment desired. These range from screening instruments to instruments to motivate the client for treatment, select appropriate treatment alternatives, and evaluate treatment progress and outcome. Depending on the clinician's interest and training, as well as time and ability to be reimbursed for assessment, the clinician may choose to pursue merely screening of substance-use and abuse issues only or may select a more comprehensive assessment.

☐ References

American Psychiatric Association. (2000). Diagnostic and statistical manual of mental disorders (4th ed., text revision). Washington, DC: American Psychiatric Association.

Babor, T. F., Brown, J., & Del Boca, F. K. (1990). Validity of self-reports in applied research on addictive behaviors: Fact or fiction? Behavioral Assessment, 12(1), 5–31.

Babor, T. F., & Del Boca, F. K. (1992). Just the facts: Enhancing measurement of alcohol consumption using self-report methods. In R. Z. Litten & J. P. Allen (Eds.), Measuring alcohol consumption: Psychological and biochemical methods (pp. 3–19). Totowa, NJ: Human Press.

Babor, T. F., Steinberg, K., Anton, R., & Del Boca, F. K. (2000). Talk is cheap: Measuring drinking outcomes in clinical trials. Journal of Studies on Alcohol, 61 (1), 5563.

Babor, T. F., de la Fuente, J. R., Saunders, J., & Grant, M. (1992). AUDIT, The Alcohol Use Disorders Identification Test: Guidelines for use in primary health care. Geneva: World Health Organization.

Ball, S., & Kosten, T. (1994). Diagnostic classification systems. In N. Miller (Ed.), Principles of addiction measure (sec. 4, ch.6, pp. 1–9). Chevy Chase, MD: American Society of Addiction Medicine.

Bien, T. H., Miller, W. R., & Tonigan, J. S. (1993). Brief interventions for alcohol problems: A review. Addiction, 88, 315–335.

Bloom, M., Fischer, J., & Orme, J. G. (1995). Evaluating practice: Guidelines for the accountable professional (2nd ed.). Boston: Allyn and Bacon, 1–681.

Brown, J., Kranzler, H. R., & Del Boca, F. K. (1992). Self–reports by alcohol and drug abuse patients: Factors affecting reliability and validity. British Journal of Addiction, 87(7), 1013–1024.

Burnam, M. A. (1996). Measuring outcomes of care for substance use and mental disorders. In H. R. Lamb (Ed.), New directions for mental health services: Using client outcomes information to improve mental health and substance abuse treatment. San Francisco, CA: Jossey-Bass.

Burns, D. D. (1993). Ten days to self-esteem. New York: William Morrow.

Butcher, J. N., Dahlstrom, W. G., Graham, J. R., Tellegen, A., & Kaemer, B. (1989). Minnesota Multiphasic Personality Inventory-2 (MMPI-2): Manual for administering and scoring. Minneapolis: University of Minnesota.

Caetano, R., & Tam. T. W. (1995). Prevalence and correlates of DSM-IV and ICD-10) alcohol dependence: 1990 U.S. National Alcohol Survey. Alcohol and Alcoholism, 30, 177–186.

Campbell, T. C., Barrett, D., Cisler, R. A., Solliday-McRoy, C., & Melchart, T. P. (2001). Reliability estimates of the Alcohol Use Disorders Identification Test revised to include other drugs (AUDIT 12). Alcoholism: Clinical and Experimental Research, 25(5, Suppl.), Abstract 242, 47A.

Campbell, T. C., Barrett, D., Brondino, M. J., Cisler, R. A., Melchart, T. P., & Solliday McRoy, C. (Under review). Alcohol Use Disorders Identification Test-Revised to Include Other Drugs (AUDIT-ID): An exploratory factor analysis of data from homeless men.

Caton, C. L., Gralnick, A., Bender, S., & Simon, R. (1989). Young chronic patients and substance abuse. Hospital and Community Psychiatry, 40, 1037–1040.

Center for Substance Abuse Treatment. (2000). A guide to substance abuse services for primary care clinicians: Treatment Improvement Protocol (TIP) Series 24 (E. Sullivan & M. Fleming, Co-Chairs). Rockville, MD: U.S. Department of Health and Human Services, Substance Abuse and Mental Health, Center for Substance Abuse Treatment.

Cisler, R. A., & Berger, L. (2001). Assessing alcoholism treatment composite outcome: Further evidence utilizing brief measures. Journal of Mental Health, 10(6), 657–672.

Cunningham, J. A., Sobell, L. C., Gavin, D. R., Sobell, M. B., & Breslin, F. C. (1997). Assessing motivation for change: Preliminary development and evaluation of a scale measuring the cost and benefits of changing alcohol or drug use. Psychology of Addictive Behavior, 11(2), 107–114.

Del Boca, T. F., & Noll, J. A. (2000). Truth or consequences: Validity of self-report data in health services research on addictions. Addiction, 95(Suppl. 3), 347–360.

De Leon, G., Melnick, G., Kressel, D., & Jainchill, N. (1994). Circumstances, Motivation, Readiness, and Suitability (The CMRS Scales): Predicting retention in therapeutic community treatment. American Journal of Drug and Alcohol Abuse, 20(4), 495–515.

Di Clemente, C. G., Carbonari, J. P., Montgomery, R. P. G., & Hughes, S. O. (1994). The alcohol abstinence self-efficacy scale. Journal of Studies on Alcohol, 55(2), 141–148.

Drake, R. E. & Wallach, M. A. (1989). Substance abuse among the chronic mentally ill. Hospital and Community Psychiatry, 40, 1041–1046.

Feragne, M. A., Longabaugh, R., & Stevenson, J. F. (1983). The Psychosocial Functioning Inventory. Evaluation and the Health Professions, 6, 25–41.

First, M., Gibbon, M., Williams, J., & Spitzer, R. (1995a). SCID screen patient questionnaire computer program (Computer software). Washington, DC: American Psychiatric Association and North Tonawanda, NY: Multi-Health Systems.

First, M., Gibbon, M., Williams, J., & Spitzer, R. (1995b). Structured clinical interview for DSM-IV Axis I disorders: Clinician version (User's guide, administration booklet and scoresheet). Washington, DC: American Psychiatric Association and North Tonawanda, NY: Multi-Health Systems.

Heather, N., Gold, R., & Rollnick, S. (1991). Readiness to Change Questionnaire: User's Manual, Technical Report 15. National Drug and Alcohol Research Centre, University of South Wales, Kensington, Australia.

Heather, N., Rollnick, S., & Bell, A. (1993). Predictive validity of the Readiness to Change Questionnaire. Addiction, 88, 1667.

Hesselbrock, M. N., & Hesselbrock, V. M. (1996). Depression and antisocial personality disorder in alcoholism: Gender Comparison. In E. L. Gomberg & T. D. Nirenberg (Eds.), Women and substance abuse (pp. 142–161). Norwood, NJ: Ablex Publishing.

Hoffman, N. G. (1995). TAAD, Triage Assessment for Addictive Disorders: Manual. Smithfield, RI: Evince Clinical Assessments.

Institute of Medicine (1990). Broadening the base of treatment for alcohol problems. Washington, D.C: National Academy Press.

Kandel, D. B., Huang, F. Y., & Davies, M. (2001). Comorbidity between patterns of substance use dependence and psychiatric syndromes. Drug and Alcohol Dependence, 64, 233–241.

Kanwischer, R. W., & Hundley, J. (1990). Screening for substance abuse in hospitalized psychiatric patients. Hospital and Community Psychiatry, 41, 795–797.

Kessler, R. C., McGonagle, K. A., Zhao, S., Nelson, C. B., Hughes, M. Eshleman, S. Wittchen, H., & Kendler, K. S. (1994). Lifetime and 12-month prevalence of DSM-III-R psychiatric disorders in the United States: Results from the National Comorbidity Study. Archives of General Psychiatry, 51, 8–19.

Kessler, R. C., Nelson, C. B., McGonagle, K. A., Edlund, M. J., Frank, R. G., & Leaf, P. J. (1996). The epidemiology of co-occurring addictive and mental disorders: Implications for prevention and service utilization. American Journal of Orthopsychiatry, 66, 17–31.

Kessler, R. C. (1997). The prevalence of psychiatric comorbidity. In S. Wetzler & W. C. Sanderson (Eds.), Treatment strategies for patients with psychiatric comorbidity (pp.23–48). New York: Wiley.

Litten, R. Z., & Allen, J. P. (Eds.). (1992). Measuring alcohol consumption: Psychosocial and biochemical methods. Totowa, NJ: Human Press.

Maisto, S. A., & Connors, G. J. (1990). Clinical diagnostic techniques and assessment tools in alcohol research. Alcohol Health and Research World, 14(3), 232–238.

Markham, M. R., Miller, W. R., & Arciniega, L. (1991) BACCHUS: Blood Alcohol Concentration Calculation System (Version 2.01) [Computer software]. Albuquerque: University of New Mexico.

Marsden, J., Gossop, M., Stewart, D., Best, D., Farrell, M., Lehmann, P., Edwards, C. & Strang, J. (1998). The Maudsley Addiction Profile (MAP): A brief instrument for assessing treatment outcome. Addiction, 93(12), 1857–1867.

Martin, G. W., Wilkinson, D. A., & Poulos, C. X. (1995). The Drug Avoidance Self-Efficacy Scale. Journal of Substance Abuse, 7(2), 151–163.

McCrady, B. S., & Epstein, E. E. (1999). Addictions: A comprehensive guidebook. London: Oxford University Press.

McLellan, A. T., Luborsky, L., O'Brien, C. P., & Woody, G. E. (1980). An improved diagnostic instrument for substance abuse patients: The Addiction Severity Index. Journal of Nervous and Mental Disorders, 168, 26–33.

McLellan, A. T., Kushner, H., Metzger, D., Peters, R., Smith, I., Grisson, G., Pettinati, H., & Argeriou, M. (1992). The fifth edition of the Addiction Severity Index. Journal of Substance Abuse Treatment, 9, 199–213.

McMurtry, S. L., Rose, S. J., & Cisler, R. A. (2003). Identifying and Administering the Most-Used Rapid Assessment Instruments. Seventh Annual Conference of the Society for Social Work and Research. Washington, D.C. (January).

Mee-Lee, D. (1988). An instrument for treatment progress and matching: The Recovery Attitude and Treatment Evaluator (RAATE). Journal of Substance Abuse Treatment, 5, 183–186.

Miele, G. M., Carpenter, K. M., Cockerham, M. S., Trautman, K. D., Blaine, J., & Hasin, D. S. (2000). Substance Dependence Severity Scale (SDSS): Reliability and validity of a clinician-administered interview for DSM-IV substance use disorders. Drug and Alcohol Dependence, 59, 63–75.

Miller, W. R. (1985). Motivation for treatment: A review with special emphasis on alcoholism. Psychological Bulletin, 98, 84–107.

Miller, W. R. (1996). Form 90: A structured assessment interview for drinking and related behaviors. In M. E. Mattson (Ed.), NIAAA Project MATCH Monograph Series (Vol. 5). Bethesda, MD: U.S. Department of Health and Human Services, National Institute on Health.

Miller, W. R., Benefield, R. G., & Tonigan, J. S. (1993). Enhancing motivation for change in problem drinking: A controlled comparison of two therapist styles. Journal of Consulting and Clinical Psychology, 61, 455–461.

Miller, W. R., & Rollnick, S. (1991). Motivational interviewing: Preparing people to change addictive behavior. New York: Guilford.

Miller, W. R., Tonigan, J. S., & Longabaugh, R. (1995). The Drinker Inventory of Consequences (DrInC): An instrument for assessing adverse consequences of alcohol abuse. In M. E. Mattson (Ed.), NIAAA Project MATCH Monograph Series (Vol. 6). Bethesda, MD: U.S. Department of Health and Human Services, National Institute on Health.

Mueser, K. T., Yarnold, P. R., Levinson, D. F., Singh, H., Bellack, A. S., Kee, K. Morrison, R., & Yadalam, K. G. (1990). Prevalence of substance abuse in schizophrenia: Demographic and clinical correlates. Schizophrenia Bulletin, 16, 31–56.

Nathan, P. E., Skinstad, A. H., & Langenbucher, J. W. (1999). Substance abuse: Diagnosis, comorbidity, and psychopathology. In T. Millon & P. H. Blaney (Eds.), Oxford textbook of psychopathology (pp. 227–248). London: Oxford University Press.

National Institute on Alcohol Abuse and Alcoholism. (In press). Combined behavioral intervention (CBI) treatment manual. Bethesda, MD: U.S. Department of Health and Human Services, Public Health Services, National Institute of Health.

National Institute on Alcohol Abuse and Alcoholism (1997). Ninth special report to the U.S. Congress on alcohol and health. Bethesda, MD: U.S. Department of Health and Human Services, Public Health Services, National Institute on Health.

National Institute on Alcohol Abuse and Alcoholism (1995a). Diagnostic criteria for alcohol abuse and dependence. Alcohol Alert, 30(October). Bethesda, MD: U.S. Department of Health and Human Services, Public Health Services, National Institute on Health.

National Institute on Alcohol Abuse and Alcoholism (1995b). The physician's guide to helping patients with alcohol problems. Bethesda, MD: U.S. Department of Health and Human Services, Public Health Services, National Institute on Health.

National Institute on Drug Abuse. (1994). Fourth triennial report to Congress on drug abuse and drug abuse research. Washington, D.C.: U.S. Department of Health and Human Services, Public Health Services, National Institute on Health.

Oppenheimer, E., Sheehan, M., & Taylor, C. (1988). Letting the client speak: Drug misusers and the process of help seeking. British Journal of Addiction, 83, 635–647.

Prochaska, J. O., Velicer, W. F., Di Clemente, C. C., & Fava, J. (1988). Measuring processes of change: Applications to the cessation of smoking. Journal of Consulting and Clinical Psychology, 56(4), 520–528.

Reiger, D. A., Farmer, M. E., Rae, D. S., Locke, B. Z., Keith, S. J., Judd, L. L., & Goodwin, F. K. (1990). Comorbidity of mental disorders with alcohol and other drug abuse: Results from the Epidemiologic Catchment Area (ECA) study. Journal of the American Medical Association (JAMA), 264(19), 2511–2518.

Rollnick, S., Heather, N., Gold, R., & Hall, W. (1992). Development of a short "Readiness to Change" questionnaire for use in brief opportunistic interventions. British Journal of Addictions, 87, 743–754.

Ross, H. E., Glaser, F. B., & Germanson, T. (1988). The prevalence of psychiatric disorders in patients with alcohol and other drug problems. Archives of General Psychiatry, 45, 1023–1031.

Rost, K., Burnam, M. A., & Smith, G. R. (1993). Development of screeners for depressive disorders and substance disorder history. Medical Care, 31(3), 189–200.

Rouse, S. V., Butcher, J. N., & Miller, K. B. (1999). Assessment of substance abuse in psychotherapy clients: The effectiveness of the MMPI-2 Substance Abuse Scales. Psychological Assessment, 11(1), 101–107.

Safer, D. J. (1987). Substance use by young adult chronic patients. Hospital and Community Psychiatry, 38, 511–514.

Schonfeld, L., Peters, R., & Dolente, A. (1993). SARA — Substance Abuse Relapse Assessment: Professional manual. Odessa, FL: Psychological Assessment Resources.

Skinner, H. A. (1982). The Drug Abuse Screening Test. Addictive Behaviors, 7, 363–371.

Skinner, H. A. & Horn, J. L. (1984). Alcohol Dependence Scale: User's Guide. Toronto: Addiction Research Foundation.

Skinstad, A. H., Eliason, M. J., Gerken, K., Spratt, K. F., Lutz, G. M., & Childress, K. (1996). Alcohol and drug abuse among Iowa women: Iowa State Needs Assessment Project. Iowa City: The Univeristy of Iowa.

Sobell, L. C., Kwan, E., & Sobell, M. B. (1995). Reliability of a Drug History Questionnaire (DHQ). Addictive Behaviors, 20(2), 233–241.

Sobell, L. C., & Sobell, M. B. (1995). Alcohol consumption measures. In J. P. Allen & M. Columbus (Eds.), Assessing alcohol problems: A guide for clinicians and researchers. Treatment handbook series 4. Bethesda, MD: National Institute on Alcohol Abuse and Alcoholism.

Sobell, L. C., Toneatto, T., Sobell, M. B., Gloria, I. L., & Johnson, L. (1992). Alcohol abusers' perceptions of the accuracy of their self-reports of drinking: Implications for treatment. Addictive Behaviors, 17(5), 508–511.

Stein, L. A. R., Graham, J. R., Ben-Porath, Y. S., & McNulty, J. L. (1999). Using the MMPI-2 to detect substance abuse in an outpatient mental health setting. Psychological Assessment, 11(1), 94–100.

Ware, J. E., Kosinski, M., & Keller, S. D. (1998). SF-12: How to score the SF-12 Physical and Mental Health Summary Scales (3rd Ed.). Lincoln, RI: Quality Metric, Inc.

Ware, J. E., & Sherbourne, C. D. (1992). The MOS 36-item short-form health status survey (SF-36): 1. Conceptual framework and item selection. Medical Care, 30, 473–483.

Wilson, G. T., Nathan, P. E., O'Leary, K. D., & Clark, L. A. (1996). Abnormal psychology: Integrating perspectives. Needham Heights, MA: Allyn and Bacon.

Tiffany M. Stewart
Donald A. Williamson

Assessment of Eating Disorders

☐ Description of the Problem

Eating disorders, as defined by the *Diagnostic and Statistical Manual of Mental Disorders*, 4th edition (American Psychiatric Association; DSM-IV, 1994), may be conceptualized as having multiple symptom domains that should be assessed. We believe that there are six essential features of eating disorders that should be measured: body size, binge eating, compensatory behavior (e.g., purging), restrictive eating, body image, and general psychopathology. To establish an eating disorder diagnosis, DSM-IV diagnostic criteria, summarized in Table 8.1, should be used.

In this review, we have selected assessment methods that can be used for specific objectives, including screening measures, diagnostic interviews, multisymptom measures, measures that assess pathological eating, body image, body weight, comorbid pathology, and special problems. Table 8.2 provides a summary of the methods reviewed in this chapter and describes the symptom domains that are measured by each procedure. Recommendations are made for an assessment battery pertaining to eating disorders.

TABLE 8.1. Summary of DSM–IV Criteria for Anorexia and Bulimia Nervosa

---

DSM- IV Criteria for Anorexia Nervosa

A. Refusal to maintain body weight at or above a minimally normal weight for age and height.

B. Despite being underweight, the person has an intense fear of gaining weight or becoming fat.

C. Body image disturbance. Denial of seriousness of low weight status.

D. The absence of atleast three consecutive menstrual cycles (in females who have past puberty).

Types:

Restricting type: The person has not regularly engaged in in binge- eating or compensatory (i.e. purging behavior).

Binge-Eating/Purging type: The person has regularly engaged in binge- eating or compensatory behavior.

DSM- IV Criteria for Bulimia Nervosa

A. Episodes of binge eating that are recurrent. An episode of binge eating has both of the following characteristics:

(1) eating in a discrete period of time an objectively large amount of food, and
(2) a sense of lack of control over eating during the episode.

B. Recurrent compensatory behavior in order to prevent weight gain (e.g., self- induced vomiting; misuse of laxatives, diuretics, enemas, or other medications; fasting; or excessive exercise).

C. The binge eating and compensatory behaviors both occur at least twice a week for 3 months.

D. Self- evaluation is strongly influenced by body shape and weight.

E. The disturbance does not occur exclusively during episodes of anorexia nervosa

Types:

Purging type: The person has regularly engaged in self- induced vomiting or the misuse of laxatives, diuretics, or enemas.

Nonpurging type: The person has used other compensatory behaviors, such as fasting or excessive exercise, but has not regularly engaged in self- induced vomiting or misuse of laxatives, diuretics, or enemas.

Note: These criteria are derived from the criteria specified by the American Psychiatric Association. (1994). *Diagnostic and Statistical Manual of Mental Disorders* (4th Ed.). Adapted with permission.

TABLE 8.2. Summary of Eating Disorder Assessment Methods and the Domains Measured by Each Method

	Body Size	Binge Eating	Compens- atory Behavior	Restrictive Eating	Body Image	General Psycho- pathology
Screening						
Eating Attitudes Test		X	X	X		
Eating Disorder Diagnostic Scale		X	X	X		
Eating Disorder Examination Questionnaire		X	X	X	X	
Diagnosis						
Eating Disorder Examination		X	X	X	X	
Interview for the Diagnosis of Eating Disorders- IV		X	X	X	X	
Multiscale						
Eating Disorder Inventory- 2		X	X	X	X	X
Multidimensional Assessment of Eating Disorder Symptoms		X	X	X	X	X
Pathological Eating Habits						
Bulimia Test Revised		X	X			
Self- monitoring		X	X	X	X	
Eating Inventory		X		X		
Binge Eating Scale		X				
Body Image						
Body Image Assessment					X	
Body Morph Assessment					X	
Body Shape Questionnaire					X	

TABLE 8.2. (Continued)

	Body Size	Binge Eating	Compens-atory Behavior	Restrictive Eating	Body Image	General Psycho-pathology
Body Mass/Weight						
Body Mass Index	X					
Body Composition	X					
Diagnosis						
Structural Clinical Interview DSM- IV						X
Minnesota Multiphasic Personality Inventory						X
Symptom Checklist-90						X
Special Problems						
Food Craving Inventory		X				
Body Checking Questionnaire					X	
Muscle Appearance Satisfaction Scale					X	

☐ Range of Assessment Strategies Available

Screening Measures

Over the past 25 years, psychologists and psychiatrists have developed a number of relatively brief screening measures for eating disorders. Some of the measures that have been established as useful and reliable and valid screening methods are described below.

Eating Attitudes Test
(EAT; Garner & Garfinkel, 1979)

The EAT is a 40-item self-report inventory that measures the symptoms of anorexia nervosa. A modified version, the EAT-26, was developed in response to factor analysis of the original EAT (Garner, Olmstead, Bohr, & Garfinkel, 1982). The EAT and EAT-26 are highly correlated ($r = .98$;

Garner et al., 1982). Test-retest reliability (Carter & Moss, 1984) and internal consistency (Garner & Garfinkle, 1979) of the EAT are satisfactory. The EAT has been found to have good concurrent validity.

A version of the EAT that is specific to pathological eating habits of children has also been developed; it is called the Children's Eating Attitude Test (ChEAT; Maloney, McGuire, & Daniels, 1988). The reliability and validity of the ChEAT have not been established. However, two factor analytic studies of the ChEAT have reported that it measures dieting, concern with eating, and social pressure to gain weight (Kelly, Riciardelli, & Clarke, 1999; Williamson et al., 1997).

Eating Disorder Diagnostic Scale
(EDDS; Stice, Telch, & Rizvi, 2000)

The EDDS is a brief self-report measure that uses the DSM-IV diagnostic criteria as the content that forms a 22-item questionnaire. The EDDS is used to screen for the presence of anorexia nervosa, bulimia nervosa, and binge eating disorder. Tests of the reliability and validity of the EDDS found strong support for its use as a brief screening device for eating disorders (Stice et al., 2000).

Eating Disorder Examination-Questionnaire
(EDE- Q; Fairburn & Beglin, 1994)

The EDE-Q follows the questions used in the interview called the Eating Disorders Examination (see below) to assess the central features of anorexia and bulimia nervosa. It can be adapted for use with binge eating disorder. The reliability and validity of the EDE-Q have been established. The EDE-Q can be used to screen for the presence of binge eating, purging, and extreme concerns related to body size, body shape, and eating.

Diagnostic Interviews for Eating Disorders

Diagnostic interviews are the most reliable and valid methods for establishing clinical diagnoses. Two semistructured interviews for eating disorders have been developed and tested. They are described next.

Eating Disorder Examination
(EDE; Cooper & Fairburn, 1987; Fairburn & Cooper, 1993)

The EDE, currently in its 12th edition, is a semistructured interview designed to assess psychopathology associated with anorexia nervosa and bulimia nervosa. It was not developed as a diagnostic interview, but it has been used for this purpose. The EDE is considered to be one of the best methods for assessing the core symptoms of eating disorders. The EDE measures two behaviors, overeating and methods of extreme weight control. It has four subscales (restraint, eating concern, shape concern, weight concern). The EDE is an interview method for measuring the severity of eating disorder symptoms. It was developed as a measure of treatment outcome. The interviewer, not the patient, rates the severity of symptoms.

Interrater reliability for individual items and the subscales of the EDE has been found to be satisfactory (Cooper & Fairburn, 1987; Wilson & Smith, 1989). Furthermore, estimated test-retest reliability (Rizvi, Peterson, Crow, & Agras, 2000) and internal consistency of the EDE (Cooper, Cooper, & Fairburn, 1989) have been found to be good. The EDE has been found to discriminate between individuals diagnosed with eating disorders and controls (Cooper et al., 1989).

Interview for Diagnosis of Eating Disorders, 4th ver.
(IDED- IV; Kutlesic, Williamson, Gleaves, Barbin, & Murphy- Eberenz, 1998)

The IDED-IV was developed specifically for the purpose of establishing a diagnosis of anorexia nervosa, bulimia nervosa, binge eating disorder, or eating disorder not otherwise specified, using the diagnostic criteria established by the American Psychiatric Association (1994). The reliability and validity of the IDED-IV has been established in a number of studies of anorexia and bulimia nervosa and it has been used to reliably differentiate binge eating disorder from simple obesity (Kutlesic et al., 1998). The most important use for the IDED-IV in clinical practice concerning eating disorders may be for differential diagnosis of anorexia nervosa, bulimia nervosa, and binge eating disorder. Unlike the EDE, the IDED-IV (Kutlesic et al., 1998) was specifically developed for the purpose of differential diagnosis of eating disorders, including Eating Disorder Not Otherwise Specified (EDNOS). The IDED-IV has good reliability and validity, and it reliably differentiates the primary eating disorder diagnoses (Kutlesic et al., 1998).

Multiscale Questionnaires for Eating Disorders

In clinical practice, it is often convenient to use a single questionnaire to measure a variety of symptom features or problem areas. Two of the most well-developed multiscale questionnaires for eating disorders are described below.

Eating Disorder Inventory-2
(EDI- 2; Garner, 1991)

The EDI-2 was developed for use with anorexia and bulimia nervosa. The EDI-2 (Garner, 1991) is a 91-item self-report measure that assesses symptom domains associated with eating disorders. The EDI-2 was developed from an earlier version of the measure (EDI; Garner, Olmstead, & Polivy, 1983), which had eight scales (drive for thinness, bulimia, body dissatisfaction, ineffectiveness, perfectionism, interpersonal distrust, interoceptive awareness, and maturity fears). The EDI-2 retained the original eight scales and added three additional scales (asceticism, impulse regulation, and social insecurity).

Test-retest reliability of the EDI subscales has been found to be satisfactory (Crowther, Lilly, Crawford, & Shepard, 1992; Wear & Pratz, 1987). The internal consistency estimates of the original scales of the EDI-2 are higher than for those of the new scales (Eberenz & Gleaves, 1994).

Multidimensional Assessment of Eating Disorder Symptoms
(MAEDS; Anderson, Williamson, Duchmann, Gleaves, & Barbin, 1999)

The MAEDS was developed for the measurement of treatment outcome with eating disorders. The MAEDS has six scales: (1) binge eating, (2) restrictive eating, (3) purgative behavior, (4) fear of fatness, (5) avoidance of forbidden foods, and (6) depression. Unlike the EDI-2, the MAEDS only measures the core symptoms of eating disorders. The MAEDS has 56 questions.

The test-retest reliability, internal consistency, and concurrent validity of the six scales of the MAEDS have been tested and found to be satisfactory (Anderson et al., 1999). A recent study supported the criterion validity of the MAEDS (Martin, Williamson, & Thaw, 2000). The MAEDS has been successfully used in one prevention study (Varnado-Sullivan, Zucker, Williamson, Reas, Thaw, & Netemeyer, 2001) and one treatment outcome study (Williamson, Thaw, & Varnado, 2001). These studies found that the scales of the MAEDS were sensitive to changes in eating disorder symptoms and the Varnado-Sullivan and colleagues (2001) study found that the total score of the MAEDS can be used as a general index of treatment outcome.

Methods for Assessing Pathological Eating Habits

A variety of methods has been developed to measure unhealthy or pathological eating habits. Included in this list is the EAT, which was discussed earlier. Other useful and widely used measures of eating habits are summarized in the next section.

Bulimia Test-Revised
(BULIT- R; Thelen, Farmer, Wonderlich, & Smith, 1991)

The BULIT-R is a 28-item questionnaire designed to measure the symptoms of bulimia nervosa, as defined by DSM-IIIR (American Psychiatric Association, 1987). Much of the psychometric research on the BULIT was conducted on an earlier version (BULIT; Smith & Thelen, 1984); however the BULIT and BULIT-R are highly correlated ($r = 0.99$; Thelen et al., 1991). The BULIT has been found reliable and valid as a measure of bulimic symptoms (Thelen et al., 1991), and it discriminates individuals diagnosed with bulimia nervosa from anorexia nervosa and from nonclinical controls (Welch, Thompson, & Hall, 1993; Williamson et al., 1991). The BULIT-R was used extensively during the 1980s and early 1990s. In recent years, multiscale questionnaires such as the MAEDS have supplanted the BULIT-R because it is specific to only one eating disorder, that is, bulimia nervosa.

Self-Monitoring

Self-monitoring of food intake is a useful method for obtaining information about eating behavior and for conducting a functional analysis of pathological eating behavior (Williamson, 1990). Information collected via self-monitoring includes: temporal eating patterns, type and amounts of food eaten, frequency and topography of binge episodes and purgative behavior, and mood before and after the meal (Crowther & Sherwood, 1997; Williamson, 1990). Self-monitoring is an essential component of cognitive-behavior therapy for eating disorders. (Williamson, 1990). Self-reported binge/purge episodes are the most common treatment outcome measures (Williamson et al., 1995a, b). However, there is controversy about the reliability and validity of self-reported binge/purge episodes and food intake (Anderson & Maloney, 2001).

Eating Inventory
(EI; Stunkard & Messick, 1988)

Stunkard and Messick (1985) developed the Three Factor Eating Questionnaire, which has been renamed the Eating Inventory (EI; Stunkard & Messick, 1988). The Eating Inventory has three scales, dietary (cognitive) restraint, disinhibition, and perceived hunger. A series of studies (Westenhoefer, 1991; Williamson et al., 1995b; Smith, Williamson, Bray, & Ryan, 1999) have reported that flexible approaches to dieting are not associated with overeating, but that rigid approaches to dieting are associated with overeating. This line of research led to the development of a revision of the Dietary Restraint scale that has two dimensions: rigid and flexible dieting. A recent study reported by Stewart, Williamson, and White (2002) found that the rigid dieting scale was associated with the presence of eating disorder symptoms, but the flexible dieting scale was not associated with the symptoms of anorexia and bulimia nervosa. For the purposes of clinical applications, the EI is useful for measuring the severity of "normal" intent to restrict eating, overeating or both.

Binge Eating Scale
(BES; Gormally, Black , Daston, & Rardin, 1982)

The BES is a 16-item questionnaire that measures the severity of binge eating. The reliability and validity of the BES has been established and it has been used in many studies of binge eating and binge eating disorder (Williamson & Martin, 1999; Williamson & O'Neil, 2004). Recent studies have found that the BES tends to overestimate the presence of binge eating disorder (Williamson & Martin, 1999; Varnado et al., 1998). The EDE and IDED-IV, described earlier, are semistructured interviews that provide a more accurate method for measuring binge eating. Therefore, the primary use of the BES is for quick measurement of binge eating severity. It should not be used for diagnostic or screening purposes.

Body Image Assessment Methods

Over the past 30 years, many methods for assessing body image concerns associated with eating disorders have been developed (Stewart & Williamson, 2004). Three of these methods were selected for review based upon their potential utility for clinical practice. These methods are described below.

Body Image Assessment
(BIA; Williamson, Davis, Bennett, Goreczny, & Gleaves, 1989)

The Body Image Assessment (BIA) is a figural stimulus test for measuring body image. The BIA is administered using nine silhouettes of different body sizes in random order. The patient selects a body size that matches their perception of current (actual) body size (CBS) and ideal body size (IBS). The discrepancy between CBS and IBS has been validated as a measure of body dissatisfaction (Williamson, Gleaves, Watkins, & Schlundt, 1993). The reliability and validity of the BIA have been established in a series of studies (Williamson, Barker, Bertman, & Gleaves, 1995; Williamson, Cubic, & Gleaves, 1993; Williamson, et al., 1989). The BIA was developed exclusively for women and was designed for use with women ranging in body size from very thin to overweight. Williamson and colleagues (2000) extended the BIA to men and women and to be applicable for obese individuals with a new procedure called the Body Image Assessment for Obesity (BIA-O). The BIA-O measures estimates of current, ideal, and reasonable body size, using pictures of body silhouettes that vary from very thin to very obese. The reliability and validity of the BIA-O was established in the study reported by Williamson and colleagues (2000). The BIA-O has been validated for use with Caucasian men and women and African-American men and women.

Body Morph Assessment
(BMA; Stewart, Williamson, Smeets, & Greenway, 2001)

Stewart, Williamson, Smeets, and Greenway developed and validated a computerized body image assessment procedure called the Body Morph Assessment (BMA). Like the BIA-O, the BMA measures estimates of current, ideal, and reasonable body size and these estimates were validated against the BIA-O. A new revision of the BMA (2.0) is much improved from the original and can be applied to men and women of Caucasian and African American descent. The reliability and the validity of the BMA 2.0 have been supported in a preliminary study (Stewart, Williamson, & Allen, 2002). The BMA 2.0 measures very small increments of changes in body size estimation. There are 100 total increments from the extremely thin endpoint on the measure to the obese endpoint. It is computer-based and self-administered. Therefore, in comparison to the BIA-O, the BMA 2.0 is a more sophisticated, automated body image assessment method. It utilizes realistic human images rather than silhouettes in its graphic representation of stimuli. The BMA 2.0 is highly recommended for clinicians who specialize in the evaluation of eating disorders.

Body Shape Questionnaire
(BSQ; Cooper, Taylor, Cooper, & Fairburn, 1987)

The BSQ is a 34-item self-report questionnaire that measures excessive concern about one's body size and shape. Williamson and colleagues (1995a) found that the BSQ measures body dissatisfaction and intention to diet and suggested that it may be a good measure for defining over-concern about body size and shape in normal weight women, which can be viewed as a type of subclinical eating disorder. Higher scores on the BSQ indicate greater concerns with body size and shape. A score of 110 or above is indicative of significant body concerns (Cooper, Taylor, Cooper, & Fairburn, 1987). Short forms of the BSQ have been developed (Evans & Dolan, 1993), including one specifically developed for use with anorexia nervosa (Dowson & Henderson, 2001). The BSQ has been shown to have good reliability and validity, and has been shown to discriminate between persons with bulimia nervosa and nonclinical controls (Cooper et al., 1987; Rosen, Jones, Ramirez, & Waxman, 1996).

Measurement of Body Weight/Mass/Composition: Body Mass Index (BMI)

Height and weight can be converted into a ratio called body mass index (BMI), which is defined as kg/m^2. BMI has become the standard method for expressing a relationship between height and weight. For purposes of classification of different body sizes, a BMI less than 18.5 is considered to be underweight and is often used as the operational definition for low weight associated with anorexia nervosa. Some clinicians use a BMI < 17.5 as a more conservative definition for anorexia nervosa. Normal weight is usually defined as BMI between 18.5 and 24.9; overweight is between 25 and 29.9; and a BMI greater than 30 is often used to define obesity (World Health Organization, 1998).

Measurement of Body Weight/Mass/Composition: Body Composition

Body mass index does not express differences in body composition, that is, percentages of lean versus fat mass. Therefore, it is preferable to also measure body composition. Unfortunately, the measurement of body composition requires the use of sophisticated and expensive equipment that is beyond the means for most clinicians. Of the options for measuring body composition, use of bioelectric impedance assessment is the most convenient and least expensive method that is currently available (Kushner, 1992).

Diagnosis and Assessment of Comorbid Psychiatric Disorders

At least half of the eating disorder cases seen in clinical practice have other psychiatric problems that are a focus of treatment (Williamson, 1990). The following section describes three methods that have been successfully used to assess for these other problem areas.

Structured Clinical Interview for the Diagnosis of DSM-IV Axis I Disorders
(SCID; First, Gibbon, Spitzer, & Williams, 1995)

The SCID is the "gold standard" for valid and objective diagnosis of comorbid psychiatric disorders. This semistructured interview format has been found to be a reliable and valid method for establishing psychiatric diagnoses based on the diagnostic criteria established by the American Psychiatric Association (1994).

Minnesota Multiphasic Personality Inventory
(MMPI- 2; Butcher, 1990)

One of the most frequently used measures of personality is the Minnesota Multiphasic Personality Inventory, second version. The MMPI-2 has three validity scales that test for "faking good" and "faking bad." The MMPI-2 also has ten clinical scales (Butcher, 1990) and hundreds of supplemental scales (Wiggins, 1966; Graham, 1987). The MMPI has been used in many studies of anorexia and bulimia nervosa (e.g., Williamson, 1990; Williamson, Kelly, Davis, Ruggeiro, & Blouin, 1985). Cases of anorexia and bulimia nervosa tend to have elevations on Scales 1 (Hs), 2 (D), 3 (Hy), 4 (Pd), 7 (Pt), and 8 (Sc), which is a common MMPI profile for neurotic disorders (Williamson, 1990).

Symptom Checklist-90
(SCL- 90; Derogatis, 1977)

One shorter screening method for general psychological problems is the Symptom Checklist-90. The SCL-90 measures nine symptom domains including depression, anxiety, obsessive-compulsive symptoms, and symptoms of psychotic disorders. The SCL-90 also has three global measures of symptom severity that may be more useful as general measures of psychopathology than the nine scales that measure specific symptom domains. The SCL-90 has been validated in a variety of studies over the past 30 years and has been used in research related to eating disorders (Williamson, 1990).

Assessment of Special Problems

Eating disorder patients often have special problems that are unique to concerns about eating and body size and body shape. In recent years, many symptom-specific measures related to these concerns have been developed. We have selected three of these measures for review and they are described below.

Food Craving Inventory
(FCI; White, Williamson, Whisenhunt, & Greenway, 2002)

The FCI was developed to measure specific food cravings. The reliability and validity of the FCI has been established (White et al., 2002) and four subscales were established: cravings for sweets, starches, fats, and fast foods. Also, the FCI yields a total score that can be used as a general index of the severity of food craving. Therefore, if food craving is a specific concern for a particular patient, the FCI is a good method for objectively evaluating the severity of this special problem.

Body Checking Questionnaire
(BCQ; Reas, Whisenhunt, Netemeyer, & Williamson, 2002)

One of the less obvious behavioral symptoms associated with eating disorders is compulsive checking of various body areas (e.g., stomach or hips,), or the entire body (e.g., observation using a mirror or compulsive weighing), to detect minute changes in fatness. The BCQ was developed to measure the severity of this set of behavioral symptoms. Reas and colleagues (2002) established the reliability and validity of this brief self-report inventory. The BCQ should be used in cases where body checking is a special problem that requires attention.

Muscle Appearance Satisfaction Scale
(MASS; Mayville, Williamson, White, Netemeyer, & Drab, 2002)

Body image concerns in men is a problem that has only recently been the focus of study. Mayville, Williamson, White, Netemeyer, and Drab (2002) developed the Muscle Appearance Satisfaction Scale (MASS) to measure excessive concern with the appearance of muscularity. Men who are obsessed with body size often perceive their bodies to be too thin and insufficiently muscular. This "reverse body image distortion" is associated with compulsive weight lifting and use of steroids to correct this appearance defect. The MASS should be used in cases that express special concerns about being too thin or those who engage in compulsive weight lifting to increase upper body size. These cases are often young men, though the problem can be found in women.

☐ Pragmatic Issues Encountered in Clinical Practice with Eating Disorders

Reimbursement for Assessment

Generally speaking, reimbursement for assessment of eating disorders is inadequate. Most often, it is not reimbursed at all. In hospital-based treatment programs for eating disorders, in order to be reimbursed for psychological assessment, the costs of assessment are typically built into the program costs. In outpatient treatment settings, one initial assessment session comprised of a brief interview, may be reimbursed. However, paper-and-pencil assessments are omitted because they are not reimbursed. Any other assessment, such as progress in treatment or outcome measures, can be built into the ongoing outpatient therapy program.

Time Required for Assessment

Time required for assessment is often a balance between time, assessment, and reimbursement. Time for thorough assessment for eating disorders can be lengthy. However, because of the reimbursement dilemma, it is wise to be efficient in data collection. It is possible to do a thorough examination in an efficient manner. Measures are often chosen for the yielding of diagnostic information in a short amount of time. However, it is important to obtain enough information about the experience of the client in order to properly develop a case formulation and treatment plan.

☐ Case Illustration

Client Description

Amy, age 21, presented at a hospital-based program for eating disorders, prompted by her parents' concern about her weight status and eating habits. It was immediately apparent that Amy could be classified as "low weight status." She reported that her mother was concerned about her difficulties with eating and persuaded her to enter a program for eating disorders. Although Amy agreed, she was apprehensive about participating in a structured treatment program that required eating meals on a scheduled basis.

History of the Problem

Amy reported that when she was a young child, her mother was overweight and often dieted. As she entered adolescence, Amy began to have some worry about being overweight. She reported that as she entered puberty, she gained weight and was teased by peers at school about her body shape and size. Additionally, her boyfriend at the time decided to break up with her and she felt that the breakup was caused by excessive body weight. She reported that this incident made her feel bad about herself and she began to think it was a good idea to try to lose weight. At first, she tried to diet and exercise to lose weight. Eventually, she lost some weight and received praise and compliments from peers about her thin body size and shape. Amy reported that there were times when she was unmotivated to exercise and that she would purge via self-induced vomiting and use laxatives to prevent weight gain. She also reported that at times she was able to sustain restrictive eating for a few days at a time. She denied significant binge eating. Amy reported that this pattern of behavior continued for several years, and that her current eating habits were the worst in her life. At the time of assessment, she no longer used laxatives or purged; she simply did not eat often. She reported that it had become easy to restrict food intake and that her body weight had dropped from 140 to 96 pounds. She reported dizzy spells, cessation of her menstrual cycle, chest pains, and intense fatigue. Her parents had begun to worry about her health, though she did not share this concern.

Presenting Complaints

In the intake interview, Amy reported fears of being fat, restrictive eating, purging occasionally via self-induced vomiting and excessive exercise, and the use of laxatives to control body weight. She reported depressed mood and symptoms of anxiety. Amy reported that she would like to stop having obsessive thoughts about food and eating and resume the life she had before worrying so much about body size and shape, however, she wanted to remain thin.

Assessment Methods Used

The IDED-IV was used in conjunction with a clinical interview of history to acquire a clear description of the history and current diagnosis. Amy expressed a fear of fatness and a denial of the seriousness of her low body weight. She endorsed restrictive eating patterns, sometimes going several days without eating at a time. The MAEDS measured a baseline level of: fear of fatness (t = 80), restrictive eating (t = 75), binge eating (t = 55), purgative behavior (t = 70), depression (t = 73), and avoidance of fear foods (t = 75). The BMA 2.0 was utilized to measure Amy's level of body dissatisfaction and body size overestimation (current = 66, ideal = 34). These data indicated that Amy overestimated her body size, had a strong drive for thinness, and was dissatisfied with her current body size, despite being significantly underweight. Based on these data, it was determined that Amy met criteria for anorexia nervosa, binge/purge type, and major depressive disorder. There was no evidence for the presence of a personality disorder. Height and weight were measured to determine BMI, which was 17.5; classifying Amy in the "low weight category." A bioelectric impedance measure of body composition showed that Amy's body fat was 13.5%.

Psychological Assessment Protocol

The history and clinical interview (IDED-IV) were conducted first, in order to establish rapport with Amy. It was apparent that she was apprehensive about disclosing personal information, so motivational interviewing techniques, such as reflective listening and open-ended questions, were used to express understanding of her situation. Amy came forth with more details as time progressed. During the interview, Amy endorsed many symptoms of an eating disorder and some level of discord with her current quality of life. The MAEDS and the BMA 2.0 were then administered to collect behavioral and attitudinal data. Amy's height, weight, and body composition were measured to complete the assessment.

Targets Selected for Treatment

Following assessment, a case conceptualization and treatment plan were outlined. Targets selected for treatment included: (1) refeeding and stabilization of nutrition, (2) weight gain and stabilization of weight between 92% and 100% of ideal body weight, (3) improvement of depressed mood, (4) reduction of fear surrounding eating, (5) reduction of anxiety related to body image and eating, (6) reduction of fears of fatness, (7) decreased drive for thinness, (8) cessation of restrictive eating, and (9) cessation of purging via self-induced vomiting and excessive exercise.

Assessment of Progress

Throughout treatment, body weight and body composition were regularly assessed through bioelectrical impedance. The MAEDS was administered each week to assess progress over time. MAEDS scores were compared over time to evaluate trends suggesting improvement, stability, or worsening on each scale, with a special interest in those elevated at baseline assessment (i.e., fear of fatness, avoidance of fear foods, restrictive eating, purging, and depression). Finally, the BMA was utilized to assess progress with overestimation of body size, drive for thinness, and dissatisfaction with body size and shape.

☐ Summary

Assessment of eating disorders is often complex; thus, it is challenging to make simple recommendations. The selection of assessment methods should be based on careful consideration of the referral questions and the psychometric properties of the assessment methods that are chosen. Within this context, we make the following recommendations.

For the purpose of screening for the presence of eating disorder symptoms, we recommend the EAT, primarily because it has been successfully used for this purpose for many years and has very well established reliability and validity. For cases suspected of clinically significant eating problems, we recommend the IDED-IV as a diagnostic interview. The IDED-IV is the only method that has been validated specifically as a diagnostic test for anorexia nervosa, bulimia nervosa, binge eating disorder, and eating disorder not otherwise specified (American Psychiatric Association, 1994). We recommend the SCID as a method for establishing comorbid psychiatric diagnoses. The MAEDS is recommended as a multiscale questionnaire to obtain an objective profile of the severity of eating disorder symptoms. For assessing body image disturbances, we recommend the relatively simple BIA or BIA-O; for clinicians seeking a more sophisticated measure of body image, we recommend the BMA 2.0. For all cases, height and weight should be carefully measured and converted to BMI, for comparison to norms for underweight, normal weight, and overweight/obese.

☐ References

American Psychiatric Association. (1987). *Diagnostic and statistical manual of mental disorders* (3rd ed. rev.). Washington, DC: American Psychiatric Association

American Psychiatric Association DSM-IV. (1994). *Diagnostic and statistical manual of mental disorders* (4th ed.). Washington, DC: American Psychiatric Association (DSM-IV).

Anderson, D. A., & Maloney, K. C. (2001). The efficacy of cognitive-behavioral therapy on the core symptoms of bulimia nervosa. *Clinical Psychology Review, 21,* 971– 988.

Anderson, D. A., Williamson, D. A., Duchmann, E. G., Gleaves, D. G., & Barbin, J. M. (1999). Development and validation of a multifactorial treatment outcome measure for eating disorders. *Assessment, 6,* 7–20.

Butcher JN. (1990). *MMPI-2 in Psychological Treatment.* New York: Oxford University Press.

Carter, P. I., & Moss, R. A. (1984). Screening for anorexia and bulimia nervosa in a college population: Problems and limitations. *Addictive Behaviors, 9,* 417–419.

Cooper, Z., Cooper, P. J., & Fairburn, C. G. (1989). The validity of the Eating Disorder Examination and its subscales. *British Journal of Psychiatry, 154,* 807–812.

Cooper, Z., & Fairburn, C. G. (1987). The Eating Disorder Examination: A semistructured interview for the assessment of the specific psychopathology of eating disorders. *International Journal of Eating Disorders, 6,* 1–8.

Cooper, P. J., Taylor, M. J., Cooper, Z., & Fairburn, C. G. (1987). The development and validation of the Body Shape Questionnaire. *International Journal of Eating Disorders, 6,* 485–494.

Crowther, J. H., Lilly, R. S., Crawford, P., & Shepard, K (1992). The stability of the Eating Disorder Inventory. *International Journal of Eating Disorders, 12*(1), 97–101.

Crowther, J. H., & Sherwood, N. E. (1997). Assessment. In D. M. Garner & P. E. Garfinkel (Eds.), *Handbook of treatment for eating disorders* (2nd ed., pp. 34–49). New York: Guilford.

Derogatis, L. (1977). *Manual for the Symptom Checklist-90, revised.* Baltimore: Johns Hopkins Press.

Dowson, J., & Henderson, L. (2001). The validity of a short version of the Body Shape Questionnaire. *Psychiatry Research, 102,* 263–271.

Eberenz, K. P., & Gleaves, D. H. (1994). An examination of the internal consistency and factor structure of the eating disorders inventory-2 in a clinical sample. *International Journal of Eating Disorders, 16,* 371–379.

Evans, C., & Dolan, B. (1993). Body Shape Questionnaire: Derivation of shortened "alternative forms." *International Journal of Eating Disorders, 13,* 315–321.

Fairburn, C.G., & Beglin, S.J. (1994). Assessment of eating disorders: Interview or self-report questionnaire? *International Journal of Eating Disorders, 16* (4), 363–370.

Fairburn, C. G., & Cooper, Z. (1993). The eating disorder examination (12th edition). In C. G. Fairburn & G. T. Wilson (Eds.), *Binge eating: Nature, assessment, and treatment* (pp. 317–360). New York: Guilford

First, M. B., Gibbon, M., Spitzer, R. L., & Williams, J. B. W. (1995). *User's guide for the structural clinical interview for DSM-IV Axis I Disorders (SCID-I, Version 2.0).* Washington, DC: American Psychiatric Press.

Garner, D. M. (1991). *Eating disorder inventory-2 manual.* Odessa, FL: Psychological Assessment Resources.

Garner, D. M., & Garfinkel, P. E. (1979). The eating attitudes test: An index of the symptoms of anorexia nervosa. *Psychological Medicine, 9,* 273–279.

Garner, D. M., & Garfinkel, P. E. (1979). The eating attitudes test: An index of the symptoms of anorexia nervosa. *Psychological Medicine, 9,* 273–279.

Garner, D. M., Olmstead, M. P., Bohr, Y., & Garfinkel, P. E. (1982). The Eating Attitude Test: Psychometric features and clinical correlates. *Psychological Medicine, 12,* 871–878.

Garner, D. M., Olmstead, M. P., & Polivy, J. (1983). Development and validation of a multidimensional eating disorder inventory for anorexia nervosa and bulimia. *International Journal of Eating Disorders, 2,* 15–34.

Geller, J., Cockell, S. J., & Drab, D. (2001). Assessing readiness for change in the eating disorders: The psychometric properties of the readiness and motivation interview. *Psychological Assessment, 13 (2),* 189–198.

Gormally, J., Black, S., Daston, S., & Rardin, D. (1982). The assessment of binge eating severity among obese persons. *Addictive Behaviors, 7,* 47–55

Graham, J. R. (1987). *The MMPI: A Practical Guide* (2nd ed.). New York: Oxford University Press.

Kelly, C., Ricciardelli, L. A., & Clarke, J. D. (1999). Problem eating attitudes and behaviors in young children. *International Journal of Eating Disorders, 25,* 281–286.

Kushner, R.G. (1992). Bioelectric impedence analysis: A review of principles and applications. *Journal of the American College of Nutrition, 11,* 199–209.

Kutlesic, V., Williamson, D. A., Gleaves, D. H., Barbin, J. M., & Murphy-Eberenz, K. P. (1998). The Interview for the Diagnosis of Eating Disorders-IV: Application to DSM-IV diagnostic criteria. *Psychological Assessment, 10,* 41–48.

Maloney, M. J., McGuire, J. B., & Daniels, S. R. (1988). Reliability testing of a children's version of the eating attitudes test. *Journal of American Academy of Child and Adolescent Psychiatry, 27,* 541–543.

Martin, K. C., Williamson, D. A., & Thaw, J. M. (2000). Criterion validity of the Multiaxial Assessment of Eating Disorders Symptoms. *International Journal of Eating Disorders, 28,* 303–310.

Mayville, S. B., Williamson, D. A., White, M. A., Netemeyer, R., & Drab, D. L. (2002). Development of the Muscle Appearance Satisfaction Scale: A self-report measure for the assessment of muscle dysmorphia symptoms. *Assessment, 9,* 351–360.

Prochaska, J. O., Di Clemente, C. C., & Norcross, J. C. (1992). In search of how people change. *American Psychologist, 47,* 1102–1114.

Reas, D. L., Whisenhunt, B. L., Netemeyer, R., & Williamson, D. A. (2002). Development of the Body Checking Questionnaire: A self-report measure of body checking behavior. *International Journal of Eating Disorders, 31,* 324–333.

Rizvi, S. L., Peterson, C. B., Crow, J. C., & Agras, W. S. (2000). Test-retest reliability of the eating disorder examination. *International Journal of Eating Disorders, 28,* 311–316.

Rosen, J. C., Jones, A., Ramirez, E., & Waxman, S. (1996). Body shape questionnaire: Studies of validity and reliability. *International Journal of Eating Disorders, 20,* 315–319.

Smith, M. C., & Thelen, M. H. (1984). Development and validation of a test for bulimia. *Journal of Consulting and Clinical Psychology, 52,* 863–872.

Smith, C. F., Williamson, D. A., Bray, G. A., & Ryan, D. H. (1999). Flexible vs. rigid dieting strategies: Relationship with adverse behavioral outcomes. *Appetite, 32,* 295–305.

Stewart, T. M. & Williamson, D. A. (2004). Assessment of body image disturbances. In J. K. Thompson (Ed.), *Handbook of Eating Disorders and Obesity.* New York: Wiley. (pp. 495–514).

Stewart, T. M., Williamson, D. A., & Allen, R. (2002). *The body morph assessment 2.0 (BMA 2.0): A psychometric study*. Paper presented at the November 2002 meeting of the Association for the Advancement of Behavior Therapy, Reno, Nevada.

Stewart, T. M., Williamson, D. A., & White, M. A. (2002). Rigid vs. flexible dieting: Association with eating disorder symptoms in nonobese women. *Appetite, 38*(1), 39–44.

Stewart, T. M., Williamson, D. A., Smeets, M. A. M., & Greenway, F. L. (2001). The Body Morph Assessment: Development of a computerized measure of body image. *Obesity Research, 9,* 43–50.

Stice, E., Telch, C. F., & Rizvi, S. L. (2000). Development and validation of the eating disorder diagnostic scale: A brief self-report measure of anorexia, bulimia, and binge eating disorder. *Psychological Assessment, 12*(2), 123–131.

Stunkard, A. J., & Messick, S. (1985). The three-factor eating questionnaire to measure dietary restraint, disinhibition, and hunger. *Journal of Psychosomatic Research, 29,* 71–83.

Stunkard, A. J., & Messick, S. (1988). *The Eating Inventory*. San Antonio, TX: Psychological Corporation.

Thelen, M. H., Farmer, J., Wonderlich, S., & Smith, M. (1991). A revision of the bulimia test: The BULIT–R. *Psychological Assessment, 3,* 119–124.

Varnado, P. J., Williamson, D. A., Bentz, B. G., Ryan, D. H., Rhodes, S. K., O'Neil, P. M., Sebastian, S. B., & Barker, S. E. (1998). Prevalence of binge eating disorder in obese adults seeking weight loss treatment. *Eating and Weight Disorders, 2,* 117–124.

Varnado-Sullivan, P. J., Zucker, N., Williamson, D. A., Reas, D., Thaw, J., & Netemeyer, S. B. (2001). Development and implementation of the Body Logic Program for adolescents: A two-stage prevention program for eating disorders. *Cognitive and Behavioral Practice, 8,* 248–259.

Wear, R. W., & Pratz, O. (1987). Test-retest reliability for the Eating Disorder Inventory. *International Journal of Eating Disorders, 6,* 767–769.

Welch, G., Thompson, L., & Hall, A. (1993). The BULIT-R: Its reliability and clinical validity as a screening tool for DSM-III-R bulimia nervosa in a female tertiary education population. *International Journal of Eating Disorders, 14,* 95–105.

Westenhoefer, J. (1991). Dietary restraint and disinhibition: is restraint a homogeneous construct? *Appetite, 16,* 45–55.

White, M. A., Williamson, D. A., Whisenhunt, B. L., Greenway, F. L., & Netemeyer, R. G. (2002). Development and validation of the Food Craving Inventory. *Obesity Research, 10,* 107–114.

Wiggins, J. S. (1966). Substantive dimensions of self-report in the MMPI item pool. *Psychological Monographs, 80*(22) (no. 630).

Williamson, D. A. (1990). *Assessment of eating disorders: Obesity, anorexia, and bulimia nervosa*. Elmsford, NY: Pergamon.

Williamson, D. A., Barker, S. E., Bertman, L. J., & Gleaves, D. H. (1995). Body image, body dysphoria, and dietary restraint: Factor structure in nonclinical subjects. *Behavior Research Therapy, 33,* 85–93.

Williamson, D. A., Cubic, B. A., & Gleaves, D. H. (1993). Equivalence of body image disturbances in anorexia and bulimia nervosa. *Journal of Abnormal Psychology, 102,* 177–180.

Williamson, D. A., Davis, C. J., Bennett, S. M., Goreczny, A. J., & Gleaves, D. H. (1989). Development of a simple procedure for assessing body image disturbances. *Behavioral Assessment, 11,* 433–446.

Williamson, D. A., DeLany, J. P., Bentz, B. G., Bray, G. A., Champagne, C. M. & Harsha, D. W. (1997). Gender and racial differences in dieting and social pressures to gain weight among children. *Journal of Gender, Culture, & Health, 2,* 231–234.

Williamson, D. A., Gleaves, D. H., & Lawson, O. J. (1991). Biased perception of overeating in bulimia nervosa and compulsive binge eaters. *Journal of Psychopathology and Behavioral Assessment, 13,* 257–268.

Williamson, D. A., Gleaves, D. H., Watkins, P. C., & Schlundt, D. G. (1993). Validation of self-ideal body size discrepancy as a measure of body dissatisfaction. *Journal of Psychopathology and Behavioral Assessment, 15,* 57–68.

Williamson, D. A., Kelley, M. L., Davis, C. J., Ruggiero, L., & Blouin, D. (1985). Psychopathology of eating disorders: A controlled comparison of bulimic, obese, and normal subjects. *Journal of Clinical and Consulting Psychology, 53,* 161–166.

Williamson, D. A., Lawson, O. J., Brooks, E. R., Wozniak, P. J., Ryan, D. H., Bray, G. A., & Duchmann, E. G. (1995). Association of body mass with dietary restraint and disinhibition. *Appetite, 25,* 31–41.

Williamson, D. A., & Martin, C. K. (1999). Binge eating disorder: A review of the literature after publication of DSM-IV. *Eating and Weight Disorders, 4,* 103–114.

Williamson, D. A., & O'Neil, P. M. (2004). Obesity and Quality of Life. In G. Bray and C. Bouchard (Eds.) *Handbook of obesity* (2nd ed.) (pp. 1005–1023). New York: Marcel Dekker.

Williamson, D. A., Thaw, J. M., & Varnado, P. J. (2001). Cost-effectiveness analysis of a hospital-based cognitive-behavioral treatment program for eating disorders. *Behavior Therapy, 32,* 459–477.

Williamson, D. A., Womble, L. G., Zucker, N. L., Reas, D. L., White, M. A., Blouin, D. C., & Greenway, F. (2000). Body Image Assessment for Obesity (BIA-O): Development of a new procedure. *International Journal of Obesity, 24,* 1326–1332.

Wilson, G. T., & Smith, D. (1989). Assessment of bulimia nervosa: An evaluation of the Eating Disorder Examination. *International Journal of Eating Disorders, 8,* 173–179.

World Health Organization. (1998). Obesity: Preventing and managing the global epidemic. Report of a WHO Consultation on Obesity, Geneva, June 3–5, 1997. (Publication No. WHO/NUT/NCD/98.1). Geneva: World Health Organization.

Barry M. Maletzky
Cynthia Steinhauser

Sexual Deviations

☐ Definition of the Problem

Among the vast majority of mental health clients to be evaluated in any setting, few are truly undertaking assessment against their will. Unfortunately, this is not true of most sexual offenders being evaluated for forensic or treatment purposes. Most such offenders would not have elected, by their own choosing, to undertake assessment or treatment. Many have been referred only after having been adjudicated, that is, charged with a crime, then either pled guilty, or been found guilty by trial. Some will have been referred by their attorneys before any charges have been formally brought, but in anticipation of being accused. Only a few, fewer than 5% in most series (Maletzky, 1991b, pp. 213–267), will present of their own free will because they believe they have a problem requiring treatment.

The largely involuntary nature of these clients creates a far different atmosphere in assessing the sexual offender; it complicates treatment even more so. Nonetheless, successful evaluations and treatment outcomes are routinely reported in the sexual offender literature (Hanson et al., 2002). In the sections which follow, we will provide a brief description of the populations presenting for evaluation and treatment, the assessment strategies routinely employed, the day-to-day clinical issues encountered with this population, and a typical case example (a homosexual pedophile), selected with an eye toward describing how a sexual treatment provider would analyze such a client, prepare him (the vast majority of such clients are male) for treatment, and assess whether treatment is attaining a successful outcome.

Any fully informed description of the paraphilias and associated deviations would overwhelm the goals of the present chapter. However, to understand the analysis of typical clients encountered in practice, a brief description is in order. Among all sexual disorders addressed in *Diagnostic and Statistical Manual of Mental Disorders*, 4th edition, revised text (DSM-IV-TR; American Psychiatric Association, 2000), just one subsection comprises the paraphilias, yet the manner in which these afflictions are presented has led to intense debate within the field (O'Donohue, Regev, & Hagstrom, 2000). Table 9.1 lists the major categorizations as they now stand, with the recognition that change is a constant in psychiatric taxonomy.

Human sexual behavior is assuredly idiosyncratic and often unpredictable, thus confounding attempts at classification. Nonetheless, DSM-IV-TR makes the apparently reasonable demand that the paraphilias conform to several basic criteria:

- That they be characterized by recurrent and intense sexually arousing fantasies, urges, or behaviors involving inappropriate objects.
- That they be of greater than 6 months' duration.
- That they cause clinically significant distress or impair day-to-day function.

As can be seen from Table 9.1, these paraphilias include exhibitionism, the pedophilias, transvestic fetishism, and voyeurism. Omitted, however, are common categories encountered in clinical practice, including men who have molested a single child and do not fulfill criteria for pedophilia, and men who rape; these latter often do not meet criteria for sexual sadism (Hucker, 1997). In addition, some authors have questioned the requirement that distress or functional impairment occur (Maletzky, 2002; O'Donhue et al., 2000), as most sexual offenders experience distress only upon discovery of their crimes and very few manifest disturbances in their social, occupational, or other important areas of functioning as a direct result of their affliction; dysfunction stems almost entirely from the legal repercussions following disclosure of their deviant behaviors. While potential solutions to the difficulties inherent in typifying sexual offense behavior have been proposed (American Psychiatric Association, 1995; Maletzky, 1997), an agreed upon taxonomy is in the distant future.

To complicate the diagnostic picture further, the clinician is often faced with a client who will not readily admit to deviant behaviors (Abel et al., 1987). Because there are no definitive tests to determine the full

TABLE 9.1. Diagnostic Criteria for the DSM-IV-R Paraphilias

These must be of at least 6 months' duration; cause significant distress or impairment in social, occupational, or other significant functions; and produce recurrent sexually arousing fantasies, urges, or behaviors involving:

1. Nonhuman objects

2. Suffering or humiliation of oneself or one's partner

3. Children or other nonconsenting individuals

Exhibitionism 302.4

Fantasies, urges, or behaviors involving the exposure of one's genitals to a stranger

Fetishism 302.81

Fantasies, urges, or behaviors involving the use of objects, not limited to articles of female clothing used in cross-dressing (as in transvestic fetishism), or devices designed for genital stimulation

Frotteurism 302.89

Fantasies, urges, or behaviors involving touching or rubbing against a nonconsenting person

Pedophilia 302.2

Fantasies, urges, or behaviors involving sexual activity with a prepubescent child by a person at least 16 years old and at least 5 years older

Sexual masochism 302.83

Fantasies, urges, or behaviors involving the act of being humiliated, beaten, bound, or otherwise made to suffer

Fantasies, urges, or behaviors involving acts in which the suffering of a victim is sexually exciting

Transvestic fetishism 302.3

Fantasies, urges, or behaviors in a heterosexual male involving cross-dressing

Voyeurism 302.82

Fantasies, urges, or behaviors involving observing unsuspecting persons who are nude, disrobing, or in sexual activity

Paraphilia not otherwise specified 302.9

Paraphilia that does not meet the above criteria

Source: Adapted from the American Psychiatric Association: Diagnostic and Statistical Manual of Mental Disorders, IV-TR, Text Revision. Washington, DC, American Psychiatric Association, 2000.

extent of deviant behaviors, treatment providers may never know all of an offender's misbehaviors which require treatment — a situation resembling that of trying to treat a depressed client who gives no history, displays no symptoms, nor reports any treatment effects. Nonetheless, successful assessment and treatment approaches have been devised over the past two decades, and an ample literature has documented success at reducing community risk.

The majority of offenders presenting to outpatient programs are classified as situational offenders; that is, they would not have raped or molested had they not found themselves in a particular situation at the time. Examples include a man who molested a stepdaughter after moving into her home, or an intoxicated college student who committed a date rape. Even in outpatient settings, however, more dangerous offenders, sometimes referred to as predatory or preferential offenders, are encountered. Most such offenders, while having served time in prison, will eventually be released, and the majority will not have been treated in a penitentiary setting. Examples of these more dangerous offenders include men who rape repeatedly and men who seek out and prefer youngsters as sexual partners. Table 9.2 displays some of the distinctions between these types of offenders.

Despite differences in opinion about the classification of sexual offenders, no one doubts the serious nature of these offenses and the need to prevent further harm. The true prevalence of sexual crimes may never be fully known, but the figures we do possess continue to astonish: between 30% and 70% of college age females have been victimized in some fashion (Russell, 1988); the majority of victims are under 16 years of age (Lutzker, 2000); among children, prevalence rates of up to 39% have been estimated (Salter, 1992). Females are not the sole gender being victimized; Salter (1992) estimates that up to 30% of boys may have been

TABLE 9.2. Distinctions between Situational and Predatory/Preferential Sexual Offenders

Situational Offender	Predatory/Preferential Offender
Single victim	Multiple victims
Living with victim	Not living with victim, or, if living with victim, having at least one other victim in the community
Well known to victim	Not well known to at least some victims
Single paraphilia, usually heterosexual	Often multiple paraphilias, and often homosexual
Often married or living with a woman	Often single and living alone

victims as well. A nationwide survey estimated that between 4% and 17% of adult males have molested children of one or both genders (Wang, 1999). Of even more startling impact, up to 55% of college males say they would use force against a woman to obtain sexual access if they were guaranteed no consequences (Malamuth, Haber, & Feshbach, 1990). Given these depressing statistics, one may truly wonder not why men rape, but why more do not.

The enormity of this problem, magnified by daily media accounts of horrific crimes, has spurred the creation of a host of assessment and treatment programs and techniques which now offer not only a clearer picture of how to analyze these disorders but how to prevent their recurrence as well. We will omit here discussions of theories of etiology, including those containing behavioral (Van Wyk & Geist, 1984) and evolutionary (Maletzky, 1996; Quinsey & Lalumiere, 1995) points of view, but would point out that such reviews in the literature (Maletzky, 2002) have not contributed to the practical management of sexual offender clients. Nonetheless, such work will continue to make important advances in our understanding of sexual abuse in general.

☐ Range of Assessment Strategies Available

Psychological Assessment Tools

No single psychologic test has been shown to delineate a sexual offender (Marshall & Hall, 1995; Schlank, 1995), undoubtedly because there is no single offender profile. Sexual offenders come from all walks of life and have as many personality styles as any other preselected groups (Maletzky, 1993). Nonetheless, a number of assessment devices have proven of immense help in characterizing these clients, especially for the purposes of predicting sexual risk, testifying in court, and devising a treatment plan.

Review of Materials

Because offenders often do not reveal the full extent of their deviant fantasies and behaviors, it is essential to review any materials available prior to the first interview. Most often, these include information in the legal file, including police reports, a presentence investigation, and institutional files. Not infrequently, previous psychological evaluations are available as well. Most crucial are reports of the current offense, but notes about prior crimes are relevant, as are indications of substance abuse and prior treatment. For the unusual cases in which the legal system has not been involved, it is equally important to make every effort to acquire similar materials, such as past evaluation and treatment records, in order to be as well prepared as possible before the initial interview.

The Clinical Interview

The value of simply building trust and eliciting information by history taking and mental status evaluation is often underestimated, yet clinicians possess uncommon skill in these areas, which proves invaluable in assessing the sexual offender. These skills are challenged in such evaluations because such offenders face assessment and treatment with distrust and trepidation. Thus, early sessions are often reserved for gentle probing only after trust can be established by not directly confronting the offender at first. Not infrequently, it can take three to five interviews to begin to break through initial denial.

Overcoming denial is considered by many therapists to be an essential step in initiating treatment, yet many offenders cannot admit their offense even when presented with irrefutable evidence. More common than outright denial, however, is minimization. Many offenders claim no memory of the events due to intoxication, or claim the offense was unintentional, or misinterpreted by the victim. Still others claim that the victim(s) concocted the story, or was induced to do so by angry adults. While a slim minority of these accounts may verge on truth, long experience with offenders who finally disclose the truth, combined with findings from the literature (Abel et al., 1987; De Young, 1988), have convinced therapists that most offenders minimize and deny. Table 9.3 lists the types of denials, minimizations, and distortions often encountered when obtaining an initial history from sexual offenders.

Although structured clinical interviews have been published for some psychiatric conditions, none exists for sexual offenders. Clinicians favor unstructured interviews in order to obtain information while building trust. At first, obtaining nonsexual information and steering clear of controversial issues may prove beneficial; later there will be time to challenge distortions. Generally, three to five sessions will be required to obtain a history sufficient to reach conclusions about danger to the community and to devise a treatment plan.

Interviews with the victim(s) and significant others, such as parents and partners, are occasionally possible, and can yield important additional information, as can reviews of victim accounts and treatment

TABLE 9.3. Examples of Distortions, Assumptions, and Justifications Employed by Different Types of Sexual Offenders

Category	Example
Misattributing blame	"She was saying no but her body was saying yes." "She would always run around half dressed."
Minimizing or denying sexual intent	"I was just teaching her about sex." "My hand must have slipped."
Blaming the victim	"The way she came on to me, she deserved it." "She always lies."
Minimizing consequences	"She'd had sex before; it was no big deal." "He's always been real friendly with me, even afterward."
Deflecting censure	"This happened years ago — why can't people forget about it?" "I only did it once."
Justifying the cause	"If I wasn't molested as a kid, I'd never have done this." "If my girlfriend gave me what I want, I wouldn't have to rape."

records, if available. It is hazardous to rely on just a single source of data collection in such evaluations.

An important part of the clinical interview is the mental status examination because it represents the therapist's systematic report of observations of the client's behavior and thought patterns. Noteworthy are issues of awareness of the impact of the offender's behavior on victims, acceptance of responsibility, feelings about treatment, and any indications of a comorbid psychiatric illness. While most offenders do not offend because of an illness, comorbidity can be a potentially treatable contributing factor (Kafka & Hennen, 2002).

It is in these initial sessions that rapport can be built and defenses gradually worn down so that further disclosures and smoother treatment can proceed. Most offenders enter assessment in a hostile and defensive mood, isolated, angry, and afraid. Nonetheless, they deserve the same respect provided as a matter of course to all clients and will appreciate their therapist's support at these early sessions.

Self-Reports

Therapists often ask clients during initial sessions to prepare a sexual autobiography and to maintain a record of ongoing sexual urges, fantasies, dreams, and behaviors, such as urges to molest, or masturbation to deviant themes. The value of these reports is questionable, given offenders' tendencies to distort information. Exhaustive reviews under guarantees of strict anonymity (Abel et al., 1987) reveal that authorities and clinicians will learn about only a trifling percentage of the actual sexual misdeeds these men have committed. Thus it is best, at present, to view such information with a skeptical eye.

Psychological Tests

In spite of a multitude of attempts to typify the sexual offender (as reviewed in Marshall & Hall, 1995), no single instrument, or combination of tests, has yielded a set of characteristic responses for sexual offenders as a group, or for any subset within it. As a corollary, the evaluator is not justified in predicting the probability of future acts on the basis of psychological tests (or physiologic ones — see below) alone. Thus, general tests such as the MMPI (Schlank,1995), tests of intelligence (Maletzky, 1991b), and even tests of general psychopathy, such as the Hare Psychopathy Checklist-Revised (Hare, 1991), have not proven helpful in evaluating the sexual offender (Serin, Mailloux, & Malcolm, 2001). The lack of correlations among tests, diagnoses, and treatment results may stem from the heterogeneity within sexual offenders in general.

Summarizing an unusually thorough review in this area, Marshall and Hall (1995) concluded that psychologic tests, "however they are scored or represented, do not satisfactorily distinguish any type of sexual offender from various other groups of subjects, including, most particularly, non-offenders" (pp. 216–217). Nothing in the more recent literature contradicts this view; indeed, further confirmation of the nonutility of standard tests has recently been reinforced (Tierney & McCabe, 2001).

However, this does not mean that psychologic testing has no place in the evaluation of the sexual offender. Rather, studies have shown that, in specialized situations, certain tests can be of value in ferreting out specific information in individual offenders, and a host of instruments can be useful as well in determining risk to be at large, a special issue to be addressed separately below. Not all the tests described in the literature can be examined here; however, we will attempt to describe the most popular and helpful tests.

Tests of Empathy

The vast majority of treatment programs rely upon instilling a sense of empathy in sexual offenders as one component of therapy (Freeman-Longo, Bird, Stevenson, & Fiske, 1995), yet a means to identify and measure this construct has proven devilishly difficult. Early approaches focused on general empathy (Cronbach,1995; Davis, 1983) and proved difficult to apply to sexual offenders specifically (Hildebran & Pithers, 1989; Marshall, Jones, Hudson, & McDonald, 1993). One reason for this difficulty may be the complex and amorphous nature of this concept. Empathy involves a number of components, including the ability to perceive another person's distress, appreciate that person's point of view, experience similar emotions, and want to assist in reducing that person's pain (Marshall, O'Sullivan, & Fernandez, 1996).

A seminal approach to a systematic analysis of empathy in sexual offenders occurred with the validation of the Empat Scale by McGrath, Cann, and Konopasky in 1998. First introduced in 1995 (McGrath, Cann, Konopasky, 1995), the Empat measures not only general empathy for others, but more specifically, sensitivity and concern for victims of sexual assault. Utilizing a 5-point Likert scale, the Empat includes 34 items specific to sexual offending drawn from clinical experience and research reports on hundreds of actual victims. Examples include, "If someone was molested 18 years ago, they should be over it by now," and "It is fair for the court to order a man to pay $5,000 to someone he molested if the money is going to be used to pay for therapy for that victim." Eighteen measures of general empathy were also included, such as "People who fought in the war usually exaggerate the injuries they got."

In their 1998 validation study, McGrath, Cann, and Konopasky involved 104 child molesters, 30 men convicted of nonsexual crimes, and 30 nonoffenders. The sexual offenders demonstrated an equal amount of empathy toward nonsexual abuse victims as did the other subjects but significantly less empathy toward victims of sexual abuse than the two other groups. Even when sexual offenders were instructed to fake their responses in a positive direction, they still demonstrated less sexual abuse empathy.

Unfortunately, these results have been difficult to replicate. Hennessy, Walter, and Vess (2002), in a sample of 108 offenders, found that rapists and child molesters scored significantly higher in empathy toward sexual abuse victims on the Empat scale than did the original group reported by McGrath and colleagues (1998); indeed, these men, all from an incarcerated population of severe offenders, scored higher than McGrath and colleague's original control group of nonoffenders, raising doubts about the construct validity of the scale. Moreover, clinicians' impressions of the Empat reflected a belief that the scale was highly transparent and easily manipulated by clients. These beliefs are further amplified by the finding that the Empat had no significant correlation with a host of other scales which measure affective and cognitive constructs found to be of importance in assessing sexual offenders (Tierney & McCabe, 2001).

Recognizing these difficulties, Marshall and his group (Fernandez, Marshall, Lightbody, & O'Sullivan, 1999) took a slightly different approach to measuring empathy in sexual offenders by constructing the Child Molester Empathy Measure (CMEM). This scale describes three vignettes: a child injured in a motor vehicle accident, a child molested by an unknown assailant, and the offender's own victim(s). A complicated scoring system was devised assessing recognition of the child's distress and general feelings about the child on a 0–10 scale across a variety of possible emotions the victim might have been experiencing. Subjects included 61 offenders in a medium security institution. Initial results indicated that the measure was reliable and stable over time.

A second part of this study, reported in the same paper, found that, among 29 child molesters and 36 nonoffenders, this measure proved valid, as shown by the molesters' relative deficiency in empathy toward an anonymous offender's victim. Of equal interest was the offenders' equivalent empathy toward the accident victim, but of crucial relevance was the finding that these offenders showed the least concern toward their own victim(s).

Some importance to these findings has been added by this group's follow-up report comparing 34 child molesters with 24 nonsexual offenders and 28 nonoffenders (Marshall, Hamilton, & Fernandez, 2001). Child molesters in this study displayed the greatest empathy deficits toward their own, as opposed to general, or anonymous, sexual abuse victims. Of additional interest, this group reported that there was no difference in the emotional component of empathy, but rather, differences emerged in the cognitive elements of the empathy measure.

It seems safe to assume, on the basis of the research reported thus far, that sexual offenders do not display empathy deficits in general, but are deficient in perceiving and appreciating the suffering of sexual abuse victims, and most specifically, these deficits are greatest when reflecting upon their own victims. Unfortunately, the clinical and scientific utility of these findings is questionable. The two scales mentioned above have been employed in small samples of disparate offenders and have reported differing results. The scales are transparent, a flaw common in assessing sexual offenders who are highly defensive, and the results from these research groups have neither been validated by other groups nor followed up by the original groups themselves. Moreover, the relationships among sexual offending, its treatment, and improving empathy in offenders, remain to be defined (Pithers, 1999). There still has been no demonstration that enhancing a client's scores on any empathy measure will lead to a reduction in the risk he poses to commit another sexual offense. As we will see, these defects represent an all too common theme in the assessment of the sexual offender.

Tests of Social Desirability

The influences of social desirability and transparency on test responses are major considerations in evaluating the validity of any measure to be employed in assessing sexual offenders. A number of studies have called into question whether any such responses can be considered accurate (Gendreau, Irvine, & Knight, 1973; McGrath et al., 1998; Stermac, Segal, & Gillis, 1990). In addition, sexual offenders have been able to fake positive responses (Abel, Becker, Blanchard, & Mavissakalian, 1975), raising the likelihood that such offenders wish mostly to present themselves in a positive light rather than answer test questions honestly.

Recently, Tierney and McCabe (2001) collected data from 36 child molesters, 31 sexual offenders against adults, 33 men who committed a nonsexual crime, and 40 community nonoffenders. These workers employed a Sexual Social Desirability Scale designed to measure the extent to which offenders attempt to present themselves in a desirable light about sexual issues (McGrath et al., 1998). Examples include statements such as "I buy magazines that have nude pictures mainly for the articles," and "There have been times when I have had sexual thoughts or fantasies about someone else, even though I am involved in a relationship." Unfortunately, the discriminative power of this instrument was relatively weak. Child molesters were the most likely group to deny negative but likely sexual behaviors, and the second most likely to attribute positive but unlikely behaviors to themselves; offenders against adults fell in the middle range on many of these attributions. Although this scale was validated to some extent in this study, its clinical utility remains questionable.

Social desirability has been repeatedly demonstrated to influence assessment outcome in sexual offenders. Baumgartner, Scalora, and Huss (2002) have recently shown that child molesters reported significantly lower levels of fantasies than college student controls, a result which again calls into question the validity of self-reports among such offenders.

One other general issue complicating these assessment techniques is the failure to distinguish among offender subtypes. It is not only possible, but likely, that pedophiles differ from situational offenders and men who rape on many of these measures (Maletzky & Steinhauser, 2002). However, it has proven difficult to engage sufficient numbers of each subgroup of offender in a single study. Future efforts are needed in this regard, along with attempts at a meta-analysis, to ensure more statistically valid results.

Assessments of Cognitive Distortions

So many attempts to analyze the distortions typical of sexual offenders have been made in recent years that only the highlights and major trends can be discussed here. This attention reflects twin concerns: sexual offenders often distort their thought patterns in order to reduce their guilt or complicity (Pithers, 1999) and helping them to alter those patterns has become an integral part of most treatment programs (Freeman-Longo et al., 1995). Indeed, many of the cognitive instruments employed focus a good deal on the concept of denial (see Table 9.3). If an instrument could accurately measure these distortions, then progress in treatment could be objectively tracked.

One of the initial instruments to assess erroneous perceptions in such offenders was formulated by Nichols and Molinder two decades ago as the Multiphasic Sex Inventory — the MSI (Nichols & Molinder, 1984). Although this scale also measures behaviors and fantasies (see below), the majority of items assess offenders' thought distortions about their crimes and about sexuality in general. Concepts addressed include accountability, responsibility, and honesty in reporting sexual behaviors. While internal consistency (Beech, Friendship, Erikson, & Hanson, 2002) and reliability (Simkins, Ward, Bowman, & Rinck, 1989) have been demonstrated, the cognitive scales on the MSI have not been shown to possess construct validity (Beech et al., 2002; Murphy, 1990); moreover, the test is lengthy and has been faulted for its transparency (Stermac et al., 1990).

Another early attempt to assess cognitive distortions was undertaken by Abel and his group with the development of the Abel and Becker Cognition Scale (Abel et al., 1984). Designed to measure the attitudes of child molesters toward sexual activities between adults and children, the ABCS contains 29 items drawn from clinical experience but subsequently validated (Murphy, 1990). A sample true or false statement from this scale is "Having sex with a child is a good way to teach the child about sex." As can be seen from the example, however, transparency has been a clinical problem with this scale (McGrath et al., 1998).

A very similar scale, the Child Molester Scale (CMS), was devised by Cann, Konopasky, and McGrath (1995) in order to surmount this difficulty by "veiling" the test statements. For example, some of the statements were reworded to seemingly justify sexual activity between adults and children. In addition, the direction of the appropriate answers was occasionally reversed so that the acceptable responses were less obvious. Compared to nonsexual offenders and nonoffenders, a group of 104 child molesters displayed significantly more cognitive distortions on this scale (McGrath et al., 1998). However, the greatest differences emerged in the group of sexual offenders promised anonymity; those whose identities were known to authorities were far less willing to disclose distortions. These identifiable men had scores similar to nonsexual offenders, again raising the likelihood that such clients can discern what is socially acceptable and can tailor their responses accordingly.

Moreover, a more recent analysis (Tierney & McCabe, 2001) failed to validate the psychometric properties of the CMS and noted that it showed only a weak correlation with the ABCS. These findings highlight the difficulties inherent in developing an opaque scale for sexual offenders.

Indeed, over the past 10 years there has been extensive media coverage of the harm sexual abuse can cause and offenders have been part of this audience. In addition, sexual offenders can easily learn, in prison or even in group therapy, the "correct" responses on many of these instruments. A more disturbing possibility, however, is that the attitudes of offenders, at least as reflected on their responses to questionnaires, do not represent a measure of their true beliefs or their actual tendencies to reoffend.

Another problem in evaluating the clinical utility of these scales is their reliance on just one subgroup of offenders to reach conclusions about all sexual offenders. For example, child molesters differ from men who rape across a number of variables (Maletzky, 1993; McConaghy, 1993) yet many studies either focus on one group or lump groups together. An early attempt to learn more about the subgroup of men who rape was made by Burt over 20 years ago when he developed the Burt Rape Myth Acceptance Scale (RMA; Burt, 1980). This scale is composed of 11 items related to justification of rape, with each item scored on a 7-point scale ranging from "strongly agree" to "strongly disagree." Studies with the RMA have shown that men with sexually aggressive histories endorse a greater number of distorted beliefs than community-based controls (Burt, 1984; Muehlenhard & Linton, 1987; Spence, Losoff, & Robbins, 1991). However, these reports have not demonstrated a vigorous difference, and other investigators have reported very little discriminative ability (for a review, see Stermac et al. [1990]).

To address these problems, Bumby (1996) devised the MOLEST and RAPE Scales. Over 30 statements on each scale are posed on a 0 to 4 scale, from "strongly disagree" to "strongly agree." Items on the MOLEST Scale include such statements as, "I believe that sex with children can make the child feel closer to adults," and "Some children can act very seductively." Examples on the RAPE Scale include "Women often falsely accuse men of rape," and "When a woman gets raped more than once, she is probably doing something to cause it."

Bumby tested 44 men convicted of a sexual assault of a child, 25 men convicted of rape, and 20 men convicted of a nonsexual offense; all men were incarcerated at the time and the sexual offenders were undergoing treatment. From their responses, Bumby was able to show that these scales were reliable and valid measures of the cognitive distortions held by sexual offenders, at least in this group of prisoners. Whether an outpatient sample would have responded in a similar fashion is still uncertain. Also of concern is the finding that, among child molesters, endorsements on the RAPE Scale were as high as those of the rapists, thus clouding the discriminant validity of these measures.

Obviously, denial has been an obstacle in the path of not only treating sexual offenders, but in evaluating them as well. Recently, Schneider and Wright (2001) have devised a scale designed to measure multiple aspects of denial, the Facets of Sexual Offender Denial (FoSOD). This scale was tested on 179 men who had had sexual contact with a minor. All were undergoing outpatient treatment at the time of assessment. Six factors were identified, including denial of the offense (for example, "The victim is the kind of person who would make up a story"), denial of extent ("I did not go as far as people think"), and denial of intent ("I was under stress"). While construct and predictive validity were demonstrated, of chief interest was the ability of the FoSOD to distinguish men early in the therapy process from those who had undergone more extensive treatment. Offenders more advanced in treatment had lower denial scores than their counterparts just beginning therapy. Thus the FoSOD holds some promise in being able to assess progress in treatment, something few other instruments have demonstrated.

Unfortunately, all these tests of cognitive distortions suffer from a number of deficiencies when held up to the scrutiny of both controlled scientific research and clinical experience. Indeed distinctions are rarely made among types of offenders. For example, predatory offenders against boys are vastly different on a number of characteristics from those who situationally offend against a single girl (Maletzky & Steinhauser, 2002), yet studies purportedly validating these instruments fail to distinguish among these groups (McGrath et al., 1998; Tierney & McCabe, 2001).

Furthermore, many of the assessment instruments employed to measure cognitive distortions have been tested mainly in nonoffender populations, such as college students (Burt, 1980; Malamuth, 1989; Schewe & O'Donohue, 1998). This has been particularly true of the sometimes ingenious tests devised to measure tendencies to sexually aggress (for a review, see Maletzky, 2000.). Whether the behaviors of psychology students on these tests can be generalized to those of sexual offenders remains to be determined.

Of equal concern is that most of these instruments have not been documented to be of clinical benefit outside of their initial publication. Other centers either have not chosen to duplicate these instruments or have found them to be of limited utility. Therefore, the limitations of assessing cognitive distortions in this group of offenders remain to be overcome. We have every confidence, however, that this will occur, given the attention devoted in recent years to the problems of discrimination among subtypes of sexual offenders and to the transparency of assessment instruments.

Assessment of Fantasies

DSM-IV-R requires "recurrent, intense sexually arousing fantasies or urges" to support the diagnosis of any paraphilia. Such fantasies strengthen deviant sexual behaviors (Knafo & Jaffe, 1984; O'Donohue, Letourneau, & Dowling, 1997) and could thus form targets for treatment. However, quantifying these inner and private events has proven difficult.

The first attempt at analyzing deviant fantasies was made by Wilson in 1978 with the development of the Wilson Sex Fantasy Questionnaire (WSFQ; Wilson, 1978). In this instrument, 40 items are divided into four subtypes: exploratory, such as group sex and mate swapping; intimate, such as kissing and oral sex; impersonal, such as sex with strangers and fetishism; and sadomasochistic, such as spanking or being forced to have sex. Although the WSFQ has been shown to distinguish among some groups of sexual offenders (Gosselin & Wilson, 1980; Wilson, 1997), it has not proven clinically useful as a measurement device, perhaps because many such offenders underreport fantasies (Baumgartner et al., 2002; Langevin, Lang, & Curnoe, 1998). Sexual offenders may have good reason to minimize their fantasies; in addition, the continued focus on fantasies in treatment programs may also have had the effect of reducing reporting. Moreover, many items on the WSFQ do not specify gender or age, thus obscuring their relevance for specific types of sexual crimes. In addition, just one question assesses pedophilic fantasies.

A second attempt to measure sexual fantasies was made by O'Donohue and colleagues (1997) with the construction of the Sexual Fantasy Questionnaire (SFQ), an instrument comprising 155 items describing sexual acts about which an individual might fantasize. Examples, to be endorsed on a 3-point scale ("never," "sometimes," "frequently"), include, "getting a blow job from a woman who is enjoying it," "Thrusting my penis into a boy's rear end," and "Rubbing myself with a pair of panties until I come." These authors found acceptable reliability and convergent validity when the SFQ was tested in 42 child molesters compared with 87 male college students.

Results indicated that the child molesters, as predicted, had higher scores on the items associated with fantasies about children. Complicating the interpretation of this finding, however, is the use of an undergraduate control group, a fact underscored by the fact that the control group actually scored higher than the child molesters on certain deviant scales, such as bondage. Moreover, other types of sexual offenders, such as exhibitionists and rapists, were not included. Finally, there has been no follow-up report on the use of the SFQ.

However, more recent attempts to assess the fantasies of sexual offenders have also not proven helpful. In an extensive analysis of the contributions various tests make to the relationship between risk and recidivism, Beech and colleagues (2002) reported that the sections on the Multiphasic Sex Inventory (Nichols & Molinder, 1984) which purportedly deal with fantasy failed to influence the overall level of risk in sexual offenders and did not assist in any significant way in the prediction of risk to commit another sexual crime. It would appear that, in being asked to report their innermost fantasies, offenders are understandably reluctant to be totally honest. It will fall to other measures to more accurately assess this crucial area in the evaluation and treatment of sexual offending.

Card Sorts

Despite the commonly held belief that sexual offenders will not self-report deviant thoughts and behaviors, a number of attempts have been made to devise tests in which prearranged answers on cards can be endorsed by the client, with the hope that selecting cards will prove less ego damaging than answering standard test questions or replying in one's own voice. Such card sorts have been employed in the main as corroborative measures of treatment progress (Abel et al.,1987; Day, Miner, Sturgeon, & Murphy, 1989). Some evidence exists that self-report measures, such as items from the Clarke Sex History Questionnaire (Langevin, Paitch, Handy, & Langevin, 1990) and the MSI (Nichols & Molinder, 1984) do provide useful additional information in distinguishing among types of child molesters.

However, these instruments have dealt with past behaviors to the relative exclusion of present interests. To correct that deficiency, Laws, Hanson, Osborn, and Greenbaum (2000) have recently analyzed whether the addition of a card sort measure enhanced the accuracy of the penile plethysmograph (PPG — see below) in the diagnosis of 124 community child molesters. This card sort identified a variety of deviant behaviors which the offender was asked to endorse on a 7-point scale, from 1, "very attractive," to 7, "very unattractive," including a number of sexual activities with children. Of interest, the card sort demonstrated its greatest accuracy in differentiating men who molested boys from those offending against girls. Taken together with the PPG findings, diagnostic accuracy was improved from the mid 80% range with any single measure to 91.7%, significantly greater than if any individual instrument was used.

While these results bolster hope that self-report measures may be useful for diagnosis in sexual offenders, optimism is tempered by this study's reliance on a small group of one type of offender; in addition, all offenders were already in treatment and had admitted to deviant behaviors. It may be difficult to replicate these findings in a less cooperative, but more typical, population of offenders without disguising the intent of these tests to a greater degree.

Sexual Offender Typologies

In a series of seminal papers devoted to elucidating sexual offender typologies, workers at the Massachusetts Treatment Center have outlined a number of characteristics typifying rapists (Knight & Prentky, 1990) and child molesters (Prentky, Knight, & Lee, 1997). For example, for rapists, four primary groups were defined based upon motivation for the offense, but these were then further subdivided into nine categories based upon offender characteristics, such as social competence. Child molesters were classified on a two-axis system, with Axis I comprising fixation and social competence and Axis II including the amount and meaning of the contact, the extent of physical injury, and the presence of sadism.

Although reliability and predictive validity of these diagnostic systems have been demonstrated (Brown & Forth, 1997), few studies have attempted to corroborate this type of classification. Barbaree, Seto, Serin, Amos, and Preston (1994), in an attempt at replication, could only classify child molesters on the fixated and social competence dimensions. Looman, Gauthier, and Boer (2001) attempted a replication with 119 child molesters. These researchers found that only the high fixation–low social competence group demonstrated a clear sexual preference for children. Differences were not found for groups when rates of sexual and violent recidivism were examined. Utilizing these typologies did not add predictive or diagnostic power to the PPG data, which were the most helpful in identifying risk.

Problems with these typologies are twofold: they are complicated and offer little additional clinical information beyond more simple diagnostic approaches, such as obtaining a history and a PPG. For example, Seto and Lalumiere (2001) have recently proposed a simple Screening Scale for Pedophilic Interests (SSPI), comprising just four historical variables: the presence or absence of male victims, multiple victims, younger victims, and extrafamilial victims. These data can be obtained from police reports, presentence investigations, and self-histories, all easily available to clinicians conducting these assessments. These investigators found, in a study of 1,113 child molesters, that SSPI scores identified pedophilic interests, as measured subsequently by the PPG, significantly better than chance, while the presence of false positives in offenders who had not molested children was minimal.

It appears that attempts to classify sexual offenders into neat bundles are frustrated by the heterogeneity of this population. Offenders, even within one subgroup such as exhibitionists or rapists, may be too diverse to classify using present-day technologies. Evidence exists, as well, that some offenders are polymorphously diverse — they may expose for some time, then molest a child (McConaghy, 1993). Moreover, attempts to classify offenders have been so complex that, in everyday clinical practice, it has proven more feasible to employ simpler measures, such as historical variables, the SSPI, and the PPG. These, as we shall see, have proven of immense help in elucidating issues of treatment and risk.

Physiologic Tests

The Plethysmograph

Originally employed to test impotence, the penile plethysmograph (PPG) has an extensive, but controversial, history in measuring sexual arousal. The first such devices measured penile volume changes (Freund, 1963), although now penile circumference is preferred because the methodology is widely available and relatively inexpensive, and the reliability (Howes, 1998) and validity (Howes, 1998; Lalumiere & Quinsey, 1994; Serin et al., 2001) well demonstrated. Figure 9.1 depicts the instrument, along with its penile gauge. Figure 9.2 demonstrates a typical office/laboratory set-up for the provision of assessment and treatment services for sexual offenders, including the PPG.

A practitioner consensus has now emerged, codified in guidelines for the use of the PPG published by the Association for the Treatment of Sexual Abusers (ATSA, 1993), on how to employ this instrument. Briefly, a mercury-in-rubber strain gauge, thin as a rubber band (but loose, not tight), is placed by the client onto the midshaft of his penis, which remains covered by clothing. The client then views explicit sexual material such as slides or videotapes, or nonexplicit material (such as clothed

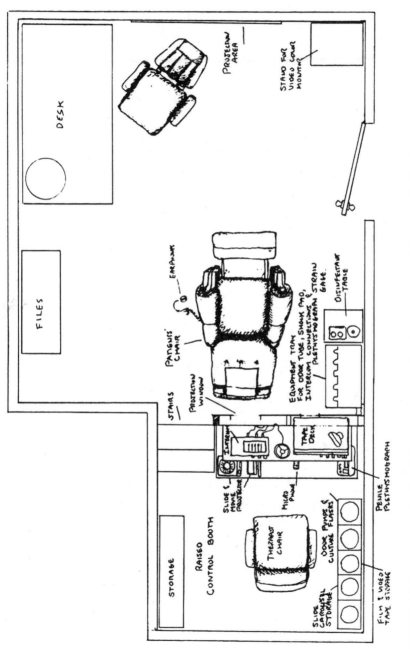

FIGURE 9.1.   A typical office/laboratory set-up for the treatment of the sexual offender.

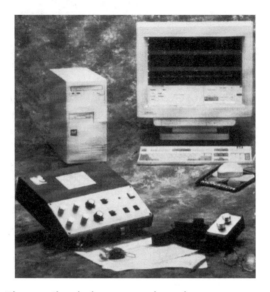

FIGURE 9.2.   The penile plethysmograph and gauge.

children) associated with his offense, or listens to descriptions of normal and deviant sexual scenes. Penile circumference is simultaneously and continuously recorded and expressed, in terms of percentage of previously determined full erection, throughout the process. GSR and respiratory rate are also routinely recorded. Clients are asked to respond to a randomly presented signal displayed on the screen as an attentional control. Changes less than 20% of full erection are considered below the level of clinical import. Testing can consume several hours.

Of surprise, under such artificial laboratory conditions, and under pressure to appear normal, many offenders demonstrate deviant arousal. A number of studies have testified to the safety, reliability, and validity of PPG testing (for a review, see Howes [1995]). These studies have reported changes in the expected directions, with many child molesters showing arousal to child-related themes and many rapists demonstrating arousal to aggressive sexuality.

For example, Card and Dibble (1995) found that the PPG strongly discriminated between offenders attracted to adults as opposed to those attracted to children. Laws, Gulayets, and Frenzel (1995) determined that the instrument could discriminate child molesters from normal subjects. Serin and colleagues (2001) demonstrated that child molesters and rapists could be differentiated on the PPG, a result echoed by Looman and Marshall (2001), who reported that audiotaped descriptions of sexual activity with children were as effective as visual stimuli (slides) in distinguishing these two groups. Moreover, distinctions have been demonstrated with this instrument in discriminating those who have molested boys as opposed to girls (Laws et al., 2000).

In addition, the PPG has been shown to be a robust predictor of recidivism in several recent studies. Serin and colleagues (2001) reported that among 68 incarcerated offenders, those who displayed higher deviant arousal on the instrument recidivated sooner and at higher rates. Moreover, the pedophile index on the PPG (a ratio of deviant to nondeviant arousal) added significantly to the prediction of a new sexual offense in a similar study of 258 offenders (Nunes, Firestone, Bradford, Greenberg, & Broom, 2002). Even adolescents have been tested on the machine, with results in a positive direction (Kaemingk, Koselka, Becker, & Kaplan, 1995) and without harm.

However, the measurement of circumference changes in sexual offenders to determine preferences and predilections has also been fraught with difficulty and controversy. Indeed, Just over 30% of men who molest children show either normal PPG readings (erections to normal material and no arousal to child material) or a "flat line," with no response to any stimulus. These figures jump to over 40% with rapists and exhibitionists (Howes, 1998; Looman, Abracen, Maillet, & DiFazio,1998). Indeed, rapists may be the most difficult group to classify on the PPG due to their heterogeneity (Looman, 2002).

The major difference between offenders and controls may be the latter group's enhanced ability to inhibit arousal (Howes, 1998). Thus, a better test for many offenders may be to elicit arousal with nondeviant stimuli first, then measure the individual's ability (as determined by latency) to lose arousal with the presentation of deviant material, a measure still not routinely incorporated into most testing paradigms. Furthermore, correlations between PPG scores and recidivism have not always been high (Nunes et al., 2002) and studies purporting to demonstrate reliability and validity have not included sufficient numbers of offenders to inspire confidence.

It is also evident that the instrument has not been sufficiently standardized. Different stimuli are used in different centers, exposure times vary, and varying measures of arousal are utilized as well. It is as if electrocardiogram electrodes were being applied at the whim of the examiner to monitor an EKG. This is exacerbated because the testing situation is highly artificial, intrusive, and, to some degree, transparent.

Meanwhile, the PPG cannot be employed within a legal framework to determine whether an individual committed a crime, even though it smacks of objectivity and could thus be disproportionately weighted. False negatives are common but, fortunately, false positives are rare (Lalumiere & Harris, 1998) and results thus far have suffered from a sampling bias because only those offenders who have been caught are evaluated. In this same vein, the PPG cannot be employed with the increasing number of female sexual offenders. However, a special gauge, the Geer Gauge, has been devised to measure female sexual arousal (Geer, Morokoff, & Greenwood, 1974).

Finally, and most seriously of all, cheating is not only possible (Wilson, 1998), but likely. When instructed to falsify results, particularly suppression of arousal, subjects have been able to use cognitive control to obscure test findings (Looman et al., 1998). However, a control may be to first present stimuli which will generate erections, then determine if an offender can detumesce with deviant stimuli (Maletzky, 2002).

Overall, the PPG has proven helpful in distinguishing some offenders from nonoffenders and in predicting the risk of recidivism in those with deviant arousal. Although most clinicians and researchers continue to employ it, the number of false negatives and the possibility of cheating cast doubt on its use in forensic settings and its overall utility. Indeed, the PPG may be as useful as an instrument of treatment in providing biofeedback to a client on his level of arousal (see below) as it is in assessment. The finding that sexual arousal can also be indicated by PET scan measurements (George, 1995) raises the at once intriguing, yet frightening, vision of peering directly into the organ determining sexual arousal: the brain. Whether such science fiction scenarios will ever become an ethically acceptable method to determine sexual arousal, only the future will tell.

The Abel Assessment

Recently, an altogether different and novel way to measure sexual interest, far less intrusive than the PPG, has been described, the Abel Assessment, or Visual Reaction Time (VRT). First proposed by Abel and coworkers almost a decade ago (Abel, Lawry, Karlstrom, Osborn, & Gillespie, 1994), this test utilizes a slide projector to present images of clothed models in a variety of categories, including children and adults and scenes of sadistic activity. Each participant is asked to view the slide as long as he likes, then to rate each on a scale of 1 (extremely repulsive) to 7 (extremely interesting). A computer then records the time each individual takes to view and rate each slide. Theoretically, subjects are unaware that this "reaction" time is being measured. It is supposed that the longer a client takes to view and rate a slide, the greater his sexual interest is in the subject depicted within it.

Indeed, Abel's group has reported acceptable reliability and validity of the VRT when compared to the PPG (Abel, Huffman, Warberg, & Holland, 1998), although technical cautions have been raised about the interpretation of the test (Fischer & Smith, 1999; Smith & Fischer, 1999) which have as yet not been clarified. However, some independent laboratories have also ascribed validity to the test (Johnson & Listiak, 1999; Letourneau, 1999). A recent study of 57 sexual offenders reported reasonable validity and clinical utility of the VRT in offenders against boys and adolescent girls, but not in men who molested younger girls or in rapists (Letourneau, 2002).

The VRT is unobtrusive and equal in expense to the PPG, but caution is advised in assuming that it can, as of the present, replace the PPG:

- The intention of the VRT is to measure sexual interest, not arousal. These may be separate constructs.
- Thus far, only small numbers of subjects have been tested in reported studies.
- As with the PPG, this test cannot determine if an individual has committed a crime.
- Unlike the PPG, no study has demonstrated a relationship between the VRT and recidivism.
- Most seriously, although a study demonstrating that subjects could not falsify results has been reported (Abel, 1997), the transparency of the VRT is worrisome. It is possible, if not likely, that offenders will learn the nature of the test and thus be able to conceal their true interests. Indeed, in our clinical experience, this is already occurring.

Despite these cautions, the VRT contains numerous strengths, especially when compared to the PPG. It employs a standardized set of visual stimuli, is easily administered, and is less intrusive and more palatable to offenders and treatment providers alike. Whether it will prove to be a valuable contribution to the assessment of the sexual offender remains for future large and collaborative studies, and extensive clinical experience, to determine.

The Polygraph

Controversy also surrounds the use of the poorly named "lie detector," or polygraph, in the assessment of sexual offenders, even though its use is almost universal in treatment programs (Freeman-Longo et al., 1995). During this test, an offender might be asked about engaging in deviant acts while recordings are made of his pulse, blood pressure, EKG, and GSR. As with the PPG, the subject is in a threatening environment, one in which he is aware that the reason for the test is the suspicion of dishonesty. The test is intrusive; moreover, it is not accorded full validity in the popular or scientific literatures (Abrams, 1991).

Polygraph examinations for sexual offenders can be full disclosure tests, in which a complete sexual history is explored, or maintenance exams, during which just a few questions about the original crime and activities during the present time period are asked. Experience with these examinations is mixed (Blasingame, 1998). While some offenders fail the test and then admit culpability for a crime, many others probably pass despite concealment, having conquered the machine and their own anxiety.

A recent study examined the polygraph in 35 inmates and 25 parolees who had committed a variety of sexual offenses (Ahlmeyer, Heil, McKee, & English, 2000). Results indicated that the polygraph elicited a greater number of admissions of additional victims and crimes than history alone. However, 84% of the inmates and 74% of the parolees showed some deception on the test. Inmates admitted a greater number of offenses and victims than did parolees, perhaps because of the greater consequences attendant upon disclosure in a community setting. Of concern, most subjects offered less offense and victim information on a second polygraph than they had on the first test. Perhaps many of these offenders experienced less apprehension about the test by the second round.

It is thus clear that polygraph results need to be interpreted with caution. The setting and prior experience with the machine must be taken into account. However, in a clinical sense, the polygraph can be an important tool in treatment. It can uncover additional areas for inquiry (Maletzky, 2003), and can be utilized almost as a placebo (as demonstrated in the case example below) to encourage the disclosure of more information before an upcoming polygraph. While this can help the client pass his next test, it can also provide valuable new data to be utilized in constructing a treatment plan.

The Assessment of Risk

While assessments for purposes of diagnosis and treatability of sexual offenders are often requested of clinicians, just as frequently, an evaluation of the level of risk to the community is required as well. Such assessments are often necessary for decisions about release from an institution, determining the level of supervision in the community, and the need for civil commitment. Unfortunately, clinical opinion about the level of risk any individual poses to reoffend is only slightly better than chance (Hanson & Bussiere, 1998). In addition, prediction of risk to reoffend sexually differs from the risk of general recidivism (Hanson & Thornton, 2000).

Fortunately, risk assessment tools have been developed which improve the predictions of a sexual reoffense considerably. One of the first widely used such instruments has been the Minnesota Sex Offender Screening Tool — Revised (MnSOST-R), developed by Epperson and colleagues (Epperson, Kaul, & Huot, 1995). Recognizing that mental health professionals hold no special expertise in the prediction of violence in general, or of sexual aggression in particular, these researchers utilized actuarial methods to retrospectively analyze which factors, taken from information routinely available to clinicians from the criminal and clinical records, are predictive of a sexual (as opposed to a nonsexual) reoffense.

Sample items on the MnSOST-R include number of prior sexual convictions, offenses while under supervision, use of force, whether the victim was a stranger, and the relative instability of employment history, all factors shown in prior clinical trials to predict recidivism (Maletzky & Steinhauser, 2002). However, Epperson's group has reported only modest reliability and validity (Epperson et al., 1995); moreover, to rank offenders on this scale requires obtaining and reviewing voluminous records which may not always be available. In addition, the scale has not been able to predict recidivism accurately in situational offenders, the largest group being treated in community-based clinics (Hanson & Bussiere, 1998).

To partially address these concerns, Hanson and colleagues have developed a briefer, more accessible scale based on several more readily obtainable MnSOST-R items and on those proven most robust in predicting risk to reoffend (Hanson, 1997). This newer scale, the Rapid Risk Assessment for Sexual Offense Recidivism (RRASOR) contains just four weighted elements: prior sexual offenses, age over or under 25, victim gender, and relationship to victim. It is based on the predictive value of knowing that offenders with more than one prior sexual conviction, who are under 25, who have offended against male victims, and who have victims outside of their immediate families, are at markedly higher risk to commit another sexual offense at some time in the future (Maletzky, 1993).

Although the RRASOR has been extensively employed to quickly gauge risk (Hanson & Harris, 2000), it may prove hazardous to rely upon a limited set of variables in helping to decide such important issues as whether an offender is safe to be released from prison or whether a parolee should be identified as requiring community notification. Indeed, the originators of the RRASOR caution that it was not intended to provide a comprehensive assessment of all the factors relevant to the prediction of risk. Of particular concern, it does not include a way to measure exposure to risk, as, for example if a child molester is again living around children. Of more serious import, it does not include two of the most significant predictors of risk to be at large — deviant arousal on the PPG (Nunes et al., 2002) and the presence of psychopathy (Serin et al., 2001). Nonetheless, the RRASOR has proven to be a widely used and easily accessible tool to arrive at a rough estimate of sexual risk. It remains, however, to be validated in large prospective trials.

To expand on the RRASOR while maintaining its ease of use, Hanson and his coworkers have described a new instrument for predicting sexual risk to reoffend, the Static-99. The name refers both to the test's use of static factors available from a records review and the year of its development (Hanson & Thornton,1999). This new scale combines elements of the RRASOR with a second, limited-use but validated scale, the Structured Anchored Clinical Judgement (Grubin, 1997). The Static-99 is composed of 10 weighted factors, including the four RRASOR items, combined with elements related to psychopathy, the presence of any stranger victims, and relationship history.

The Static-99 is now widely used and has demonstrated reasonable reliability (Hanson & Thornton, 2000) but only moderate validity (Nunes et al., 2002). Despite its limitations, including the lack of inclusion of deviant arousal on the PPG and the absence of a way to measure changes in risk based upon environmental and treatment variables, it remains a valuable and easily scoreable instrument if access to criminal and clinical data can be assured.

One instrument which does include PPG data is the Sex Offender Risk Appraisal Guide (the SORAG), developed by Quinsey and colleagues to predict sexual and violent recidivism in sexual offenders (Quinsey, Harris, Rice, & Cormier, 1998). The SORAG incorporates a wide range of historical and arousal information, including living with biological parents, history of alcohol problems, age at first offense, presence of a psychiatric disorder, presence of antisocial traits, and presence of deviant arousal on the PPG.

Recently, Nunes and coworkers (Nunes et al., 2002) compared the Static-99 with the SORAG in a sample of 258 sexual offenders with a variety of types of offense. Both instruments demonstrated moderate levels of accuracy in predicting sexual reoffenses, but only deviant sexual arousal, as measured by the PPG, added significantly to the prediction of sexual recidivism. The authors concluded that, while the Static-99 is the easier test to administer, the addition of a PPG would markedly enhance its predictive accuracy.

This result is consistent with an earlier study finding that, among a variety of psychological instruments attempting to predict recidivism, only the PPG demonstrated accuracy in distinguishing who would go on to repeat a sexual crime (Proulx et al., 1997). Indeed, in a recent attempt to predict which offenders might need the antitestosterone medication, depo-Provera, used only in the most dangerous of sexual offenders, deviant arousal, along with other historical factors described above, was found to be among the strongest predictors of the need for the drug (Maletzky & Field, 2003).

A completely different approach to predicting recidivism has been described by Nicholaichuk (Nicholaichuk, Gordon, Gu, & Wong, 2000), in which a Career Criminal Profile (CCP) is plotted. The CCP is a graphic representation of the time in years that an offender has been incarcerated. The steeper the slope, the greater the ratio of time the offender has been in jail or prison as opposed to being in the community. Although data now show that the CCP can differentiate treated from untreated offenders (Looman, Abracen, & Nicholaichuk, 2000), and the information needed to construct the test is usually available, reoffense rates of situational offenders were not well predicted using the CCP, perhaps because these rates are low to begin with (Barbaree, 1997), and these men may not spend much time incarcerated (Maletzky, 1991b). Moreover, recent results from an analysis of 579 offenders (Nicholaichuk et al., 2000) demonstrated that CCP slopes were lower following a specified time delay for both treated and untreated offenders, although the degree of change was marginally greater for the treated group. Again, situational offenders were not well differentiated and PPG data, probably crucial to predicting relapse rates, were not included in the CCP.

One problem with all the predictive tests thus far described is their reliance upon historical, or static, factors, such as number and gender of, and relationship to, prior victims, or employment and relationship histories. While these factors have been demonstrated to reliably predict future sexual offenses (Maletzky, 1993), they do not take into account variables that could change over a treatment course or with a change in environment. Such factors could include improvements in disclosure, empathy, or self-esteem, reductions in deviant arousal on the PPG, or moving into a home where there are no children.

In order to assess the benefits of treatment in predicting recidivism, Studer and Reddon (1998) contrasted 150 treatment completers with 127 noncompleters. While static variables, such as prior sexual offenses, were related to recidivism in noncompleters, successful treatment completion removed this correlation. The authors concluded that treatment not only was successful in reducing repeat offending, but that reliance on historical, static factors alone could prove misleading in that it ignores progress in treatment.

Indeed, in a recent study of 95 community-based offenders by Dempster and Hart (2002), variable, or dynamic factors proved as robust as historical, or static factors, in predicting the risk of a sexual reoffense. Such dynamic factors included improvements in relationship and employment situations, reductions in minimization and denial, and altering attitudes condoning sexual offenses, all changes which could be brought about through treatment and social support, perhaps through the correctional system itself (Harris & Hanson, 1999). These dynamic variables possessed incremental value when added to the standard static factors described above.

This finding is echoed in a recent report by Thornton (2002) who reported that, in a group of 158 incarcerated sexual offenders with a mixture of types of crimes, factors such as the presence of cognitive distortions, the level of socioaffective functioning, and the degree of self-management skills, were all related to propensity to reoffend. These factors are changeable through treatment; thus, these findings point to a need to identify the extent to which such change is occurring within a treatment program.

Because no standard existed to evaluate these changes in risk, especially in offenders undergoing treatment, Hanson and Harris (2001) have recently developed the Sex Offender Need Assessment Rating (SONAR). This scale includes items which might change during, or as a result of, treatment and are believed to correlate with a reduced risk of reoffense, such as intimacy deficits, sexual attitudes, substance abuse, and victim access. In this initial study, the SONAR demonstrated adequate internal consistency and a moderate ability to distinguish men who would go on to reoffend while in the community. A particularly strong effect was found on the item of self-regulation or impulsivity.

These are encouraging results as they engender some optimism about the treatment of offenders, especially because of an improving ability to identify those offenders progressing in treatment. However, the extent to which these results will generalize is, as yet, uncertain, as other groups have not yet replicated these results. In addition, it is possible that some dynamic factors are simply proxies for enduring propensities, such as a tendency to act impulsively or to abuse alcohol. It seems safe to say, however, that, based upon research and clinical experience, the addition of changeable, dynamic factors to the already proven predictive power of static, historical ones, will improve our ability to identify those offenders most at risk to reoffend.

Summarizing the research and clinical experience in this area, Table 9.4 lists what we now believe are the most salient predictors of risk of sexual recidivism. These factors assume special importance as they are drawn from both extensive clinical experience (Maletzky, 1993; Maletzky & Steinhauser, 2002) and actuarial and statistical procedures (Hanson & Thornton, 2000); yet, both sources of data appear to yield the same sets of factors. While obviously, historical factors take precedence in the current prediction of the tendency to reoffend, dynamic factors which might change as a result of treatment or environmental alterations are being accorded increasing prominence.

TABLE 9.4. Static and Dynamic Risk Factors in Predicting a Sexual Reoffense

Static risk factors	Dynamic risk factors
-Multiple victims	Continuing presence of deviant sexual arousal
-Multiple paraphilias	Lack of participation in a treatment program
-Extrafamilial victims	Persistence of denial
-Stranger victims	Persistence of poor impulse control
-Predatory pattern	Probation or parole violation
-Use of force in the crime	Victim access
-Deviant sexual arousal	
-Minimization or denial	
-Unamenability to treatment	
-History of nonsexual antisocial behavior	
-Presence of neurologic impairment	
-Prior treatment failure	
-History of employment instability	
-History of unstable relationships	

In analyzing these factors, it is important to keep in mind the following caveats:

- While the actuarial tools described here have proven more accurate than clinical judgement alone, they depend upon the quality of the data available; in sexual offender assessments, historical data are often suspect or incomplete.
- No instrument is currently able to predict *when* an offender might commit a new crime.
- Scales cannot take into account all intervening variables; for example, a child molester might have few predictors of reoffense, yet announce an intention to commit a new crime; a rapist might suffer a stroke and be relatively immobilized.
- Few of these assessments include tests of IQ, a factor that has been shown to lower self-control and increase risk of reoffense (Maletzky, 1993).
- All such predictions are statistical in nature, and cannot prove that any single individual will commit any paricular crime in the future.
- While an offender with many risk factors is at high risk, and an offender with few is at low risk, most sexual offenders carry a moderate number of such factors; assessing this risk in a quantitative fashion poses a serious challenge to researchers, now being met by

large ongoing studies (Hanson et al., 2002), which, hopefully will provide even more accurate predictions in the future.

☐ Pragmatic Issues in Assessing the Sexual Offender

The most serious issue encountered in evaluating and treating sexual offenders is, unfortunately, the lack of financial resources in providing services. Despite the sometimes sensationalized media coverage of sexual crimes and the political outcries against them, very few government sponsored programs exist. State institutions, which house growing numbers of such offenders, rarely provide adequate assessment and treatment facilities (Freeman-Longo et al., 1995) and those which do exist are being severely curtailed or discontinued (Gordon & Hover, 1998). Moreover, county correctional and mental health services are being stretched ever more thinly over a burgeoning patient population to the extent that sexual offender services are essentially nonexistent. Thus offenders in jail or prison are being released without the benefit of adequate assessment and treatment services.

This dire picture is aggravated by the lack of funding for outpatient treatment as well. Most community-based offenders are hardly wealthy and need to rely on the generosity of county corrections departments or treatment providers to subsidize their treatment. They often have just been released from incarceration and have not secured well-paying jobs. To compound the problem, private and governmental insurance programs have, until now, refused to even partially cover the costs of evaluation and treatment in this population due, in part, to the perception that sexual offending is not a disease, but a choice. There is, unfortunately, no vocal constituency to advocate for coverage equivalent to that which was so effective in ensuring coverage for drug and alcohol abuse a decade ago.

Payments for assessments are more often assured than for the lengthier process of treatment because agencies are under pressure to ascertain safety to be at large. In this plight, clinicians can help by spreading whatever payments are required from an offender (for testing or treatment) over a longer period of time and by rewarding progress in treatment with fee reductions (Maletzky & Steinhauser, 1998). Fortunately, many therapists, recognizing the financial difficulties of their clients, have made these generous sacrifices to assist in the important tasks of evaluating and treating this clientele.

A second pragmatic issue in treating sexual offenders, alluded to above, is their resistance to change. These clients rarely admit everything

TABLE 9.5. Percent Recidividism Among Patients Who Did, and Did Not, Successfully Complete Treatment (N=7,275)

Type of Offender(N)	Completed treatment		Recidivated*		Terminated treatment		Recidivated*	
	n	%	n	%	n	%	n	%
CM, FV (2,196)	1,675	76.3	4	0.24	521	23.7	9	1.7
CM, MV (765)	514	67.2	3	0.58	251	32.8	5	2.0
Het ped (1,011)	851	84.2	4	0.47	160	15.8	12	7.5
Homo ped (1,251)	1,067	85.3	19	1.80	184	14.7	32	17.1
Exhib (1,604)	1,102	68.7	8	0.73	502	31.3	40	8.0
Rapists (448)	397	88.6	39	9.80	51	11.4	38	74.5
Totals (7,275)	5,606	72.1	77	1.4	1,669	22.9	136	8.1

Note: CM, FV = child molesters, female victim; CM, MV = child molesters, male victim; Het ped = heterosexual pedophiles; Homo ped = homosexual pedophiles; Exhib = exhibitionists.
*Recidivated means being charged with a new sexual crime.

they have done, and often do not want to give up pleasurable, if deviant and harmful, behaviors. Contrary to clinical lore, however, offenders are eminently treatable (see treatment results in Table 9.5). By creating trust and refraining from directly challenging and confronting such offenders at first, and by including them in an assessment and treatment plan, even those offenders in absolute denial can be successfully treated utilizing the behavioral and cognitive methods developed over the past 20 years, and briefly described below in the case illustration.

☐ Case Illustration

Mr. G., a 45-year-old accountant, had a history of attraction to boys in the age ranges of 10 to 13; it dated back to his teenage years. While no testable theories of the etiology of this disorder, homosexual pedophilia, exist, many researchers believe that a combination of biological (Ellis, 1993) and developmental (Malamuth et al., 1990) factors may play a role.

In G's case, early sexual play with other boys had occurred, although to what extent these were formative is uncertain.

G had molested a 9-year-old cousin when he was 13 and had mutually consenting sexual activity with other male teenagers throughout his adolescent years, but continued to fantasize about young boys during this time. He dated girls as well, although he later admitted this was mostly a ruse to avoid being labeled as a homosexual. As is not uncommon in such cases, he married in his early 20s, but continued to fantasize about boys, purchase pornography about them, and take advantage of situations in which he could gain access to them.

Over the course of 23 years, G molested nine boys, usually by first getting to know them and their families, establishing trust, buying them gifts, and appearing to be almost a substitute father; in many cases, he chose boys without an actual father figure in the home. His typical method of operation was to offer to watch these boys while their mothers were busy, then take them shopping, then go on trips and campouts with them. He would make sexual overtures to these boys by first discussing sexual matters with them, then show them pornographic videos, and finally attempt fondling and mutual oral sexual activity with them. While some of the boys consented, others resisted; G usually did not use physical force or restraint, but he would cajole and use verbal pressure to obtain sexual access. On several occasions, however, he became threatening, and certainly his size and adult presence were factors securing some compliance. On most occasions he warned the boys not to tell others, and occasionally he would threaten harm to them or their families should they do so.

Several of these victims did tell their parents or other authoities, however, and G had been arrested twice before for sexual abuse. He had, however, received only probation on the first occasion, then escaped treatment by delaying entering a program. His probation officer did not extend his period of supervision and allowed him to complete probation without graduating from a treatment program, something fortunately rarely allowed in the present day.

Following his second conviction for sexual abuse 4 years later, G received a 3-year prison sentence, but received no treatment as all prison-based programs had been discontinued due to budget cuts. He therefore presented to a sexual abuse clinic in the community following release from prison with many of the danger signs listed in Table 9.4, yet never having received the benefit of treatment.

When first seen in the clinic, G's wife had divorced him and he had found work at an accounting firm. It is important to understand that G was not a thoroughly evil person. He had not committed nonsexual crimes, was neither antisocial nor insensitive, and, indeed, had contributed to his family and community in a variety of worthwhile ways. This is not atypical of many offenders, who, were we unaware of their offending, might appear to be upstanding members of their communities. As is true of many people, they have committed many honorable acts, along with a few very harmful ones.

G had married mostly to appear conventional, but during his prison term he had formed an adult homosexual relationship and wished to pursue this upon release. He believed he was fully homosexual and treatment personnel agreed that this lifestyle was healthier than his attraction to boys; it did not appear feasible nor ethically justifiable to force heterosexuality upon him.

Requirements of supervision prevented G from associating with children or having access to pornography (or a personal computer), but he remained potentially dangerous; in addition, his period of supervision would only extend another 3 years. Beyond that time, no legal restrictions could prevent his access to children. Therefore, it was urgent to continually assess his risk while providing him the modern treatment techniques proven to reduce risk in such cases.

Based upon static variables, G scored a 6 on the Static-99 and a 13 on the MnSOST, placing him in the high risk group to be at large. The dynamic test instruments described above, such as the SONAR, were not developed at the time of these evaluations and thus were unavailable for use in his case. (However, a retrospective SONAR was administered — see below.) A full disclosure polygraph done on admission to treatment, however, revealed deception on questions relating to number of victims and ongoing fantasies; this led to additional disclosures and subsequent successful completion of polygraphs later in treatment.

G was afforded individual as well as group therapy, both on a weekly basis, although to hold costs down, the group was offered free of charge as long as G completed homework assignments in his relapse prevention workbook (Eldridge, 1998) regularly. In group, G reviewed the antecedents of his offending behavior and how to intervene at the earliest possible steps in the chains leading to a reoffense. He also was effectively confronted by offenders more experienced in therapy about his typical minimizations and distortions and he learned more about some of the cognitive errors he used to justify his sexual misdeeds. Moreover, he was confronted by videotapes and letters produced by victims of sexual abuse and hence gained some empathy for what harm his own offenses might have caused.

G failed his first polygraph on questions of additional victims. His therapist helped G prepare for his second polygraph several months later by reviewing with him all possible victims and encouraging him to be as open in this area as possible. When G then admitted to additional crimes (not to be adjudicated), he was able to pass his next test, and, as a bonus, the clinic gained valuable new information upon which to construct more scenarios useful in treatment.

In G's individual therapy, more personalized relapse prevention measures were implemented. Of even greater importance, individualized behavioral therapy was accomplished, including aversive conditioning utilizing foul odors (Maletzky, 1991b), assisted covert sensitization (Maletzky, 1985), PPG biofeedback (Maletzky & Steinhauser, 1998), aversive behavior rehearsal (Wickramaserka, 1980), masturbatory reconditioning (Laws & Marshall, 1991), vicarious sensitization (Weinrott, Riggan, & Frothingham, 1997), and alternative behavior completion (McConaghy, 1993).

It is beyond the scope of this chapter to describe these techniques further, but those interested should consult the references noted above. G was treated weekly with these techniques over a period of 20 months while continuing group therapy. Although somewhat resistant at first, through trust building with his therapist and support from his group, he participated with increasing enthusiasm and eventually became a facilitator in one of the clinic's support groups. Even after his term of supervision ended, and even after his formal letter of successful termination from the clinic was delivered to his parole officer (after 22 months of active therapy), he continued to participate in groups as a senior member.

Of significance in G's case was his high risk to be at large. The clinic director determined that he was an appropriate candidate for the testosterone reducing medication, depo-Provera. This drug was administered intramuscularly at the clinic every two weeks upon the mandate of G's parole officer but with G's consent as well, as he recognized that his libido might well be out of control during the early phases of treatment. This medication has been shown to markedly reduce (although not eliminate) sexual drive (Prentky, 1997), yet has not inhibited the effects of cognitive and behavioral treatments (Maletzky, 1991a). The medication was continued over a period of 9 months, until the impact of the other treatment methods could be observed and it was felt safe to discontinue it. depo-Provera leaves no lasting effects but should generally not be continued indefinitely; it is employed as a temporary aid and adjunct to a behavioral and cognitive treatment program (see Maletzky & Field, 2003, for a review). G believed it was of marked help at first in reducing sexual drive, thus freeing more energy to pursue other social interests and therapy as well.

Most crucial in evaluating the effects of these treatments were PPG recordings taken at the beginning of the program, then at monthly intervals thereafter. (The Abel Assessment, or VRT, was not employed in G's case.) Although the PPG was used at times weekly as a biofeedback device during conditioning sessions, its use for assessment was more

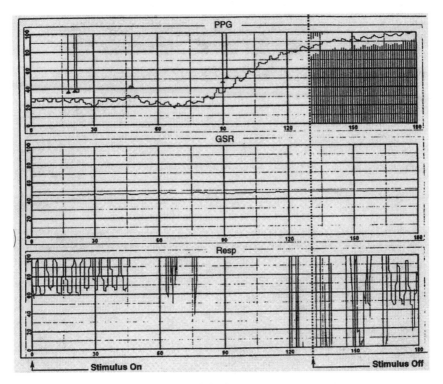

FIGURE 9.3. G's plethysmograph before treatment.

structured. Three visual stimuli (videotapes) and three auditory stimuli (scenes) depicting sex with boys were withheld from aversive conditioning sessions and used as test stimuli uncontaminated by the noxious odors employed in treatment. Figure 9.3 and Figure 9.4 depict pre- and posttreatment PPG's utilizing these scenes.

In Figure 9.3, the PPG before active treatment shows a slow but steady increase in penile circumference as this particular stimulus (a story about a man seducing a 12-year-old boy) unfolds. By 90 seconds into the story, an erection begins to grow, even though G probably was trying to suppress this at that time. While the GSR is not helpful in this particular tracing, the respiratory rate shows a definite irregularity suggesting efforts to suppress. Of particular concern, even when the story stopped, indicated by "Stimulus Off" in the figure (or when a slide or videotape was discontinued or followed by a neutral stimulus, such as a nature scene), he continued to manifest arousal and was unable to detumesce. Of note, G also demonstrated arousal to adult males, but none to girls or adult women.

By 16 months into treatment, however, G's PPG shows significant change, as demonstrated in Figure 9.4. No significant arousal is seen with

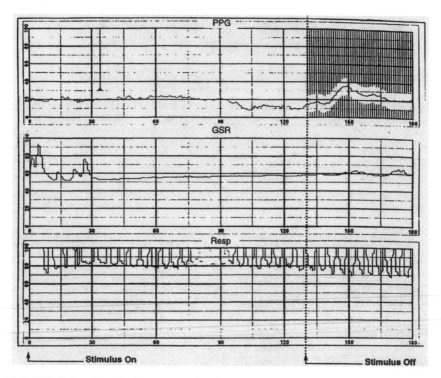

FIGURE 9.4. G's plethysmograph after treatment.

a similar stimulus, and no GSR or respiratory irregularities are present. While not incontrovertible proof of absence of risk, these PPG findings offer the most direct and reassuring evidence that progress has been made. To boost confidence in these results, a retrospective SONAR assessment revealed clinically significant improvements in the areas of intimacy deficits (he was involved in a close relationship with an adult male and active in a number of social activities); attitudes; cognitive distortions (as measured by the Child Molester Scale (Cann et al., 1995) and the MOLEST Scale (Bumby, 1996); and victim access (he actively avoided any activities and environments associated with children). He passed all remaining polygraphs as well. While not offering indisputable proof of complete treatment success, these multiple measures ensured much greater safety to be at large.

Perhaps the greatest reassurance, however, is the absence of a reoffense. An ongoing check of the Criminal Justice LEDS System, designed to detect criminal recidivism, failed to reveal any repeat offenses (sexual or nonsexual) by G during treatment or over a 9-year period of follow-up. The clinic has also tested G on the PPG annually over that period of time with no evidence of recurrence of deviant sexual arousal but with continuing arousal to adult men. Thus, conditioning was stimulus specific and did not reduce overall arousal.

☐ General Assessment of Treatment Results

Any clinic can point to single success stories; however, the results of modern-day treatment programs in reducing recidivism are greatly improved and stand as testimony against the common notion that sexual offenders cannot be treated. Indeed, recent large clinical trials (Alexander, 1999; Aytes, Olsen, Zakrajsek, Murray, & Ireson, 2001; Maletzky & Steinhauser, 2002; Studer & Reddon, 1998) and two comprehensive meta-analyses (Hall, 1995; Hanson et al., 2002) have demonstrated significant reduction in risk to reoffend among treated sexual offenders, as opposed to those either untreated or those who did not complete a treatment program.

All, however, is not as sanguine as these data would indicate. Success rates are greatest with situational rather than predatory or preferential offenders, and rapists and homosexual pedophiles, among the most dangerous of these men, have the highest rates of recidivism, although still much lower than those who remain untreated. Table 9.5 provides the recidivism rates among different offenders based upon their primary type of victim and whether they completed, or prematurely terminated, treatment. It can be seen that men who molest girls or boys (usually situational offenders) and exhibitionists have the greatest success rates, but these rates are reduced in men attracted to boys (homosexual pedophiles) and rapists. In this latter group, almost 10% of those completing treatment go on to reoffend.

Of greater concern, among men who do not successfully complete treatment, 17% of homosexual pedophiles and 75% of rapists will proceed to commit another such crime. Rapists may be more difficult to treat due to their greater heterogeneity (Maletzky, 1991b). Clearly, there is considerable room for improvement; fortunately, researchers and clinicians are hard at work refining techniques for these more intractable cases (Hanson et al., 2002).

Of interest, several studies have described female sexual offenders (Allen, 1991; Kaplan & Green, 1995; Mathews, Mathews, & Speltz, 1989). However, no study has systematically defined assessment protocols for this population, and none has published replicable and quantitative outcome data. The same can be said for juvenile offenders. While this population has been extensively described (Campbell & Lerew, 2002; Worling,

2001), no large-scale study has investigated the psychometric properties of teenage offenders.

☐ Summary

Considerations in the assessment of the sexual offender can be categorized as follows:

- Diagnostic assessments — these have been accomplished largely on the basis of symptomatic and historical factors and either follow the DSM-IV-R or rely on complicated typologies that have not proven to be of immediate clinical utility.
- Cognitive assessments — these have been well constructed and often validated, but have been criticized for their transparency and unwieldy nature. None of these instruments, such as the Empat, the ABCS, the SFQ, or the CMS, have been employed in large replications of the original studies nor, by and large, in centers outside of those where they were devised.
- Physiological measurements — The polygraph, PPG, and VRT have all proven of immense help in the assessment of sexual interests. While not perfect, and often intrusive, they have been of benefit not only for evaluation but for purposes of treatment as well.
- The assessment of risk — Fortunately, forensic necessity has created a number of instruments, such as the Static-99 and SONAR, which can, with acceptable statistical accuracy, predict which offenders will be at the highest risk to reoffend.

However, despite successes in treatment, crucial challenges in assessment remain:

- No test has been able to unambiguously distinguish a sexual offender from a nonoffender, despite ample attempts.
- Current tests, especially those assessing cognitive distortions and visual reaction times, are highly transparent: Offenders have learned the "correct" responses. Many rely upon self-report, highly suspect in sexual offenders. There remains a need for more sophisticated tests.
- Most such tests do not distinguish among types of offenders, yet typology can be crucial in determining response to treatment, as, for example, in considering the differences between prognoses for men who molest a single child because of that child's availability, as opposed to men who prefer to have sex with boys, or who have

bonded sexual arousal with aggression and thus serially rape women.

- The physiological tests now available are intrusive and produce an unacceptably high rate of false negatives.
- Psychologic and physiologic tests have been validated mostly for adult men; findings are too sparse to generalize assumptions to adolescent and female offenders.
- No current test can accurately predict which offenders will succeed in treatment, nor can any test ferret out the characteristics to target in treatment to ensure that offenders stay involved in, and complete, a program, one of the most crucial factors predicting the tendency to reoffend.

Researchers are now tackling these challenges and there remains every hope that more ingenious and sophisticated tests will be devised in the future. Some have gone so far as to predict a direct physiologic measurement of sexual arousal in the central nervous system. Indeed, PET scans are believed to be capable of now detecting some evidence of such arousal (George, 1995). Whether such mind reading will ever be acceptable ethically, however, is another matter. Regardless, we can be confident that the future will see assessment devices both better designed and more thoroughly validated than those currently available. Public opinion and clinical concern will, in all likelihood, keep the issue of sexual offending in the forefront of research efforts and hopefully spur even more effective tools for evaluation and treatment of these disorders, among our darkest of dysfunctions.

☐ References

Abel, G. G. (1997). *Abel Assessment for Sexual Interest: Judges' product information*. Atlanta, GA: Abel Screening Press.

Abel, G. G., Becker, J. V., Blanchard, E., & Mavissakalian, M. (1975). Measurement of sexual arousal in male homosexuals: Effects of instructions and stimulus modality. *Archives of Sexual Behavior, 4*, 623–629.

Abel, G. G., Cunningham-Rathner, J., Rouleau, J. L., Kaplan, M., & Reich, J. (1984). *The treatment of child molesters*. Atlanta, GA: Behavioral Medicine Institute.

Abel, G. G., Becker, J. V., Mittelman, M. S., Cunningham-Rathner, J., Rouleau, J. L., & Murphy, W.D. (1987). Self-reported sex crimes of nonincarcerated paraphiliacs. *Journal of Interpersonal Violence, 2*, 3–25.

Abel, G. G., Huffman, J., Warberg, B., & Holland, C. L. (1998) Visual reaction time and plethysmography as measures of sexual interest in child molesters. *Sexual Abuse: A Journal of Research and Treatment, 10*, 81–95.

Abel, G. G., Lawry, S. S., Karlstrom, E. M., Osborn, C. A., & Gillespie, C. F. (1994). Screening tests for paraphilia. *Criminal Justice and behavior, 21*, 115–131.

Abrams, S. (1991). The use of polygraphy with sex offenders. *Annals of Sex Research, 4,* 239–263.

Ahlmeyer, S., Heil, P., McKee, B., & English, K. (2000). The impact of polygraphy on admission of victims and offenses in adult sexual offenders. *Sexual Abuse: A Journal of Research and Treatment, 12,* 1223–1238.

Alexander, M. A. (1999). Sexual offender treatment efficacy revisited. *Sexual Abuse: A Journal of Research and Treatment, 11,* 101–116.

Allen, C. (1991). *Women and men who sexually abuse children: A comparative analysis.* Orwell, VT: Safer Society Press.

American Psychiatric Association. (2000). *Diagnostic and statistical manual of mental disorders IV-TR.* Washington, DC: American Psychiatric Association.

American Psychiatric Association. (1995). *Fact sheet on pedophilia.* Washington, DC: American Psychiatric Association.

Association for the Treatment of Sexual Abusers. (1993). *The Association for the Treatment of Sexual Abusers' practitioners' handbook.* Portland, OR: The Association for the Treatment of Sexual Abusers.

Aytes, K. E., Olsen, S. S., Zakrajsek, T., Murray, P., & Ireson, R. (2001). Cognitive/behavioral treatment for sexual offenders: An examination of recidivism. *Sexual Abuse: A Journal of Research and Treatment, 13,* 223–231.

Barbaree, H. E. (1997). Evaluating treatment efficacy with sexual offenders: The insensitivity of recidivism studies to treatment effects. *Sexual Abuse: A Journal of Research and Treatment, 9,* 111–128.

Barbaree, H. E., Seto, M. C., Serin, R. C., Amos, M. L., & Preston, D. L. (1994). Comparison between sexual and nonsexual rapist subtypes. *Criminal Justice and Behavior, 21,* 95–114.

Baumgartner, J. V., Scalora, M. J., & Huss, M. T. (2002. Assessment of the Wilson Sex Fantasy Questionnaire among child molesters and nonsexual forensic offenders. *Sexual Abuse: A Journal of Research and Treatment, 14,* 19–30.

Beech, A., Friendship, C., Erikson, M., & Hanson, R. K. (2002). The relationship between static and dynamic risk factors and reconviction in a sample of U. K. child abusers. *Sexual Abuse: A Journal of Research and Treatment, 14,* 155–167.

Blasingame, G. D. (1998). Suggested clinical uses of polygraphy in community-based sexual offender treatment programs. *Sexual Abuse: A Journal of Research and Treatment, 10,* 37–45.

Brown, S. L., & Forth, A. E. (1997). Psychopathy and sexual assault: Static risk factors, emotional precursors and rapist subtypes. *Journal of Consulting and Clinical Psychology, 65,* 848–857.

Bumby, K. M. (1996). Assessing the cognitive distortions of child molesters and rapists: Development and validation of the MOLEST and RAPE scales. *Sexual Abuse: A Journal of Research and Treatment, 8,* 37–54.

Burt, M. (1980) Cultural myths and supports for rape. *Journal of Personality and Social Psychology, 38,* 217–230.

Burt, M. (1984). Justifying personal violence: A comparison of rapists and the general public. *Victimology: An International Journal, 8,* 131–150.

Campbell, J. S., & Lerew, C. (2002). Juvenile sexual offenders in diversion. *Sexual Abuse: A Journal of Research and Treatment, 14,* 1–17.

Cann, S., Konopasky, R. J., & McGrath, M. L. (1995, June). Chi-mo: A new measure of cognitive distortions in sexual offenders. Presented at the annual convention of the Canadian Psychological Association, Prince Edward Island, Canada.

Card, R. D., & Dibble, A. (1995). Predictive value of the Card/Farrell stimuli in discriminating between gynephilic and pedophilic sexual offenders. *Sexual Abuse: A Journal of Research and Treatment, 7,* 129–141.

Cronbach, L. J. (1995). Processes affecting sores on "understanding of others" and "assumed similarity." *Psychological Bulletin, 52,* 177–193.

Davis, M. H. (1983). Measuring individual differences in empathy: Evidence for a multidimensional approach. *Journal of Personality and Social Psychology, 44,* 113–126.

Day, D., Miner, M. H, Sturgeon, V. H., & Murphy, J. (1989). Assessment of sexual arousal by means of physiological and self-report measures. In D. R. Laws (Ed.), *Relapse prevention with sexual offenders* (pp. 115–123). New York: Guilford.

Dempster, R. J., & Hart, S. D. (2002). The relative utility of fixed and variable risk factors in discriminating sexual recidivists and nonrecidivists. *Sexual Abuse: A Journal of Research and Treatment, 14,* 121–138.

DeYoung, M. (1988). Issues in determining the veracity of sexual abuse allegations. *Children's Health Care, 17,* 50–57.

Eldridge, H. (1998). *Maintaining change: A personal relapse prevention manual.* Thousand Oaks, CA: Sage.

Ellis, L. (1993). Rape as a biosocial phenomenon. In G. C. Nagayama-Hall, R. Hirschman, J. N. Graham, & M. J. Zaragoza (Eds.), *Sexual aggression: Issues in etiology, assessment, and treatment* (pp. 17–41). Washington, DC: Taylor and Francis.

Epperson, D. L., Kaul, J. D., & Huot, S. J. (1995, October). Predicting risk for recidivism for incarcerated sex offenders: Update on development of the Sex Offender Screening Tool (SOST). Paper presented at the annual meeting of the Association for the Treatment of Sexual Abusers, New Orleans, LA.

Fernandez, Y. M., Marshall, W. L., Lightbody, S., & O'Sullivan. C. (1999). The Molester Empathy Measure: Description and examination of its reliability and validity. *Sexual Abuse: A Journal of Research and Treatment, 11,* 17–31.

Fischer, L., & Smith, G. (1999). Statistical adequacy of the Abel Assessment for Interest in Paraphilias. *Sexual Abuse: A Journal of Research and Treatment, 11,* 195–205).

Freeman-Longo, R., Bird, S. Stevenson, W., & Fiske, J. (1995). *1994 nationwide survey of treatment programs and models: Serving abuse-reactive children and adolescent and adult sexual offenders.* Brandon, VT: Safer Society Press.

Freund, K. (1963). A laboratory method of diagnosing predominance of homo- or hetero-erotic interest in the male. *Behaviour Research and Treatment, 12,* 355–359.

Geer, J. H., Morokoff, P., & Greenwood, P. (1974). Sexual arousal in women: The development of a measurement device for vaginal blood volume. *Archives of Sexual Behavior, 3,* 559–564.

Gendreau, P., Irvine, M., & Knight, S. (1973). Evaluating response set styles on the MMPI with prisoners: Faking good adjustment and maladjustment. *Canadian Journal of Behavioral Sciences, 5,* 183–193.

George, M. S. (1995). The clinical use of SPECT in depressive disorders. *Journal of Clinical Psychiatry, 56,* 539–546.

Gordon, A., & Hover, G. (1998). The Twin Rivers Sex Offender Treatment Program. In W. L. Marshall, Y. M. Fernandez, S. M. Hudson, & T. Ward (Eds.), *Sourcebook of treatment programs for sexual offenders* (pp. 3–15). New York: Plenum.

Gosselin, C., & Wilson, G. (1980). *Sexual variations.* London: Faber and Faber.

Grubin, D. (1997). Predictors of risk in serious sex offenders. *British Journal of Psychiatry, 170,* 17–21.

Hall, G. C. N. (1995). Sexual offender recidivism revisited: A meta-analysis of recent treatment studies. *Journal of Consulting and Clinical Psychology, 63,* 802–809.

Hanson, R. K. (1997). *The development of a brief actual risk scale for sexual offense recidivism.* (User Report 97–04). Ottawa: Department of the Solicitor General of Canada.

Hanson, R. K., & Bussiere, M. T. (1998). Predicting relapse: A meta-analysis of sexual offender recidivism studies. *Journal of Consulting and Clinical Psychology, 66,* 348–362.

Hanson, R. K., Gordon, A. Harris, A. J. R., Marques, J. K., Murphy, W., Quinsey, V. L., & Seto, M. C. (2002). First report of the collaborative outcome data project on the effectiveness of psychological treatment for sex offenders. *Sexual Abuse: A Journal of Research and Treatment, 14,* 169–194.

Hanson, R. K., & Harris, A. J. R. (2000). Where should we intervene? Dynamic predictors of sex offense recidivism. *Criminal Justice and Behavior, 27,* 6–35.

Hanson, R. K., & Harris, A. J. R. (2001). A structured approach to evaluating change among sexual offenders. *Sexual Abuse: A Journal of Research and Treatment, 13,* 105–122.

Hanson, R. K., & Thornton, D. (1999). *Static-99: Improving actuarial risk assessments for sex offenders.* (User Report 99–02). Ottawa: Department of the Solicitor General of Canada.

Hanson, R. K., & Thornton, D. (2000). Improving risk assessments for sex offenders: A comparison of three actuarial scales. *Law and Human Behavior, 24*, 119–136.

Hare, R. D. (1991). *Manual for the Revised Psychopathy Checklist.* Toronto: Multi-Health Systems.

Harris, A. J. R., & Hanson, R. K. (1999). Dynamic predictors of sex offense recidivism — New data from community supervision officers. In B. K. Schwartz (Ed.), *The sex offender: Theoretical advances, treating special populations and legal developments* (Vol. 3, pp. 9-1 to 9-12). Kingston, NJ: Civic Research Institute.

Hennessy, M., Walter, J. S., & Vess, J. (2002). An evaluation of the Empat as a measure of victim empathy with civilly committed sexual offenders. *Sexual Abuse: A Journal of Research and Treatment, 14*, 241–251.

Hildebran, D., & Pithers, W. D. (1989). Enhancing offender empathy for sexual abuse victims. In D. R. Laws (Ed.), *Relapse prevention with sex offenders* (pp. 237–243). New York: Guilford.

Howes, R. J. (1995). A survey of plethysmographic assessment in North America. *Sexual Abuse: A Journal of Research and Treatment, 7*, 9–24.

Howes, R. J. (1998). Plethysmographic assessment of incarcerated sexual offenders: A comparison with rapists. *Sexual Abuse: A Journal of Research and Treatment, 10*, 183–194.

Hucker, S. J. (1997). Sexual sadism: Psychopathology and theory. In D. R. Laws & W. O'Donohue (Eds.), *Sexual deviance: Theory, assessment, and treatment* (pp. 194–209). New York: Guilford.

Johnson, S. A., & Listiak, A. (1999). The measurement of sexual preference — A preliminary comparison of phallometry and the Abel Assessment. In B. K. Schwartz (Ed.), *The sexual offender: Theoretical advances, treating special populations and legal developments* (Vol. 3, pp. 26-1 to 26-20). Kingston, NJ: Civic Research Institute.

Kaemingk, K. L., Koselka, M., Becker, J. V., & Kaplan, M. S. (1995). Age and adolescent sexual arousal. *Sexual Abuse: A Journal of Research and Treatment, 7*, 249–257.

Kafka, M. P., & Hennen, J. (2002). A DSM-IV Axis I comorbidity study of males (N = 120) with paraphilias and paraphilia-related disorders. *Sexual Abuse: A Journal of Research and Treatment, 14*, 349–366.

Kaplan, M. S., & Green, A. (1995). Incarcerated female sexual offenders: A comparison of sexual histories with eleven female nonsexual offenders. *Sexual Abuse: A Journal of Research and Treatment, 7*, 287–300.

Knafo, D., & Jaffe, Y. (1984). Sexual fantasizing in males and females. *Journal of Research in Personality, 18*, 451–462.

Knight, R. A., & Prentky, R. A. (1990). Classifying sexual offenders: The development and corroboration of taxonomic models. In W. L. Marshall, D. R. Laws, & H. E. Barbaree (Eds.), *Handbook of sexual assault: Issues, theories and treatment of the offender* (pp. 23–52). New York: Plenum.

Lalumiere, M. L., & Harris, G. T. (1998). Common questions regarding the use of phallometric testing with sexual offenders. *Sexual Abuse: A Journal of Research and Treatment, 10*, 227–237.

Lalumiere, M. L., & Quinsey, V. L. (1994). The discriminability of rapists from nonsexual offenders using phallometric measures. *Criminal Justice and Behavior, 21*, 150–175.

Langevin, R., Lang, R., & Curnoe, S. (1998). The prevalence of sexual offenders with deviant fantasies. *Journal of Interpersonal Violence, 13*, 315–327.

Langevin, R., Paitch, D., Handy, N., & Langevin, A. (1990). *The Clarke Sex History Questionnaire.* Oakville, Ontario: Juniper Press.

Laws, D. R., Gulayets, M. J., & Frenzel, R. R. (1995). Assessment of sex offenders using standardized slide stimuli and procedures: A multisite study. *Sexual Abuse: A Journal of Research and Treatment, 7*, 45–66.

Laws, D. R., Hanson, R. K., Osborn, C. A., & Greenbaum, P. E. (2000). Classification of child molesters by plethysmographic assessment of sexual arousal and a self-report measure of sexual preference. *Journal of Interpersonal Violence, 15*, 1297–1312.

Laws, D. R., & Marshall, W. L. (1991). Masturbatory reconditioning with sexual deviates: An evaluative review. *Advances in Behavior Research and Therapy, 13*, 13–25.

Letourneau, E. J. (1999, September). A comparison of the plethysmograph with the Abel Assessment for Sexual Interest on incarcerated military sex offenders. Paper presented at the annual conference of The Association for the Treatment of Sexual Abusers, Lake Buena Vista, FL.

Letourneau, E. J. (2002). A comparison of objective measures of sexual arousal and interest: Visual reaction time and penile plethysmography. *Sexual Abuse: A Journal of Research and Treatment, 14,* 207–223.

Looman, J. (2002). Sexual arousal in rapists as measured by two stimulus sets. *Sexual Abuse: A Journal of Research and Treatment, 12,* 235–248.

Looman, J. Abracen, J., Maillet, G., & DiFazio, R. (1998). Phallometric nonresponding in sexual offenders. *Sexual Abuse: A Journal of Research and Treatment, 10,* 325–336.

Looman, J., Abracen, J, & Nicholaichuk, T. P. (2000). Recidivism among treated sexual offenders and matched controls. *Journal of Interpersonal Violence, 15,* 179–190.

Looman, J., Gauthier, C, & Boer, D. (2001). Replication of the Massachusetts Treatment Center Child Molester Typology in a Canadian sample. *Journal of Interpersonal Violence, 16,* 753–767.

Looman, J., & Marshall, W. L. (2001). Phallometric assessments designed to detect arousal to children: The responses of rapists and child molesters. *Sexual Abuse: A Journal of Research and Treatment, 13,* 3–13.

Lutzker, J. R. (2000). Child abuse. In V. B. Van Hasselt & M. Hersen (Eds.), *Aggression and violence: An introductory text* (pp. 54–66). Needham Heights, MA: Allyn and Bacon.

Malamuth, N. M. (1989). The attraction to sexual aggression scale: Part 1. *Journal of Sex Research, 26,* 26–49.

Malamuth, N. M., Haber, S., & Feshbach, S. (1990). Testing hypotheses regarding rape: Exposure to sexual violence, sex differences and the "normality" of rapists. *Journal of Research in Personality, 14,* 121–137.

Maletzky, B. M. (1985). Assissted covert sensitization. In A. S. Bellak & M. Hersen (Eds.), *Dictionary of behavior therapy techniques* (pp. 10–11). New York: Pergamon.

Maletzky, B. M. (1991a). The use of medroproxyprogesterone acetate to assist in the treatment of sexual offenders. *Annals of Sex Research, 4,* 117–129.

Maletzky, B. M. (1991b). *Treating the sexual offender.* Newbury Park, CA: Sage.

Maletzky, B. M. (1993). Factors associated with success and failure in the behavioral and cognitive treatment of sexual offenders. *Annals of Sex Research, 6,* 241–258.

Maletzky, B. M. (1996). Evolution, psychopathology, and sexual offending: Aping our ancestors. *Aggression and Violent Behavior: A Review Journal, 1,* 369–373.

Maletzky, B. M. (1997). Defining our field: I. *Sexual Abuse: A Journal of Research and Treatment, 9,* 261–265.

Maletzky, B. M. (2000). Sexual assault. In V. B. Van Hasselt & M. Hersen (Eds.), *Aggression and violence: An introductory text* (pp. 152–197). Boston, MA: Allyn and Bacon.

Maletzky, B. M. (2002). The paraphilias: Research and treatment. In P. E. Nathan & J. M. Gormon (Eds.), *A guide to treatments that work* (2nd. Ed., pp.525–557). New York: Oxford University Press.

Maletzky, B. M. (2003). A serial rapist treated with behavioral and cognitive techniques and followed for 12 years. *Clinical Case Studies, 1,* 1–27.

Maletzky, B. M., & Field, G. (2003). The biological treatment of dangerous sexual offenders: A review and preliminary report of the Oregon pilot depo-Provera program. *Aggression and Violent Behavior: A Review Journal, 8,* 391–412.

Maletzky, B. M., & Steinhauser, C. (2002). A 25-year follow-up of cognitive/behavioral therapy with 7,275 sexual offenders. *Behavior Modification, 26,* 123–147.

Maletzky, B. M., & Steinhauser, C. (1998). The Portland Sexual Abuse Clinic. In W. L. Marshall, Y. M. Frenandez, S. M. Hudson, & T. Ward (Eds.), *Sourcebook of treatment programs for sexual offenders* (pp. 105–116). New York: Plenum.

Marshall, W. L., & Hall, G. C. N. (1995). The value of the MMPI in deciding forensic issues in accused sexual offenders. *Sexual Abuse: A Journal of Research and Treatment, 7,* 205–219.

Marshall, W. L., Hamilton, K., & Fernandez, Y. K. (2001). Empathy deficits and cognitive distortions in child molesters. *Sexual Abuse: A Journal of Research and Treatment, 13,* 123–130.

Marshall, W. L., Jones, R., Hudson, S. M., & McDonald, E. (1993). Generalized empathy in child molesters. *Journal of Child Sex Abuse, 2,* 61–68.

Marshall, W. L., O'Sullivan, C., & Fernandez, Y. L. (1996). The enhancement of victim empathy among incarcerated child molesters. *Legal and Criminological Psychology, 1,* 95–102.

Mathews, R. Mathews, J. K., & Speltz, K. (1989). *Female sexual offenders: An exploratory study.* Brandon, VT: Safer Society Press.

McGonaghy, N. (1993). *Sexual behavior: Problems and management* (pp. 303–363). New York: Plenum.

McGrath, M. L., Cann, S., & Konopasky, R. J. (1995, June). The Sexual Social Desirability Scale: A new measure of denial and acquiescence. Paper presented at the annual conference of the Canadian Psychological Association, Prince Edward Island.

McGrath, M. L., Cann, S., & Konopasky, R. J. (1998). New measures of defensiveness, empathy, and cognitive distortions for sexual offenders against children. *Sexual Abuse: A Journal of Research and Treatment, 10,* 25–36.

Muehlenhard, C. L., & Linton, M. A. (1987). Date rape and sexual aggression in dating situations: Incidence and risk factors. *Journal of Counseling Psychology, 34,* 186–196.

Murphy, W. D. (1990). Assessment and modification of cognitive distortions in sex offenders. In W. L. Marshall, D. R. Laws, & H. E. Barbaree (Eds.), *Handbook of sexual assault: Issues, theories, and treatment of the offender* (pp. 3331–3342). New York: Plenum.

Nicholaichuk, T. P., Gordon, A., Gu, D., & Wong, S. (2000). Outcome of an institutional sexual offender treatment program: A comparison between treated and matched untreated offenders. *Sexual Abuse: A Journal of Research and Treatment, 12,* 139–153.

Nichols, H. R., & Molinder, I. (1984). *Multiphasic Sex Inventory Manual: A test to assess the psychosexual characteristics of the sexual offender.* Tacoma, WA: Nichols and Molinder.

Nunes, K. L., Firestone, P., Bradford, J. M., Greenberg, D. M., & Broom, I. (2002). A comparison of modified versions of the Static-99 and the Sex Offender Risk Appraisal Guide. *Sexual Abuse: A Journal of Research and Treatment, 14,* 253–269.

O'Donohue, W., Letourneau, E. J., & Dowling, H. (1997). Development and preliminary validation of a paraphilic sexual fantasy questionnaire. *Sexual Abuse: A Journal of Research and Treatment, 9,* 167–178.

O'Donohue, W., Regev, L. G., & Hagstrom, A. (2000). Problems with the diagnosis of pedophilia. *Sexual Abuse: A Journal of Research and Treatment, 12,* 95–105.

Pithers, W. (1999). Empathy: Definition, enhancement, and relevance to the treatment of sexual abusers. *Journal of Interpersonal Violence, 14,* 257–284.

Prentky, R. A. (1997). Arousal reduction in sexual offenders: A review of antiandrogenic interventions. *Sexual Abuse: A Journal of Research and Treatment, 9,* 335–347.

Prentky, R. A., Knight, R. A., & Lee, A. (1997). Risk factors associated with recidivism among extrafamilial child molesters. *Journal of Consulting and Clinical Psychology, 65,* 141–149.

Proulx, J., Pellerin, B., Paradis, Y., McKibben, A., Aubut, J., & Ouimet, M. (1997). Static and dynamic predictors of recidivism in sexual aggressors. *Sexual Abuse: A Journal of Research and Treatment, 9,* 7–27.

Quinsey, V. L., Harris, G. T., Rice, M. E., & Cormier, C. A. (1998). *Violent offenders: Appraising and managing risk.* Washington, DC: American Psychological Association.

Quinsey, V. L., & Lalumiere, M. L. (1995). Evolutionary perspectives on sexual offending. *Sexual Abuse: A Journal of Research and Treatment, 7,* 301–315.

Russell, D. E. H. (1988). The incidence and prevalence of intrafamilial and extrafamilial sexual abuse of female children. In L. E. A. Walker (Ed.), *Handbook on sexual abuse of children* (pp. 19–36). New York: Springer.

Salter, A. C. (1992). Epidemiology of child sexual abuse. In W. T. O'Donohue & J. H. Gear (Eds.), *Sexual abuse of children: Theory and research* (Vol. 1, pp. 108–138). Hillsdale NJ: Erlbaum.

Schewe, P. A., & O'Donohue, W. (1998). Psychometrics of the rape conformity assessment and other measures: Implications for rape prevention. *Sexual Abuse: A Journal of Research and Treatment, 10,* 97–112.

Schlank, A. M. (1995). The utility of the MMPI and the MSI in identifying a sexual offender typology. *Sexual Abuse: A Journal of Research and Treatment, 7,* 185–194.

Schneider, S. L., & Wright, R. C. (2001). The FoSOD: A measurement tool for reconceptualizing the role of denial in child molesters. *Journal of Interpersonal Violence, 16,* 545–564.

Serin, R. C., Mailloux, D. L., & Malcolm, P. B. (2001). Psychopathy, deviant sexual arousal, and recidivism among sexual offenders. *Journal of Interpersonal Violence, 16,* 234–246.

Seto, M. C., & Lalumiere, M. L. (2001). A brief screening scale to identify pedophilic interests among child molesters. *Sexual Abuse: A Journal of Research and Treatment, 13,* 15–25.

Simkins, L., Ward, W., Bowman, S., & Rinck, C. M. (1989). The Multiphasic Sex Inventory as a predictor of response in child abusers. *Annals of Sex Research, 2,* 205–226.

Smith, G., & Fischer, L. (1999). Assessment of juvenile sexual offenders: Reliability and validity of the Abel Assessment for Interest in Paraphilias. *Sexual Abuse: A Journal of Research and Treatment, 11,* 207–216.

Spence, J. T., Losoff, M., & Robbins, A. S. (1991). Sexually aggressive tactics in dating relationships: Personality and attitudinal correlates. *Journal of Personality and Social Psychology, 10,* 289–304.

Stermac, L. E., Segal, S. V., & Gillis, R. (1990). Social and cultural factors in sexual assaults. In W. L. Marshall, D. R. Laws, & H. E. Barbaree (Eds.), *Handbook of sexual assault: Issues, theories, and treatment of the offender* (pp. 143–160). New York: Plenum.

Studer, L. H., & Reddon, J. R. (1998). Treatment may change risk prediction for sexual offenders. *Sexual Abuse: A Journal of Research and Treatment, 10,* 175–181.

Thornton, D. (2002). Constructing and testing a framework for dynamic risk assessment. *Sexual Abuse: A Journal of Research and Treatment, 14,* 139–153.

Tierney, D. W., & McCabe, M. P. (2001). An evaluation of self-report measures of cognitive distortions and empathy among Australian sex offenders. *Archives of Sexual Behavior, 30,* 495–519.

Van Wyk, P. H., & Geist, C. S. (1984). Psychosexual development of heterosexual, bisexual, and homosexual behavior. *Archives of Sexual Behavior, 13,* 505–544.

Wang, C. (1999). *Current trends in child abuse reporting and fatalities: The results of the 1997 annual fifty state survey.* Chicago: Prevent Child Abuse America.

Weinrott, M. R., Riggan, M., & Frothingham, S. (1997). Reducing deviant arousal in juvenile sexual offenders using vicarious sensitization. *Journal of Interpersonal Violence, 12,* 704–728.

Wickramaserka, I. (1980). Aversive behavior rehearsal: A cognitive-behavioral procedure. In D. J. Cox & R. J. Daitzman (Eds.), *Exhibitionism: Description, assessment, and treatment* (pp. 123–149). New York: Garland.

Wilson, G. (1978). *The secrets of sexual fantasy.* London: J.M. Dent.

Wilson, G. (1997). Gender differences in sexual fantasy: An evolutionary analysis. *Personality and Individual Differences, 22,* 27–31.

Wilson, R. J. (1998). Psychophysiological signs of faking in the phallometric test. *Sexual Abuse: A Journal of Research and Treatment, 10,* 113–126.

Worling, J. R. (2001). Personality-based typology of adolescent male sexual offenders: Differences in recidivism rates, victim selection characteristics, and personal victimization histories. *Sexual Abuse: A Journal of Research and Treatment, 13,* 149–166.

CHAPTER 10   Steven L. Sayers

Marital Dysfunction

☐ Description of Marital Dysfunction

Marital dysfunction, as in most clinical problems, is best described from a variety of perspectives. Spouses can behave in a spiteful way toward one another — they criticize, accuse, and stomp away angrily. At times, they fight physically, and some relationships are characterized by one spouse, usually the male, dominating and controlling the other through violence and intimidation. Marital dysfunction, however, is more than the unpleasant behavior we see or that is reported to us by unhappy spouses. Research over the last several decades has documented characteristic ways that an unhappy spouse is likely to think about his or her partner and relationship. In addition, unhappy spouses have characteristic ways of feeling and responding emotionally to conflict that are different from those of spouses who report being happy with their relationships. Furthermore, attachment theory suggests that long-held dispositions toward relationships might have an influence on one's current marital relationship. Thus, marital dysfunction is multidimensional, and the astute clinician considers a variety of ways of understanding and describing couples. Correspondingly, there is a wide range of choices for the assessment of couples. First, however, marital dysfunction is described below on several important dimensions.

Functional and Dysfunctional Behavior

Several decades of research indicates that unhappy couples often have a common appearance. While trying to resolve disagreements, unhappy spouses display more hostility, even from the beginning of the discussion, and they tend to reciprocate their partners' negative statements (Heyman, 2001). For example, when the wife criticizes her husband, the husband tends to respond with a complaint of his own, a look of disgust, or by withdrawing from the discussion with probability greater than the base-rate of negative behavior alone. Unhappy couples tend to escalate in conflict when they try to resolve a problem, leading to more and more intensely negative behavior. They are also less likely to "edit" out their negative comments than happy couples. Some research suggests that in the context of low levels of negativity, negative reciprocity may represent that spouses are successfully pressing their concerns to the other spouses. Negative reciprocity predicts increases in satisfaction when the couple shows a decrease in negativity as a result of marital therapy (Sayers, Baucom, Sher, Weiss, et al. 1991).

Unhappy couples are also likely to show a pattern of conflict known as the demand-withdraw pattern (Christensen & Heavey, 1990; Raush, Barry, Hertel, & Swain, 1974). This pattern is exemplified by a wife's complaints to her husband about "always" being late for their social engagements, which are responded to with the husbands' silence, or an attempt to discuss another topic. The demand-withdraw pattern, also called the engage-avoid style of interaction, is typically observed with the husband of the couple in the withdraw role and the wife in the demand role. Some research, however, suggests that this pattern is most affected by the choice of problems under discussion; a spouse who seeks change in a specific problem tends to be in the demand role while the partner who likes the status quo tends to be in the withdraw role (Christensen & Heavey, 1990).

Cognitions

The ways spouses think and perceive their problems are significantly associated with their status as happy or unhappy couples. Several types of cognitions about marriage have been examined in empirical studies, although marital attributions have received the most substantial focus in the literature. Marital attributions, or explanations that spouses have about the marriage and events occurring within the marriage, are highly associated with marital distress. A review of this literature (Bradbury & Fincham, 1990) indicated that maritally unhappy spouses tend to attribute negative events to global and stable characteristics of their spouse (e.g., the spouse's "objectionable personality"). In addition, spouses making attributions of responsibility to their partner for problems in the relationship tend to be less satisfied with their relationship, both in the present and in the future from the time the attributions are assessed.

Baucom, Epstein, Sayers, and Sher (1989) suggested that unhappy spouses exhibit selective attention to negative events, also known as "negative tracking" (Epstein, 1984). Distressed spouses in fact tend to underestimate frequency of pleasurable events by 50% (Robinson & Price, 1980). Related to this, Weiss (1980) hypothesized that the primary sentiment in a marital relationship would influence the spouses' perceptions, such that unhappy couples would (mis)perceive and interpret marital events as negative and happy couples would tend to perceive more positive events and give greater weight to positive events in relationships. Several empirical studies have found support for this hypothesis (Flora & Segrin, 2000; Floyd, 1988; Hawkins, Carrere, & Gottman, 2002; Vanzetti, Notarius, & NeeSmith, 1992).

Unhappy spouses also tend to endorse unrealistically high standards or beliefs about their relationship (Eidelson & Epstein, 1982). Specifically, unhappy spouses tend to endorse the belief that one's partner should be able to read one's mind in preferences, needs, and desires, as well as believe that it is inherently destructive to a marriage for the spouses to disagree (Bradbury & Fincham, 1993). On the other hand, more recent research suggests that extremely positive, relationship-oriented standards about marriage are also associated with couples who have particularly high relationship satisfaction (Baucom, Epstein, Rankin, & Burnett, 1996); additional research is needed to clarify this counterintuitive finding.

Emotional Experiences and Other Important Dimensions

Naturally, spouses tend to experience negative affect during and after marital conflict. Sayers, Kohn, Fresco, Bellack, and Sarwer (2001) found that maritally dissatisfied spouses, compared to maritally satisfied spouses, experienced greater increases in negative emotion as a consequence of discussing marital problems (see also Whisman, Weinstock, & Uebelacker, 2002). Nonverbal and paralinguistic expressions of emotion tend to discriminate distressed from nondistressed couples even more reliably than negative verbal interaction (Gottman, Markman, & Notarius, 1977; Gottman, 1998; Gottman, Coan, Carrere, & Swanson, 1998).

Depression is a consistent correlate of marital distress. In an epidemiological study of married couples, marital dissatisfaction was associated with increased incidence of major depression (Whisman & Bruce, 1999). In this study, maritally dissatisfied spouses were about 3 times more likely than maritally satisfied spouses to develop major depression in the 12-month follow-up period. Nearly 30% of the new occurrences of major depression were associated with marital dissatisfaction (Whisman & Bruce, 1999). This relation between marital discord and depression appears to be less consistent for men than for women (Fincham, Beach, Harold, & Osborne, 1997; Rounsaville, Prusoff, & Weissman, 1980; Rounsaville, Weissman, Prusoff, & Herceg-Baron, 1979; Whisman, 2001), whereas for men it appears that depression may lead to marital discord (Fincham et al., 1997). In any event, clinicians treating marital discord will often need to assess depression and take the treatment of this disorder into account.

Two individual difference characteristics, negative affectivity and insecure attachment styles, are associated with spouses who are maritally distressed or unhappy. There is evidence that the tendency to experience negative affect is associated with relatively low marital satisfaction (Karney & Bradbury, 1997). In addition, insecure attachment style has been identified as a correlate of low marital satisfaction as well as the tendency to stay in unhappy relationships (Davila & Bradbury, 2001). Indeed, the stable tendency to experience negative affect may mediate the relationship between insecure attachment style and marital satisfaction (Davila, Bradbury, & Fincham, 1998). These findings have supported marital therapies that were developed to address the emotional experiences of spouses whose marital dysfunction may be based on an insecure attachment style (Greenberg & Johnson, 1988).

☐ Range of Assessment Strategies Available

There are many commercially available measures of marital functioning, and many more measures in the public domain are available in the empirical literature. Over the last several decades, global indices of marital functioning have been the most commonly researched construct in this area. Global marital functioning has been measured for many purposes, including as an indicator of the status of the relationship, as a way to validate measures of specific constructs such as destructive communication, and as a predictor of stability in the relationship. Global marital functioning is perhaps the most common aspect of marriage assessed by clinicians when evaluating a couple for treatment.

Many other aspects of marital functioning can also be assessed using measures designed specifically for that construct, including communication patterns (Communication Patterns Questionnaire; Christensen, 1988), intimacy (Personal Assessment of Intimacy in Relationships; Schaefer & Olson, 1981), attachment (Adult Attachment Inventory; Collins & Read, 1990), marital cognition (Marital Attitude Survey; Pretzer, Epstein, & Fleming, 1991), cohesion and adaptability (Family Adaptability and Cohesion Evaluation Scales; Olson, 1986), and marital aggression (Conflict Tactics Scale; Straus, 1979). Only a few of these measures will be discussed here, in that some of these measures provide limited information that would directly guide clinical work with couples. In addition, inventories that are illustrated in the case example presented below will be described in somewhat more detail than others.

There is a long traditional of observational measurement methods used to characterize couples' interaction in a laboratory or home-based problem-solving session (see Gottman & Notarius [2002] for a review). These methods involve the development of a detailed coding system, training coders to rate spouses' communication behavior, and laborious data entry and data analysis. Needless to say, these steps are impractical for routine clinical work. Some familiarity with these coding systems, however, is a benefit to clinicians. Most importantly, some communication checklists are based on this empirical observational research (i.e., Response to Conflict Scale; Birchler & Fals-Stewart, 1994). Also, the breadth of detailed description of interactional behavior and empirical information on the affective correlates of conflict behavior can guide clinicians on the most problematic type of conflict resolution behavior. It is possible to request that couples enact their own problem-solving style during assessment sessions in order to get firsthand observation of communication patterns. Although spouses sometimes report feeling uncomfortable discussing a problem with the clinician observing and not guiding the interaction, they often report that their general style of solving problems during such an assessment is similar (but less intense) than arguments occurring at home. Similarities and differences between in-session communication samples and arguments at home can lead to productive discussions using interview methods as described below.

A great deal of information about communication and conflict patterns can be obtained through a behavioral assessment style of clinical interview. This type of interview often begins with an explanation about the scope of the interview and general approach of the interviewer. The primary complaints are identified in dialogue with each spouse, with an explicit focus on each spouse's own subjective view of the problems or conflicts, after requesting that the other spouse refrain from interjecting. The clinician coaches each spouse to provide his or her best description of the temporal development of conflicts, specifying the conditions that give rise to a particular conflict, the precipitants of the conflict, the sequence of events as the conflict unfolds, and his or her own feelings and perceptions of the events. Although the spouse's partner may have some difficulty listening without interrupting, the negative impact of this assessment on each spouse is lessened if the clinician emphasizes that each spouse has an important and valid view of the couples' problems. A more detailed description of behavioral interviewing for couples is beyond the scope of this chapter but can be found in Sarwer and Sayers (1998) and Sayers and Sarwer (1998).

Global Evaluations of Marital Functioning

The primary domain to assess when preparing to treat couples is each spouse's global judgment about his or her degree of satisfaction with the relationship. A measure that quantifies this global judgment in relation to population norms provides the clinician a sense of how much distress a spouse is in, the level of distress one spouse relative to another, and in the case of many measures, provides global satisfaction judgments about several areas of the relationship (e.g., communication, sex, raising of children).

Some of the research literature discusses the concept of marital quality or marital adjustment (Fincham & Bradbury, 1987; Spanier & Lewis, 1980), but for several reasons it may not matter much whether a clinician uses a measure of marital quality or a measure of marital satisfaction to characterize spouses' general marital functioning. First, the Dyadic Adjustment Scale (DAS; Spanier, 1976), which is the dominant measure of marital adjustment, shares approximately 80% variance with measures of marital satisfaction (Heyman, Sayers, & Bellack, 1994). This leaves little room for arguing that the two types of measures assess radically different constructs. Second, factor analyses have inconsistently supported the underlying structure of the DAS. Perhaps the largest empirical evaluation to date found that a hierarchical structure fits the DAS best — four lower-order content factors and a second-order satisfaction factor (Eddy, Heyman, & Weiss, 1991). Third, from a face-validity standpoint the global evaluations spouses make on marital quality measures are very similar to the judgments made on marital satisfaction measures, and the items on the two types of measures often cover similar content areas, such as communication, financial matters, friends, and sexual relations. It is perhaps best to view most global measures as assessing spouses' subjective estimation of their current sentiment about their relationship.

Useful measures that fall into this domain include the DAS, as mentioned above, and its forbearer, the Marital Adjustment Test (Locke & Wallace, 1959). The DAS is a 32-item self-report measure with very favorable psychometric properties, including high test-retest reliability, internal consistency, and discriminant validity (Heyman et al., 1994; Spanier, 1976). Jacobson and colleagues (1994) used empirical methods to determine the cutoff points for the DAS that optimally distinguished between clinic (i.e., treatment-seeking) and nonclinic couples. A spouse who scores 98 or less on the measure is typically regarded as being dissatisfied with his or her relationship. Most volunteer community samples score approximately 115 on the DAS, which is close to 1 standard deviation higher than this cutoff. A 7-item short form is available; some preliminary data suggests that scores above 25 indicate nondistressed status and scores below 19 suggest distressed marital status (Hunsley, Best, Lefebvre, & Vito, 2001), although a single cutoff for marital distress has not been tested at this point. Heyman, Feldbau-Kohn, Ehrensaft, Langhinrichsen-Rohling, and O'Leary (2001), however, cautioned that using self-report global measures and their standard cutoff scores may overidentify dysfunctional relationships in comparison to in-depth interviews. The DAS is in the public domain and can be obtained in an article by its author (Spanier, 1976).

There are also less well-known alternatives to the DAS for measuring spouses' global evaluations of their marriage, but few of these measures are widely tested or cited outside the developers' own studies (Heyman et al., 1994). There has been some interest in developing measures that assess "pure" satisfaction, as opposed to the constructs of adjustment or quality. Heyman and colleagues (1994) argued that items on the DAS assess frequency of disagreements and others assess behavior such as "leaving the house after a fight," thereby confounding global judgments about one's sentiment toward the marriage with reports of marital behavior. One alternative, the Relationship Satisfaction Questionnaire (RSAT; Burns & Sayers, 1988), is a 13-item self-report measure that includes only judgments about satisfaction in 13 areas of the relationship (e.g., communication and openness, handling of finances). It has high internal consistency (alpha = 0.97), favorable 6-week test-retest reliability (r = 0.72), and high positive correlations with the DAS (r = 0.89 for males, and r = 0.90 for females). The usual cutoff scores for identifying marital dysfunction are approximately 46 for husbands and wives (Heyman et al., 1994). The RSAT also has a briefer 7-item version that correlates highly with the 13-item version.

A related class of marital assessment tools purports to assess multiple domains or dimensions of marital functioning, primarily, but not exclusively, from the standpoint of satisfaction about these domains.

The best example of this type of measure is the Marital Satisfaction Inventory (MSI-R; Snyder & Aikman, 1999), now in a revised version that is commercially available. A partial list of MSI-R subscales includes those that measure global distress, dissatisfaction with affection and understanding expressed by the partner, dissatisfaction with sexual relations, disagreement about finances, as well the spouse's advocacy for traditional versus egalitarian gender roles. In addition, two other subscales assess response inconsistency and distortion in the spouse's appraisal of the marriage. The questionnaire is well normed using a large national sample of over 1000 couples and has an automated scoring system that provides T-scores and interpretive paragraphs from the profile of subscale scores that are supported by validation research (Hoover & Snyder, 1991). The inventory also has been validated in gay and lesbian populations (Means-Christensen, Snyder, & Negy, 2003). The cost to the increased amount of information provided by the MSI-R, however, is that this 150-item inventory requires approximately 25 minutes to complete, compared to the 5–15 minutes for brief global measures.

Measures of Marital Communication and Marital Interaction

Communication and other types of marital interaction are often important domains of assessment. As discussed above the demand-withdraw, or engage-avoid, style of couples' interaction has received increasing focus in the empirical literature (Christensen & Heavey, 1990; Raush et al., 1974). This engaging-avoiding style forms the basis of the subscales of the Styles of Conflict Inventory (SCI; Metz, 1993). The SCI is a 126-item commercially available self-report measure that organizes conflict styles along two orthogonal dimensions: engaging versus avoiding styles, and constructive versus destructive styles. Behaviors categorized as constructive and engaging include assertion, for example, whereas an example of a destructive and engaging style would be physical aggression. In addition to scales that describe the report of one's own behavior, another scale assesses the perceptions of the spouse's behavior. Similar item content of these scales allows for an index that represents the discrepancies between spouses' perceptions. Cognitive scales assess the respondent's thoughts about the relationship conflict in terms of engaging and avoiding styles, similar to the categories used with behaviors on the inventory. The measure is well validated and shown to have adequate reliability (Metz, 1993). The SCI is computer scored, and the automated report generates T-scores based on a standardization sample of 156 couples, as well as a listing of critical items responded to with "Very Often." The conflict styles have been shown to be similar across heterosexual, gay and lesbian couples, with differences based on gender rather than role-orientation (Metz, Rosser, & Strapko, 1994). The SCI is an explicitly cognitive-behavioral measure based on a well-researched pattern of couples' interaction. Similar to the MSI, the SCI requires more time to complete than brief global measures, although it is based on a small regional, rather than national, normative sample.

The Communication Patterns Questionnaire (CPQ; Christensen, 1988; Christensen & Sullaway, 1984; Heavey, Larson, Zumtobel, & Christensen, 1996) is another measure of the demand-withdraw pattern of interaction. The CPQ is unique in assessing spouses' self-reports of their interaction behavior in three phases of conflicts: (a) as a problem arises (4 items), (b) during the conflict (18 items), and (c) after the conflict (13 items). Similar to the SCI, discrepancies between spouses' perceptions can be scored. Generally, the interspousal agreement is similar to other behavioral checklists in the marital literature with correlations ranging from r = 0.57 to r = 0.74 (Christensen, 1988; Heavey et al., 1996), and interclass correlations (ICC's) ranging from ICC = 0.73 to ICC = 0.80 (Christensen, 1987, 1988). The internal consistency for the subscales is variable, with Chronbach alpha's ranging from alpha = 0.50 to alpha = 0.91, depending on the specific subscale, reporting source (i.e., husband vs. wife) and whose behavior is being rated (Christensen, 1988; Heavey et al., 1996).

Several subscales can be derived from the CPQ, most notably for demand and withdraw patterns of behavior (e.g., "Woman nags and demands while Man withdraws, becomes silent or refuses to discuss the matter further"). Each of the items in this domain represents complementary patterns, in that both spouses' behavior is presented, although the items are not meant to express sequences of demand and withdraw behavior. Indices can be obtained for the total amount of demand-withdraw communication, man demands/woman withdraws, woman demands/man withdraws, roles in demand-withdraw (i.e., who has the most demand and least withdraw behavior), and mutual avoidance and withholding. In addition, a Constructive Communication (CC) subscale can be scored (Heavey et al., 1996). Items representing constructive communication (e.g., "Both members try to discuss the problem") are summed, and the sum of items representing destructive communication (e.g., "Both members threaten each other with negative consequences") are subtracted from the constructive sum to obtain the CC score. There are other items on the CPQ representing the degree to which the spouses feel understood, feel the problem was solved, and the degree of support sought from others after the discussion for which no subscale has been fully evaluated.

There is evidence to support the criterion validity of the Constructive Communication subscale (Heavey et al., 1996; Noller & White, 1990). One study examined associations of spouses' ratings on the CPQ with objective coders' ratings of videotaped interactions of these same couples and found supportive correlations, ranging from r = 0.62 to r = 0.72 (Heavey et al., 1996). Rankin-Esquer and colleagues (1997) developed optimal cutoff scores for the subscales, and have found that the wives' Constructive Communication subscale scores of zero or below, in particular, differentiates between clinic and community couples.

The Response to Conflict scale (RTC (Birchler & Fals-Stewart, 1994) is a 24-item paper and pencil measure of destructive conflict strategies. The RTC requires the respondent to check identical behaviors, such as "yelling or screaming," "swearing," and "criticizing" for both the husband and wife, which allows a check of interspousal agreement. The measure has high internal consistency and temporal stability, and factor analyses confirm the presence of Active and Passive Subscales, with a common factor measuring general distress. The total score ranges from 0–192, with a cutoff point of 62 empirically differentiating distressed and nondistressed couples. The measure correlates highly with other measures of marital conflict and global measures of marital satisfaction. The primary benefits of the measure include its availability (Birchler & Fals-Stewart, 1994), its brevity, and the ability for clinicians to examine items reflecting physical aggression quickly.

In some clinical contexts it may be important to assess marital violence in a very detailed fashion. Several of the measures above have items that bear on marital violence, although the Conflict Tactics Scale (CTS; Straus, 1979), and its revision (CTS2; Straus, Hamby, Boney-McCoy, & Sugarman, 1996), are the most widely used measures. The CTS has the benefit of being used in hundreds of studies on marital and family violence and much is known about its correlates and reliability in detecting physical aggression (Heyman et al., 2001; Heyman & Schlee, 1997). The measure detects behaviors representing negotiating as well as coercive methods of influence in intimate relationships, such as psychological and physical aggression. In addition, the CTS2 has scales to measure sexual coercion and physical injury. The CTS has been criticized for not taking the context of marital violence into account (i.e., self-defense), the level of injury that males versus females inflict upon the other spouse, and the 1-year retrospective time frame for reporting events (Gelles, 1990); the revision of the CTS addresses these concerns to some extent.

At times clinicians may need a measure of couples' interaction behavior to obtain an ongoing account of events within the home. Using this type of measure can help spouses improve observations of their own communication behavior, develop alternative responses, and gain a better appreciation of the impact of their behavior. The Peterson Interaction Record (Peterson, 1979) is a self-report form that asks spouses to describe in writing the most important event of the day, the conditions under which it took place, how it started, and then any subsequent behavior, events, thoughts, and feelings. These data can then be used clinically to examine exchanges between spouses, and if spouses are directed to describe the same event, it can be used to show the differences in their perceptions. This, in turn, can be used to address spouses' cognitions, specifically, selective attention, that may be limiting their ability to resolve these conflicts.

Marital Cognitions

Most of the studies of marital cognition have focused on attributions spouses have about their spouse, their conflicts, and their relationship. Several inventories that have adequate psychometric characteristics have received substantial support for their association to marital discord. These measure share the same problem — they are limited by the lack of national norms against which spouses' scores could be compared, or lack well-accepted cutoff scores that designate the dysfunctional range of the scores. Nevertheless, clinicians can use subscale means published by the developers of these inventories for groups of discordant couples, or use the trends of the scores over time to determine the extent to which spouses are responding to marital therapy with a change in their attributions.

Two marital attribution measures deserve mention: the Relationship Attribution Measure (RAM; Fincham & Bradbury, 1992) and the Marital Attitude Survey (MAS; Pretzer et al., 1991). The RAM has been examined in a number of studies and the subscales have adequate internal consistency, test-retest reliability and validity (Bradbury, Beach, Fincham, & Nelson, 1996; Bradbury & Fincham, 1992; Fincham, Harold, & Gano-Phillips, 2000). The RAM assesses causal attributions as well as responsibility attributions. It is correlated with measures of marital satisfaction and maladaptive problem-solving behavior, and longitudinal studies suggest that the RAM assesses attributional patterns that lead to increased marital discord over time.

The Marital Attitude Survey (MAS; Pretzer et al., 1991) uses more colloquial concepts for the attributional dimensions it assesses. For example, in addition to the subscale Attribution of Causality to Own Behavior, the measure includes the subscales of Attribution of Malicious Intent to Spouse and Attribution of Lack of Love to Spouse. These latter dimensions are highly associated with marital distress, and there is evidence from qualitative research that supports that the dimensions may more directly represent how spouses think about problems in the relationship (Sayers & Baucom, 1995). This may make interpretation of findings on the measure easier and more easily conveyed to spouses for clinical purposes. The subscales on the measure have adequate internal consistency and are highly negatively correlated with marital satisfaction (Pretzer et al., 1991).

Sexual Functioning and Sexual Disorders

A brief self-report measure can be used to determine the degree to which the couples' level of sexual functioning has decreased and to screen for the existence of a sexual dysfunction. The Arizona Sexual Experiences Scale (ASEX; McGahuey, Gelenberg, Laukjes, Moreno, Deldago, McKnight, & Manber, 2000) is a 5-item self-report scale that can also be interviewer administered. Its brevity derives from assessing only five core elements of sexual dysfunction: drive, arousal, penile erection/vaginal lubrication, ability to reach orgasm, and satisfaction from orgasm. Although the scale was originally developed to assess sexual dysfunction due to medications, the scale is brief enough to examine individual responses in order to detect nonmedication-related disorders such as premature ejaculation (i.e., the answer "extremely easy," in response to the item "ability to reach orgasm"). The scale has adequate internal consistency, validity, and sensitivity for detecting sexual dysfunction. If sexual dysfunction is detected, then a longer multidimensional interview tool, such as the Derogatis Sexual Functioning Index (Derogatis & Melisaratos, 1979), can be used to specify the nature of the dysfunction.

☐ Pragmatic Issues Encountered in Clinical Practice with the Assessment Marital Dysfunction

Many clinicians do not routinely use standardized psychological assessment methods with couples, relying on clinical interview and in-session observation as their only methods. Although these approaches are certainly essential, the initial assessment phase of treatment could benefit from some of the self-report measures described above. The most immediate reasons clinicians are likely to cite for not using these techniques include time constraints, the perceived relevance of the assessments, compliance of spouses in completing the assessments, and the lack of third-party payment for the assessment of marital dysfunction. These barriers, however, can be overcome with some forethought and preparation prior to meeting with a couple the first time.

A busy clinical practice in which a provider spends a great deal of time securing third-party payment might find little extra effort for formalized psychological assessment, especially when that assessment is highly unlikely to be reimbursed by insurers. Although a systematic search of insurers might be difficult to conduct, third-party payment for marital assessments is virtually unheard of among practitioners. Nevertheless, assessment can be conducted quickly and can be individualized to each couple so that the clinician does not feel that substantial resources are being used in an uncompensated activity.

For many spouses, there is considerable week-to-week variability in their overall evaluation of the relationship when there is ongoing conflict. Multiple brief assessments of satisfaction may be warranted in the initial phases of assessment and treatment in order to obtain a realistic view of the couple. Spouses can be asked to complete forms mailed to their home prior to treatment, although this procedure comes with some risks. Spouses who are not enthusiastic about coming to couples therapy will be much less likely to complete them, which may lead to the other spouse's increased exasperation and pessimism, as well as the inability of the practitioner to compare the spouses' scores. It may be important to have at least one face-to-face meeting to provide the opportunity to engage hesitant spouses in the assessment and treatment process. It also provides the therapist opportunity to introduce the purpose of the assessment and to answer any concerns voiced by either of the spouses. In particular, discussing any additional charges spouses incurred by using commercial measures would be important to couples. If completed forms are mailed back to the therapist or scored quickly prior to the second assessment session, the results can then be integrated into the ongoing battery of information being gathered. The therapist can significantly individualize the assessment when he or she meets with the couple once before selecting the domains to assess.

Subsequent, ongoing assessment can be integrated into the routine of the therapy practice. Office staff can ask patients to complete self-report measure of marital satisfaction or marital communication, using the past week as the reference period. This works best when the couple is encouraged to come a few minutes in advance of the session and the measure is fairly brief. Couples often arrive at sessions from different locations (i.e., from their respective workplaces) with different levels of promptness. Consistent, gentle attention to the procedural aspects of treatment can often produce better adherence to meeting times allowing pretherapy assessment to occur on a regular basis.

As alluded to above, spouses often attend to their partner's compliance with the therapist's expectations and requests in order to gauge the partner's level of commitment to therapy, and ultimately, to the relationship itself. Response of a noncompliant partner might be to demonstrate his or her resistance to change by not fulfilling requests to complete assessments. The general line of thinking by spouses when these dynamics unfold might be expressed as, "You don't care enough about the marriage to simply fill out a questionnaire," and "You can't make me change by bringing me to this therapist and you can't make me fill out his stupid questionnaires." The therapist should always take care to intervene on nonadherence to requests to complete assessments so that the request does not become co-opted by the couple as part of this struggle. Two simple messages from the therapist to each spouse can mitigate this potential problem: (1) The measures completed by each spouse helps the therapist understand each of their individual perspectives better, and (2) the therapist maintains responsibility for the request and it is the therapist's job to try to help each spouse adhere to the request. These sentiments might be expressed verbally as follows: "I know I've asked you to do extra work by filling out this form, but it will really help me understand you as individuals more quickly than questions I can ask in our sessions," and "Remember that it's my job to ask about filling out and bringing the questionnaires from home; please resist the temptation to bug each other about it. I like to do that" [stated humorously].

☐ Case Illustration

History of the Problem

Brenda and Greg (pseudonyms) had been married for 15 years prior to entering treatment. They reported being increasingly dissatisfied over the several years before coming to therapy. Brenda also reported several periods of depression, including the present, and both spouses thought that their difficulties increased when Brenda was depressed.

Greg and Brenda met while working for a transportation company. They began dating after Greg left a serious romantic relationship and after Brenda had separated and divorced from her husband at the time, although they also dated others. After a time, Greg became much more attentive because of the competition of another man who Brenda was dating; this culminated in his asking her to marry him. She fended off these offers for 2 years because she enjoyed being single. They lived together for 3 years after meeting before they married, and reported initial conflicts from that time concerning housekeeping and Greg's waning attention to Brenda.

The couple's problems started early in their relationship. Brenda described their recurrent marital conflicts as occurring because of Greg's decreasing attention, and Greg's increased focus on work. Greg acknowledged that he sometimes adopted a "traditional" singular focus on his work, describing it as "putting blinders on." He stated he became unhappy that he had to assert himself too vigorously (e.g., "I had to go to the mat for everything"). Other stressors during the first several years of their marriage included career changes, the birth of their two children, and Brenda's recurrent depression.

Presenting Complaints and Individual Histories

The focus of the couple's complaints were their verbal conflicts, especially when Brenda was depressed and had taken a few drinks. Brenda focused a great deal on the interference of Greg's job, and the long and erratic work hours. Complicating this problem was Greg's avoidance of discussing problems with Brenda, his procrastination, and from Brenda's point of view, his lack of punctuality at most family events or appointments. Brenda acknowledged that her drinking was often problematic, and often resulted in her worsening mood and an argument between them.

Greg is the youngest of three children, but he was essentially raised as an only child because his siblings were at least 10 years older than he. He described his parents as supportive but overprotective (i.e., no football). His father was "traditional" and stubborn, and his mother had a "wicked" temper. Because of his size and self-imposed isolation, he was assumed to be a "bully"; his academic success and outside interests (e.g., playing classical piano) were in contrast with his reputation. Greg tended to use clumsy metaphors to express himself (e.g., Brenda was a solid person, "like a battleship"). He often monopolized conversations with topics of interest only to himself (e.g., WW II airplanes). He reported no psychiatric history, but reported current dysphoria and occasional back pain. He had not been married prior to his marriage to Brenda, although he had broken an engagement because of severe conflicts with his future mother-in-law at the time.

Brenda is the oldest of three children; her siblings are 2 and 3 years younger. She described her family role as a "goody-two-shoes" especially in contrast to her younger sister. She described her father as authoritarian and the sole provider, whereas her mother "actually ran everything." Her niche in high school was as a cheerleader. Brenda reported several periods of depression — as a child, around the time of her separation and divorce from her first husband, while she was at home with two young children, and at the time of her current treatment. She was treated with psychotherapy during the first two reported depressive episodes while she was an adult. Brenda described her first husband as a "pathological liar" who pursued her actively, then built up huge financial debts and was unfaithful with a friend of hers. In her current treatment, Brenda presented as very dysphoric and angry with Greg for his decreased attention, but attributed much of her emotionality to her depression. She met diagnostic criteria for a moderately severe clinical depression. Her alcohol use was moderate (3–4 glasses of wine 3 times/week), and often led to a worsening of her mood.

Psychological Assessment Protocol

Greg and Brenda initially provided data relevant to their treatment in the context of an assessment study conducted by the author. Subsequently, they entered treatment and agreed to provide the self-report and clinical data reported here. The assessment targeted several domains, including the spouses' marital satisfaction (RSAT), their current levels of depressive symptoms (Beck Depression Inventory, [BDI]; Kendall, Hollon, Beck, Hammen, et al., 1987), and their perceptions of marital conflict (CPQ). Because clinical interview suggested that the couple exhibited a demand-withdraw pattern of interaction, with the wife in the "demand" role and the husband in the "withdraw" role, we examined the corresponding Demand-Withdraw subscale as well as the Mutual Problem Solving subscale. A diagnostic interview was conducted to assess whether either of the spouses met criteria for any psychiatric disorder. In order to simplify the presentation, the results of other measures also obtained at the time have been excluded.

Pretreatment values on the assessment battery suggested that the spouses were dissatisfied with the relationship, moderately dysphoric, and exhibited a mix of dysfunctional communication and functional communication as rated by the spouses. As shown in Figure 10.1, the initial self-report values for relationship satisfaction and depression were provided well in advance (i.e., treatment day = -56) of the initiation of the clinical assessment (i.e., treatment day = -8). The wife's and husband's initial self-report scores were as follows: wife — RSAT = 29, BDI = 32; husband — RSAT = 40, BDI = 21. The spouses' RSAT scores were well below the cutoff for marital distress (i.e., approximately 46 for husbands and wives, Heyman et al., 1994) and both spouses had BDI scores above

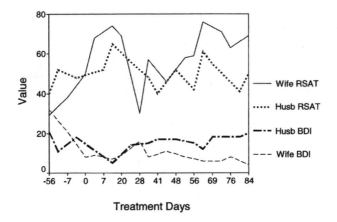

FIGURE 10.1. Marital satisfaction (RSAT) and depression (BDI) for husband and wife.

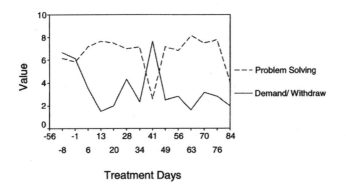

FIGURE 10.2. Wife Demand, husband withdraw and mutual problem solving; self-report CPQ subscales.

the usual cutoff of 16 that indicates a moderately high level of depressive mood (Kendall et al., 1987; see Figure 10.1). In addition, the spouses' CPQ subscale for Demand-Withdrawal was 6.7, and their subscale score for Mutual Problem Solving was 6.2. These scores were assessed at the time of the initiation of the clinical assessment, and are close to the "very likely" (i.e., "9") end of the dimension on which each CPQ item is rated (see Figure 10.2).

Couple Interaction Patterns and Conceptualization

Brenda and Greg exhibited an extreme "demand-withdraw" pattern of interaction. Brenda expressed her discontent vociferously and Greg withdrew and avoided conflicts, with occasional outbursts of anger. Greg had difficulty identifying, labeling, and expressing his own emotions effectively, and instead justified his position, or expressed somatic complaints. Brenda had difficulty moderating her anger, and her depression interfered with finding adequate solutions to her mood problems or to the marital conflicts. She was frustrated and hurt regarding Greg's minimal attention to their relationship and lack of effort in addressing their conflicts. The couple spent little leisure time with one another and had periodic verbal outbursts. Both of their teenage children were concerned about their parents divorcing.

Greg often lapsed into a defensive position when Brenda was angry and vocal in her criticisms about a specific issue. Brenda's depression and irritability was also exacerbated by alcohol use. Greg somewhat consistently adopted a victim's role, acknowledging having difficulty with confronting conflict. Early learning that possibly contributed to these roles included Brenda's adopting from her mother the role of the active problem solver, as well as her anger at twice being pursued by men only to be ignored after assenting to a committed relationship. Greg's belief in the traditional role of the father as provider and Greg's mother's angry style may have contributed to his own tendency to withdraw from conflict. Their lack of communication skill inhibited them from addressing relatively basic concerns such as work and home schedules, home responsibilities, and the maintenance of relationship intimacy.

Targets Selected for Treatment

After two assessment sessions, the couple received nine treatment sessions using a behavioral couples approach for depressed spouses (e.g., Beach, Smith, & Fincham, 1994). The first step in treatment consisted of discussing the conceptualization of their problems, the treatment rationale, and building a collaborative set. The early emphasis in treatment was on increasing positive interaction using a simple clinical form in which each spouse listed the other's positive behavior and their own verbal response to it. In addition, the couple was encouraged to engage in other shared positive events, and these events were extensively discussed and tracked. In later sessions the couple was taught reflective listening skills and problem-solving skills. Brenda was also taking Prozac (20 mg) when couples therapy started and then switched to Paxil (20 mg) 63 days after initiating treatment. The issue of how the spouses were attributing changes or improvements in their relationship to medication versus shifts in communication patterns was discussed throughout treatment.

☐ Assessment of Progress

Brenda and Greg showed an initial boost in optimism, an increase in marital satisfaction, and rapid improvement in Brenda's mood (see Figures 10.1 and 10.2). However, Brenda was becoming more aware that she was highly critical but she could not always moderate her expression of anger. Greg had difficulty identifying and expressing feelings without being defensive. Both spouses had difficulty staying focused on solutions during problem solving. An important shift occurred between therapy sessions at 34 and 41 days after initiating treatment, when Greg expressed a great deal of anger at Brenda's high criticism. This event was accompanied with both a temporary decrease in satisfaction and changes in perceived interaction style. It also stimulated useful discussions about their styles of handling anger, and ways of handling these types of critical events. The couple continued to improve from that point, terminating when Greg's work schedule made appointments difficult for them to keep.

Data showed significant variability across the assessment and treatment sessions, primarily because of the instructions to the spouses to complete the forms in reference to the time period since the last assessment; thus, spouses did not provide global impressions of a longer period of time. However, it is possible to see how having the completion of brief measures prior to each session can provide a "snapshot" of the couples' week prior to the session. Having this information can help the therapist prepare his or her approach to session management when it is possible that the couple is experiencing a rapid positive shift in their relationship, or is currently in a crisis. Data for spouses for the current case example provide documentation for positive changes the couple experienced. Moreover, data added support to the informal impression of their progress. Furthermore, data for Greg also demonstrated that he continued to have uncomfortable levels of depressive symptoms, probably associated with somatic problems he described during treatment. If continued treatment were possible, it might have focused on these problems in order to ensure improved functioning on his part as well as long-term stability of the relationship.

□ Summary

Marital dysfunction is a multifaceted clinical syndrome. Unhappy spouses have characteristically negative communication and interactional behavior, they tend to blame their partner's for their marital problems, and often feel hostile and depressed after trying to bring a problem to a resolution. Discordant spouses, especially wives, are at increased risk for subsequent major depressive episodes. Inversely, there is some evidence that depression in husbands results in increased risk of marital discord in the future. For both husbands and wives, depression may be an important contextual factor when assessing and treating marital discord.

There are many choices in marital assessment methods available to practitioners who treat couples. Measure of spouses' global evaluations of the relationship are by far the most common, although a number of other measures have been constructed to measure communication and other conflict behavior, intimacy, as well as marital cognitions. Other constructs of interest, such as attachment, can be measured with well-constructed measures. Few measures have been normed using national probability samples that are representative of the U.S. population as a whole. These measures tend to be available only through commercial firms and require a significant time investment from spouses to complete.

A variety of forces work against the utilization of marital assessments in regular clinical practice. These include low likelihood that practitioners would receive third-party payment for the administration and interpretation of the measures, the time it takes to organize the regular use of the measures, and the potential noncompliance of spouses. These barriers can be successfully overcome with some minimal care in the selection of assessments, as well as some attention to preparing and supporting spouses in their completion of these forms.

Use of regular, systematic marital assessments can enhance therapy with couples. Regular assessment keeps the therapy focused on original treatment goals and can help prepare the therapist for fluctuations in treatment response over time. In addition, documenting areas of improvement and lack of improvement helps therapy be responsive to the needs of the couple. Most spouses gladly complete self-report forms they feel will be helpful with treatment. When the couple can be shown a chart of their progress, their experience and appreciation of therapy will often be enhanced.

□ References

Baucom, D. H., Epstein, N., Rankin, L. A., & Burnett, C. K. (1996). Assessing relationship standards: The Inventory of Specific Relationship Standards. *Journal of Family Psychology, 10*(1), 72–88.

Baucom, D. H., Epstein, N., Sayers, S. L., & Sher, T. G. (1989). The role of cognitions in marital relationships: Definitional, methodological, and conceptual issues. *Journal of Consulting & Clinical Psychology, 57*(1), 31–38.

Beach, S. R. H., Smith, D. A., & Fincham, F. D. (1994). Marital interventions for depression: Empirical foundation and future prospects. *Applied & Preventive Psychology, 3*(4), 233–250.

Birchler, G. R., & Fals-Stewart, W. (1994). The Response to Conflict Scale: Psychometric properties. *Assessment, 1*(4), 335–344.

Bradbury, T. N., Beach, S. R. H., Fincham, F. D., & Nelson, G. M. (1996). Attributions and behavior in functional and dysfunctional marriages. *Journal of Consulting & Clinical Psychology, 64*(3), 569–576.

Bradbury, T. N., & Fincham, F. D. (1990). Attributions in marriage: Review and critique. *Psychological Bulletin, 107*(1), 3–33.

Bradbury, T. N., & Fincham, F. D. (1992). Attributions and behavior in marital interaction. *Journal of Personality & Social Psychology, 63*(4), 613–628.

Bradbury, T. N., & Fincham, F. D. (1993). Assessing dysfunctional cognition in marriage: A reconsideration of the Relationship Belief Inventory. *Psychological Assessment, 5*(1), 92–101.

Burns, D. D., & Sayers, S. L. (1988). Development and validation of a brief relationship satisfaction scale. Unpublished manuscript, Presbyterian Medical Center of Philadelphia.

Christensen, A. (1987). Detection of conflict patterns in couples. In K. Hahlweg & M. J. Goldstein (Eds.), *Understanding major mental disorder: The contribution of family interaction research* (pp. 250–265). New York: Family Process Press.

Christensen, A. (1988). Dysfunctional interaction patterns in couples, In P. Noller, M. A. Fitzpatrick (Eds.), *Perspectives on marital interaction: Monographs in social psychology of language, No. 1.* (pp. 31–52). Clevedon, Avon, England: Multilingual Matters.

Christensen, A., & Heavey, C. L. (1990). Gender and social structure in the demand/withdraw pattern of marital conflict. *Journal of Personality & Social Psychology, 59*(1), 73–81.

Christensen, A., & Sullaway, M. (1984). *Communication Patterns Questionnaire.* University of California, Los Angeles.

Collins, N. L., & Read, S. J. (1990). Adult attachment, working models, and relationship quality in dating couples. *Journal of Personality & Social Psychology, 58*(4), 644–663.

Davila, J., & Bradbury, T. N. (2001). Attachment insecurity and the distinction between unhappy spouses who do and do not divorce. *Journal of Family Psychology, 15*(3), 371–393.

Davila, J., Bradbury, T. N., & Fincham, F. (1998). Negative affectivity as a mediator of the association between adult attachment and marital satisfaction. *Personal Relationships, 5*(4), 467–484.

Derogatis, L. R., & Melisaratos, N. (1979). The DSFI: A multidimensional measure of sexual functioning. *Journal of Sex & Marital Therapy, 5*, 244–281.

Eddy, J. M., Heyman, R. E., & Weiss, R. L. (1991). An empirical evaluation of the Dyadic Adjustment Scale: Exploring the differences between marital "satisfaction" and "adjustment." *Behavioral Assessment, 13*(3), 199–200.

Eidelson, R. J., & Epstein, N. (1982). Cognition and relationship maladjustment: Development of a measure of dysfunctional relationship beliefs. *Journal of Consulting & Clinical Psychology, 50*(5), 715–720.

Epstein, N. (1984). Depression and marital dysfunction: Cognitive and behavioral linkages. *International Journal of Mental Health, 13*(3–4), 86–104.

Fincham, F. D., Beach, S. R. H., Harold, G. T., & Osborne, L. N. (1997). Marital satisfaction and depression: Different causal relationships for men and women? *Psychological Science, 8*(5), 351–357.

Fincham, F. D., & Bradbury, T. N. (1987). The assessment of marital quality: A reevaluation. *Journal of Marriage & the Family, 49*(4), 797–809.

Fincham, F. D., & Bradbury, T. N. (1992). Assessing attributions in marriage: The Relationship Attribution Measure. *Journal of Personality & Social Psychology, 62*(3), 457–468.

Fincham, F. D., Harold, G. T., & Gano-Phillips, S. (2000). The longitudinal association between attributions and marital satisfaction: Direction of effects and role of efficacy expectations. *Journal of Family Psychology, 14*(2), 267–285.

Flora, J., & Segrin, C. (2000). Affect and behavioral involvement in spousal complaints and compliments. *Journal of Family Psychology, 14*, 641–657.

Floyd, F. J. (1988). Couples' cognitive/affective reactions to communication behaviors., *Journal of Marriage & the Family, 50*, 523–532.

Gelles, R. J. (1990). Methodological issues in the study of family violence, In G. R. Patterson (Ed.), *Depression and aggression in family interaction: Advances in family research* (pp. 49–74). Eugene, OR: Oregon Social Learning Center.

Gottman, J., Markman, H., & Notarius, C. (1977). The topography of marital conflict: A sequential analysis of verbal and nonverbal behavior. *Journal of Marriage & the Family, 39*(3), 461–477.

Gottman, J. M. (1998). Psychology and the study of the marital processes. *Annual Review of Psychology, 49*, 169–197.

Gottman, J. M., Coan, J., Carrere, S., & Swanson, C. (1998). Predicting marital happiness and stability from newlywed interactions. *Journal of Marriage & the Family, 60*(1), 5–22.

Gottman, J. M., & Notarius, C. I. (2002). Marital research in the 20th century and a research agenda for the 21st century. *Family Process, 41*(2), 159–197.

Greenberg, L. S., & Johnson, S. (1988). *Emotionally focused therapy for couples*. New York: Guilford.

Hawkins, M. W., Carrere, S., & Gottman, J. M. (2002). Marital sentiment override: Does it influence couples' perceptions? *Journal of Marriage & the Family, 64*(1), 193–201.

Heavey, C. L., Larson, B. M., Zumtobel, D. C., & Christensen, A. (1996). The Communication Patterns Questionnaire: The reliability and validity of a constructive communication subscale. *Journal of Marriage & the Family, 58*(3), 796–800.

Heyman, R. E. (2001). Observation of couple conflicts: Clinical assessment applications, stubborn truths, and shaky foundations. *Psychological Assessment, 13*(1), 5–35.

Heyman, R. E., Feldbau-Kohn, S. R., Ehrensaft, M. K., Langhinrichsen-Rohling, J., & O'Leary, K. D. (2001). Can questionnaire reports correctly classify relationship distress and partner physical abuse? *Journal of Family Psychology, 15*(2), 334–346.

Heyman, R. E., Sayers, S. L., & Bellack, A. S. (1994). Global marital satisfaction versus marital adjustment: An empirical comparison of three measures. *Journal of Family Psychology, 8*(4), 432–446.

Heyman, R. E., & Schlee, K. A. (1997). Toward a better estimate of the prevalence of partner abuse: Adjusting rates based on the sensitivity of the Conflict Tactics Scale. *Journal of Family Psychology, 11*(3), 332–338.

Hoover, D. W., & Snyder, D. K. (1991). Validity of the computerized interpretive report for the Marital Satisfaction Inventory: A customer satisfaction study. *Psychological Assessment, 3*(2), 213–217.

Hunsley, J., Best, M., Lefebvre, M., & Vito, D. (2001). The Seven-Item Short Form of the Dyadic Adjustment Scale: Further evidence for construct validity. *American Journal of Family Therapy, 29*(4), 325.

Jacobson, N. S., Follette, W. C., Revenstorf, D., Baucom, D. H., Hahlweg, K., & Margolin, G. (1994). Variability in outcome and clinical significance of behavioral marital therapy: A reanalysis of outcome data. *Journal of Consulting and Clinical Psychology, 52*(4), 497–594.

Karney, B. R., & Bradbury, T. N. (1997). Neuroticism, marital interaction, and the trajectory of marital satisfaction. *Journal of Personality & Social Psychology, 72*(5), 1075–1092.

Kendall, P. C., Hollon, S. D., Beck, A. T., Hammen, C. L., et al. (1987). Issues and recommendations regarding use of the Beck Depression Inventory. *Cognitive Therapy & Research, 11*, 289–299.

Locke, H. J., & Wallace, K. M. (1959). Short marital-adjustment and prediction tests: Their reliability and validity. *Marriage & Family Living, 21*, 251–255.

McGahuey, C. A., Gelenberg, A. J., Laukes, C. A., Moreno, F. A., Deldago, P. L., McKnight, K. M., & Manber, R. (2000). The Arizona Sexual Experiences Scale (ASEX): Reliability and Validity. *Journal of Sex & Marital Therapy, 26*, 25–40.

Means-Christensen, A. J., Snyder, D. K., & Negy, C. (2003). Assessing nontraditional couples: Validity of the Marital Satisfaction Inventory-Revised with gay, lesbian, and cohabiting heterosexual couples. *Journal of Marital & Family Therapy, 29*(1), 69–83.

Metz, M. E. (1993). *Manual for the Styles of Conflict Inventory*. Palo Alto, CA: Consulting Psychologists Press.

Metz, M. E., Rosser, B. R. S., & Strapko, N. (1994). Differences in conflict-resolution styles among heterosexual, gay, and lesbian couples. *Journal of Sex Research, 31*(4), 293–308.

Noller, P., & White, A. (1990). The validity of the Communication Patterns Questionnaire. *Psychological Assessment, 2*(4), 478–482.

Olson, D. H. (1986). Circumplex Model VII: Validation studies and FACES III. *Family Process, 25*(3), 337–351.

Peterson, D. R. (1979). Assessing interpersonal relationships by means of interaction records. *Behavioral Assessment, 1*, 221–236.

Pretzer, J., Epstein, N., & Fleming, B. (1991). Marital Attitude Survey: A measure of dysfunctional attributions and expectancies. *Journal of Cognitive Psychotherapy, 5*(2), 131–148.

Rankin-Esquer, L. A., Baucom, D. H., Christensen, A., Epstein, N. B., Burnett, C. K., & Harris, L. (1997). Communication Patterns Questionnaire: Discriminating between community, clinic, and divorcing couples. Unpublished manuscript.

Raush, H. L., Barry, W. A., Hertel, R. K., & Swain, M. A. (1974). *Communication Conflict and Marriage*. San Francisco: Jossey-Bass.

Robinson, E. A., & Price, M. G. (1980). Pleasurable behavior in marital interaction: An observational study. *Journal of Consulting & Clinical Psychology, 48*, 117–118.

Rounsaville, B. J., Prusoff, B. A., & Weissman, M. M. (1980). The course of marital disputes in depressed women: A 48-month follow-up study. *Comprehensive Psychiatry, 21*, 111–118.

Rounsaville, B. J., Weissman, M. M., Prusoff, B. A., & Herceg-Baron, R. L. (1979). Marital disputes and treatment outcome in depressed women. *Comprehensive Psychiatry, 20*, 483–490.

Sarwer, D. B., & Sayers, S. L. (1998). Behavioral interviewing. In A. S. Bellack & M. Hersen (Eds.). *Behavioral assessment: A practical handbook* (4th ed., pp. 63–78). Boston: Allyn & Bacon.

Sayers, S. L., & Baucom, D. H. (1995). Multidimensional scaling of spouses' attributions for marital conflicts. *Cognitive Therapy & Research, 19*(6), 667–693.

Sayers, S. L., Baucom, D. H., Sher, T. G., Weiss, R. L., & Heyman, R. (1991). Constructive engagement, behavioral marital therapy, and changes in marital satisfaction. *Behavioral Assessment, 13*(1), 25–49

Sayers, S. L., Kohn, C. S., Fresco, D. M., Bellack, A. S., & Sarwer, D. B. (2001). Marital cognitions and depression in the context of marital discord. *Cognitive Therapy & Research, 25*(6), 713–732.

Sayers, S. L., & Sarwer, D. B. (1998). *Assessment of marital dysfunction, Behavioral assessment: A practical handbook* (4th ed., pp. 293–314). Boston: Allyn and Bacon.

Schaefer, M. T., & Olson, D. H. (1981). Assessing intimacy: The PAIR Inventory. *Journal of Marital & Family Therapy, 7*(1), 47–60.

Snyder, D. K., & Aikman, G. G. (1999). Marital Satisfaction Inventory–Revised. In M. E. Maruish, (Ed). *The use of psychological testing for treatment planning and outcomes assessment* (2nd ed., pp. 1173–1210). Mahwah, NJ: Lawrence Erlbaum Associates.

Spanier, G. B. (1976). Measuring dyadic adjustment: New scales for assessing the quality of marriage and similar dyads. *Journal of Marriage & the Family, 38*(1), 15–28.

Spanier, G. B., & Lewis, R. A. (1980). Marital quality: A review of the seventies. *Journal of Marriage & the Family, 42*(4), 825–839.

Straus, M. A. (1979). Measuring intrafamily conflict and violence: The Conflict Tactics (CT) Scales. *Journal of Marriage & the Family, 41*(1), 75–88.

Straus, M. A., Hamby, S. L., Boney-McCoy, S., & Sugarman, D. B. (1996). The revised Conflict Tactics Scales (CTS2): Development and preliminary psychometric data. *Journal of Family Issues, 17*(3), 283–316.

Vanzetti, N. A., Notarius, C. I., & NeeSmith, D. (1992). Specific and generalized expectancies in marital interaction. *Journal of Family Psychology, 6,* 171–183.

Weiss, R. L. (1980). Strategic behavioral marital therapy: Toward a model for assessment and intervention. In J. P. Vincent (Ed.), *Advances in family intervention, assessment, and theory* (Vol. 1, pp. 229–271). Greenwich, CT: JAI Press.

Whisman, M. A. (2001). The association between depression and marital dissatisfaction. In S. R. H. Beach (Ed). *Marital and family processes in depression: A scientific foundation for clinical practice* (pp. 3–24). Washington, DC: American Psychological Association.

Whisman, M. A., & Bruce, M. L. (1999). Marital dissatisfaction and incidence of major depressive episode in a community sample. *Journal of Abnormal Psychology, 108*(4), 674–678.

Whisman, M. A., Weinstock, L. M., & Uebelacker, L. A. (2002). Mood reactivity to marital conflict: The influence of marital dissatisfaction and depression. *Behavior Therapy, 33*(2), 299–314.

SECTION III

Evaluation of Children and Adolescents

Wendy K. Silverman
Barbara Lopez

Anxiety Disorders

☐ Description of the Disorder

Anxiety disorders are one of the most prevalent disorders of childhood and adolescence with epidemiological studies showing that between 8% to 12% of youths experience anxiety problems severe enough to interfere with their functioning (Costello et al., 1996; Fergusson, Horwood, & Lynskey, 1993). If untreated, areas of interference relating to anxiety disorders include school drop out, arrests, and psychopathology extending into late adolescence and adulthood (e.g., Brown & Harris, 1993; Costello, Angold, & Keeler, 1999). Consistent and strong research evidence has accumulated in the past decade showing that anxiety disorders in youth can be successfully reduced with the use of exposure-based cognitive behavioral treatment procedures (see Silverman & Treffers [2001] for review). Given the cumulative evidence, it would seem incumbent on clinicians to become knowledgeable about and experienced in the use of exposure-based cognitive behavioral treatment procedures so that they might deliver interventions most likely "to work."

Equally important is for clinicians to become knowledgeable about and experienced in the use of psychological assessment strategies for use with childhood anxiety disorders. Knowledge about and experience in using psychological assessment strategies would enable clinicians to accurately ascertain whether a child is experiencing anxiety disorders and would thereby benefit from receiving an anxiety reduction intervention program. Knowledge about and experience in using psychological assessment strategies would also enable clinicians to accurately identify specific symptoms and maintaining factors (e.g., parental reinforcement of child avoidant behavior) that might be targeted in treatment.

There are a number of complex issues involved, however, in the psychological assessment of anxiety and its disorders in children and adolescents. This chapter aims to shed light on some of these issues. For example, assessing whether a child has impairing anxiety disorders is complicated by high rates of comorbidity found in clinic samples (see Saavedra & Silverman, 2002). In addition, children and parents frequently disagree on the presence or absence of anxiety symptoms and the extent to which symptoms are impairing child functioning (e.g., Grills & Ollendick, 2002; Jensen et al., 1999). Moreover, child-parent (dis)agreement is influenced by myriad of factors, such as children's developmental level and parental psychopathological conditions (Grills & Ollendick, 2002). Time, finances, and resources also can influence psychological assessment of children and adolescents with anxiety disorders.

This chapter thus summarizes the range of psychological assessment strategies available for anxiety disorders in children. This is followed by a discussion of pragmatic issues that arise in using these psychological assessment strategies with anxiety disorders in youth. A case example is provided to illustrate several of the issues. The chapter begins first, however, with a brief description of the anxiety disorders. (For ease of presentation, "child" or "children" are used hereafter to refer to "children and adolescents.")

Several different subtypes of anxiety disorders are described in the Diagnostic and Statistical Manual of Mental Disorders, 4th edition (DSM-IV; American Psychiatric Association, 1994). These subtypes along with their key clinical features are summarized in Table 11.1. As the table shows, the object or situation that provokes anxiety, fear, or both in the individual varies across the anxiety disorders. For a child with social phobia, for example, social evaluative situations provoke anxiety; for a child with separation anxiety disorder, situations involving child separation from parents or loved ones provoke anxiety.

Although different objects or situations provoke anxiety, fear, or both, the manner in which "anxiety" is manifested in the individual is similar across the anxiety disorders, albeit with variation in the extent to which that manifestation is a clinically significant problem. Anxiety disorders are generally manifested by behavioral avoidance in which the child often avoids or attempts to avoid the fear or anxiety provoking object or situation (e.g., a child with a specific phobia of dogs would likely avoid situations where dogs might be present). Anxiety disorders also are

TABLE 11.1. DSM- IV Anxiety Disorders

Disorder	Clinical Features
Separation anxiety disorder	Excessive and developmentally inappropriate anxiety concerning separation from home or attachment figures that begins prior to 18 years old, has been present for at least 4 weeks, and causes clinically significant distress or impairment in important areas of functioning (e.g., social, academic).
Specific phobia	Marked, excessive, and persistent fear in either presence or anticipation of a circumscribed object or event that is developmentally inappropriate, leads to avoidance or attempts at avoidance of object or event, not due to a recent stressor, present for at least 6 months, and causes clinically significant distress or impairment.
Social phobia	Marked and persistent fear circumscribed (e.g., school) or pervasive (e.g., school, family, and friends) of situations in which there is likelihood of social evaluation present for at least 6 months, leads to avoidance or attempts at avoidance of situation, and causes clinically significant distress or impairment.
Generalized anxiety disorder	Excessive anxiety and worry that is difficult to control, not focused on a specific situation or object, unrelated to a recent stressor, occurs more days than not, at least one physical symptom (e.g., restlessness, stomach and muscle aches), present for at least 6 months and causes clinically significant distress or impairment.
Panic disorder	Sudden occurrence of a cluster of symptoms that peak within 10 minutes (e.g., palpitations, sweating, trembling, feelings of shortness of breath, chest pain, nausea, dizziness). Reoccurs unexpectedly, associated with at least 1 month of chronic worry or fear about future attacks and consequences regarding attacks and leads to avoidance or attempts at avoidance. Can occur either independently or with agoraphobia.
Posttraumatic stress disorder	Exposure to a traumatic event leads to persistent reexperiencing (e.g., intrusive thoughts or images), persistent avoidance of situations/persons associated with event or lack of responsiveness (e.g., avoid thoughts, feelings, conversations associated with or a reminder of event), and increased arousal (e.g., hypervigilance, sleep disturbance). Present for at least one month and causes clinically significant distress or impairment.
Obsessive-compulsive disorder	Obsessive thoughts, impulses, or images, compulsions or both that lead to marked distress, last over 1 hour a day, and causes clinically significant distress or impairment. Attempts are made to ignore obsessions; relieve distress by performing compulsions.

generally manifested by excessive or recurrent thoughts that frequently involve harm befalling either the child or a loved one (e.g., a child with separation anxiety disorder may often think, "I might get kidnapped or my parents might leave and never come back."). Finally, anxiety disorders are generally manifested by physiological or somatic symptoms (e.g., a child with generalized anxiety disorder may report having stomach aches or headaches).

☐ Range of Assessment Strategies Available

Structured and Semistructured Diagnostic Interview Schedules

Table 11.2 presents an evaluative summary of the most widely used semi-structured and structured diagnostic interview schedules available for use with children and adolescents for assessing anxiety disorders. All of the interview schedules indicated in the table are based on the DSM and have child and parent versions. One interview schedule, the DICA, has a separate child and adolescent version. Most of the interview schedules are designed for use with children as young as 6 years of age and adolescents as old as 18 years of age. Most require minimal verbal expressive skills to answer questions (e.g., either "yes" or "no").

Unlike the unstructured clinical interview, semistructured and structured interviews are standardized with respect to the types of questions that are asked of informants, with the former being less standardized and more flexible than the latter. Standardization results in reduced interviewer variance and increased diagnostic reliability. In addition, because of the interviews' detailed coverage of each symptom that comprises each anxiety disorder as well as other disorders (e.g., depression, attention deficit hyperactivity), semistructured and structured interviews are particularly useful in reliably differentiating among the wide range of possible comorbid conditions with which children may present. Through such detailed coverage and questioning, clinicians can better determine and prioritize the various problems children display. This is of particular benefit when assessing children who present with anxiety-related concerns because there is considerable overlap in symptomatology and clinical features of anxiety and other disorders (e.g., affective disorders, attention deficit hyperactivity disorder).

Several of the interview schedules also contain rating scales to assist in determining and prioritizing the range of disorders presented by a child. For example, using the Anxiety Disorders Interview Schedule for Children (Silverman & Albano, 1996; Silverman & Nelles, 1988), clinicians ask the child and parent to rate on a 0–8 point "Feelings Thermometer" how each disorder for which the child meets diagnostic criteria interferes with the child's functioning with respect to school, friends, and family. The interview schedules' focus on DSM disorders is of further utility in the climate of managed care, which usually requires clinicians to report the results of their assessments and treatments using DSM diagnoses.

TABLE 11.2. Structured and Semistructured Interview Schedules for Diagnosing DSM-IV Anxiety Disorders in Youth

Diagnostic Interview Schedule	Ages (years)	Versions	Structured or Semistructured	Reliability of Anxiety Diagnoses (Kappa coefficients)
Anxiety Disorders Interview Schedule for DSM-IV: Child and Parent Versions (ADIS for DSM-IV: C/P; Silverman & Albano, 1996; Silverman et al., 2001)	6 to 18	C/P	SS	Child: .78 SAD; .71 SOP; .80 SP; .63 GAD Parent: .88 SAD; .86 SOP; .65 SP; .72 GAD Combined: 84 SAD; .92 SOP; .81 SP; .80 GAD
Schedule for Affective Disorders and for School-Age Children (K-SADS; Ambrosini, 2000)	6 to 18	C/P	SS	Combine C/P: .78 OAD; .80 SP
NIMH Diagnostic Interview Schedule for Children Version IV (NIMH DISC-IV; Shaffer et al., 2000)	9 to 17	C/P	S	Child: .68 SP; .25 SOP; .46 SAD. Parent: .96 SP; .54 SOP; .58 SAD; .65 GAD Combine: .86 SP; .48 SOP; .51 SAD; .58 GAD
Child and Adolescent Psychiatric Assessment (CAPA; Angold & Costello, 2000; Angold et al., 1995)	10 to 18	C/P	S	Child: .74 OAD; .79 GAD
Diagnostic Interview for Children and Adolescents (DICA; Herjanic & Reich, 1997; Reich, 2000; Schwab-Stone et al., 1994)	6 to 17	C/A/P	SS	Child: .55 OAD; .60 SAD; .65 SP. Adolescent: .72 OAD; .75 SAD (past)

Note: DSM-IV= Diagnostic and Statistical Manual of Mental Disorders, 4th ed. C=child. P=parent. A=adolescent. S= structured. SS = semistructured.

TABLE 11.3. Child Rating Scales for Assessing Anxiety in Youth

Instrument	Brief Description	Psychometric Properties
General Symptoms		
Youth Self Report (Achenbach & Edelbrock, 1987)	102 items; assesses positive and problem behaviors. Includes broadband factors (externalizing, internalizing) and anxious/narrow band factors (withdrawn, somatic complaints, depressed, social problems, thought problems, attention problems, delinquent behavior, and aggressive behavior)	Internal Consistency: Alpha coefficients range from .64 to .92 Test-retest reliability: .78 to .85
Revised Children's Manifest Anxiety Scale (RCMAS; Reynolds & Richmond, 1985)	37 items; assesses anxiety symptoms and yields total anxiety and lie scores and three factor scales: physiological, worry/oversensitivity, and social concerns/ concentration	Internal Consistency: Alpha coefficients >.80 Test-retest reliability: .64 to .76
State–Trait Anxiety Inventory for Children (STAIC; Speilberger, 1973)	20 items in two subscales (A-Trait and A-State). A-Trait assesses chronic cross-situational anxiety and A-State assesses acute, transitory anxiety	Internal Consistency: Alpha coefficients .80 to.90 for A-State; ~.80 for A-Trait Test-retest reliability: .65 to .71 for A-Trait; .31 to .47 for A-State
Specific Features		
Social Anxiety Scale for Children Revised (SASC-R; La Greca & Stone, 1993)	22 items; yields total score and three factor scales: fear of negative evaluation, social avoidance and distress in new situations, general social avoidance and distress	Internal Consistency: Alpha coefficients >.65 Test-retest reliability: .69 to .86
Social Phobia Anxiety Inventory for Children (SPAIC; Beidel et al., 1995, 1999b)	26 items; yields total score and three factor scales: assertiveness/general conversation, traditional social encounters, and public performance	Internal Consistency: Alpha coefficient for total score = .95 Test-retest reliability: ranges from .63 to .86

Measure	Description	Reliability
Child Anxiety Sensitivity Index (CASI; Silverman et al., 1991)	18 items; assesses aversiveness of experiencing anxiety symptoms. Yields four factor scales: disease concerns, unsteady concerns, mental incapacitation concerns, and social concerns	Internal Consistency: Alpha coefficient = 0.87 Test-retest reliability: .62 to .78
Test Anxiety Scale for Children (TASC: Sarason et al., 1958)	30 items; assess child's anxiety in test-taking situations	Internal Consistency: Alpha coefficients range .82 to .90 Test-retest reliability: .44 to .85
Fear		
Fear Survey Schedule for Children-Revised (FSSC-R; Ollendick, 1983)	80 items; assesses subjective levels of fear and yields total score and five factor scales: fear of failure and criticism, fear of the unknown, fear of danger and death, medical fears, and small animals	Internal Consistency: Alpha coefficients range from .92 to .95 Test-retest reliability: .82
DSM-Based		
Multidimensional Anxiety Scale for Children (MASC; March et al., 1997; March & Sullivan, 1999)	39 items; assesses anxiety in four domains: physical symptoms, social anxiety, harm avoidance, and separation/panic	Internal Consistency: Alpha coefficients range from .60 to .90 Test-retest reliability: range from .79 to .93
Screen for Child Anxiety Related Emotional Disorders (SCARED; Birmaher et al., 1997)	38 items; yields five factors: panic/somatic, generalized anxiety, separation anxiety, social phobia, school phobia	Internal Consistency: Alpha coefficients range .74 to .89 Test-retest reliability: .86
Spence Children's Anxiety Scale (Spence, 1997)	44 items; yields six factors: separation anxiety, social phobia, obsessive-compulsive disorder, panic-agoraphobia, generalized anxiety and fears of injury	Internal Consistency: Alpha coefficient= .70 Test-retest reliability: .63

TABLE 11.4. Parent and Teacher Rating Scales for Assessing Anxiety in Youth

Instrument	Versions	Brief Description	Psychometric Properties
Child Behavior Checklist (CBCL; Achenbach, 1991a) Teacher Report Form (TRF: Achenbach, 1991b)	P/T	118 items (P) and 120 items (T); assesses positive and problem behaviors. Includes broadband factors, externalizing, internalizing, and narrow band factors (withdrawn, somatic complaints, anxious/depressed, social problems, thought problems, attention problems, delinquent behavior, and aggressive behavior)	Internal Consistency: Alpha coefficients range from .54 to .96 Test-retest reliability: .86 to .89
Conner's Rating Scales-Revised (CRS-R; Conners, 1997)	P/T	48 items (P) and 59 items (T); assesses behavior problems and includes five factors: conduct problems, learning problem, psychosomatic, impulsive-hyperactive, and anxiety	Internal Consistency: Alpha coefficients range from .70s to .90s Test-retest reliability: .47 to .88
Behavior Assessment System for Children (BASC: Reynolds & Kamphaus, 1992)	P/T	126–148 items; assesses behavior problems. 20 scales and subscales (e.g., internalizing, anxiety)	Internal Consistency : Alpha coefficients range from .78 to .90 Test-retest reliability: .70s to .80s
Devereux Behavior Rating Scale-School Form (Naglieri et al., 1993)	T	40 items; assesses behavior problems. 4 subscales: interpersonal problems, inappropriate behaviors/feelings, depression, physical symptoms, and fears	Internal Consistency: Alpha coefficients range from .92 to .97 Test-retest reliability: 69 to .85

Note: P = Parent. T = Teacher.

Rating Scales

Table 11.3 presents a brief evaluative summary of the most widely used child self-rating scales; Table 11.4 presents the parent and teacher rating scales; and Table 11.5 presents the clinician rating scales. Most of these scales were devised for use in identifying and quantifying symptoms of anxiety. Several of the recently developed child self-rating scales were devised to assess features or symptoms of specific types of anxiety problems (e.g., anxiety sensitivity); others were devised to assess features of anxiety in terms of the DSM-IV nosologic scheme (e.g., Multidimensional Anxiety Scale for Children). There also are several rating scales that can be used to identify and quantify possible factors that relate to the maintenance of anxiety problems, such as child social skills. A sampling of these types of scales is presented in Table 11.6. As the tables indicate, the scales have been evaluated with respect to issues of reliability and validity.

Rating scales provide a total summary score several provide factor scale scores. Summary scores represent quantitative indexes of the degree to which a total set of symptoms are relevant to a child or that the child will emit a class of behaviors (Jensen & Haynes, 1986). Factor scale scores similarly represent quantitative indexes, but of specific aspects or features of anxiety-related symptoms (e.g., worry/oversensitivity on the Revised Children's Manifest Anxiety Scale). Most rating scales have normative data and provide clinical cutoffs that can be used to evaluate clinical significance by comparing the target child's score to normative scores based on children of the same age and gender (Barkley, 1988). Departures from the norm usually can be determined based on standard deviation units that define a particular percentile of the sample (Silverman & Serafini, 1998).

Rating scales offer several advantages in the assessment of anxiety in children. They require minimal professional training, and are easy and inexpensive to administer. They may be used in a wide range of settings (schools, clinics) and with a wide range of populations. In addition, because rating scales exist for use with a variety of informants (e.g., parent, child, teacher), they allow for an assessment of the child's symptoms via multiple perspectives. This type of multisource assessment has been noted as critically important in clinical child research and practice (see Achenbach, 1991a, b; Achenbach, McConaughy, & Howell, 1987; Silverman & Rabian, 1999; Silverman & Serafini, 1998). Rating scales also are useful in identifying and quantifying low-frequency symptoms or behaviors (e.g., "All of a sudden I feel really scared for no reason at all"; Spence Children's Anxiety Scale) that may not be emitted by the child during time-limited direct observations nor reported by the parent or child during the interview.

TABLE 11.5. Clinician Rating Scales Used for Assessing Anxiety in Youth

Instrument	Brief Description	Psychometric Properties
NIMH OCD Global Scale (Insel et al., 1983)	One- item anchored clinician rating. Assesses OCD severity. Score of >6 indicates clinically significant OCD.	No published reports found
Children's Yale- Brown Obsessive Compulsive Scale (CY- BOCS; Goodman et al., 1989)	Semistructured clinical interview administered to parent and/ or child. Assesses OCD severity. Two sections (obsessions, compulsions) yielding separate scores. Symptoms rated on frequency/ duration, interference, distress, resistance, and control. Score of > 15 indicates clinically significant OCD.	Internal consistency: .89 Inter- rater reliability: .98
Pediatric Anxiety Rating Scale (PARS; RUPP Anxiety Study Group, 2002)	Semistructured clinical interview administered to parent and/ or child. 50- item checklist assesses anxiety symptoms in six areas (Separation, Social Interactions or Performance Situations, Generalized, Specific Phobia, Physical Signs & Symptoms, Other). Clinician rates severity in each of seven dimensions (number of symptoms, frequency, severity of distress associated with anxiety symptoms, interference at home, interference out of home, severity of physical symptoms, avoidance) on 6- point scale. Score of > 2 indicates clinically significant interference.	Internal consistency: .64 Inter- rater reliability: .97 Test- retest reliability: .55

TABLE 11.6. Sampling of Rating Scales to Assess Variables Maintaining Anxiety in Youth

Variable	Rating Scale	Description
Parent-child relationship	Parenting Behavior Inventory Child Report/Parent Report (CRPBI & PRPBI; Schluderman & Schluderman, 1970).	30 items; assesses perceptions of parent's behaviors toward child from child and parent report. Includes three subscales: psychological control, acceptance, and firm control. Internal consistency: alphas ranging from .65 to .74
Parent-child relationship	Conflict Behavior Scale (CBQ; Prinz et al., 1979).	20 items; assesses problem areas (i.e., conflict) and positive and negative parent-child communications from child and parent report. Internal consistency: alphas ranging from .88 to .95
Peer relationships/social skills	Friendship Questionnaire (FQ; Bierman & McCauley, 1987).	40 items (8 open-ended); assesses peer interactions from child report. Includes 3 factors: positive interactions, negative interactions, and extensiveness of peer network. Internal consistency: alphas ranging from .72 to .82
Social skills	Social Skills Rating System Child & Parent Version (SSRS P/C; Gresham & Elliot, 1990).	34 items (C), 38 items (P); assesses social skills. Includes 5 subscales: empathy, cooperation, assertion, responsibility, and self-control. Internal consistency: alphas ranging from .83 (C) to .87 (P)
School refusal behavior	School Refusal Assessment Scale (Kearney & Silverman, 1993)	16 items; assesses factors maintaining school refusal behavior from parent and child report. Includes 4 subscales: avoidance of fear-provoking situations, escape from aversive social evaluative situations, attention-getting behavior, and positive tangible reinforcement. Test-retest reliability: subscales range from .44 to .87
Negative cognitions	Children's Negative Affectivity Self-Statement Questionnaire (Ronan, Kendall, & Rowe, 1994)	11 items for 7–10 year olds & 31 items for 11–15 year olds; assesses frequency of self-statements in past week. Test-retest reliability: .73

Finally, several rating scales were designed for use in assessing, maintaining or controlling factors of child anxious behavior. For example, the School Refusal Assessment Scale (Kearney & Silverman, 1999) assesses whether a child's school refusal behavior may be maintained due to one or more of the following factors: (1) avoidance of stimuli provoking specific fearfulness or general anxiousness, (2) escape from aversive social or evaluative situations, (3) attention-getting behavior, and (4) positive tangible reinforcement. An intervention could be prescribed based on the child's profile on the scale (e.g., train parents in providing less positive tangible reinforcement such as television watching when their child displays school refusal behavior as determined by elevations on the positive tangible reinforcement subscale [Kearney & Silverman, 1999]).

Direct Observations

In addition to using rating scales to help in identifying and quantifying anxiety symptoms and behaviors, and the maintaining factors of anxiety, direct observations also can be used for these purposes. Direct observations can be conducted in children's naturalistic settings (e.g., school) but given practical constraints, observations also can be conducted in the clinic setting. That is, an analogue situation may be devised in the clinic that closely corresponds to the situation that elicits the child's anxiety problems in the natural environment. If the child has social phobia, for example, the child might be asked to talk about him or herself in front of unfamiliar people (e.g., staff members in the clinic setting). Alternatively, following the procedures used in Beidel, Turner, and Morris (2000), children could be asked to read aloud a story in front of a small group. If possible, the practitioner could also set up an interaction between the target child and a peer. These situations could last for 5 to 10 minutes. Although it is important that children be told that they can stop these types of observation tasks at any time, they also should be encouraged to "try as hard as they can."

Direct observations allow for an assessment of the various anxiety symptoms that the child may frequently display (e.g., avoidance) as well as the severity of the child's symptoms. For example, the child might adamantly refuse to do the task; this would be a revealing observation in terms of showing a high level of avoidant behavior. Alternatively, the child might show initial hesitation, but then perform the task with surprisingly good skills and minimal display of anxiety behaviors. This too would be a revealing observation, and could serve as a launching pad for fruitful discussion in session (e.g., the child might think she looks anxious and that everyone notices this, but actually the child does not appear anxious at all).

To obtain quantifiable indexes, behavior codes used in Kendall (1994), adapted from Glennon and Weisz (1978), could be used. The behaviors that could be coded would include: (a) gratuitous vocalizations (e.g., stating a physical complaint, desire to leave, dislike for the task), (b) gratuitous body movements (e.g., leg kicking or shaking, rocking body, biting lips), (c) trembling voice (e.g., shaking speech, stuttering, volume shifts), and (d) absence of eye contact. The child's level of anxiety also might be rated using a similar 5-point rating scale, used in Kendall (1994): (a) 1 = "no signs of anxiety," 5 = "subject appears to be in crisis", (b) fearful facial expression: 1 = "no tears, tension, or biting of lips," 5 = "tearful, facial tension, clenching of jaws", and (c) problematic performance: 1 = "composed, nonavoidant behavior," 5 = "disjointed and difficult-to-understand."

The 5-point rating scale used by Beidel et al. (2000) also could be considered for use. Here the focus is on the child's effectiveness in the peer interaction or reading out loud task (1 = completely ineffective and 5 = very effective.) In addition, children might be asked to self-rate their own anxiety using the following 5-point scale (1 = very relaxed and 5 = very anxious or distressed).

Direct observations also can be used to assess factors that are hypothesized as maintaining children's anxiety disorders or symptoms. For example, parent-child interaction tasks, such as those used by Barrett, Dadds, and Rapee (1996) could be adapted, in which ambiguous situations (e.g., parents have called and they will be late coming home from work) are given to the parent-child dyad and they are asked to discuss how the child might handle the ambiguous situations. Whether they generate solutions such as, "worry that my parents were killed in a car crash," versus "the traffic must be bad," can provide a revealing picture about the extent that the parent-child interaction may be serving to maintain children's anxious thoughts and behaviors.

Self- Monitoring

Another way anxiety in childhood can be assessed is through self-monitoring. In self-monitoring, the child, sometimes with the assistance of the parent, records aspects of the anxiety behavior (e.g., frequency of avoidance or negative thoughts). Generally these records are brought to the clinician's office at an agreed upon time interval; early in treatment this might be each weekly visit (McGlynn & Rose, 1998). Self-monitoring can be particularly useful in the assessment process to obtain information that may not be readily accessible via direct observation (e.g., worried thoughts). Self-monitoring also can be helpful in identifying antecedents and possible maintaining factors of the child's anxiety symptoms. For example, the child could be asked to record the situations that are occurring "right before" she or he began feeling anxious. The child also could be asked to record, "what happens afterward?" Finally, self-monitoring at the assessment phase can provide a baseline that can later be used to document behavior change during the treatment phase.

Physiological Measures

Physiological measures to assess anxiety in children generally focus on heart rate, electrodermal activity, and respiration (see McGlynn & Rose [1998] for details). Although physiological measures have been used in assessing childhood anxiety in research (e.g., Beidel, Turner, & Morris, 1999a), the cost and specialized training of the equipment reduces the likelihood of their wide usage in clinical practice. More importantly, the utility of physiological assessment with respect to treatment planning and implementation remains to be demonstrated.

☐ Pragmatic Issues Encountered in Clinical Practice with This Disorder

This section discusses pragmatic issues clinicians are likely to encounter when assessing anxiety disorders. Although additional issues are likely to arise beyond these, the authors have selected the subsequent ones for discussion because they are particularly salient when dealing with anxiety disorders. Despite the saliency of these issues with aspect to anxiety disorders, they are by no means unique to anxiety disorders — many are likely to be relevant when assessing the types of other disorders covered in this volume.

Selecting the Assessment Strategy to Be Used

The assessment strategy that should be selected for use would depend on one's assessment goals. As outlined by Silverman and Kurtines (1996), the most common goals are: (1) screening, (2) differential diagnosis, (3) identifying and quantifying anxious symptoms, and (4) identifying and quantifying maintaining factors of anxiety. Thus, apparent from the preceding sections, rating scales appear to be best to use for screening; semistructured and structured interviews appear to be best to use for differential diagnosis. Various assessment strategies can be used to attain goals (3) and (4), including interview schedules, rating scales, direct observations, and self-monitoring.

In addition to selecting an assessment strategy that would best achieve a particular goal, the strategy that should be selected for use is influenced as well by the setting or context in which the assessment will take place. For example, in school settings, self-rating scales are preferable for use due to their low cost and ease and timely administration. Direct observations, particularly naturalistic ones, also are preferable for use in school settings because they can be done with little intrusion on children's daily activities (i.e., children can just do "what they typically do" and observers can observe). Research further shows that concerns about reactivity are generally unwarranted: children and teachers readily habituate to being observed by others. In clinic settings, particularly those that depend on third party payments, interview schedules are likely to be preferred in light of the need to obtain DSM-IV diagnoses for reimbursement purposes in most of these types of settings. Self-monitoring forms can also be very helpful to use in clinic settings, especially when the child is being seen weekly by the clinician, because the information that the child records on the form each week can be used to launch specific topics for discussion in session.

Dealing with Child- Parent Disagreement in Their Reports of Anxiety Symptoms

As noted earlier, it is recommended that information about the child's anxiety problems be obtained from a number of individuals who are familiar with the child in a variety of settings. In clinic settings, children and parents usually are most readily available. Obtaining information from both sources is particularly important in assessing internalizing problems such as anxiety because agreement between children and parents is significantly lower for childhood internalizing problems than childhood externalizing problems (e.g., Achenbach et al., 1987).

Recent studies have further demonstrated high child-parent discordance, particularly with regard to parent and child reports on interview schedules (i.e., Anxiety Disorders Interview Schedule for Children for DSM-IV; Child and Parent Versions; Silverman & Albano, 1996; Choudhury, Pimentel, & Kendall, 2003; Grills & Ollendick, 2003; Rapee, Barrett, Dadds, & Evans, 1994). Choudhury and colleagues, for example, recently reported that in 45 children (ages 7 to 14 years) and parents who presented to a childhood anxiety disorders specialty clinic, levels of agreement were low for all the major anxiety disorders presented by the children. This was true for both the primary and the principal diagnosis as well as whether the anxiety diagnosis was present anywhere in the child's clinical picture.

Low levels of agreement between informants do not necessarily mean that one informant is "right" and the other is "wrong." Oftentimes it mainly reflects the fact that different sources see the child in different settings, and different levels of anxiety symptoms and problems may be displayed in those settings. Moreover, the child's anxiety problems may not be directly observable to parents and teachers, especially if the child manifests his or her anxiety primarily via the cognitive response system. This is all the more reason why it is critical to obtain information from the children. Conversely, some children are reluctant to report that they are experiencing anxiety difficulties; this is all the more reason why it is critical to also obtain information from parents, teachers, or both.

Given high levels of disagreement found between informants, one might ask whether it helps to consider the child's age in deciding how to handle this disagreement. Research findings are mixed, however, on the influence of age in child-parent (dis)agreement. Rapee and colleagues (1994) found no difference in parent-child agreement based on age, but there was significantly greater agreement between parents and children for diagnoses of social phobia. Choudhury and colleagues (2003) also found no difference based on age.

However, age has been found to influence reliability (retest) of child and parent anxiety reports. Edelbrock (1985), for example, found that among younger children (aged 6–9 years), parent reports of internalizing symptoms were more reliable than child self-reports. This finding could thereby support the suggestion that when resources are limited and when working with a young child, clinicians might wish to focus on obtaining information from the parent (e.g., parent diagnostic interview, parent rating scales), because it might prove more reliable than information obtained from the child. If the young child can be assessed, clinicians might wish to administer a time and cost efficient assessment method, namely, a child self-rating scale, rather than an interview schedule.

On the other hand, among older children (10 years and above), Edelbrock (1985) found that child self-reports of their own internalizing symptoms were more reliable than parent reports. This finding could thereby support the suggestion that when resources are limited and when working with an older child, the clinician might wish to focus on obtaining information from the child (e.g., child diagnostic interview, child self-report rating scales) and give only a small number of anxiety rating scales to the parent.

Parental levels of anxiety and depression also might be considered to help decide how to handle child-parent discordance. Research has shown that anxious and depressive symptoms in parents are associated with parental under- and overreporting of their child's anxiety symptoms (Krain & Kendall, 2000). Thus, a source other than the parent might be considered when assessing for childhood anxiety, especially when the clinician knows prior to the actual assessment, perhaps from the referral source or from the initial intake form, that anxiety or depressive problems are present in the parent. This might include obtaining information from another adult who is knowledgeable about the child's functioning, such as the teacher, or rounding out the child report with direct behavioral observations.

Dealing with Low Correspondence among Child Anxiety Responses

As noted earlier, some children may display their anxiety problems via overt behavior such as avoidance. Other children may display their anxiety less via overt behavior, but more via reports of negative thoughts and worries. Other children may experience high physiological arousal such as rapid heartbeats or sweating. There also are children who experience a combination of all three types of responses when faced with anxiety-provoking situations.

In light of the different types of responses that children may display when experiencing anxiety and its disorders, a multimethod assessment, which would include each of the different strategies summarized in the earlier sections of the chapter, might be used (i.e., interviews and rating scales to assess the subjective components; direct observations to assess the behavioral; and, if the child reports high physiological reactivity, a physiological assessment or at least a subjective rating from the child about his or her physiological reactions). A multimethod assessment strategy thus helps to obtain a fuller picture of the child's problems and functioning, and can help determine the key areas (e.g., child worry, child avoidance behavior) that might be most appropriately targeted in treatment (e.g., cognitive therapy to reduce worry; behavioral contracting to reduce avoidant behavior; see Eisen & Silverman [1998] for example).

Although ideal, it may not be feasible in some clinical practice settings to conduct multimethod assessments. If this is the case, it might be useful to consider the child's age. Given what was said earlier about younger children's reports not being as reliable as older children's (Edelbrock, 1985), it might make sense to administer a direct observation procedure with the young child, but administer interviews or rating scales with the older child. There also is the pragmatic issue of time and resources. If they are minimal, it makes more sense to use child self-rating scales then interview schedules and direct observations.

Determining Child Anxiety Diagnoses When Time and Resources Are Limited

The administration time needed to conduct interview schedules is approximately 60 to 90 minutes with the child and parent, respectively. The time spent administering the full schedules is likely to save time in the long run in that it will more likely lead to accurate and reliable differential diagnosis. This is because having an accurate diagnosis is important for therapeutic implementation of exposure-based cognitive behavioral treatment. That is, accurate diagnosis informs the clinician about what the content of the exposures should be in therapy (e.g., social evaluative situations for children with social phobia). Nevertheless, the amount of time needed to conduct full interviews with both the child and parent may be difficult in some clinical practice settings, especially if third party payers do not reimburse for such services.

One way to resolve this difficulty is to use the interview schedules as templates, or guides, for one's questioning rather than as scripts that must be precisely followed (Silverman & Kurtines, 1996). In this way, there is allowance for flexibility such as skipping questions or even entire modules (e.g., the OCD module). Such skipping may make practical sense if the clinician has full confidence that particular questions or modules are not relevant for that particular child. In other words, the clinician might use the various modules and interview questions selectively. By having on hand an interview schedule, however, the clinician has available a full range of DSM-oriented questions to which he or she can refer, if necessary. This can serve to maximize the probability that diagnoses derived are accurate and reliable.

We also have found that if children and parents understand the rationale for administering the interview schedule, they usually do not mind the time spent. We usually explain that because children typically display many different types of anxiety problems as well as other types of problems, we need to leave no stone uncovered in order to be fully confident that an anxiety treatment reduction program is what would be most helpful to the child at this time. We have found that children, and parents especially, are delighted that such a comprehensive set of questions about the child's anxiety symptoms and behaviors are "finally" being inquired about in such a comprehensive and systematic manner.

Nevertheless, there are likely to be settings and circumstances where even the above-mentioned strategy is not feasible. Under such conditions when an initial administration child and parent interview schedules (either the full versions or certain modules) is not possible, we would recommend using one of the rating scales that were designed along the DSM criteria, such as the Multidimensional Anxiety Scale for Children. For the subscales on which the child shows elevations (e.g., separation anxiety, social anxiety) the interview modules for those disorders might then be administered to help confirm these are the problem areas for that child.

Considering Children Who Show Impairment in Functioning, but Do Not Meet Diagnostic Criteria for an Anxiety Disorder

The diagnostic interview schedules emphasize DSM symptoms and psychopathology and are in line with the evidence-based treatment approaches' emphasis on targeting specific DSM symptoms and psychopathology. However, research has found that a substantial proportion of children who present to community mental health clinics do not meet criteria for a DSM disorder, but they do in fact evidence impaired functioning (Angold et al., 1999). Anxiety was an area that was particularly likely to lead to impairment, but not necessarily a diagnosis (Angold et al., 1999).

In addition, in working with children with anxiety disorders, there are particular challenges in trying to determine whether the child's anxiety symptoms are causing impairment. This is because certain types of fear, worry, and anxiety are normative for particular ages (e.g., separation anxiety in a toddler). And even if the fear, worry, and anxiety displayed or reported by the child are not normative (e.g., separation anxiety in an adolescent), it may be challenging to ascertain whether the problem is causing impairment. A common situation we have seen, for example, is the older child with separation anxiety, but is attending school and the parent does not present separation situations to the child. Impairment is not immediately apparent. In determining whether the separation anxiety is impairing requires careful probing of developmental tasks that children are expected to master (e.g., developing peer relationships). To the extent that the child may not be mastering such tasks, then the separation anxiety might be deemed as impairing functioning.

The above highlights the importance in obtaining some type of index to assess children's level of (dys)function. Obtaining such an index, and moving beyond symptoms and diagnoses, would seem to be in the best interest of youth: in this way clinical services might still be made available to children who are impaired but do not meet full diagnostic criteria.

We noted earlier in the chapter that several of the interview schedules, such as the Anxiety Disorders Interview Schedule for Children for DSM-IV (Silverman & Albano, 1996) contains a 0–8 point rating scale to assess interference or impairment. Although the scale is primarily used to assess how much interference each disorder for which the child meets diagnostic criteria interferes with the child's functioning, the scale can be adapted for use to assess interference of anxiety symptoms, even if diagnostic criteria are not met. This could be done by asking children and parents a few simple questions. For example, for a child who does not meet full criteria for separation anxiety disorder, but cannot sleep alone at night without mother being in the bed with her until the child falls asleep, one could ask: "You just told me that sometimes you have trouble sleeping alone at night without your mother. How does not being able to go to sleep by yourself mess things up for you in terms of how you now are doing in school? How about in terms of things with your family? And how much does it affect things with friends? And how much does it make you feel very upset (personal distress)?"

In addition, there exists the Children's Global Assessment Scale (Shaffer et al., 1983), perhaps the most widely used measure for assessing children's level of functioning. The Children's Global Assessment Scale requires clinicians to provide a rating of the child's overall functioning on a 1–100 point scale with higher scores reflecting higher levels of functioning. To make this rating, it is important to obtain information about the extent that the child's symptoms are interfering in various settings as well as how they may be leading to personal distress in the child.

Handling Anxious Children Who Strive to Always "Look Good"

Anxious children have been observed as showing high levels of social desirability or in wanting to always "look good" and "never making mistakes." Research further suggests that the manifestation of social desirability in anxious children (using school samples as in Dadds, Perrin, & Yule [1998] and clinic samples as in Pina, Silverman, Saavedra, & Weems [2001]) is influenced by age and ethnicity. Specifically, using the "Lie" Scale of the RCMAS, younger children score significantly higher than older children (Dadds et al., 1998; Pina et al., 2001); African-American children score significantly higher than Euro-American children (Dadds et al., 1998) and Hispanic/Latino-American children score significantly higher than Euro-American children (Pina et al., 2001).

This quality therefore of anxious children, and particularly of younger ethnic minority children, to present themselves in a favorable light, underscores the need for clinicians to highlight to these children that there are "no right or wrong answers" and they need to answer the questions as "honestly and truthfully as possible" during administration of assessment measures. In general, upon child completion of rating scales, it is a good idea to carefully review the responses and ensure, for example, that the full range of items on a scale have been used (not just the anchors). As noted, the RCMAS also contains items that comprise a Lie Scale (e.g., "I never get angry"). A perusal of the items on the Lie Scale (every fourth item on the questionnaire) can serve as "red flags" for clinicians that the child may not be answering accurately.

Similarly, during direct observations, there may be pressure on children with anxiety disorders to present themselves in a positive light. Similar instructions to those mentioned earlier are useful in this situation to minimize this possibility.

☐ Case Illustration

Client Description

Amy, a 10-year-old, Euro-American girl was referred to a childhood anxiety disorders specialty clinic by one of her teachers. She was referred for increasing nervousness during gymnastics practice, particularly prior to gymnastics competitions.

History of the Disorder or Problem

Although Amy had been involved in gymnastics since she was 6 years old, she reported that she recently had become increasingly nervous prior to practices and competitions. She reported becoming so nervous at one meet about a year ago that she vomited during the competition. According to Amy, no one in the audience noticed her vomit because she was off to the side on the stage; however, the other gymnasts noticed and asked if she was okay. Amy vomited again 2 months later during another competition. Since that competition, Amy feared she would vomit during each competition and at practices. As a consequence, Amy was no longer attending competitions, her attendance at practices was increasingly sporadic, and she was seriously considering discontinuing gymnastics all together.

Presenting Complaints

Amy complained that she felt nauseous in the preceding hours of competitions and practices and worried about vomiting. She was careful to eat only light meals for breakfast and lunch on the days of competitions and practices. Despite such precaution, Amy continued to feel nauseous prior to competitions and practices and she continued to have frequent and uncontrollable worry about vomiting during competitions and practices. As noted, she also was showing increasing avoidance behavior of practices and total avoidance of competitions.

Psychological Assessment Protocol

Amy and her mother were interviewed using the Anxiety Disorders Interview Schedule for Children. The child also was asked to complete the RCMAS and the CASI. The CASI was administered because of its focus on assessing the level of distress associated with anxiety-related physiological symptoms. Amy's mother was asked to complete the CBCL.

In addition, because mother reported during the interview that she did not attend Amy's practices because watching her child made her "nervous" because she worried about Amy making a mistake, we obtained permission from mother to obtain information from Amy's gymnastics instructor. Although more designed for use by classroom teachers, we nevertheless asked the gymnastics instructor to complete the Teacher Report Form.

A final part of the assessment protocol was to have Amy participate in a behavioral observation. She was asked to perform a gymnastics routine for 5 minutes in front of a small audience (i.e., clinic staff). Rating codes discussed in Beidel and colleagues (2000) were used. Amy's gymnastics performance was rated 4; where 5 is the highest score for "very effective." However, Amy's own self-rating of anxiety was 5 (very anxious or distressed). Amy also reported that her stomach felt "funny," and that she was feeling increasingly nauseous. Her face also turned pale. In addition, during the observation, Amy started and stopped her routine several times, noting that she had "made a mistake" though no one in the audience noticed any mistake. We also conducted another observation with the mother present. During this observation, mother averted her eyes from her daughter and clenched her fist and made other overt signs of anxiety.

Results from the assessment protocol indicated that Amy's self-rating scores on the CASI were high, but her scores on the RCMAS were low.

She scored high, however, on the Lie Scale. However, the parent and teacher scores were all elevated and above the normative means. In addition, based on the interview information, mother endorsed a diagnosis of Social Phobia — specific type (gymnastics competitions/practices) on the parent version of the interview; Amy endorsed a Specific Phobia (vomiting). Both child and mother rated interference a 5 on the 0–8 point Feelings Thermometer. Upon discussing with Amy and her mother their respective views on Amy's problem, we discerned that Amy's primary fear focused on vomiting. However, Amy also expressed severe fear about social evaluation and that she might be embarrassed if she vomited. Consequently, Amy was assigned comorbid diagnoses of Social Phobia — specific type (gymnastics competitions/practices) and Specific Phobia (vomiting). In addition, the results from the interviews, self-rating scales, and behavioral observation task were compiled and a C-GAS rating of 60 was assigned during a clinical staff meeting. A clinical cutoff for the C-GAS is 67 and so Amy's score was below this cutoff, indicating that this was a significant clinical problem. In light of this, coupled with her receiving DSM diagnoses, she was deemed appropriate for treatment.

Targets Selected for Treatment

Based on the information obtained on the assessment protocol, it was evident that Amy experienced significantly high levels of anxiety in a specific situation — gymnastics, both practices and competitions. What particularly bothered Amy was a fear of vomiting in this specific situation. What also was apparent was that Amy thought she needed to be "perfect" during her gymnastics routines and not being perfect compounded her nervousness. This was despite the fact that raters did not view Amy as nervous or her performance as having any errors. In addition, it was evident that mother's own anxiety was serving to maintain Amy's anxiety about gymnastics and vomiting during gymnastics practices and competitions.

Hence, Amy's treatment involved an exposure-based cognitive behavioral treatment. Exposures included having Amy do simulated gymnastics routines in the clinic (in front of small audiences) as well as in her imagination (wherein Amy actually imagined vomiting during a practice). These in-session exposures successfully elicited anxiety and the "funny" feelings in Amy's stomach assessed via Beidel and colleagues (2000) behavior codes. In addition, Amy wrote contracts with the therapist for attending her gymnastics practice out-of-session and "small steps" were taken each week in terms of what Amy had to do in the practice (e.g., first time just watch the others perform gymnastics routines to Amy fully participating in the gymnastics practices and competitions). Amy kept track of her behaviors and thoughts during each class through self-monitoring records. Amy learned to handle her anxiety and physiological distress symptoms as well as to be "less hard on herself," through a variety of therapeutic strategies, including relaxation techniques and cognitive self-control and restructuring procedures. Several meetings also were held with Amy's mother and her role in possibly maintaining Amy's difficulties were discussed. Suggestions were made to mother regarding how she might better handle her own worries and anxiety about her daughter's gymnastics performances.

Assessment of Progress

Amy's progress in treatment was assessed through out treatment using the self-monitoring forms and with ratings during the observation tasks. In addition, at midtreatment the rating scales were administered to Amy, her mother, and the gymnastics instructor. Progress was evident on these measures. As treatment continued, further progress was evident by increased attendance and activity in gymnastics practice, assessed via self-monitoring and external ratings from the instructor. By the end of 16 sessions, Amy was fully attending practices and was participating in competitions.

To assess Amy's progress at the end of treatment, the specific phobia and social phobia sections of the interview schedules were administered to Amy and her mother. Neither Amy nor mother endorsed any symptoms. Their ratings of interference were 2 and 1, respectively, on the 0–8 point scale. Amy's CASI scores also had improved dramatically, as did the internalizing subscale score of the CBCL and the teacher version, with all scores being below the clinical range. Mother also reported that she was now able to attend Amy's gymnastics competitions with decreased anxiety.

☐ Summary

This chapter provided a summary of childhood anxiety disorders and the range of assessment strategies available to assess the disorders. Pragmatic issues involved in the use of the strategies were discussed, and recommendations were offered regarding how to handles these issues. The case of Amy served to illustrate several of these strategies and issues.

☐ References

Achenbach, T. M. (1991a). *Manual for the Child Behavior Checklist 14-18 and 1991 profile.* Burlington, VT: University of Vermont, Department of Psychiatry.

Achenbach, T. M. (1991b). *Manual for the Teacher Reporting Form and 1991 Profile.* Burlington, VT: University of Vermont, Department of Psychiatry.

Achenbach, T. M., & Edelbrock, C. S. (1987). *Manual for the Youth Self-Report and profile.* Burlington: University of Vermont, Department of Psychiatry.

Achenbach, T. M., McConaughy, S. H., & Howell, C. T. (1987). Child/adolescent behavioral and emotional problems: Implications of cross-informant correlations for situational specificity. *Psychological Bulletin, 101,* 213–232.

Ambrosini, P. J. (2000). Historical development and present status of the Schedule for Affective Disorders and Schizophrenia for School-Age Children (K-SADS). *Journal of the American Academy of Child and Adolescent Psychiatry, 39,* 49–58.

American Psychiatric Association (1994). *Diagnostic and Statistical Manual of Mental Disorders* (4th ed.). Washington, DC: American Psychiatric Association.

Angold, A., Prendergast, M., Cox, A., Harrington, R., Simonoff, E., & Rutter, M. (1995). The child and adolescent psychiatric assessment (CAPA). *Psychological Medicine, 25,* 739–753.

Angold, A., & Costello, E. J. (1995). A test-retest reliability study of child-reported psychiatric symptoms and diagnoses using the child and adolescent psychiatric assessment (CAPA). *Psychological Medicine, 25,* 755–762.

Angold, A., Costello, E. J., Farmer, E. M. Z., Burns, B. J., & Erkanli, A. (1999). Impaired but undiagnosed. *Journal of the American Academy of Child and Adolescent Psychiatry, 38,* 129–137.

Barkley, R. A. (1988). *Hyperactive children: A handbook for diagnosis and treatment.* New York: Guilford.

Barrett, P. M., Dadds, M. R., & Rapee, R. M. (1996). Family treatment of childhood anxiety: A controlled trial. *Journal of Consulting and Clinical Psychology, 64,* 333–342.

Beidel, D. C., Turner, S. M., & Morris, T. L. (1995). A new inventory to assess childhood social anxiety and phobia: The Social Phobia and Anxiety Inventory for Children. *Psychological Assessment, 7,* 73–79.

Beidel, D. C., Turner, S. M., & Morris, T. L. (1999a). Psychopathology of childhood social phobia. *Journal of the American Academy of Child and Adolescent Psychiatry, 38,* 643–650.

Beidel, D. C., Turner, S. M., & Morris, T. L. (1999b). A new inventory to assess childhood social anxiety and phobia: The Social Phobia and Anxiety Inventory for Children. *Psychological Assessment, 7,* 73–79.

Beidel, D. C., Turner, S. M., & Morris, T. L. (2000). Behavioral treatment of childhood social phobia. *Journal of Consulting and Clinical Psychology, 68,* 1072–1080.

Bierman, K. L., & McCauley, E. (1987). Children's descriptions of their peer interactions: Useful information for clinical child assessment. *Journal of Clinical Child Psychology, 16,* 9–18.

Birmaher, B., Khetarpal, S., Brent, D., Cully, M., Balach, L., Kaufman, J., & McKenzie Neer, S. (1997). The screen for child anxiety related emotional disorders (SCARED): Scale construction and psychometric characteristics. *Journal of the American Academy of Child and Adolescent Psychiatry, 36,* 545–553.

Brown, G. W., & Harris, T. O. (1993). Etiology of anxiety and depressive disorders in an inner-city population: I. Early adversity. *Psychological Medicine, 23,* 143–154.

Choudhury, M. S., Pimentel, S. S., & Kendall, P. C. (2003). Childhood anxiety disorders: Parent-child (dis)agreement using a structured interview for the DSM-IV. *Journal of the American Academy of Child and Adolescent Psychiatry, 42,* 957–964.

Conners, C. K. (1997). *Conners rating scales-revised technical manual.* Toronto: Multi-Health Systems.

Costello, E. J., Angold, A., Burns, B. J., Stangl, D. K., Tweed, D. L., Erkanli, A., et al. (1996). The Great Smoky Mountains study of youth: Goals, designs, methods, and the prevalence of DSM-III-R disorders. *Archives of General Psychiatry, 53,* 1129–1136.

Costello, E. J., Angold, A., & Keeler, G. P. (1999). Adolescent outcomes of childhood disorders: The consequences of severity and impairment. *Journal of the American Academy of Child and Adolescent Psychiatry, 38*, 121–128.

Dadds, M. R., Perrin, S., & Yule, W. (1998). Social desirability and self-reported anxiety in children: An analysis of the RCMAS Lie Scale. *Journal of Abnormal Child Psychology, 26*, 311–317.

Edelbrock, C. S. (1985). Age differences in the reliability of the psychiatric interview of the child. *Child Development, 56*, 265–275.

Eisen, A. R., & Silverman, W. K., (1998). Prescriptive treatment for generalized anxiety disorder in children. *Behavior Therapy, 29*, 105–121.

Fergusson, D. M., Horwood, J., & Lynskey, M. T. (1993). Prevalence and comorbidity of DSM-III-R diagnoses in a birth cohort of 15 year olds. *Journal of the American Academy of Child and Adolescent Psychiatry, 32*, 1127–1134.

Glennon, B., & Weisz, J. R. (1978). An observational approach to the assessment of anxiety in young children. *Journal of Consulting and Clinical Psychology, 46*, 1246–1257.

Goodman, W. K., Price, L. H., Rasmussen, S. A., Mazure, C., Fleischmann, R. L., Hill, C. L., et al. (1989). The Yale-Brown Obsessive Compulsive Scale. *Archives of General Psychiatry, 46*, 1006–1016.

Gresham, F. M., & Elliot, S. N. (1990). *Social skills rating system: manual*. Circles Pines, MN: American Guidance Service.

Grills, A. E., & Ollendick, T. H. (2002). Issues in parent-child agreement: The case of structured diagnostic interviews. *Clinical Child and Family Psychology Review, 5*, 57–82.

Grills, A. E., & Ollendick, T. H. (2003). Multiple informant agreement and the Anxiety Disorders Interview Schedule for Parents and Children. *Journal of the American Academy of Child and Adolescent Psychiatry, 42*, 30–40.

Herjanic, B., & Reich, W. (1997). Development of a structured psychiatric interview for children: Agreement between child and parent on individual symptoms. *Journal of Abnormal Child Psychology, 25*, 21–31.

Insel, T., Murphy, D. Cohen, R., Alterman, I., Kilts, C., & Linnoila, M. (1983). Obsessive-compulsive disorder in five US communities. *Archives of General Psychiatry, 40*, 605–612.

Jensen, B. J., & Haynes, S. N. (1986). Self-report questionnaires and inventories. In A. R. Ciminero, K. S., Calhoun, & H. E. Adams (Eds.), *Handbook of behavioral assessment* (pp. 150–175). New York: Wiley.

Jensen, B. J., Rubio-Stipec, M., Canino, G., Bird, H. R., Dulcan, M. K., Schwab-Stone, M. E., et al. (1999). Parent and child contributions to diagnosis of mental disorder: Are both informants always necessary? *Journal of the American Academy of Child and Adolescent Psychiatry, 38*, 1569–1579.

Kearney, C. A., & Silverman, W. K. (1999). Functionally based prescriptive and nonprescriptive treatment for children and adolescents with school refusal behavior. *Behavior Therapy, 30*, 673–695.

Kendall, P. C. (1994). Treating anxiety disorders in children: Results of a randomized clinical trial. *Journal of Consulting and Clinical Psychology, 62*, 100–110.

Krain, A. L., & Kendall, P. C. (2000). The role of parental emotional distress in parent report of child anxiety. *Journal of Clinical Child Psychology, 29*, 328–335.

La Greca, A. M., & Stone, W. L. (1993). Social Anxiety Scale for Children — Revised: Factor structure and concurrent validity. *Journal of Clinical Child Psychology, 22*, 7–27.

March, J. S., Parker, J. D. A., Sullivan, K., Stallings, P., & Conners, K. (1997). The mulitidimensional anxiety scale for children (MASC): Factor, structure, reliability, and validity. *Journal of the American Academy of Child and Adolescent Psychiatry, 36*, 554–565.

March, J. S., & Sullivan, K. (1999). Test-retest reliability of the multidimensional anxiety scale for children. *Journal of Anxiety Disorders, 13*, 349–358.

McGlynn, F. D., & Rose, M. P. (1998). Assessment of anxiety and fear. In A. S. Bellack & M. Hersen (Eds.) *Behavioral assessment: A practical handbook* (pp. 179–209). Needham Heights, MA: Allyn and Bacon.

Naglieri, J. A., LeBuffe, P. A., & Pfeiffer, S. I. (1993). *Devereux Behavior Rating Scale-school form*. San Antonio, TX: Psychological Corporation.

Ollendick, T. H. (1983). Reliability and validity of the Revised Fear Survey Schedule for Children (FSSC-R). *Behaviour Research and Therapy, 21,* 395–399.

Pina, A. A., Silverman, W. K., Saavedra, L. M., & Weems, C. F. (2001). An analysis of the RCMAS lie scale in a clinic sample of anxious children. *Journal of Anxiety Disorders, 15,* 443–457.

Prinz, R. J., Foster, S. L., Kent, R. N., & O'Leary, K. D. (1979). Multivariate assessment of conflict in distressed and nondistressed mother-adolescent dyads. *Journal of Applied Behavior Analysis, 12,* 691–700.

Rapee, R. M., Barrett, P. M., Dadds, M. R., & Evans, L. (1994). Reliablity of the DSM-III-R childhood anxiety disorders using structured interview: interrater and parent-child agreement. *Journal of the American Academy of Child and Adolescent Psychiatry, 33,* 984–992.

Reich, W. (2000). Diagnostic interview for children and adolescents (DICA). *Journal of the American Academy of Child and Adolescent Psychiatry, 39,* 59–66.

Reynolds, C. R., & Kamphaus, R. W. (1992). *Behavior assessment system for children.* Circle Pines, MN: American Guidance Service.

Reynolds, C. R., & Richmond, B. O. (1985). *Revised Children's Manifest Anxiety Scale: Manual.* Los Angeles: Western Psychological Services.

Ronan, K. R., Kendall, P. C., & Rowe, M. (1994). Negative affectivity in children: Development and validation of a self-statement questionnaire. *Cognitive Therapy and Research, 18,* 509–528.

RUPP Anxiety Study Group. (2002). The pediatric anxiety rating scale (PARS): Development and psychometric properties. *Journal of the American Academy of Child and Adolescent Psychiatry, 41,* 1061–1069.

Saavedra, L. M., & Silverman, W. K. (2002). Classification of anxiety disorders in children: What a difference two decades make. *International Review of Psychiatry, 14,* 87–100.

Sarason, S. B., Davidson, K., Lighthall, F., & Waite, R. (1958). A test anxiety scale for children. *Child Development, 29,* 105–113.

Schludermann, E., & Schludermann, S. (1970). Replicability of factors in children's report of parent behavior (CRPBI). *Journal of Psychology, 76,* 239–249.

Schwab-Stone, M., Fallon, T., Briggs, M., & Crowther, B. (1994). Reliability of diagnostic reporting for children aged 6–11 years: A test-retest study of the diagnostic interview schedule for Children-Revised. *American Journal of Psychiatry, 151,* 1048–1054.

Shaffer, D., Fisher, P., Christopher, P., Dulcan, M. K., & Schwab-Stone, M. E. (2000). NIMH diagnostic interview schedule for children version IV (NIMH DISC-IV): Description, differences from previous versions, and reliability of some common diagnoses. *Journal of the American Academy of Child and Adolescent Psychiatry, 39,* 28–38.

Shaffer, D., Gould, M. S., Brasic, J., Ambrosini, P., Fisher, P., Bird, H., et al. (1983). A children's global assessment scale. *Archives of General Psychiatry, 40,* 1228–1231.

Silverman, W. K., & Albano, A. M. (1996). *Anxiety disorders interview schedule for children for DSM-IV: (child and parent versions).* San Antonio, TX: Psychological Corporation.

Silverman, W. K., Fleisig, W., Rabian, B., & Peterson, R. A. (1991). Child anxiety sensitivity index. *Journal of Clinical Child Psychology, 20,* 162–168.

Silverman, W. K., & Kurtines, W. M. (1996). *Anxiety and phobic disorders: A pragmatic approach.* New York: Plenum Press.

Silverman, W. K., & Nelles, W. B. (1988). The anxiety disorders interview schedule for children. *Journal of the American Academy of Child and Adolescent Psychiatry, 27,* 772–778.

Silverman, W. K., & Rabian, B. (1999). Rating scales for anxiety and mood disorders. In D. Shaffer & C. P. Lucas (Eds), *Diagnostic assessment in child and adolescent psychopathology* (pp. 127–166). New York: Guilford.

Silverman, W. K., Saavedra, L. M., & Pina, A. A. (2001). Test-retest reliability of anxiety symptoms and diagnoses using the anxiety disorders interview schedule for DSM-IV: child and parent versions (ADIS for DSM-IV: C/P). *Journal of the American Academy of Child and Adolescent Psychiatry, 40,* 937–944.

Silverman, W. K., & Serafini, L. T. (1998). Assessment of child behavior problems: Internalizing disorders. In A. S. Bellack & M. Hersen (Eds.), *Behavioral assessment: A practical handbook* (4th ed., pp. 342–360). Needham Heights, MA: Allyn and Bacon.

Silverman, W. K., & Treffers, P. D. A. (2001). *Anxiety disorders in children and adolescents: Research, assessment and intervention.* Cambridge, UK: Cambridge University Press.

Spence, S. H. (1997). The structure of anxiety symptoms among children: a confirmatory factor analytic study. *Journal of Abnormal Psychology, 106,* 280–297.

Spielberger, C. D. (1973). *Manual for the state-trait anxiety inventory for children.* Palo Alto, CA: Consulting Psychologists Press.

CHAPTER 12   Helen Orvaschel

Depressive Disorders

☐ Description of the Disorders

According to the *Diagnostic and Statistical Manual of Mental Disorders*, 4th edition (DSM-IV; American Psychiatric Association, 2000) criteria, a diagnosis of Major Depression (MDD) requires a total of five symptoms, at least one of which is depression and/or anhedonia, and another four (three if both depression and anhedonia are present) symptoms from the following: appetite or weight disturbance (decrease or increase in appetite, weight, or both, or failure to make expected gains), sleep disturbance (insomnia or hypersomnia), psychomotor disturbance (agitation or retardation), fatigue or loss of energy, feelings of worthlessness or excessive or inappropriate guilt, concentration difficulties or indecisiveness, and suicidality (thoughts or behavior). Irritability is a mood equivalent for children and adolescents and may therefore be used instead of depressed mood. Depressed/irritable mood and (most of the) other symptoms need to be present most of the day, almost every day for at least 2 weeks and anhedonia (if present) should be marked. The syndrome requires presence of clinically significant distress, impaired functioning, or both. The disorder may have an acute or insidious onset, may be single or recurrent, melancholic or atypical, psychotic or nonpsychotic, and transitory or chronic.

Dysthymia, on the other hand, is by definition a chronic, nonpsychotic, major mood disorder, generally viewed as less severe than MDD. The DSM-IV criteria specify that depressed/irritable mood be present most of the day, more days than not, and be accompanied by two or more additional symptoms. Potential symptoms for dysthymia include appetite problems (poor appetite or overeating), sleep problems (insomnia or hypersomnia), low energy or fatigue, low self-esteem, poor concentration or difficulty making decisions, and feelings of hopelessness, resulting in clinically significant distress and/or impaired functioning. Mood disturbance and symptoms must be present for at least 1 year (compared with 2 years for adults), with no remissions lasting longer than 2 months during the first year.

Some symptoms of dysthymia are either the same (i.e., depression/irritability, fatigue) or similar (i.e., low self-esteem rather than worthlessness) to MDD. Others are specific to each disorder (i.e., anhedonia, suicidality, psychomotor disturbance for MDD; hopelessness for dysthymia). Clearly, the two disorders are phenomenologically similar and viewed as related syndromes. The literature supports this relationship with greater than expected comorbidity between the two and higher morbid risks for both disorders in family psychiatric history studies of depressed probands (Weissman, Kidd, & Prusoff, 1982). Additionally, dysthymia provides a risk factor for MDD and is associated with recurrence of MDD in children and adolescence (Kovacs, Feinberg, Crouse,-Novak, Paulauskas, Pollock, & Finkelstein, 1984; Lewinsohn, Rohde, Seeley, & Hops, 1991).

While criteria for child and adolescent depressions are very similar to those of adults, with very few noted modifications (i.e., irritability as a mood equivalent; 1 rather than 2 years for dysthymia), developmental issues relevant to diagnosis have been largely ignored. Nowhere is this more evident than in the assessment of mood in preadolescent children. Mood lability in this population is considerably more notorious than in adults, but no effort is made to recognize this difference in disorder criteria or assessment. Inasmuch as the typical (nondepressed) 8 or 9 year old is likely to maintain a consistent mood for less than five minutes, remarkably few in this age group will be depressed (or its equivalent) "most of the day, nearly every day," but they may still be appropriate candidates for MDD. From a developmental perspective, flexibility in interpretation of this (time frame) criterion is needed for children between the ages of about 5 to 11. For a 7 or 8 year old, 3 hours of consistent sadness in a day often qualifies as a minimal screen for depressed mood, while in an older child (e.g., 13 or 14 year old) a lengthier time depressed, approximating that of adults, may be expected. Clearly, clinical judgment is an essential feature in the diagnostic process, and the need for a knowledgeable developmental perspective is apparent.

Clinical judgment and developmental considerations are also essential facets of the differential process. MDD and dysthymia must be differentiated from each other, as well as from adjustment problems, parent-child/family issues, transitory mood lability of nonclinical significance, bipolar disorders, anxiety disorders, and sometimes even disruptive disorders such as attention deficit hyperactivity disorder (ADHD) or oppositional defiant disorder (ODD). If younger children pass a minimal screen for depression, with mood disturbance of 3 or more hours, the distinction between MDD and dysthymia becomes more complicated. A 1 year time frame is not a sufficient basis for diagnosing dysthymia, because even younger children may suffer from longer-term (or more chronic) MDD. Determining the more appropriate diagnosis must be based on an integrative evaluation of severity, duration, specific symptomatology, and impairments, all within a developmental context. Also, presence of MDD superimposed on an underlying dysthymic disorder (or double depression) must be considered, as this designation has particular significance for length of episode, treatment response, and probability of recurrence (Kovacs et al., 1984). Those with double depression are likely to have been depressed for a longer period of time when compared with children who present with MDD and no prior history of mood disorder, and they may have more extensive functional impairments. They are also likely to have a more mitigated response to treatment, inasmuch as a return to baseline for these children may mean a return to a dysthymic rather than a euthymic state. Not only is response to treatment more refractory, but their increased risk for subsequent episodes of MDD suggests that therapeutic efforts should provide some emphasis on relapse prevention as well as early identification of onset of pathology in the event of recurrence.

While MDD and dysthymia are major mood disorders with established prognostic significance, adjustment disorder with depressed mood (Adj-D) in children is generally self-limited and has little established risk associated with subsequent morbidity (Kovacs et al., 1984). These children will recover from Adj-D whether or not they are treated, and do not show the increased risk for subsequent major mood disorders characteristic of those with MDD, dysthymia, or double depression. Many clinicians assume that presence of a stressor is sufficient reason to assign adjustment disorder with depressed mood, but this should be done only when symptoms are insufficient to meet criteria for either of the other (major) mood diagnoses. The differential is not trivial, and should be based on the most essential hierarchal criterion, that is, whether criteria for MDD or dysthymia are met, irrespective of the presence or absence of a significant stressor. A diagnosis of depression-NOS (D-NOS) is made when a mood disorder is present, but has not met criteria for any of the previous categories. For example, a child who meets all criteria for dysthymia except the 1 year duration or who meets all but one criterion of MDD may best be characterized as D-NOS. Increasingly, evidence suggests that the NOS state may be a precursor to MDD. Therefore, the symptoms of these children/adolescents should be monitored as they may be at increased risk for a major mood disorder.

With respect to the issue of bipolar disorder, noninduced manic episodes in prepubertal children remain infrequent, but adolescent onsets represent about one-third of all bipolar cases. Complicating the matter further, bipolar adolescents often appear with mixed states, rapid cycling, or both, which may be overlooked when considering depression because of the lack of clear mood delineation. Such an adolescent bipolar presentation may also be confused with substance use or disruptive behaviors. Even more difficult is the determination of mood in bipolar cases, since irritability is a documented part of manic syndromes, but is also a mood equivalent of depression in children and adolescents.

Finally, depressive disorders must be distinguished from anxiety disorders, with which they are often comorbid. For example, MDD has been found to co-occur with separation anxiety disorder (SAD) in about 75% of 6- to 9-year-old (referred) cases (Puig-Antich, Blau, Marx, Green-hill, & Chambers, 1978). Also, depressed mood is a significant part of SAD, inasmuch as children with this disorder experience sadness and distress when separated; nevertheless, MDD children often report feeling worse (sadder) if they are not with their primary attachment figure. For the differential, the clinician should consider that a child with MDD may feel somewhat better in the presence of a major attachment figure, but will generally retain significant depressed mood. A child with SAD should feel little or no residual depressed mood when reunited with the major attachment figure since it is the separation or its anticipation that is creating the negative affect.

Clearly, if criteria for mood and anxiety disorders are met, both should be noted. However, a clinician must determine if the child presents with an agitated mood disorder, or if an additional diagnosis such as SAD, generalized anxiety (GAD), obsessive compulsive disorder (OCD), and the like is a more accurate descriptor. Given the myriad of potential complexities, a careful evaluation of mood, accompanying symptoms, impairments, functioning, and a thorough history, conducted by a clinician experienced with children and adolescents, is necessary for appropriate diagnosis and consideration of differential issues.

☐ Range of Assessment Strategies Available

Standard clinical evaluation is a term that means different things to many people. When this is translated as "unstructured clinical interview," there are problems with reliability, as well as comprehensiveness and comparability. Those in the field of research have been compelled to develop alternative assessment procedures because they must demonstrate reliability and thoroughness needed for appropriate group assignment, as well as for funding competitiveness. Their efforts have resulted in the development of a handful of structured and semistructured diagnostic interviews and a number of paper-and-pencil inventories, most frequently used in empirical investigations and often in academic settings. Several reviews of these instruments exist and will not be repeated here (Edelbrock & Costello, 1988; Orvaschel, 1988; Orvaschel, Sholomskas, & Weissman, 1980). Instead, we will examine some specific types of assessment strategies available, in order to determine their appropriateness, utility, and feasibility.

Using a standard assessment protocol in clinical practice has many advantages, but the practitioner must determine which tools are most appropriate to the setting and task at hand. Few clinicians are likely to use a structured diagnostic interview (i.e., DISC; Schaffer, Fisher, Piacentini, Schwab-Stone, & Wicks, 1989), as they may be awkward, result in unnecessary burden, and fail to use the skills of the clinician. Fully structured interviews were intended, after all, to be used by lay interviewers and were designed to eliminate the need for clinical judgment. On the other hand, the introduction of a semistructured interview may appear similarly superfluous, but results in many benefits beyond the customary procedures used in office practice.

Use of a semistructured diagnostic interview allows the clinician to utilize his or her judgment and skills, while providing a mechanism for the systematic gathering of data. Rather than focusing only on the often ambiguous reports of patient and family, the practitioner is compelled to follow an established format for assessing signs and symptoms of psychopathology. The result is a far more comprehensive evaluation that attends to the identification of specific problem symptoms, and documents not only which symptoms are present but which are absent. Semistructured assessments provide an organized format for determining current psychopathology and past episodes of the same or a different disorder. A routine corollary is the appraisal of comorbid disorders that may be overlooked in less rigorous examinations.

The efficient, orderly, and methodical information-gathering and classification procedures employed by semistructured diagnostic interviews provide a more reliable product because of the reduction of information variance (Endicott & Spitzer, 1978). Outcome is better comparability in measurement and evaluation of children's behavioral disturbances and enhanced ability to establish explicit targets for treatment. Some interview procedures also provide a mechanism for managing informant variance (Kashani, Orvaschel, Burk, & Reid, 1985) that result from the use of multiple informants needed with this population (Orvaschel, Puig-Antich, Chambers, Tabrizi, & Johnson, 1982). Children and adolescents can rarely be adequately assessed with one reporter, as is more typical with adults. In fact, it is not unusual to gather information from the designated patient, the mother, the father, both, or other regular caretakers, and school personnel (e.g., child's teacher). When data are assembled from more than one source, disagreement is the rule and not the exception (Weissman, Orvaschel, & Padian, 1980). Therefore, the clinician must exercise judgment on how best to combine disparate information so as to most accurately ascertain a practical "truth" for the scenario presenting. While disruptive behaviors can realistically be established by caretakers, such as parents and teachers, the child is the better source of information on internal emotional states such as depression (Orvaschel, Weissman, Padian, & Lowe, 1981).

The end product of what may initially be an unfamiliar and painstaking process is a more thorough, precise, and accurate evaluation than would be likely with the more standard (unstructured) clinical interview. Many of these (semistructured) instruments allow for the measurement of onsets and offsets of episodes, and differential diagnosis questions are more easily resolved because of the scrupulous adherence to systematic inquiry. This is especially important in the assessment of mood disorders, generally, and depression, specifically, because of problems with differential diagnosis discussed above. Additionally, the diagnostic process is not hampered by preexisting biases or assumptions generated by sometimes misleading initial impressions. Finally, use of such tools assists in a methodical appraisal of suicidality and risk assessment.

Despite the many benefits of semistructured interviews, they remain only a part of the clinical evaluation process needed for the assessment of depression in youth. Another component of measurement should be paper-and-pencil inventories, such as the Children's Depression Inventory (CDI, Kovacs, 1980/1981) or for older adolescents, the Beck Depression Inventory (BDI, Beck, Ward, Mendelsohn, Mock, & Erbaugh, 1961) and the Beck Hopelessness Scale (BHI, Beck, Weissman, Lester, & Trexler, 1974), and possibly ancillary instruments such as a problem behavior checklist (i.e., CBCL; Achenbach & Edelbrock, 1981), self-esteem scales (i.e., Coopersmith Self-Esteem Inventory [Chiu, 1988]; Piers-Harris Children's Self-Concept Scale [Piers & Harris, 1964]), anxiety measures, family interaction measures (i.e., FES; Moos & Moos, 1981), and the like. The purpose of these inventories is not diagnostic and was never intended to be, even though they are sometimes used in this manner. They are, however, very valuable for assessing overall severity, establishing baseline measures for specific symptoms, evaluating effects of implemented interventions, and progress or the lack of it over time. By and large, paper-and-pencil self-reports are easy to administer and inexpensive to evaluate. They can be given frequently and to sources the clinician may not be able to interview, thereby expanding the information available. For example, while teachers may be an important resource for evaluating areas of impairment and changes in functioning, rarely is it convenient for practitioners to meet with these individuals in an interview format, making checklists an essential supplement. Furthermore, determining if symptoms are abating is best evaluated with periodic administration of such inventories for patients and their caretakers, rather than with more time-consuming interviews. Therefore, these measures should be administered at the beginning of treatment to assist in the targeting of specific problems and symptoms and at specific intervals to provide ongoing monitoring of treatment progress.

Despite the aforementioned advantages, use of some evaluation procedures can result in complexities when administered in traditional clinical practice. Prominent issues include convenience and control of costs. These in turn are connected with time expended and staffing needs, all of which are related to reimbursement. Practitioners cannot expect to conduct diagnostic evaluations that take 3 or more hours of their time for every patient that presents, because such efforts are not likely to be compensated in today's marketplace. Similar concerns are present if the evaluation requires extensive additional training or supplementary staff. Nevertheless, a comprehensive evaluation should be viable within these parameter limitations.

Because semistructured instruments encourage and expect clinical judgment, training in their use is limited to procedural instruction rather than a reeducation in developmental psychopathology or diagnosis. The clinician need learn only how to administer and score these interviews, not how to conduct a diagnostic evaluation. For those with experience in their use, most of these interviews can be completed in less than 2 hours. Personnel whose time is less valuable than that of the clinician can be used to administer and sometimes score paper-and-pencil inventories. Their costs are generally limited to the price of ordering the copyrighted materials from their publishers and sometimes scoring, although this is more often done in the office. Because of their comprehensiveness, these evaluations can replace unstructured practices of the past which often required two or three visits to complete. They may also help meet new practice requirements for written documentation of assessments and diagnosis.

☐ Pragmatic Issues in Assessing Depression

In clinical practice, the practitioner must be able to obtain reliable information from child informants who may be quite young or from adolescents who may be reluctant to respond to specific questions. Also of concern is how to combine the child's information with that obtained from the caretaker(s). Even children as young as 4 or 5 are capable of answering questions about internal states such as mood, if these questions are asked properly. As a rule, parents and children should initially be evaluated separately, with the parent (adult informant(s)) interview preceding that of the child. This will allow the clinician to establish the caretaker's perception of the presenting problem, its time frame, and a historical context, as well as information on child development, health, and family history, areas on which the child is lacking in knowledge or inappropriate to the task. Of course, many parents do not endorse depressed mood (or its equivalent) in their children because they do not believe young children would have any reason to feel depressed and many believe, erroneously, that only adults can experience such a disorder.

When interviewing the child, the clinician must determine level of vocabulary and specific words used to describe the moods of interest. Young children may not know what depression is, but they do know words like sad, unhappy, cranky, grouchy, crabby, or mad (remember: irritability is a mood equivalent for depression). For young children, such terms are often synonymous with feelings of clinical depression. The clinician should begin by asking the child what word he or she uses (to describe) when they feel really bad, like when they get in trouble or when they are scolded. Identifying terms is the first step and is then followed by inquiry about mood using those words supplied by the child. The assessment can then proceed to questions about whether the child always knows why he/she feels "that way" in order to establish context. Depressed and irritable moods should be assessed first, followed by the other mood screen item, anhedonia. Children may use or equate the term boredom for anhedonia, but the practitioner should make certain that this boredom is present even when there are activities available to the child. One or both mood (depression/irritability and/or anhedonia) symptoms must be present in order to determine the likelihood of an episode.

Once mood is ascertained, the inquiry should establish how long those feelings last. This must be assessed carefully, since how long is too vague a concept for many children. The child should more appropriately be asked if they feel that way (e.g., bad, sad, cranky, mad, etc.) for a few minutes, or a long time, like all morning, or all afternoon, or all day at school, and so on. This can then be followed with questions about whether this is true today, was true yesterday, the whole week, since school started, since his or her birthday, Christmas, summer vacation, and so forth. Starting with small time frames and building from there is particularly helpful with younger children who are less likely to provide reliable information involving time past a few days, particularly for inquiries about mood and behaviors. Grounding time to events likely to be noted by children (e.g., birthdays, school, holidays, and the like) will always yield better results than vague or open-ended questions like how long did that last or was that for 2 weeks or 1 month, which are times with little meaning for the younger child.

Since depression is an episodic disorder, additional symptoms and criteria items should be investigated within the context of the time frame established for the presenting episode. It is useful, therefore, to try to find out if the episode in question is particularly lengthy, that is, one or more years, or has been true for months or weeks, so that the interviewer can investigate the possibility that the disorder may be dysthymia, MDD, or MDD superimposed on an underlying dysthymia. If the episode has been particularly long, all other symptoms should be ascertained for the "worst" part of the episode or, if this impractical because it cannot be easily established or results in other problems, questions should focus on the previous month. If the presenting episode is lengthy and turns out to be MDD, the clinician can follow up with questions about whether the mood and symptoms are worse now than they were when they started, allowing for the differential between a long MDD or a preexisting dysthymia. Questions about onsets are more easily answered by older children and adolescents, so information on the starting point of psychopathology in younger children may need to be supplemented from parents.

Care in assessing other symptoms should also be noted. For example, children (of all ages) can answer questions about whether they feel hungry (loss of appetite), but younger children are unlikely to be useful informants on weight loss or gain (or failure to make appropriate weight gains). Instead, children can be asked if their clothes have become especially loose (or tight), or parents can be targeted for this piece of the puzzle. For the assessment of sleep problems, children are often better informants than parents since awareness of insomnia by caretakers may be limited unless the child has been vocal about the problem. The term worthlessness should be avoided and questions should focus instead on whether the child is down on him or herself, such as feeling stupid, or ugly, or unlovable, and the like. Parents who endorse this item should be able to document that they have heard the child make such comments rather than just the assumption that the child feels this way.

With respect to guilt, parents rarely endorse this item because few parents seem to believe that their children experience it. On the other hand, depressed children do acknowledge feelings of excessive or inappropriate guilt, sometimes even of psychotic proportion, despite parental ignorance on the matter. However, younger children may not understand the term "guilt" so the clinician should use examples that provide gradations of guilt from appropriate (e.g., doing something wrong and feeling bad about it) to excessive (e.g., feeling really bad even after saying you're sorry and getting punished) to inappropriate (e.g., feeling bad even when not in any way at fault), to psychotic (e.g., believing you cause bad things to happen to other people). Assessing symptoms of psychomotor agitation and difficulty concentrating may be difficult with children because these items may be part of ADHD. If a child does have a history of ADHD, psychomotor agitation and difficulty concentrating should be exacerbated during episodes of depression in order to be considered as symptoms for this disorder. Otherwise, every child with ADHD begins as positive for at least two symptoms of depression and this would intensify an artificial rate of comorbidity.

Finally, suicidality must be assessed and this is best done with the child, irrespective of age. Many depressed children have suicidal thoughts and many have attempted suicide without the knowledge of their parents. Really young children often make poor attempts (i.e., little likelihood of success), but this is generally the result of ignorance of how to die or avoidance of pain. For example, some children attempt suicide by holding their breath, putting their head under water in the tub, or putting their head in a pillowcase. While such behavior may not appear serious, they may nonetheless represent serious intent on the part of these children who should always be carefully evaluated, as their suicidal efforts unfortunately become more effective with practice. For older children and adolescents, rates of suicide have steadily escalated over the past 3 decades and are viewed as a major public health problem. All children and adolescents should be asked if they feel so bad that they have wished they were dead or had never been born, and whether they have thought about hurting themselves. These questions should be followed by inquiry on frequency of ideation, the presence of a specific plan, attempts now and in the past, and a determination of availability of means. This investigation produces the information needed for appropriate risk assessment, so that the clinician can take steps necessary to ensure the child's safety.

Adolescents present fewer challenges with respect to language comprehension, but may be reluctant to cooperate with a process they often view as instigated by and for the benefit of the parent. Here, establishing trust and an understanding of the role of the therapist becomes a more essential aspect of the assessment process. In fact, establishing a working relationship with the adolescent should be done within the first half hour to maximize likelihood of a successful collaboration between patient and therapist. Recognizing the adolescent's concerns and asking him or her to participate in the solution are important steps in the collaborative process. Striking agreements can also be a useful strategy, so that the adolescent does not feel as if an unending commitment has been made, but rather that a contract of cooperation is negotiated that is time-limited and open to renegotiation by either party. Moreover, a clear delineation of confidentiality, its parameters and limitations, is another important component in working with this age group. Once a good working relationship has been established, the assessment process is likely to proceed quite successfully.

Following the interview with parent and child or adolescent, the clinician must evaluate how to combine the information from different sources. It is not a good idea to simply add positively endorsed items from all informants. While no absolute rules for combining information are available, some conventions can be offered. As already noted above, parents are better informants on child health, development, and historical data. They also do better on observing disruptive behaviors, including those that create difficulties with others in the home or at school. Children are likely to provide more accurate information on internal states which include mood and affect, sleep problems, changes in attention, energy level, guilt feelings, and suicidal thoughts and behaviors. When a symptom is indicated to be present, the clinician should ask for (recent) examples to ensure an accurate appraisal and then document evidence of impaired function. Difficulties in one or more primary areas of functioning should be present if the child is actually suffering from a mood disorder, and the onset of these difficulties should coincide with the episode of mood disturbance. If discrepancies in information cannot be adequately resolved during the child or adolescent interview, the interviewer can have informants reunite and then inquire about inconsistencies with all parties present, so that resolution becomes partly the responsibility of the child and parent(s).

☐ Case Illustration

Client Description

Susan is a 9-year-old Caucasian female who was brought in by her mother. She attends a local elementary school, is in the 4th grade, and lives with her biological mother, Mrs. M, her stepfather, Mr. M, and her older sister, Maria, age 12. She is an attractive child of average height and weight who was neatly groomed and appeared her stated age. While a little anxious during the interview, she interacted in a cooperative manner and was verbally articulate for her age. Her presentation was coherent and oriented, with no evidence of thought disorder or impaired cognitive function. She manifested a full affective range, sad mood, and fluent speech, with no signs of pressure, overproduction, perseveration, or oddities, and she was clearly able to understand and respond to the interaction as required.

Presenting Complaint

Both Susan and her mother were the primary informants for the intake. Mrs. M indicated that she was seeking treatment for Susan because of concerns about her decline in academic functioning, increased irritability, difficulties most mornings due to escalating school reluctance, and mounting oppositional behavior in the home. Further questioning yielded additional concerns about Susan's somatic complaints, frequent crying, anxious statements, and disputes with her stepfather.

According to Mrs. M, Susan has always been a "high-strung" child, but that many of the problems noted have escalated, although some are of more recent origin. Her irritability has led to increased arguments with all family members and she has become far less compliant with requests. Initially a good student, her grades had shown a marked decline and she was barely passing 4th grade. Her school performance was made worse by repeated days missed because of her unwillingness to attend on many mornings. The school informed Mrs. M that they believed Susan has attentional problems, but her parents believed that Susan was a behavior problem, although their efforts at enhanced discipline were met with failure.

Susan acknowledged many of the concerns articulated by her mother but stated that she was feeling "really bad" and that her family didn't understand her. She believed that everyone would be better off without her and that her parents did not love her. She reported feeling sad, mad, and tired, and that she did not go to school because she was sick many mornings. She said she was not having any fun, that she did not have any friends, and that nobody liked her. She also said that she felt really nervous when she was in school, because she was afraid she might become sick and that there would be no one around to take care of her. Recent and historical medical evaluations were negative.

History of the Problem

Mrs. M reported that Susan had a history of "hypochondrias," often complaining about minor aches and pains in order to get attention. Susan began school when she was 5 and displayed a fair amount of anxiety at the time, but this was viewed as developmentally appropriate. She eventually made an adequate transition and did well in school until about a year and a half ago. In the 3rd grade, Susan again began to have difficulty going to school and staying in school although her grades did not notably suffer. By the time she began the 4th grade, however, going to school was a daily struggle and her academic functioning has significantly deteriorated. The school requested that Mrs. M have Susan evaluated for ADHD. Irritability and family arguments followed a similar time line. During the past few months, Susan had become unpleasant to be around, no longer showed interest in many activities, and had stopped spending time with friends after school. Efforts to discipline her did not work because she said she didn't care if she lost privileges.

Mrs. M was married to Susan's father, Mr. S, for 14 years. Dissolution of their relationship was gradual, but Mr. S finally left the household when Susan was age 7. This was a difficult time because Susan was close to her father; nevertheless, she received a lot of emotional support during that time and continued to see her father on a regular basis. Mrs. M met and married her current husband, Mr. M, when Susan was 8. Mrs. M believes the transition has been more difficult for Susan given that "she is high strung" and because the new family arrangement led to decreased contact with her father. In addition, Mrs. M mentioned that Mr. S may also be remarrying in the coming months, and that Susan was aware of this. Clearly, many of the complaints about Susan's behavior coincided with the events surrounding her parents' divorce and their subsequent new relationships.

Assessment Methods Used

The evaluation began with a 15-minute discussion that yielded much of the information thus far presented. The intake then proceeded to separate Schedule for Affective Disorders and Schizophrenia for School-Age Children-Epidemiologic Version 5 (K-SADS-E; Orvaschel, 1995) interviews with Mrs. M and Susan. While the clinician interviewed Mrs. M, Susan was asked to complete the CDI, and anxiety and self-esteem checklists. During Susan's interview, Mrs. M was asked to complete the CBCL. Following Susan's interview, the two were brought together to resolve a few discrepancies. A determination on obtaining additional information from Susan's teacher was postponed, as initial impressions suggested that this source may not be needed or may require a somewhat specific line of inquiry.

The evaluation focused on both current and past behaviors and a systematic determination of chronology. The K-SADS-E was administered first to the mother, and her responses to each item were recorded. This was followed by an interview with the child and notation of her responses. During Susan's interview, summary ratings were also made and these summary ratings provided the primary data for the resulting diagnostic impressions. The K-SADS-E interview also afforded the assessment of Susan's suicidal ideation and behavior. Information on the psychiatric history of Susan's first degree relatives and that of her stepfather was obtained from Mrs. M.

The decision to include a paper-and-pencil depression scale was based on the inference by the clinician that the complaints made by Mrs. M and the statements made by Susan may be the result of a mood disorder. Therefore, obtaining ratings from the child on a symptom checklist would be useful for assessing baseline severity and the ongoing evaluation of treatment progress. Similarly, a self-report anxiety measure was included because initial impressions suggested the potential presence of significant anxiety or even a separate anxiety disorder. The CBCL is a comprehensive checklist, and was administered as a means of obtaining an overview of Mrs. M's concerns in multiple symptom domains. Readministration of all symptom checklists over the course of treatment would also allow for the evaluation of interventions from the mother's and child's perspectives.

Psychological Assessment Protocol

Administration of the K-SADS-E lasted 45 minutes with Mrs. M and 35 minutes with Susan. Sample page items of the K-SADS-E Interview and

Scoring Form are provided that display examples of questions and notation of informant responses (Figures 12.1–12.4). Mrs. M endorsed symptoms of Susan's irritability, fatigue, and concentration problems. There were no reported manic or psychotic symptoms, nor evidence of panic, clinically significant fears, obsessive compulsive disorder, trauma, eating disorder, substance abuse, or conduct disorder. There were, however, complaints of oppositional behavior (i.e., often loses temper, often argues with adults, is touchy or easily annoyed, and is often angry or resentful), ADHD (i.e., difficulty sustaining attention, difficulty with sustained mental effort, easily distracted, and fidgety/squirms), and separation anxiety (i.e., worry about harm befalling mother and harm befalling child when separated, school reluctance or refusal, reluctance to sleep alone, physical complaints when anticipating separation, excessive distress when separated). Based on the reports of Mrs. M, Susan met criteria for ODD, SAD, and possibly dysthymia. Onset of all the problems noted appeared to be about 14 to 16 months prior to intake, with significant increases in symptom severity and impairment during the previous 3 months.

The interview with Susan clarified a number of questions and yielded a somewhat different clinical picture. Susan disclosed feelings of depression in addition to irritability for at least the last 16–18 months. Figure 12.1 provides a sample page that screens for episodes of depression. Since the last 2 or 3 months were the most severe, symptoms of depression were assessed for the past month. In addition to mood disturbance, symptoms rated positively for the current episode included moderate anhedonia, initial and terminal insomnia (of at least 1 hour duration), fatigue, psychomotor agitation, feelings of worthlessness, difficulty concentrating, and recurrent suicidal ideation with no plan or attempts. Figure 12.2 provides a sample page of MDD symptoms, including questions on suicide. These problems resulted in increased arguments at home, a decline in school performance, and social withdrawal. Susan admitted that some of the mood problems began early in the previous school year, but that they were not as severe. A separate assessment for dysthymia produced positive symptoms of depressed/irritable mood, fatigue, low self-esteem, concentration problems, and feelings of hopelessness. Figure 12.3 provides a sample chronology page for dysthymia. The escalating irritability during the past 15 months led to many of the arguments reported by Susan's mother, as well as her perceived hypersensitivity. Susan acknowledged feelings associated with SAD and endorsed most of the symptoms of this disorder reported by her mother. Since her feelings of depression were worse in the morning, a careful evaluation was needed to distinguish melancholic symptoms from those of separation anxiety such as somatic

DEPRESSION

EPISODES OF ILLNESS CHARACTERIZED BY PERSISTENTLY DYSPHORIC (DEPRESSED, IRRITABLE, OR ANHEDONIC) MOOD AND ACCOMPANYING SYMPTOMS SPECIFIED BELOW. DIAGNOSTIC OPTIONS INCLUDE MAJOR DEPRESSIVE DISORDER (MDD) WITH OR WITHOUT MOOD CONGRUENT OR INCONGRUENT PSYCHOTIC FEATURES (AND SUBTYPING FOR MELANCHOLIA AND ATYPICAL), DYSTHYMIA (DYS), DEPRESSIVE DISORDER NOT OTHERWISE SPECIFIED (D-NOS), ADJUSTMENT DISORDER WITH DEPRESSED MOOD (ADJ-D) AND …
THIS SECTION BEGINS WITH A GENERAL SCREEN FOR DYSPHORIC MOOD, IRRITABILITY, AND ANHEDONIA. IF THE SCREEN IS POSITIVE, THE INTERVIEWER SHOULD INQUIRE ABOUT DURATION(S), ONSET(S), AND OFFSET(S) BEFORE ASSESSING SPECIFIC SYMPTOMS.

SYMPTOMS ARE ASSESSED SEPARATELY FOR EPISODES OF DYSTHYMIA AND DEPRESSION. SYMPTOM SEVERITY RATINGS CAN BE MADE FOR CURRENT EPISODES. SYMPTOMS FOR PAST EPISODES ARE RATED AS ONLY POSITIVE OR NEGATIVE.

I. Depressed or Irritable Mood

How have you been feeling? Mostly happy (or OK) or mostly sad (moody, down, mad, cranky, like crying, OR CHILD'S EQUIVALENT*)? When you feel sad (etc.), how long does it last? How many days of the week do you feel sad (etc.) for that long? Do you know why? How many weeks in a row?*

Has there even been a (another) time when you felt sad, cranky, mad (etc.) for _____ (AT LEASE 3 HOURS A DAY FOR 3 DAYS A WEEK)? *Have you ever felt that way for longer? What was the longest? How many weeks in a row? When was that? Did you know why? Any other time?*

RECORD DURATION, SEVERITY, AND CHRONOLOGY.

Notes:

	Past Episode			Current				
	NA/No			NA/No				
	Info	No	Yes	Info	No	Mild	Mod	Severe
1a. Depressed mood (at least 2 weeks)	X	1	2	X	1	2	3	4
1b. Irritable mood (at least 2 weeks)	X	1	2	X	1	2	3	4

FIGURE 12.1. Depressive disorders' screens on K- SADS- E interview.

During this (that) time		Most Severe		**Rate severity for current episode only.**				
When you feel (felt) _____		Past				Current		
	NA/No			NA/No				
8. **Concentration/Thinking/Indecision**	Info	No	Yes	Info	No	Mild	Mod	Severe
a. Concentration/Slowed Thinking	X	1	2	X	1	2	3	4

Is (was) it harder to keep your mind on things than usual? Harder to concentrate? A lot? Is (was) it harder to think, when doing homework or remembering something?

b. Indecision	X	1	2	X	1	2	3	4

Is (was) it harder to make your mind up? Like you don't know what to do? Or can't make a decision?

9. **Suicidality**

a. Recurrent Thoughts of Death	X	1	2	X	1	2	3	4

Do (did) you feel so bad that you think (thought) about death or dying? A lot?

b. Suicidal Ideation	X	1	2	X	1	2	3	4

Do (did) you think about hurting or killing yourself? A lot?

c. Suicidal Plan	X	1	2	X	1	2	3	4

What do (did) you think of doing?
Interviewer Rate for Method

d. Suicide Attempt	X	1	2	X	1	2	3	4

Did you try to kill yourself? What did you do?

FIGURE 12.2. MDD and suicide symptom items on K- SADS- E interview.

Chronology of Dysthymia	**NA/NO Info**	**No**	**Yes**
Currently in an episode	X	1	2
Current episode meets DSM-IV diagnostic criteria	X	1	2
Current episode meets Alternative Research Criteria	X	1	2
Current episode most severe (of dysthymia)	X	1	2
Duration of current episode (in months) OR Age at onset of last episode	___	___	___
Duration of last episode (in months)	___	___	___
Past episode followed by remission (no mood disorder)	X	1	2
Past episode followed by MDD	X	1	2
Duration of most severe episode (in months)	X	1	2
Age of Onset of (first episode) of dysthymia	___	___	
Pubertal Status at Onset of dysthymia (circle)	Prepubertal		Postpubertal
Total number of episodes of dysthymia (separated by at least 2 months)	___	___	

Treatment

Out-patient treatment for dysthymia	X	1	2
Duration of out-patient treatment (total in weeks)	___	___	___
Medication (Specify: _____)	X	1	2

Rate Most Severe Episode		
Rating should be based on the number and nature of symptoms and the degree of associated functional impairment.	Mild	1
	Moderate	2
	Severe	3

FIGURE 12.3.   Chronology section of dysthymia on K- SADS- E interview.

A. <u>DEPRESSIVE EPISODES</u>   **MOTHER**   **CHILD**   **SUMMARY**

EVIDENCE OF DEPRESSIVE EPISODE(S) |X   1| 2 |X   1| 2 |X   1| 2
                                                                                          >
                                                              SKIP TO DYSTHYMIA

NOTES:

Rate symptom severity for current episode only

SYMPTOM RATING CODES ARE:
    MOST SEVERE PAST (MSP)   AND   **FOR CURRENT EPISODE (CE)**
    NA/NO   **NA/NO**

Info	No	Yes			Info	No	Mild	Mod	Severe
X	1	2			X	1	2	3	4

<u>SYMPTOMS</u>	Mother		Child		Summary	
	MSP	**CE**	**MSP**	**CE**	**MSP**	**CE**
3a. Appetite Loss	___	___	___	___	___	___
b. Weight Loss	___	___	___	___	___	___
c. Increased Appetite	___	___	___	___	___	___
d. Weight Gain	___	___	___	___	___	___
4a. Initial Insomnia	___	___	___	___	___	___
b. Middle Insomnia	___	___	___	___	___	___
c. Terminal Insomnia	___	___	___	___	___	___
d. Hypersomnia	___	___	___	___	___	___
5. Fatigue/Loss of Energy	___	___	___	___	___	___
6a. Psychomotor Agitation	___	___	___	___	___	___
b. Psychomotor Retardation	___	___	___	___	___	___
7a. Worthlessness/Low Self-Esteem	___	___	___	___	___	___
b. Excessive Guilt	___	___	___	___	___	___

FIGURE 12.4. Depressive disorders symptoms on K- SADS- E Scoring Form.

complaints on school days and difficulty concentrating when separated. In addition, despite feeling somewhat less depressed when she was not in school, Susan admitted that she remained sad and irritable, even when she was not separated (from her mother). No other significant psychopathology was recounted by the child. Information from both informants was recorded on the K-SADS-E Scoring Form. Figure 12.4 provides a sample page of the depression section in the Scoring Form.

During the interview with Susan, summary ratings were also noted and formed the basis of the diagnostic assessment. Based largely on information from the child, Susan was diagnosed with MDD superimposed on an underlying dysthymic disorder. Information from both informants also resulted in an additional diagnosis of SAD, as the symptoms of this disorder were viewed as sufficiently independent of those for either of the depressions. An inadequate number of symptoms was reported for a diagnosis of ADHD, and those symptoms that were reported were consistent with both mood disorder syndromes identified. While accounts from Mrs. M provided sufficient symptoms for Susan to meet criteria for ODD, this diagnosis was not assigned because several behaviors (i.e., often loses temper, touchy/easily annoyed, and often angry or resentful) in this category were already accounted for as part of the mood disturbance and, in the clinician's judgment did not warrant an additional diagnosis. Results from the paper-and-pencil inventories administered to both informants confirmed impressions that Susan experienced significant depression and anxiety, and that her mother was distressed by her negative behavior at home and at school.

Targets Selected for Treatment

In addition to a diagnostic evaluation, the assessment provided considerable information on behaviors requiring intervention and objectives for treatment. Primary targets selected for immediate attention were mood related, and included depression, irritability, worthlessness, social withdrawal, and the ongoing assessment of suicidality and associated risk. Reducing Susan's depression was likely to have positive affects on school performance, improved behavioral compliance, social relationships, and family interaction. Nevertheless, family relations and communication were selected for specific action and efforts to increase Susan's contact with peers were also initiated. Finally, a specific course of treatment was instigated to focus on Susan's separation concerns and difficulties attending school.

Assessment of Progress

Improvement was evaluated by multiple methods and on a number of dimensions. Verbal reports by parent and child were routinely noted and periodic readministration of symptom inventories (e.g., depression, anxiety, self-esteem, CBCL) provided a systematic appraisal of overall and specific symptom reduction. Somewhat more objective measures of progress were obtained by monitoring Susan's attendance at school and her test grades and report cards. In addition, therapeutic progress was assessed by evaluation of family relationships (e.g., number of arguments per week), increased contacts with peers, and improved self-esteem.

Utilization of standardized measures in combination with evaluations designed for the unique problems presented by a specific patient is generally optimal. This approach allows the clinician to gather data with established norms, while also developing measures that capture the distinct difficulties in an individual presentation. Diversity in strategies and behavioral targets yields flexibility in what is measured, how frequently it is measured, and the manner of measurement. In Susan's case, symptom checklists were administered about once a month and showed a gradual but regular reduction in all symptom categories over the course of 5 months of treatment. However, these measures were not sufficiently detailed to capture a number of the problems noted for this case. Reports on school attendance and academic performance were useful adjuncts in the evaluation process, but additional efforts to assess areas such as family communication, peer relationships, and overall functioning were also valuable.

☐ Summary

The case of 9-year-old Susan exemplifies the importance of a systematic and thorough evaluation, utilizing information from adult and child informants. If a diagnosis was made on the basis only of information from Mrs. M, an inaccurate determination would have been the result, likely missing the mood disorder because of the mother's emphasis on disruptive behaviors. Combining data from all sources available will result in a more valid appraisal, particularly when the child in question is judged to be a reliable informant.

Although onset of a mood disturbance appeared related to important changes in the family structure of the child (i.e., mother's remarriage, father's impending remarriage), a diagnosis of Adj-D was not appropriate in this case because the child met criteria for two more specific mood disorders. Instead, notation of the events likely to have impacted the presentation should be listed on Axis IV as (chronic) stressors. The co-occurrence of SAD in a child this age is also a frequent comorbid disorder. The clinician must consider whether presentation is depression with significant concomitant anxiety or whether symptoms are sufficient to meet criteria for both (mood and SAD) diagnoses.

Differentials must also made for ADHD and ODD, also common comorbid pathologies for this age group. Concentration/attentional problems and restlessness often suggest ADHD, but may simply be part of the symptom picture in MDD (e.g., trouble concentrating, psychomotor agitation). Making an accurate determination must be based on the historical context of the behaviors and any additional symptoms present suggesting alternative or additional psychopathology. Similarly, an additional diagnosis of ODD may be warranted, but only if symptoms are not simply a duplication of previously assessed behaviors presenting exclusively during an episode of MDD. Of course if depression is treated but oppositional behaviors remain problematic, an additional diagnosis of ODD would be justified. Finally, the assessment of suicidal thoughts and behaviors should be emphasized whenever mood disorders are presented. They are more frequently problematic in adolescents, but occur in even the youngest of cases and present dangers requiring persistent monitoring and intervention.

☐ References

Achenbach, T. M., & Edelbrock, C. S. (1981). Behavior problems and competencies reported by parents of normal and disturbed children aged four to sixteen. *Monographs for the society for research in child development, 46*, 1–82.

American Psychiatric Association (2000). *Diagnostic and statistical manual of mental disorders* (4th Ed., revised text). Washington, DC: American Psychiatric Press.

Beck, A. T., Ward, C. H., Mendelsohn, M., Mock, J., & Erbaugh, J. (1961). An inventory for measuring depression. *Archives of General Psychiatry, 4*, 561–571.

Beck, A. T., Weissman, A., Lester, D., & Trexler, L. (1974). The measurement of pessimism: The hopelessness scale. *Journal of Consulting and Clinical Psychology, 42*, 861–865.

Chiu, L. H. (1988). Measurements of self-esteem for school-age children. *Journal of Counseling and Development, 66*, 298–301.

Edelbrock, C., & Costello, A. J. (1988). Structured psychiatric interviews for children. In M. Rutter, A. H. Tuma, I. S. Lann (Eds.) *Assessment and diagnosis in child psychopathology* (pp. 87–112). London: David Fulton Publishers.

Endicott, J., & Spitzer, R. L. (1978). A diagnostic interview. *Archives of General Psychiatry, 35*, 837–844.

Kashani, J. H., Orvaschel, H., Burk, J. P., & Reid, J. C. (1985). Informant variance: The issue of parent-child disagreement. *Journal of the American Academy of Child Psychiatry, 24*, 437–446.

Kovacs, M. (1980/1981). Rating scales to assess depression in school aged children. *Acta Paedopsychiatry, 46*, 305–315.

Kovacs, M., Feinberg, T. L., Crouse-Novak, M. A., Paulauskas, S. L., Pollock, M., & Finkelstein, R. (1984). Depressive disorders in childhood II. A longitudinal study of the risk for a subsequent major depression. *Archives of General Psychiatry, 41*, 643–649.

Lewinsohn, P. M., Rohde, P., Seeley, J. R., & Hops, H. (1991). Comorbidity of unipolar depression: I. major depression with dysthymia. *Journal of Abnormal Psychology, 200*, 205–213.

Moos, R. H., & Moos, B. S. (1981). *Family environment scale manual.* Palo Alto: Consulting Psychologists Press.

Orvaschel, H. (1988). Structured and semi-structured psychiatric interviews for children. In C. J. Kestenbaum & D. T. Williams (Eds.), *The handbook of clinical assessment of children and adolescents* (Vol. 1; pp. 31–42). New York: University Press.

Orvaschel, H. (1995). *Schedule for affective disorders and schizophrenia for school-age children-epidemiologic version 5 (K-SADS-E).* Ft. Lauderdale, FL: Nova Southeastern University.

Orvaschel, H., Puig-Antich, J., Chambers, W., Tabrizi, M. A., & Johnson, R. (1982). Retrospective assessment of child psychopathology with the Kiddie-SADS-E. *Journal of the American Academy of Child Psychiatry, 21*, 392–397.

Orvaschel, H., Sholomskas, D., & Weissman, M. M. (1980). *The assessment of psychopathology and behavioral problems in children: A review of scales suitable for epidemiological and clinical research, (1967–79).* Monograph for NIMH Series AN No. 1, DDHS Publication No. (ADM) 80–1037. Washington, DC: Superintendent of Documents, U.S. Government Printing Office.

Orvaschel, H., Weissman, M. M., Padian, N., & Lowe, T. (1981). Assessing psychopathology in children of psychiatrically disturbed parents: A pilot study. *Journal of the American Academy of Child Psychiatry, 20*, 112–122.

Piers, E. V., & Harris, D. B. (1964). Age and other correlates of self-concept in children. *Journal of Educational Psychology, 55*, 91–95.

Puig-Antich, J., Blau, S., Marx, N., Greenhill, L., & Chambers, W. (1978). Pre-pubertal major depressive disorder; a pilot study. *Journal of the American Academy of Child Psychiatry, 17*, 695–707.

Schaffer, D., Fisher, P., Piacentini, J., Schwab-Stone, M., & Wicks, J. (1989). *Diagnostic interview schedule for children (DISC 2.1).* Rockville, MD: National Institute of Mental Health.

Weissman, M. M., Kidd, K. K., & Prusoff, B. A. (1982). Variability in the rates of affective disorders in the relatives of severe and mild major nonbipolar depressives and normals. *Archives of General Psychiatry, 39*, 1397–1403.

Weissman, M. M., Orvaschel, H., & Padian, N. (1980). Children's symptoms and social functioning self-report scales: Comparison of mothers' and children's reports. *Journal of Nervous and Mental Disease, 168*, 736–740.

CHAPTER

Allen G. Sandler
Clifford V. Hatt

Mental Retardation

☐ Description of the Disorder

Psychological assessment of children with mental retardation is most commonly required for purposes of educational decision-making. Decisions include whether a student meets eligibility criteria for special education services as provided by federal law under the Individuals with Disabilities Education Act (IDEA, 1997), and, if so, what type of educational placement and program are appropriate. A second common reason children with mental retardation are referred for psychological consultation is for assistance regarding the management of behavior problems. Conduct problems, including aggression and other disruptive behavior, are estimated to occur in 12%–45% of individuals with mental retardation (Bregman, 1991). Severe behavior problems in individuals with mental retardation, such as self-injury, are less common, but represent a significant treatment challenge. Effective behavioral treatment of behavior problems in children with mental retardation will be based upon a comprehensive assessment of the environmental factors associated with maintenance of the problem behavior.

This chapter will have two parts. In the first part we will review assessment procedures for purposes of identification and classification of children with mental retardation. In the second part, functional assessment strategies for the design of effective behavioral interventions will be described. In each part we will discuss pragmatic issues that might confront the practitioner working in a typical school or clinic setting. Finally, a case illustration will be provided that demonstrates use of both assessment approaches with a child having mental retardation.

For purposes of identification, classification, and school placement, mental retardation is defined in federal legislation (IDEA, 1997) as "significantly subaverage general intellectual functioning existing concurrently with deficits in adaptive behavior and manifested during the developmental period that adversely affects a child's educational performance" (34 C.F.R., Sec.300.7 [b][5]). Two systems are presently in use to operationalize this definition and to classify children according to their level of intellectual functioning, or, in the case of the American Association on Mental Retardation (AAMR) classification system, their need for varying levels of support. The more commonly used system is based upon the American Psychiatric Association definition of mental retardation found in the text revision of the 4th edition of its *Diagnostic and Statistical Manual of Mental Disorders* (DSM-IV-TR; American Psychiatric Association, 2000). Although the DSM-IV-TR definition of mental retardation requires deficits in adaptive functioning in at least two areas, classification according to level of mental retardation — an important factor in determining classroom placement — is based solely on the intelligence level of the individual. Mild mental retardation is present if the IQ level falls within the range of 50–55 to approximately 70; moderate mental retardation if the IQ level is between 35–40 to 50–55; severe mental retardation if the IQ level is between 20–25 and 35–40; and profound mental retardation if the IQ level is below 20–25.

The other, less commonly used system for the identification and classification of children with mental retardation is based upon the AAMR definition of mental retardation found in the 10th edition of its manual on definition and classification — Mental Retardation: Definition, Classification and Systems of Supports (Luckasson et al., 2002). As is the case when the DSM-IV-TR system is used, identification of mental retardation requires an IQ score of approximately 70 or below, as well as significant limitations in adaptive behavior. However, the AAMR bases its classification system not on IQ, but on the presumed level of support needed by an individual to function more effectively in society. Levels of mental retardation associated with various IQ scores are replaced with a hierarchy of support levels ranging from: (a) intermittent or "as-needed" support, to (b) time-limited support, to (c) extensive support, to (d) pervasive, lifelong support. The level of support required by an individual is determined through evaluating the individual's specific needs within various environments. Based upon this evaluation, supports are recommended that might enhance the personal well-being of the individual and promote the development of new skills, greater knowledge, and expanded interests (Luckasson et al., 2002).

Identification and classification of children with mental retardation using either the AAMR or the DSM-IV-TR approach requires the assessment of both intellectual and adaptive functioning. Psychologists who specialize in the assessment of school-aged children have a wide range of strategies available. A brief review of selected strategies will be provided next.

Range of Assessment Strategies Available

Assessment of Intellectual Functioning

Standardized intelligence tests are most appropriately used with children suspected to be within the mild to moderate range of mental retardation. There are measures available based upon a traditional view of intelligence, as well as other measures that are based upon more contemporary theories. When selecting an assessment instrument, the clinician must consider how appropriate the potential tool is given the age, cultural background, primary language, and means of communication of the person being assessed (Luckasson et al., 2002).

The Wechsler Scales are the most widely used intelligence measure, and most familiar to psychologists in clinical practice. The Wechsler Intelligence Scale for Children-Third Edition (WISC-III; Wechsler, 1991) provides useful diagnostic information for the assessment of children from elementary age to high school age who are functioning within four standard deviations of the mean (standard scores from 40 to 160).

The Wechsler Preschool and Primary Scale of Intelligence-Third Edition (WPPSI-III; Wechsler, 2002) is a recent revision of the earlier edition with an expanded age range (from 2–6 years old to 7–3 years old). It is more developmentally appropriate than earlier versions, and is a better choice than the WISC-III for children with developmental delays who are between the ages of 6–0 and 7–3, when the age range of the two instruments overlap (Sattler, 2001).

Another traditional measure to assess intelligence is the Stanford-Binet Intelligence Scale: Fourth Edition (SB-IV; Thorndike, Hagen, & Sattler, 1986). It can be used with individuals between 2 and 23 years of age, and contains 15 subtests, although not all subtests are used at every age level. Methodological problems associated with the fourth edition of the Stanford Binet, including the domains of intelligence it purports to measure, and concerns about the normative sample used to standardize the test, suggest that it might be most appropriately used as a supplement in conjunction with other major tests (Kaufman, 1990). A new fifth edition of the Stanford-Binet is expected to address many of the shortcomings of the present edition.

The Cognitive Assessment System (CAS; Naglieri & Das, 1997) is a more recently developed tool based upon a cognitive processing model called PASS. Planning, attention, simultaneous cognitive processes, and sequential cognitive processes are measured through a basic battery of 8 subtests and a standard battery of 12 subtests. Naglieri (1999) suggests that the CAS can be especially useful in the differential diagnosis of children who might have mental retardation due to the minimal acquired knowledge required and the broad range of cognitive processes it measures. The CAS can be used to assess children between 5 and 17 years of age.

The Comprehensive Test of Nonverbal Intelligence (CTONI; Hammill, Pearson, & Wiederholt, 1996) is a short measure of nonverbal intelligence that can be useful in distinguishing children with mental retardation from those with language problems. It consists of six subtests that use either pictorial objects or geometric designs to measure three aspects of nonverbal intelligence. Although designed for ages 0–6 to 11–18, the CTONI cannot be used to differentiate levels of mental retardation in children under age 8 (Sattler, 2001).

The Universal Nonverbal Intelligence Test (UNIT; Bracken & McCallum, 1998) is another nonverbal measure of intelligence in children and adolescents from 5 to 17 years of age. The UNIT is entirely nonverbal in administration and response. Bracken & McCallum (1998) indicate that the UNIT is useful in the identification of children with mild to moderate mental retardation because it includes both memory and reasoning measures, thereby extending the more traditional single dimensional measures of nonverbal assessment. The nonverbal administration will be useful with those children whose language is affected by mental retardation, and may assist in the differential diagnosis of severe speech and language impairment and mental retardation.

A third nonverbal intelligence test is the Leiter International Performance Scale-Revised (Leiter-R; Roid & Miller, 1997). The Leiter-R was designed to assess cognitive functioning in children with communication disorders, cognitive delay, hearing impairment, motor impairment, traumatic brain injury, attention-deficit disorder, certain types of learning disabilities, as well as those who use English as a second language. It consists of two batteries: a visualization and reasoning battery, and an attention and memory battery. The Leiter-R may be especially useful for the assessment of children who have little or no functional speech or who have limited motor coordination (Sattler, 2001). However, Roid and Miller (1997) caution against use of the Leiter-R in isolation when identifying individuals with mental retardation. They point out the limitations associated with assessment of global intelligence exclusively through the use of nonverbal tasks, even though this practice might reduce bias due to cultural and linguistic differences.

There are several advantages, however, of using the Leiter-R in conjunction with other instruments to identify children with mental retardation. The scale covers a wide age range (0–2 to 11–20) in which consistent abilities (factors) are measured across the scale. The full scale IQ scores provide for lower range standard scores in the severe range of mental retardation (down to 30), which are not provided in other intellectual measures. It is also possible to derive "growth" scores that provide ability estimates sensitive to small increments of improvement in cognitive ability, making it useful as a measure of individual program progress (Roid & Miller, 1997).

The Bayley Scales of Infant Development—Second Edition (BSID-II; Bayley, 1993) was designed for assessment of mental and motor development in infants and young children 1 month to 42 months of age. Because the standardization sample for the BSID-II includes norms for children with standard scores above 50, it may be used to assess infants and young children with mild mental retardation. For young children with more significant degrees of delay, the examiner can report a developmental age and describe the child's ability level through indicating his or her response to test items (Black & Matula, 2000). The BSID-II may also be useful for assessing older, out-of-norms children with severe to profound mental retardation. While the norms cannot be used, the item performance and the age equivalent scores may be helpful for purposes of monitoring progress. Although not a recommended practice, psychologists often use the age equivalent and chronological age to calculate a ratio IQ or standard score for their clients, which is then provided to governmental agencies to help in determining eligibility for services.

The Differential Ability Scales (DAS; Elliott, 1990) may be especially useful in assessing preschool-aged children suspected of cognitive delays. The DAS includes scales at lower preschool (ages 2–6 to 3–5), upper preschool (ages 3–6 to 6–11) and school-age (ages 6–11 to 11–17) levels. It yields a general cognitive ability score, a special nonverbal composite score, and verbal and nonverbal cluster scores. Despite limited assessment of verbal expression at the preschool level, the DAS is highly recommended, especially for 2 to 3 year olds (Sattler, 2001).

Another measure that can be used with young children is the Kaufman Assessment Battery for Children (K-ABC; Kaufman & Kaufman, 1983). It consists of a battery of tests that measure intelligence and achievement in children 2 to 12 years of age. The K-ABC has a number of desirable features for the assessment of preschool children, including developmentally appropriate materials, limited language demands, and the inclusion of teaching items to ensure the child understands and can practice a task prior to test administration. However, the K-ABC has a limited range of standard scores at certain ages, making it difficult to use for evaluating children with mental retardation at these ages (Sattler, 2001). Also, there is a heavy reliance on short-term memory and attention tasks. Although the K-ABC may have benefits when assessing specific strengths and weaknesses, Sattler (2001) suggests that it not be used as a primary instrument for assessing intellectual ability in children. The K-ABC is currently being revised and restandardized.

Assessment of Adaptive Behavior

Adaptive behavior must also be assessed to determine the presence of mental retardation in children. Adaptive behavior is comprised of conceptual, social, and practical skills needed by an individual to meet the demands of everyday life (Luckasson et al., 2002). According to the DSM-IV-TR definition of mental retardation, deficits in adaptive functioning must be present in at least two areas. The American Association on Mental Retardation (AAMR) definition of mental retardation requires the presence of "significant" limitations in adaptive behavior, operationally defined as a score at least two standard deviations below the mean on a measure of adaptive behavior. Presence of significant limitations may be indicated through either the overall score, or performance on one or more of the three areas of adaptive functioning — conceptual, social, or practical skills (Luckasson et al., 2002).

Norm-referenced instruments typically used with children include the Vineland Adaptive Behavior Scales (Sparrow, Balla, & Cicchetti, 1985), the AAMR Adaptive Behavior Scale-School: Second Edition (Lambert, Nihira & Leland, 1993), the Adaptive Behavior Evaluation Scale — Revised (McCarney, 1995), and the Adaptive Behavior Assessment System (ABAS; Harrison & Oakland, 2000). These rating scales use parents and teachers as informants and focus on rating adaptive skills that occur at home, in school, and in the community.

Due to limitations associated with use of norm-referenced measures to assess adaptive behavior (Harrison & Boney, 2002) it is recommended that these measures be supplemented through the use of additional assessment procedures. Other procedures might include informal interviews with parents and teachers; structured observations in home, classroom, or other natural settings; social skills assessment; use of sociometric techniques; and direct testing of adaptive skills. Data from these additional sources are integrated with the results of norm-referenced testing to obtain a more valid and reliable measure of adaptive functioning (Harrison & Boney, 2002).

Pragmatic Issues Encountered in Clinical Practice with the Disorder

There is a range of pragmatic issues related to the assessment of children who may have mental retardation. These include a tendency to overemphasize the importance of intellectual functioning when identifying children, use of assessment instruments based on availability rather than appropriateness, limited clinical experience with children having mental retardation, assessment of children from culturally diverse backgrounds, and assessment of children with a sensory, motor, or language impairment, or with a suspected psychiatric disorder. These issues will be reviewed next.

Pragmatic factors sometimes lead to an overemphasis upon intellectual functioning during the assessment process, and a lack of emphasis on adaptive functioning. Practicing psychologists generally use the diagnostic criteria for mental retardation found in the DSM-IV-TR discussed earlier. The DSM-IV-TR includes clear, objective diagnostic criteria for determining an individual's level of intellectual functioning, but the criteria for adaptive behavior deficits needed for a diagnosis of mental retardation are less clearly stated, and relatively deemphasized. Also, many governmental agencies that provide services for individuals with mental retardation neglect adaptive behavior and require only an IQ score to determine eligibility for services. They consequently only reimburse practitioners for intellectual assessment. This raises ethical, professional, and financial issues for the practitioner and can lead to the inappropriate and exclusive use of intellectual measures to diagnose mental retardation, with the associated risk of misidentification.

Appropriateness of the intellectual assessment measure selected by the clinician becomes especially critical if it is used exclusively in reaching a diagnosis. Most psychologists, however, are limited to using whatever assessment instruments are available in their practice setting. While the WISC-III may be an appropriate test to use with children with suspected mild or moderate mental retardation, the clinician may lack an instrument that is appropriate for children with more significant intellectual deficits. Also, for example, it may be necessary to distinguish between children with mental retardation and those with severe speech and language deficits. It would be helpful to have a measure of nonverbal intelligence like the CTONI or a nonverbal measure of intelligence such as the UNIT available for such a purpose.

Selection of test instruments for assessing children with severe or profound mental retardation may be especially problematic. Standardized norm-referenced testing may be of limited value. Test directions and test items are likely to be too difficult, and the derived standard scores from these tests are not sensitive enough to measure the small developmental changes that tend to occur in children with severe or profound mental retardation (Browder, 2001; Sattler, 2002). Use of raw scores to indicate change may be more appropriate if standardized measures must be used. An alternative to using a standardized approach would involve use of a developmental scale, with performance on relevant skills used to provide an overall picture of the child's level of cognitive ability.

Another practical issue facing clinicians may be their own lack of training in mental retardation and limited exposure to children with mental retardation. Nezu (1994) reported that 75% of clinical graduate programs and 67% of counseling graduate programs failed to include mental retardation in their curriculum. Practitioners may lack familiarity with the characteristics of children with mental retardation and lack knowledge of potentially useful testing adaptations. Characteristics of children with mental retardation, including short attention span, distractibility, difficulty establishing rapport, lack of confidence, and distrust of strangers (Sattler, 2002) may make it necessary to modify assessment techniques. Sattler (2002) suggests that the practitioner avoid asking open-ended questions, ask simple structured questions, provide examples and frequent prompts, and be ready to repeat or rephrase questions. Because children with mental retardation also tend to have higher rates of acquiescence than children without mental retardation, there may be a tendency for affirmative responses to yes or no questions, which should, therefore, not be overused.

Among the rights afforded children with disabilities under federal law (IDEA'97) is the right to a fair, unbiased assessment (Turnbull, Turnbull, Shank, Smith, & Leal, 2002). This guarantee was included in special education law in response to concerns related to the disproportionate number of children from culturally diverse backgrounds identified and placed in special education programs for children with mental retardation (Artiles & Duran, 1997; Harry, 1994). To reduce the risk of bias when evaluating children from diverse cultural, racial, and socioeconomic backgrounds, it may be helpful to administer a second intellectual measure that is based upon a different theory of intelligence than the initial measure used, particularly when a child scores within the upper range of mild mental retardation on the initial measure. Some of the newer intellectual measures discussed earlier, such as the CAS, DAS, UNIT, and CTONI are based on theories of intelligence that incorporate multiple abilities and information processing strategies and differ significantly from more traditional measures (Harrison, Flanagan, & Genshaft, 1997). The chance of bias is reduced if results from a second instrument confirm the results obtained with an initial measure. Cultural variables should also be taken into account when evaluating adaptive behavior, as the value placed on independent functioning is sometimes culturally influenced.

Another challenge facing clinicians involves the accurate assessment of children with mental retardation who have sensory, motor, and/or language impairments. Accommodations will probably be needed when administering standard measures of intelligence. A description of these accommodations should be included in the clinician's report, as well as an indication of how the child benefited from the accommodations. Specific adaptations will depend on the type and severity of the child's impairment. If a child has poor attention, the clinician might introduce additional structure and provide frequent orienting prompts. Other adaptations might involve providing tangible reinforcers, calling the child's name before presenting an item, tapping the stimulus materials, or physically guiding a child's face toward the materials. If a child has a visual impairment or visual processing problem, stimulus materials may need to be altered by enlarging materials, reducing the number of items presented on a page, or altering the visual plane in which the materials are presented. For a child with a physical disability, additional time might be allowed to complete a task, or more complex adaptations of materials or response methods might be provided. For example, a child with an impaired pointing response may be able to respond more accurately if allowed to use a more gross response, such as placing a card or block over the desired choice, or if test materials are spread farther apart to allow for a fisted or eye-gaze response. If the clinician has access to an assistive technology department, more sophisticated adaptations of printed materials and use of computer-assisted devices may be possible (Newsom, personal communication, February 27, 2003).

Psychologists are sometimes called upon to assess children with mental retardation who may also have a psychiatric problem. Psychiatric problems are more common among individuals with mental retardation. For example, affective or mood disorders occur among 2%–5% of the nondisabled population, but among an estimated 5%–15% of individuals with mental retardation (Reber & Borcherding, 1997). These problems can be difficult to recognize and are often overlooked (Hurley, 1996). When psychiatric problems are suspected, a clinical interview with the child and parents should be conducted, and supplemented with other behavioral and clinical measures (King, DeAntonio, McCracken, Forness, & Ackerland, 1994). Use of a psychiatric rating scale designed for individuals with mental retardation, such as the one developed by Reiss and Valenti-Hein (1994), may help confirm information obtained from the interview. If the clinician lacks experience in the assessment of children with mental retardation who have a suspected psychiatric problem, referral should be made to a specialized tertiary care center where the input of a multidisciplinary team is available (Reber & Borcherding, 1997). When conduct problems or more severe behavior problems like self-injury are present, a functional assessment, as described in the next section, should be carried out.

☐ Functional Assessment

Description of the Problem

Traditional psychological assessment of children referred for behavioral difficulties has occurred primarily in the clinician's office, and involved informal interviews, and tools such as behavior rating scales and personality measures. The source of a child's problem has been thought to rest within the child or his or her family, and the result of assessment has usually been a label, with this label only having a general influence upon the recommended treatment (Horner, Albin, Sprague, & Todd, 2000; Kerr & Nelson, 2002). Assessment based upon a behavioral model has in the past also had little direct bearing upon treatment, and typically involved determining the precise nature of a target behavior and formulating an operational definition, then collecting baseline data on the behavior's occurrence. Interventions were usually selected in a trial-and-error fashion, or reflected the experience or personal bias of the clinician (Repp, 1999; Singh, 1997). When the intent was to weaken a behavior, behavioral interventions typically involved use of punishment (Kazdin, 2001).

Current best practice in the field of mental retardation has evolved from the traditional behavioral approach, and now involves a far greater emphasis upon the role of assessment in determining the context in which a problem behavior occurs, its immediate antecedents, and its consequences (Horner et al., 2000; Westling & Fox, 2000). Informal observation of a child by the psychologist, associated with more traditional models, is replaced by a detailed, systematic examination of the environmental factors responsible for the initiation and maintenance of problem behavior (Singh, 1997). This more comprehensive assessment, especially the information gained through assessment of a problem behavior's context and its antecedents, has allowed for the use of more positive interventions that are designed based upon hypotheses derived from the results of assessment. Comprehensive, systematic assessment has become a cornerstone of "positive behavioral support," a widely accepted model for treating behavior problems in individuals with developmental disabilities such as mental retardation (Sugai et al., 2000; Turnbull, Wilcox, Stowe, & Turnbull, 2001).

The term functional assessment is used to describe the systematic assessment procedures used to identify factors responsible for a problem behavior. Early studies involving use of functional assessment (Carr, 1977; Iwata, Dorsey, Slifer, Bauman, & Richman, 1982), and the bulk of later studies in support of its use, included individuals with severe behavior problems, such as self-injury. In an effort to intervene effectively without resorting to use of punishment, researchers developed hypotheses regarding the function of a problem behavior, then verified these hypotheses through conducting a "mini-experiment" called a functional analysis. Interventions were then based upon efforts to teach new skills to serve the same function that had been served previously by the problem behavior, and either antecedents, consequences, or both were modified so that the problem behavior was no longer useful or necessary. For example, a child with severe mental retardation who bit her hand during periods when the caregiver had directed her attention to another child would be taught an appropriate communication response to request adult attention, and thereby have the means to achieve the same function appropriately that she had earlier achieved through hand-biting. Continued hand-biting would be ignored. Or if a child engaged in head-banging to escape a non-preferred task, the nature of the task, or perhaps the reinforcement provided contingent upon task completion would be modified so that there was no longer motivation to escape.

Usefulness of functional assessment procedures has now been documented with other populations displaying less severe behavior problems (Repp, 1999; Smith, 2001; Wacker, Cooper, Peck, Derby, & Berg, 1999), and functional behavioral assessment has become part of federal law governing educational services for children with disabilities. IDEA 1997 requires that whenever the behavior of a child with a disability results in suspension for more than 10 days, or necessitates a change in a child's educational placement, a functional behavior assessment is necessary (20 U.S.C. Sec. 1414 [k] [1] [B], 1999). In addition, the law requires that positive behavioral interventions be considered whenever the behavior of a child with a disability impedes his or her learning, or that of other children (20 U.S.C. Sec. 1414 [d] [3] [B] [i], 1999). Because positive behavioral interventions are most appropriately designed based upon results of a functional assessment, this provision of the law provides support for the primary role played by functional assessment in work with children who display behavior problems and have disabilities such as mental retardation (Turnbull et al., 2001).

Further support for the importance of functional assessment lies in its documented effectiveness. Kazdin (2000) indicates that of more than 550 therapy techniques used with children and adolescents, most have never been shown to be effective. In this era of rising health-care costs, third party payers are increasingly vigilant about the effectiveness of treatments they are asked to reimburse, and efforts have been made to identify evidence-based treatments. Behavioral interventions rank high among the evidence-based treatments studied (Kazdin, 2001). Results of a recent synthesis of behavioral research studies that involved the use of positive behavioral support strategies with individuals having mental retardation and other developmental disabilities indicated that the use of functional assessment to design interventions was associated with success rates nearly double those otherwise obtained (Carr et al., 1999).

Use of functional assessment procedures in everyday settings requires that the clinician adapt strategies initially designed for use in well-controlled laboratory settings. In the next section, a range of functional assessment strategies will be described, with particular attention to pragmatic issues involved in use of this approach in applied settings.

Range of Functional Assessment Strategies and Pragmatic Issues

The purpose of functional assessment is to develop a hypothesis regarding a behavior's function, or purpose, which can then be used as a guide in designing an intervention. Three levels of functional assessment are available: indirect methods, such as interviews and rating scales; direct observation; and functional analysis. Although functional analysis is often considered a separate, but closely related strategy designed to verify hypotheses derived from a functional assessment, we include it as a form of functional assessment because it will most likely be used in applied settings to formulate or refine a hypothesis, and not to verify a hypothesis as in research applications. Functional assessment methods vary according to the amount of time and expertise they require, the extent to which they interfere with everyday activities in the treatment setting, and the likelihood that they will provide accurate results (Carr, Langdon, & Yarbrough, 1999; Feldman & Griffiths, 1997). We endorse Feldman and Griffiths's practice of using the least intrusive assessment procedure necessary to collect sufficient information to formulate a hypothesis that can guide intervention.

Whichever functional assessment methods are used, the data collection phase of the assessment process is focused upon clearly defining the problem behavior and identifying its antecedents and consequences. Antecedents precede behavior, and influence its likelihood. Some act as environmental triggers (Kazdin, 2001). Common events that trigger problem behavior in children include commands, activities that are boring or disliked, schoolwork that is too difficult, loss of a desired item or activity, and being teased, or provided with insufficient attention. Identifying consistent patterns between certain antecedents and problem behavior, as well as identifying relationships between other antecedents and desirable behavior, comprise an important step in the development of a hypothesis regarding a behavior's function and subsequent design of an intervention plan.

Consequences follow behavior and have traditionally been the focus when a behavioral approach has been used. Positive consequences strengthen behavior, and when behavior is no longer followed with a positive consequence, or followed with a negative consequence, it is weakened (Kazdin, 2001). Common consequences associated with problem behavior include: positive reinforcers such as attention, repeated commands, and tangible items; negative reinforcers such as escape from a demand, or termination of an ongoing activity; and sensory stimulation, such as the proprioceptive input associated with hand-flapping, or the vestibular input derived from rocking (Sandler & McLain, 1987). Identifying the consequences that maintain a problem behavior is a critical step in determining the behavior's function.

In addition to identifying a problem behavior's consequences and immediate antecedents, factors that set the stage for a problem behavior, called setting events, are also evaluated. Setting events are antecedents that influence the likelihood that some immediate trigger will be followed by a problem behavior. They do this by altering the value of reinforcers and punishers, and making what would otherwise be a neutral or only mildly aversive stimulus, like a command from the teacher, more aversive (Artesani, 2001; Chandler & Dahlquist, 2002). For example, a teacher's request to complete a math assignment will more likely be followed by a loud outburst if a child has just received back a math test with a failing grade. Return of the math test with a failing grade is the setting event in this example. The promise of a reward for completing the math assignment, or the threat of punishment if the assignment is not completed, are less likely to motivate the child following exposure to this setting event.

Setting events include environmental factors, such as a hot or noisy classroom; social factors, such as an argument with a parent before school; and biological/medical factors, such as a headache or ear ache

(Kerr & Nelson, 2002). Careful attention to possible biological/medical factors is especially important in the case of children with mental retardation. Collection of assessment data should include steps to determine the possible effects of medication, including side effects, long-term effects, or withdrawal reactions; possible changes in sleep or eating patterns; and the presence of conditions that might cause pain, such as dental or menstrual problems, infection, allergies, constipation, and hemorrhoids (Feldman & Griffiths, 1997). Behavior problems in children with mental retardation may also be associated with various genetic disorders, such as Lesch-Nyhan, Rett, fragile X, and Prader-Willi syndromes (Reber & Borcherding, 1997) or occur in conjunction with CNS dysfunction (Lewis, Baumeister, & Mailman, 1987).

Indirect assessment methods, including interviews and rating scales, are the simplest and least time-consuming of the functional assessment techniques, and usually represent the first step in the functional assessment process. Interviews range from informal conversations aimed at determining the specific nature of a problem behavior and its antecedents and consequences, to more complex, highly structured interviews. An excerpt from an informal interview between a classroom teacher and a school psychologist intended to determine the function of a problem behavior follows:

> Jacki: I'm just curious. When she does get angry and grabs another child or spits at you, how do you react?
>
> Joan: I'll tell you. I don't tolerate it. I lay down the law and let her know this is not how a young lady behaves in my classroom!
>
> Jacki: When you say, "lay down the law," do you mean that you tell her "No," or is there more to it?
>
> Joan: Oh, much more. I tell her that we do not allow that kind of behavior here. I ask her how she would feel if I spit at her and grabbed her hair. And I tell her I know she is capable of much better behavior and that I expect her to act more grown up from now on.
>
> Jacki: How long do you talk to her like this?
>
> Joan: Oh, not long, maybe three or four minutes.
>
> —— **Carr, Langdon, et al., 1999, p. 15**

An example of a more complex interview format is the Functional Assessment Interview (FAI; O'Neill et al., 1997). The FAI is designed to gather detailed information in 11 areas, including functional communication skills, medical factors, and potential reinforcers. Although the FAI is recommended for severe behavior problems with complex causation (Artesani, 2001), the time required to complete it may make its use impractical in some contexts (Chandler & Dahlquist, 2002). A brief functional assessment interview called FACTS (March & Horner, 1998, as cited in Horner et al., 2000), designed to take only 15 to 20 minutes and providing information similar to that provided by the FAI, may be more practical in some situations. An interview format that includes students as their own informants is also available (Student Guided Functional Assessment Interview, O'Neill et al., 1997).

Rating scales, another indirect assessment method, provide more quantitative information than interviews. Respondents indicate their level of agreement with items designed to identify the function of a problem behavior, and the function with the highest cumulative rating is presumed to be the maintaining function. A commonly used rating scale is the Motivation Assessment Scale (MAS; Durand & Crimmons, 1992), which includes 16 items for identifying four potential functions. Although easy to use, methodological problems associated with the MAS suggest that its results be verified through direct observation (Chandler & Dahlquist, 2002). Other functional assessment rating scales include the Problem Behavior Questionnaire (Lewis, Scott, & Sugai, 1994), the Questions about Behavioral Function (Matson & Vollmer, 1995), and the Functional Analysis Screening Tool (Iwata & DeLeon, 1996).

Included in the indirect assessment process should be a review of a child's records to identify other strategies that may have been used in the past, identify any medical conditions that might be related to the problem behavior, and any family factors that might serve as setting events for the behavior (Chandler & Dahlquist, 2002). Information should also be collected on the conditions associated with desirable behavior, both during this phase of data collection and the direct observation phase that follows. This information will be helpful in designing effective interventions later, and also help verify the relationship between the problem behavior and its hypothesized antecedents (Artesani, 2001; Chandler & Dahlquist, 2002; Repp, 1999). For example, information indicating not only that a child displays disruptive behavior during passive activities, but also that he is cooperative during active tasks, will lend support to the hypothesized relationship between passive activities and disruptive behavior (Repp, 1999).

Using the information gathered through indirect assessment, an initial hypothesis should be developed regarding a problem behavior's function (Horner et al., 2000). The functions of problem behavior are usually conceptualized as falling into two or three broad categories. In the positive reinforcement category are behaviors that provide the child with positive or negative attention from others, access to a tangible reinforcer, or to an enjoyable activity. In the negative reinforcement category are behaviors that result in escaping or avoiding, delaying the onset of, or attenuating the effect of some undesired event (Feldman & Griffiths, 1997). Some behaviors in children with mental retardation, such as rocking or hand-flapping, may occur because they provide sensory stimulation (Sandler & McLain, 1987). Sensory stimulation is therefore sometimes included as a third category, but because this stimulation is presumed to provide positive reinforcement, others include this function in the positive reinforcement category.

Other functions might also be operative. Repp (1999), for example, adds sensory regulation — the drive to maintain an optimal level of activity — as a third category, and reports that training school personnel to use functional assessment is easier when this function is included. Some forms of self-injury and stereotypy may serve the function of releasing endogenous opiates that provide the individual with biochemical reinforcement (Thompson, Hackenberg, Cerutti, Baker, & Axtell, 1994). Some aberrant behavior, however, especially in children with severe or profound mental retardation, serves no apparent purpose, and may, for example, occur in conjunction with an obsessive-compulsive disorder (King, 1993), or otherwise occur as a result of neurological dysfunction (Lewis et al., 1987). The utility of behavioral assessment is likely to be limited in these cases, and close coordination with medical professionals is important (Chandler & Dahlquist, 2002; Sandler, 2001). The reader is referred to the biobehavioral model of Mace and Mauk (1999) for more information regarding the assessment of behaviors that occur without any apparent social function and which may have a neurological cause.

An example of an initial hypothesis regarding a problem behavior's function, as well as its presumed antecedents, follows: "When Jen is asked to wash her hands and brush her teeth after lunch she screams and bites her hand. Her problem behavior seems to be maintained by escape, and is more likely on days when she appears tired after partici-pating in community-based training." Practical constraints might require that this hypothesis based upon the results of indirect assess-ment will be used without further investigation to design an interven-tion (Kazdin, 2001). As pointed out by Carr, Langdon, and colleagues (1999), a hypothesis based upon indirect assessment will often lead to effective treatment. However, additional direct observation measures are recommended to identify controlling variables that may not have been identified through indirect assessment methods, and to help verify the information obtained through these indirect methods (Carr, Lang-don, et al., 1999; Gable, Quinn, Rutherford, Howell, & Hoffman, 1998).

For example, interview data obtained from a teacher may indicate that disruptive behavior is ignored, but when observed, it turns out that the teacher responds to disruptive behavior with eye contact and a stern look (Artesani, 2001). Or a caregiver may be embarrassed to admit in an interview that she sometimes responds to a tantrum by withdrawing a demand, which becomes apparent only upon direct observation (Carr, Langdon, et al., 1999).

The collection of direct observation data might begin with a scatter plot (Touchette, MacDonald, & Langer, 1985), a simple chart that is filled in at regular intervals, e.g., every 30 minutes, indicating if a problem behavior has occurred. If not already apparent, this technique might be used to pin down more clearly the conditions under which a problem behavior typically occurs, and make more obvious the time- or environment-dependent nature of a problem behavior (Feldman & Griffiths, 1997). More time-consuming data-keeping procedures might then be used at these times.

The initial hypothesis derived from indirect assessment should be used to guide the collection of additional direct observation data to help reduce likelihood that the data collection process might overburden those involved in collecting data (Horner et al., 2000). Some form of ABC (antecedent-behavior-consequence) assessment would typically be carried out. This could be accomplished through collecting narrative data regarding the events surrounding a problem behavior. Data would be charted so that consistent patterns between a behavior and its presumed antecedents and consequences become clear, thus helping to confirm the behavior's hypothesized function (Kazdin, 2001). Alternately, a prepared data sheet might be used that includes coded notations to facilitate the data collection process. A commonly used tool is the Functional Assessment Observation Form (O'Neill et al., 1997), which includes options to code presumed functions of behavior, as well as a behavior's antecedents and consequences. Other functional assessment data collection systems based upon an ABC format are provided by Fad, Patton, and Polloway (2000), and Smith and Heflin (2001).

ABC data should be recorded until a consistent relationship among antecedents, the behavior, and its consequences has been established. This may range from a period as short as a half-day to several weeks (Chandler & Dahlquist, 2002). O'Neill and colleagues (1997) suggest that data be collected for at least 2 to 5 days, and that data on at least 10 to 15 occurrences of the problem behavior will be necessary to identify consistent patterns. More complex data-keeping approaches, such as lag sequential analysis and computation of conditional probabilities (Repp, 1999), require the use of computers and additional personnel, and are not realistic in most applied settings (Chandler & Dahlquist, 2002).

In the majority of cases, data collected through direct observation will lead to confirmation of an initial hypothesis or development of a revised hypothesis that can be used in the design of an intervention (Dyer & Larsson, 1997). As suggested by Horner and colleagues (2000), in many cases further analysis will not be required, and use of interviews, rating scales, and direct observation for functional assessment purposes will represent a practical option for practitioners. However, if indirect assessment and direct observation methods fail to provide information needed to identify clear patterns among the variables maintaining a problem behavior, as is especially likely in the case of a behavior that serves multiple functions (Kerr & Nelson, 2002; Repp, 1999), functional analysis procedures might be used to help identify these patterns (Dyer & Larsson, 1997). Although typically used to verify hypotheses derived from a functional assessment, functional analysis might be used in this case to gain additional information that might lead to the formulation of a hypothesis (Atresani, 2001; Dunlap & Kern, 1993). Functional analysis procedures are complex, however, and their use will only be feasible when well-trained staff with sufficient time and expertise in applied behavior analysis are available (Horner et al., 2000; Kazdin, 2001). Feldman and Griffiths (1997) recommend their use only as a last resort, as they require that conditions be set up that will be associated with an increase in the problem behavior. This may be questionable from an ethical standpoint (Artesani, 2001), and require informed consent and human subjects' approval in some cases (Horner et al., 2000).

When use of functional analysis is feasible, and warranted for purposes of assessment, it is recommended that a brief functional analysis be conducted in the natural environment. This involves the systematic manipulation of antecedents and consequences in the home or classroom to determine the subsequent effect upon a problem behavior. Analog situations might be employed (Wacker et al., 1999), although analog conditions have most typically been associated with laboratory research. Examples of naturalistic functional analysis procedures can be found in Repp, Felce, and Barton (1988), Dunlap, Kern-Dunlap, Clarke, and Robbins (1991), and Lewis and Sugai (1996).

Is there a need in applied settings to conduct a functional analysis to verify the hypothesis derived from a functional assessment? This is a matter of controversy (Chandler & Dahlquist, 2002), and probably the most significant of the practical issues related to functional assessment that face clinical personnel. Gable and colleagues (1998), for example, in a document vetted by the U.S. Office of Special Education Programs, warn against the temptation to design an intervention plan based upon a functional assessment without in most cases first engaging in the experimental manipulation of variables needed to establish the accuracy of the hypothesis upon which the intervention would be based. We agree with Carr, Langdon, and colleagues (1999), however, that it is not realistic to expect every practitioner to be a researcher. In most applied settings verification of a hypothesis prior to intervention, and the evidence of a causal relationship between a problem behavior and its antecedents and consequences that such verification provides, is not necessary, and a functional analysis will only be advisable for assessment purposes as described earlier. Ongoing assessment of an intervention's effectiveness is an essential aspect of a behavioral approach (Kazdin, 2001). If data collected during treatment indicates that a hypothesis-based intervention is not effective, a functional analysis might then be conducted to help identify additional causal factors, and lead to revision of the original hypothesis, and an alternate treatment approach (Carr, Langdon, et al. 1999).

☐ Case Illustration

The following case illustration provides an example of psychological assessment for purposes of both identifying a child with mental retardation and developing a hypothesis to guide in the design of a behavior intervention plan to remediate his problem behavior.

Client Description

Jeff was a 9-year-old African-American male who lived with his aunt and received special education services in an inclusive general education classroom. He had recently moved from another state where he was enrolled in a self-contained EMR classroom for students with mild mental retardation.

History of the Problem

Jeff had been labeled with mild mental retardation based upon his scores on the WISC-III. A year earlier he had obtained a Verbal IQ of 60, a Performance IQ of 68, and a Full Scale IQ of 60. While these scores are clearly within the mild range of mental retardation, it was reported that he was culturally and educationally deprived, which may have negatively influenced his scores. His records included no mention of scores on a measure of adaptive behavior. Jeff had a history of behavior problems and had been suspended from school the previous year following a fight with another student.

Presenting Complaints

Jeff's teacher requested assistance in managing his disruptive behavior in class, and complained that his "belligerent, disrespectful attitude" created a classroom environment that interfered with her other students' ability to learn. Jeff's aunt requested that he be reevaluated because she felt he was not mentally retarded, and that the stigma and shame associated with this label was the cause of his behavioral difficulties in school.

Assessment Methods Used

Jeff's intellectual performance and adaptive skills were assessed with the Universal Nonverbal Intelligence Test (UNIT) and the Adaptive Behavior Assessment System (ABAS). A functional assessment interview that included completion of the Motivation Assessment Scale (MAS) was carried out, and classroom observations were conducted using the Functional Assessment Observation Form designed by O'Neill and colleagues (1997).

Assessment Protocol

Since prior language assessment indicated deficits in auditory processing, and there were concerns about possible cultural bias related to his earlier testing with the WISC-III, the UNIT was selected to reassess Jeff's intellectual ability. A full scale IQ of 66 was obtained, and his other UNIT composite scores fell within this same range.

Adaptive behavior was assessed with the ABAS, using Jeff's aunt and teacher as informants. His aunt's ratings (adaptive composite score of 68) were higher than his teacher's ratings (adaptive composite score of 56), but still within a range compatible with the diagnosis of mental retardation. This result, coupled with the result of intellectual assessment, supported the earlier diagnosis of mild mental retardation.

Functional assessment included an informal interview with Jeff's teacher to identify the specific problem behaviors that were of concern. Jeff refused to follow his teacher's commands to complete assignments, especially in the area of language arts, and responded to her repeated requests by sometimes throwing his notebook and making comments such as, "If you want it done, you do it," and "Back off, teacher!" During the interview the MAS was completed to help determine the function of Jeff's behavior. It was hypothesized that his behavior provided escape from tasks he found too difficult. Classroom observations conducted with the Functional Assessment Observation Form confirmed this hypothesis and also indicated that Jeff's outbursts were more likely if his teacher threatened him with disciplinary action or transfer to a "more appropriate" class.

Targets Selected for Treatment

A behavior intervention plan was designed based upon the results of the functional assessment. Target behaviors included compliance with teacher commands to complete assignments, throwing classroom materials, and disrespectful comments to the teacher. To address the hypothesized function of Jeff's disruptive behavior the difficulty level and length of his assignments were adjusted, and a positive reinforcement program was set up to reward him for completed assignments. To address the antecedents that triggered Jeff's behavior, commands to complete assignments were to be repeated only once after the initial request and teacher warnings would no longer be provided.

Assessment of Progress

Ongoing data collection procedures were set up in the classroom to assess the effectiveness of the intervention. The assistant teacher recorded frequency data on the number of assignments given and completed daily, the number of objects thrown in class, and the number of disrespectful comments made to the teacher. A meeting was scheduled in 30 days to review these data, and consider the need for modifications in the treatment plan.

☐ Summary

In this chapter we have reviewed psychological assessment procedures used to identify and classify children with mental retardation and develop hypotheses to guide in the design of behavioral interventions to remediate behavior problems. Measures of intellectual and adaptive functioning were reviewed, as well as pragmatic issues related to their use in applied settings. Functional assessment procedures were described, including the use of interviews and rating scales, direct observation, and functional analysis. Among the pragmatic issues discussed was the need to conduct a functional analysis as part of the functional assessment process. This review should be of assistance to practitioners engaged in the assessment of children with mental retardation who must work within the practical constraints of typical school and clinic settings.

☐ References

American Psychiatric Association. (2000). *Diagnostic and statistical manual of mental disorders* (4th ed., text revision). Washington, DC: American Psychiatric Association.

Artesani, A. J. (2001). *Understanding the purpose of challenging behavior: A guide to conducting functional assessments.* Upper Saddle River, NJ: Merill/Prentice Hall.

Artiles, A., & Duran, G. Z. (1997). *Reducing disproportionate representation of culturally diverse students in special and gifted education.* Reston, VA: Council for Exceptional Children.

Bayley, N. (1993). *Bayley scales of infant development* (2nd ed.). San Antonio, TX: Psychological Corporation.

Black, M. M., & Matula, K. (2000). *Essentials of Bayley scales of infant development — II: Assessment.* New York: Wiley.

Bracken, B. A., & McCallum, R. S. (1998). *Universal nonverbal intelligence test.* Itasca, IL: Riverside.

Bregman, J. D. (1991). Current developments in the understanding of mental retardation: Part I. Psychopathology. *Journal of the American Academy of Child and Adolescent Psychiatry, 30,* 861–872.

Browder, D. M. (2001). *Curriculum and assessment for students with moderate and severe disabilities.* New York: Guilford.

Carr, E. G. (1977). The motivation of self-injurious behavior: A review of some hypotheses. *Psychological Bulletin, 84,* 800–816.

Carr, E. G., Horner, R. H., Turnbull, A. P., Marquis, J. G., Magito McLaughlin, D., McAtee, M. L., et al. (1999). *Positive behavior support for people with developmental disabilities: A research synthesis* (American Association on Mental Retardation Monograph Series). Washington, DC: American Association on Mental Retardation.

Carr, E. G., Langdon, N. A., & Yarbrough, S. C. (1999). Hypothesis-based intervention for severe problem behavior. In A. C. Repp & R. H. Horner (Eds.), *Functional analysis of problem behavior: From effective assessment to effective support* (pp. 9–31). Belmont, CA: Wadsworth.

Chandler, L. K., & Dahlquist, C. M. (2002). *Functional assessment: Strategies to prevent and remediate challenging behavior in school settings.* Upper Saddle River, NJ: Merill/Prentice Hall.

Dunlap, G., & Kern, L. (1993). Assessment and intervention for children within the instructional curriculum. In J. Reichle & D. P.Wacker (Eds.), *Communication alternatives to challenging behavior: Integrating functional assessment and intervention strategies* (pp. 177–204). Baltimore, MD: Paul H. Brookes.

Dunlap, G., & Kern-Dunlap, L., Clarke, S., & Robbins, F. R. (1991). Functional assessment, curricular revision, and severe behavior problems. *Journal of Applied Behavior Analysis, 24,* 387–397.

Durand, V. M., & Crimmins, D. (1992). *The motivation assessment scale (MAS).* Topeka, KS: Monoco & Associates.

Dyer, K., & Larsson, E. V. (1997). Developing functional communication skills: Alternatives to severe behavior problems. In N. N. Singh (Ed.), *Prevention and treatment of severe behavior problems: Models and methods in developmental disabilities* (pp. 121–148). Pacific Grove, CA: Brookes/Cole.

Elliott, C. D. (1990). *Differential ability scales.* San Antonio, TX: Psychological Corporation.

Fad, K., Patton, J., & Polloway, E. (2000). *Behavioral intervention planning.* Austin, TX: Pro-Ed.

Feldman, M. A., & Griffiths, D. (1997). Comprehensive assessment of severe behavior problems. In N. N. Singh (Ed.), *Prevention and treatment of severe behavior problems: Models and methods in developmental disabilities* (pp. 23–48). Pacific Grove, CA: Brookes/Cole.

Gable, R. A., Quinn, M. M., Rutherford, R. B., Howell, K. W., & Hoffman, C. C. (1998, May). *Addressing student problem behavior—Part II: Conducting a functional assessment.* Washington, DC: Center for Effective Collaboration and Practice.

Hammill, D. D., Pearson, N. A., & Wiederholt, J. L. (1996). *Comprehensive test of nonverbal intelligence.* Austin, TX: Pro-Ed.

Harrison, P. L., & Boney, T. L. (2002). Best practices in the assessment of adaptive behavior. In A. Thomas & J. Grimes (Eds.), *Best practices in school psychology IV* (pp. 1167–1179). Bethesda, MD: National Association of School Psychologists.

Harrison, P. L., Flanagan, D. P., & Genshaft, J. L. (1997). An integration and synthesis of contemporary theories, tests, and issues in the field of intellectual assessment. In D. P. Flanagan, J. L.Genshaft, & P. L. Harrison (Eds.), *Contemporary intellectual assessment: Theories, tests, and issues* (pp. 533–561). New York: Guilford.

Harrison, P. L., & Oakland, T. (2000). *Adaptive behavior assessment system.* San Antonio, TX: Psychological Corporation.

Harry, B. (1994). *The disproportionate representation of minority students in special education: Theories and recommendations. Project FORUM: Final report* (pp. 8–11, 43–48). Alexandria, VA: National Association of State Directors of Special Education (ED374637).

Horner, R. H., Albin, R. W., Sprague, J. R., & Todd, A. W. (2000). Positive behavior support. In M. E. Snell & F. Brown (Eds.), *Instruction of students with severe disabilities* (5th ed.; pp. 207–243). Upper Saddle River, NJ: Merill/Prentice Hall.

Hurley, A. D. (1996). Identifying psychiatric disorders in persons with mental retardation: A model illustrated by depression in Down syndrome. *Journal of Rehabilitation, 15,* 6–31.

Individuals With Disabilities Education Act (IDEA; 1997). 20 U.S.C. Secs. 1400 et seq.

Iwata, B., & DeLeon, I. (1996). The functional analysis screening tool. The Florida Center on Self-Injury. Gainesville: University of Florida.

Iwata, B., Dorsey, M., Slifer, K., Bauman, K., & Richman, G. (1982). Toward a functional analysis of self-injury. *Analysis and Intervention in Developmental Disabilities, 2,* 3–20.

Kaufman, A. S. (1990). *Assessing adolescent and adult intelligence.* Needham, MA: Allyn and Bacon.

Kaufman, A. S., & Kaufman, N. L. (1983). *Kaufman assessment battery for children.* Circle Pines, MN: American Guidance Service.

Kazdin, A. E. (2000). *Psychotherapy for children and adolescents: Directions for research and practice.* New York: Oxford University Press.

Kazdin, A. E. (2001). *Behavior modification in applied settings* (6th ed.). Belmont, CA: Wadsworth.

Kerr, M. M., & Nelson, C. M. (2002). *Strategies for addressing behavior problems in the classroom* (4th ed.). Upper Saddle River, NJ: Merill/Prentice Hall.

King, B. H. (1993). Self-injury by people with mental retardation: A compulsive behavior hypothesis. *American Journal on Mental Retardation, 98,* 93–112.

King, B. H., DeAntonio, C., McCracken, J. T., Forness, S. R., & Ackerland, V. (1994). Psychiatric consultation in severe and profound mental retardation. *American Journal of Psychiatry, 151,* 1802–1808.

Lambert, N., Nihira, K., & Leland, H. (1993). *AAMR adaptive behavior scale-school* (2nd ed.). Austin, TX: Pro-Ed.

Lewis, M. H., Baumeister, A. A., & Mailman, R. B. (1987). A neurological alternative to the perceptual reinforcement hypothesis of stereotyped behavior: A commentary on "self-stimulatory behavior and perceptual reinforcement." *Journal of Applied Behavior Analysis, 20,* 253–258.

Lewis, T., Scott, T., & Sugai, G. (1994). The problem behavior questionnaire: A teacher-based instrument to develop functional hypotheses of problem behavior in general education classrooms. *Diagnostique, 19,* 103–115.

Lewis, T., & Sugai, G. (1996). Functional assessment of problem behavior: A pilot investigation of the comparative and interactive effects of teacher and peer social attention on students in general education settings. *School Psychology Quarterly, 11,* 1–19.

Luckasson, R., Borthwick-Duffy, S., Buntinx, W. H. E., Coulter, D. L., Craig, E. M., Reeve, A., et al. (2002). *Mental retardation: Definition, classification, and systems of supports* (10th ed.). Washington, DC: AAMR.

Mace, F. C., & Mauk, J. E. (1999). Biobehavioral diagnosis and treatment of self-injury. In A. C. Repp & R. H. Horner (Eds.), *Functional analysis of problem behavior: From effective assessment to effective support* (pp. 78–97). Belmont, CA: Wadsworth.

Matson, J., & Vollmer, T. (1995). *User's guide: Questions about behavioral function (QABF).* Baton Rouge, LA: Scientific Publishers.

McCarney, S. B. (1995). *Adaptive behavior evaluation scale, revised: School version.* Columbia, MO: Hawthorn Educational Services.

Naglieri, J. A. (1999). *Essentials of CAS assessment.* New York: Wiley.

Naglieri, J. A., & Das, J. P. (1997). *Cognitive assessment system interpretive handbook.* Itasca, IL: Riverside.

Nezu, A. M. (1994). Introduction to special section: Mental retardation and mental illness. *Journal of Consulting and Clinical Psychology, 62,* 4–5.

O'Neill, R., Horner, R., Albin, R., Sprague, J., Storey, K., & Newton, J. S. (1997). *Functional assessment and program development for problem behavior* (2nd ed.). Pacific Grove, CA: Brookes/Cole.

Reber, M., & Borcherding, B. R. (1997). Dual diagnosis: Mental retardation and psychiatric disorders. In M. L. Batshaw (Ed.), *Children with disabilities* (4th ed.; pp. 405–424). Baltimore, MD: Paul H. Brookes.

Reiss, S., & Valenti-Hein, D. (1994). Development of a psychopathology rating scale for children with mental retardation. *Journal of Consulting and Clinical Psychology, 62,* 28–33.

Repp, A. C. (1999). Naturalistic functional assessment with regular and special education students in classroom settings. In A. C. Repp & R. H. Horner (Eds.), *Functional analysis of problem behavior: From effective assessment to effective support* (pp. 238–258). Belmont, CA: Wadsworth.

Repp, A. C., Felce, D., & Barton, L. E. (1988). Basing the treatment of stereotypic and self-injurious behaviors on hypotheses of their causes. *Journal of Applied Behavior Analysis, 21,* 281–289.

Roid, G. H., & Miller, L. J. (1997). *Leiter international scale — Revised.* Wood Dale, IL: Stoelting.

Sandler, A. (2001). Sensory reinforcement strategies for the treatment of nonsocially mediated self-injury. *Journal of Developmental and Physical Disabilities, 13*(3), 303–317.

Sandler, A., & McLain, S. (1987). Sensory reinforcement: Effects of response-contingent vestibular stimulation on multiply handicapped children. *American Journal of Mental Deficiency, 91,* 373–378.

Sattler, J. M. (2001). *Assessment of children: Cognitive applications* (4th ed.). San Diego, CA: Jerome M. Sattler.

Sattler, J. M. (2002). *Assessment of children: Behavioral and clinical applications* (4th ed.). San Diego, CA: Jerome M. Sattler.

Singh, N. N. (1997). Enhancing quality of life through teaching and habilitation. In N. N. Singh (Ed.), *Prevention and treatment of severe behavior problems: Models and methods in developmental disabilities* (pp. 1–22). Pacific Grove, CA: Brookes/Cole.

Smith, M. A. (2001). Functional assessment of challenging behaviors in school and community. In S. Alper, D. L. Ryndak, & C. N. Schloss (Eds.), *Alternate assessment of students with disabilities in inclusive settings* (pp. 256–272). Boston: Allyn and Bacon.

Smith, M., & Heflin, L. J. (2001). Supporting positive behavior in public schools: An intervention program in Georgia. *Journal of Positive Behavior Interventions, 3,* 39–47.

Sparrow, S. S., Balla, D. A., & Cicchetti, D. V. (1985). *Vineland adaptive behavior scales, classroom edition.* Circle Pines, MN: American Guidance Service.

Sugai, G., Horner, R. H., Dunlap, G., Hieneman, M., Lewis, T. J., Nelson, C. M., et al. (2000). Applying positive behavior support and functional behavioral assessment in schools. *Journal of Positive Behavior Interventions, 2,* 131–143.

Thompson, T., Hackenberg, T., Cerutti, D., Baker, D., & Axtell, S. (1994). Opioid antagonist effects on self-injury in adults with mental retardation: Response form and location as determinants of medication effects. *American Journal on Mental Retardation, 99,* 85–102.

Thorndike, R. L., Hagen, E. P., & Sattler, J. M. (1986). *Guide for administering and scoring the Stanford-Binet intelligence scale* (4th ed.). Chicago: Riverside.

Touchette, P. E., MacDonald, R. F., & Langer, S. N. (1985). A scatter plot for identifying stimulus control of problem behavior. *Journal of Applied Behavior Analysis, 18,* 343–351.

Turnbull, R., Turnbull, A., Shank, M., Smith, S., & Leal, D. (2002). *Exceptional education in today's schools* (3rd ed.). Upper Saddle River, NJ: Merill/Prentice Hall.

Turnbull, R., Wilcox, B., Stowe, M., & Turnbull, A. (2001). IDEA requirements for the use of PBS. *Journal of Positive Behavior Interventions, 3,* 11–18.

Wacker, D. P., Cooper, L. J., Peck, S. M., Derby, K. M., & Berg, W. K. (1999). Community-based functional assessment. In A. C. Repp & R. H. Horner (Eds.), *Functional analysis of problem behavior: From effective assessment to effective support* (pp. 32–56). Belmont, CA: Wadsworth.

Wechsler, D. (1991). *Wechsler intelligence scale for children — Third edition: Manual.* San Antonio, TX: Psychological Corporation.

Wechsler, D. (2002). *Wechsler preschool and primary scale of intelligence — Third edition: Technical and interpretive manual.* San Antonio, TX: Psychological Corporation.

Westling, D. L., & Fox, L. (2000). *Teaching students with severe disabilities.* Upper Saddle River, NJ: Merrill/ Prentice Hall.

Lara Delmolino
Sandra L. Harris
Heather Jennett
CHAPTER   Megan Martins

Pervasive Developmental Disorders

☐ Description of the Disorders

The term pervasive developmental disorders (PDD) refers to a continuum of disorders that are characterized by severe impairments in three areas of functioning: social behavior, verbal and nonverbal communication, and the presence of stereotyped, repetitive patterns of behavior, according to the *Diagnostic and Statistical Manual of Mental Disorders*, 4th edition, revised text (American Psychiatric Association; DSM-IV-TR, 2000). The terms Autistic Spectrum Disorders and Pervasive Developmental Disorders are used interchangeably to describe this cluster of disorders that includes autistic disorder, Asperger's disorder, pervasive developmental disorder — not otherwise specified (PPD-NOS), Retts disorder, and childhood disintegrative disorder. PDD should be distinguished from the broader term of developmental disability that includes a range of disorders (e.g., cerebral palsy, epilepsy, and mental retardation) that have an impact on development of processes such as language, learning, mobility, and self-care (Olley & Guttentag, 1999). Although procedures outlined in this chapter apply to the full range of pervasive developmental disorders, there is currently very little literature addressing the differential diagnosis of Rett's disorder and childhood disintegrative disorder based on psychological assessments. The current chapter will focus primarily on the use of psychological assessments in autistic disorder, Asperger's disorder, and PDD-NOS.

Autistic Disorder

The term "autism" is sometimes used to encompass the range of PDD and is sometimes used more narrowly to mean autistic disorder (AD). For the sake of clarity we will use the precise diagnostic terms such as autistic disorder or Asperger's disorder, and when we use the word "autism" we intend it to encompass the PDDs broadly. Although estimates vary, prevalence rates now suggest that approximately 10–20 per 10,000 children meet criteria for AD, indicating that the disorder is more common than previously thought and should not be considered a rare occurrence (Filipek et al., 1999). According to DSM-IV-TR, the disorder must manifest itself before the age of 3 in the form of significant impairment in social interaction, language use, or symbolic or imaginative play. The lifelong disorder is approximately four to five times more common in males than females and is often associated with mental retardation.

AD is usually diagnosed in early childhood and it is generally assumed that the disorder is present at or acquired soon after birth. Parental report and home videos from children's infancy have revealed that symptoms of AD and PDD-NOS can be seen as early as the first few months of life (Adrien et al., 1991; Osterling & Dawson, 1994). Parents will often have concerns about their child's development before the second birthday, yet the disorder is not diagnosed for up to 2 years in many cases (Filipek et al., 1999). Most often, parents initially become concerned when they have observed delays in speech development, lack of social behavior, or loss of skills that the child previously demonstrated.

Social Deficits in Autistic Disorder

Children with AD demonstrate qualitative impairments in reciprocal social interaction. It is often stated that these social deficits are the hallmark and core feature of autism and are the most difficult of the symptoms to treat. The social impairments are qualitative in that they are relative to the child's chronological or mental age, and thus, they manifest themselves differently according to the developmental age of the child and may change over time (American Psychiatric Association; DSM-IV-TR, 2000). However, deficits in social understanding and interactions still persist in high functioning and older individuals with the disorder.

Children with AD display impairment in the use of nonverbal behaviors during social interaction, such as eye contact, facial expressions, body postures, and gestures. It is often reported that children with AD do not mold to their parents' body or engage in eye-to-eye gaze, as typical infants do when they are held. Some children with AD might not raise their arms to be held or change their body posture in anticipation of being picked up (Filipek et al., 1999). Further, children with AD fail to demonstrate a range of joint attention behaviors (Grossman, Carter, & Volkmar, 1997). Joint attention is the capacity to use social-communicative skills to regulate another person's experience with an object or an event. An example of joint attention is when a child uses a finger point to show a parent a balloon in the sky. Some children with AD only use these behaviors to gain aid in obtaining an object (e.g., when the child would like her mother to purchase a balloon for her) and not for the purely social reason of sharing the experience of an object or event with another person (e.g., when the child would like her mother to share her enjoyment in seeing the balloon).

Children with AD tend to show limited interest in children and adults with whom they are not familiar. Many children display such social avoidance by not approaching other children in attempts to interact or play and preferring to play alone (Hauck et al., 1995). Other children indicate a desire to have friendships with peers but do not understand the social conventions that are necessary to develop friendships. Children with AD have difficulty understanding the unique intentions, beliefs, and motivation of others (Baron-Cohen, 1995). As a result, children with AD are often observed to treat a person as an object or a means to an end because they do not understand that the person has his own beliefs and thoughts (Grossman, Carter, & Volkmar, 1997). These social deficits can be obstacles to establishing friendships with peers because of the associated difficulty in developing and displaying empathy toward peers.

Communication Deficits in Autistic Disorder

Children with AD demonstrate a variety of language and communication deficits. Most children exhibit a delay in or total lack of language development, despite evidence that the physiological and structural components necessary for language have developed appropriate to chronological age (Charlop-Christy, Schreibman, Pierce, & Kurtz, 1998). In past years it was reported that up to 50% of children with AD do not develop functional speech (Rutter, 1978), however, more recent estimates are thought to be closer to 35%–40% (Mesibov, Adams & Klinger, 1997).

In individuals who develop functional language, certain abnormal speech characteristics are common (Schreibman, 1988). Children with AD may display both immediate and delayed echolalia, the repetition of words or phrases spoken by others. Immediate echolalia is the repetition of words just spoken, such as when a teacher asks a child, "How are you?" and the child repeats, "How are you?" Delayed echolalia is the repetition of words heard at some time in the past. An example of delayed echolalia is when a child repeats part of a television program or a conversation that occurred a few days or a few hours before. Further, children with AD might demonstrate pronomial reversal, the tendency to use an incorrect or opposite pronoun when speaking, such as requesting a drink of water by saying "May you have a glass of water?"

Children who develop sufficient language abilities will still display problems associated with conversation and interactive play (American Psychiatric Association; DSM-IV-TR, 2000). Some children will display impairment in the ability to initiate or sustain conversation with others. Children with AD rarely initiate conversation or engage in any other form of spontaneous speech with peers or adults. During conversation, some children with AD have difficulty introducing new topics or building off the conversation of others. In these cases, a child will approach and initiate a conversation with ease using common phrases such as "Hi! How are you?" and "What's your name?" Despite an obvious desire to engage in conversation with another individual, the same child may have difficulty taking the next step and be unable to participate in a more complex conversation and interaction.

Restricted and Repetitive Interests and Behaviors

Children with AD also demonstrate restrictive, repetitive, and ritualistic patterns of behavior (American Psychiatric Association; DSM-IV-TR, 2000). This can include an unusual preoccupation with an object or concept that is abnormal in either intensity or focus. These preoccupations range from interests in concepts such as numbers and shapes, to the study of political science, to a particular video game. Children with AD may demonstrate their preoccupation by discussing the concept or object repetitively or developing an attachment to the object and becoming upset if separated from the object (Schreibman, 1988). Some children with AD become preoccupied with parts of objects, such the wheel of a truck, the door of a toy car, or the handle on a talking toy. They may also display a restricted range of interests and preferred items compared with other children the same age.

Children with AD often engage in stereotyped and repetitive motor mannerisms, such as hand-flapping, rocking, or spinning objects. These behaviors appear to serve no other purpose than the experience of the sensory input they provide and appear to be highly preferred activities. Also, many children follow highly specific routines and appear inflexible to changes in these routines (Mesibov, Adams, & Klinger, 1997). A child may appear distressed and upset when new furniture is installed in the home, a disruption in the bedtime ritual occurs, or when a parent chooses to drive a different route to school. Since some children with AD resist such changes, parents may spend considerable time and energy maintaining routines in order to prevent upsetting their child.

Asperger's Syndrome and PDD-NOS

Aperger's disorder and PDD-NOS share characteristics with autistic disorder but can also be distinguished based upon DSM-IV-TR criteria. Individuals with Asperger's disorder display similar social deficits and restricted range of behaviors as seen in individuals with AD. However, Asperger's disorder differs from autistic disorder in that individuals with Asperger's disorder must not display any significant deficit in language or communicative skills or cognitive development and onset may be after 3 years of age. PDD-NOS is diagnosed in the presence of significant impairment in social skills, impairment in communicative skills or in the presence of restrictive, repetitive behaviors, despite not meeting diagnostic criteria for any other pervasive developmental disorder. The label PDD-NOS, also referred to as atypical autism, is often given to individuals due to subthreshold symptomatology or onset after 3 years of age.

Range of Assessment Strategies Available

Assessing a child with a pervasive developmental disorder should include a comprehensive evaluation of multiple areas including behaviors diagnostic of autism, cognitive development, developmental functioning, and adaptive behavior. The information from this broad-based assessment will result in a diagnosis, a picture of the child's patterns of strengths and weaknesses in several important areas of functioning, information for educational planning, and a method to track progress over time.

Diagnostic Assessments

The diagnosis of autism is behavioral in nature and based on a variety of behavioral deficits and excesses as defined by the DSM-IV-TR and described above. There is a range of standardized diagnostic tools available consisting of standardized interviews with caregivers, direct observational measures, and psychometric screening questionnaires.

The Autism Diagnostic Interview — Revised (ADI-R; Lord, Rutter, & LeCouteur, 1994) is a semistructured interview for caregivers focusing on the child's behavior in the areas of social relatedness, communication, and repetitive behaviors. The interview questions are based on DSM-IV and ICD-10 criteria and the results determine a diagnosis and the severity of an autism spectrum disorder. It can be used for children with mental ages of at least 18 months through adulthood. The interview takes about 90 minutes to administer but the length varies depending on the age of the participant. The ADI-R has good reliability and validity and is currently considered the gold standard for diagnosing children with autism for research purposes. However, it takes considerable training to administer and score for a valid diagnosis.

The Autism Diagnostic Observation Schedule (ADOS; Lord, Risi, et al., 2000; Lord, Rutter, DiLavore, & Risi, 2001) is a semistructured observational assessment during which the evaluator directs activities intended to elicit behaviors that are diagnostic of autism. The main focus of the ADOS is on social and communicative behavior and it taps into areas such as social interactions, communication, and play or imaginative use of materials. There are four modules to choose among, based on the participants' chronological age and expressive language abilities and the activities in each are designed to be interesting and provide natural opportunities for target behaviors to occur. Thus, a strength of the ADOS is that the items are designed to elicit relevant behaviors across developmental levels regardless of the language level of the individual. It takes about 30–45 minutes to administer. Like the ADI-R, the ADOS is a gold standard in diagnosis for research purposes and requires training and practice in observation, administration, and scoring for a valid diagnosis.

The Childhood Autism Rating Scale (CARS; Schopler et al., 1988) is a 15-item observational rating scale consisting of items such as relating to people, imitation, adaptation to change, verbal and nonverbal communication, and consistency of intellectual response. Information for the ratings can come from a variety of sources, such as an observation of the participant during psychological testing or during other activities, or from parental report of observed behaviors. The ratings result in a total score as well as a pattern of impairments that will determine the autism diagnosis. The CARS has acceptable reliability and validity (Schopler et al., 1988) as well as sensitivity to changes across development (Mesibov et al., 1989). Researchers have recommended the CARS for screening for autism or in combination with other diagnostic procedures (Mesibov et al., 1989).

There are several other psychometrically strong behavioral questionnaires available as screening tools for autism. Because these are best used for screening, they should not be used in isolation for the diagnosis of autism (e.g., Volkmar et al., 1988). The Gilliam Autism Rating Scale (GARS; Gilliam, 1995) is a behavioral checklist that can be completed by parents or professionals who know the child well. It contains autism-relevant items, such as communication and socialization abilities, stereotyped behaviors, and questions regarding the child's development during the first three years of life. The resulting score indicates the probability that the individual has autism and the severity of the autism. It can be used with participants from 3 years to 22 years old and takes 5–10 minutes to complete. The Autism Behavior Checklist (ABC; Krug, Arick, & Almond, 1980) is a parent or teacher checklist of behavioral characteristics common in the diagnosis of autism. It contains descriptors in five areas, sensory, relating, body and object use, language, and social and self-help skills. It is easy to administer and score and the result indicates the likelihood of the autism diagnosis.

The Checklist for Autism in Toddlers (CHAT; Baron-Cohen, Allen, & Gillberg, 1992) is designed for early detection of autism at 18 months by pediatricians and contains interview questions for parents to endorse as well as brief observational probes. It covers nine developmental areas, such as pretend play, protodeclarative pointing, and joint attention, and takes approximately 15 minutes to complete. In initial studies, the CHAT correctly predicted at 18 months those children who were later diagnosed with autism and those who were not (Baron-Cohen et al. 1992; Baron-Cohen et al. 1996). However, follow-up to this research found the CHAT to have relatively low sensitivity for mild symptoms of autism at an early age, which may limit its utility as a screening instrument (Baird et al., 2000).

Cognitive and Developmental Assessments

In addition to using diagnostic instruments specific to autism, cognitive and developmental assessments are valuable pieces of the assessment because they provide information about the child's pattern of intellectual development and can assist in setting goals for educational placements.

The uneven nature of the pattern of development makes this kind of assessment especially important.

The most widely used cognitive assessment instruments for children in general are the Stanford-Binet Intelligence Scale — Fourth Edition (Thorndike, Hagen, & Sattler, 1986), the Wechsler Intelligence Scale for Children — Third Edition (WISC-III; Wechsler, 1991), and the Wechsler Preschool and Primary Scale of Intelligence — Revised (WPPSI-R; Wechsler, 1989). All of these scales have high reliability and validity with typically developing populations and therefore represent the gold standard for intellectual assessment in general.

The Stanford-Binet Intelligence Scale — Fourth Edition (Thorndike et al., 1986) is a norm-referenced measure of general intelligence that taps into four general areas: verbal reasoning, quantitative reasoning, abstract-visual reasoning, and short-term memory. It can be administered to individuals between 2 and 23 years old and is especially useful for assessing children with autism because of its broad age range. One study suggests that children with autism tend to demonstrate a certain profile on the Stanford-Binet, with the lowest score on the Absurdities Subtest and a relative strength on the Pattern Analysis Subtest (Harris, Handleman, & Burton, 1990). However, this work requires replication.

The WISC-III is a standardized instrument assessing mental abilities in both verbal and perceptual-motor areas, such as abstract reasoning skills, memory, and perceptual skills. It can be used with children from age 6 through 16 years, 11 months and takes about 60–90 minutes to administer. The WPPSI-R is a similar battery of tests for use with children between 3 and 7 years old. Some researchers report that children with autism show a profile on the Weschler scales in which their performance IQ (PIQ) is greater than their verbal IQ (VIQ), the highest performance subtest score is on Block Design and the lowest is on Picture Arrangement, and the highest verbal subtest score is on Digit Span and the lowest is on Comprehension (e.g., Allen, Lincoln, & Kaufman, 1991). In contrast, Siegel and colleagues (1996) found no significant difference between VIQ and PIQ in the majority of their sample of high-functioning individuals with autism, and when there was a significant difference it was in either direction. Additionally, although they found a scatter of skills similar to the reports of previous researchers, it was not statistically outside the range of variability of the standardization sample. Therefore, although particular profiles have been found on both the Wechsler scales and the Stanford-Binet, these profiles may vary within the population and are not diagnostic.

Each of the instruments described above requires language, sustained attention, and includes timed tasks, all which are often difficult for children with autism. Thus, for many children with autism the resulting IQ may not be the best indicator of their actual cognitive abilities. These tests have been recommended for higher functioning individuals with autism (Sattler, 1992). There are other standardized measures of cognitive development to use with less verbal children or those with attentional deficits.

The Leiter International Performance Scale — Revised (Leiter-R; Roid & Miller, 1997) is a nonverbal test of intelligence which requires no speech from the evaluator or the participant. This may be a good alternative for some children with autism because it is entirely nonverbal, the items cover a broad age range, it does not have timed tests so that children with short attention spans or interfering behaviors are not penalized, it is brief, and the administration is fairly flexible (Shah & Holmes, 1985). However, because it relies on nonverbal skills it provides a different estimate of intelligence than the Stanford-Binet and the Weschler scales and may overestimate IQ for children with autism (Shah & Holmes, 1985). Additionally, it does not allow a comparative analysis of different skills.

The Merrill Palmer Scale of Intelligence (Stutsman, 1948) is a norm-referenced test of intelligence for children from 18 months through 78 months. Some clinicians use this scale because of its wide age range, its nonverbal materials, and the limited language and abstract problem-solving requirements. However, the Merrill-Palmer seems to overestimate IQ compared to other cognitive scales (Magiati & Howlin, 2001) and relies on outdated norms. It is particularly a good test for measures of visuo-spatial development but emphasizes different areas than other traditional cognitive instruments (Magiati & Howlin, 2001).

The Differential Ability Scales (DAS; Elliott, 1990) is a battery of cognitive and achievement tests for children between 2 and 17 years old containing a variety of subtests dependent on age. Many different skills, such as comprehension, nonverbal reasoning, and quantitative concepts, are measured and the test yields a profile of the child's strengths and weaknesses, as well as giving diagnostic information about learning difficulties. Many of the tasks have nonverbal components that can be helpful for children with autism.

The Bayley Scales of Infant Development — Second Edition (BSID-II; Bayley, 1993) measure developmental functioning in children from 2 months through 42 months and tap into mental development, psychomotor development, and have scales to rate behaviors observed during the testing such as social orientation and general emotional tone. The relatively low age limit may make this a valuable tool for assessing lower functioning children with autism and the results provide information about the child's pattern of mental development.

The Psychoeducational Profile — Revised (PEP-R; Schopler, Reichler, Bashford, Lansing, & Marcus, 1990) is a standardized developmental assessment designed to identify variations in patterns of learning and yields results that can be used for educational programming. Items are presented within structured play activities and comprise seven scales of developmental functioning: imitation, perception, fine motor, gross motor, eye-hand integration, cognitive performance, and cognitive verbal skills. Each item is scored as passed, failed, or emerging, which results in a developmental score for each area and an overall developmental score, and presents a profile of the child's strengths and weaknesses. Use of the emerging score is especially helpful, as it can serve as the basis for educational programming. In addition to developmental scores, the PEP-R consists of items designed to identify the degree of abnormality in four behavioral areas (relating and affect, sensory, play and interest in materials, and language) and thus the severity of autism. The PEP-R is designed for children functioning between 6 months and 7 years old and takes about 60–90 minutes to administer. The test materials were selected for their appeal to young children and can help to establish rapport with children who may be challenging to assess. Order of administration of the test items is also flexible and therefore allows the administrator to intersperse easier and more appealing items with more difficult items.

Adaptive Behavior Assessments

In addition to an evaluation of cognitive development, an assessment of adaptive behavior is important to assessing a child with autism. Adaptive behavior is defined as the skills needed for successful life functioning and focuses on personal independence and social responsibility (American Association on Mental Retardation, 1992). An assessment of adaptive behavior can provide a profile of the child's strengths and needs which can lead to educational planning. Interventions geared toward adaptive behaviors are important in the education of a child with autism as they increase ability to function independently in life.

The Vineland Adaptive Behavior Scales (Sparrow, Balla, & Cicchetti, 1984) assess social competence within four domains: communication, daily living, socialization, and motor skills, as well as a maladaptive behavior assessment. It is administered in an interview format to parents or professionals familiar with the child. Research shows that the instrument is sensitive to changes in the level of adaptive functioning over time with children with autism (Harris et al., 1995) and can be a useful tool for educational planning. It can serve as a way to gather important information about the child's level of development without relying on cooperation from the child (Harris et al., 1995).

The Scales of Independent Behavior — Revised (SIB-R; Bruininks, Woodcock, Weatherman, & Hill, 1996) is a comprehensive assessment of adaptive and problem behaviors in individuals from early infancy through adulthood. It covers areas such as motor skills, social interaction and communication skills, personal living skills, community living skills, and problem behavior. It is administered to parents or professionals familiar with the child's development and the full-scale form takes about 1 hour to complete.

Other Assessments

The cognitive, developmental, and adaptive tests described above provide valuable information about the child's pattern of strengths and weaknesses and can assist the educator, psychologist, or other professional in identifying areas for educational programming and measuring the progress of the individual. In addition to these standardized tests, there are other tools that may be helpful in gathering this information. A couple of these are described below.

The Assessment of Basic Language and Learning Skills (ABBLS; Partington & Sundberg, 1998) provides an assessment of the presence or absence of the skills necessary to communicate and learn successfully in children with autism and then serves as a curriculum guide and a method of tracking new skill acquisition. The main focus of the ABBLS is on language skills but it also includes skills necessary for learning such as the child's motivation to respond, the ability to attend to multiple stimuli, and the ability to generalize skills. It provides criterion-referenced information about the child's current skills and is designed to help select educational objectives. Once completed the assessment yields a visual display of the child's strengths and weaknesses, as well as opportunities to update the child's progress over three subsequent assessment periods. One weakness of the ABBLS is that although it sets up a curriculum guide by highlighting areas of deficit, it does not provide a method for selecting the order of the skills to be taught, nor are there age norms. However, there is a companion book that explains the methodology for teaching language to children with autism (Sundberg & Partington, 1998).

The Early Learning Accomplishment Profile (E-LAP; Glover, Preminger, & Sanford, 1988) and the Learning Accomplishment Profile (LAP; Sanford & Zelman, 1981) are other useful assessment tools providing help in developing educational goals and programming as well as in tracking progress. Both are criterion-referenced instruments that examine skills in areas such as gross motor, fine motor, cognition, language, and self-help. The E-LAP assesses these skills in children functioning at the birth to 36-month-old age range and the LAP assesses them from birth through 72 months. Information can be gathered through observation or direct interaction with the child.

Pragmatic Issues Encountered in Clinical Practice

Psychological assessment of a person with autism requires two kinds of special skills. The first of these is an intimate familiarity with the instruments one uses. People with autism, especially young children or those with significant mental retardation or behavior problems, are not likely to be patient while the novice fumbles with materials. One needs to know the test kit well enough that the procedures are almost automatic and require little reflection. This frees the examiner to attend closely to the client. A skilled examiner can be flexible during test administration and thereby take advantage of the immediate interests of the person with autism. An examiner should not begin to do psychological assessments with this population until he or she is fluent in the use of the test materials and understands the instruments well enough to know what must be done in standardized order and what can be switched, repeated, or reworded while not violating standardization.

The second set of skills one needs to do an effective assessment is an understanding of autism. The effective examiner has a knowledge of the spectrum of autism and the special needs of people with autism including, for example, the need for a motivational system to maintain the person's attention, an understanding of how the lack of a "theory of mind" impacts on the ability of the person with autism to anticipate the needs of the examiner, and the intrusive impact of stereotypic behavior on attending.

It can take time to build sufficient rapport with a person with autism to enable one to obtain meaningful test results. This is not a population with whom one can routinely expect to schedule a session and complete testing in a straightforward fashion. At our Center we often do our formal assessments of new students only after they have had some time to settle into their classrooms. Even after the examiner has become familiar to the child, he or she may do a series of short testing sessions rather than a single longer one. These multiple sessions may help maintain attention and motivation. For some children with autism such precautions may not be needed, but for other children careful planning may make a major difference in permitting the child to demonstrate his or her skills. Knowing the individual also allows one to select tests that are most appropriate; for example, using a nonverbal test for the client whose expressive language is too limited to verbally communicate effectively.

A developmental perspective enriches any psychological assessment, but nowhere is it more central than in evaluation of persons with autism. A significant number of these clients will have mental retardation co-occurring with autism and as a result it becomes key to consider the individual's mental age as well as chronological age in interpreting test results. Understanding the interplay between the cognitive deficits related to mental retardation and those of autism requires an experienced examiner.

Global test scores are of limited use in understanding the functioning of people with autism. It is not usual for them to demonstrate a jagged test profile, which diminishes the value of a summary score. Although some variability in skills is part of typical human behavior, for people with autism these variations are greater. In our study of the responses of children with autism to the Stanford Binet (Harris, Handleman, & Burton, 1990) we noted patterns of variation such as the challenge these youngsters faced in dealing with the Absurdities Subtest and their relative strength on Pattern Analysis. Although there was a general pattern among the children as a group, there was also considerable variability among individuals, and it is these individual profiles that are most meaningful in clinical practice. We found similar variation from one domain to another on the Vineland Adaptive Behavior Scales (Harris, Handleman, Belchic, & Glasberg, 1995) where prior to treatment the children at our Center showed their greatest strength in the Motor Domain, followed by Daily Living, Communication, and Socialization. After 2 years of intensive treatment there were gains in every area, but most striking was the increase in communication skills making that the strongest domain while socialization remained the weakest of the four domains. Understanding the strengths and weakness of the person with autism is a crucial piece of using the test data to help in intervention planning.

Another important aspect of the assessment is an understanding that this is a team effort. The clinical or school psychologist has a role, as does the speech and language professional, the psychiatrist or neurologist, and other professionals depending on the specific needs of the client. None of these assessments stands alone. The skilled clinician working with this population must learn how to integrate his or her findings with those of colleagues from other disciplines to generate a coherent description of the person with autism. Often, diagnostic assessments are completed as part of a medical evaluation process. When completed by licensed clinical psychologists or other medical professionals (e.g., pediatric neurologist, developmental pediatrician) with expertise in pervasive developmental disorders, cost for diagnostic evaluations are routinely submitted through a parent's health insurance. Additional psychological and educational assessment is often required by the child's school, and may be completed as part of an enrollment process or may be reimbursed if a parent seeks independent evaluation. In other geographic areas, such team evaluations may be completed at state or county evaluation centers. Third party reimbursement procedures vary significantly depending on the specifics of individual children, insurance companies, schools, and community agencies.

Standardized test data alone do not paint a sufficient picture of the person with autism, just as those data would fail to do for any other person. Although test scores can contribute to our understanding of the individual, it is also essential that one observe the client in natural settings. How do the skills and deficits that are reflected in the formal assessment play out in the life of the individual? Social behavior in particular can be hard to assess outside of the natural environment and if we are to understand people with autism in context we need to see them in those settings as well as talking with the people with whom they live, study, and work.

☐ Case Illustration

Steve and Kelly Matthews first noticed things that concerned them about their son's development in the months following his 18-month visit to the pediatrician. Until that time, Joseph had been showing typical development, and was meeting all milestones according to schedule. In fact, his parents had been particularly impressed with Joseph's relatively early development of motor skills and his use of simple words such as Ma-Ma, Da-Da, cookie, juice, doggie, and other familiar labels. In addition, Joseph was showing an interest in letters and numbers on his toy blocks, and was beginning to identify them in objects around him.

As their son approached his second birthday, Steve and Kelly Matthews began developing some minor concerns, although friends and family often reassured them. Joseph's initial spurt in language development slowed and eventually seemed to plateau. His use of words was no longer consistent, and he did not seem to be acquiring new words. Steve and Kelly noticed that words they had heard at one time no longer seemed to be a part of Joseph's vocabulary.

After Joseph turned 2, the Matthews's concerns became more intense. Joseph began having tantrums, and it was difficult for Steve and Kelly to identify the cause of the tantrums or to calm him. At times, it seemed that he wanted something, although the Matthews were unable to figure out what it was. Sometimes, Joseph pulled one of his parents by the wrist to the refrigerator or cabinets, and put their hand on the handle as if asking them to open it, or using their hand as his own. When this happened, Steve and Kelly tried to identify the item Joseph wanted by presenting him with choices, which he pushed away until the correct one was presented.

Joseph did not show much interest in other children and often played alone with toys at family gatherings or at neighborhood playgroups. He spent much of his playtime with books, carefully turning and looking closely at the pages. He arranged toy cars or crayons in rows, and could become distressed if his arrangement were disturbed. Sometimes he held items up and looked at them out of the corner of his eyes. Often, when Joseph's parents tried to play with him by driving the cars or doing other things with the objects, he became upset or left the play area to use other toys on his own.

At times, Joseph seemed so engrossed in his play activities that he did not respond when his name was called or when people walked into the room. The Matthews thought that Joseph might have a hearing impairment, although he clearly seemed to hear other sounds from a distance, such as a theme to a favorite television show from another room in the house.

Although Steve and Kelly Matthews began to read about disorders in child development, they did not consider autism or pervasive developmental disorders as a possibility, because Joseph continued to be an affectionate little boy, who liked to be held or cuddled by his parents. They were also encouraged by his precocious interest in letters and numbers.

At the age of 30 months, Joseph's language had begun to develop again, although it largely consisted of single words and short phrases that seemed to be echoed from television shows, videotapes, and from favorite books that had been read to him repeatedly. Since Joseph used language in that repetitive way, it was difficult for his parents to have conversations with him. He often brought favorite books or videotapes to his parents to watch or have them read to him. However, he did not bring or show other items to his parents unless he needed assistance, and he did not bring his parents to watch him or see something he had done.

After sharing their concerns with their pediatrician, Steve and Kelly Matthews were referred to a specialist. A physical examination of Joseph indicated that he was showing typical physical development. Other medical testing did not reveal any apparent genetic or physical abnormality. A review of Joseph's developmental history and symptoms was conducted, and the specialist indicated that Joseph was showing symptoms of a pervasive developmental disorder, based on a preliminary review of the diagnostic criteria in the DSM-IV.

A full battery of diagnostic, psychological, and other developmental assessments was recommended. The Matthews brought Joseph to a specialized children's medical center, where Joseph was evaluated. A clinical psychologist completed the diagnostic assessment. The Autism Diagnostic Interview — Revised (ADI-R) was administered to Steve and Kelly Matthews. During the 3-hour interview, the Matthews recounted their early concerns and experiences with Joseph in the areas of social interaction, communication, and repetitive behaviors and stereotyped patterns. Based on the ADI-R algorithm, Joseph met criteria for autism in all of these areas of behavior.

In coordination with the ADI-R, a clinician also completed the Autism Diagnostic Observation Schedule with Joseph and his parents. A series of interactive play activities was completed, with specific tasks designed to elicit social and communicative behavior. Based on the behavior Joseph exhibited during the assessment, he was classified as meeting the autism criteria on the ADOS as well.

Using data obtained from the ADI-R, the ADOS, and other information obtained through observation and interview with his parents, it was determined that Joseph met DSM-IV criteria for autistic disorder. He received this diagnosis at the age of 36 months.

Until this time, the Matthews had worked with the pediatrician and the local early intervention services to obtain services with a speech and language specialist to facilitate Joseph's development of speech. Following his diagnosis, the Matthews pursued additional evaluations in order to identify further education and treatment services for Joseph, and to make decisions regarding the type of education experience that would suit his needs at the preschool level.

A cognitive assessment was one of the first components of this extended evaluation. A clinical psychologist with experience testing children with autism administered the Stanford-Binet Intelligence Scales to Joseph, (See Table 14.1). The Stanford-Binet was selected because Joseph demonstrated adequate prerequisite skills, such as sitting, attending to materials, and responding to simple requests to engage in the assessment. Joseph' composite score of 76 on this instrument falls in the Slow Learner category for the Stanford-Binet (Thorndike, Hagen, & Sattler, 1986, p. 127). Joseph also demonstrated an uneven pattern of development. His score in the Quantitative Reasoning domain was statistically greater that his Composite Score, Verbal Reasoning, and Short-Term Memory standard scores at the 5% levels of significance. This level of significance means that a difference of this magnitude could only

TABLE 14.1. Stanford-Binet Scores

Domain/Subtest	Raw Score	Standard Score	Composite Score
Verbal Reasoning			75
Vocabulary	4	38	
Comprehension	5	42	
Absurdities	1	37	
Abstract/Visual Reasoning			80
Pattern Analysis	6	46	
Copying	1	37	
Quantitative Reasoning			90
Quantitative	2	45	
Short-Term Memory			74
Bead Memory	2	40	
Memory for Sentences	2	38	
Test Composite			76

be expected in 5% of cases by chance, indicating 95% confidence that the difference in score reflects a true cognitive difference.

This information was explained to the Matthews in relation to their son's diagnosis and development. The psychologist explained the relationship between Joseph's performance on this instrument and how this compared to the performance of typically developing children of his chronological age. Joseph's scores on similar assessments in the future will continue to reflect the relationship between his skills to his age peers. It was explained to the Matthews that a steady IQ score in future years would indicate that Joseph is making progress at the same rate as other children his age, although he continues to be somewhat delayed in the development of his skill level. An increase in IQ score on this instrument in subsequent years is likely to represent the fact that Joseph is acquiring skills at a very rapid rate, in essence "catching up" to his peers in some areas. Research has demonstrated that this may occur when children with autism receive intensive instruction at a very early age (e.g.,

TABLE 14.2. Vineland Adaptive Behavior Scales

Domain/Subtest	Raw Score	Standard Score	Age Equivalent
Communication		61	**1–3**
Receptive	12		1–0
Expressive	14		1–6
Written	0		1–6
Daily Living Skills		63	**1–6**
Personal	25		1–8
Domestic	0		1–4
Community	1		1–0
Socialization		56	**0–10**
Interpersonal Relationships	18		0–10
Play and Leisure Time	6		0–5
Coping Skills	0		0–11
Motor Skills		85	**2–7**
Gross	30		2–9
Fine	16		2–4
Adaptive Behavior Composite		61	

Handleman & Harris, 2000; Lovaas, 1987). Similarly, a lower IQ score in subsequent years might reflect that Joseph continues to be behind his same-age peers, and may be becoming further behind in some areas. This, however, would not indicate that Joseph was not acquiring new skills; rather, it would only reflect the relationship to skills demonstrated by other individuals his age.

The clinical psychologist also completed an assessment of Joseph's current level of adaptive skills by administering the Vineland Adaptive Behavior Scales (VABS) to Steve and Kelly (See Table 14.2). Joseph's Adaptive Behavior Composite score of 61 indicates that he is showing considerable delays in his demonstration of adaptive skills compared to other children his age. Among the four domains assessed with the VABS, Joseph was demonstrating the strongest skills in the Motor Skills domain, with a standard score of 85. Joseph showed considerable challenges in the socialization and communication domain (Standard Score = 56). Steve and Kelly Matthews noted that it was difficult to assess Joseph's abilities in those areas. Specifically, they noted that Joseph was capable of performing a number of skills, but felt that he lacked the motivation or interest in participating in typical social activities and in types of social communication. They also commented that although Joseph was skilled in using speech when reciting from books or videotapes, he was not as likely to use language to communicate with others or respond when others where speaking to him. It seemed particularly frustrating for the Matthews to observe that although Joseph appeared to have skills at one level, that he lacked the ability to use and apply those skills functionally, independently, and spontaneously. Joseph's scores on the remaining areas of the VABS also showed considerable delay, with standard scores of 61 in Communication and 63 in Daily Living Skills.

Several educationally related items were presented to Joseph throughout the assessment process to identify specific strengths and weaknesses related to preschool and early learning skills. Joseph was noted to have very strong letter and number skills, and he also showed some ability to name colors and shapes. However, there were also times when he labeled a particular toy car "red" while playing with it, yet did not name the color when asked, or when shown a different car of the same color. Systematic assessment of these inconsistencies in his skills was conducted throughout the evaluation process in order to identify the variables related to his learning and the circumstances under which he was able to demonstrate the skills. At times, it was noted that Joseph was able to demonstrate a skill only if it was requested in a specific way. This information was important in identifying educational goals to expand his skills and his ability to demonstrate and apply those skills.

Information obtained via psychological assessment was discussed at length with Joseph's parents. He had demonstrated a profile with significant strengths and significant challenges, consistent with the diagnosis of autism. It was also noted that Joseph's demonstration of skills was often highly dependent on specific circumstances, and his abilities were often inconsistent. Together with a psychologist, other specialists (e.g., speech therapist) and educators from Joseph's new school, an educational plan was developed. Careful consideration was paid to Joseph's interests and strengths in developing strategies to address his more difficult areas of development. Detailed information was obtained on the variables influencing Joseph's performance of skills, and strategies were developed to address each of these systematically. Communication skills were addressed intensively, as an important prerequisite to continued development across other areas.

Follow-up assessment of Joseph's level of adaptive behavior and cognitive skills will be an important component in evaluating his progress and planning future educational and therapeutic intervention.

☐ Summary

Comprehensive assessment of individuals with Pervasive Developmental Disorders is a complex endeavor. It requires knowledge of a wide range of assessment instruments and the ability to select those instruments that are most relevant for a particular child, and those that would provide the information that is most relevant for a given question. In addition, skilled assessment demands familiarity with the instruments so that administration can be flexible as needed. Extensive knowledge and experience working with individuals with autism is also necessary for both administration and interpretation of test findings. A combination of these factors is needed to ensure that an assessment of a child with PDD produces valuable information that is presented in a useful and informative way. Ongoing assessment is critical in providing a baseline measure against which progress can be measured and as a mechanism for obtaining information to guide treatment decisions.

☐ References

Adrein, J., Faure, M., Perrot, A., Hameury, L., Garreau, B., Barthelemey, C., & Sauvage, D. (1991). Autism and family home movies: Preliminary findings. *Journal of Autism and Developmental Disorders, 21*, 43–49.

Allen, M. H., Lincoln, A. J., & Kaufman, A. S. (1991). Sequential and simultaneous processing abilities of high-functioning autism and language-impaired children. *Journal of Autism and Developmental Disorders, 21*(4), 483–502.

American Association on Mental Retardation. (1992). *Definition, classifications, and systems of supports.* Washington DC: American Association on Mental Retardation.

American Psychiatric Association (DSM-IV-TR). (2000). *Diagnostic and statistical manual of mental disorders* (4th ed., text revision). Washington, DC: American Psychiatric Association.

Baird, G., Charman, T., Baron-Cohen, S., Cox, A., Sweetenham, S., Wheelwright, S., & Drew, A. (2000). A screening instrument for autism at 18 months of age: A 6-year follow-up study. *Journal of the American Academy of Child and Adolescent Psychiatry, 39*(6), 694–702.

Baron-Cohen, S., Allen, J., & Gillberg, C. (1992). Can autism be detected at 18 months? The needle, the haystack, and the CHAT. *British Journal of Psychiatry, 161*, 839–843.

Baron-Cohen, S., Cox, A., Baird, G., Swettenham, J., Nightingale, N., Morgan, K., Drew, A., & Charman, T. (1996). Psychological markers in the detection of autism in infancy in a large population. *British Journal of Psychiatry, 168*, 158–163.

Baron-Cohen, S. (1995). *Mindblindness.* Cambridge, MA: MIT Press.

Bayley, N. (1993). *Bayley scales of infant development* (2nd ed.). San Antonio, TX: Psychological Corporation.

Bruininks, R. H., Woodcock, R. W., Weatherman, R. F., & Hill, B. K. (1996). *Scales of independent behavior — revised (SIB-R).* Itasca, IL: Riverside Publishing Company.

Charlop-Christy, M., Schreibman, L., Pierce, K., & Kurtz, P. (1998). Childhood autism. In R. J. Morris & T. R. Kratochwill (Eds.) *The Practice of child therapy* (3rd Ed.; pp. 271–302). Needham Heights, MA: Allyn and Bacon.

Elliott, C. (1990). *Differential ability scales.* San Antonio, TX: Psychological Corporation.

Filipek, P., Accardo, P., Baranek, G., Cook Jr., E., Dawson, G., Gordon, B., Gravel, J., Johnson, C., Kallen, R., Levy, S., Minshew, N., Prizant, B., Rapin, I., Rogers, S., Stone, W., Teplin, S., Tuchman, R., & Volkmar, F. (1999). The screening and diagnosis of autistic spectrum disorders. *Journal of Autism and Developmental Disorders, 29,* 439–484.

Gilliam, J. E. (1995). *Gilliam autism rating scale.* Austin, TX: Pro-Ed.

Glover, M. E., Preminger, J. L., & Sanford, A. R. (1988). *Early LAP: The Early learning accomplishment profile for young children: Birth to 36 months.* Chapel Hill, NC: Chapel Hill Training-Outreach Project.

Grossman, J. B., Carter, A., & Volkmar, F. R. (1997). Social behavior in autism. In C. S. Carter (Ed.). *Annuals of New York Academy of Sciences Vol. 807* (pp. 440–454). New York: New York Academy of Sciences.

Handleman, J. S., & Harris, S. L. (2000). *Preschool education programs for children with autism* (2nd ed.). Austin, TX: Pro-Ed.

Harris, S. L., Handleman, J. S., Belchic, J., & Glasberg, B. (1995). The Vineland adaptive behavior scales for young children with autism. *Special Services in the Schools, 10,* 45–54.

Harris, S. L., Handleman, J. S., & Burton, J. L. (1990). The Stanford Binet profiles of young children with autism. *Special Services in the Schools, 6,* 135–143.

Hauck, M., Fein, D., Waterhouse, L., & Feinstein, C. (1995). Social initiations by autistic children to adults and other children. *Journal of Autism and Developmental Disorders, 25,* 579–596.

Krug, D. A., Arick, J., & Almond, P. (1980). Behavior checklist for identifying severely handicapped individuals with high levels of autistic behavior. *Journal of Child Psychology and Psychiatry, 21,* 221–229.

Lord, C., Risi, S., Lambrecht, L., Cook, E. H., Leventhal, B. L., DiLavore, P. C., Pickles, A., & Rutter, M. (2000). The autism diagnostic observation schedule-generic: A standard measure of social and communication deficits associated with the spectrum of autism. *Journal of Autism and Developmental Disorders, 30*(3), 205–223.

Lord, C., Rutter, M., DiLavore, P. D., & Risi, S. (2001). *Autism diagnostic observation schedule.* Los Angeles: Western Psychological Services.

Lord, C., Rutter, M., & LeCouteur, A. (1994). Autism diagnostic interview — revised: A revised version of a diagnostic interview for caregivers of individuals with possible pervasive developmental disorders. *Journal of Autism and Developmental Disorders, 24*(5), 659–685.

Lovaas, O. I. (1987). Behavioral treatment and normal educational functioning in young autistic children. *Journal of Consulting and Clinical Psychology, 55,* 3–9.

Magiati, I., & Howlin, P. (2001). Monitoring the progress of preschool children with autism enrolled in early intervention programmes: Problems in cognitive assessment. *Autism, 5*(4), 399–406.

Mesibov, G., Adams, L., & Klinger, L. (1997). *Autism: Understanding the disorder.* New York: Kluwer Academic/Plenum.

Mesibov, G. B., Schopler, E., Schaffer, B., & Michal, N. (1989). Use of childhood autism rating scale with autistic adolescents and adults. *Journal of the American Academy of Child and Adolescent Psychiatry, 28*(4), 538–541.

Olley, J. G., & Gutentag, S. S. (1999). Autism: Historical overview, definition, and characteristics. In D. B. Zager (Ed.) *Autism: Identification, Education, & Treatment* (pp. 3–22). Mahwah, NJ: Erlbaum.

Osterling, J., & Dawson, G. (1994). Early recognition of children with autism: A study of first birthday home videotapes. *Journal of Autism and Developmental Disorders, 24,* 247–257.

Partington, J. W., & Sundberg, M. L. (1998). *The assessment of basic language and learning skills (The ABBLS).* Pleasant Hill, CA: Behavior Analysts, Inc.

Roid, G., & Miller, L. (1997). *Leiter international performance scale — revised.* Wood Dale, IL: Stoelting.

Rutter, M. (1978). Diagnosis and definition of childhood autism. *Journal of Autism and Childhood Schizophrenia, 8,* 131–161.

Sanford, A. R., & Zelman, J. G. (1981). *The learning accomplishment profile.* Winston-Salem, NC: Kaplan.

Sattler, J. M. (1992). *Assessment of children — revised and updated Third Edition*. San Diego: Jerome M. Sattler.

Schopler, E., Reicher, R. J., Bashford, A., Lansing, M. D., & Marcus, L. M. (1990). *Psychoeducational Profile Revised (PEP-R)*. Austin, TX: Pro-Ed.

Schopler, E., Reichler, R. J., Devellis, R. F., & Daly, K. (1988). *The childhood autism rating scale (CARS)*. Los Angeles: Western Psychological Services.

Schreibman, L. (1988). *Autism*. Newbury Park, CA: Sage.

Shah, A., & Holmes, N. (1985). The use of the Leiter international performance scale with autistic children. *Journal of Autism and Developmental Disorders, 15*(2), 195–203.

Siegel, D. J., Minshew, N. J., Devellis, R. F., & Daly, K. (1996). Weschler IQ profiles in diagnosis of high-functioning autism. *Journal of Autism and Developmental Disorders, 26*(4), 389–406.

Sparrow, S. S., Balla, D. A., & Cicchetti, D. V. (1984). *Vineland adaptive behavior scales*. Circle Pines, MN: American Guidance Service.

Stutsman, R. (1948). *Merrill-Palmer scale of mental tests*. Los Angeles: Western Psychological Services.

Sundberg, M. L., & Partington, J. W. (1998). *Teaching language to children with autism and other developmental disabilities*. Pleasant Hill, CA: Behavior Analysts, Inc.

Thorndike, R. L., Hagen, E. P., & Sattler, J. M. (1986). *Stanford-Binet intelligence scale — fourth edition*. Chicago: Riverside Publishing Co.

Volkmar, F. R., Cicchetti, D. V., Dykens, E., Sparrow, S. S., Leckman, J. F., & Cohen, D. J. (1988). An evaluation of the autism behavior checklist. *Journal of Autism and Developmental Disorders, 18*(1), 81–97.

Wechsler, D. (1989). *Weschler preschool and primary scale of intelligence — Revised*. San Antonio, TX: Psychological Corporation.

Wechsler, D. (1991). *Weschler intelligence scale for children — third edition*. San Antonio, TX: Psychological Corporation.

Kurt A. Freeman

Conduct Disorders

☐ Description of the Disorders

Conduct problems (CP) in children and adolescents include a wide range of behavioral disruptions ranging from relatively minor problems, such as whining, crying, sassing or talking back, temper tantrums, and passive defiance or noncompliance to more significant challenges such as active defiance, property destruction, truancy, and verbal and physical aggression (McMahon & Wells, 1998). Research suggests that oppositional and defiant behaviors (e.g., noncompliance, sassiness) may serve as precursors to more serious forms of antisocial behavior (Beiderman et al. 1996; Loeber, Green, Keenan, & Lahey, 1995). Although historically CP were conceptualized along a one-dimensional bipolar scale of overt-covert behavior (Loeber & Lahey, 1989; Loeber & Schmaling, 1985), more recent evidence suggests a multidimensional approach with two bipolar dimensions, overt-covert and nondestructive-destructive (Frick et al., 1993). Using such an approach, CP have been categorized into four quadrants: (1) oppositional behavior (e.g., stubborn, angry, touchy), (2) aggression (e.g., bullies, fights, blames others), (3) property violations (e.g., vandalism, fire setting, cruelty to animals), and (4) status violations (e.g., substance use, truancy).

Typically, CP do not occur alone, but rather are part of a constellation of behaviors that may constitute a behavioral syndrome or disorder.

When a sufficient number co-occur, children may be diagnosed with oppositional defiant disorder (ODD) or conduct disorder (American Psychiatric Association, 2000). ODD is characterized by a pervasive pattern of negativistic, argumentative, defiant, and hostile behavior directed primarily toward authority figures. In order to meet *Diagnostic and Statistical Manual of Mental Disorders*, 4th edition, revised text (DSM-IV-TR) criteria for ODD, at least 4 of 8 specific behavioral symptoms must be present for at least 6 months. Conduct disorder is diagnosed when the youth engages in a persistent and pervasive pattern of behavior in which the basic rights of others, and societal norms and rules, or both are violated. To diagnose this disorder, at least 3 of 15 symptoms must have occurred during the past 12 months, with at least 1 symptom occurring during the past 6 months.

CP are the most frequently occurring behavior disorders in children, with a prevalence of between 2%–9% for Conduct Disorder and 6%–10% for ODD in nonclinical samples (see Costello, 1990). Further, CP constitute the most common referral to outpatient mental health clinics, accounting for one-third to one-half of all child referrals (Kazdin, 1995; Sholevar & Sholevar, 1995). Existing evidence shows that prevalence rates vary as a function of age and gender of the child, as well as by type of CP. For instance, younger children are more likely to engage in overt behavior problems such as oppositional behavior, whereas older children and adolescents are more likely to engage in covert problems (e.g., stealing). Further, evidence demonstrates that boys are more likely to engage in CP earlier and at higher rates than girls throughout childhood. However, this gender difference decreases significantly during adolescence, which seems to be accounted for by the large number of girls who engage in covert CP (McMahon & Wells, 1998).

CP are often comorbid with a variety of other psychiatric conditions, particularly for girls (McMahon & Wells, 1998). Most notably, research has consistently shown a high co-occurrence of CP and ADHD (e.g., Loeber & Keenan, 1994; Waschbusch, 2002). Current evidence suggests that ADHD often predates CP, with some researchers suggesting that the essential features of ADHD (impulsivity or hyperactivity) seem to facilitate the development of early onset CP (see McMahon & Wells, 1998). Children with comorbid ADHD and CP have been found to demonstrate more significant risk factors during infancy (Shaw, Owens, Giovannelli, & Winslow, 2001). Further, coexisting ADHD and CP predict a more negative life outcome than does CP alone (for review, see Hinshaw, Lahey, & Hart, 1993). In addition to being comorbid with ADHD, CP have been associated with internalizing disorders such as anxiety and affective disorders (Hinden, Compas, Howell, & Achenbach, 1997), academic underachievement (Hinshaw, 1992), suicidal behavior

(Renaud, Brent, Birmaher, Chiappetta, & Bridge, 1999), and substance-use disorders during adolescence (Hawkins, Cataldo, & Miller, 1992; Loeber, 1988).

Range of Assessment Strategies Available

Given the prevalence of CP, it is not surprising that there are myriad assessment tools available to better understand the severity of CP, as well as the collateral variables that may be impacting those problems. An exhaustive review of tools available to facilitate clinical assessment of CP is beyond the scope of this chapter. Instead, information presented focuses primarily on well-researched, commonly used assessment methods. Readers interested in more extensive reviews are referred to McMahon and Estes (1997) and Hinshaw and Nigg (1999). In this section, assessment strategies will be organized by the level of focus of the method (i.e., broadband versus narrowband) and will include reviews of interviews, behavioral rating scales (including self- and other person-report), direct observation methods, and assessment strategies to evaluate associated and comorbid conditions.

Broadband Measures

Broadband measures are designed to gather information about multiple areas that are potentially problematic for any given client. Strategies classified as broadband typically are multidimensional, in that they are designed to ascertain whether clinically relevant problems exist in various areas. There exist several types of broadband measures, including clinical interviews, structured interviews, and behavior rating scales.

Unstructured Clinical Interviews

Extensive literature exists as to content and processes involved in conducting effective unstructured clinical interviews, which will not be reviewed here. Instead, the focus is on two main factors important when using unstructured clinical interviews to evaluate children with CP. First, when conducting parental interviews, it is useful to involve both parents if a two-parent household (McMahon & Estes, 1997). Ensuring that both parents are present allows for an assessment of (a) parent-child interaction patterns with both parents, (b) degree of consistency in child-rearing attitudes and practices, and (c) marital interactions. Second, attention should be given to the issue of whether to interview the entire family together, or to interview the parents and child separately. Currently differences of opinion exist, with some (e.g., Haley, 1987) suggesting that you should interview family members together, whereas others suggest that it may be advantageous to interview parents separately (McMahon & Estes, 1997). Because empirical data demonstrating which approach is most advantageous do not exist, clinicians are left to make their own decisions based on personal views, as well as the characteristics of a given child with CP and his or her family.

Structured Diagnostic Interviews

Increasingly, there is a focus on use of structured diagnostic interviews in clinical and research settings as a means of improving the reliability and validity of the diagnostic processes and outcomes (Shaffer, Fisher, & Lucas, 1999). The two most common diagnostic interviews used with children with CP are the National Institute of Mental Health Diagnostic Interview Schedule for Children (DISC; for review of history and development, see Shaffer et al. [1999]) and the Diagnostic Interview for Children and Adolescents (DICA). Both instruments share several common features, including versions for multiple informants (e.g., parent, child), assessment of a broad range of psychological problems that correlate with DSM-IV-TR diagnoses, and explicit guidelines regarding administration and scoring.

The DISC is a highly structured, respondent-based interview that covers over 30 diagnoses listed in the DSM-IV-TR. The term "respondent-based interviews" refers to those interview approaches in which "there is a precise script that obtains clinically relevant information through carefully worded and ordered questions that are read to the informant as written" (Shaffer, Fisher, & Lucas, 1999, p. 4). This type of strategy is contrasted against "interviewer-based interviews" in that the latter allows the clinician to vary the order or wording of questions and does not constrain the respondent to simply answer with "yes," "no," or "sometimes."

Interviewers are required to read questions verbatim and record whether respondents answered with "yes" or "no." Separate parent and youth interview versions exist. Multiple administration versions are available, including a computerized and voice versions. The Computerized-DISC is administered by a trained interviewer, who reads questions verbatim as they are presented on the computer screen. The Voice-DISC allows for independent administration, as the respondent is able to simply listen to the questions being presented via headphone while the questions are simultaneously presented visually on the computer screen and then respond appropriately. The parent versions of the DISC are appropriate for use with care providers of children ages 6 through 17, whereas the child versions are appropriate for use with youth ages 9 through 17. Although frequent revisions and format changes have occurred since its original inception, the DISC has been shown to be a reliable and valid instrument (e.g., Friman et al., 2000; Rubio-Stipec et al., 1996; Shaffer et al., 1999).

Although the DICA started as a paper-and-pencil instrument, multiple revisions and format changes throughout it's over 20-year history have resulted in the development of an interviewer-based interview. Multiple versions of the DICA are available, including a computerized version (the computerized version of the DICA is a respondent-based interview [Reich, Cottler, McCallum, Corwin, & VanEerdewegh, 1995]) as well as versions for multiple informants. Self-report versions are available for children as young as 6 years of age, and different versions are available for children ages 6–12 and 13–17 (Angold & Fisher, 1999). Like the DISC, the DICA is designed to gather information about specific presenting concerns in order to determine diagnostic classification.

Behavioral Rating Scales

Currently, there are several multi-informant (e.g., self, parent, teacher) broadband behavioral rating scale systems available. These systems are preferred over single-informant systems because they allow for a comprehensive assessment of a particular child's presenting concerns. Perhaps the most commonly used multi-informant systems are the Child Behavior Checklist System (CBCL; Achenbach, 2001a, b), the Behavioral Assessment System for Children (BASC; Reynolds & Kamphaus, 1992), and the Conners Rating Scales (Conners, Sitarenios, Parker, & Epstein, 1998a, b).

The CBCL is perhaps the most widely used broadband measure of child and adolescent behavior. Currently, there are versions available ranging from 1.5 to 18 years of age. Additionally, there are parent, teacher, and self-report instruments, as well as a direct observation system, although the ages for which these different versions are appropriate varies. Derived via empirical methods, the CBCL originally had different factors based on gender, age, and informant (Hart & Lahey, 1999). Based on revisions done in 1991 (Achenbach, 1991a, b, c), the different systems now share common syndrome categories, as well as several that are unique to particular forms. Syndrome categories are divided into "externalizing," "internalizing," and "other problems" categories. Additionally, the CBCL versions for children ages 6–18 (including the teacher and self-report versions) allow for an assessment of competence (i.e., social and academic). Recently, the CBCL system was updated, resulting in more recent norms and slightly different factor structures (Achenbach, 2001a, b).

The BASC is a multi-informant broadband instrument used for evaluation of children and adolescents from the ages of 2–18. Like the CBCL system, there are versions available for parents and teachers, as well as self-report versions for youth ages 8–18. Given that the BASC scales were developed through a focus on content and construct validity, the subscales are consistent across genders, age of child, and informants (parent and teacher only). This allows for easy interpretation across informants. Interpretation may be based on norms from a national, normative sample or a clinical sample. Both sets of norms are divided by age and gender. Like the CBCL, the BASC provides information about clinical problems in a variety of domains, as well as adaptive behaviors.

The Conners Rating Scales were originally developed through research conducted in the late 1960s and early 1970s (Conners 1969, 1970). These scales include both a parent and a teacher version (CPRS and CTRS, respectively). There are long and short versions of the CPRS and CTRS, both of which were revised in 1997 (Conners et al., 1998a, b). Research on the revised versions resulted in factors that signify both internalizing (e.g., psychosomatic complaints) and externalizing (e.g., oppositional behavior, hyperactivity) and behavioral and emotional problems. Previous reviewers (e.g., Kamphaus & Frick, 1996) cautioned against use of the Conners Rating Scales as broadband measures because of the confusion regarding the multiple versions available, inconsistently demonstrated psychometric properties, and the availability of other instruments (e.g., CBCL). However, research on the revised versions has demonstrated that the newer versions do not necessarily suffer from the same problems (Conners et al., 1998a, b).

Narrowband Measures

In contrast to broadband measures, narrowband measures are designed to gather information about occurrence and causal mechanisms of specific presenting problems. In this section, both behavioral rating scales and behavioral observation approaches appropriate when assessing youth with CP are discussed.

Behavior Rating Scales

The Eyberg Child Behavior Inventory (ECBI; Eyberg, 1992; Eyberg & Pincus, 1999) is a 36-item parent-report form that was specifically developed for use with children ages 2–16 with CP. Completion takes approximately 5–10 minutes and involves reading a series of statements that describe potential behavioral characteristics of a child and (a) rating the frequency of occurrence on a 7-point scale (resulting in the Intensity Score) and (b) identifying whether the behavior is a problem for the parent (resulting in the Problem Score). Current research supports the reliability and validity of the ECBI for assessing CP, as well as for an analysis of the covariation between Intensity and Problem scores (for review, see Eyberg & Pincus, 1999; McMahon & Estes, 1997). Regarding the latter issue, a high Intensity score coupled with a low Problem Score suggests a parent who may be overindulgent of the child's behavior problems, whereas the opposite pattern may indicate a parent who has unrealistic expectations and standards for the child's behavior (Eyberg, 1992).

The Sutter-Eyberg Student Behavior Inventory (SESBI; Eyberg, 1992; Eyberg & Pincus, 1999) uses a format identical to the ECBI to assess CP in school settings. Teacher responses result in an Intensity and Problem Score. Items on the ECBI not related to the school environment were replaced with 13 new items that specifically addressed school-based concerns. The SESBI has been normed with children from kindergarten to sixth grade (for review, see Eyberg & Pincus, 1999). Although there may be a low correlation between scores on the ECBI and SESBI, changes in scores are positively correlated (McNeil, Eyberg, Eisenstadt, Newcomb, & Funderburk, 1991).

CP-specific self-report forms also exist for use in clinical assessment. Examples of such instruments are the Self-Report Delinquency Scale (SRD; Elliott, Huizinga, & Ageton, 1985) and the Self-Reported Antisocial Behavior Scale (SRA; Loeber, Stouthamer-Loeber, Van Kammen, & Farrington, 1989). The SRD is normed for youth ages 11–19 and consists of 47 items that cover a wide variety of antisocial and delinquent behaviors. The SRA is a downward extension of the SRD and has been used with children in the 1st through 4th grades (McMahon & Estes, 1997).

Behavioral Observation

To assess interaction patterns between youth with CP and care providers (e.g., parents, teachers), use of behavioral observation is encouraged.

While interviewing care providers, clinicians have naturally occurring opportunities to observe child misbehavior and care provider reactions. Such instances provide important data regarding strategies used to address CP. When appropriate and possible, clinicians may also choose to conduct unstructured observations in the school and home environment. By doing so, one can learn about the general structure of those settings, as well as about interaction patterns with people other than care providers (e.g., peers).

Structured observations may be conducted to ensure opportunity to learn about the influence of particular situations on child behavior and the reactions that parents have to behavior problems. Currently there are several different approaches described in the literature for conducting structured behavioral observations of children with CP in clinic-based assessments (Roberts, 2001). While variations in specific procedures exist, there are several general approaches described in the literature. Each is described next.

Parent-Child Interaction Observations

Three common approaches to conducting structured parent-child interaction observations include the free-play analog, parent-directed play analog, and the parent-directed chore or clean-up analog situations (Roberts, 2001). Necessary requirements for conducting these observations include several age-appropriate toys, a parent and one or more children, a therapy room, and an observation or coding system. While potentially beneficial as a method of reducing reactivity to the presence of a clinician, having the ability to observe the parent-child interactions behind a one-way mirror is not essential.

Free-play analog observations, the two most common types being the "Child's Game" (e.g., Forehand & McMahon, 1981) and "Child-Directed Interactions" (Hebree-Kigin & McNeil, 1995), involve allowing the care provider and the child to play together with enjoyable toys while instructing the parent to (a) allow the child to pick what she or he wants to play with and (b) simply follow along with the play. The goal of free-play analog situations is to assess a parent's ability to allow the child to direct the play (Hebree-Kigin & McNeil, 1995), assess a parent's misguided attention (e.g., ignoring appropriate behavior, responding to misbehavior), and evaluate the frequency of commands and negative verbalizations made by the parent when instructed to allow the child to lead the play (Roberts, 2001).

Parent-directed play analog observations involve instructing the parent to guide the interaction by selecting activities in which to engage and attempting to have the child play along (Hebree-Kigin & McNeil, 1995;

Roberts, 2001). The goal is to assess child compliance with parental expectations, as well as the parenting strategies used in order to gain compliance. Typical behaviors targeted for assessment include the type (e.g., indirect versus direct) and frequency of parental commands, frequency of child compliance and misbehavior, and frequency and probability of parental attention contingent upon compliance or noncompliance.

Finally, clean-up or parent-directed chore analogs may be conducted. Most commonly, this involves instructing the parent to have the child clean up the session room by putting toys away without assistance. No other instructions are given regarding how the parents should obtain compliance. Roberts and Powers (1988) developed a variation of this approached called the Compliance Test. This approach eliminates the confound of instructional quality on compliance by standardizing the types and methods of instructions given by parents (Roberts, 2001). With this approach, the parent is instructed to issue 30 two-step commands, one at a time with a 5-second pause between instructions. The parent is instructed to remain silent otherwise. In clean-up/parent-directed chore analogs, parent and child behaviors coded are identical to those assessed during the parent-directed play analog. Assessment is limited to child behavior codes in the Compliance Test (Roberts, 2001).

Analog Functional Analysis

With the exception of the Compliance Test, parent-child interaction observations typically involve structuring the setting and activity in which the dyad interact while not prompting specific parent or child behavior. In this manner, typical interaction patterns are assessed. In contrast to such an approach, one may choose to structure both the setting and parental behaviors in order to assess the influence of specific variables on child behavior. Such an approach is called an analog functional analysis.

The goal of conducting an analog functional analysis is to assess which environmental variables (e.g., parental reaction, escape from tasks) are reinforcing or maintaining the occurrence of problematic behavior (Iwata, Dorsey, Slifer, Bauman, & Richman, 1982/1994; O'Neill et al., 1997). This approach is based on the hypothesis that problematic behavior serves a particular function, or purpose. In other words, it is assumed the child is attempting to either obtain or avoid certain environmental stimuli. Typically, an analog functional analysis involves exposing the child to several conditions designed to mimic naturally occurring situations and potentially provoke problematic behavior. Then, the clinician compares rates of behavior across conditions. The condition during which the child exhibited the highest rate of behavior is said to contain the maintaining variables and treatment is then designed to address those.

While there is a long tradition of using functional analysis and related strategies with children and adults with developmental disabilities who exhibit significant behavior problems (Ervin et al., 2001; Iwata, Vollmer, & Zarcone, 1990), use of this technology with typically developing children with CP is relatively new, and thus little is known about the applicability of this technology to this population (Sasso, Conroy, Peck Stichter, & Fox, 2001). Recently Wacker and colleagues (e.g., Cooper, Wacker, Sasso, Reimers, & Donn, 1990; Harding, Wacker, Cooper, Millard, & Jensen-Kovalan, 1994; Reimers et al., 1993) have evaluated various analog functional analysis techniques with typically developing children within an outpatient clinic setting. For example, Reimers and colleagues (1993) described an analog approach to assessing the maintaining variables for noncompliance of six school-aged children, five of whom were typically developing, using analog conditions. The first condition, free play, involved the parent and the child in a room with preferred toys. The parent was instructed to avoid giving commands, ignore any misbehavior, and provide praise every 30 seconds. In the second condition, attention, the parent delivered a series of instructions every 30 seconds. If the child was noncompliant or engaged in misbehavior, the parent was instructed to provide a brief verbal rationale as to why compliance was expected. This condition was designed to mimic parental reactions of "nagging" or reasoning with children and assessed whether access to attention served as a maintaining variable for problematic behavior. In the third condition, escape, the parent issued instructions using a three-step procedure. If, at any time during the prompting sequence, the child became noncompliant, the parent was instructed to stop instructions for 20–30 seconds. Results showed that children demonstrated differential rates of noncompliance and other problematic behavior across conditions, and that rates of inappropriate behavior decreased when the contingency (i.e., escape, attention) was no longer applied contingent upon misbehavior.

Observational Strategies with Older Children and Adolescents

Observations strategies discussed thus far are primarily appropriate for use with young children (e.g., 8 years old and younger) who display CP. When working with older children and adolescents, conducting structured observations may be developmentally inappropriate. However, other approaches may be potentially beneficial. For instance, clinicians may ask parents and adolescents to discuss topics that typically produce arguments, allowing for an evaluation of interaction patterns. Alternatively, parents and adolescents may be asked to solve a problem, resulting in the ability of the clinician to evaluate several important parent (e.g., limit setting, negotiation) and child (e.g., appropriate language, acceptance of limits) behaviors, as well as general interaction patterns (e.g., frequent interruptions, raising of one's voice).

☐ Evaluation of Associated Features

Given that CP may be comorbid with a variety of conditions (e.g., McMahon & Wells, 1998), screening for other types of clinical concerns may be necessary. Many of the broadband instruments described earlier (e.g., diagnostic interviews, broadband behavioral rating scales) allow for a determination of whether comorbid problems exist. Additionally, use of narrowband measures can serve an important function to better understanding psychological concerns beyond CP. For example, if broadband measures indicate depressive symptoms may be present, then use of the Children's Depression Inventory (CDI; Kovacs, 1992) or some other child or adolescent depression measure may be warranted.

In addition to assessing for other areas of child psychopathology, use of tools that allow for an investigation of variables that may co-occur with CP may be warranted. For example, a significant body of literature demonstrates the role of parenting practices in the development and/or maintenance of CP (e.g., Patterson, Reid, Dishion, 1992). As such, relying on strategies to investigate specific parenting practices may be beneficial (e.g., Arnold, O'Leary, Wolff, & Acker, 1993). Other issues that may be important to assess include parental stress, parental psychopathology, parent-adolescent conflict, family environment and cohesiveness, marital relationships, and so forth, all of which have been shown to relate directly or indirectly to CP.

☐ Pragmatic Issues Encountered in Clinical Practice with This Disorder

As is evident, there is a wide variety of assessment strategies available for clinicians when assessing children with CP and their families. While each has its own strengths and weaknesses, overarching practical considerations need to be considered when selecting assessment approaches. These include: (a) the intent of the assessment, (b) the time allotted for assessment, (c) accessibility of collateral reporters and direct observation opportunities, and (d) issues related to obtaining reimbursement for assessment services. Each will be explored next.

Intent of the Assessment

Psychologists are increasingly serving in a variety of roles and functioning within multiple environments. As a result, they are asked to provide assessment services to meet the needs of the setting in which they are working. For example, a psychologist working in a juvenile detention center may be asked to assess the risk that a youth will engage in violent behavior. Such an assessment likely would be broad in nature in order to understand the youth within context and might involve multiple methods (e.g., interview, behavior rating scales) across multiple informants. A psychologist working in a school setting may be asked to gather data to help make determinations for academic placement. This professional may conduct an assessment that is more focused in nature that relies primarily on results of intellectual and achievement testing. Finally, a psychologist consulting in a medical setting may be asked to help design interventions to help children cope with painful procedures and thus may limit assessment data-gathering to this specific task at hand.

Further, regardless of setting, the goal of conducting clinical assessment may vary depending on the particular situation of any given client. Mash and Terdal (1997) summarized four main reasons for conducting psychological assessment: (1) diagnosis, or determination of the cause of presenting problems; (2) prognosis, or the generation of hypotheses regarding the course of clinical problems and the likelihood of positive outcome given certain conditions; (3) treatment design, or the gathering of information to determine the best course of intervention for a given client; and (4) evaluation, or the determination of the effects of treatment efforts. Depending on the goal of any given assessment, different types of assessment strategies may be selected.

Time Allotted for Assessment

In most clinical settings, a balance between the need to conduct a thorough assessment of presenting problems and pragmatic constraints such as time must be reached. Different clinical settings have varying constraints regarding the time that one may spend on clinical assessment prior to moving toward therapeutic endeavors. Thus, one must select from the array of available assessment instruments those that can be completed within existing constraints. Although no single assessment protocol approach is best for all clients, in general an approach that utilizes at least one broadband interview and rating scale and then appropriate follow-up measures appears best (McMahon & Estes, 1997). In this way, presence of significant conduct problems can be documented while screening for other mental health concerns. Using an assessment approach that blends a combination of approaches allows for collection of significant sources of information within a relatively short period of time.

Accessibility of Collateral Reporters and Direct Observation Opportunities

Another factor influencing assessment strategy selection is the accessibility of different reporters, as well as the ability to conduct observations. In some situations (e.g., residential placement), gaining access to individuals who can provide an adequate report about a child's behavior problems may be difficult. Thus, clinicians working with children recently placed in out-of-home care may need to rely less on other-report instruments. However, in most other settings at least one (e.g., parent), and possibly several (e.g., teacher, day care provider) care providers will be readily available to contribute during the assessment. In these situations, accessing report from each care provider to develop a comprehensive understanding of the clinical problems seems most prudent.

When using other report instruments, be they broad- or narrowband in nature, informants should have sufficient history with the individual to provide a valid representation of ongoing behavioral concerns. Currently, there is no specific guideline to determine the length of time that qualifies for "sufficient history." I recommend that, for children who exhibit overt CP that are relatively frequent in nature (e.g., daily), clinicians consider 1 month of frequent (e.g., several times per week) contact between a youth and an informant as "sufficient history." It may be necessary for informants to have a more extended history of interactions with youth who demonstrate covert behavior or less frequent behavior in order for their report to be a valid representation of presenting concerns.

One must also consider pragmatic constraints when entertaining the use of clinic- or other setting-based direct observation methods. Any combination of home-, school-, or community-based assessments are potentially difficult due to constraints such as time, inability to travel off site due to constraints of agency, or unwillingness of site to allow observations. Further, if a clinician has already developed a therapeutic relationship with a youth, then the child may purposefully alter his or her behavior during the observation period. While clinic-based observations are likely to be more easily accomplished than school- or home-based observations, there are still potential constraints that one must consider. For example, when conducting structured parent-child observations, ideally the clinician would be able to observe through a one-way mirror. In this way, the potential influence of an observer may be diminished. However, not all clinical settings have such capabilities. While observations can still be done with the clinician in the room, the influence of the observer must be considered when analyzing the results.

Reimbursement for Services

In the current context of changes within the health-care environment, psychologists are increasingly being asked to provide services for reduced rates, within shorter time frames, or both. Capitated systems of coverage that authorize only certain types and durations of services require that clinicians maximize both their assessment and service provision, and the likelihood of obtaining reimbursement for services. While variations potentially exist within individual insurance and managed care systems, this author has not experienced difficulties in obtaining reimbursement for utilizing the assessment tools described above based on the strategies per se. Rather, likelihood of reimbursement may depend more on whether assessment is provided through an evaluation versus through ongoing treatment provision. When one is conducting an evaluation only, insurance providers may require that clinicians submit a priori requests and justifications for each assessment to be completed. In situations when one is providing ongoing treatment services, and assessment is completed as part of that process, insurance companies may not allow separate billing and reimbursement for outcome assessment, instead conceptualizing that as part of the cost of providing treatment. Some insurance plans also may differentiate between clinic-based and community-based assessment, and may not be willing to pay for services provided in certain settings (e.g., home-based or school-based observations). Given variations that exist in how reimbursement processes will occur, communicating with prospective clients the role that they need to play in ensuring payment for services (e.g., contacting insurance company prior to initial appointment to learn about reimbursement issues) is important.

☐ Case Illustration

Given the diversity of behavioral disruptions categorized as CP it is difficult to select one clinical case that demonstrates the "typical" or "usual" assessment approach. The case presented here is that of a young child with significant CP. The protocol selected matched well with the developmental level and presenting concerns of this individual. While this case illustrates a multimethod approach that can be quite useful with younger children with CP, markedly different assessment strategies may occur with older children and adolescents.

Client Description

Tina was a 5-year-6-month-old Caucasian female referred to an outpatient clinic focused on the assessment and treatment of children with disruptive behavior problems. Tina lived with her adoptive father and biological mother, Mr. and Ms. A. According to Ms. A., Tina had had no contact with her biological father since birth and his whereabouts were unknown. Mr. and Ms. A had been together since Tina was 2 months old, and thus Mr. A. was considered by Tina to be her father. Tina was the only child of both her mother and adoptive father.

Range and History of the Disorder or Problem

Tina presented with a variety of problematic and disruptive behaviors. She reportedly was frequently noncompliant with parental instructions, often with active defiance (e.g., yelling "no"). Further, she was often possessive and would not share well with other children. She also frequently bossed others around and wanted to be in control (e.g., of play or other activities). Her parents reported that she engaged in frequent tantrums (e.g., stomping her feet, screaming, slamming doors). Mr. and Ms. A. also reported that she frequently dawdled, whined, and engaged in back talk. These problems reportedly had been present for some time and occurred in both home and school settings. Further, these problems appeared to be escalating during the past 6 months, despite no obvious stressor or triggering event.

Mr. and Ms. A. reported using various parenting strategies to improve Tina's behavior, with limited success. Ms. A. reported attempts at using time out. Initially attempts were made to have Tina sit in a chair. According to report, this was ineffective. Thus, Ms. A. attempted to have her stand in a corner, again with ineffective results. Mr. A. spanked Tina in response to several of her problematic behaviors, particularly her back talk. Additionally, both Ms. and Mr. A. reported raising their voices at Tina when she engaged in problematic behaviors. In general, Mr. and Ms. A. reported using discrepant approaches to discipline, and each experienced limited success.

Assessment Methods Used

To fully assess the breadth, frequency, and severity of Tina's presenting concerns, a multimethod assessment using unstructured and structured interviews, broadband and narrowband behavior rating scales, and direct observations was completed. The unstructured clinical interview was used to gather general background information (e.g., developmental and medical history) as well as specifics about the presenting concerns. A structured interview designed to gather information about the presence of symptoms consistent with DSM-IV-TR diagnoses of ODD, CD, ADHD, or any combination thereof was also completed, based on the methodology described by Campbell Ewing, Breauz, and Szumowksi (1986). Tina's parents independently completed the CBCL and the ECBI. Further, her kindergarten teacher completed the CBCL-Teacher Report Form (CBCL-TRF) and the SESBI. Finally, each of Tina's parents independently interacted with her during three different dyadic parent-child interactions (i.e., child-directed play analog, parent-direct play analog, and clean-up; Hebree-Kigin & McNeil, 1995). The therapist observed the interactions behind a one-way mirror and documented both child and parent behavior using a structured coding system.

Psychological Assessment Protocol

During dyadic parent-child interactions, Tina engaged in dawdling and whining behaviors, as well as noncompliance (e.g., saying "no"), which were reportedly milder in form than what Mr. and Ms. A. experienced at home. Both Ms. and Mr. A. demonstrated genuine positive regard for Tina through positive physical interactions and nonspecific praise when Tina engaged in appropriate behaviors. They did, however, give many indirect commands as well as direct commands without allowing Tina an opportunity to respond. Approximately 75% of all commands given were indirect. Additionally, they both demonstrated trouble in allowing Tina to lead the activities when asked to do so by frequently asking her questions or directing her play. Finally, they often responded with verbal attention when Tina dawdled or whined.

On the standardized behavior rating scales (i.e., CBCL and ECBI), Ms. and Mr. A.'s responses resulted in discrepant findings. Ms. A. responses on the CBCL indicated borderline significant internalizing ($t = 65$) and clinically significant externalizing ($t = 73$) problem behaviors. Specific subscales that were in the clinical range were the delinquent and aggressive factors ($t = 73$ and $t = 72$, respectively). In contrast, Mr. A. responses on the CBCL suggested that Tina was not experiencing any clinically significant problems, given that no composite or subscale scores were significantly elevated.

On the ECBI, Ms. A. indicated that 22 of the 36 items were problematic for Tina. The intensity score of 153 was higher than would be expected of children Tina's age and suggested she exhibited CP at a frequency likely to cause moderate disruptions in her functioning. According to Mr. A., only 10 of the 36 items were problematic for Tina, with an intensity score of 78. These results are obviously discrepant from those obtained from Ms. A. and suggest Tina may not engage in as many behavior problems in the presence of Mr. A. Alternatively Mr. A.'s responses may indicate that he does not identify many of Tina's disruptive behaviors as problematic.

To further assess Tina's functioning, both Ms. and Mr. A. participated in the structured DSM-IV-TR interview for disruptive behavior disorders. They indicated that Tina was engaging in several oppositional and inattentive behaviors of significant intensity, frequency, or both. However, results of the interviews were inconclusive as to a diagnosis.

To assess Tina's behavioral functioning at school, her kindergarten teacher, Mrs. M., completed the CBCL-TRF and the SESBI. According to her responses on the CBCL-TRF, Tina experienced borderline significant externalizing behavior problems at school ($t = 67$). Also, she indicated on the SESBI that 14 of the 36 items were problematic for Tina. Her intensity score of 110 suggests that Tina is having mild behavioral difficulties at school.

Taken together, assessment results suggested that Tina was experiencing clinically significant oppositional and defiant behavior problems both at home and at school. Additionally, results indicated that Tina may have been experiencing some internalizing behavior problems, as indicated by Ms. A. Although discrepant reports were provided by Ms. and Mr. A., they did state during the interview that Tina displayed more problems with Ms. A. Additionally, Mrs. M.'s responses on the

CBCL-TRF and SESBI suggested that Tina was experiencing difficulties at school. Together, assessment data resulted in a diagnosis of ODD.

Targets Selected for Treatment

The initial assessment with Tina and her parents indicated a variety of externalizing behavioral concerns, including passive and active noncompliance, back talk, bossiness, and possessiveness. Further, her mother's report on CBCL suggested that she may have been experiencing some internalizing/emotional concerns as well. The assessment also revealed that her parents utilized approaches that were minimally effective at best, and related to the continuation of the behavior problems at worse. Specifically, her parents were observed to use indirect commands (e.g., "Would you please pick that up?" or "Why don't we clean this up?") that are unlikely to promote compliance in young children who tend to be noncompliant. Additionally, Mr. A. reported reacting to behaviors such as back talk with verbal and physical consequences, which may have perpetuated a coercive parent-child interaction (Patterson, 1982; Patterson et al., 1992). Further, time out approaches utilized in the past were not effective.

Based on the assessment results, several child and parent behaviors were selected as targets of treatment. Specifically, child behaviors targeted to increase included compliance with adult instructions and appropriate verbalizations. Child behaviors targeted to decrease included tantrums, back talk, and whining. Parent behaviors targeted for decrease included verbal and physical reactions to certain child behaviors and use of indirect commands. Parent behaviors targeted for increase included selective ignoring skills, giving direct instructions, providing labeled praise, and implementing time out effectively.

Assessment of Progress

To evaluate progress as a result of treatment, several assessment measures were utilized. Because therapy involved behavioral parent training, determining if intervention affected both parent and child behaviors was necessary. Further, evaluating whether Tina's parents learned to effectively implement strategies targeted in treatment was a goal of outcome assessment. Thus, both ongoing assessment and pre-post assessment was conducted.

To evaluate whether Tina's parents were learning specific parenting strategies taught during behavioral parent training, child-directed play analog observations were conducted for 5 minutes at the beginning of each session during the first phase of treatment. This allowed for an assessment of whether Mr. and Ms. A. were increasing their ability to create a positive, loving interaction with Tina. Both parent and child behaviors were coded using a structured coding system, and the data were shared with Mr. and Ms. A. to help them focus on skills requiring additional attention. Tina's parents also collected data on whether they practiced the parenting skills in the home environment during prescribed situations throughout therapy.

Pre-post outcome evaluation involved completing the core original assessment instruments at the end of treatment (i.e., ECBI, CBCL, CBCL-TRF, SESBI, structured parent-child interactions). This allowed for: (a) documentation of change in child behavior, (b) documentation of change in parenting behavior, and (c) assessment of generalization of behavioral improvements to the school setting.

☐ Summary

In this chapter, four main issues were discussed: (1) characteristics, prevalence, and comorbidity of CP, (2) instruments available to assess CP, (3) pragmatic constraints of assessing CP, and (4) case presentation. Methods described to assess this clinical problem, the main focus of the chapter, included both broadband and narrowband measures involving multiple assessment types (e.g., interviews, rating scales, observations). While information presented is not exhaustive, a review of well-researched, commonly used instruments available is provided.

The process of assessing CP can be an interesting and challenging task. Given that multimodal, multimethod assessment is often recommended when dealing with CP (McMahon & Estes, 1997), clinicians are encouraged to utilize various strategies to better understand the severity of CP and the contextual variables influencing them. McMahon and Estes discuss an approach referred to as "multiple-gating." This involves using less costly procedures (e.g., interviews, behavior rating scales) to screen all children referred for CP. Clinicians could then follow up with more costly procedures (e.g., observations) for those children for whom the initial screening suggested a need for further detail. A similar approach is also recommended for assessment of comorbid conditions, family variables, and other contextual influences (McMahon & Estes, 1997).

As research continues to provide information about the presentation of CP, and the variables impacting their development and maintenance, researchers also continue to focus on psychometrically sound, clinically relevant assessment instruments and practices. For example, some researchers (e.g., Hinshaw, Heller, & McHale, 1992; Kolko & Kazdin, 1989) have focused on assessment strategies applicable to covert CP, whereas others (e.g., Walker, Severson, & Feil, 1995) have focused on how to utilize assessment tools to screen and identify young children at risk for developing CP. These, and other similar, research efforts help inform clinicians of best practices in the assessment of CP. As a result, there are a wide variety of assessment strategies available for clinicians to use to better understand the severity of CP, as well as the collateral and contextual variables impacting those problems.

☐ References

Achenbach, T. M. (1991a). *Manual for the child behavior checklist/4-18 and 1991 profile.* Burlington: University of Vermont, Department of Psychiatry.

Achenbach, T. M. (1991b). *Manual for the teacher's report form and 1991 profile.* Burlington: University of Vermont, Department of Psychiatry.

Achenbach, T. M. (1991c). *Manual for the youth self-report and 1991 profile.* Burlington: University of Vermont, Department of Psychiatry.

Achenbach, T. M. (2001a). *Manual for the Achenbach system of empirically based assessment school-age forms & profiles.* Burlington: University of Vermont, Department of Psychiatry.

Achenbach, T. M. (2001b). *Manual for the Achenbach system of empirically based assessment pre-school forms & profile.* Burlington: University of Vermont, Department of Psychiatry.

American Psychiatric Association. (2000). *Diagnostic and statistical manual* (4th ed., text revision). Washington, DC: American Psychiatric Association.

Angold, A., & Fisher, P. W., (1999). Interviewer-based interviews. In D. Shaffer, C. P. Lucas, & J. E. Richters (Eds.), *Diagnostic assessment in child and adolescent psychopathology* (pp. 34–64). New York: Guilford.

Arnold, D. S., O'Leary, S. G., Wolff, L. S., & Acker, M. M. (1993). The parenting scale: A measure of dysfunctional parenting in discipline situations. *Psychological Assessment, 5,* 137–144.

Beiderman, J., Faraoen, S. V., Milberger, S., Jetton, J. G., Chen, L., Mick, E., Greene, R. W., & Russell, R. L. (1996). Is childhood oppositional defiant disorder a precursor to adolescent conduct disorder? Findings from a four-year follow-up study of children with ADHD. *Journal of the American Academy of Child & Adolescent Psychiatry, 35,* 1192–1204.

Campbell, S. B., Ewing, L. J., Breauz, A. M., & Szumowksi, E. K. (1986). Parent-referred problem three-year-olds: Follow-up at school entry. *Journal of Child Psychology and Psychiatry, 27,* 473–488.

Conners, C. K. (1969). A teacher rating scale for use in drug studies with children. *American Journal of Psychiatry, 126,* 884–888.

Conners, C. K. (1970). Symptom patterns in hyperkinetic, neurotic, and normal children. *Child Development, 41,* 667–682.

Conners, C. K., Sitarenios, G., Parker, J. D. A., & Epstein, J. N. (1998a). Revision and restandardization of the Conners parent rating scale (CPRS-R): Factor structure, reliability, and criterion validity. *Journal of Abnormal Child Psychology, 26,* 257–268.

Conners, C. K., Sitarenios, G., Parker, J. D. A., & Epstein, J. N. (1998b). Revision and restandardization of the Conners teacher rating scale (CTRS-R): Factor structure, reliability, and criterion validity. *Journal of Abnormal Child Psychology, 26,* 279–291.

Cooper, L. J., Wacker, D. P., Sasso, G. M., Reimers, T. M., & Donn, L. K. (1990). Using parents as therapists to evaluate appropriate behavior of their children: Application to a tertiary diagnostic clinic. *Journal of Applied Behavior Analysis, 23,* 285–296.

Costello, E. J. (1990). Child psychiatric epidemiology: Implications for clinical research and practice. In B. B. Lahey & A. E. Kazdin (Eds.), *Advances in clinical child psychology* (Vol. 13, pp. 53–90). New York: Plenum Press.

Elliott, D. S., Huizinga, D., & Ageton, S. S. (1985). *Explaining delinquency and drug use.* Beverly Hills, CA: Sage.

Ervin, R. A., Radford, P. M., Bertsch, K., Piper, A. L., Ehrhardt, K. E., & Poling, A. (2001). A descriptive analysis and critique of the empirical literature on school-based functional assessment. *School Psychology Review, 30,* 193–210.

Eyberg, S. M., (1992). Parent and teacher behavior inventories for the assessment of conduct problem behaviors in children. In L. VandeCreek, S. Knapp, & T. L. Jackson (Eds.), *Innovations in clinical practice: A sourcebook* (Vol. 11, pp. 261–270). Sarasota, FL: Professional Resources Exchange.

Eyberg, S., & Pincus, D. (1999). *Eyberg child behavior inventory and Sutter-Eyberg student behavior inventory: Professional manual.* Lutz, FL: Psychological Assessment Resources.

Forehand, R., & McMahon, R. J. (1981). *Helping the noncompliant child: A clinician's guide to parent training.* New York: Guilford.

Frick, P. J., Van Horn, Y., Lahey, B. B., Christ, M. A. G., Loeber, R., Hart, E. A., Tannenbaum, L., & Hanson, K. (1993). Oppositional defiant disorder and conduct disorder: A meta-analytic review of factor analyses and cross-validation in a clinical sample. *Clinical Psychology Review, 13,* 319–340.

Friman, P. C., Handwerk, M. L., Smith, G. L., Larzelere, R. E., Lucas, C. P., & Shaffer, D. M. (2000). External validity of conduct and oppositional defiant disorders determined by the NIMH Diagnostic Interview Schedule for Children. *Journal of Abnormal Child Psychology, 28,* 277–286.

Haley, J. (1987). *Problem-solving therapy* (2nd ed.). San Francisco, CA: Jossey-Bass.

Harding, J., Wacker, D. P., Cooper, L. J., Millard, T., & Jensen-Kovalan, P. (1994). Brief hierarchical assessment of potential treatment components with children in an outpatient clinic. *Journal of Applied Behavior Analysis, 27,* 291–300.

Hart, E. L, & Lahey, B. B. (1999). General child behavior rating scales. In D. Shaffer, C. P. Lucas, & J. E. Richters (Eds.), *Diagnostic assessment in child and adolescent psychopathology* (pp. 65–87). New York: Guilford.

Hawkins, J. D., Cataldo, R. F., & Miller, J. Y. (1992). Risk and protective factors for alcohol and other drug problems in adolescence and early adulthood: Implications for substance abuse prevention. *Psychological Bulletin, 112,* 64–105.

Hebree-Kigin, T. L., & McNeil, C. B. (1995). *Parent child interaction therapy.* New York: Plenum.

Hinden, B. R., Compas, B. E., Howell, D. C., & Achenbach, T. M. (1997). Covariation of the anxious-depressed syndrome during adolescence: Separating fact from artifact. *Journal of Consulting & Clinical Psychology, 65,* 6–14.

Hinshaw, S. P. (1992). Externalizing behavior problems and academic underachievement in childhood and adolescence: Causal relationships and underlying mechanisms. *Psychological Bulletin, 111,* 127–155.

Hinshaw, S. P., Heller, T., & McHale, J. P. (1992). Covert antisocial behavior in boys with attention-deficit hyperactivity disorder: External validation and effects of methylphenidate. *Journal of Consulting and Clinical Psychology, 50,* 274–281.

Hinshaw, S. P., Lahey, B. B., & Hart, E. L. (1993). Issues of taxonomy and comorbidity in the development of conduct disorder. *Development and Psychopathology, 5,* 31–49.

Hinshaw, S. P., & Nigg, J. T. (1999). Behavior rating scales in the assessment of disruptive behavior problems in childhood. In D. Shaffer, C. P. Lucas, & J. E. Richters (Eds.), *Diagnostic assessment in child and adolescent psychopathology* (pp. 91–126). New York: Guilford.

Iwata, B. A., Dorsey, M. F., Slifer, K. J., Bauman, K. E., & Richman, G. S. (1994). Toward a functional analysis of self-injury. *Journal of Applied Behavior Analysis, 27,* 197–209. (Reprinted from Analysis and Intervention in Developmental Disabilities, 2, 3–20, 1982).

Iwata, B. A., Vollmer, T. R., & Zarcone, J. R. (1990). The experimental (functional) analysis of behavior disorders: Methodology, applications and limitations. In A. C. Repp & N. N. Singh (Eds.), *Perspectives on the use of nonaversive and aversive interventions for persons with developmental disabilities* (pp. 301–330). Sycamore, IL: Sycamore Publishing.

Kamphaus, R. W., & Frick, P. J. (1996). *Clinical assessment of child and adolescent personality and behavior*. Needham Heights, MA: Allyn and Bacon.

Kazdin, A. E. (1995). *Conduct disorders in childhood and adolescence* (2nd ed). Thousand Oaks, CA: Sage.

Kolko, D. J., & Kazdin, A. E. (1989). Assessment of dimensions of childhood firesetting among patients and nonpatients: The firesetting risk interview. *Journal of Abnormal Child Psychology, 17,* 157–176.

Kovacs, M. (1992). *Children's depression inventory manual*. North Tonawanda, NY: Multi-Health Systems.

Loeber, R. (1988). Natural histories of conduct problems, delinquency, and associated substance use: Evidence for developmental progression. In B. B. Lahey & A. E. Kazdin (Eds.), *Advances in clinical child psychology* (Vol. 11, pp. 73–124). New York: Plenum.

Loeber, R., Green, S. M., Keenan, K., & Lahey, B. B. (1995). Which boys will fare worse? Early predictors of the onset of conduct disorder in a six-year longitudinal study. *Journal of the American Academy of Child & Adolescent Psychiatry, 34,* 499–509.

Loeber, R., & Keenan, K. (1994). Interaction between conduct disorder and its comorbid conditions: Effects of age and gender. *Clinical Psychology Review, 14,* 497–523.

Loeber, R., & Lahey, B. B. (1989). Recommendations for research on disruptive behavior disorders of childhood and adolescence. In B. B. Lahey & A. E. Kazdin (Eds.), *Advances in clinical child psychology* (vol. 12, pp. 221–251). New York: Plenum Press.

Loeber, R., & Schmaling, K. B. (1985). Empirical evidence for overt and covert patterns of antisocial conduct problems: A meta-analysis. *Journal of Abnormal Child Psychology, 13,* 337–352.

Loeber, R., Stouthamer-Loeber, M., Van Kammen, W. B., & Farrington, D. P. (1989). Development of a new measure of self-reported antisocial behavior for young children: Prevalence and reliability. In M. W. Klein (Ed.), *Cross national research and self-reported crime and delinquency* (pp. 203–225). Dordrecht, Netherlands: Kluwer-Nijhoff.

Mash, E. J., & Terdal, L. G. (1997). Assessment of child and family disturbance: A behavioral-systems approach. In E. J. Mash & L. G. Terdal (Eds.), *Assessment of childhood disorders* (3rd ed., pp. 3–68). New York: Guilford.

McMahon, R. J., & Estes, A. M. (1997). Conduct problems. In E. J. Mash & L. G. Terdal (Eds.), *Assessment of childhood disorders* (3rd ed., pp. 130–193). New York: Guilford.

McMahon, R. J., & Wells, K. C. (1998). Conduct problems. In E. J. Mash & R. A. Barkley (Eds.), *Treatment of childhood disorders* (2nd ed., pp. 111–207). New York: Guilford.

McNeil, C. B., Eyberg, S., Eisendstat, T. H., Newcomb, K., & Funderburk, B. (1991). Parent-child interaction therapy with behavior problem children: Generalization of treatment effects to the school setting. *Journal of Clinical Child Psychology, 20,* 140–151.

O'Neill, R. E., Horner, R. H., Albin, R. W., Sprague, J. R., Storey, K., & Newton, J. S. (1997). *Functional assessment and program development for problem behavior: A practical handbook.* Pacific Grove, CA: Brooks/Cole.

Patterson, G. R. (1982). *A social learning approach: 3. Coercive family process.* Eugene, OR: Castalia.

Patterson, G. R., Reid, J. B., & Dishion, T. J. (1992). *Antisocial boys.* Eugene, OR: Castalia.

Reimers, T. M., Wacker, D. P., Cooper, L. J., Sasso, G. M., Berg, W. K., & Steege, M. W. (1993). Assessing the functional properties of noncompliant behavior in an outpatient setting. *Child and Family Behavior Therapy, 15,* 1–15.

Reich, W., Cottler, L., McCallum, I., Corwin, D., & VanEerdewegh, M. (1995). Computerized interviews as a method of assessing psychopathology in children. *Comprehensive Psychiatry, 37,* 40–45.

Renaud, J., Brent, D. A., Birmaher, B., Chiappetta, L., & Bridge, J. (1999). Suicide in adolescents with disruptive disorders. *Journal of the American Academy of Child & Adolescent Psychiatry, 38,* 846–851.

Reynolds, C. R., & Kamphaus, R. W. (1992). *Behavioral assessment system for children.* Circle Pines, MN: AGS Publishing.

Roberts, M. W. (2001). Clinic observations of structured parent-child interactions designed to evaluate externalizing disorders. *Psychological Assessment, 13,* 46–58.

Roberts, M. W., & Powers, S. W. (1988). The compliance test. *Behavioral Assessment, 10,* 375–398.

Rubio-Stipec, M., Shrout, P. E., Canino, G., Bird, H. R., Jensen, P., Dulcan, M., & Schwab-Stone, M. (1996). Empirically defined symptom scales using the DISC 2.3. *Journal of Abnormal Child Psychology, 24,* 67–83.

Sasso, G. M., Conroy, M. A., Peck Stichter, J., & Fox, J. J. (2001). Slowing down the bandwagon: The misapplication of functional assessment for students with emotional or behavioral disorders. *Behavioral Disorders, 26,* 282–296.

Shaffer, D., Fisher, P. W., & Lucas, C. P. (1999). Respondent-based interviews. In D. Shaffer, C. P. Lucas, & J. E. Richters (Eds.), *Diagnostic assessment in child and adolescent psychopathology* (pp. 3–33). New York: Guilford.

Shaw, D. S., Owens, E. B., Giovannelli, J., & Winslow, E. B. (2001). Infant and toddler pathways leading to early externalizing disorders. *Journal of the American Academy of Child and Adolescent Psychiatry, 40,* 36–43.

Sholevar, G. P., & Sholevar, E. H. (1995). Overview. In G. P. Shovelar (Ed.), *Conduct disorders in children and adolescents* (pp. 3–26). Washington, DC: American Psychiatric Press.

Walker, H. M., Severson, H. H., & Feil, E. G. (1995). *The early screening project: A proven child-find process.* Longmont, CO: Sopris West.

Waschbusch, D. A. (2002). A meta-analytic examination of comorbid hyperactive-impulsive-attention problems and conduct problems. *Psychological Bulletin, 128,* 118–150.

Kenneth C. Winters
Michael D. Newcomb
Tamara Fahnhorst

Substance-Use Disorders

☐ Description of the Problem

Adolescent alcohol and other drug (AOD) use continue to be a significant public health concern for this country. Extensive social and economic ramifications are evident as a direct result of adolescent substance
abuse including increased legal issues, educational problems, and risky
sexual behavior (Children's Defense Fund, 1991; Johnston, O'Malley, &
Bachman, 1992; Newcomb & Bentler, 1988). Since 1992, AOD use among
adolescents has increased in America despite reduction or stabilization
in use of some drugs (Johnston, O'Malley, & Bachman, 2003). In fact,
drinking alcohol, smoking cigarettes, and less frequently, smoking
marijuana in a social context is quite typical (Clark, Kirisci, & Moss, 1998;
Kandel, 1975; Yamaguchi & Kandel, 1984), and may be part of the
"normal developmental trajectory for adolescents" (Shedler & Block,
1990). Unfortunately, use of AOD goes beyond experimentation and
evolves into a debilitating disorder of abuse or dependence for a number
of adolescents. Accurate assessment of adolescent substance use is,
therefore, a key to understanding prevalence of this serious problem,
and is beneficial in providing communities, researchers, and clinicians
the knowledge and tools necessary for effective prevention and intervention initiatives. The following chapter will present an overview of adolescent AOD use and abuse rates in this country, address complexities

associated with diagnosis of substance-use disorders (SUD) with this age group, outline the best practices for assessment of adolescent AOD use or abuse, and summarize a case presentation of an adolescent who struggles with addiction.

Adolescent AOD Use

It is evident that experimentation with AOD by adolescents is commonplace. The National Institute of Drug and Alcohol (NIDA), in collaboration with Monitoring for the Future (Johnston et al., 2003), recently reported nationwide rates of substance use for over 43,000 8th, 10th, and 12th grade youth. Their results revealed that over one-third (38.7%) of 8th graders drank alcohol in the past year, 19.6% drank in the past month, and less than 1% drank daily. In comparison, nearly three-quarters of 12th graders (71.5%) drank in the past year, almost one-half (48.6%) drank in the past month, and 3.5% drank daily. Further examination into the quantity of alcohol that American youth are drinking suggests that 12.5% of 8th graders and 28.5% of 12th graders reported having five or more drinks in the last 2 weeks on one or more occasions (Substance Abuse and Services Administration; SAMHSA, 2001).

Rates of use for marijuana identified that 14.6% of 8th graders reported using marijuana in the past year, 8.3% used in the past month, and 1.2% used daily. For 12th graders, rates of marijuana use are even more alarming, with 36.2% reporting use in the past year, 21.5% used in the past month, and a concerning 6% used daily (National Institute of Drug Abuse; NIDA, 2002).

Abuse and Dependence Rates

Although many youth outgrow their use of AOD, some go on to face problems associated with their AOD use and progress toward the development of a substance-use disorder (Brown, D'Amico, McCarthy, & Tapert, 2001; Clark, Parker, & Lynch, 1999; Kandel, 1975; Martin & Winters, 1998; Shedler & Block, 1990). Results from the 2001 National Household Survey on Drug Abuse reveal that, within an epidemiological sample of 12–17 year olds, 8% of the sample was diagnosed with a substance abuse or dependence disorder in the past year (SAMHSA, 2001). In a sample of 74,000 Midwestern students who admitted to substance use over the past year, 13.8% of 9th graders and 22.7% of 12th graders met *Diagnostic and Statistical Manual of Mental Disorders*, 4th edition (DSM-IV; American Psychiatric Association, 1994) criteria for substance abuse. Dependence criteria were met by 8.2% of 9th graders and 10.5% of 12th graders (Harrison, Fulkerson, Beebe, 1998). In another study of students, Lewinsohn and colleagues (1996) reported that 23% of 14- to 18-year-old students had at least one DSM-IV alcohol abuse or dependence symptom.

☐ Assessment Issues

The substantially high rates of substance use among youth emphasize the importance of the accurate, obtainable substance use assessment instruments for adolescents. The measurement of adolescent substance use is multifaceted and involves dimensions that are unique to adolescents, including important developmental considerations.

Measurement of AOD Use

Naturally, any assessment of AOD involvement requires attention to multiple factors of AOD use history. First, it is important to identify the specific categories of drugs used (i.e., hard liquor, beer, amphetamines, crack, etc., including "club" drugs such as Ecstasy, Rohypnol, and GHB); the age at which they first used and at which they were regularly used (e.g., on a monthly basis) for each substance; how often each substance has been used during a given time point; and the number of months or years they have been using each substance also needs to be substantiated. Furthermore, in order to improve validity of alcohol assessment, the instrument should have provisions to specify the amount of a substance used by utilizing standard unit of measurements such as a 12-ounce glass of beer (Martin & Nirenberg, 1991). Utilization of nonstandardized units of measurement can also be beneficial for the accurate account of some illicit drugs such as marijuana use (i.e., hit, joint, blunt, etc.) over time.

Distinguishing "Typical" Use from Abuse and Dependence

With experimentation of "gateway" drugs, such as alcohol, cigarettes, and to a lesser extent marijuana, being almost universal by adolescents (Johnston et al. 2003), determining normative versus "clinical" or "problem" use becomes more challenging. Researchers have found that age of onset for AOD use is an important consideration in distinguishing typical adolescent experimentation from problematic use. For example, Clark and colleagues (Clark, Kirisci & Moss, 1998) found that preadolescent cigarette use predicts early adolescent marijuana use. Furthermore, use of marijuana in early adolescence leads to development of use of other illicit substances (Kandel & Davies, 1996).

DSM-IV outlines two diagnostic categories of substance misuse that is beyond normative: abuse and dependence. Symptoms of abuse are comprised of substance use that increases risk for negative health and social consequences. Specifically, abuse is characterized by a maladaptive use of a substance that leads to significant impairment over a one-year period that includes a reoccurrence of one or more of the following: (a) a failure to fulfill work, school, or home obligations; (b) placing oneself in a physically hazardous situation (e.g., driving while intoxicated); (c) legal problems or; (d) social or interpersonal distress.

Dependence, on the other hand, incorporates psychological and physiological characteristics that perpetuate substance use despite significant negative personal consequences while simultaneous tolerance and withdrawal symptoms make a substantial biological impact. A diagnosis of substance dependence occurs if three or more of the following symptoms are endorsed over a one-year period: (a) tolerance for a substance develops whereby increased amounts of the drug are needed for the same effect, (b) withdrawal symptoms for a substance occur, (c) substance is taken in larger amounts or for longer periods, (d) persistent desire or unsuccessful attempts to cut down or control use, (e) significant amount of time spent obtaining substance, (f) social activities are abandoned, and (g) use is continued despite physical or psychological problems.

Diagnostic Criteria and Developmental Considerations

Of notable concern in the diagnosis of substance-use disorders is the applicability of these adult criteria to adolescents (Martin & Winters, 1998). Diagnostic symptomatology of abuse and dependence may have limited utility with adolescents. Kaminer (1991) found that most adolescents do not manifest the same psychological, behavioral, and physiological attributes that are seen with adults. For example, withdrawal symptoms and medical problems are seen at very low rates among adolescents (Winters, 2001). These symptoms are more in keeping with an adult who has been using for several years rather than with an adolescent's relatively short period of use. Furthermore, differences exist in the rate at which AOD use progresses. It has been reported that some adolescents can be diagnosed with an SUD within as little as 1 or 2 years after their initial use while the progression to abuse or dependence for adults takes much longer (Martin, Kaczynski, Maisto, Bukstein, & Moss, 1995). Symptom distinctions between abuse and dependence may be quite different for such rapid onset cases.

In addition to limitations the diagnostic criteria pose with adolescents compared to adults, there are other weaknesses pertaining to SUD diagnostic criteria when applied to youth. For one, there is the limited utility of two of the four symptoms of abuse: harmful use and substance-related legal problems. These symptoms are rarely endorsed in early adolescence and, when endorsed, they are highly correlated with male gender, increased age, and symptoms of conduct disorder (Langen-bucher & Martin, 1996). Another problem with the abuse criteria is that, contrary to the normative progression seen in the severity of a diagnosis, abuse symptomatology does not always precede symptoms of dependence (Martin, Kaczynski, Maisto, & Tarter, 1996). A related problem is that approximately 10%–30% of AOD using adolescents are missed diagnostically because they only have two dependence symptoms (thus falling short of meeting criteria for a dependence disorder) and no symptoms of abuse. Among those in the substance-use field, these cases are termed "diagnostic orphans" (Hasin & Paykin, 1998; Pollock & Martin, 1999).

Other Developmental Considerations

Researchers have shown that many adolescents are developmentally delayed in social and emotional functioning (Noam & Houlihan, 1990) and may lack the insight needed to honestly report their use of AOD (Winters, 2001). Common adolescent beliefs and behaviors, such as egocentrism, defiance of authority, and risk taking may not be conducive to accurate reporting of substance use.

Several cognitive factors are also pertinent to the assessment process. It has been shown that adolescents who hold normative beliefs about AOD use have an elevated risk for the development of SUD (Christiansen, Smith, Roehling, & Goldman, 1989). For example, typical negative drug use–related expectancies for adolescents include harmful physical and psychological health consequences (Brown, Christiansen, & Goldman, 1987). However, Botvin and Tortu (1988) revealed that it was customary for teenagers to minimize or overlook the negative sequelae from the use of AOD or have the illusion that they can control their use and stop at any time. Therefore, the degree to which an adolescent adheres to these beliefs may be predictive of subsequent problems with AOD use.

Several psychosocial risk factors need to be assessed given their importance in understanding onset, maintenance, and desistance of adolescent AOD use and SUD. Family environment, peer drug use, family AOD use, school functioning, and comorbid psychiatric disorders have been found to exacerbate the risk for adolescent AOD abuse. For example, researchers have found that inadequate monitoring by parents and inconsistent discipline practices contribute to adolescent AOD use and antisocial behavior (Barnes, Reifman, Farrell, Uhteg, & Dintcheff, 1994; Gorman-Smith, Tolan, Loeber, & Henry, 1998; Peterson, Hawkins, Abbott, & Catalano, 1995; Steinberg, Fletcher, & Darling, 1994). Other family factors, such as childhood maltreatment, have also been associated with the development of an SUD (Stewart, 1996). Adolescent AOD use has been found to be influenced by peers. Farrell and Danish (1993) reported higher rates of AOD use among adolescents whose friends used substances compared to those whose friends did not. Finally, comorbid mental health problems have also been correlated with adolescent substance use. Adolescents with attention deficit/ hyperactivity disorder (ADHD) or conduct disorder, for example, have higher rates of substance use. Further discussion of the assessment of psychiatric comorbidity and its correlation with AOD use will be detailed in a later section.

A final developmental consideration pertains to utilization of appropriate tools. The supporting reliability and validity evidence of tools need to be based on samples for which the instrument's use was intended. Assessment measures should be normed appropriately for differing ages of adolescents, written at an appropriate age level, and limited in length. Given the likelihood of high rates of learning and reading problems occurring among drug-abusing adolescents (Latimer, Winters, & Stinchfield, 1997), assessment tools for adolescents have to be sensitive to utility concerns.

☐ Range of Assessment Strategies Available

Several information sources may be relevant when evaluating an individual's drug-abuse problems. Self-report and laboratory testing are methods based on information provided by the client. Other main sources of information important in measuring adolescent drug abuse include direct observation, archival records, and parent and peer report.

Self-Report

Among the most common assessment tools is self-report, including diagnostic interviews, timeline follow-back, and questionnaires. Debate about the validity of this technique has been rampant in the literature. Researchers have found that among adolescents in a clinical or legal setting, underreporting of drug use is common, while other researchers have found an exaggeration of use (Babor, Stephens, & Marlatt, 1987; Harrison, 1995; Magura & Kang, 1997). Stinchfield (1997) found that adolescent treatment completers reported greater use of substances and related problems in the past at time of departure compared to their report at intake. Similar findings exist in the adult literature. Despite these findings, there is a substantial amount of data that refutes these results and supports the use of self-report in the assessment of adolescent substance abuse (Johnston & O'Malley, 1997; Maisto, Connors, & Allen, 1995; Winters, Anderson, Bengston, Stinchfield, & Latimer, 2000; Winters, Stinchfield, Henly, & Schwartz, 1990–1991).

Laboratory Testing

Urinalysis is the most common laboratory method utilized to detect substance use and validate self-report. Unfortunately, although validation of presence of THC found in marijuana or hashish has been substantiated, its overall correlation with self-report of drug use is limited. Multiple conditions may also alter the test results making them invalid. Factors such as length of time between sample collection and analysis, ingestion of other substances that interfere with the results such as poppy seeds and medications, and dilution of the sample may all alter the results of the test.

Direct Observation

Documentation of the presence of physical and behavioral characteristics by a clinician is one of the most objective and valid methods of collecting information on an adolescent's drug use. Identification of signs, such as needle marks, slurred or incoherent speech, unsteady gate, shaking and twitching of hands and eyelids, and the smell of alcohol or marijuana are some examples of symptoms easily documented on a checklist included in an AOD use assessment protocol.

Archival Records

Obtaining information from schools, employers, physicians, and state and government sources can be beneficial in understanding the severity of an individual's AOD use and its ramifications, and can impact the treatment plan and subsequent long-term abstinence from AOD. Inappropriate school conduct, including fighting and possession of AOD, is one example of an archival record. Other forms include: arrest records, bankruptcy notification, and physical and mental health records. Unfortunately, obstacles such as documentation error, lack of cooperation by an agency, and the inability to obtain a release of information by the client can inhibit the attempt to collect this type of data.

Parent Report

The utility of corroborating parent report in adolescent AOD use has been controversial. Although parent testimony of youth behavior for many psychiatric conditions is especially valuable for assessment of SUDs, parents commonly do not have unmitigated knowledge of their child's substance use and may frequently underreport AOD use when compared to the child's self-report (Winters et al., 2000). In fact, Weissman and colleagues (1987), found 17% agreement between youth and parent report of AOD use while others found 63% agreement (Edelbrook, Costello, Dulcan, & Kalas, 1986). Thus, while collateral reporting may be useful in therapeutic and psychiatric conditions, its value as an adolescent AOD assessment tool is questionable.

Peer Report

A peer who is not abusing substances or one who is in recovery may provide a valid account of a friend's use of AOD. Even a friend who may be using AOD and who is candid about their own involvement with substances may be beneficial in providing corroborating information about their friend's use.

Instrument Classification

Since the 1980s, extensive research in teenage substance use has provided adolescent mental health researchers and clinicians with a substantial number of valid assessment tools for measuring adolescent substance use (Lecesse & Waldron, 1994). Multiple instruments have been researched extensively and found to have solid psychometric properties, and, as a result, the subsequent publication of several handbooks and review articles has facilitated easy access to the selection of appropriate assessment measures. Winters, Latimer, and Stinchfield (1999) provide a descriptive list of multiple clinical adolescent AOD assessment measures ranging from screening tools to comprehensive diagnostic interviews. Additional references have been detailed by Leccese and Waldron (1994), and by federal agencies including the Center for Substance Abuse Treatment (CSAT), the National Institute on Drug Abuse (NIDA), and the National Institute on Alcohol Abuse and Alcoholism (NIAAA).

There are two main types of tools used to assess adolescent AOD use: screening instruments and comprehensive measures. Of the various screening instruments, some assess alcohol use only, while others assess all drugs including alcohol. Still others serve as "multiscreen" instruments that address several domains in addition to AOD exposure. Advantages of utilizing screening tools include brief administration time and ease of administration by a wide range of professionals, as well as producing quick highlights of an adolescent's AOD use frequency and age of onset. Screening tools also briefly assess for other critical risk factors associated with mental health and well-being.

The comprehensive measures can be divided into three subtypes: diagnostic interviews, problem-focused interviews, and multiscale questionnaires. Diagnostic interviews are DSM-based and usually follow a structured format outlining criteria for a wide range of psychiatric disorders including SUDs. Using standardized questions and follow-up queries, the diagnostic interview can quite precisely and reliably elicit information needed to make a diagnosis. For these tools, interviewers should be thoroughly trained and have adequate knowledge of psychiatric symptomatology. Some of these interviews are designed to be completed with the youth while others utilize interviews for both youth and parent.

A second type of comprehensive assessment measure includes the problem-focused interview, an instrument that has been developed from the adult Addiction Survey Index (ASI; McLellan, Luborsky, Woody, and O'Brien, 1980). Drug-use history, drug-use related consequences, and other psychosocial life skills including compliance with authority and interpersonal relations are commonly assessed by this type of measure (Winters, 2001).

The multiscale questionnaire is the final type of comprehensive instrument. Although these self-report instruments range in terms of length, they commonly measure both drug-use problem severity and psychosocial risk factors, have strategies for detecting rater misrepresentation, are normed on a clinical sample, and can be administered and scored via the computer (Winters, 2001).

In addition to the screening tools and comprehensive assessment measures, another type of instrument has been widely utilized recently and found to be beneficial and reliable in measuring retrospective drug use: the systematic Timeline Follow-Back (TLFB; Sobell and Sobell, 1992).

This interview procedure allows an in-depth look at a client's daily usage, including the types of substances used, amount used, and patterns of use (e.g., binge drinking on weekends).

Measuring Comorbidity

The co-occurrence of SUDs and other psychiatric illnesses is not uncommon (Clark & Bukstein, 1998), and can significantly impact the development of effective treatment plans and subsequent outcomes. Therefore, supplemental assessment of comorbid psychiatric problems such as ADHD, major depression, and conduct disorder is relevant. Certain types of psychopathology conceptualized in three distinct forms of dysregulation are most highly correlated with SUDs. Tarter and colleagues (1999) report that a deficiency or delay in the acquisition of behavioral, emotional, or cognitive regulation is hypothesized to result in psychopathology when the demands and expectations of the social environment exceed the individual's adaptive capacities.

Behavioral dysregulation is evidenced by antisocial behavior. Disorders that are relevant to this type of dysregulation include conduct disorder and oppositional disorder. Numerous researchers have reported correlations among children with these disorders and SUDs. For example, children of parents with SUDs are commonly found to have antisocial behavior and related disorders (Earls, Reich, Jung, & Cloninger, 1988; Clark, Moss, Kirisci, Mezzich, Miles, & Ott, 1997; Zucker, Fitzgerald, & Moses, 1995). Furthermore, community and clinical samples of adolescents with SUDs have shown elevated rates of behavior disorders. Finally, antisocial behaviors in childhood and early initiation of substance use predict later substance involvement (Boyle, Offord, Racine, Szatmari, Fleming, & Links, 1992; Clark et al., 1999).

A second type of dysregulation, emotional, is correlated with affective disorders such as anxiety and depression and may pose risk factors associated with SUD (Clark & Sayette, 1993). Researchers have found that parents with SUD have children who suffer from affective disorders and related symptoms at a higher rate than parents without SUD (Clark et al., 1997; Earls et al., 1988; Hill & Muka, 1996). In addition, adolescents with SUDs report higher rates of affective disorders and symptomatology, with females affected more frequently than males (Deykin, Levy, & Wells, 1987; Martin, Lynch, Pollock, & Clark, 2000). Finally, diagnosis of major depression as a child is associated more with adolescent-onset, rather than adult-onset, of SUD. It is important to note, however, these associations between childhood affective disorders and later SUD do not represent causal pathways, and more research in this area is needed.

Finally, the third type of dysregulation is cognitive, which is commonly associated with ADHD. Multiple researchers have found that individuals with a history of ADHD are more likely than those without an attention disorder to develop substance-abuse and substance-related problems (Mannuzza, Klein, Bessler, Malloy, & LaPadula, 1993; Milberger, Biederman, Farone, Chen, & Jones, 1997; Thompson, Riggs, Mikulich, & Crowley, 1996). However, other studies have shown that conduct disorder has either a mediating or interacting effect on the risk for substance abuse (Clark, Parker, & Lynch, 1999; Flory & Lynam, 2003; Molina, Smith, & Pelham, 1999). Contrary to these findings, other studies have found no relationship between ADHD and SUD (Hechtman & Weiss, 1986), leaving some uncertainty regarding the causal pathway between ADHD and SUD.

☐ Case Illustration

Stacy turned 17 in the spring of 2000. She grew up in a picturesque middle-class neighborhood in the suburbs of a Midwestern major metropolitan area. She was of Asian decent and adopted by a Caucasian family as an infant. Her mother worked as a school teacher and her father owned a small business. When Stacy was in 1st grade she was identified through a research study as having ADHD and oppositional defiant disorder based on DSM-III-R. At that time, Stacy's academic achievement in math and reading fell in the average range. Results from a brief measure of intelligence indicated an average IQ. As her performance declined over the early school years she was assessed by her school and identified as having a learning disability. Special educational services at school soon followed. Socially, friendships did not come naturally to Stacy and, in addition to educational assistance, she also participated in social skills groups at school. Stacy continued to struggle during the middle and high school years despite efforts by her parents, the school, and medication interventions. Mother reported that her daughter's response to Ritalin in elementary school was good but that it was discontinued because they decided it was no longer needed. Trials of Prozac and Adderall were introduced in middle school but medication follow-through was incomplete.

Stacy reported that she started smoking cigarettes in 8th grade. She became intoxicated with alcohol for the first time when she was 14, and soon thereafter started using marijuana. When she was 15 she first tried her eventual "drug of choice," Ecstasy. Her use of alcohol increased dramatically over the next 2 years, regularly drinking a 25-ounce bottle of hard liquor along with her Ecstasy use. Family pressures mounted at home when her father lost his job. Stacy's behavior escalated and she started to engage in serious physical fights at school.

Stacy was treated for her drug problem at age 17. The hospitalization was triggered by an Ecstasy overdose and alcohol poisoning. She was diagnosed with major depressive disorder, along with alcohol, marijuana, and Ecstasy dependence. As with many teenagers, Stacy minimized the devastating effects of drug use. Nonetheless, she stayed abstinent for a short period after completing treatment, but trying to finish high school and working part-time as a sales clerk was difficult and she slipped back into using AOD.

Stacy had just turned 19 when she was interviewed again. Upon completing high school from a nontraditional setting, she attended a local community college for cosmetology. Stacy continued to socialize with her former peer group and use alcohol, marijuana, and Ecstasy. She reported being arrested for participating in physical altercations while brandishing a weapon. She also stated that she engaged in shoplifting, risky sexual behavior, extensive lying, and was fired from several jobs. Stacy remained nonchalant during the interview and continued to minimize the ramifications of her actions.

Reflecting on Stacy's AOD use history, she progressed from use of more socially acceptable drugs (alcohol and cigarettes) to polydrug use (alcohol, marijuana, and Ecstasy). Her comorbid psychiatric problems aggravated her pattern of use. She faced increasing family pressures and legal problems, and treatment for drug dependence did little except temporarily slow down her drug use. This glimpse into Stacy's life illustrates some of the debilitating ramifications of AOD use that an adolescent may experience during such a significant transitional period in their life.

☐ Summary

Considerable sophistication has transpired in the field of adolescent AOD assessment since the mid-1980s. Significant attention has been directed toward accurately distinguishing typical adolescent AOD experimentation from substance abuse, highlighting differences in the clinical manifestations of SUD between adults and adolescents, developing and psychometrically evaluating screening tools and the large group of well-researched comprehensive instruments, and understanding and identifying the role psychosocial risk factors have on the development, maintenance, and desistance of adolescent AOD use and SUD.

Nonetheless, much work needs to be done. There is nearly not as much psychometric research on screening tools as compared to the larger instruments, and the clinical arena would benefit from the development of very brief drug-abuse screens for use in settings that need a quick and accurate measure. An excellent example of progress in this area is the CRAFFT, a brief screen that has been validated in pediatric clinics (Knight, Sherritt, Shrier, Harris, & Chang, 2002).

There is also a significant lack of empirical evidence pertaining to how assessment profiles can translate to statistical predictions in order to improve the efficiency and effectiveness of treatment referral decisions. Current referral models are not informed by statistical rules based on assessment data. Such research has potential to clarify with precision the extent to which the severity and nature of a problem complex can lead to treatment-client matching models. Many matching research questions come to mind, including how severe should a drug problem be to optimally benefit from intensive treatment? Can mild-to-moderate drug abusing teenagers benefit from a brief intervention? Are there indications when the intensity of family therapy can be minimal in the treatment regimen and when its intensity should be maximized?

Despite these needs for further growth and sophistication, clinicians and researchers have many resources and strategies from which to choose when faced with challenges of problem identification, referral, and treatment for adolescents suspected of drug abuse.

☐ References

American Psychiatric Association. (1994). *Diagnostic and statistical manual of mental disorders* (4th ed.). Washington, DC: American Psychiatric Association.

Babor, T. F., Stephens, R. S., & Marlatt, G. A. (1987). Verbal report of methods in clinical research on alcoholism: Response bias and its minimization. *Journal of Studies on Alcohol, 48,* 410–424.

Barnes, G. M., Reifman, A. S., Farrell, M. P., Uhteg, L., & Dintcheff, B. A. (1994). Longitudinal effects of parenting on alcohol misuse among adolescents. *Alcoholism: Clinical and Experimental Research, 18,* 507.

Botvin, G. J., & Tortu, S. (1988). Peer relationships, social competence, and substance abuse prevention: Implications for the family. In R. H. Coombs (Ed.), *The family context of adolescent drug use* (pp. 245–273). New York: Haworth Press.

Boyle, M. H., Offord, D. R., Racine, Y. A., Szatmari, P., Fleming, J. E., & Links, P. (1992). Predicting substance use in late adolescence: Results of the Ontario child health study follow-up. *American Journal of Psychiatry, 149,* 761–767.

Brown, S. A., Christiansen, B. A., & Goldman, M. S. (1987). The Alcohol expectancies questionnaire: An instrument for the assessment of adolescent and adult alcohol expectancies. *Journal of the Studies on Alcohol, 48,* 483–491.

Brown, S. A., D'Amico, E. J., McCarthy, D. M., & Tapert, S. F. (2001). Four-year outcomes from adolescent alcohol and drug treatment. *Journal of Studies on Alcohol, 62,* 381–388.

Children's Defense Fund. (1991). *The adolescent and young adult fact book.* Washington, DC: Children's Defense Fund.

Christiansen, B. A., Smith, G. T., Roehling, P.V., & Goldman, M. S. (1989). Using alcohol expectancies to predict adolescent drinking behavior after one year. *Journal of Consulting and Clinical Psychology, 57,* 93–99.

Clark, D. B., & Bukstein, O. G. (1998). Psychopathology in adolescent alcohol abuse and dependence. *Alcohol Health & Research World, 22*(2), 117–121.

Clark, D. B., Kirisci, L., & Moss, H. B. (1998). Early adolescent gateway drug use in sons of fathers with substance use disorders. *Addictive Behaviors, 23,* 561–566.

Clark, D. B., Moss, H., Kirisci, L., Mezzich, A. C., Miles, R., & Ott, P. (1997). Psychopathology in preadolescent sons of substance abusers. *Journal of the American Academy of Child and Adolescent Psychiatry, 36,* 495–502.

Clark, D. B., Parker, A., & Lynch, K. (1999). Psychopathology and substance-related problems during early adolescence: A survival analysis. *Journal of Clinical Child Psychology, 28,* 333–341.

Clark, D. B., & Sayette, M. A. (1993). Anxiety and the development of alcoholism: Clinical and scientific issues. *American Journal on Addictions, 2,* 59–76.

Deykin, E. Y., Levy, J. C., & Wells, V. (1987). Adolescent depression, alcohol and drug abuse. *American Journal of Public Health, 77,* 178–182.

Earls, F., Reich, W., Jung, K. G., & Cloninger, C. R. (1988). Psychopathology in children of alcoholic and antisocial parents. *Alcoholism: Clinical and Experimental Research, 12,* 481–487.

Edelbrook, C., Costello, A. J., Dulcan, M. K., & Kalas, R. (1986). Parent-child agreement on child psychiatric symptoms assessed via structured interview. *Journal of Child Psychology and Psychiatry, 27,* 181–190.

Farrell, A. D., & Danish, S. J. (1993). Peer drug associations and emotional restraint: Causes and consequences of adolescents' drug use? *Journal of Consulting and Clinical Psychology, 61,* 327–334.

Flory, K., & Lynam, D. (2003). The relation between attention deficit hyperactivity disorder and substance abuse: What role does conduct disorder play? *Clinical Child and Family Psychology Review, 6*(1), 1–16.

Gorman-Smith, D., Tolan, P. H., Loeber, R., & Henry, D. B. (1998). Relation of family problems to patterns of delinquent involvement among urban youth. *Journal of Abnormal Child Psychology, 26,* 319–333.

Harrison, L. D. (1995). The validity of self-reported data on drug use. *Journal of Drug Issues, 25,* 91–111.

Harrison, P. A., Fulkerson, J. A., & Beebe, T. J. (1998). DSM-IV substance use disorder criteria for adolescents: A critical examination based on a statewide school survey. *American Journal of Psychiatry, 155,* 486–492.

Hasin, D., & Paykin, A. (1998). Dependence symptoms but no diagnosis: Diagnostic orphans in a community sample. *Drug and Alcohol Dependence, 50,* 19–26.

Hechtman, L., & Weiss, G. (1986). Controlled prospective fifteen-year follow-up of hyperactives as adults: Non-medical drug and alcohol use and anti-social behavior. *Canadian Journal of Psychiatry, 31,* 557–567.

Hill, S. Y., & Muka, D. (1996). Childhood psychopathology in children from families of alcoholic female probands. *Journal of the American Academy of Child and Adolescent Psychiatry, 31,* 1024–1030.

Johnston, L. D., & O'Malley, P. M. (1997). The recanting of earlier reported drug use by young adults. *NIDA Research Monograph, 167,* 59–80.

Johnston, L. D., O'Malley, P. M., & Bachman, J. G. (1992). *National survey results on drug use from the monitoring the future study, 1975–1992: Vol. 1: Secondary School Students.* Rockville, MD: National Institute on Drug Abuse.

Johnston, L. D., O'Malley, P. M., & Bachman, J. G. (2003). *Monitoring the future national survey results on drug use, 1975–2002: Volume 1: Secondary School Students* (NIH Publication No. 03-5375). Bethesda, MD: National Institute on Drug Abuse.

Kaminer, Y. (1991). Adolescent substance abuse. In R. J. Frances & S. I. Miller (Eds.), *The clinical textbook of addictive disorders* (pp. 320–346). New York: Guilford.

Kandel, D. B. (1975). Stages in adolescent involvement in drug use. *Science, 90,* 912–914.

Kandel, D. B., & Davies, M. (1996). High school students who use crack and other drugs. *Archives of General Psychiatry, 53,* 71–80.

Knight, J. R., Sherritt, L., Shrier, L. A., Harris, S. K., & Chang, G. (2002). Validity of the CRAFFT substance abuse screening test among general adolescent clinic patients. *Archives of Pediatric Adolescent Medicine, 156,* 607–614.

Langenbucher, J., & Martin, C. S. (1996). Alcohol abuse: Adding context to category. *Alcoholism: Clinical and Experimental Research, 20* (Suppl.), 270a–275a.

Latimer, W. W., Winters, K. C., & Stinchfield, R. D. (1997). Screening for drug abuse among adolescents in clinical and correctional using the problem oriented screening instrument for teenagers. *American Journal of Drug and Alcohol Abuse, 23,* 79–98.

Leccese, M., & Waldron, H. B. (1994). Assessing adolescent substance use: A critique of current measurement instruments. *Journal of Substance Abuse Treatment, 11,* 553–563.

Lewinsohn, P. M., Rohde, P., & Seeley, J. R. (1996) Alcohol consumption in high school adolescents: Frequency of use and dimensional structure of associated problems. *Addiction, 91,* 375–390.

Magura, S., & Kang, S. Y. (1997). The validity of self-reported cocaine use in two high-risk populations. *National Institute on Drug Abuse (NIDA) Research Monograph, 167,* 227–246.

Maisto, S. A., Connors, G. J., & Allen, J. P. (1995). Contrasting self-report screens for alcohol problems: A review. *Alcoholism: Clinical and Experimental Research, 19,* 1510–1516.

Mannuzza, S., Klein, R. G., Bessler, A., Malloy, P., & LaPadula, M. (1993). Adult outcome of hyperactive boys' educational achievement, occupational rank, and psychiatric status. *Archives of General Psychiatry, 50,* 565–576.

Martin, C. S., Kaczynski, N. A., Maisto, S. A., Buckstein, O. M., & Moss, H. B. (1995). Patterns of DSM-IV alcohol abuse and dependence symptoms in adolescent drinkers. *Journal of Studies on Alcohol, 56,* 672–680.

Martin, C. S., Kaczynski, N. A., Maisto, S. A., & Tarter, R. E. (1996). Poly drug use in adolescent drinkers with and without DSM–IV alcohol abuse and dependence. *Alcoholism: Clinical and Experimental Research, 20,* 1099–1108.

Martin, C. S., Lynch, K. G., Pollock, N. K., & Clark, D. B. (2000). Gender differences and similarities in the personality correlates of adolescent alcohol problems. *Psychology of Addictive Behaviors, 14,* 121–133.

Martin, C. S., & Nirenberg, T. D. (1991). Alcohol content variation in the assessment of alcohol consumption. *Addictive Behaviors, 16*(6), 555–560.

Martin, C. S., & Winters, K. C. (1998). Diagnosis and assessment of alcohol use disorders among adolescents. *Alcohol Health and Research World, 22*(2), 95–105.

McLellan, A. T., Luborsky, L., Woody, G. E., & O'Brien, C. P. (1980). An improved diagnostic evaluation instrument for substance abuse patients: The addiction severity index. *Journal of Nervous and Mental Disease, 186,* 26–33.

Milberger, S., Biederman, J., Faraone, S. V., Chen, L., & Jones, J. (1997). ADHD is associated with early initiation of cigarette smoking in children and adolescents. *Journal of the American Academy of Child and Adolescent Psychiatry, 36,* 37–44.

Molina B.S.G., Smith, B.H., & Pelham, W.E. (1999). Interactive effects of attention deficit hyperactivity disorder and conduct disorder on early adolescent substance use. *Psychology of Addictive Behaviors, 13,* 348–358.

National Institute on Drug Abuse. (2002). High school and youth trends. Retrieved July 30, 2003, from www.nida.nih.gov/infofax/hsyouthtrends.html.

Newcomb, M. D., & Bentler, P. M. (1988). *Consequences of adolescent drug use: Impact on the lives of young adults.* Beverly Hills, CA: Sage.

Noam, G. G., & Houlihan, J. (1990). Developmental dimensions of DSM-III diagnoses in adolescent psychiatric patients. *American Journal of Orthopsychiatry, 60,* 371–378.

Peterson, P. L., Hawkins, J. D., Abbott, R. D., & Catalano, R. F. (1995). Disentangling the effects of parental drinking, family management, and parental alcohol norms on current drinking by black and white adolescents. In G. M. Boyd, J. Howard, & R. A. Zucker (Eds.), *Alcohol Problems among Adolescents: Current Directions in Prevention Research* (pp. 33–57). Hillsdale, NJ: Erlbaum.

Pollock, N. K., & Martin, C. S. (1999). Diagnostic orphans: Adolescents with alcohol symptoms who do not qualify for DSM-IV abuse or dependence diagnoses. *American Journal of Psychiatry, 156,* 897–901.

Shedler, J., & Block, J. (1990). Adolescent drug use and psychological health. *American Psychologist, 45,* 612–630.

Sobell, L. C., & Sobell, M. B. (1992). Time-line follow-back: A technique for assessing self-reported alcohol consumption. In R. Z. Litten & J. P. Allen (Eds.), *Measuring Alcohol Consumption* (pp. 73–98). Totowa, NJ: Humana Press.

Steinberg, L., Fletcher, A., & Darling, N. (1994). Parental monitoring and peer influences on adolescent substance abuse. *Pediatrics, 93,* 1060–1064.

Stewart, S. H. (1996). Alcohol abuse in individuals exposed to trauma: A critical review. *Psychological Bulletin, 120,* 83–112.

Stinchfield, R. D. (1997). Reliability of adolescent self-reported pretreatment alcohol and other drug use. *Substance Use and Misuse, 32,* 63–76.

Substance Abuse and Mental Health Services Administration. (2001). 2001 National Household Survey on Drug Abuse. Retrieved July 30, 2003, from www.samhsa.gov/oas/nhsda/2k1nhsda/vol1/toc.htm.

Tarter, R., Vanyukov, M., Giancola, P., Dawes, M., Blackson, T., Mezzich, A., & Duncan, B. (1999). Etiology of early age onset substance use disorder: A maturational perspective. *Development & Psychopathology, 11* (4), 657–683.

Thompson, L. L., Riggs, P. D., Mikulich, S. K., & Crowley, T. J. (1996). Contribution of ADHD symptoms to substance problems and delinquency in conduct-disordered adolescents. *Journal of Abnormal Child Psychology, 24*(3), 325–347.

Weissman, M. M., Wickramaratne, P., Warner, V., John, K., Prusoff, B. A., Merikangas, K. R., & Gammon, G. D. (1987). Assessing psychiatric disorders in children: Discrepancies between mothers' and children's reports. *Archives of General Psychiatry, 44,* 747–753.

Winters, K. C. (2001). Adolescent assessment of alcohol and other drug use behaviors. In J. P. Allen & V. Wilson (Eds.), *Assessing alcohol problems: A guide for clinicians and researchers* (2nd ed.). Rockville, MD: National Institute on Alcohol Abuse and Alcoholism.

Winters, K. C., Anderson, N., Bengston, P., Stinchfield, R. D., & Latimer, W. W. (2000). Development of a parent questionnaire for the assessment of adolescent drug abuse. *Journal of Psychoactive Drugs, 32,* 3–13.

Winters, K. C., Latimer, W., & Stinchfield, R. D. (1999). The DSM-IV criteria for adolescent alcohol and cannabis use disorders. *Journal of Studies on Alcohol, 60*(3), 337–344.

Winters, K. C., Stinchfield, R. D., Henly, G. A., & Schwartz, R. (1990–1991). Validity of adolescent self report of substance involvement. *International Journal of the Addictions, 25,* 1379–1395.

Yamaguchi, K., & Kandel, D. B. (1984). Patterns of drug use from adolescence to young adulthood-III: Patterns of progression. *American Journal of Public Health, 74,* 673–681.

Zucker, R. A., Fitzgerald, H. E., & Moses, H. D. (1995). Emergence of alcohol problems and the several alcoholisms: A developmental perspective on etiologic theory and life course trajectory. In D. Cicchetti, & D. J. Cohen (Eds.), *Developmental Psychopathology Vol. 2: Risk, Disorder, and Adaptation* (pp. 677–711). New York: Wiley.

Author Index

A

Aasland, O.G., 68
Abbott, R.D., 398
Abel, G.G., 198, 202, 204, 207–208, 212, 218–219
Abracen, J., 217–218, 223
Abrams, S., 219
Abramson, L.Y., 86, 96
Accardo, P., 348–349
Achenbach, T.M., 8–9, 274, 276–277, 283, 302, 370, 373–374
Acierno, R., 71
Acker, M.M., 379
Ackerland, V., 329
Adams, L., 350–351
Addis, M.E., 98
Adler, A.B., 65
Adrein, J., 348
Ageton, S.S., 375
Agras, W.S., 96, 180
Ahern, J., 73
Ahlmeyer, S., 220
Ahrens, A., 47
Aikman, G.G., 250
Akiskal, H.S., 87, 89
Albano, A.M., 272–273, 283, 288
Albin, R.W., 97, 330, 334–335, 337–338, 340, 377
Albrecht, J.W., 71
Albrecht, N.N., 71
Alexander, M.A., 233
Alexopoulos, G.S., 90
Alicke, M.D., 4
Allen, C., 233
Allen, J., 353

Allen, J.P., 162, 165, 399
Allen, M.H., 354
Allen, R., 184
Alloy, L.B., 86, 89
Almond, P., 353
Alterman, A.I., 159
Alterman, I., 278
Ambrosini, P.J., 273, 288
American Association on Mental Retardation (AAMR), 356
American Educational Research Association, 31
American Psychiatric Association, 35–37, 66, 86–88, 120, 148–149, 157, 175–176, 180, 182, 186, 192, 198–199, 270, 297, 322, 347–348, 350, 370, 394
American Psychological Association Committee on Psychological Tests and Assessment, 23, 25–26, 31
American Psychological Association, 5, 22, 24, 26, 28, 31, 100
Americans with Disabilities Act (ADA), 21, 30
Amos, M.L., 213
Anastasi, A., 22–23
Anderson, D.A., 181–182
Anderson, N., 399–400
Anderson, R.L., 86
Andreasen, N.J.C., 96
Andreski, P., 62
Andrews, B., 63–64, 134
Angold, A., 269, 273, 287, 373

G

L

M

Subject Index

A

Abel and Becker Cognition Scale, 208, 209
Abel Assessment, *see* Visual Reaction Time
Acute stress disorder
    assessment methods, 65
    diagnostic criteria, 61–62
    differential diagnosis, 62–64, 78
    early treatment intervention, 65–66
    incidence, 62
    justification for, 64
Acute Stress Disorder Interview, 65
Acute Stress Disorder Scale, 65
Adaptive Behavior
    assessment of, 326
    in pervasive developmental disabilities, 356–357
Adaptive Behavior Assessment System 326, 340
Adaptive Behavior Evaluation Scale-Revised, 326
Addiction Severity Index, 153, 158, 401
ADIS-IV-L, *see* Anxiety Disorders Interview Schedule for DSM-IV: Lifetime Version
Adjustment disorder, with depressed mood, 299
Administration, supervision in, 23, 24
Adult Attachment Inventory, 247
Affective Control Scale, 47

Agoraphobia, *see* Panic disorder with agoraphobia
Agoraphobic Cognitions Questionnaire, 40, 51–52
Albany Panic and Phobia Questionnaire, 40, 51–52
Alcohol Abstinence Self-Efficacy, 153, 165
Alcohol abuse, case illustration, 163–168
Alcohol and Drug Consequences Questionnaire, 154, 159
Alcohol Dependence Scale, 152, 165
Alcohol use disorders, *see also* Substance use disorders
    case illustration, 74–78
    comorbidity with PTSD, 71
    treatment, 77–78
Alcohol Use Disorders Identification Test, 68
    in PTSD assessment, 75–76
    in substance use assessment, 152, 156, 165, 167
American Association on Mental Retardation, *see also* Mental retardation
    Adaptive Behavior Scale-School-II, 326
    classification system, 322, 326
American Psychological Association
    code of ethics, *see* Ethics code, APA
    Guidelines for Test User Qualifications, 22, 31